D0713194

A World We Have Lost: Saskatchewan Before 1905

A WORLD WE HAVE LOST: SASKATCHEWAN BEFORE 1905

BILL WAISER

FIFTH
HOUSE

Published in Canada by Fifth House Limited, 195 Allstate Parkway, Markham, ON L3R 4T8
Published in the United States in 2016 by Fifth House Limited, 311 Washington Street,
Brighton, Massachusetts 02135

Fifth House acknowledges with thanks the Canada Council for the Arts, and the Ontario Arts Council
for their support of our publishing program. We acknowledge the financial support of the
Government of Canada through the Canada Book Fund (CBF) for our publishing activities.

Library and Archives Canada Cataloguing in Publication
Waiser, Bill, 1953-, author
A world we have lost : Saskatchewan before 1905 / Bill Waiser.

Includes bibliographical references and index.
ISBN 978-1-927083-39-0 (hardback)
1. Native peoples--Saskatchewan--History. 2. Fur trade--Saskatchewan--History. 3. Native peo-
ples--Colonization--Saskatchewan--History. 4. Saskatchewan--History. I. Title.

FC3206.W35 2016   971.24'01   C2016-901492-4

Publisher Cataloging-in-Publication Data (U.S.)
Waiser, W. A., author.
A world we have lost : Saskatchewan before 1905 / Bill Waiser.
Markham, Ontario: Fifth House Limited, 2016. | Includes bibliography and index. | Summary:
"A World We Have Lost examines the early history of Saskatchewan through
an Aboriginal and environmental lens" – Provided by publisher.
ISBN 978-1-92708-339-0 (hardcover)
LCSH: Saskatchewan -- History. | BISAC: HISTORY / Canada / General.
LCC   F1072.W357 | DDC 971.24 – dc23

All colour photographs, except those credited in block letters,
are by John L. Perret, Light Line Photography, Saskatoon.
Proofreader: Penny Hozy
Text and cover design: Kerry Designs

For Owen, Quinn, Dylan, and Taylor,
children of the new Saskatchewan
and inheritors of the province of yesterday.

CONTENTS

VII

Maps

TABLES

AUTHOR'S NOTE

A World We Have Lost tells the history of the region that became the province of Saskatchewan in 1905. Because the province has completely artificial boundaries, the focus of the book must necessarily deal with a much larger geographical area, including the northern United States, in order to provide an appreciation and understanding of that history. A special effort is made to use Saskatchewan-based examples whenever possible.

The term "Indians" is used throughout the book for First Nations or Native people. It was the term used during the time period covered by the book. The commonly used names for tribes are also employed throughout the text: Cree, Assiniboine, Blackfoot (Blackfoot, Blood, and Peigan), and Chipewyan. Métis peoples are identified as either Métis or mixed-descent peoples. It took one or more generations before people of mixed descent formed a cultural identity as Métis and the experience was not the same across the region. Grammar and spelling in the quotations from fur trade sources have not been corrected.

All units of measurement are expressed in imperial—except for Chapter One ("Invariably Variable") where both the metric and imperial system are used.

It is not possible to provide an exhaustive history of pre-1905 Saskatchewan. *A World We Have Lost* is an introduction to that history. It also seeks to avoid as much as possible overlap with the centennial history of the province, *Saskatchewan: A New History*. Some topics, themes, and issues from the pre-1905 period are already covered in that book. The two books are intended to complement one another.

For further information about particular topics, issues, or themes, readers should consult the notes.

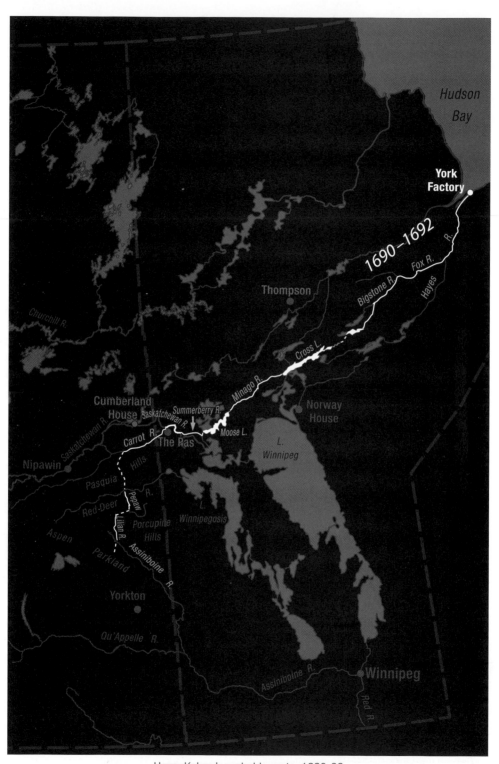

Henry Kelsey's probable route, 1690-92

INLAND COUNTRY
OF GOOD REPORT

HE WAS AN OUTSIDER. HE WAS ONLY THERE BECAUSE HE HAD BEEN TAKEN INLAND FROM Hudson Bay. He could never have made the trip on his own, even though he is celebrated today as an adventurer. It was the summer of 1691. The place, likely somewhere north of present-day Yorkton in east-central Saskatchewan. Twenty-four-year-old Henry Kelsey, a Hudson's Bay Company (HBC) servant, had been dispatched a year earlier on a special mission "to call, encourage and invite, the remoter Indians to a Trade with us."[1] It was the first time that an employee of the British trading monopoly had left the relative safety of York Factory on the southwest coast of Hudson Bay to visit the home territory of the company's Indian trading partners, the Cree (called Southern Indians in the records) and the Assiniboine (also known as Nakota/Nakoda, Stony, or Asinoe Poets or *Asinipwāt* [Stone Sioux]). It

was a remarkable feat. Kelsey spent the better part of two years in the interior, becoming the first newcomer to North America to walk the prairies of western Canada and see first-hand the bison. And he has been recognized today in any number of ways—from the name

In 1970, on the 280th anniversary of Kelsey's inland trip, Canada Post honoured "the first explorer on the plains" with a six-cent stamp.

of the Saskatoon campus of the Saskatchewan Institute of Applied Science and Technology to the call letters of CBC radio in Saskatchewan (CBK) to a rosebush in the "explorer" series developed by Agriculture Canada to singer Stan Rogers's "Northwest Passage." But the greater significance of Kelsey's much-heralded trip is that it demonstrated how any early European activity in what would become the future province of Saskatchewan was entirely dependent on the

C. W. Jefferys's *Kelsey Sees the Buffalo*, 1691, portrays the Hudson's Bay Company servant as superior to his Indian escorts.

goodwill and cooperation of the Indian peoples of the region. Kelsey, as their guest, was the fortunate beneficiary.

Probably the most famous portrait of Henry Kelsey—at least for school kids who studied Canadian history after the Second World War—was prepared by artist and illustrator C. W. Jefferys around 1927.[2] *Kelsey Sees the Buffalo*, 1691, features a tall, auburn-haired Kelsey, in a full deerskin suit and scarlet bandana with white polka dots, resting his hands on the barrel of his gun, watching a grazing herd of bison from the nearby shelter of an aspen grove. Around him are a handful of copper-coloured, half-naked Indian men, one kneeling, others crouching, staring at the animals in the distance. Jefferys has deliberately painted Kelsey's clothing in a brighter hue of brown, so that he stands out as the dominant figure in the portrait. After all, it was a momentous event in Canadian history.

Jefferys was not alone in portraying Kelsey in such romantic terms. A 1955 biography, *First in the West*, lauded Kelsey as the "Discoverer of the Canadian Prairies."[3] It was as if the Indian peoples who had been living there for generations were simply part of the flora and fauna. A. S. Morton, long-time professor of western Canadian history at the University of Saskatchewan, was equally effusive about Kelsey's legacy. "The spirit of the great prototype of the coureurs-des-bois had descended upon him," Morton observed in his monumental *A History of the Canadian West to 1870–71*. "He is our first example of that comparatively rare species, the Indianized Englishman."[4] Morton's intended compliment, however, was unwittingly undermined in the same paragraph by his use of the term "savages" to describe Indians.

What is particularly ironic about this heroic treatment of Henry Kelsey is that little is known about him, despite his lengthy HBC career, and that even less is known about where he actually went in the western interior during his now-famous expedition. Morton, for example, refers to Kelsey as "a character as interesting as [he] is illusive [sic]," while one of his biographers, who incorrectly puts Kelsey near the junction of the Battle and North Saskatchewan Rivers, claims that the "problem" of his route is "like that presented by a jigsaw puzzle."[5] Others in the search for clues to his exact whereabouts have politely called his travel descriptions "vague."[6] Indeed, several people have painstakingly tried to decipher Kelsey's location references, while tramping through east-central Saskatchewan and talking to old-timers who settled the district, in a valiant effort to match them to particular places.[7]

The mystery is further compounded by the fact that Kelsey's original journal did not surface until 1926 when it was found in Northern Ireland among the papers of Arthur Dobbs, an avowed eighteenth-century critic of the HBC.[8] Until then, there was reason to question whether Kelsey had ever taken the trip, and if he had, his motives for doing so. Maybe, as one former company employee suggested, the young man was really running away from his job at bayside.[9] Even then, the discovery of Kelsey's papers did not clear up the confusion beyond confirming that the two-year trip had been officially sanctioned and rewarded with a sizeable thirty-pound bonus. The first part of his journal deals largely with his departure from York Factory in June 1690 until he reached the northern prairies. It serves as a kind of prologue. The remainder of the document covers the second year of his inland trip, the period from 15 July to 12 September 1691 (based on the Julian calendar). Kelsey makes no other entries, including the date of his return to York Factory in 1692. This lack of information, by a servant working for a company otherwise obsessed with record keeping, is puzzling at best.[10]

What is not disputed is Kelsey's remarkable thirty-eight-year career (1684–1722) with the Hudson's Bay Company (founded 1670), during which he was absent from the bay region for only three years. He spent the better part of his adult life in the subarctic, serving with distinction as the company struggled to consolidate its control over the northwestern fur trade. Born in East Greenwich, England, in 1667, and probably the son of a mariner, Kelsey joined the HBC in 1684 as a seventeen-year-old apprentice. He was not, as the story goes, a street waif or an illiterate orphan or he would never have found employment with the company. Nor was he a "boy explorer" as some writers have dubbed him. He was at least twenty-three and had already completed one term of service when he embarked on his famous trip inland in 1690. Kelsey quickly impressed Governor George Geyer at York Factory as "a very active Lad Delighting much in Indians Compa., being never better pleased than when hee is Travelling amongst them."[11] That was certainly the case during the winter of 1688–89 when he carried the mail packet about two hundred miles south from York Factory along the coastal lowlands to New Severn when three local Indians had failed at the task. He added to his growing reputation the following summer when, with a young Indian companion, he walked several hundred miles northward along the western shore of Hudson Bay in an effort to encourage the Chipewyan (also known as Northern Indians or Dene) to trade at a new post that the HBC hoped to establish at the mouth of the Churchill River.

Kelsey's wanderlust was unusual for company servants at that time. When King Charles II granted the Hudson's Bay Company a monopoly in 1670 over the trade and commerce of all lands that drained into Hudson and James Bays (called Rupert's Land), the expectation was that the English would quickly outflank their French competitors by sailing into the northern heart of the continent. This revolutionary approach to the fur trade, initiated by disaffected Frenchmen Pierre Esprit Radisson and his brother-in-law Médard Chouart Des Groseilliers in the late 1660s, had several advantages over the French route to the interior, the most important being that it provided the HBC with direct access to Indian trappers and their fine northern furs. But instead of pursuing its advantage and venturing inland, the HBC chose to establish permanent posts, or "factories" as they were called, on the rim of the bay and encourage Indian traders to come there by canoe each spring. This rather unimaginative strategy enabled the company, fearful of illicit activity, to exercise a kind of tight-fisted control over its operations, especially its employees. It also meant that company success largely depended on its ability to attract Indians to the bay to trade. Posts were located on rivers best suited for canoe navigation to and from the interior. At York Factory, for example, ocean-going ships from England had to anchor several miles offshore, at Five Fathom Hole, because the harbour was too shallow for large vessels. In a sense, then, the HBC posts were like downtown department stores, only in this case at bayside.

Most company servants, working under this rigid regime in Rupert's Land, were little more than clerks, receiving furs from inland and trade goods and other supplies from overseas, while keeping inventories of the kind and quantity of furs exchanged for particular trade items. They rarely ventured any distance from the posts unless it was to hunt or secure fuel—and that was because the landscape was completely foreign to them. The Hudson Bay lowlands, where the HBC decided to set up its North American operations, were bleak, forbidding, and swampy. Winter was marked by deep snows, frigid temperatures, and even colder, biting winds off the bay. Summer was little better, maybe even more unpleasant, what with the presence of surface water almost everywhere and countless blood-sucking insects that made life outside almost unbearable. Henry Kelsey found a home here, though. As a

Came up with them six tents of wch they kill'd
This ill news kept secrett was from me

Nor none of those same Indians did I see
Untill that they their murder all had done
And the Chief actor was he yt called ye Sun
So far I have spoken concerning of the spoil
And now will give acco.t of that same Country soile
Which hither parts is very thick of wood
Affords small nutts wth little cherryes very good
Thus it continues till you leave ye woods behind
And then you have beast of severall kind
The one is a black a Buffillo great
Another is an outgrown Bear wch is good meat
His skin to gett I have used all ye ways I can
He is mans food & he makes food of mans
His hide they would not me it preserve
But said it was a god & they should Starve
This plain affords nothing but Beast & grass
And over it in three days time we past
getting unto ye woods on the other side
It being about forty six miles wide
This wood is poplo ridges with small ponds of water
There is beavour in abundance but no Otter
with plains & ridges is the Country throughout
Their Enemies many is whom they cannot resist
But now of late they hunt their Enemies
And with our English guns do make ym flie
At deering point after the frost
I set up their a Certain Cross
In token of my being there
Cut out on it ye date of year
And Likewise for to verifie the same
added to it my master sir Edward deerings name
So having not more to trouble you is all I am
Sir your most obedient & faithfull Servt at command
Henry Kelsey

A page from Henry Kelsey's journal

teenaged apprentice from greater London, he revelled in his new environment and took in all he could about the land and its wildlife, including the shaggy muskox. He also enjoyed spending time with the local Cree people, picking up words and phrases in their language, while learning about their ways. These interests, when combined with his two walking expeditions, made him the perfect candidate to go inland, at Governor Geyer's request, to bring new Indian customers into the York Factory trading network.

Kelsey left for the interior on 12 June 1690 with the captain of a group of Assiniboine (Asinoe Poets or *asinipwāt* [Stone Sioux]) headed back up the Hayes River after their annual trade session at the fort. He carried with him a sampling of trade goods that were otherwise available at bayside. From his surviving account, written in rhyming couplets probably during the winter of 1690–91, Kelsey approached the trip with a mixture of fear and determination; he was anxious, if not somewhat distressed, about being separated from his fellow Englishmen for such a long time, yet looked forward to seeing the more rugged forested country, upriver in the interior:

> In the sixteen hundred & ninety'th year
> I set forth as plainly may appear
> Through Gods assistance for to understand
> The natives language & to see their land
> And for my masters interest I did soon
> Sett from ye house ye twealth of June
> Then up ye River I with heavy heart
> Did take my way & from all English part
> To live amongst ye Natives of this place
> If god permits me for one two years space
> The Inland Country of Good report hath been
> By Indians but by English yet not seen[12]

By 10 July, almost a month after departing from York Factory, the Assiniboine reached the edge of their territory. Kelsey reckoned that they had travelled some six hundred miles, including some thirty-three portages or "carriages," to

A group of Assiniboine Indians took Kelsey inland from York Factory through present-day northwestern Manitoba.

the southwest. Here, probably at a bend in the Saskatchewan River, he named "Deerings Point" in honour of Sir Edward Dering, the HBC deputy governor.

Deerings Point has been called "the critical hinge location in Kelsey's travels."[13] He not only sent a message to York Factory from here, but as prearranged, picked up new supplies and instructions from Governor Geyer for his second year inland. And it is now generally accepted that it was probably at The Pas, near the junction of the Carrot River and Saskatchewan River, just on the eastern side of the Manitoba/Saskatchewan interprovincial boundary. What is not fully appreciated, however, is that it was the Assiniboine and Cree who chose the places to stop and camp on the way inland—in effect, assisting Kelsey in his "discovery" of the interior by serving as guides and sharing their knowledge about the land[14] The Deerings Point location, for example, was clearly a favourite rendezvous site for those going and returning from the bay and may even have served as a place to make canoes for the trip. There is also a tendency to focus on Kelsey's bravery and forget that his initial apprehensions about leaving York Factory—as the only non-Native—were largely unfounded because he had been accepted into the Assiniboine group as a guest.[15] The arduous trip inland from the bay would not have been possible on his own: Kelsey did not know where he was going, let alone where he might find the people he was supposed to bring into the trade. Besides, even though he worked on ships in the bay, negotiating the rivers of the Canadian Shield, including stringing canoes around rapids, was beyond his capabilities. Simply put, the HBC servant was a passenger, not a pathfinder. He did, however, attempt to learn the local customs.

Under the guiding hand of his Indian escort, Kelsey entered a landscape never encountered before by another European. Sometime during the summer of 1690, at some point in east-central Saskatchewan, he left behind the boreal woodlands and walked out into a new world, at least to him, featuring gently undulating grasslands, small isolated groves of aspen poplar, chains of wetlands, and occasional dense brush-filled ravines. The transition from forest to prairie parkland would have been dramatic, if not a little startling, even for someone who had become accustomed to the subarctic tundra. "Which hither part is very thick of wood/Afford small nuts wth little cherryes very good," Kelsey recounted. "Thus it continues till you leave ye woods behind/And then you have beast of severall kind/The one is a black a Buffillo great/Another is an outgrown Bear wch, is good meat."[16] This clumsy poetry was the first written record of the bison, the prairie grizzly, and maybe, the Saskatoon berry. Kelsey was also the first European visitor to the region to remark on the monotony of the prairies—"This plain affords nothing but Beast & grass"[17]—after it took a full three days to cross a particular section of open grassland. This simple passage has been described as "an important text of early Canadian literature,"[18] in part because he was the first non-indigenous person to distinguish the major vegetation zones of western Canada. What is unfortunate is Kelsey's brevity, a shortcoming only compounded by his amateurish verse. It takes some imagination to get a sense of what he experienced.

Kelsey's Indian escorts probably stopped at this "God Stone" on the Red Deer riverbank along the Pasquia Hills–Nut Mountain trail in present-day east-central Saskatchewan.

Kelsey spent his first inland Canadian winter probably in the Upper Assiniboine River area on the edge of the northern parklands. To the north, the Saskatchewan River delta was the territory of the Basquia Cree. Further up the Saskatchewan River toward present-day Nipawin and the Saskatchewan forks were the Pegogamaw Cree. And in an area stretching from the mouth of the Saskatchewan River to the upper Assiniboine River lived the Sturgeon Cree. Some of this same territory, around the Porcupine and/or Duck Mountains of the Manitoba escarpment, was also apparently co-occupied by the Assiniboine, identified as the Mountain Poets by Kelsey. These Indian peoples, unlike their English visitor from the bay, had a knowledge of the local environment that was "extensive in scope and deep in history."[19] Their prairies were not an empty wilderness but alive with history and the experiences of generations. Written in the land were the stories of their lives. They also enjoyed kinship ties with one another, whether through blood, marriage, or trade, mostly at the band level.

Once or twice a year, usually in early spring, but sometimes fall as well, the regional bands would come together at a favourite rendezvous or "ingathering" centre. These aggregation places had special cultural and spiritual significance that transcended the size of the group. Some were located along the Saskatchewan River Valley, others strategically located throughout their territory—wherever there was convenient access and sufficient food and firewood for the bands involved. Connecting them all together, like a web, was a regional trail system. Walking was an efficient form of travel through the southern boreal forest and adjoining prairie parkland in summer because of the general lack of navigable streams, and some of these travelways came to be heavily used. Resting places sometimes featured offering stones. One of the more well-known in the area today is the "God Stone," located on the bank of the Red Deer River along the old trail from the Pasquia Hills to Nut Mountain (about fifteen miles northeast of Archerwill).[20]

In the spring of 1691, Kelsey sent a message to Governor Geyer at York Factory with a group of trading Cree. He reported on his efforts to increase the Indian trade, complaining that this work was hampered by constant fighting among various groups, and then asked for a number of specific trade items, considerably more than he had brought with him the year before. Kelsey seemed to have a better understanding, now that he had spent a year inland, of what goods were desired. Some of the things—from scissors to rings to combs— might have been gifts for his host families. There is also some speculation that he may have even taken a wife, something that went against HBC policy. He apparently insisted that the woman be allowed to enter York Factory upon his return there in 1692 and refused to enter the fort without her.[21]

The Cree returned to Deerings Point weeks later with the supplies and new instructions from Geyer. This time, in addition to his original assignment, Kelsey was "to search diligently for mines, minerals or drugs of what kind soever." He was also ordered to return to York Factory the following year "with as many Indians as he can."[22] It was Geyer's hope, according to a letter that he sent to the HBC London committee, that he would learn from Kelsey "the humour and nature of these strange people [that] I may know the better how to manage them at their arrival [at the bay]." The governor was also already planning to follow up on the Kelsey "example" and told the company that if he found "other young men qualified to undertake such a journey" that he would give them "all suitable encouragement."[23]

Kelsey did not leave Deerings Point until mid-summer, 15 July 1691. According to the first page of his daily journal, he set out "to discover & bring to a Commerce the Naywatame Poets."[24] Kelsey planned to travel with the Assiniboine again, perhaps the same group that had brought him inland from the bay the previous year, but they had left Deerings Point ten days earlier. He consequently headed after them with a group of trading Cree up the Saskatchewan River through the maze of channels and marshlands that make up the river delta. They soon portaged south to the Carrot River and resumed their travel westward to the Sipanok Channel, where on 18 July, Kelsey cached some of the trade supplies. The next day, the group set off on foot, a trip imperilled by their having "very little victuals." Even Kelsey's shooting of three (now extinct) passenger pigeons on 24 July did little to still their hunger.[25]

Over the next few days, Kelsey found "good footing for all yt [that] we had passed before was heavy mossy going." The hunters with the party, always on foraging side trips, also killed several "beasts." And he finally caught up with "our Indians [the Assiniboine]" who were "very glad … I was returned according to my promise."[26] But where was Kelsey? And how did he get there? There are no easy answers to these questions, but it becomes even more complicated because of the mileage Kelsey reported in his daily log. These distances, if miscalculated, can make sorting out his route even more challenging. It would appear that Kelsey generously overestimated the mileage covered, especially when compared to the experience of other travellers in the region.[27]

To try to resolve the question of where Kelsey went in the latter part of July, it is best to remember that he was part of an Assiniboine group—effectively, being led. His escorts would naturally have followed the extensive system of trails that crossed Indian territories and have been used for generations. The other clue is found in the invitation that Kelsey received from some "Indian strangers" to meet them at "Waskashreeseebee" (Red Deer [Elk] River *waskesiw sipiy)*, the only Cree place name found in Kelsey's 1691 journal. He and his companions reached there on 1 August. Based on what is known about these travelways today from archaeological research, Kelsey must have walked along the historic Greenbush Trail, the major north-south travelway that ran from the Shoal Lake area (south of the Saskatchewan delta/Carrot River) through the Pasquia Hills to the Red Deer Forks (where the Fir and Etomani Rivers meet). Some trail features nicely match his journal descriptions, especially his comments about going from wet to drier ground.[28]

The Indians that Kelsey was supposed to meet at the Red Deer Forks were not there by the time he arrived and so his group "followed their track." For the next two weeks, Kelsey and his party walked the trailways that paralleled the streams through the region, first south, then west and then south again to the Upper Assiniboine River, arriving at the aspen parklands near Sturgis, Saskatchewan. Throughout his travels, Kelsey met "strangers" but never the elusive Naywatame Poets who were apparently afraid of the Cree and Assiniboine because of the constant "warring" between them. He also experienced days where they were forced to "lye still" in camp because of the heavy summer showers that regularly rolled through the region, often accompanied by thunder. But what he found most striking was the transition to open prairie as they continued south towards the Touchwood Hills. On 20 August 1691, Kelsey's group pitched their tents on the "outtermost Edge of ye woods this plain affords Nothing but short Round sticky grass[29] & Buffillo." Two days later, they crossed "barren ground it being very dry heathy land &

BILL WAISER

During the summer of 1690, Kelsey entered the prairie parkland in
east-central Saskatchewan.

no water but here & there a small pond ... could not see ye woods on ye
other side."

These were long summer days that seemed to have no end, and Kelsey
and his companions feasted on bison that were killed in great numbers on the
prairie. One of the most effective hunting techniques, and one that Kelsey was
fortunate to witness, was the bison surround. "Now ye manner of their hunting
these Beast on ye barren ground," he explained in his journal, "is when they
see a great parcel of them together they surround them wth men wch done
they gather themselves into a smaller Compass Keeping ye Beast still in ye
middle & so shooting." Once the bison had been killed, it was "for the women
to fetch home ye meat & Dress it."[30]

On 25 August, Kelsey was joined by the Mountain Poets, an Assiniboine
group from the Porcupine Hills area of the Manitoba escarpment. He identified
their leader or "captain" as Washa, only one of two Aboriginal people named
in his journal. With the addition of the Mountain Poets, Kelsey's group now
numbered eighty tents. That so many people, perhaps as many as five hundred

BILL WAISER

Kelsey travelled with a group of trading Cree up the Saskatchewan River through the maze of channels and marshlands that make up the river delta.

to eight hundred, could come together in a single camp was made possible because of the great bison herds. Kelsey also learned to his chagrin that the Cree and Assiniboine planned to go to war against their enemies and he did everything possible to discourage them, even threatening that the HBC governor would henceforth refuse to trade with them. Worried that his mission to secure more trading partners would be spoiled, Kelsey made arrangements to meet with another unnamed Indian group with only a small escort party on 6 September, probably somewhere east of the Touchwood Hills or what he described as "their Enemies Country." Formally unwrapping a pipe that he brought from York Factory, Kelsey played the role of peacemaker and urged the Indians to hunt beaver and come to trade at the bay. "But all my arguments prevailed nothing," he confided in his journal. The Indians "knew not ye use of Cannoes & were resolved to go to wars."[31]

16

Kelsey had no sooner rejoined his group than he received word that the leader of the Naywatame Poets would meet with him. He first went to the Assiniboine, getting them to promise "not to disturb nor meddle" with their enemies, before travelling two days to meet with the group that he had been trying to contact for almost two months. On 12 September, Kelsey met with the Naywatame Poets' leader, participating in a pipe ceremony to confirm his friendly purpose and promising that the English would do all that they could to end tribal fighting. He then presented the captain with a coat and sash and several other presents, including one of his own guns. The leader, "very well pleased" by the gesture, accepted the invitation to meet at Deerings Point the following spring and travel with Kelsey to the bay.[32] But the Naywatame Poets never made the trip, according to Kelsey's last journal entry, because of a skirmish with the Cree that winter. The exact identity of this Indian group, in the meantime, has been subject to speculation. It was initially assumed that the Naywatame Poets were Gros Ventre (Fall or Rapid Indians), but more recently, it has been proposed that they were likely the Siouan-speaking Hidatsa. The confusion likely arises because the Gros Ventre and Hidatsa occupied present-day southwestern and southeastern Saskatchewan, respectively, at this time.[33] This uncertainty is just another example of how much of Kelsey's trip remains open to debate, even after three hundred years.

Kelsey returned to York Factory sometime in the late spring in 1692. His whereabouts over the winter, his second inland, and the identity of his companions are unknown. But he evidently used the time to prepare a brief account of Nayhaythaway (Cree) beliefs and customs, or "superstitions" as he termed them.[34] Kelsey approached the subject in a matter-of-fact manner, identifying several practices based on his observations over a two-year period. He noted how the sacred pipe stem had deep ritualistic purposes, how there were special songs for certain occasions, how men wore feathered bonnets when they went to war, and how a talisman was used to improve hunting. He also reported on gender relations—how women were treated little better than dogs and forbidden from certain ceremonies—but said little about the place of children. Nor did he mention anything about the Cree propensity for humour. His most interesting comments, based on discussions he had with his hosts, concerned the afterlife, the significance of the sun and its position in the sky, the centrality of dreams and visions, and the role of shamans. It was evident that these were religious people whose world and surroundings were filled with spiritual meanings. It also appears that Kelsey was skeptical of some of the things he had been told, suggesting that his informants would "pretend" at times, such as when they spoke about heaven.[35]

Kelsey went home to England in the fall of 1693, having completed his contract with the HBC, but signed on again the following spring and sailed back to York Factory with the summer supply ships. He was there for less than two months when the French, fighting the English in other parts of North America during the War of the Grand Alliance (1688–97), decided to extend the struggle to the Bay region. In early October 1695, Canadian Pierre le Moyne d'Iberville easily captured York Factory (renamed Fort Bourbon) and pitched Kelsey and other company employees outside the fort to fend for themselves over the winter. Repatriated to England by 1696, Kelsey was part of the Royal Navy force that retook York Factory late that summer. But in 1697, d'Iberville was back again in the *Pélican* and, after beating a larger English force in the greatest arctic sea battle in Canadian history, accepted the surrender of the garrison at York Factory, including Kelsey. French control of the entire west side of Hudson Bay was subsequently confirmed in the 1697 Treaty of Ryswick.

Kelsey's career with the HBC was not over though. He returned to the bay in 1698, only this time to Fort Albany on the west coast of James Bay, and spent the better part of the next fifteen years developing the trade of the region, especially the nearby East Main. September 1714 found him back at York Factory as deputy governor to accept the handover of the fort under the terms of the Treaty of Utrecht, which formally ended the War of Spanish Succession (1702–13) and awarded the English control of the entire bay region. Kelsey oversaw the rebuilding of York Factory and then worked at expanding the trade north of the Churchill River, while investigating rumours about possible

BILL WAISER

Kelsey was part of a large Cree and Assiniboine camp that feasted on the bison of the northern plains during the summer of 1691.

copper deposits in the region. He was named governor of the post in 1717 and then head of all the HBC bay settlements the following year; at that point in his HBC career, he had served the company for almost thirty-five years. Kelsey was recalled to England in 1722 and died in East Greenwich two years later, at age fifty-seven, survived by his wife Elizabeth and three children. He had lived two-thirds of his life in subarctic Canada.

It is not certain whether Kelsey had ever intended to write a fuller account of his inland trip. His death, so soon after his retirement from the HBC, prevented him from doing so—if he planned to do it. He certainly had the opportunity to prepare a more complete chronicle of his two years in the western interior during one of his many winters at bayside, but again, never did so. During his time as governor at York Factory, he also never commented about being acquainted with the inland Cree and Assiniboine or being familiar with their country. The only known reference to the trip in his later correspondence came in 1722 when he was recalled to England: "I was sent away wt ye stone Indians in whose Country I remaind 2 years Enduring much hardships."[36] This silence on Kelsey's part might seem peculiar, if not surprising, but the company had no desire to pursue the young servant's initiative. It preferred to continue to concentrate its trading activities at the bay. After all, the reason Governor Geyer had sent him inland was to persuade more Indian groups to make the annual spring trading trip to York Factory—and not open a new post on the southern edge of the boreal forest. That is why Kelsey was instructed to meet with the Naywatame Poets—they were supposed to become new bayside trading partners—and why he tried to discourage intertribal fighting in favour of expanding the area that the bayside trade drew upon.

Kelsey, for his part, seemed prepared to go back inland when he returned to York Factory in the summer of 1694 after spending the winter in England. But he sensed that the HBC leadership was against these kinds of endeavours. "[F]or my own part," he wrote rather cryptically in August 1694, "I shall neither do nor act on any discovery untill I receive further orders from my masters in England."[37] Such orders were not forthcoming, and Kelsey never engaged in any exploratory activity until much later, when as governor of all the bay posts, he made two sailing trips along the northwest coast of Hudson Bay in 1719 and 1721, ostensibly to bring the Inuit of the region into the trade. Nor did the HBC send anyone else to the prairie parkland in the following decades to follow up Kelsey's lead. Any information that he may have brought back about the interior geography never appeared on company maps at that time.[38]

Even the commercial success of Kelsey's trip—the very reason for sending him inland—was shortlived. There may have been a dramatic boost in trade upon his return to York Factory—the total number of beaver skins traded at all HBC posts nearly quadrupled (from 24,236 to 92,117 Made Beaver) between 1692 and 1693[39]—but he generally failed in his efforts to bring about peace among the warring tribes and get more groups directly involved in the fur trade. The French capture of the post in the fall of 1694, moreover, ushered in a period of instability and uncertainty. It would be another two decades before the HBC regained absolute control of the bay trade. The hiatus did nothing to change the company's bayside business strategy, and it simply resumed its traditional trade in 1714. Kelsey faithfully supported the policy, and by the time he became governor of all Canadian operations, York Factory stood out in the constellation of bay posts. The growing volume of trade never blinded Kelsey to the importance of maintaining good relations with the HBC's Indian partners. He once reprimanded a fellow officer for being discourteous. In an apparent effort to facilitate trade relations, he also prepared a pamphlet, *A Dictionary of Hudson's Bay Indian Language*, that the company printed and distributed to all posts in the expectation that servants would learn Cree.[40] This alertness to Aboriginal sensibilities may have been cultivated during Kelsey's two years inland, but it likely had as much to do with the fact that he lived more than half his life in Indian territory during his HBC tenure.

In summing up Henry Kelsey's 1690–92 trip, one historian has called the journey "an isolated feat."[41] A respected geographer, on the other hand, has suggested that his travels were "just brief highlights" in a Canadian career that should be considered in its entirety, an extraordinary thirty-eight years, punctuated by only short absences in England.[42] But it would be equally instructive to look at Kelsey's odyssey from the inside, to open the lens and shift the focus to consider a different perspective rather than that perpetuated in the Jefferys portrait. In other words, who he went with and how he went are just as important as where he went and what he saw. It must also be remembered that because Kelsey was a stranger, the landscape did not speak to him the same way that it spoke to his Indian companions. As an outsider, someone new to the unfamiliar prairie environment, he lacked the experience, the understanding, but above all the stories, that gave meaning to the "inland country of good report."[43]

Kelsey was allowed to enter an Aboriginal world that had its own distinct territories, nations, traditions, and legends. Much like nation-states of Europe at the time, the Cree and the Assiniboine actively cooperated as allies and fought enemy groups, depending on changing circumstances and how they perceived their interests and needs. They were also pedestrian societies—there were no horses in the region—who knew the land and its rhythms intimately and successfully exploited a rich and diverse range of natural resources, especially the great bison herds, from season to season and from place to place. Nor did these resilient, adaptive people squander opportunities. In the two decades since the establishment of the HBC in 1670, the Cree and Assiniboine had deliberately altered their annual cycle to make the difficult two-to-three-week canoe trip to York Factory on the southwest coast of Hudson Bay and secure trade goods that were readily incorporated into their material culture. Welcoming Kelsey and taking him into their lives on their home ground was also seen to be in their interest, not just for trade purposes but for what they might learn about his world and why the English were there on their doorstep. At the same time, they shrewdly sought to take advantage of their geographic position by controlling, if not preventing, access to English trade items, especially guns, by other inland Indian groups. Kelsey's failure to get the Naywatame Poets to travel to the bay was largely the result of Cree resistance, something that he did not seem to comprehend. There would be other misunderstandings, sometimes painful difficulties, if not outright disputes, between Natives and newcomers. But Henry Kelsey's 1690–92 visit served notice that Indian and mixed-descent peoples would be the dominant force, not supporting actors, in the early history of Saskatchewan and that this story would be as much about the environment as it would about the players involved.

In places, the South Saskatchewan River occupies an ancient glacial spillway.

RELIABLY UNRELIABLE

IT WAS A PRISTINE ENVIRONMENT. SO THOUGHT HUDSON'S BAY COMPANY SERVANT Henry Kelsey when he visited Saskatchewan's prairie parkland over three hundred years ago. He breathed in air that was clear, fresh, and invigorating, quite unlike that of his home in England. He tramped across vast, open grasslands that were swallowed up by the distant horizon. And he came upon great gatherings of animals, whose numbers defied imagination, from bison herds that stretched for miles to flocks of waterfowl that filled the sky. Kelsey is generally regarded as one of the first European newcomers to the region who was lucky enough to see the land in its natural condition, an Eden-like setting that seemed to have been made just the day before. The apparent perfection, a place undisturbed and untouched, was illusory. What Kelsey actually experienced during his travels was a natural world quite different from the one that existed when humans first arrived in the western interior some ten thousand to twelve thousand years earlier. The region's ecosystems were never static, as if fixed in time and space, but dynamic and always changing, even without human interference, because of their continuous response to changing physical conditions, especially climate. "Disturbance is the natural state," one environmental historian has observed, "and adjustment to it is ongoing and fundamental."[1] Kelsey's encounter with the natural world of west-central Saskatchewan is consequently best understood as a snapshot of a particular place at a particular time.

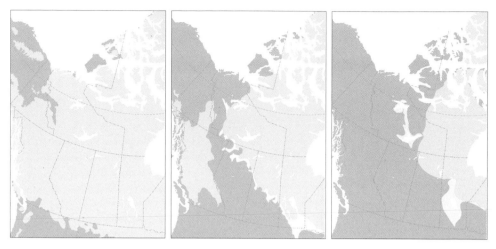

Wisconsinan glacier over western Canada (18,000 years BP [maximum],
11,000 years BP, and 9,000 years BP)

Step back some eighteen thousand years ago to what is known as the late
Pleistocene interval, and most of present-day Saskatchewan was under a
mantle of ice as much as a mile thick in places. The only areas that escaped the
southward reach of the Laurentide Ice Sheet were the summits of the Cypress
Hills and possibly Wood Mountain because the ice likely flowed around them
rather than over them. This last interval of glaciation, the Wisconsinan, was
nothing less than an extreme makeover of the face of the land. Or as one
specialist observed, "Glaciation essentially 'reset the clock' for soils, plants, and
animals ... by scraping clean the land surface."[2]

In advancing southwestward from Hudson Bay, the heavy ice gradually
scraped and smoothed out the Precambrian bedrock of the Canadian Shield.
Thousands of years later, water from the melting ice sheet filled any scoured-
out depressions and channels to create a maze of hundreds of lakes amidst
irregular bedrock ridges, all interlaced by rivers, many with rapids and the
occasional waterfall. From above, the drainage pattern seems fractured, almost
jumbled—what geomorphologists refer to as "deranged" drainage-—but a
glance at the map shows that the lakes generally align with the northeast to
southwest direction of the ice flow, except where intercepted by fault lines.
The impact of the ice sheet on the southern interior plains, by contrast, was
largely depositional.

BILL WAISER

Erratics litter the landscape today in the western block of Grasslands National Park in southwestern Saskatchewan.

Around seventeen thousand years ago, as the ice sheet began to melt away, any ice-carried debris was left behind, stacked as it were, in a series of drift deposits from 330 to 980 feet (100 to 300 m) in thickness—a kind of "unmade bed of glacial rubble ... lying exactly where it dropped."[3] Today, the most obvious reminder of the last Ice Age are bands of moraines, like the rolling Eagle Hills between Purdue and Biggar. These high, often elongated, ridges stand out from the plains throughout southern Saskatchewan and often run parallel to the former position of the ice sheet's retreating margin. Elsewhere, ice-thrust bedrock has formed prominent uplands, such as the Cactus and Dirt Hills south of Regina—a vivid testament to the ice sheet's enormous power to erode and configure the land. This ice-sculpted terrain gives the lie to the popular belief that the province is uniformly flat. The other telltale remnant of glaciation are erratics, large boulders that were carried great distances by the ice sheet and then deposited here and there in isolation about the landscape

29

BILL WAISER

Grasslands are exceedingly resilient, not only to changing climatic conditions but also to fire.

as the ice melted. Their name derives from the fact that the lithology or rock type of these big stones often differs from the local bedrock—hence erratic. The most famous in the province was probably Mistaseni (from the Cree *mistasiniy*) that had been left lying in the Qu'Appelle Valley near the elbow of the South Saskatchewan River. Thought to resemble a resting buffalo, the massive four hundred-ton erratic was a sacred Aboriginal site for millennia until it was blown up in 1966 during construction of the South Saskatchewan River Dam project.

Glaciation also influenced the course of rivers in the region. Although the land gradually sloped to the northeast toward Hudson Bay, meltwater along the ice margin was initially blocked from flowing in that direction by the massive ice sheet. Because the rapidly accumulating water could not be contained and had to go somewhere, it carved deep, trench-like spillways that ran roughly parallel to the margin of the receding ice front. The North Saskatchewan and Qu'Appelle Rivers, with their steep, seemingly oversized valley running east-west in places, are good examples of these ancient glacial channels. As new terrain was uncovered, meltwater also began to collect in huge proglacial lakes. The largest in North America was Agassiz, which at its maximum extent covered much of central Saskatchewan and southern Manitoba and held a greater volume of water than all of the Great Lakes today. Because of the volatile conditions, the size, shape, and location of Lake Agassiz was constantly in flux. It drained, for example, in different directions at different times, creating spillways across the western interior that were eventually occupied by the rivers of the region—from the Battle, Frenchman, and Souris to the Qu'Appelle and South Saskatchewan. Where the silt-laden meltwaters flowed into the lake, meanwhile, large deltas formed, which gradually evolved into low-lying marshy areas, such as between Nipawin and Cumberland House in west-central Saskatchewan or at the north end of Last Mountain Lake. When the lake finally emptied, it left behind the level, seemingly perfectly flat plains (glacial-lacustrine deposits) commonly associated with Saskatchewan, especially in the Regina area. Sand dunes found here and there throughout the province are also a relic of Agassiz, because of strong winds that whipped up and reworked the dried lake sediments.[4]

Once the ice sheet had melted away, the landscape began to stabilize and the frozen ground began to thaw, so that by around ten thousand to twelve thousand years ago, soils began to develop, while plants and animals re-colonized the region. Humans also made an appearance as hunter-gatherers. What this world looked like at the time, before the existence of documentary and instrumental records, is largely based on information that can be unlocked from "proxy" indicators of climate. These records, ranging from lake sediments to peatland deposits, provide snapshots of the vegetation in the distant past by capturing and preserving biophysical data. Ancient pollen samples from lake bottoms, for example, suggest that plant populations took root immediately after deglaciation, during what is known at the early Holocene interval, but that new vegetation cover was sparse and patchy because of varying soil and moisture conditions. Whereas grasses, forbs, and shrubs were initially limited to the present-day southwestern part of Saskatchewan, most of the province was covered by open boreal forest, dominated by conifers, especially white spruce, because of the cool climate. It was not until the climate moderated, became warmer and drier, that the coniferous forest became confined to more northern areas, while grassland vegetation became established in the south. Remnants of this coniferous forest, occasional patches of spruce and pine, can be found today stranded at higher elevations throughout the prairie west.[5]

Much of the animal life of the late Pleistocene interval experienced a different fate—extinction. When palaeontologists started to unearth fossils from this interval in western Canada, they found that "the hugest, and fiercest, and strangest forms"[6] were all gone. These megafauna, as they were called, had included mammoths and mastodons, several types of horses, two kinds of giant bison, a sabretooth cat (*Smilodon*) and lion (*Panthera*), a ground sloth, and the appropriately named Yesterday's Camel. In all, close to fifty distinct species, representing more than half the genera of large mammals, disappeared across North America by about eleven thousand years ago. It is all the more perplexing because many of the plants, shrubs, and trees on which they grazed and browsed were still there.

Several theories have been put forward to explain this mass extinction. The most recent—and strongly criticized—contends that a comet or some other object smashed into northern Canada 12,900 years ago, precipitating a cataclysmic event that the large terrestrial animals that once roamed central Saskatchewan could not survive. But if the great woolly mammoth and other megafauna were wiped out, then why not other smaller species, especially because they would have fallen victim to the same trauma? A more plausible explanation is that the climatic changes at the end of the last ice age created environmental stresses that proved too much for the large land animals. The warmer, drier climate introduced a new vegetation pattern, one where the central mixed woodlands gave way to vast open grasslands. But here again, one wonders why only certain species could not cope with the new climatic

Bison was the dominant species on the northern Great Plains.

BILL WAISER

regime, while others readily adjusted to the new emerging ecosytems. The other likely trigger was people, whose arrival at the end of deglaciation just happened to coincide with the sudden disappearance of several large grazing species and their predators. Could these hunters have driven their prey into extinction? This hypothesis has proven controversial, if not unpalatable, for it calls into question the popular notion that early peoples lived in harmony with nature. Something happened to these Pleistocene animals. Maybe it was a combination of both factors: habitat change made the great beasts vulnerable and, as a consequence, it did not take much for humans to push them over the precipice.[7] The loss of so many mega-mammals reduced or better yet simplified the number of animal species dominant in the region to a select few.

No animal has a closer association in the historical consciousness with the western environment than do the bison (*Bison bison*). But people get their name wrong, incorrectly calling them buffalo, a species native to Africa and Asia. This champion ruminant, which first appeared around 5000 BP [Before Present], was a more compact or dwarf version of its North American ancestors: the massive *Bison latifrons*, which was not only twice the size of the modern bison but equipped with six-foot-long curving horns, and *Bison antiquus*, a slightly smaller animal with a distinctive hairy mane. It also did not move into western Canada from the north, but was already in southern North America (having migrated earlier from northeast Asia) and dispersed northward to re-occupy the land after glaciation. Recent genetic research indicates that all modern bison are descendants of the population that once lived south of the continental ice sheets.[8]

The modern bison was a perfect fit for the plains environment because of the ready availability of forage and water. What it had lost in size from its ancient ancestors, it made up in speed and agility. Reaching speeds of thirty-five miles an hour, the bison was a locomotive on legs. Add its keen sense of smell, and it is easy to understand why it had few natural predators. Ironically, what often determined the animal's life span—usually thirty to forty years—was the wear of its teeth from the intense grazing of coarse grasses. The bison also came equipped to deal with the harsh climate. Its horns could be used to crater snow—swinging its head from side to side—to get at grass and forbs. Bulls also had smaller scrotums to prevent their testes from freezing, while cows had a shorter gestation period so that calves were more likely to survive the cold winters.

The bison soon spread throughout the southern half of present-day Saskatchewan because conditions were ideal for its emergence as *the* dominant species. Not only had the late Pleistocene extinctions created vacant grazing niches, but also the warming conditions had expanded the area to be grazed. But what really enabled the bison to proliferate and flood the open grasslands by the hundreds of thousands, soon to be millions, was its high reproductive rate, about 15 to 20 per cent per year. One western historian has even argued that it is best to think of the bison at this time as a "weed species."[9] Others have more accurately called it a "keystone species"[10] because it was not only

The Great Sand Hills in southwestern Saskatchewan were re-activated during intervals of prolonged drought.

superbly adapted to the post-glacial prairie environment, but more important, its grazing habits and movements were absolutely fundamental to the operation of the ecosystem.

What sustained this great biomass were the grasslands, something that does not seem possible to those, especially outsiders, who associate the peculiar plains environment with deficiency. How could a region devoid of trees satisfy the daily dietary requirements of so many animals? But the native grasses that had evolved were "an expression of the drought-prone prairie climate and a living response to the geography of the midcontinent."[11] Because of the rain shadow cast by the Rocky Mountains, precipitation was generally sparse in the western interior, usually falling during the summer months, when not a drought year. The amount of rainfall was further influenced by the northeast-to-southwest rise in elevation from below 650 to about 3,900 feet (200 to 1,200 m); annual precipitation levels tended to decline along this east-west gradient in direct opposition to elevation, ranging on average from more than 20 inches (500 mm) in the northeast to less than 12 inches (300 mm) in the southwest. The other complicating factor was the region's location in the centre of the continent, well away from the moderating influence of any ocean. Temperature extremes were consequently the norm rather than the exception. Winters were mercilessly long and quite cold at times under the influence of arctic high pressure ridges, while in summer, daytime heating often generated late-day menacing thunder heads that led to convective storms, complete with lightning and strong winds and sometimes hail. In general, the overall moisture deficit in the climate ledger meant that evaporation exceeded precipitation on an annual basis.

The open southern grasslands responded best to these climate limitations, while the boreal forests were confined to the north. The leaves and stems of the grassland plants above the ground were dwarfed by the amount of root growth below the surface, which comprised as much as 80 per cent of the organism's weight. Prairie grasses were therefore exceedingly resilient, not only to episodes of prolonged drought, but also to the constant fires that swept

The boreal forest covers half of present-day Saskatchewan.

indiscriminately through the region. When it rained or when burned-over sections cooled, seemingly dead or otherwise withered plants were poised, ready to green up, flourish, and flower. The grasslands were like a mosaic "with patches of vegetation of varying sizes in varying stages of recovery ... a system that achieve[d] stability by responding constructively to continual challenges."[12]

The specific kinds of grass communities were also a reflection of local conditions, especially rainfall. In the southern short-grass prairie district, bison could graze on wheat grass, June grass, blue grama, and spear grasses, often stunted by the moisture-starved climate, but still rich in carbohydrates. Farther north, in the mixed-grass prairie, as the name implies, they fed on a denser mixture of tall and short grass species—ranging from blue grama to spear and wheat grasses to fescues—that provided much-needed protein in winter. Even with the heavy grazing, droughts, and fires, the grasses produced surplus root fibres that gradually broke down over time to provide the organic matters in soils. The density, colour, and richness of the earth was a reflection of the plant cover and, of course, the climate. The most fertile soils were found along the edge of the boreal forest or in the moister east where tall grasses thrived.[13]

Bison grazing habits were deeply attuned to this dynamic interplay between grasses, climate, and fire, and their movement through the region was rarely the same. But bison simply did not wander from place to place, indiscriminately grazing here and there. They remembered exactly where the best grasses were to be found and revisited favourite sites through a season to create distinct boundaries between grazed and ungrazed areas. They also fed only upon certain dominant grasses, even in burned-over areas, leaving behind forbs and woody plants to thrive in areas that had otherwise been defoliated. Nor did bison remain on the same grazing ground year after year but migrated to feed on grasses in nearby areas; they soon came back to the same grazed-over patches because the new plant growth had been enhanced by nitrogen-rich urine from their last visit. Even the bison habit of wallowing, rubbing, and rolling around the ground on their backs to create shallow depressions produced micro-habitats that supported vegetation different from the surrounding prairie. Bison consequently had a profound influence on the biodiversity of the grasslands—so much so that their grazing activities over space and time have been characterized as "landscape-level forces."[14] Remove the bison and the whole ecology of the grasslands changes.

Even though bison were the undisputed masters of the grasslands environment, the great herds were probably not prepared for what has become known as the Hypsithermal interval (also called the Holocene Thermal Maximum [HTM]), a period of centuries-long aridity, as long as four thousand years, that held the region in a stranglehold from about nine thousand to five thousand years ago during the Middle Holocene period. The exact cause of this dramatic climate change is not known. It might have been increased sunspot activity. More recently, it has been attributed to changes in the earth's orbit, which in turn affected what happened at the earth's surface, such as a decided shift in Pacific air masses and wind patterns. What is known with greater certainty, though, is that average annual temperatures rose as much as three degrees Celsius higher than current values, while humidity and moisture levels decreased dramatically. The upshot was a general northward shift in vegetation patterns. These changes, moreover, were time-transgressive. It not only took time for the climate change to be reflected in the vegetation, but the timing and impact of the change varied across the western interior.[15]

Once again, plant and tree pollen assemblages, painstakingly secured from ancient sediments dating back to the Hypsithermal, have been analyzed to reconstruct the vegetation record. In the northern half of the province, warmer summer temperatures encouraged the boreal forest to move into the region now occupied by tundra in the Northwest Territories. The boreal forest, meanwhile, experienced a pronounced increase in jack pine, a species that needs fire to crack open its seed cones and regenerate. Along the southern margin of the forest, in the transitional zone, the greatest vegetation change took place. Here, in the open aspen parkland, fires constantly consumed any tree and brush cover, while the prairie grasslands infiltrated burned-over areas. Warmer, drier weather also inhibited peat production in low-lying, normally marshy areas, as well as reduced the size and depth of sloughs; most closed water bodies increased in salinity. Over time, the Hypsithermal drove a dramatic shift from grassland to forest across the central region of the province. It was as if there was an imaginary line demarking where one ecotone abruptly ended and another abruptly started.[16]

These drier conditions favoured the grasslands, which used the arid conditions to extend northward into parkland and forested areas. But the persistent drought also took its toll on the prairies. Grasses were thinned out or replaced outright by drought-tolerant plants that were better adapted to the desert-like conditions. Shallow sloughs dried up and became desiccated, much like the surrounding landscape. Hot, drying winds scooped up the dry loose ground and whipped it into dust storms that deposited the churning soil along ridges or any other obstacle that stood in the way of the swirling dust. There is an on-going debate whether the Hypsithermal drove the bison from the interior plains. The poor range conditions, it has been argued, could not support millions of grazing animals; there was simply not enough forage for them. But whether the bison disappeared completely from the region for two thousand years is extremely doubtful, especially because the mountain-fed Saskatchewan River continued to flow and the zone of short-grass prairie probably increased. It is more likely that the herds altered their seasonal grazing patterns to deal with the drier conditions, as well as decreased in size in response to the reduced carrying capacity of the land.[17] This reduction was probably accelerated by the now extinct Rocky Mountain locust, a large grasshopper whose numbers darkened the sky as it descended to chew its way through drought-stricken grasses.

Around fifty-five hundred to two thousand years ago, the climate of the western interior changed again, this time becoming wetter and cooler, in many respects much closer to the climate that existed when Henry Kelsey visited

BILL WAISER

The Missouri Coteau plateau is normally drier than the rest of Saskatchewan because of limited precipitation.

the region. These new conditions, once again time-transgressive across the western interior, reversed the earlier northward shift of the boreal forest in the northeast part of the province, and the woodland became more open with a greater frequency of bogs and fens between sparse black spruce stands. The forest, at the same time, evolved into two roughly distinct zones. The northern boreal region, running in a band across the Canadian Shield, was predominately a dense or "closed" coniferous forest, featuring jack pine, with some white spruce and a scattering of white birch and other hardwoods on higher ground, and black spruce and tamarack on the lower wetlands. The southern boreal region, by contrast, became mixed-wood forest, with trees often in pure stands, consisting of white spruce, aspen, balsam poplar, white birch, and balsam fir. The richer soils, unlike the thin soil layer in the shield country, combined with the longer, warmer growing season, supported bigger trees. Giant white spruce could boast a girth of more than three feet (1 m) and reach over eighty feet (25 m) in height. Marshes, muskegs, and fens were also more common because of wide, open stretches of wet, low-lying terrain, sometimes intercepted by lazy, winding streams or punctuated by the occasional shallow lake, surrounded by brush and scrubby jack pine. Lightning remained a major threat, and fire the major regenerative force.

The boreal forest, covering half of the present-day province, was populated by large hoofed animals or ungulates, from moose and woodland caribou, particularly in the north, to deer, elk (wapiti), and bison, which wintered in sheltered areas along the southern edge. It was also prime real estate for beaver and muskrat and other fur-bearing animals like the squirrel, snowshoe hare, and timber wolf, the north's major year-round predator. Fish were equally abundant—mostly walleye (pickerel), whitefish, arctic grayling, lake trout, and northern pike—and thrived in the clear waterways of the shield country. What was perhaps most surprising was the great number of different species of plants and birds found in the region. Not only were there, for example, from four hundred to five hundred different kinds of vascular plants, but a diverse number of avifauna during the breeding season—one survey has pegged the number of bird species at over two hundred.[18]

The aspen parklands, which straddled the boundary between forest and prairie, likely expanded and became more densely treed under the influence of the cooler, wetter climate. But the aspen, poplar, and green ash were still suppressed by repeated fires that swept in from the grasslands. Even then, trembling aspen, so named because of the shaking or quaking nature of its leaves, could readily recover because new tree shoots arose from the extensive root system even when the above-ground growth had been killed.[19] Aspen stands were hardier near the southern edge of the forest and then thinned out to the south, where they were largely restricted to north-facing slopes in depressions and moraine-based uplands. These same sites, if particularly moist, were often shared with tall shrubs, such as saskatoon and chokecherry. Grasslands, on the other hand, were generally limited to sunnier and drier south-facing slopes at the northern edge of the parkland and then became more pronounced towards the drier regions of the south. The dominant grass was fescue, a taller, denser, and rougher species than found in the mixed and dried-mixed grasslands. This fescue prairie was nutritious for grazers and attracted foraging animals from out of the forest and in from the grasslands. The region's wetlands also sustained a rich faunal life, but unlike the boreal forest to the north, water levels were prone to greater fluctuations because of the generally drier climate. It is worth noting that the region where Kelsey travelled in July 1691—in east-central Saskatchewan probably between Endeavour and Preeceville—supports the greatest bird diversity in North America.[20]

The end of the Hypsithermal finally released the southern grasslands from the grip of centuries-long aridity. The grasses became thicker and more diverse, while water bodies, like Kenosee Lake in the southeastern part of the province, became deeper and less saline.[21] Whether the land was covered in mixed-grass prairie or short-grass prairie depended on the soil, the elevation, but mostly precipitation. Mixed-grass prairie generally covered the more northern and northeasterly regions of the grassland, while only short-grass prairie grew in the southwest, beyond the Missouri Couteau or third prairie steppe, where

The Cypress Hills has a microclimate that is both cooler and wetter because of its higher elevation.

the terrain was higher and considerably drier. Trees—in this case, aspen, birch, poplar, and cottonwood—were largely confined to more sheltered and moister locales such as river valleys, bottom lands, and coulees. The one exception was the Cypress Hills in the southwest corner of the province, a prairie oasis that had escaped glaciation, which at 3,900 feet (1,200 m) elevation, towered over the surrounding plains by more than 1,300 feet (400 m). The higher elevation produced a microclimate that was both cooler and wetter. The vegetation was different, too. Fescue prairie, more common to the parkland, skirted the bottom of the hills. Higher up, there were forests of white spruce and lodgepole pine, species that flourished in the Rocky Mountain foothills, several hundred miles away to the west. These distinctive characteristics certainly made the Cypress Hills an anomaly on the open, dry short-grass prairies. For the people and animals that secured food and shelter there, it was a refuge.

Apart from fire and climate, the major transformative force on the prairies remained the great bison herds. Their passage through a region decimated the vegetation to a few isolated stands of ravaged grass, forbs, and shrubs. What forage they did not consume got trampled by the millions of hooved feet or flattened by their wallowing on the ground. Grasses were able to cope with this trauma by immediately growing new shoots. The other dominant prairie animal was the pronghorn (*Antilocapra americana*).[22] A survivor of the great extinctions and the only species in its family—it is not related to the African antelope— the pronghorn rivalled the bison in number. There might have been as many as thirty-five million in the Great Plains region at Kelsey's time. Fortunately, they did not compete with bison for the same food, preferring shrubs and forbs to grass. They were also much swifter, able to run up to sixty miles an hour for great distances. This speed, the fastest of any animal in North America,

The prairie pothole region of central and southern Saskatchewan is a prime waterfowl breeding ground.

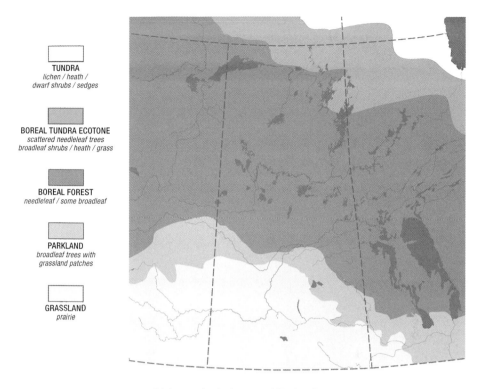

TUNDRA
*lichen / heath /
dwarf shrubs / sedges*

BOREAL TUNDRA ECOTONE
*scattered needleleaf trees
broadleaf shrubs / heath / grass*

BOREAL FOREST
needleleaf / some broadleaf

PARKLAND
*broadleaf trees with
grassland patches*

GRASSLAND
prairie

Major ecological zones of Saskatchewan

when combined with their sharp eyesight, kept pronghorn out of the clutches of prairie predators, such as wolves, coyotes, cougars, and grizzlies. But what often proved their undoing was their curiosity. A pronghorn would no sooner run away from trouble than return to investigate anything different or unusual. Their congregation after the rut in large herds for the winter months also made them targets for communal hunting.[23]

Dominance by a few species on the prairies did not extend to birds. More than two hundred species used the region for breeding grounds, among them a dozen or so songbirds that deliberately colonized the grasslands, nesting on the open bare ground, in a clump of grass, or in the shade of some shrub. These species included Baird's sparrow, lark bunting, and bobolink, but probably not the mountain bluebird, which is only a recent migrant to the region.[24] Their voices, rising above a carpet of wildflowers or sung from the skies overhead, belied the notion that the prairies were a barren, deficient place. The prime bird-breeding area, meanwhile, was the prairie pothole region of central

45

DROUGHT AS RECORDED BY TREE RINGS

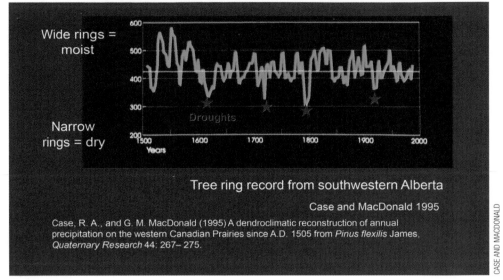

Tree ring record from southwestern Alberta

Case and MacDonald 1995

Case, R. A., and G. M. MacDonald (1995) A dendroclimatic reconstruction of annual precipitation on the western Canadian Prairies since A.D. 1505 from *Pinus flexilis* James, *Quaternary Research* 44: 267– 275.

Tree ring data has been used to document continual climatic variability.

and southern Saskatchewan, so named because of the shallow, water-filled depressions—like potholes in a road in spring—left behind by the retreating glaciers. These small sloughs or ponds might appear inconsequential, but their location, on the major north-south migratory flyway, and their numbers, in the tens of thousands, made them ideal breeding grounds for waterfowl. It is not too exaggerated to suggest that they served as the "duck factory" of the continental interior.[25]

The prairie pothole region was one of the best indicators of the climate variability experienced by the western interior. Ephemeral ponds always disappear during the summer, but exactly when depended on the snow-melt runoff and rainfall. Semi-permanent ones might survive the entire summer, but if not recharged by winter snowfall, dry up late the next spring. Precipitation and evaporation also had a direct bearing on salinity; if the pond was not continually recharged each season, then the water became brackish (less drinkable) and able to support only certain kinds of aquatic life. These kinds of changes were not predictable from year to year according to some master schedule. Instead, the ecological reality across the region was dynamic and random change. Even though the climate two thousand years ago came to more closely approximate the climate today, variability remained the defining characteristic—not simply from season to season, but also from place to place.[26] One writer has half-jokingly summed up the weather situation as "reliably unreliable."[27]

This idea of constant variability goes against the practice of dividing recent worldwide climate shifts into the Medieval Warm Period (sometimes known as the Medieval Climatic Anomaly), when the climate was notably warmer and drier for about four centuries (1000 to 600 BP), followed by the Little Ice Age, which marked some five centuries of cooler, unstable climate (until about 150 years ago). These broad climatic patterns can certainly be read in the proxy data collected in western Canada. There were clearly defined periods of extreme drought, lasting several decades (between 950 and 1350 AD), contrasted with bouts of climatic severity, especially low summer temperatures, colder winters, and glacier advances in the Rocky Mountains (from about 1350 to 1880 AD). Indeed, the climate appears to "flip" from one state (arid) to another (moister) quite rapidly around 1200 AD. But these climate "intervals" can be too simplistic because they fail to account for variability, if not complexity. Ancient tree-ring sequences that capture growing conditions of the past few centuries, especially precipitation variability during the so-called Little Ice Age, point to periods of warm climate, even intense, multi-year droughts (1670s, 1720s, and 1790s) that were considerably worse than the 1930s. Nor were climatic conditions always the same across the entire region, but localized in terms of timing, intensity, and duration. Tree-ring data indicate that some areas escaped drought, whereas other areas suffered. In other words, there were both north-south and east-west variations in the incidence of drought on the Great Plains. That was certainly the case for Henry Kelsey's inland trip. He had the pleasure of visiting western Canada during the coldest twenty-year period (1685–1704) in the past one thousand years, but at the same time, climatic conditions varied across the region: a severe dry spell gripped the eastern prairies, while cooler summers descended on western Alberta.[28]

Kelsey, for his part, was oblivious to this climatic variability, having spent only two years in the western interior. Besides, as a visitor, he was reacting to the environment for the first time and, unlike his Indian hosts, did not possess any long-term perspective over several lifetimes. He could not place himself in the landscape, let alone begin to know and read its ways. Nor did he realize that the land and its history were actually quite old. Instead, it was all new and strange to him. That was certainly the case when Kelsey encountered the open grasslands. In his 1691 journal, he repeatedly used the term "barren ground" to describe the unfamiliar prairie landscape. But this same barren region was home to the great bison herds that fed him and his companions. Kelsey never seemed to appreciate this apparent contradiction—that the supposedly empty grasslands generously supported Indian peoples—but rather complained at one point that his group had lost its way "by reason of so many beaten paths wch ye buffillo makes."[29] All he could see was what was not there. If he had stayed longer, he might have come to a better understanding of the diverse and rich environment and how its dynamic nature was partly "choreographed by the rhythms of earth, weather, fire, and buffalo."[30] He would have also learned that Indians were essential partners in this dance and manipulated and controlled the landscape in sophisticated ways to ensure their survival and future welfare.

The Clovis culture used elongated, fluted projectile points on their hunting weapons.

CHAPTER TWO

I SHALL HOWL

IN APRIL 1963, FARMER EARL GRAY WAS OUT WALKING HIS LAND NORTHWEST OF Swift Current, checking whether it was dry enough for seeding. On a south-facing hillside, where the wind had carved out a depression in the sandy soil, he spotted a human skull. Gray alerted the local Royal Canadian Mounted Police detachment, and it was determined that the remains were quite ancient. Excavations over several years revealed that the Gray homestead sat atop a burial ground that had been used for over two thousand years, starting around five thousand years ago, and that it contained the remains of probably more than five hundred people. In many instances, bones from the skeletal remains of the dead had been bundled and buried together, sometimes on top of other bone bundles. The people in the graveyard had also died young. Few of the remains were older than forty years, while more than half of the bones were those of children and infants. Some of the burials included dogs, whose skeletal remains showed distinct signs of stress from hauling loads on travois. Other grave materials included fire-cracked rocks (from stone-boiling), scrapers, mauls, and hammerstones, and native copper and marine shell items.[1]

Earl Gray had stumbled upon the oldest known cemetery in the Canadian prairie west—recognized today as a place of national historic significance. But the accidental find is only part of the story of indigenous societies that reach back more than three hundred generations in Saskatchewan. During those millennia, they had developed an intimate, spiritually informed relationship with the diverse ecosystems, a sense of place that allowed them to adjust successfully to change and challenge, especially the vagaries of the climate.

Nor were these early peoples simply opportunistic, living on whatever resources they chanced upon. As one western historian has aptly observed, the environment may have "regulated human activity, but it left considerable latitude for human innovation."[2] This innovation meant that successive Indian generations "settled" into the different Saskatchewan regions to become increasingly sophisticated and more complex by the time Europeans like Kelsey arrived on the scene.[3]

In 1823, George Nelson, a twenty-year veteran of the fur trade, then working as a clerk for the Hudson's Bay Company at Lac la Ronge post in present-day northern Saskatchewan, decided to keep a journal about the spiritual beliefs and practices of the local Cree. One of the stories he collected on 29 March concerned the making of human beings:

> Now after some time he [*Wīsahkēcāhk*] became very lonesome and bethought himself of making Indians, i.e., human beings. He in consequence took up a stone and fashioned it into the form of a man; but whilst at this work it struck him that by forming them of so strong and hard a substance that in time when they would become to know their nature, they would grow insolent and rebellious and be a great annoyance to each other and of course also would never die. "This will not do, I must make them of a more weak and fragile substance, so that they may live a reasonable time and behaves as becomes humans beings." Upon this he took up a handful of common Earth and made the form of a man, and blew into his nostrils *the breath of life.*[4]

This creation story and others like it suggest that Indian peoples were "made" in the West, that they were not immigrants but have always been part of the New World since time immemorial. Even the earth, according to Cree oral tradition, had been created by *Wisahkecahk*, the trickster-transformer who used primal mud, retrieved by a muskrat diving to the ocean's bottom, to fashion the world. "Now Weesuck took this earth," Nelson recorded his journal, "and made a ball of it, and blew in it a considerable time and sent off the Wolf to make its circuit to see if it was large enough." The wolf returned after only four days, prompting Weesuck to make the world larger before sending the Wolf away again: "But before he went off, he said, 'My Elder, the Earth now must be very large, and I shall possibly be too much wearied to make its circuit; I shall travel, and if I find any thing to assure me of its being large enough I shall howl.'"[5]

These kinds of Aboriginal stories are rarely included in history and archaeology texts. Instead, the standard explanation for the peopling of the Americas maintains that the earliest newcomers migrated from Siberia to present-day Alaska and Yukon over a dried-up Bering Strait about twelve thousand years ago. Ocean levels dropped dramatically during the last Ice Age, exposing a broad, more than 620-mile-wide, plain between the two continents (Beringia), and big-game hunters simply travelled from one continent to another in pursuit of their prey. Temporarily stalled in Yukon by the ice sheets, these first peoples eventually worked their way south through an ice-free corridor along the eastern edge of the Rocky Mountains and then spread out over the two continents all the way to the bottom of South America. This overland migration theory has recently been called into question, however, by the discovery of several archaeological sites that pre-date the arrival of the Siberian peoples by at least one thousand years. There might have been an earlier group of first Americans, maybe some fifteen thousand years ago, who used skin boats to ply the waters of the North Pacific. They gradually made their way south along the ancient North American coastline (now submerged under water) to South America, before moving inland east along the southern margin of the great ice sheet. These peoples would have witnessed the disintegration of the immense Laurentide ice sheet—a time of dynamic, at times violent, environmental change. It is probably no coincidence that flood stories are part of Aboriginal oral history.[6]

Even though if, when, and how humans came to the New World is open

Archaeologists excavating evidence of past cultures in the riverbank of the
Saskatchewan River (below the forks).

to debate, there is no uncertainty about when they arrived in Saskatchewan.
Paleo-Indian peoples moved into the western interior in concert with the
withdrawal of the ice sheet. By around 11000 BP, with ice now covering only the
northern half of the province, big-game hunters roamed the newly available
terrain, stalking in small bands the large grazing animals of the region—
mammoths, bison, horses, and camels. Collectively, these people have become
known as the Clovis culture, so named because of their leaf-shaped, fluted
spear points, first found near the community of Clovis, New Mexico. What they
actually called themselves is not known. Nor, as a nomadic hunting society,
did they leave behind much of a footprint on the landscape. Only limited
evidence of their existence has been recovered in artifact assemblages—either

it has eroded away or not been found because it lies deeply buried. Describing the lives of these early people is consequently not only difficult but open to considerable speculation, sometimes quite divergent interpretations. And that is because archaeologists have largely come to identify prehistoric peoples and separate them into distinct complexes, traditions, or phases by meticulously studying their projectile points and denoting any modification or innovation.[7] Clovis hunters, for example, sought out fine-grained stone, such as chert or chalcedony, to expertly craft large spear points, with flaked (sharp) sides for greater penetrating efficiency and a fluted, thinner base for better adhesion to the shaft. Several of these points have been identified among surface finds in the Battleford–Lloydminster area of Saskatchewan.[8]

Clovis people have been blamed for the "over-killing" of the megafauna of the late Pleistocene period—what one author has called "the first of a series of human-caused ecological collapses on the American plains."[9] It is something that is entirely possible because these large animals had lived in isolation before the arrival of the first humans and could have been easily ambushed by the newcomers, armed with their lethal spear points, as they made their way into the region. But the evidence is inconclusive at best. The changing climate, and the accompanying stress on habitat, could also have been a deciding factor in the mass extinctions, especially when the low reproduction rate of some of the animals like the mammoth is taken into account.[10] A recent re-examination of several Clovis sites also suggests that these people did not survive only on big game, but depended on a more diverse subsistence base.[11] The picture emerging from the archaeological record is of a highly mobile and efficient people, the first "pioneers" or "colonizers" as it were, finding their way in a new environment marked by instability and change.[12]

The Clovis people were followed by those of the Folsom phase (10,000 BP), this time identified on the basis of their long-fluted, extremely thin, and deadly sharp projectile points—what one archaeologist has called the "pinnacle of lithic craftsmanship on the Northern Plains."[13] The exquisite workmanship that went into Folsom stone-flaked points may have been a reflection of the spiritual or supernatural powers that ancient peoples attached to them. Hunting societies followed sacred protocols, including a respect for the animals that were being pursued. There was also a very good practical reason for ensuring that the weaponry was "state of the art." The projectile had to slice through the tough exterior hide of the prey and penetrate the body to inflict a mortal wound. An improperly designed or poorly maintained point increased the chances of an unsuccessful hunt, particularly in those circumstances where there was only one brief moment to bring down an animal. The speed and force at which the blow was delivered was enhanced by the use of the atlatl or spear thrower, which effectively extended the reach of the human arm, thereby enabling small spear-like darts to be hurled at greater velocity for higher impact.[14]

Because of the loss of other Pleistocene large mammal species, Folsom people pursued the ancient bison, a much larger, heavier beast with longer, more menacing horns. It is not known whether these animals behaved the same as the modern bison—whether, for example, they herded together or tended to be more solitary. It was because of their fearsome size, though, that Folsom groups stalked bison individually or in small groups, often making use of natural traps such as a steep-banked arroyo (also known as a wash or gulch). This procurement strategy required hunters to come to know the habits of the bison intimately, to know what to anticipate in any given situation—as one author has commented, to make "a way of life that was predictable, not precarious."[15] It also demanded great perseverance, to wait patiently, often for hours, and to know exactly when to strike with surprise and speed. Many an ancient hunter went through a long apprenticeship, learning from more experienced elders and honing their spear-throwing skills through constant practice. When the kill was made, there was still hard work ahead for women, who had to use large flake tools to skin and butcher the bison and process the meat and hide.[16]

Folsom phase occupations have never been excavated in Saskatchewan. Surface finds have, however, been made near Bromhead and Mortlach at sites usually associated with bison killing and butchering in the southern part of

ARCHAEOLOGICAL PERIODS AND CULTURES
BY VEGETATION ZONE

	Years BP*	Prairie/Parklands	Boreal forest	Subarctic woodland
Late Period		Mortlach, Moose Jaw	Selkirk	Late Taltheilei
	1,000	Old Women's	Laurel	
		Avonlea		Middle Taltheilei
	2,000	Besant	Taltheilei	
Middle Period		Pelican Lake	Pelican Lake	Early Taltheilei
	3,000	Hanna	?	
		McKean	McKean points	
	4,000	Oxbow	Oxbow points	
	5,000	Mummy Cave	Mummy Cave points	Mummy Cave points
	6,000			
	7,000			
Plano Period		Late Plano Late	Plano points	Late Plano
	8,000	Cody complex		
	9,000	Hell Gap		
		Agate Basin	ice covered	ice covered
Palaeo-Indian Period	10,000	Folsom		
			ice covered	ice covered
		Clovis		
	11,000		ice covered	ice covered

*Radiocarbon years before present.

Saskatchewan periods and cultures arranged by time period and vegetation zones.

MEYER AND RUSSELL

the province. These materials suggest that Folsom people lived in small multi-family units in keeping with their hunting methods. It is also apparent that they had a greater familiarity with the landscape, as it stabilized, and used local resources in their tool manufacturing.[17] But their numbers were still relatively low, and as hunting societies, they constantly moved from campsite to campsite in the continuous search for game. "The harsh reality of the Plains," noted one archaeologist, "kept social groups smaller and more fluid."[18]

Folsom people never occupied northern Saskatchewan because of the continuing presence of glacial ice there until about 9000 BP. There were, however, other groups—the Agate Basin, Hell Gap, Alberta, and Cody cultural complexes—active in the largely deciduous forest that once existed between the North Saskatchewan and Churchill Rivers. These Middle to Late Paleo-Indian peoples are more readily associated with the plains, where excavated sites tell a story of intensive bison processing. Not only did they hunt bison more systematically and in greater numbers, as evidenced by the remnant bone beds, but they did so communally, usually building corral-like barriers across arroyos and maneuvering the animals along the valley into the enclosures and their death.[19] So why, then, have several of their spear points been found well to the north along the upper Churchill River (Buffalo Narrows region)? These people likely moved into the region from the south, their migration encouraged by the beginning of a warming trend, known as the Hypsithermal interval, starting around nine thousand years ago. Higher temperatures not only moved the boundaries of the grasslands and parkland northward, but also the range of prehistoric bison. Because these Paleo-Indian peoples had come to specialize in bison procurement, they naturally followed the herds to the southern edge of the boreal forest and began to exploit the resources found there. Over time, they adapted their already considerable hunting skills to include caribou.[20]

Only one Paleo-Indian group is known to have occupied the Churchill River system. That distinction belongs to the Angostura culture, who probably hunted bison, moose, and caribou, as well as other smaller game. Little if anything is known about their subsistence activities in the boreal forest because no campsites have been located in the region—only their spear points, especially around Buffalo Narrows. The other barrier to understanding the lives of these peoples is the environment. Unlike the grasslands, where evidence of past cultures is found in neat, distinct layers, such strata deposition is rare to absent in northern Saskatchewan with its shallow soils. Instead, several millennia of occupation are often found jumbled together as surface deposits, while the bones of the animals that the Angostura and other cultures lived on have long since disintegrated because of the acidic soils, making it impossible to determine with any accuracy their seasonal movements, let alone their diet.[21]

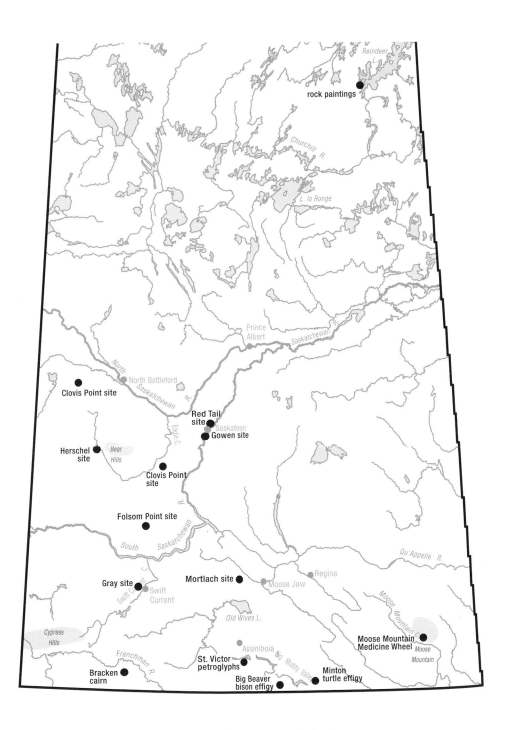

Selected archaeological sites in Saskatchewan

The next major period of human occupation was the Archaic, lasting from about seventy-five hundred to two thousand years ago. These cultural groups—moving forward in time from the Early Side-notched, Mummy Cave, Oxbow, McKean, Hanna, and finally, the Pelican Lake complex—were more sophisticated than their Paleo-Indian predecessors and represented a clear break from past cultures because of their "variety, inventiveness, and adaptability."[22] For starters, they had a different tool kit, most likely a consequence of technological advances from outside the region. Hunters now chipped side notches at the base of smaller spear points in order to lash the projectile head to the atlatl dart shaft. Gone were the larger, lance-shaped points with centre grooves or flutes of the big-game days.

Early to Middle Archaic peoples did not live solely on bison. As they perfected their understanding and appreciation of the resource base available to them, they pursued a broader, more diverse subsistence pattern that took advantage of entire ecosystems. That meant more plant foods in their diet (as evidenced by the appearance of grinding stones in the artifact assemblage). To do so, they mastered what each regional environment had to offer in the way of tubers, seeds, nuts, greens, and fruits, as well as learning when and where these resources could best be harvested. They did not practice horticulture. They also consumed pronghorn, elk, and deer, as well as smaller game, such as rabbits and waterfowl (including their eggs), and of course, fish and waterfowl from rivers and lakes. These hunting and harvesting activities were intended to supplement, and not displace, the reliance on bison. But in the search for variety, they became efficient, if not "affluent foragers."[23]

Archaic societies were severely tested during the worst centuries of the Hypsithermal, around seventy-five hundred to five thousand years ago, when the climate became decidedly warmer and drier. Indeed, the archaeological community initially believed that plains people had vacated the western interior—in the case of Saskatchewan, probably moving north. This "cultural hiatus" theory seemed to be supported by the lack of archaeological deposits from this period, suggesting that the extremely arid conditions had effectively

BILL WAISER

The view from the top of the cliff at the St. Victor petroglyph site

led to the forced abandonment of the plains by both humans and bison. But then, new evidence was discovered, including a major find in Saskatoon in 1977, when a heavy equipment operator unearthed an ancient campsite along the South Saskatchewan River that was radiocarbon-dated to around 6000 BP.

The Gowen site, named for its discoverer, confirmed that people (Early Side-notched or Mummy Cave culture) still lived in the northern plains and still hunted bison during the Hypsithermal, but that the camp was occupied for only a short duration because of the low number of animal remains uncovered. It would appear, then, that the severity of the prolonged dry spell was not synchronous throughout the region—it was localized or site-specific—and

THOMAS KEHOE

A combination bison jump and pound was used to hunt bison in the Gull Lake area.

that humans continued to occupy the plains, albeit sporadically in many places, maybe for only one or two seasons. Some Archaic people persisted in hunting the thinning bison herds, relying more on communal killing practices; others adopted a widely diverse subsistence lifestyle, increasingly on the move, foraging in smaller groups for any food source, especially along major waterways where there was still fresh water to be found; while still others might have lived near groundwater-fed sites like springs where it might have been possible to store food for times of scarcity. These adaptive strategies varied throughout the western interior and, in that sense, reflected the uneven impact of Hypsithermal conditions from district to district and from generation to generation. Clearly, people sought out places of refuge. But there was no Biblical-like exodus from the northern plains of North America. Nor could the region in any sense of the word be considered "empty." If anything, these hunter-gatherer societies became better attuned to their local environment, learning how to interpret and respond to changing climatic conditions.[24]

The grip of the Hypsithermal on the region began to lessen around five thousand years ago, grudgingly giving way to a climate that was both wetter and cooler, more in keeping with the conditions that characterize the climate today. The boreal forest reversed its retreat and gradually moved southward to reclaim areas once taken over by grasslands during the preceding dry centuries. The modern bison also made its appearance around this time, as did bison-hunting societies that occupied and dominated the plains region in successive waves. These Middle Archaic peoples were quite adept at killing bison in great numbers, especially when this "dwarf" version was more gregarious and congregated in large herds. They also boasted higher populations than their predecessors because of the vast number of bison at their disposal—more food on the hoof meant more mouths could be fed—and outnumbered their counterparts in the boreal forest and shield country. Plains Archaic cultures even had a direct influence on those living in northern Saskatchewan. Plains Archaic points have been recovered north of the parklands, suggesting that some hunting societies from the south expanded into the boreal forest and took full advantage of the resources found along the Churchill River system. The projectile points of the more northerly Shield Archaic were also similar to those employed by grasslands complexes.[25]

Middle Archaic peoples in the grasslands and parklands hunted bison by stalking them—what might seem like an unfair struggle between the swift, agile bison with their sharp sense of smell and humans on foot on the open plains. Archaic hunters found any number of ways to bring down their quarry, from ambushing them at water sites, to running them into deep snow or onto ice, to driving them into dead-end ravines.[26]

Bison might have known where the best forage was to be found, but hunters, armed with their knowledge of bison habits, knew where to find the bison and what to do when they found them. They were keenly aware, for example, that bison sought winter shelter in wooded coulees and that the males were first out on the plains in the spring, while cows remained behind with their calves. They were also selective hunters. Recognizing the need for fat in their diets, Middle Archaic peoples deliberately sought out cows rather than the larger bulls, whose meat could be tough and musky, especially during the

GEORGE TOSH

The Roy Rivers medicine wheel in southwest Saskatchewan

rut. It was no coincidence that more animals were taken in the fall, when cow/ calf herds were easier to manipulate and females were in prime condition with layers of fat along the ribs, back, and hump (often affecting hair colour). Bones from the slaughtered bison were broken up and boiled in hide-lined pits, where the water was heated by hot rocks—a major cultural innovation at this time. The grease that was rendered during this new process was mixed with dried, pounded meat to produce pemmican, a high-energy food that could be stored for months.

The most remarkable Oxbow complex site in Saskatchewan was the burial ground found by Earl Gray on his land northwest of Swift Current in 1963. Given the length of time that the cemetery was used (over two thousand years), it may have been the hub of Oxbow culture in Saskatchewan.[27] But such an interpretation is largely speculative. One of the best McKean sites, on the other hand, is found on the outskirts of Saskatoon at Wanuskewin Heritage Park. The Red Tail site along the South Saskatchewan River features multiple levels of McKean complex occupation, including a possible house pit, dating from 4200 to 3500 BP.[28]

ROYAL SASKATCHEWAN MUSEUM

A petroglyph found in the Beaver Hills

The stalking of bison eventually gave way to different hunting methods, especially pounds and jumps, by people who produced projectile points of the Pelican Lake complex. These new Middle Archaic peoples, first appearing in the archaeological record around 3000 BP, systematically and continuously used these procurement techniques whereas their past employment had been largely episodic. Both strategies took advantage of the local landscape, and both hunting methods followed certain spiritual protocols to ensure that the hunt was successful. Pounds, corral-like structures, sometimes shrouded to keep the penned-up animals from seeing out, were established in natural depressions, much like the earlier arroyo traps. Jumps sent bison over cliffs, but only if the animals could be calmly coaxed along specially prepared

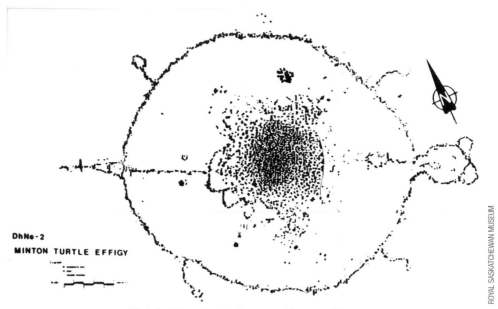

DhNe-2
MINTON TURTLE EFFIGY

ROYAL SASKATCHEWAN MUSEUM

Sketch of the giant turtle stone effigy near Minton

driving lanes by "runners" disguised in hides, before being stampeded to their death at the last moment. These communal hunts brought more people together into large camps at favoured locations for longer periods of time. The procurement of bison required a larger workforce, especially women, who faced the onerous task of butchering and preparing several thousand pounds of meat[29] Women were also responsible for putting up and taking down and transporting the teepees, the conical-shaped, hide-and-pole dwellings that were developed around this time. The supporting poles typically came from the aptly named lodgepole pine stands, while the covering was made from the more supple bison cow hides. The doorway of the teepee always faced east and the rising sun.[30]

Evidence of Archaic people can be found throughout southern Saskatchewan. The most common—in the tens of thousands—are teepee rings, stones that once held down the sides of the skin dwellings, left behind in irregular circles, partially embedded today in the ground. Some have been unwittingly gathered up into rock piles over the years by homesteaders anxious to clear their fields. Archaic people also used stones to mark out effigies in the shape of animals, such as the giant turtle near Minton, Saskatchewan, and in a

ROYAL SASKATCHEWAN MUSEUM

The bison effigy, outside Big Beaver, Saskatchewan, is the only known bison effigy
on the northern plains

few instances, anatomically correct men. Their spiritual meaning is uncertain. Equally puzzling, given the central importance of the animal to their lives, is why there is only one known bison effigy in North America—just outside Big Beaver in south-central Saskatchewan. Then there are the so-called medicine wheels, a strange term because early peoples in North America never used the wheel. These circular stone formations, as old, if not older than Stonehenge in England, have been laid out on with central cairns and radiating arms on high ground. No two are alike, except that they all provide an unobstructed 360-degree view of the surrounding landscape and are usually located near a reliable source of water. Perhaps the most famous medicine wheel, because of its sprawling size, straddles Moose Mountain. Several theories have been advanced to explain their purpose—from observatories to temples to burial sites—but they remain a mystery. Most of these stone features are difficult to fully appreciate at ground level and are best viewed from the air. Although frowned upon today, one popular trick is to spread a light dusting of flour over each stone and then take a photograph from an airplane.

Archaic peoples also produced rock art—a seemingly simplistic form of cultural expression, but one that nonetheless infuses the lives of early Saskatchewan people with "different layers of meaning and spiritual significance" that may not be readily accessible from the rigorous study of projectile points.[31] The largest single collection of petroglyphs in Saskatchewan is found on a single cliff in the sandstone bluffs south of St. Victor. Besides the number of images in one place—roughly three hundred—what makes the site so unusual is that the artwork is carved on the top of the cliff, on the horizontal, rather than along the vertical face. There are faces, animals, handprints, and an assortment of tracks (both bison and grizzly), all intermingled with symbols. Because of erosion, many of the carvings are now difficult to make out, let alone comprehend, and are best viewed during the rising and setting of the sun, when the light strikes the bluff at the right angle. This characteristic has led to the conclusion that it might have been a "vision quest" site, where young men sought guidance from the spiritual world, after fasting and praying for several days, and then recorded their experience.[32] The other popular canvases for artwork were the erratics scattered about the landscape. Just outside Herschel, Saskatchewan, above Coal Mine Ravine, in a perfect place for a campsite, are three ribstones (rock carvings) that have been meticulously carved with grooves and cupules. The most distinctive of the three, a large slab of dolomite

ROYAL SASKATCHEWAN MUSEUM

Pictographs found along the Clearwater River

that was dropped on the spot during the retreat of the last glacier, resembles a bison, complete with a backbone, ribs, and row-upon-row of cupules between the ribs. Archaeological excavations have unearthed an assortment of offerings around the base of the ribstones, suggesting that it might have once been a ceremonial site, especially since there is a bison jump nearby.[33]

Death was also steeped in ritualism, as evidenced by the findings in the Bracken Cairn in southwestern Saskatchewan, a Pelican Lake burial site dating to about twenty-five hundred years ago. First discovered in 1936 but not formally investigated for almost another half century, the grave was prominently situated on a hill overlooking the deep valley of the Frenchman River. Inside a shallow pit overlain with rocks were the carefully arranged skeletal remains of five individuals, all heavily stained with red ochre, as was the surrounding soil. Buried with them were decorative animal bones, a spear point, tools, a shell pendant or gorget, and even some native copper from western Lake Superior. Whether or not it was a nuclear family is debatable, but clearly, interment was not something that was hurried, but performed with solemnity.[34]

Around 2000 BP, new cultural groups (Late Archaic to Late Prehistoric) appeared in the province—often identified today by the technological innovations that accompanied them. The most northerly part of present-day Saskatchewan, extending south to the upper Churchill River basin, was home to the Taltheilei tradition. These people were the ancestors of the Athapaskan-speaking Chipewyan, the forerunners of the same people that the Hudson's Bay Company tried to involve in the fur trade in the late seventeenth and early eighteenth centuries. The Taltheilei subsistence economy was largely based on the migratory caribou herds of the barren lands, a lifestyle that necessitated the use of stone hide-working tools (chithos) and the bow and arrow (with small notched points made of bone or local copper). In fact, it was from the Arctic that the bow and arrow, that quintessential weapon most often identified with plains Indians, was introduced to North America—and not until about two thousand years ago!

The Taltheilei might be considered poor by today's standards because they were constantly on the move, seeking out resources as the season dictated, and hence had few personal possessions. But material things were an encumbrance and would only slow down early societies. To survive in the northern Saskatchewan environment, the Taltheilei developed a material culture that was determined in part by portability. They kept baggage to a minimum and travelled from place to place with only those things that were absolutely necessary. It could even be argued that the wealth of the Taltheilei was what they carried in their heads and not on their backs. They had this extraordinary ability to take bone, stone, wood, and skins and transform them into tools,

Aerial view of teepee rings, after first snowfall, in the Cabri Hills

TED DOUGLAS

72

shelter, and clothing. Something as simple as a rabbit snare, for example, was constructed when needed and perfectly met their needs. That was the real genius of these early Saskatchewan peoples. Whereas later Euro-Canadian settlement was tied down to a particular place and what was available there, the mobility and resourcefulness of Indian groups, a kind of innate flexibility, enabled them to respond to climatic forces and environmental change.[35]

By the time of Kelsey's visit to the western interior in the early 1690s, the Taltheilei had formed two distinct Chipewyan groupings. The more northerly people, known as Caribou Eaters, followed the Beverly caribou herd as it migrated over two thousand miles annually, alternating between the barren grounds of present-day Nunavut and the Northwest Territories during the summer and the boreal forest of northern Saskatchewan and Manitoba during the winter. The second group of Chipewyan lived in the northwest, between Lake Athabasca and the upper Churchill River. In summer, they gathered at large fishing camps along the Churchill, in places such as Patuanak, and then dispersed throughout the forest into smaller bands, often extended families, for the winter months. Here, they hunted caribou that had also taken refuge in the northern woods. For both Chipewyan groups, though, pursuing the caribou was "a hit-or-miss proposition" and they "either flourished or starved as conditions dictated."[36]

Further south in the boreal forest, in the eastern half of the Churchill River system, the Laurel culture flourished. These people, originating in the upper Great Lakes, brought the first pottery (Middle Woodland) to the region about fifteen hundred years ago—conical vessels made by coiling and then decorated with pressed-in designs or punctates. Another distinct pottery-making complex, termed the River House people, occupied the upper Saskatchewan River district at the outer edge of the boreal forest and extending into the parkland in Manitoba, where they had interacted with bison-hunting peoples of the region. Both these groups were followed, first by the Blackduck culture, migrants from the western Lake Superior region, and then by the Selkirk (Cree) culture, another Woodland group that quickly expanded throughout the entire

Churchill River network and into the northern edge of the parklands, often residing near major fisheries. Selkirk people, probably the ancestors of the Algonquian-speaking Cree of the boreal forest, were known for their elaborate globular pottery vessels, featuring constricted necks, sometimes with outward-curving rims, and decorated by impressing fabric against the exterior. They also employed an array of stone and bone tools—from knives, axes, and scrapers to awls and barbed harpoon heads—to better exploit the resources of the boreal forest. And they readily adapted to the changing seasons, switching from toboggans and snowshoes to birchbark canoes. Sherds (pottery fragments) from Selkirk ceramics, sometimes covering several acres in places, constitute the most common artifacts recovered from this period, and suggest that their population was comparably larger than previous cultures in the region.[37]

Selkirk people were most likely the artists who did the rock-face paintings, more correctly called pictographs, found throughout the Saskatchewan shield country, usually near rapids (portages) or other significant locations on rivers and lakes. To date, over seventy rock-art sites have been recorded in the northern half of the province, most of them ranging from four to eight drawings in any one place, normally on adjoining rock surfaces just above the waterline. An unusually high concentration—nine sites in total—is found in southwestern Reindeer Lake.[38] Iron oxide pigment, otherwise known as ochre, that was dug from the earth and then heated with some kind of gelatin to make the paintings, gives them a rich rusty-red or rusty-brown hue. Although their vibrancy has faded with time, they remain striking, especially given their locations, forcing the passing canoeist to look up. They are also heavy with meaning because of their simplicity and their spiritual significance. Oral history collected from Saskatchewan elders suggests that the images depict extraordinary events in an individual's life, such as contact with a guardian spirit or a powerful vision, or some unusual occurrence, even a crisis. Those who visited the sites, meanwhile, left offerings on a nearby rock shelf because of the belief that spirits resided there.[39] That was the experience of renowned fur trader Alexander Mackenzie, who paused on an island while crossing Sandfly

TED DOUGLAS

An anatomically correct human effigy in the Cabri Hills

Lake in the late eighteenth century to see "a very large stone, in the form of a bear, on which the natives have painted the head and snout of that animal; and here they also were formerly accustomed to offering sacrifices."[40]

Pictographs were only one aspect of Selkirk spirituality. In reading HBC trader George Nelson's Lac la Ronge journal, it becomes readily apparent that he was dealing with complex societies with deeply rooted belief systems. His informants not only had their own creation stories about the origins of the earth, humans, and animals, but explained how they looked to supernatural beings for direction. Young males embarked on vision quests, fasting and dreaming, in order to get in touch with their guardian spirits. This relationship was not one-directional but carried with it certain obligations, such as showing respect and providing offerings. Another way to contact the spirits was through the shaking lodge, where the diviner served as a kind of conduit between the audience and the spirits. Conjuring was undertaken to help heal the sick or secure guidance for the future, while sorcery was practised to drive away unwelcome beings. European observers often scoffed at these activities,

BILL WAISER

The remains of a Sun Dance lodge on the One Arrow First Nation reserve

dismissing them as superstitions, but really, how different were they from the religious practices of Old World civilizations?[41]

In the eastern parklands, as in the boreal forest during the Late Precontact period, the Selkirk culture was the dominant group, especially along the Saskatchewan River valley east of the forks. Their descendants were the Cree whom Kelsey had encountered during his inland journey, living on the edge of the northern prairies. The land these people occupied was as much a cultural landscape as a physical one. The names they gave geographical features had special significance or served as important reference points. Birch Hills (*waskway waciy*), for example, provided a source of building materials for their canoes, while the Eagle Hills (*mikisiw waciy*) were favoured wintering grounds. These landforms were connected by a network of trails that did more than get people from one site to another or facilitate communications with other bands. The pathways also served to reinforce Cree identity, to provide a sense of place and a sense of history, all the more so since stories were told along the way and offerings were left at sacred places. At least once a year in the spring, for a few intense days, the various bands in a particular region came together

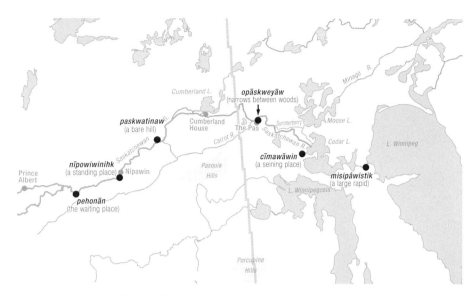

Cree rendezvous sites in east-central Saskatchewan

at an ingathering centre to hold religious ceremonies, find partners, visit with extended family members, or exchange items and ideas. Several of these rendezvous sites in east-central Saskatchewan and west-central Manitoba have been identified and confirmed through archaeological field work and oral testimony: *misipâwistik* (Grand Rapids), *cîmawāwin* (the entrance to Cedar Lake), *opāskweyāw* (The Pas), *nîpowiwinihk* (Nipawin), and *pêhonân* (Fort à la Corne area). The excavated debris suggests they were used for centuries, if not thousands of years. Fur trade posts were later deliberately established at these gathering places.[42]

Because these people lived in the zone between one ecosystem and another, the boundary or edge between forest and grassland, they enjoyed a rich and varied diet. It was a prime hunting, trapping, and harvesting area—a veritable cornucopia of fish, fowl, large and small mammals, and plants. And even though any of these resources might be scarce one year, there was always something else to eat. HBC servant Anthony Henday would later describe the parklands as "a pleasant and plentyful country." Métis interpreter Peter Erasmus said much the same thing: "It was an ideal life of abundance."[43] But in order to maintain and enhance the resource base to ensure harvesting success, the Selkirk people intentionally intervened in ecological systems. They pruned saskatoon and chokecherry patches and thinned out edible roots such as wild parsnip in order to improve next year's crop. Or they burned along the margins of meadows to stimulate new vegetation to attract elk and moose. Or they built fish weirs along creeks to trap fish. These and other measures were undertaken to ensure that the land remained productive for their purposes. They did not simply consume what was "naturally" available and move on, but sought a sustainable relationship with the land.[44]

Most of southern Saskatchewan, if not all of the northern plains, on the other hand, was occupied by people who produced points identified with the Besant phase about two thousand years ago (from 200 BC to 500 AD). These migrants to the region, probably from the eastern woodlands, were bison-hunting peoples, who used the atlatl with side-notched points. They might also have been the first on the Saskatchewan grasslands to make pottery, but that is uncertain because few ceramic sherds have been found in the province; they are more common to the south at Besant sites in the Middle Missouri River region. They, in turn, were displaced, beginning around 500 AD, by the Avonlea Horizon, so named because of the initial identification of a projectile point type—small, thin, delicate, triangle-shaped, and side-notched—found outside Avonlea, Saskatchewan, in 1958. What made the point so distinctive, if not revolutionary, was that it came from a bow and arrow and thereby marked the arrival of a new weapon on the plains from the northwest. The Avonlea people were also skilled potters, and the net- and fabric-pressed ceramics they produced exhibited regional variations.[45]

Unlike the Besant people whose activities were largely confined to the plains,[46] the Avonlea ranged over a much larger area, pushing north across the parklands to the southern edge of the boreal forest. Avonlea components have been uncovered in the Nipawin area along the lower Saskatchewan River valley. They also harvested a greater variety of foodstuffs and did not restrict themselves to a bison diet. Near the village of Lebret in the Qu'Appelle Valley, for example, archaeological salvage work in 1984 made necessary by a new cottage development found a large spring fishery dating back to about 500

DAVID MEYER

The nīpowiwinihk gathering site was one of several along the Saskatchewan River valley.

AD.[47] Another popular staple was the prairie turnip or breadroot. Similar to a potato, the tuber was an important source of carbohydrates and its availability influenced seasonal movement. Women harvested the plant in the early summer, and after removing the tough outer brown husk, either dried and ground it into a kind of flour or cut it into chunks and boiled it; it was also eaten raw or toasted in campfire embers.[48]

The mainstay of the Avonlea subsistence economy, however, was the bison. Despite the lack of horses, this formidable hunting society tackled the procurement of bison with a sophistication and intensity that resulted in the killing of the animal in numbers never matched before. One of the most heavily used sites was a combination bison jump and pound near Gull Lake along the Missouri Couteau.[49] Another was located in the Big Muddy Lake at Roan Mare Coulee. The Avonlea people also took advantage of natural features, such as sand hills, to build pounds, or in some instances, stampeded bison over a low bluff into a pound below. These communal hunts demanded considerable organization, preparation, and coordination. Bison were not easily fooled. To lure them into the trap, spiritual leaders performed religious ceremonies, such as prayers and chanting, as well as directed the placement of offerings, before the hunt.[50] What also helped was the Avonlea understanding of bison behaviour and movements—something they probably learned in part by watching wolf packs hunt bison. This knowledge not only meant that their procurement techniques were effective but also ensured that the herds could be continually exploited in the same general area on an annual basis.[51]

In moving about the region in pursuit of the herds, these plains hunters deliberately avoided the rivers in favour of walking along the valley margins. Water travel was fraught with difficulties—from low volumes and sandbars to meandering courses and deep-sided channels. There was also limited access to boat-building and repair materials on the prairies. It was more practical to use overland trails that were set back from the rivers and roughly paralleled the valleys. Travel was not only faster, but also more efficient, in that people and their work dogs were spared the extra exertion of going down and up ravines. There was also more to be seen from the uplands, especially bison and other game. When rivers had to be forded, to move from one watershed to the next, the hunters sought out shallow crossings that doubled as campsites. Over time, the repeated use of these and other locations along the trails led to the naming of places in recognition of the resources found in the vicinity.[52]

The great bison herds of the Saskatchewan plains spent their summers on the open grasslands, but come fall and colder weather, migrated north to the parklands or sought shelter and feed in the valleys and coulees along the edge of the plains; only a few bison remained on their summer range through the winter months. Avonlea people followed them. They moved into the valley complexes to exploit the range of resources found there, and then, like the bison in the spring, moved back out onto the grasslands, thereby allowing local ecosystems to recover.[53] Others took up temporary residence in the parklands for the fall, winter, and early spring, where they found a ready supply of wood for fuel and pounding. But it is unlikely that Avonlea and Laurel/River House populations converged on the region—one from the south, the other from the north—and co-occupied the parklands for the winter. Instead, the archaeological record indicates that the parklands were really an extension of the grasslands for the Avonlea peoples and the bison they lived on, and that they moved in concert from one ecotone to the other. Any interaction between bison hunters and northern peoples was consequently limited to the forest edge because northern peoples preferred their boreal refuge during the winter months. The only likely time that forest-adapted peoples and plains-adapted people were together in the parklands was during the spawning season in the spring.[54]

About 1000 AD, the Old Women's phase, with its prairie side-notched arrow heads and late variant pottery, replaced the Avonlea Horizon on the Saskatchewan plains. They were another bison-hunting society based on their pounding activities near Gull Lake, at the confluence of the South Saskatchewan and Red Deer Rivers, and in the Dunfermline sand hills west of Saskatoon. The presence of foetal bones among the faunal assemblage at the kill sites also suggests that they remained at the edge of the grasslands in the late winter and early spring rather than migrating from the region.[55] A little more than two hundred years later, a new cultural group, known as the Mortlach phase, swept across the Saskatchewan grasslands and pushed the Old Women's people to the west-central part of the province. That was about the same time, around one thousand years ago, that sedentary groups practising agriculture along the Mississippi River moved into the upper Missouri River region in the present-day Dakotas.

The Mortlach people were bison hunters who wintered in wooded coulees in such places as the Qu'Appelle Valley, Last Mountain Lake, Wood Mountain, and the Big Muddy—wherever the herds could be found. Come spring, they travelled south across what is now the international border with the United States to trade with the horticultural villages on the Missouri, Knife, Heart, and James Rivers. Archaeological excavations at Mortlach sites demonstrate that there were strong linkages between the hunting and farming peoples. The pottery is not only similar, but large quantities of Mortlach projectile points were made from Knife River flint derived from the Middle Missouri region. Even gaming discs, identical to those used at the villages sites, have been found among Mortlach artifacts.[56] One archaeologist has even speculated that these late pre-contact northern plains peoples "were either descended from … horticultural groups to the south and east or were in regular and close contact with them and were strongly influenced by them."[57]

If contact and interchange between the two groups were so extensive, then why did the Mortlach peoples not adopt agriculture, or at the very least, try to grow a few domesticated plants from seed secured from their trading partners? Why did the spread of farming not extend into the northern Saskatchewan plains? It apparently did in neighbouring Manitoba, where gardening was underway along the upper Red River Valley around 1200 AD, presumably by horticultural groups who had moved north into the province. There is no evidence, however, that maize (corn) or any other domesticated crop was ever deliberately planted and grown in Saskatchewan before the arrival of Europeans.[58]

An obvious explanation is that the Mortlach people secured whatever foodstuffs they required from the Missouri/Mississippi villages through trade, and that the prized items they could offer in return were bison meat and other bison products. This exchange network enabled them to take advantage of a renewable resource—the great herds at their disposal-—and the geography of the region. A glance at a map of southern Saskatchewan, for example, shows that the Big Muddy Valley, with its series of bison jumps, was part of a natural conduit to the southern trade. Even without the horse, bison procurement on the interior plains was a lucrative lifestyle, prompting some groups, like the ancestors of the Crow and Cheyenne, to abandon agriculture to become hunters.[59]

The Mortlach concentration on the pursuit of the bison for trade, and not simply subsistence, had a decided impact on how and where they lived. Artifact deposits are quite deep over sizeable areas, indicating

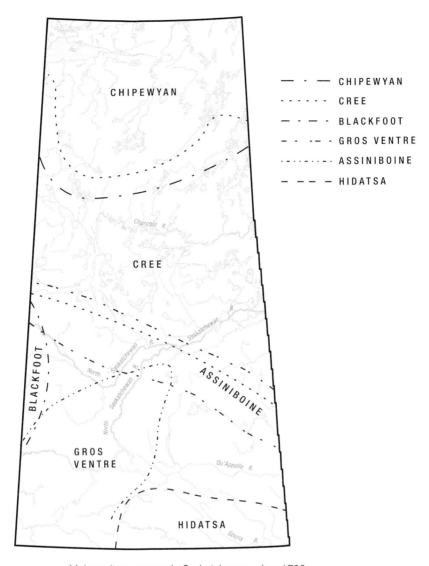

Major culture groups in Saskatchewan, circa 1700

that several hundred people lived together for perhaps as long as eight months in one place. Their communal existence might even be described as "semi-sedentary." The emergence of these larger communities, a new development in the human occupation of the Saskatchewan plains, was a direct response to the bison trade. The Mortlach peoples were not only feeding themselves, but also preparing pemmican, robes, and other bison products for exchange. And this intensive, almost industrial-like, production required more people performing these tasks in one place over longer periods, usually in the fall, winter, and spring. The larger camps were also necessary for defensive purposes. Because peoples to the south and east were organized tribally, normally in fortified villages, the Mortlach took similar precautions to avoid being overrun or evicted by the other groups seeking to move out onto the plains—just as they had done to the people of the Old Women's phase. That is probably why agriculture never moved north from the Dakotas or west from Manitoba into Saskatchewan. The large bison-hunting communities actively resisted any invasion of their lands in the interests of protecting not only their lifestyle, but also their position in the trade network.[60] As a consequence, only one other group, the Cluny phase, is known to have briefly occupied Old Women's territory in southwestern Saskatchewan in the late pre-contact period. This temporary encroachment probably came about because the Cluny peoples were prevented from taking up agricultural land in the south and turned to a hunting-gathering lifeway on the northern plains.[61]

The larger aggregations of people on the Saskatchewan plains or rendezvous places in the parklands and boreal forest facilitated the development of more complex societies in the western interior. Groups became increasingly conscious of their tribal identity, an identity that was defined and reinforced by their relationship with the environment and their sense of territory. When Henry Kelsey travelled inland with the Assiniboine, for example, his escorts cautioned him at one point in 1692 that they were entering an area where they might encounter their enemies. Warfare was not unknown—it did not arrive with Europeans—and conflict often arose between competing groups over access to resources, in some cases because of fluctuating game populations brought about by environmental change.[62] Trade also served to reinforce territorial boundaries, as well as help structure the relationship between different tribal groups. Alliances were forged to take advantage of regional resource specialization and promote the exchange of diverse goods over great distances. They were also a spiritual people with a belief system rooted in the world around them, rich in history and cultural significance.

Such was the situation that Europeans encountered in Saskatchewan in the late seventeenth century.[63] The two dominant groups were the Cree, descended from the Selkirk culture, and the Assiniboine, who probably represented the Mortlach phase. Contrary to the belief that these cultures had not yet migrated west into the province,[64] the Cree resided in the parklands of the lower Saskatchewan River valley, perhaps as far west as the forks, and the east-central boreal forest. They were already allied and trading with the northern Assiniboine, who lived in the eastern parklands on the edge of the northern plains. The southern Assiniboine, meanwhile, inhabited the northeastern plains and were more closely associated with the Mandan–Hidatsa villages in the Dakotas, a consequence of the earlier interchange between these farming and hunting societies; a Hidatsa subgroup was probably present in southeastern Saskatchewan. The Gros Ventre, on the other hand, were to the west, centred on the South Saskatchewan River, and may have co-occupied southwestern Saskatchewan with the Blackfoot.[65]

What newcomers like Henry Kelsey and others that followed him never realized was that these tribal groups were just the latest cultures to thrive in the region and that the human occupation of the western interior was actually quite ancient. Like other early societies throughout the world, they had struggled to meet the challenges of the environment, constantly adapting and finding ways to survive and flourish. Nor were they any different from other peoples with their traditions and stories, their spiritual beliefs and practices, their diplomacy and warfare, their interactions and trade, and their pleasures and their grief. It is actually something of a disservice to these first Saskatchewan peoples to call them "prehistoric" and describe their timeline as "prehistory" for it conjures up images of primitive, if not backward peoples. Nor do these terms help in imagining who they were and how they lived. Because their cultures are identified on the limited evidence of what they left behind and where it was found and by whom, it will never be known, for example, what they called themselves.

During their first encounters, newcomers regarded Indian groups as a seemingly "simple" people. They appeared to be lacking in specialization and sophistication, especially in comparison to the Europeans' home civilizations. Henry Kelsey probably thought this way. One of the curious omissions in the account of his 1690–92 trip inland were the names of his Indian hosts. Here was a Hudson's Bay Company employee who spent an unprecedented two years alone in the company of the Cree and Assiniboine, essentially as their guest, travelling with them in all seasons, sharing their food and sometimes their hunger, learning their ways and hearing their stories, and maybe even fathering a child. Yet these same people, especially Kelsey's host family, remained nameless—their existence is not even mentioned in his journal. But even though Europeans considered themselves superior, they quickly learned—as Kelsey did during his time inland—that Indian peoples could not be ignored or discounted. From the time of their arrival on the edge of the western interior, newcomers came to rely on Indians in ways that made them crucial partners. Quite simply, Europeans needed Indians.

A Cree hunter and his family on Hudson Bay

CHAPTER THREE

BY ALL FAIR PERSUASION

WHEN THE ASSINIBOINE AND CREE TOOK ENGLISHMAN HENRY KELSEY INLAND from Hudson Bay in the early 1690s, most Indian people living in what would become Saskatchewan had never met a European. It is not surprising, then, that past writers have glorified Kelsey as "first in the west."[1] But his trip to the east-central part of the province should really be viewed from the inside looking out. The interior of the continent was not a new world, but Indian country, occupied and controlled by people with their own customs, values, and history. And if Kelsey was going to secure the allegiance of the various inland bands for the Hudson's Bay Company—the reason for his inland mission—then he and other European newcomers had to become part of this Indian world and not simply expect Indian peoples to embrace the new trade opportunities at the expense of their own ways and traditions. Recognizing and responding to these Indian realities, however, would not be easy because the company deliberately chose to confine its presence in northern North America to the shores of Hudson Bay and consequently had a limited knowledge of the interior geography and a limited understanding of the peoples who lived there. The working out of a relationship between Indian traders and company servants was to be further complicated by competition from the French in eastern North America. Indeed, the imperial rivalry between the two European nations in the late seventeenth and early eighteenth centuries not only produced instability in the fur trade, but eventually turned Indian territory into contested land. Both Natives and newcomers had to adapt and change, but not at the same pace nor to the same extent. Together, they created a different world, both old and new, neither Indian nor European, but one that bridged both worlds.[2]

Henry Kelsey might have been the first Englishman to visit the interior plains of North America but his trip lagged significantly behind both Spanish and French initiatives. In the early sixteenth century, Spain ambitiously pushed north from its Central American empire and began its assault on Indian America, driving towards the central interior in a pincer movement from the southeast and southwest. In the 1540s, Hernando De Soto cut a bloody swath from present-day Florida across the Mississippi River to eastern Texas, while Francisco Vásquez de Coronado swept northeast into what is now central Kansas in a bid to extend the northern frontier of New Spain (Mexico). Both expeditions reached the southern Great Plains almost 150 years before Kelsey's inland journey. They were also the forerunners of a brutal colonization policy that eventually drove many Indian nations into open rebellion against their Spanish oppressors. At the very time that Kelsey returned to York Factory in 1692, for example, the Spanish were preparing to re-conquer New Mexico after being forcibly driven out by the 1680 Pueblo revolt. This fierce Indian resistance, collectively known as the Great Northern Rebellion, gave way to an uneasy peace that served to underscore the weakness of Spain's presence along the southern edge of the interior plains.[3]

The French at this same time were equally active in the southern Mississippi region, including Texas, and even threatened to drive a wedge between Spanish colonies on the southeast and southwest coasts of America.[4] Following the Iroquois destruction of Huronia in present-day southwestern Ontario in 1649 and the smashing of the Huron–New France alliance, the French sought to rebuild their trading network by reaching across the top of the Great Lakes and directly engaging the Ottawa and Ojibway peoples. But this expansion into the middle of the continent did not end at Lake Superior. Taking advantage of the waterways of the interior and with encouragement from New France officials, Father Jacques Marquette and trader Louis Joliette headed down the Mississippi River in 1673 to its juncture with the Arkansas River. Nine years later (and another eight before Kelsey was escorted inland), explorer Robert de la Salle completed the trip downriver to the Gulf of Mexico, and by doing so, laid claim to the entire Mississippi River basin for France. La Salle wanted to build a string of inland posts, in a kind of arc, from the St. Lawrence, along the Great Lakes, and down the Mississippi to Louisiana—a plan officially sanctioned by Louis XIV in 1701 in order to restrict England's American colonies to the Atlantic seaboard. That was the same year as the Great Peace of Montreal, when New France concluded a treaty with its great enemy, the Iroquois, and about forty other Indian nations from northeastern North America. Thus, by the beginning of the eighteenth century, while Spain enjoyed a tenuous toehold on the southern Great Plains, France seemed poised to dominate the interior of the continent by pushing inland from the Great Lakes and north from Louisiana along the Mississippi and its tributaries.

The arrival of Europeans in the North American interior did not mark the beginning of Great Plains history but rather connected "two worlds of equal maturity."[5] Indian society was as old as its European counterpart and had its own history dating back many generations. Perhaps the best expression of that maturity was the production of corn. This plant, indigenous to the new world, had reached the northern limits of its cultivation range by the time Europeans reached the shores of the western hemisphere. Indian farmers had developed several hundred varieties of corn during thousands of years of careful selection and experimentation. They even produced varieties that yielded crops in areas where corn agriculture seemed unpromising. Over time, corn became a staple for many southern and eastern Aboriginal societies, and together with squash and beans, the two other "sisters" of North American agriculture, led to the adoption of a semi-sedentary lifestyle and the emergence of settlements along the Mississippi Valley.[6]

The most remarkable of these early, corn-based communities was the city of Cahokia (near present-day St. Louis) at the junction of the Mississippi and

Missouri Rivers. A planned community, featuring elaborate temples, grand plazas and elevated terraces, and huge earthen burial mounds, Cahokia numbered more than thirty thousand people during its heyday around 1000 AD, coincidentally the same time that the Norse were attempting to colonize Newfoundland. It was the largest settlement north of the Rio Grande, and its population would not be surpassed until the late seventeenth century by the cities of New York

A beaver lodge along the shore of a northern lake

and Philadelphia (and until the 1830s by Montreal). The first archaeologists who investigated the site did not believe that Cahokia was Aboriginal in origin. By the time the French reached the site in the 1670s, Cahokia was gone and its population dispersed. What precipitated the community's decline and its eventual abandonment, starting around 1300, is uncertain. Climate change and the accompanying resource stress might have been the culprit.[7]

BILL WAISER

Castor du Canada

The Canadian beaver

Even though corn and other domesticated plants allowed development of the large Mississippian centres, these settlements flourished because of trade conducted with other Indian groups. Cahokia, situated in the heart of the continent, oversaw an immense trade network, primarily dealing in foodstuffs from the field and the hunt, but also including such valuable items as shells, mica, copper, obsidian—and slaves. So too did the Mandan–Hidatsa horticultural villages along the Missouri River banks and two of its tributaries, the Knife and Heart Rivers, in present-day North and South Dakota. These exchange economies in Indian country, knit together by a system of well-established trails and travel ways, allowed for the diffusion of trade items over great distances. They also facilitated the spread of technology, ideas, and information. Indian peoples consequently came to know about Europeans and experience the rippling impact of their goods, diseases, and wars long before Europeans reached the interior.[8]

The reasons for trade, moreover, were not simply to access particular goods from a particular region, but had as much, if not more, to do with renewing friendships, creating alliances, or preventing wars. Indian peoples generally traded with those with whom they had some kind of "kinship" connection, be it through birth, marriage, adoption, or agreement, or with whom they wanted to establish ties. These relationships have been described as "a vital social glue,"[9] in that they were fundamental to peaceful, amicable relations between groups and therein essential to the smooth functioning of trade. As such, they had to be regularly and continuously renewed through formal ceremonies and gift-giving before any transactions commenced. In the Indian world, goodwill was a required prerequisite to trade, especially in dealing with rivals and strangers.

Europeans, wishing to trade with interior Indian peoples, found a pre-existing system of alliances and exchange networks and had no choice but to try to fit into it. To do so, they had to recognize and respect trade protocols and adopt these symbolic practices and the obligations that went along with them as their own.[10] One author has likened the process to "learn[ing] new codes of behaviour."[11]

That was the situation that Henry Kelsey faced in the early 1690s when he reached the northern prairies of the western interior in his search for new trading partners—it is why he brought along a pipe for ceremonial purposes. Local Assiniboine and Cree had certainly heard about Europeans, probably even before the Hudson's Bay Company was established, because of Spanish activities in the south and French expansion into the Great Lakes–upper Mississippi country. They also likely had limited access to European goods either through French trading partners to the east or Mandan–Hidatsa trade centres to the south. But Indian hunting and gathering societies living in what would become Saskatchewan still remained relatively unaffected by the European presence in North America by the end of the seventeenth century. Kelsey did not find a people under stress from outside forces—abandoning traditional territories or merging with other groups, as they were along the southern edges of the Great Plains in response to the Spanish incursion. Nor did he enter Indian country as an invader or conquerer. In fact, it is debatable how much the Assiniboine, Cree, and other groups actually changed or migrated once the Hudson's Bay Company began operations from York Factory on the west coast of Hudson Bay.

The beaver trade brought the English to Hudson Bay. In the sixteenth century, the felted beaver hat, high-crowned and broad-brimmed, sometimes

NATIONAL FILM BOARD

The making of a beaver felt hat

derided as foppish, swept across Europe as the latest fad—much like fitted designer ball caps of today. Not to be left behind, England readily embraced the new style from the continent and by the 1600s, "the beaver hat was a social necessity."[12] Beaver was perfectly suited for the felting process because the soft underfur of the pelt—the beaver wool or *duvet*—was barbed and hence naturally cohesive. Beaver wool was removed from the pelt, processed into felt, and then moulded and shaped into a hat. The finished product was not only waterproof but also resilient. Felted beaver hats held their shape longer than those made from any other fur or woven cloth product on the market. For any fashion-conscious man or woman, there was no substitute. Hat styles might change over the decades, becoming smaller with turned-up brims, but the best absolutely had to be made of beaver felt.

European settlement and development of North America, especially by the French in the northern half of the continent, coincided with the growing European demand for beaver pelts to produce hat felt at a time when Baltic sources were being exhausted. Here was a renewable natural product that was not only plentiful in the forested Canadian landscape, but the animals sported a

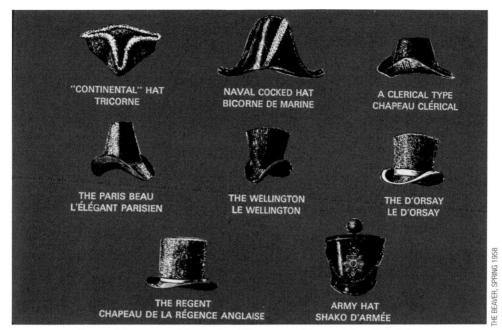

"CONTINENTAL" HAT
TRICORNE

NAVAL COCKED HAT
BICORNE DE MARINE

A CLERICAL TYPE
CHAPEAU CLÉRICAL

THE PARIS BEAU
L'ÉLÉGANT PARISIEN

THE WELLINGTON
LE WELLINGTON

THE D'ORSAY
LE D'ORSAY

THE REGENT
CHAPEAU DE LA RÉGENCE ANGLAISE

ARMY HAT
SHAKO D'ARMÉE

THE BEAVER, SPRING 1958

Beaver felt, renowned for its durability, was used in a variety of hat styles.

denser, more luxurious coat because of the colder climate. And the local Indians were more than willing to exchange furs for European trade goods. Producing beaver felt, however, required an extra or secondary step in the processing of the pelts because the softer, shorter underfur was overlain by longer, coarser guard hairs. Before shaving off the beaver wool, felters first had to remove the outer hairs. This requirement resulted in the designation or recognition of two distinct kinds of beaver pelts in the trade. *Castor sec* or "parchment" beaver was a skin that had been dried and stretched with the guard hairs still intact. *Castor gras d'hiver* or "coat" beaver, on the other hand, was a skin that had been worn by the Indians during the winter so that the pelt was not only supple and greasy but the guard hairs had been rubbed off. Coat beaver was preferred by hat-makers in Europe because it was immediately ready for the felting process. But parchment beaver (also known as *castor de moscovie*) also enjoyed a strong market because the Russians had perfected a secret process of combing the beaver wool from the skin for felting, while leaving behind the guard hairs for a fine fur pelt.[13]

The Canadian beaver trade drove the economy of New France. In the seventeenth century, trade was initially concentrated at Tadoussac, where the Saguenay River flows into the St. Lawrence River, until the French allied themselves with the agricultural-based Huron (Wendat) and became part of an existing Indian trade network centred in southwestern Ontario. This lucrative relationship ended when the Iroquois, in a bold bid to seize control of the trade, wiped out Huronia in 1649. The French were forced to move inland from the St. Lawrence, beyond Lake Huron, into the so-called *pays d'en haut*, in order to revive the shattered Huron network with the help of the Ottawa Indians and any surviving Huron. Two of the hundreds of French traders or *coureurs de bois* who helped establish new commercial ties with Great Lakes bands were Pierre Esprit Radisson and his brother-in-law Médard Chouart Des Groseilliers. They were the ones who learned, while travelling and trading along the north shore of Lake Superior in 1659–60, that the finest beaver pelts came from the Cree living near a large bay to the north. It did not take much of a mental leap to conclude that trade could best be prosecuted from Hudson Bay instead of the long, treacherous, overland route from Montreal. The pair returned to New France with this revolutionary concept, only to be rebuffed by colonial officials who were more interested in confining the colony to the St. Lawrence. Dismayed, if not stung, by their treatment, they took their idea to the English.

Radisson and Groseilliers found a receptive audience at the court of King Charles II. These were heady days for Restoration England—what one historian has called "a period in which the spirit of adventure moved along with sophisticated manners, elaborate dress, scientific inquiry, and financial acumen."[14] The scheme nicely dovetailed with the general English desire to expand and consolidate colonial trade by holding out the opportunity of becoming involved in the international trade in beaver skins. If Radisson and Groseilliers were right, the English could directly challenge the French fur trade in North America, perhaps even gaining the upper hand in their imperial rival's backyard. And that was the other attractive feature of the proposal. It offered the English a new trade route, one that enabled large ocean-going ships to sail into the heart of the continent and bring back rich cargoes of prime beaver pelts. The sailing time from London to the entrance to Hudson Bay was almost equal to the sailing time to Montreal. No wonder, then, that influential figures were intrigued by the idea, including Prince Rupert, the king's cousin, and financier George Cateret, reportedly the richest man in England. Forming themselves into a consortium, they sponsored an expedition to the bay in 1668–69 to test the theory. When the diminutive *Nonsuch* triumphantly returned,[15] laden with furs, negotiations with the Crown began in earnest to secure a royal charter. "The Governor and Company of Adventurers of England trading in Hudson's Bay," more popularly known as the Hudson's Bay Company or HBC, officially came into being on 2 May 1670.[16]

Much has been made of the seven-thousand-word HBC charter and the huge amount of territory over which the company ("true and absolute Lordes and Proprietors") was granted "sole Trade and Commerce." Rupert's Land (named after the first HBC governor and applied to the region well into the nineteenth century) apparently included all land within the Hudson Bay drainage basin—in other words, about 1.5 million square miles or 40 per cent of modern Canada. To put this area into perspective, the bay itself is almost the same size as the Mediterranean Sea. Or, as an early overseas governor mused, "Our patant is verry darke in that it is not bounded with any line of latitude or longitude."[17] The HBC steadfastly maintained its claim to this vast territory for the next two centuries. It is an interpretation repeated by fur trade histories. But the HBC never tested its rights in the courts. That might be because the wording of the charter is ambiguous in defining the reach of Rupert's Land. The charter actually gives the company a monopoly over the navigation of Hudson Strait for the purposes of trade, as well as control over coastal lands accessed via Hudson Strait.[18] Does that mean the entire Hudson Bay watershed? No mention is made, moreover, about access to the western interior via the St. Lawrence and Great Lakes. Why, then, were French and later Canadian traders characterized as interlopers and trespassers?

The charter has been rightly criticized for not allowing Indians to choose

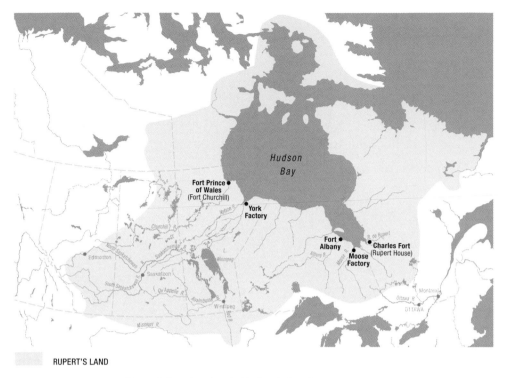

RUPERT'S LAND

Rupert's Land and early Hudson's Bay Company posts

their own trading partners, and, more significantly, for not recognizing existing occupancy rights of Indian nations. But the charter must be understood in its time, not read through today's lens. Since private investors in the company were taking on the risk in developing trade through the bay, it was fairly standard for them to request and be granted monopoly protection. The Crown, in turn, did not have to shoulder any expense, but stood to benefit from any new English influence in the area, whether it be new markets or subjects.[19] There is also a tendency to misread the obligations of the company. Although the charter mentioned settlement and exploration as possible company responsibilities, these activities were not required, nor were they the primary purpose. The charter, in the words of one fur trade expert, was "a magnificent grant of rights and privileges, not a specification of duties."[20] These rights and privileges, documented on vellum (made from sheepskin) and approved by the Great Seal of England, were no match for the realities of Indian country. The Hudson's Bay Company had to master "the essentials of its trade" if it was

102

Hudson's Bay Company ships faced a short shipping season in arctic waters.

going to survive, let alone pay a dividend to its shareholders, and not rely on its trade monopoly for protection.[21]

From its beginning, the Hudson's Bay Company was "free to adopt whatever trading methods it thought best."[22] How it ran its operations, however, went a long way in determining its relationship with Indian peoples and how they responded to the coming of the beaver trade. In addition to Charles Fort (later Rupert House) where the *Nonsuch* had successfully overwintered in 1668–69, the HBC established new posts at the mouths of the Moose (Moose Factory, 1673) and Albany (Fort Albany, 1674) Rivers at the southern end or bottom of James Bay. These coastal posts or factories, to be re-supplied on an annual basis by ships sent out from England, were intended to be the hub of company activities in North America. In living along the rim of the bay year-round, HBC servants maintained continuous contact with their Indian customers, when not handling trade goods, preparing cargoes, and dealing with inventories. Their location, however, on the open, poorly drained Hudson Bay lowlands, where even local Indians refused to live year-round because of the harsh conditions, meant that the posts were akin to "lunar colonies" in some future century.[23] It would have made more sense to have relocated company operations into the forest, if only during the winter, to seek out shelter and game resources. But the London directorship was obsessed with minimizing costs while maximizing revenue and believed that expenses could be contained by confining operations to the immediate vicinity of the bay. It was equally worried about competitors, including private trading by company servants, and sought to limit any losses by keeping company operations as contained and secretive as possible, while exercising a firm hand over its employees at controlled locations.

These few bayside posts made the company dependent on the Indians. By not moving inland, the HBC had to get the trading Indians to come to the bay posts; otherwise, the company would not have been in business for very long. It consequently had to offer quality goods that the Indians wanted or quickly came to demand. At first, acting on advice from Radisson, the company inventory featured trade items that were similar, if not identical, to those from the French. Within a few years, though, it had developed its own distinctive line of products in response to Indian tastes and complaints. In 1685, for example, the London committee confidently told Overseas Governor Henry Sergeant that the latest shipment of goods should silence any complaints: "We doubt not but the Guns we sent you … will prove well … & be very acceptable to the Indians."[24] Similar assurances were made the following year: "Our Guns are all Engelish guns, the best though they cost us the Dearer … and the right sort of Brazeele tobacco which they [Indians] soe much desire."[25] The London Committee had clearly come to appreciate the need for "good wares" that were both "serviceable and strong," especially if it was going to entice remote Indians to come down to the bay to trade, and wanted to hear from its servants "should any thing be over looked by us."[26]

The HBC also sought to accommodate Indians by introducing an official standard of trade, a kind of barter system that equated all trade goods to prime winter skins or "Made Beaver" (MB) units. Two hatchets, for example, could be "purchased" for one MB at Albany in 1700. This standard removed the guesswork for Indian traders. Before heading to the company posts, they

METROPOLITAN TORONTO LIBRARY BOARD 2329

York Factory was the Hudson's Bay Company's pre-eminent post.

had some sense of what they might be able to obtain for their furs and the exchange rate. Trade could also be conducted more expeditiously under such a system, an important consideration for groups who travelled longer distances to the bay and had limited time to spend there before returning inland. It was even contemplated—at least by HBC shareholders anxious to see their first dividend—that "such quick dispatch" would allow "some of the neerest Indians may make two returnes in a season."[27] But this system, once it became ingrained in the trading process, could work against the company, in that it did not account for fluctuating prices for beaver pelts or trade goods. Indians proved resistant to having to provide more pelts or accepting fewer goods than they had become accustomed to under the standard. Not all furs, moreover, were prime beaver pelts or the kind of pelts that the company desired. But the servants had to accept them, usually at discounted prices, rather than turning Indians away and losing customers.[28] That was the case in the first few decades of the HBC's operations when both coat and parchment beaver were traded even though the London Committee wanted only parchment. When Governor James Knight was later directed to burn all coat beaver at his post, he balked at the order, fearing it would send the wrong message to the Indians.[29]

These measures helped the HBC market its first furs in Europe in 1680. It was also a fortuitous coincidence that Fort Albany was situated at the mouth of the second longest river in present-day Ontario and drew Ojibwa and Cree to James Bay, probably from as far away as the north shore of Lake Superior. But the great promise of the Radisson and Groseilliers scheme was never to be realized as long as the company concentrated its operations in James Bay and ignored the vast fur hinterland that could be tapped by a post on the west coast of Hudson Bay. Putting a factory at the mouth of the Nelson River had been planned as early as 1670, when on 1 September, the first overseas governor arrived to take formal possession of the region on behalf of the company. But the lateness of the season and the threat of the approaching winter convinced company servants to retreat to the bottom of the bay. Three years later, the HBC started a summer trade at Port Nelson, but again deferred settling there. This vacillation finally ended in 1682 when the company dispatched John Bridgar to build a post at the mouth of the Nelson in a determined effort to uphold its charter against French traders. Radisson, in the meantime, had not only switched allegiances, but also occupied the nearby Hayes River on the southern side of the peninsula, and easily subdued the English traders. The HBC did not regain control of the Nelson–Hayes estuary until 1684, the same year it decided to relocate its temporary post on the Nelson to the other side of the peninsula on the north bank of the Hayes River. The move was for the benefit of Indian traders. Whereas the Nelson carried a huge volume of water, flowing over steep drops through the Shield country, the smaller, quieter Hayes was better suited for canoe travel.

Like other bay posts, York Factory was situated on desolate, marshy lowlands, prompting one future occupant to describe life there as "nine months of winter, varied by three months of rain and mosquitoes."[30] As at Albany, ocean-going vessels had to anchor several miles offshore because of the tidal flats. Despite these shortcomings, York Factory (known to the Cree as *kihci-wâskahikan* or "great house" because of the main depot building) would become the oldest European settlement in the future province of Manitoba and hence western Canada. More importantly, for the sake of the beaver trade, it provided access to an immense watershed that reached as far south as the Red River and as far west as the Rocky Mountains. Strategically, it was the perfect place for a post, especially because the company was not going to move inland. Within a few decades, the trade there equalled the trade at all the HBC posts combined.

The same year that York Factory was established was the same year that company shareholders enjoyed their first dividend. Better returns were anticipated in the coming decades now that the country southwest of Hudson Bay had been added to the company orbit. To ensure that Indians patronized the new post and to counter rival French claims to the territory, the HBC instructed the servant responsible for the trade there "to make such Contracts with the Natives for the River in & above Port Nelson as may in future times ascertain to us a right & property therein and the Sole Liberty of trade & Commerce there, and to make Leagues of friendship & peaceable Cohabitation with such Ceremonies as you shall finde tobee most Sacred and Obligatory amongst them."[31]

This directive did not simply apply to the new Nelson–Hayes sphere of trade. Virtually identical instructions had been issued to company employees at other posts since at least 1680. It is apparent, then, that whatever the charter might have said about rights and privileges, the HBC directors realized that the French presence called for some kind of formal agreement with the local Indian population, particularly in opening up a new regional territory. The company, through its overseas representatives, consequently desired not only to enter into commercial compacts with Indian groups to secure monopoly trade rights, but to do so in a way that captured the solemnity of these agreements.[32] To guarantee the continuing loyalty of its trading partners, moreover, company servants were to do whatever was necessary to ensure that the Indians became steady company customers. The annual instructions for 1688, for example, implored Governor Geyer at York Factory to "give the Indians all manner of Content and Satisfaction and in Some goods Under Sell the French that they may be incouraged to Come to our Factory's and to bring their Nations Downe." To ensure that the full import of these directions was appreciated by Geyer, the last part of the sentence was written in italics: "*Wee ought to Trade with the Indians Soe as that Wee may Trade with them againe, and to make them willing to Come to us and not for Once and never See them more.*"[33]

The HBC adopted these various measures to initiate and consolidate trade with the Indian population in the face of the French challenge. But the company still had to address the fundamental challenge of getting more distant Indians to come to the coast in the first place. The most obvious solution, as long as posts were to be confined to the rim of the bay, was to send servants inland to advertise and promote trade with the new English enterprise. The London committee certainly sized up the situation this way and chastised the overseas governor in 1682 for not showing more initiative along these lines. "It would bee worth your Consideration," it pushed Governor John Nixon, "if you imitated the Industrie of the French by sending some of your men up into the Countrey to meet the Indians, and by all faire persuasion. & kinde usage to Invite them to come downe & trade onely at our Factories, which indeed is a thing Wee wonder you have not in all this time put in practice."[34]

John Bridgar was told much the same thing as he prepared to establish a settlement on the Nelson River, as was the new overseas governor upon taking up his duties in 1683. And when servants, fearing danger or the unknown, proved unwilling to travel up country, the London committee promised to reward them.[35] That might have been one of the reasons why Henry Kelsey agreed to go inland in 1690. He could also have been inspired by previous trips. In 1682, while siding with the French, Radisson and his nephew and Groseilliers's son, Jean-Baptiste Chouart, journeyed about one hundred miles up the Hayes River to encourage the Indians to come down to the estuary to trade. The following year, Chouart went upriver again for the same reason. In fact, just as Kelsey is credited for being the first European to see the Saskatchewan prairies, Chouart may have been the first to visit Lake Winnipeg

A woman from the Hudson Bay region   A man from the Hudson Bay region

in present-day Manitoba when he headed inland for a third time, this time on behalf of the English in 1685.[36] That, coincidentally, was the same year that a young Kelsey was working at York Factory.

Radisson's temporary defection back to the French—he switched sides several times—was part of a larger problem that the HBC potentially faced in the bay region. The 1670 Royal Charter may have reserved the area for the English traders, but early company correspondence is riddled with references to the so-called French threat. "You must looke upon them as a standing Enemey," the HBC Committee once admonished its North American servants, "alwaies be on your guarde to prevent any of their Designes either of fraude or force."[37] Such warnings might appear exaggerated, if not unnecessary, because the northern English posts were intended to be beyond the reach of New France. But in 1672, only two years after the founding of the HBC, a small reconnaissance expedition from New France, sent to confirm the rumours of English activity on the bay, reached Charles Fort at the mouth of

109

The cover of the York Factory journal for the period September 1714 to September 1715

the Rupert River. This discovery caused the French to build a string of small trading huts on the rivers leading to the English James Bay posts in order to intercept Indians on their way to the bay to trade. To the west, a similar advance action was mounted in the following decade. In 1684, the same year that York Factory was established, Greysolon Dulhut built two new French posts, one at Kaministiquia at the extreme western end of Lake Superior, the other on Lake Nipigon in northwestern Ontario. Four years later, Jacques de Noyon pushed farther west than any previous Canadian and reached the Rainy River district. Both *coureurs de bois* sought to trade directly with the local Cree and Assiniboine, close to their trapping grounds, and thereby discourage them from taking their furs to the English at the bay.

This commercial struggle between two imperial rivals over the northwestern fur trade deepened in 1689 when France and England, after sparring for a few years, finally went to war (King William's War, 1689–97). The bay region saw no fighting until 1694, when Canadian Pierre le Moyne d'Iberville easily captured York Factory, the new jewel in the HBC trade. Henry Kelsey was among the prisoners. The English struck back in 1696 and retook the fort, only to lose it again the following year to d'Iberville, who directed a punishing mortar bombardment to force the garrison to surrender. French control of the west coast of Hudson Bay, including York Factory (renamed Fort Bourbon), was confirmed in the 1697 Treaty of Ryswick. Thereafter, no posts changed hands into the new century, even during the War of Spanish Succession (1702–13), and it fell to diplomats to sort out ownership of the bay region at the peace table. Article 10 of the 1713 Treaty of Utrecht "restored" Hudson Strait and Hudson Bay to England—a concession that has been described as part of the "catalog of French losses" in its North American colonial world.[38] But even though the article effectively recognized HBC title, it never defined the boundary between Rupert's Land and French Canada. That matter was left to a future commission to decide—a commission that never met. What might have been a "triumph" for the English trading company, then, was actually a "triumph accompanied by anxieties."[39] As long as the boundary remained fuzzy and the charter not tested in the courts, the French could continue to seek out trading opportunities in what may or may not have been the HBC hinterland. Besides, the French questioned how the bay could be "restored" to the English if the HBC had not possessed it. And even if the English did have any territorial rights in the region, the French claimed, they were limited to the rim of the bay, where the posts were located.

The French in 1713, however, had no immediate desire to challenge the English in the northwest. That was because their own beaver trade had just gone through a difficult period. In April 1697, a glut of furs on the market had convinced the French to close the western trade of the Great Lakes and upper Mississippi country. No *congés* or permits to trade in the interior were issued for almost the next two decades. That still left the problem of what to do about York Factory (Fort Bourbon). Much like their English counterparts before them, the French took in whatever furs the Indians brought down the Nelson and Hayes Rivers. Because of the limited wartime market for beaver skins, most went unsold, rotting in warehouses instead of being made into hat felt. Their ignoble fate matched the wretched conditions that the English found at York Factory when the HBC formally resumed control on 10 September 1714. Governor Knight complained that the French interlude had reduced the fort to "nothing but a confused heap of old rotten houses without form or strength," while the place where he was to spend the winter was "not half so good as [a] cowhouse."[40]

Governor Knight had been in charge of York Factory for only one day when the local Cree requested a council. For three hours on Sunday, enveloped by what Knight described as a "great Deal of ceremony," the two sides exchanged gifts, smoked the calumet, and made lengthy speeches to renew their trade relationship. Invoking the presence of the Creator, the leading chief talked about the importance of their friendship in words "straightforward and true"—how his people were miserable, needed the company's generosity, and would repay them with gratitude and loyalty. Knight, in turn, encouraged the Indians to bring their furs to the English post on the understanding that they could expect "fair dealing." Three days later, he repeated his promise when he entered into a "solemn pact" with another band of Indians.[41] These ceremonies stand in stark contrast to the international treaty that had confirmed HBC title to the bay region. Whereas European treaties were based on one-time negotiations between the representatives of centralized monarchies, the HBC at York Factory had to enter a series of alliances with band societies—alliances that required constant attention, if not regular renewal—if the Utrecht award was going to mean anything.[42] The company could not strike a trading partnership with one group of Cree and expect it to apply to all Cree people. Nor could it simply expect to displace the French on the Nelson–Hayes estuary and resume trade with the Indians after an absence of nearly twenty years.

But how much inland trade was being conducted? In 1684, the year that York Factory was established, the French reported that some three hundred canoes, manned by Cree and Assiniboine, had come down to the bay to trade. It is likely that they made the trip because of the new post at the mouth of the Hayes River and the novelty or excitement of such an adventure. Up to then, if Indians living in the northwest wanted to trade directly with the HBC, they had to travel to the bottom of the bay. They also likely came in such initial numbers because of the promotional efforts of Radisson and his nephew who had travelled upland to cajole Indian bands into trading. Thereafter, it has been estimated that there were on average as many as 420 canoes arriving at York Factory each year between 1689 and 1694. But it is questionable whether these numbers constituted "major trading expeditions" by the Cree and Assiniboine living in the Saskatchewan country.[43] If that were the case, then why did the HBC send Henry Kelsey inland to the northern prairies in 1690, as well as try to find other servants who were willing to duplicate his example? Even the French during their occupation of the post from 1697 to 1714 occasionally sent men into the interior to convince the Indians to trade at Fort Bourbon. The number of canoes is also not that large, given the huge drainage basin area of the Nelson–Hayes Rivers. Four hundred canoes might represent no more than eight hundred men from the entire region west of the trade area

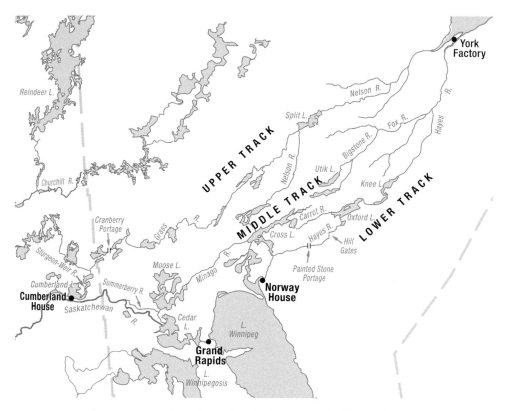

Major canoe routes between York Factory and central Saskatchewan

of the HBC James Bay posts—even less when it is realized that women often accompanied their partners, in part because they were skilled in steering and lining the canoes. It could even be argued, then, that the interior Indians were actually under-represented during the early years of the bay trade.[44]

One reason that the Cree and Assiniboine were reluctant to make the trip to York Factory was the distances involved. Indians travelling from the Saskatchewan country had the choice of three possible canoe routes, all starting in the east-central part of the province. The "Upper Track," as it was known, started from Cumberland Lake, up the Sturgeon–Weir River, over the Cranberry Portage, and then down the Grass River to the Nelson River just before Split Lake. From this point, it was only about two hundred miles to York Factory, but the dangerous Nelson was usually avoided in favour of detouring over to the canoe-friendly Hayes. The "Middle Track" started on the Saskatchewan River just below The Pas, continued down the Summerberry River to Moose Lake, and then down the Minago River to Cross Lake. Here, the route branched, one way (north branch) leading across Utik Lake to the Bigstone, Fox, and the Hayes Rivers, the other way (south branch) passed through Walker Lake, the Carrot River, and then Oxford Lake on the Hayes River. Finally, the "Lower Track" started near the mouth of the Saskatchewan River at Grand Rapids, continued across the top of Lake Winnipeg, and then down the Hayes River. Indians living in eastern Saskatchewan preferred the Lower Track, while those travelling down the Saskatchewan used the Upper and Middle Tracks.[45]

When Kelsey travelled inland with the Assiniboine in June 1690, probably along the south branch of the Middle Track, it required almost a full month (12 June to 10 July) for the group to return upriver to their home territory near present-day The Pas. Even allowing for less time going downriver because of the current, the total bay trading trip probably required a minimum of eight to ten weeks when the time needed for trading at the post is also included. Other trips required even more time. In June 1715, some Assiniboine had travelled thirty-nine days to York Factory, the farthest for any group that trading season.[46] These were demanding trips that took Indians to the edge of their survival abilities because of the need to move quickly along waterways with dangerous sections. Any delay or error could lead to misfortune. Their prolonged absence from their home territories also meant that subsistence activities were neglected, and that, too, threatened their well-being and that of their families. The likely response by distant groups was to go every second or third year or never again, while those bands living closest to York Factory absorbed most of the trade items by default.

Another factor discouraging Indians from tackling the arduous trip to the bay was a shortage of trade goods at the posts. During the French tenure, the fort was poorly supplied, especially for the period from 1708 to 1713 when it was never re-stocked. One of the "Mountain Indians" (probably Assiniboine from the Manitoba escarpment region) told HBC Governor Knight in 1716 that his people had not been to the bay for over a decade because of the lack of supplies. This problem was not peculiar to the French. No sooner had the

English—promising generous treatment—resumed command of York Factory than the 1715 fall supply ship failed to arrive. Those Indians who had come to trade in 1716, ironically including those who had not been to York Factory for more than ten years, consequently had to make do with the few trade items that were available or remain there until the early fall for the next supply ship. This delay proved deadly for some of the Indian traders who headed upriver too late in the season; others endured great suffering. The repercussions were spelled out the following trade season. The number of Indians who arrived at the post to trade in 1717, according to Knight, had fallen by two-thirds.[47]

The beaver trade was only one aspect of Indian life at that time. In the summer of 1715, for example, only 172 canoes came to the post.[48] This disappointing number could be explained by the fact that the English had only resumed control of York Factory after the Utrecht settlement and the HBC trade there was just getting re-established. But Kelsey's trip inland with sample goods, when combined with similar French initiatives, meant that Indian groups probably as far south as the Missouri River and west to the Canadian prairies knew about the traders at York Factory and the goods that could be secured there. What kept them away, besides the distance involved and the supply problems, were other opportunities, such as raiding expeditions or communal hunts.[49] This reality is not to suggest that the Cree and Assiniboine were not ready and willing to be trade partners with the English or that they did not welcome European goods and incorporate them into their daily subsistence activities. An examination of HBC account books reveals that Indians were heavy consumers of knives, kettles, hatchets, ice chisels, and especially guns, shot, and powder—an incredible 510 guns in 1691 alone.[50] They also had a special liking for the Brazil tobacco that the English traded by the pound. But the trade did not dominate Indian lives in the interior. Nor did trade items completely replace traditional tools and weapons. The bow and arrow, for example, were not jettisoned in favour of the gun. Part of the explanation was that the gun could not be easily repaired or replaced when it broke—or used when powder ran out. Guns were also in limited supply because Indian traders from the northwest, faced with the very real challenge of getting to and from York Factory safely and expeditiously, initially secured goods for their own needs. They were reluctant to part with these items, even when used or worn out, because they might not be able to replace them later at the bay due to supply problems. By the early eighteenth century, then, the diffusion of HBC trade goods across Rupert's Land was limited at best.[51]

Perhaps the biggest impediment to the expansion of the HBC beaver trade into the western interior was caused by the blockading activities of the Cree and Assiniboine. Once York Factory was established on the western shore of Hudson Bay, these two Indian groups used their locational advantage and their tribal alliance to prevent other Indians from securing trade goods—by force if necessary, ironically with the very guns that they had secured from the English. Kelsey learned of this gatekeeper role played by the Cree and Assiniboine when he travelled inland as a trade emissary and found his efforts undermined by the constant warring. "But now of late they [the Cree] hunt their Enemies," he recorded in 1690. "And with our English guns do make Ym, flie."[52] When he finally did arrange to meet with the mysterious Naywatame Poets the following summer and convince them to come to the bay to trade, the understanding quickly came undone at the hands of the Cree. Kelsey's experience confirmed what company servants had been complaining about as early as 1682 at the James Bay posts.[53]

But did the Cree and Assiniboine seek to expand this middleman role by migrating from present-day northwestern Ontario/southeastern Manitoba into east-central Saskatchewan? In other words, were they relative newcomers to the region, responding to the coming of the beaver trade by aggressively moving into other territory? Once again, Kelsey's trip is instructive—as is recent archaeological work. Keeping in mind that it was only eight years after the English had established a post on the Nelson–Hayes estuary (and just six after the founding of York Factory), his journal suggests that the Cree and Assiniboine were not only already there in east-central Saskatchewan, but well-established. They behaved and acted like it was their home ground.[54]

117

Clearly, then, the idea of the Cree and Assiniboine in the late seventeenth century embarking on what has been portrayed as a "triumphant march westward with their guns" needs to be reconsidered.[55] Indian life in this period was certainly mobile, if not fluid, but the Cree and Assiniboine did not push farther westward, up the North Saskatchewan, until decades later.

There is little doubt, though, that some Indian bands used their new European weapons to prevent other groups from trading with the English. Company records regularly mention how the York Factory Cree waged war against the Chipewyan or Northern Indians—robbing them of furs, preventing access to the English, and wantonly killing them. A thoroughly exasperated Kelsey once refused to trade with a group of Cree fresh from a raiding expedition. He bluntly informed them, "We did not bring guns, powder and other necessaries to destroy mankind."[56] This terrorization of the Northern Indians also went against Governor Knight's plan to expand the western Canadian beaver trade after the Utrecht settlement. In particular, he wanted to push the company trade beyond the reach of its French rivals and the best way to do that, from the vantage point afforded by the bay, was to tap the vast region north of York Factory via the Churchill River watershed. It was no easy undertaking.

Knight's expansion of the northwestern beaver trade was rooted in two complementary initiatives. First, he sought to bring an end to the incessant fighting between Indian groups, especially the Cree and Chipewyan. He confided to the York Factory post journal in May 1716 that he was "endeavoring to make a peace in the whole Country Round from N to S Wt for a 1000 miles."[57] To do so, Knight admonished visiting Indians, especially local Cree who were known to harass the Chipewyan at every opportunity, to busy themselves "working beaver" and not making war. But he exercised no control over them once they left the post. He also naively sent trade goods inland with returning Indians, who were supposed to act as peace emissaries and make treaties with their enemies. Here, too, he was helpless, because existing animosities were stubbornly resistant to the wishes of distant traders, especially when HBC guns were upsetting the balance of power in the interior.[58]

HUDSON'S BAY COMPANY ARCHIVES P-228

Prince of Wales Fort, along the west coast of Hudson Bay, was intended to extend the fur trade to the northwest, beyond the reach of the HBC's French rivals.

Knight's best hope in securing peace between the Cree and the Chipewyan appeared to be his decision to send one of the company servants, William Stuart (sometimes spelled Stewart), inland in June 1715. The Cree-speaking Stuart had apprenticed at York Factory when Kelsey was inland in 1691, and had also been a member of the party (including Kelsey) that had accepted the formal transfer of the post from the French in 1714. He was therefore well aware of Kelsey's experience in the interior. Maybe that was why he did not volunteer for the assignment but had to be ordered to do it. Stuart headed north from York Factory in the company of about 150 coastal Cree (or Home Indians because of their connection to the post) and a Chipewyan captive, known as Thanadelthur or the Slave Woman, who was to serve as his interpreter. His mission was to broker a peace with the Northern Indians so that they were no longer afraid of coming to the coast to trade. Within weeks, sickness and then starvation had overtaken the expedition, forcing it to splinter into smaller groups, some of whom straggled into the post with tales of hardship and hopelessness. Stuart's party fought through bitter cold and deep snow as it crossed the open barrens, only to discover to its horror that an advance group of Home Cree had attacked a camp of Northern Indians. Thanadelthur intervened at this point and proposed to make contact with the Chipewyan—on her own—and try to undo the damage that had been done. She returned over a week later with about 150 Northern Indians and at her persuasive best, helped secure a truce, made more palatable by the distribution of trade goods and the prospect of more in the future. Upon his return to York Factory in May 1716, Stuart claimed to have travelled a thousand miles and reached a latitude of sixty-seven degrees north, above the arctic circle. Several fur trade scholars have since suggested that his party probably visited the wooded country south of Great Slave Lake (about sixty-one degrees north) in the present-day Northwest Territories.[59] A more recent assessment places the HBC servant only halfway to Great Slave Lake, around Kasba Lake, near the Saskatchewan–Manitoba border.[60] In any event, Stuart was the first known European to travel across the barrenlands and visit the region that is now near the top of the province of Saskatchewan.

Stuart had promised the Chipewyan during his 1715–16 peace expedition that the HBC would build a post at the Churchill River—the second part of Governor Knight's strategy to extend the beaver trade to the northwest. It was not the first attempt to locate a settlement there. An earlier half-hearted initiative had failed in 1689. A similar outcome seemed likely this second time. The failure of the 1715 supply ship to reach York Factory meant that the establishment of the new Churchill post had to be delayed a year. Northern Indians who had come, at Stuart's urging, to the coast to trade in the summer of 1716 consequently left in frustration. Thanadelthur might have been expected to rescue the situation, as she had done earlier to get her people to come to the bay to trade, but she died in February 1717. Another Slave Woman—this one nameless—whom Knight had purchased for sixty skins from the Home Indians to serve as his Chipewyan interpreter replaced Thanadelthur.[61]

The new post, originally named Prince of Wales, was located in June

1717 on the same spot where Dane Jens Munk had been forced to spend a calamitous winter almost one hundred years earlier. It was a "miserable site"— with no natural shelter, no timber, and no harbour because of the stony tidal flats. But because it was open on all sides, it was defensible, a must for Knight who seemed deathly worried about depredations from the local Inuit.[62] The Churchill post might not seem to make good business sense because it took away some of the trade that had gone to York Factory in the past. From a larger perspective, though, it was representative of the HBC's desire to consolidate its presence in the bay region following the Utrecht settlement and bring more Indians—in this case, the Chipewyan and the Cree of the Upper Churchill— into the beaver trade. That is why no sooner had the site for the new fort been selected than sixteen-year-old apprentice Richard Norton was dispatched with a few Northern Indians "into thare own country" in July 1717.[63] He was brought back, or more accurately, rescued, frostbitten and starving, sometime the following winter. Because the post journal for that period has not survived, it is not known where Norton went. But his experience, like that of Stuart before him, confirmed that "although the prospects of trade to the northwest might be good the difficulties were proportionately great[er]."[64]

These "difficulties" did not concern Governor Knight. Instead, he had become absorbed with tales of large quantities of gold and copper in the interior and asked to be recalled to England where he might convince the HBC governing committee to sponsor a major expedition to investigate the rumours while looking for a northwest passage across the top of the continent. Knight got his wish and left with two ships in June 1719 to explore the region north of sixty-four degrees latitude. The expedition sailed directly to the far northwest of Hudson Bay, without stopping at any of the company posts, and then disappeared. The fate of Knight and his men—how they perished on Marble Island near Rankin Inlet—would not be confirmed for another fifty years. The limited evidence at the time suggested that the ships had been wrecked and the HBC quietly wrote them off as losses in its financial books in 1722. The company also decided against any more expeditions, whether by land or sea.

William Stuart died the same year that Knight went missing, reduced to a raving "lunatick"[65] who had to be physically restrained the last few months of his life. Richard Norton fared little better. Even though he continued to serve at Churchill, it was found that nothing about his trip "remained on his memory, but the danger and terrour he underwent."[66]

These two sorry cases, along with the Knight fiasco, were certainly the exception in the five-decade history of the HBC at bayside, but they raised the larger question of the wisdom of trading inland, of sending servants into the interior, especially when there appeared to be "no urgent necessity" to do so after the Utrecht victory. At the beginning of the 1720s, then, the HBC re-dedicated itself to its aseptic business strategy of pursuing its trading operations from the shores of Hudson Bay. It was something of a gamble because the success of the policy depended entirely on getting Indian peoples to come to the coastal posts. It also assumed that Indians would deal with the English company rather than its French competitors encroaching from the east. But the company was never more confident, never more convinced that its "monopoly of knowledge and experience was its greatest asset."[67]

A Saulteaux family travelling in winter near Lake Winnipeg

Trading Indians were greeted with presents upon their arrival at the Hudson's Bay Company posts.

CHAPTER FOUR

A MERE MATTER
OF PADDLING

THE NEWS HERALDED THE BEGINNING OF A PROFOUND SHIFT IN THE PLAYING FIELD of the fur trade and the rules regarding the struggle for beaver skins. In the spring of 1728, Indians wearing French clothing arrived at York Factory for the annual trading season. They told Governor Thomas Macklish of the Hudson's Bay Company that French traders were just "four Days paddling from the Great Lake [Winnipeg] that feed this River [Nelson]." Nor were the Montreal-based traders simply content to skim off some of the English beaver trade. "Several of the french," Macklish learned, "goes Yearly with the *Poits* [Sioux] to Warr with most of our Indians here" to prevent them from trading at the bay posts.[1] Other disturbing accounts of French activity in the interior were forthcoming over the next few years. In 1732, Macklish advised London that the Sturgeon Cree, normally regular customers, had not come down to York Factory that spring but had apparently been intimidated into trading with the French. Then, three years later, Indians reported that the French now had a settlement somewhere near Lake Winnipeg.[2]

This enemy activity—and that's how the HBC regarded the French—had initially been restricted in the early eighteenth century to the trading hinterland at the bottom of the bay. But now, the French seemed to be pushing into the rich beaver country of present-day Manitoba and eastern Saskatchewan, once the exclusive reserve of York Factory and Fort Churchill. It was the kind of bold move that, if left unchecked, could destroy the HBC trading system in

Rupert's Land. Equally important for those Indian bands living in the region, it signalled a new phase in Native-newcomer relations. English traders had rarely ventured inland—the one notable exception being Henry Kelsey in 1690–92. If Indian peoples wanted to participate in the beaver trade, they either traded with groups travelling to the English posts or made the trip to Hudson Bay themselves. Now, French *coureurs de bois*, or woodrunners as they were known to the English, were on their doorstep, whether Indians wanted to participate in the trade or not. No longer would the European presence be felt only from a distance.

It is not known with any great certainty which Indian groups living in the western interior traded at York Factory or Fort Churchill following the Treaty of Utrecht in 1713. One suggestion is that Indians occupying a sweeping arc of territory from Great Slave Lake to the Missouri River *may* have made the trip to the bay at some time in the 1710s and 1720s.[3] Determining HBC customers is difficult since trading Indians did not linger long at the bay, because of limited food supplies, but hurried back inland to rejoin their bands. HBC servants therefore had little opportunity to get to know Indian individuals except for the trade "captains." They also had at best only a vague idea of where they had come from, in large part because the company's horizon never extended beyond the rim of the bay. The problem is further compounded by what is not found in the post journals and account books. English traders might have been good accountants—recording the number of canoes that came to the bay, the distance travelled (usually expressed in days of canoe travel), and the length of stay—but they were generally negligent in naming the particular bands and leaders in those canoes.[4] In its defence, the company did not want, probably did not care, about these kinds of details, just the trade volume and what was in demand.

The terminology used by HBC employees also does not provide much direction in identifying trading Indians. When the company set up operations on the shores of Hudson Bay, the Cree, or the Southern Indians (Keskachewan) as they were sometimes called, were the dominant, resident people. HBC employees consequently came to use the Cree language to describe other, non-resident Indian groups. The Assiniboine or Nakota, for example, were known by the Cree word, Assinipoet (or Poet), in company records. "Archithinue," on the other hand, was the Anglicized Cree term for stranger, and it was normally applied to all trading groups and individuals who were neither Cree nor Assiniboine—mainly, the Blackfoot (Niitsitapi) groups (Blackfoot [Siksika], Blood [Kainai] and Peigan [Piikani]). Indeed, the HBC seemed to regard the Cree as a generic group—often called "Southern Indians," "our Indians," or "English Indians" in company records—when, in fact, there were several distinct Cree regional bands living throughout the boreal forest and parklands. These differences were not fully appreciated by bay men in the mid-eighteenth century. Nor did they come to understand them over time because some of these Cree bands who once traded at the bay would disappear during the 1781–82 smallpox epidemic.[5]

Who, then, traded at English posts on the western or Manitoban shore of Hudson Bay? The Blackfoot, descendants of people associated with the Old Women's cultural phase in west-central Saskatchewan and southern Alberta, are said to have travelled there in response to Governor Knight's trade invitation and peace initiative on the heels of the Utrecht settlement. So too, apparently did the Mandan and Hidatsa from their settlements on the upper Missouri River. It beggars belief, though, that the Blackfoot tribes, totally inexperienced with canoes, made such a long, arduous trip—even if, as it has been suggested, the Cree and Assiniboine accompanied them.[6]

The presence of Mandan and Hidatsa at the bay is even more problematic. In 1715, Governor Knight welcomed thirty canoes of "Mountain" Indians who had once traded at the bottom of the bay and had now made their first trip—thirty-nine days—to York Factory. They reportedly came from "Country ... of (such) a Prodigious height," where there was bison and elk, corn and nuts, and even precious metals.[7] It has widely been assumed that this mysterious group was from the Mandan–Hidatsa fortified settlements in present-day North Dakota.[8] But these Siouan-speaking people were important brokers in an extensive intertribal trade network, and it made little sense for them to travel over one thousand miles, especially when they too had little experience with canoes.[9] Besides, as Henry Kelsey learned in 1692, the Cree regularly skirmished with the Mandan and Hidatsa, making any trip to the bay a perilous undertaking. So, if the Mountain Indians were probably neither Mandan nor Hidatsa, then, who were they? In all likelihood, they were a Cree group from the Manitoba escarpment region. Their home ground, with its wealth of game resources and eastward facing slopes standing high above the Manitoba lakes region, loosely fit the exaggerated description that so intrigued Governor Knight. Given their location in southwestern Manitoba, they also had a ready familiarity with the Mandan and their corn-based lifestyle. The other telltale indicator was their apparent ability to communicate with the traders—Knight made no mention of language problems—suggesting that they were Cree speakers.[10]

The Mountain Indians appear to be one of several Cree and Assiniboine groups that dominated the western interior beaver trade by the 1720s. And they came to assume such a major role because they were already resident in the vast Hudson Bay watershed in the present-day three prairie provinces before the coming of the HBC.[11] Archaeological fieldwork over the last three decades suggests that they not only lived in the Manitoba interlake region, but west of the escarpment into Saskatchewan. Precise locations are not possible because their territories were so fluid. The Susuhana Cree occupied the Swan River–Good Spirit Lake region (along and west of the Manitoba escarpment), while the Sturgeon Cree were found to the north, along the Swan, Red Deer, and upper Assiniboine Rivers. In central Saskatchewan, and moving westward, there were the Basquia Cree in the forested area of the Saskatchewan River delta, the Pegogamaw Cree west of the forks of the north and south branches, and the Beaver Cree in the Eagle Hills and between the North Saskatchewan and Beaver Rivers. To the north, west of the Hayes and Nelson Rivers, the

Hudson's Bay Company trading partners in early 1700s

Missinipi Cree lived along the Churchill River and the Athabasca Cree around the lake of the same name.

The Assiniboine, meanwhile, consisted of two distinct groups, a northern and southern group, distinguished by their parkland and plains lifestyles. Although they did not participate in the beaver trade to the same extent as their Cree neighbours after Utrecht—as suggested by the number of Assiniboine canoes coming to the Bay[12]—those who traded at York Factory resided in west-central Manitoba and east-central Saskatchewan. In fact, the northern Assiniboine were the same people who in 1690–92 took Kelsey inland to their territory in and around Touchwood Hills on the northern edge of the open grasslands. These people were reluctant to venture into southeastern Saskatchewan because of the Hidatsa presence there—the mysterious

131

Naywatame Poets whom Kelsey wanted to involve in the bay trade. They also appear to have had an alliance with the Gros Ventre, sometimes known as the Fall or Rapid Indians, around the Eagle Hills and into the southwest part of the province. Still, the Assiniboine were probably farther west, at least in southern Saskatchewan, than the Cree, and were the largest group in the northeastern plains and parklands at this time.[13]

With their Cree and Assiniboine partners, the HBC settled down to a steady though unimaginative trade in the 1720s. The beaver skin remained the mainstay of company operations, completely overshadowing other trade and resource opportunities—and for good reason. Parchment beaver (and the beaver wool it provided for felting) was in great demand by the English hat-making industry, and pelts were shipped from the bay posts to the London market in the tens of thousands.[14] Company shareholders gladly pocketed the profit. This prosperity, however, did not extend to Fort Churchill. Even though the HBC constantly advocated peace among the various tribes, the Athapascan-speaking Chipewayan (or *wechepowuck* in Cree) did not trade regularly at the post because of their fear of the Cree. Those living north of the Churchill River, in the transitional region at the southern edge of the barrenlands from Nueltin and Wollaston Lakes to Lake Athabasca, had to circle north across Missinipi Cree territory to reach Churchill. That they had to travel on foot, carrying furs there and trade goods back, only added to the difficulty. Not even a series of HBC-sponsored trips inland between 1715 and 1721, led by the Cree leader Captain Swan or Waupisoo to secure an alliance with distant Chipewyan groups, did much to remedy the situation.[15] Trade at Churchill consequently remained a poor second to York Factory, never bringing in enough to cover operating costs; expenses exceeded returns for five consecutive trading seasons from 1722 to 1726.[16] The local governor repeatedly questioned the value of keeping the post open, but the company ignored the recommendation and persisted in its efforts to try to tap the fur-rich region to the west.

To secure the trade allegiance of its Indian partners, while ensuring that they returned year after year, the HBC adopted elaborate Aboriginal pre-

To secure and maintain the allegiance of its trading partners, the Hudson's Bay Company adopted elaborate Aboriginal pre-trading ceremonies.

trading ceremonies. The fluid nature of Indian societies was something new, if not frustrating and even perplexing, to the English who wanted to regularize the trade to ensure a stable business in the face of French competition. But in trying to turn Indian peoples into steady customers at the bayside posts, the traders ironically had to adhere to Indian traditions and protocol. As later documented by Andrew Graham, a long-time company servant in the mid-eighteenth century, pre-trade ceremonies were steeped in ritual and governed by formality. They were necessary both to maintain, as well as renew, the relationship between the Indians and the English. Some have insisted that the intention of these pre-trade activities became increasingly commercial over time—that they served the economic interests of Indian peoples in securing the most favourable exchange rates and the best quality trade items for their furs. But even if Indians engaged in "higgling and haggling" with the English traders,[17] that does not detract from the larger purpose of the ceremonies. "Trade, even within a commercial compact," one historian has noted, "was not a casual, purely businesslike transaction." The relationship, and the way it was established and renewed, was akin to a "treaty."[18]

The observance of pre-trade rituals commenced as soon as the Indian canoe flotillas, sometimes numbering more than fifty boats, neared the post. The Indian trading parties put ashore at an accessible spot, where the men put on their finest clothes and organized their descent on the fort, while the women gathered spruce boughs for their tent bottoms. Once everything had been arranged, the fleet would form up, with several canoes abreast and the trading captain in the lead vessel. A volley of musket fire announced their arrival, which, in turn, was answered by the post's guns. Once the canoes had been hauled up onto the banks of the river, an invitation was extended to the trading captain and his lieutenants to meet the governor, while the women set up camp nearby. The assembly was silent at first as pipes were solemnly smoked to set the proper atmosphere. Then, the trading captain announced how many canoes he had brought with him and any other news about the trip. The governor welcomed them in response, assuring them that they would be well treated and that they would be pleased with the trade goods. He then presented the captain and his lieutenants with new suits of brightly coloured clothing, including shoes and ornate hats, often adorned with feathers. These presents, and the status conferred by them, were a reward for the service performed by the trading captains—a form of public recognition that the success of the trading season was dependent on them. But the position came with heavy responsibilities.[19] The captains not only had to satisfy the governors' wishes, in bringing as many fur-laden canoes as possible to the posts each trading season, but were also under tremendous pressure to represent trading interests of their followers and voice any concerns. They also had to satisfy those band members who chose not to make the trip with the flotilla, but had sent their furs by proxy.

With the first round of ceremonial presentations complete, the governor offered gifts for the entire party of visiting Indians—from bread and prunes (because of their sweetness) to brandy to tobacco and pipes. The food was

The pipe ceremony was essential to setting the proper trade atmosphere.

particularly welcome because many groups arrived hungry, especially if they got delayed on their way down to the bay. The governor and post servants then formed themselves into a procession, complete with flags and drummer, and smartly marched the trading captain and his leading men to the Indian encampment. Taking his place on the floor of a specially prepared tent, the leader briefly addressed his followers before directing that the HBC presents be distributed. Trading did not commence, however, for at least another day and not until the smoking of the calumet was performed. This traditional ceremony, involving all members of the Indian trading party, including women and any children, was meant to affirm and renew their relationship with the HBC. With his calumet laid prominently before the gathering, the trading captain presented the governor with a gift of furs collected just before the Indians' arrival at the post. The governor was then assisted in lighting the pipe and solemnly pointed it to the four directions and up and down, before passing it around for each man to take a few puffs. The calumet-smoking gave way to lengthy speeches by both sides. Quite often, the trading captain harangued the governor. "We lived hard last winter and hungry ... take pity on us," one captain implored. "We paddle a long way to see you. We love the English ...

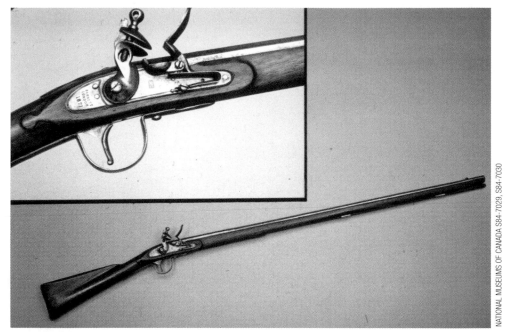

Guns were popular trade items.

take pity on us."[20] This call for "pity" did not mean that Indians had become dependent on European goods but was a bargaining tactic.[21] And the English traders accepted this demand for better terms as part of pre-trade negotiations and responded accordingly. The end of the speeches brought the distribution of more prunes and bread. Women also used the occasion to gather information about European medicines, learning the ingredients and securing samples.[22]

Trading took place over the next few days but only during daylight hours and only through a window into the warehouse, with the Indian and his furs on one side, the traders and his wares on the other. Women often exchanged small furs for bracelets, beads, and other personal items. There was no shortage of complaints about the quality of trade goods. James Isham, governor at York Factory in 1739, once provided the London Committee with a detailed listing of all that the Indians found wrong with HBC products and why they were "few or none traded and lying useless in the factory."[23] These "dislikes" included beads being too large and heavy, kettles being the wrong shape, blankets being too short, and twine being weak and uneven. The faulty items were shipped back to London with the fur packets. Indians also found fault with the specific amounts they were supposed to receive, especially for goods traded by volume or length, and demanded that the official standard of trade be observed—as one captain plaintively told Isham, "Give us good measure."[24] Once trading was concluded, the governor rewarded the captain with more presents, calculated on the volume of business that had been transacted. These going-away gifts could be quite substantial and included a wide assortment of trade items available at the post—and, of course, more prunes, only this time, mixed with oatmeal. The visitors then set off in their canoes, back upriver, to the thunderous applause of the post cannon. The traders were likely relieved to see them away because they too were often short of food before the supply ship arrived in late summer or early fall—or sometimes not at all.

These trade ceremonies helped make York Factory the most profitable HBC post in North America. Returns climbed dramatically with the restoration of the fort to English control in 1714, peaking at 43,132 Made Beaver (parchment, half parchment, and coat) in 1727; beaver skins represented 94 per cent of the total post returns that year. Churchill, by comparison, brought in only 7,422 MB that same year, but here as well, beaver was the dominant trade commodity.[25] It would be a mistake, if not presumptuous, though, to look at these fur returns and simply conclude that trade with the HBC had become an integral part of Indian annual routine. Certainly, English traders wanted it to be that way, but their perspective was coloured by their self-interest, if not skewed by the fact that contact with Indians was limited to those who were prepared to make the long trip to the bay. As a consequence, company men had only a vague idea of the inland Indian world. They knew that Indians had to be constantly encouraged to come to the bay but did not fully appreciate why some groups did not come every trading season; it was simply assumed that Indians did not come to the bay because they were lazy or necessarily dissatisfied with the trade goods or terms. Traders did not seem to comprehend that Indians consciously chose to pursue other activities in the interior, such as bison hunting or raiding, that were even more important to their lives than the beaver trade—not just to their survival, but their cultural well-being. In the words of one author, "the arrival of Westerners and Western goods" did not make "Indian-newcomer relations … the centre of Indian life" at that time.[26] Trade with Europeans was for many Indian individuals a peripheral activity, all the more so because the HBC restricted its presence to the outer edge of the region. Getting there was not easy, and required access to big or old-growth stands of white or paper birch (*Betula papyrifera*) for canoe-making. It was no coincidence that many of the HBC customers came from the Saskatchewan River delta region, the best source for canoe birch. When Indian groups did travel to the bay, moreover, they employed various strategies and rhetoric to make the trip worthwhile. An exasperated Governor Macklish reported from York Factory in August 1728: "Never was any man so upbraided with our powder, kettles and hatchets, than we have been this summer."[27]

A more pressing concern for Indians living in Rupert's Land during this period was drought. Although the early eighteenth century falls in the climatic interval known as the Little Ice Age, a time of generally cooler, moister conditions, tree-ring data suggest that the western prairies experienced an exceptionally severe dry spell in the 1720s (and more than two decades after a similar climatic event had gripped the eastern prairies). Stream flow reconstructions for the South Saskatchewan River support this finding. The lowest flow period for the past five hundred years occurred between 1700 to 1725, while the years of lowest mean flow were 1717, 1720, and 1721.[28] What this drought probably meant for Indians, already living in a semi-arid environment, is that they had to work harder, expending more energy, to secure stressed and sparser resources. Dealing with these difficult conditions left no time for a demanding trading expedition. The drought likely discouraged some groups from trading at the Bay because most trips there and back already travelled a fine line between survival and starvation, and lower water levels made things more difficult, especially returning inland. Perhaps this situation explains why the Assiniboine, living on the northern plains, did not travel to York Factory in the same numbers as the Cree.

The other major development, not only for Indians but particularly for the Hudson's Bay Company, was the arrival of competitors from the upper Great Lakes in the mid-eighteenth century. The revival of French interest in the western interior following the 1713 Treaty of Utrecht was ostensibly propelled by the search for the western sea (*La Mer de'Ouest*), an imagined water body in the heart of the continent that supposedly led to the Pacific Ocean. But going hand-in-glove with the eventual push into present-day Manitoba and then Saskatchewan was the French desire to capture the lion's share of the lucrative western beaver trade at the expense of the HBC posts. In 1717, Zacharie de La Noue re-established Kaministiquia at the western end of Lake Superior as the first in a chain of French posts leading to Lake of the Woods. It was anticipated that these *Postes du Nord* would serve as a springboard from which the French would easily reach the western sea, somewhere to the west, in the vicinity of Lake Winnipeg (Ouinipigon, to the French). La Noue's advance was stalled, however, by fighting between the Dakota Sioux and a northern alliance of Cree, Assiniboine, and Monsoni (Ojibwa) over access to the region's resources, in particular wild rice and furs. The situation became only worse when the Fox Indians, an Algonquian people, declared war on the French in the Upper Mississippi country. These hostilities bogged down the French for the next few years, effectively undermining the plan to break out directly westward to Lake Winnipeg. Instead, it was decided to bypass the war region by finding an alternative, more southerly, route to the enigmatic western sea. But French efforts to gather information from the Sioux were undermined by Fox harassment, even preventing attempts to broker a peace between them and the northern alliance.

Such was the sorry state of French affairs in the North-West when Pierre Gaultier de Varennes, sieur de La Vérendrye assumed control of the Postes du Nord in 1728. Born in Trois-Rivières in 1685 and a soldier by profession, La Vérendrye has been favourably compared to Samuel de Champlain, the celebrated founder of New France. Whereas "Champlain made the East," one historian maintained, "La Vérendrye grasped the West for the French." Another called "the two of them quintessential French explorers."[29] This praise

139

for the lesser known La Vérendrye might seem exaggerated, but only because what he gained for the French was soon lost at the peace table and "with it the perspective in which to see [his] real greatness."[30] Like Champlain before him, he had an overarching master plan, involving trade, exploration, settlement, and Indian relations that came close to snatching the western half of the North American continent from under the noses of the English. But despite these accomplishments, La Vérendrye and his sons "remain the least documented, least publicized explorers of North America."[31]

Upon assuming his new duties, La Vérendrye set up headquarters at Kaministiquia, with secondary posts at Nipigon and Michipicoten (near Wawa today), and tried to learn as much as possible about the interior country from Indian informants. The most tantalizing news came from an Indian, named Auchagah, who drew a map on a piece of birchbark showing the waterways and portages to the west. It was apparent from the crude sketch that the western sea actually lay beyond Lake Winnipeg, but there still remained the question of what water body emptied into the ocean. That could be determined only through exploration, and with the blessing of the French government to establish a post on Lake Winnipeg, La Vérendrye took up the quest in 1731 to find the answer. His efforts were handicapped, however, by the lack of financial support, forcing him to depend on trade to cover his field costs. French officials, in particular the Minister of Marine, did not "understand realistically the extent of the western wilderness and … thought it could be opened by a mere matter of paddling."[32]

At first, La Vérendrye made remarkable progress, setting up Fort St. Pierre on Rainy Lake (Ontario) in 1731 and a more substantial post and his new headquarters, St. Charles, on the west shore of Lake of the Woods, the following year. Two years later, one of his sons built Fort Maurepas on the lower Red River, just south of Lake Winnipeg (near present-day Selkirk). Then, the wind seemed to go out of La Vérendrye's sails, and he stayed in what is known today as the border lake country. His hesitation was partly attributable to the continuing Indian wars. In moving beyond Lake Superior, La Vérendrye had

The Winnipeg monument to La Vérendrye, who pushed the French fur trade into present-day
Manitoba and up the Saskatchewan River

allied himself with the Cree and Assiniboine, who normally traded at the bay
posts. This union may have made commercial sense, but it encouraged the
Cree and Assiniboine, now directly supplied by the French, to intensify their
attacks on the Sioux in order to drive them from the region's forests and lakes.
Any movement westward was now placed in jeopardy, and La Vérendrye tried
unsuccessfully to keep hostilities in check.[33]

141

The other inhibiting factor, and one that dogged any future Montreal trade into the interior, was the distance involved. It was one thing to explore westward to Lake Winnipeg and beyond, but La Vérendrye had to finance these operations through trade. He consequently had to organize the bringing of supplies and food into present-day northwestern Ontario, as well as improve canoe routes, including adoption of Grand Portage over Kaministiquia on Lake Superior. These activities caused his critics, annoyed by his inaction on the western sea front, to conclude that La Vérendrye was "a stark fur-trader in the guise of an explorer."[34] Or as the Minister of Marine put it more dismissively, he was more obsessed with the "sea of beaver."[35] It certainly appeared that way because of the huge volume of furs being brought out of the region. Although La Vérendrye remained hunkered down at his St. Charles headquarters, *coureurs de bois* had fanned out from the new French posts to win over the beaver trade of the Indians who travelled to the bottom of the bay or York Factory. In fact, when and if La Vérendrye resumed his advance westward, he would find that the *coureurs de bois* had been there first, sometimes several years ahead of him.[36] This trade, moreover, unlike the English posts, was not restricted to beaver skins. The other major "commodity" were slaves, Indian people taken prisoner during the wars in the region and later sold to New France households.[37]

It was not until February 1737 that La Vérendrye continued west to Fort Maurepas and the future province of Manitoba. He immediately held a grand council, urging the Cree and Assiniboine to stop trading with the English. He also used his time on the ground to secure a better understanding of the geography of the Lake Winnipeg basin, as reflected in a new map that now featured a Rivière Blanche, so named because of the churning Grand Rapids into Lake Winnipeg. But instead of pursuing this route up the Saskatchewan River, the French commandant chose to head south to investigate the mysterious Mandans and possibly find a shorter, more direct route to the western sea. He may have also been looking for a food source—in this case, corn—to lessen his reliance on supplies from New France.[38] His first step, though, in October 1738, was to erect Fort la Reine on the Assiniboine River, near the site of Portage la Prairie and situated purposefully on the trail used by the Assiniboine to travel south to the Mandan/Hidatsa villages and north to York Factory. His party, including two sons, his slave, and possibly his Indian partner,[39] and supplemented by a number of *engagés* and Assiniboine, then set off on foot for the Upper Missouri River. La Vérendrye's arrival there in early December predated the more famous American-sponsored Lewis and Clark expedition by sixty-five years. But he was disappointed that the Mandan, rumoured to be bearded white men, were simply another Indian group. La Vérendrye also realized that the Missouri, flowing south below the villages, did not hold the answer to the western sea riddle. He did not even bother to walk over to look at the river, even though it was just a short distance from the Mandan villages.[40] One commentator neatly summed up the trip this way: "The Sea of the West must have seemed ... ever to recede as [he] advanced towards it."[41] Sick, tired, and dispirited, La Vérendrye returned to Fort la Reine that winter to plot his next move.

The early 1740s brought a renewed commitment to exploration, a full decade after La Vérendrye had started his quest. While stationed at la Reine, intent on wresting the beaver trade of the Manitoba interlake region away from the English, he sent two of his sons in 1742–43 on a reconnaissance into the country west of the Mandan villages towards the Big Horn Mountains. A lead plate that they buried during their travels, claiming the region for France, was found by a young girl in 1913 on the path to her home in Pierre, South Dakota.[42] La Vérendrye also directed the establishment of another three posts to the west of Lake Winnipeg: Fort Dauphin (1741) near present-day Winnipegosis, Manitoba; Fort Bourbon (1741) near Grand Rapids and the mouth of the Saskatchewan River; and Fort Paskoya (1743), northwest of Cedar Lake, near the Summerberry River and the beginning of the Middle Track route to the bay. At least one of these new posts was built at the repeated urging of the Indians of the region. At the 1737 council at Maurepas, a Cree chief had reminded La Vérendrye "to keep [his] word and to take measures for establishing a fort at the end of Lake Winnipeg, at the entrance to the great English [Saskatchewan] river."[43]

These new posts provided the French with the means to push even deeper into the North-West along the Saskatchewan River, while interfering with the Indian trade at York Factory. And that is exactly what La Vérendrye was poised to do when he was forced to resign his position in 1744 because French officials had tired of his continuing failure to find the western sea. His replacement fared little better, and La Vérendrye was restored as commandant in 1746. He died in Montreal three years later before he could make his triumphant return west to investigate the Saskatchewan River. Ironically, that was the same year that one of his sons, Louis-Joseph, known as the Chevalier, learned from the Cree gathered at the Saskatchewan forks that the source of the river "came from very far, from a height of land where there were very lofty mountains" and that there was a "great lake on the other side … the water of which was undrinkable."[44] It would require two years, though, to get there from Montreal.

La Vérendrye's gradual advance westward to the Saskatchewan Valley may have been fuelled by the search for the ever-elusive western sea, but the chain of posts he established from St. Pierre on Rainy Lake to Paskoya near The Pas threatened the English beaver trade by cutting across the major routes to the bay posts. This outcome might have been different had La Vérendrye not had to pay for his exploration through the profits from trade. But it also made little sense to the commandant not to take steps to consolidate the French presence in the region. He did everything he could, then, to secure the allegiance of the Indians, especially as trade partners. When La Vérendrye learned in April 1739, for example, that a party of Assiniboine had assembled on the shores of Lake Manitoba to build canoes for their annual trip to the bay, he intercepted them and traded for their furs.[45] By such means, he was able to send out literally hundreds of bundles of furs to Montreal every year. In 1735 alone, nearly one hundred thousand beaver skins were shipped east from the Postes du Nord.[46]

La Vérendrye's activities siphoned off the English trade, first at the bottom of the bay and then York Factory. As long as the French remained

French trading posts in western Canada

outside Manitoba, the returns at the company's most lucrative post on the west side of Hudson Bay were out of reach. But in 1732, the number of parchment beaver traded at York Factory dropped by almost fifty-five hundred skins or 20 per cent from the previous year.[47] That was the same year that the French had apparently dissuaded the Sturgeon Indians from going down to the bay. This decline in trade was certainly troubling to the HBC, but nothing to fret about unless it was the beginning of a downward trend. But more worrisome, and not even known to the English, was that La Vérendrye was still in northwestern Ontario and would not build his first post on the prairies—Fort Maurepas—for another year. Instead, it was the French *coureurs de bois* who were disrupting the bay trade. They were the ones who were active throughout the Manitoba interlake area, seeking out Indians who were HBC customers. They were also the ones who encouraged the Assiniboine to forcibly prevent other Indian groups from travelling to York Factory. It could have been much worse. The *coureurs de bois* could carry only so many trade items into the interior and bring back only so many beaver skins. But that changed dramatically once French posts were established inland.

The English, hugging the rim of the bay, did not appreciate the nature of the La Vérendrye threat—or how devastating it could be. As the company historian noted, "we remained within sight of tidal water, tied to the coast."[48] The HBC consequently had to turn to the Indians to find out what the French were doing inland. And the news was increasingly unsettling. The York Factory journal for 1739 reported that the French posts upriver now numbered three.[49] Then, the following year, trading Indians handed a letter to the governor at York Factory that they had carried from a French settlement they "reckon … to be about 400 miles … from us."[50] This brazen gesture capped more than a decade of warnings to the company. All that it had done in the interim was try to improve post defences, especially at Churchill, where it decided in 1731 to build a stone fort because of the strategic significance of the harbour. But any attack from the French was not going to be staged in the bay. The unfolding drama was already underway in the interior, where *coureurs de bois* were on the offensive—taking the beaver trade directly to the Indians, undercutting the HBC official standard of trade, and making the trip to the bay unnecessary.

Company inactivity in the face of French initiative in Rupert's Land soon elicited complaints in England. The epicentre of the opposition was Arthur Dobbs, an Irish member of the British Parliament whose interest in expanding international trade caused him to cast a querulous eye on the secretive HBC and its North American operations. Dobbs was thoroughly convinced that the company had escaped official scrutiny—gone "unnoticed and undisturbed"—because it had fallen asleep by the edge of a frozen sea.[51] It was a stinging indictment, but one that was borne out by his reading of the royal charter and its generous terms. Dobbs initially challenged the company's supposed lethargy by sponsoring his own unsuccessful search for the North-West passage through Hudson Bay in the early 1740s. He then formally petitioned Parliament to strip the HBC of its exclusive trading privileges. The resultant House of Commons inquiry questioned a number of witnesses, including several former and current servants, about what the company had done to advance British interests in the region since 1670. In its defence, the HBC was forced for the first time to make its organization and practices public, including its stubborn opposition to inland trade. These disclosures, however, were not enough to dissolve the monopoly, in large part because the HBC requested neither financial nor military support from the British government and yet still managed to supply the London market with a decent trade in beaver skins.[52] When the matter was finally put to a vote in May 1749, Dobbs's request was denied and "the affair was dropt."[53]

This reprieve did not mean that the company was safe from competition. Even though the La Vérendrye family's association with the West ended rather ignominiously around the same time that Dobbs lost his HBC charter challenge, the French continued to push into the interior. In fact, the French occupation of the Saskatchewan River valley in the 1750s had nothing to do with exploration and larger imperial interests, but was "a fur-trade presence only."[54] In 1751, the new commandant of the Postes du Nord established Fort la Jonquière somewhere downstream from present-day Nipawin in central Saskatchewan. Two or possibly three years later, another post, known initially as des Prairies (but also called St. Louis and then à la Corne), was built just below the forks of the river. Fort Paskoya was also moved around this time from the entrance to Cedar Lake to The Pas. Not much more is known about these posts because the French traders in the North-West, unlike the English at the bay, were not obsessed with record-keeping. If not for HBC information-gathering, there might be even less documentation; sometimes the company is the only historical source. What is certain, though, is that the widely repeated claim that wheat was grown at la Corne in 1754 was nothing but a hoax, a story made up over 150 years later by a Saskatchewan booster trying to promote the agricultural potential of the Melfort district.[55]

With this growing network of posts, the French were able to intercept Indians who were headed to York Factory by way of the lower Saskatchewan River delta or Cumberland Lake. But it was their location that was even more telling. Four French forts along the Saskatchewan River system were deliberately placed at centuries-old Cree "ingathering centres": Fort Bourbon at *mīsiapāwistik* (a large rapid), Fort Paskoya at *cīmawāwin* (a seining place), Paskoya 2 at *opāskweyāw* (narrows between woods), and Fort à la Corne at *pêhonânihk* (the waiting place). Another French post, Fort la Jonquière, was located roughly halfway between two other aggregating centres, *nīpowwinihk* (a standing place) and *paskwatinaw* (a bare hill). It would appear, then, that Cree activities determined the location of the French posts, or perhaps even that the Cree had a voice in deciding where the French should place their trading settlements. The French, for their part, would have been foolhardy not to use the ingathering places, for it was here that the Cree assembled each spring to build the canoes that took them to the bay. If the French wanted to advance their relationship with Cree bands, including through possible intermarriage, it made sense to occupy these sites.[56]

The French also continued to support, if not advance, the trade in people. In 1742, a combined Assiniboine–Cree war party had attacked the "Sioux of the Prairies," killing at least one hundred and taking an even larger number of prisoners—a line of captives four arpents long (more than eight hundred feet).[57] It was no coincidence that later that same year the governor of New France reported that La Vérendrye had traded for "more slaves than bundles of fur."[58] Far from trying to play down such a legacy, the commandant of the Postes du Nords regarded the procurement of slaves—as opposed to captive taking—as one of the major benefits to the colony.[59] What Montreal provided in return, though, was disease. In the early 1730s, smallpox broke out in New England and soon spread northeast into New France. Because of the trade traffic between Montreal and the upper Mississippi country, the sickness, known today as a "virgin soil epidemic" because of the lack of resistance to the disease in the affected population, quickly extended its reach to the Sioux along the northeastern edge of the Great Plains. It then struck some of the Cree and Assiniboine who had attended the La Vérendrye council at Maurepas in March 1737. The following year, it decimated the Monsoni Ojibway of

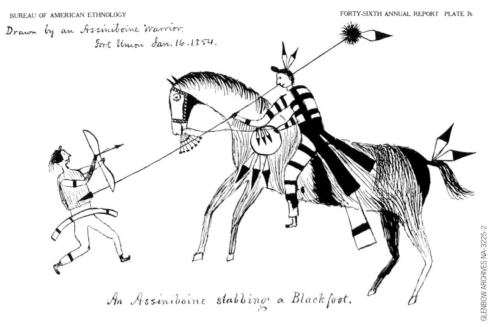

BUREAU OF AMERICAN ETHNOLOGY

FORTY-SIXTH ANNUAL REPORT PLATE 76

Drawn by an Assiniboine Warrior.
Fort Union Jan. 16. 1854.

An Assiniboine stabbing a Blackfoot.

GLENBOW ARCHIVES NA-3225-2

The horse changed Indian warfare on the northern plains.

Lake of the Woods–Rainy River district, the same area where La Vérendrye was headquartered at the time. There were even reports of smallpox—what James Isham described in 1739 as "a very remarkable sickness"—among the coastal Cree at York Factory. Somewhat surprisingly, this outbreak did not move beyond the Lake Winnipeg region into the North-West. Nor did it find its way to the Mandan–Hidatsa villages south of the forty-ninth parallel.[60] It still had a terrible toll, though, especially among the Assiniboine of east-central Manitoba. What seemed to be empty lands to future newcomers were actually emptied lands: depopulated, not unpopulated.[61]

Whereas smallpox was probably new to the region in the late 1730s,[62] the horse re-appeared in the future province of Saskatchewan around the same time. The oldest form, the dog-sized *Protohippus*, evolved in North America about 55 million years ago. Ancestral forms of the modern horse (*Equus*) migrated from North America into northeast Siberia about 2.6 million years ago and then spread throughout the Old World.[63] Horses in North America, in the meantime, disappeared from the continent at the end of the last Ice Age about ten thousand years ago. What caused this extinction—and that of other large animals at the same time—is a hotly contested topic in palaeontology. The Spanish reintroduced the animal to the southwestern part of North America (the future states of New Mexico, Arizona, and Texas) in the late sixteenth century, and it was not long before the Indians of that region, the Pueblo, Utes, and Apaches, secured the horse through trade or raiding and incorporated it into their lifeways. Over the next century, horses spread north through the existing trade network of the Numic-speaking peoples along the western plains and over the Rocky Mountains. Their acquisition vaulted the Comanches from relative obscurity to the powerhouse nation of the southwestern plains, while their Snake (*Gens de Serpents*) kin soon became the dominant force on the northwestern plains. (It is not certain whether the Snake Indians were Shoshone.)[64] The diffusion of the horse northeastward from Spanish territory, by contrast, was much slower because of the limited breeding stock and a general desire by emerging equestrian societies to keep the animal away from enemy tribes. When La Vérendrye visited the Mandan–Hidatsa villages in 1738, there were no horses present, only stories of Indians on horseback who came from the southwest to trade. Two years later, his son made a second visit to the horticultural centre and returned with two horses, likely the first pair to be brought into Manitoba's Assiniboine Valley.[65]

The arrival of the horse did not simply mean that Indian peoples had a stronger, more helpful "big dog" at their disposal. Nor should Indian cultures on the Great Plains after 1700 be merely divided into those with horses and those without. "Not since the spread of corn," one author has argued, "had the West seen such a powerful force of change ... horses changed how many people lived their lives, saw their world, and organized their societies."[66] Travel by horseback shortened distance and compressed time in much the same way the locomotive did a few centuries later. Horses could also carry more than dogs or people and probably led to greater material accumulation and trade possibilities. Perhaps the horse's greatest impact, though, was how it intensified and accelerated Indian exploitation of the great bison herds. The wary, speedy bison now had to contend with the mobile, mounted hunter, whose horse was not only equally fast and agile but also versatile. Horses could bring riders right up alongside their quarry—what became known as bison running—or drive bison into traps such as pounds or over jumps.

It is little wonder, then, why the horse became the most important trade item in the Great Plains region and the cause of so much raiding and counter-raiding by bands that did not have the animal or wanted more. The horse encouraged the emergence of tribal societies who forsook agriculture or a more diversified subsistence lifestyle to specialize in bison-hunting year-round. These mounted peoples used the horse to expand their territory into the bison-rich grasslands and often came into conflict with groups already there or moving into the same region for the same reasons. Warfare was consequently more frequent, more fearsome, as competing groups sought to consolidate their claim over territory and resources. Horse-based societies also had to be organized and ever vigilant to protect their breeding stock. They were regularly forced to relocate their camps for grazing purposes or start spring fires to promote new grass growth, while ensuring there was an adequate source of water. The horse placed a new strain on local ecosystems. It was an intruder in an environment where the horse had been absent over thousands of years. Finally, horses meant more work for women. They not only had to do more butchering and hide-processing because of the larger number of bison taken, but were now expected to tend to the horses in camp.[67] "The price paid to keep the horse was large," one western historian had observed, "but it was more than balanced by the benefits the animal brought."[68]

The impact of the horse and how it revolutionized plains Indian warfare was documented by trader David Thompson when he collected a story from Peigan elder Saukamappee (Young Man), estimated to be about seventy-five or eighty years old, during the winter of 1787–88. Although originally Cree from the Saskatchewan country, Saukamappee had joined the Peigan early in his life and participated in two battles between his adopted tribe and the Snake. In the first encounter when Saukamappee was about sixteen (*circa* 1725–30), somewhere near Saskatchewan's Eagle Hills, the Peigan and Snake lined up facing one another, sitting behind large leather shields, and fired arrows at one another. "On both sides several were wounded," Saukamappee recalled, "but none lay on the ground; and night put an end to the battle." He continued, "In those days such was the result, unless one party was more numerous than the other."[69] What Saukamappee could have added was that the skirmish ended in a stalemate only because the Snake did not bring their horses. Because of their distance from horse-trading nations to the south, they probably had too few to risk in battle and decided they were best saved for bison-hunting.[70]

By the time of the second meeting, apparently ten years later (*circa* 1735–40), some of the Snake warriors were mounted and used the advantage to terrorize the Peigan. "Our enemies the Snake Indian … had Misstutim (Big Dogs, that is horses) on which they rode, swift as the Deer, on which they dashed at the Peeagans, and … knocked them on the head," Saukamappee recounted. "This news we did not well comprehend and it alarmed us, for we had no idea of Horses and could not make out what they were."[71] But when it came to the actual battle, the two sides lined up in traditional fashion again. The Snake may have had more horses by this date but remained wary of using them for warfare, especially when they lacked protective armour for their mounts. Still, their ownership of horses and the mobility they provided had enabled them to drive the Blackfoot tribes, as well as the Gros Ventres, north to the North Saskatchewan River. The Snake's fearsome reputation as mounted raiders also caused La Vérendrye's sons, travelling on foot, to cut short their 1742–43 exploration of the country west of the Mandan–Hidatsa villages.[72]

The change brought by the horse was one of many developments in present-day Saskatchewan in the mid-eighteenth century. In the southern third of the province, horses were remaking Indian cultures, creating a state of flux as mounted and pedestrian groups jostled, sometimes fought bitterly, over access to territory and resources. The emergent mounted hunting societies focused almost exclusively on bison and their grazing range, a subsistence specialization that became even more pronounced with the acquisition of guns. Along the Saskatchewan River, meanwhile, the French were gradually advancing west in order to bring the beaver skin trade directly to the Indians of the region and undercut English competition from the distant bayside posts.

The convergence of the rival trade networks in the North-West introduced a new dynamic to the Native-newcomer relationship that went far beyond trade. But the HBC still balked at establishing inland posts and meeting the Montreal challenge head on. Since 1720 and the restoration of the trade after Utrecht, the London committee had carefully managed its overseas operations to generate income by keeping a tight rein on its costs and limiting capital expenditures. And by the 1750s, the HBC was doing quite well financially— despite the presence of the French in its backyard—because of the price of furs on the London market.[73] The company also recognized that its policy had been predicated on the Indians coming to them, and it realized that its employees were not positioned to move beyond its well-entrenched "habits of trade." Despite its vulnerability, then, the company chose "defence rather than attack, security rather than penetration."[74] As for the French, those who replaced the La Vérendrye family initially complained about the distance from Montreal, the difficulties of supplying the North-West posts—even, ironically, the competition from the English at the bay.[75] But once individual French traders became attuned to the interior trade and how to press their advantage, they extended their reach along the lower Saskatchewan River, forcing the HBC to respond. The Cree and Assiniboine adjusted to the changed circumstances—as past generations had been doing for centuries—ensuring that traders remained dependent on them.

The horse and gun enabled the Blackfoot to become a dominant force on the northern plains by the late eighteenth century.

CHAPTER FIVE

ALL TO NO PURPOSE

THEY WERE "TROUBLESOME," SOMETIMES "INSOLENT."[1] THAT'S HOW THE HUDSON'S
Bay Company had come to regard the Basquia and Pegogamaw Cree in the
mid-eighteenth century. The Indian groups had earned these uncomplimentary
epithets because of their assertiveness in the western Canadian fur trade. The
English traders did not like it. But they knew better than to alienate them or
risk losing their affection, or they would take their business elsewhere. Indeed,
if not for the Basquia and Pegogamaw—some of the Indian bands actually
known by name—the HBC system of relying on the inland Indians to come to
the bay to trade would have collapsed. Their home territory—the Basquia were
in the Saskatchewan River delta region and the Pegogamaw along the lower
north and south branches of the river, including the forks—was the gateway to
the lucrative beaver skin trade of the North-West. They willingly incorporated
company trade into their seasonal cycle and travelled regularly to York Factory
in the late spring. They also assumed a dominant middleman's role, exchanging
European goods at inflated prices for the furs trapped by other, more distant
Indian groups who either refused to travel to the bay or did not have the means
to get there. Trade, at the same time, was only one aspect of their lives and did
not necessarily define them. Drawing their identity and vitality from the land
and its resources, the Pegogamaw and Basquia were exceedingly protective
of their position, and their interests, and exerted their will to the chagrin of
the traders. Newcomers, whether from Hudson Bay or Montreal, entered an
Indian world on Indian terms and travelled and traded there only with the
acquiescence and cooperation of the Cree.[2]

On 26 June 1754, Attickasish, also known as Little Caribou, a leading Pegogamaw trading captain[3] headed back inland from York Factory with an additional person in his party—HBC servant Anthony Henday. It had been more than sixty years since the English company had dispatched one of its bayside employees to the interior with the returning Indians—the last and only one being Henry Kelsey in 1690. Since that time, the HBC had steadfastly pinned its fortunes on the rather unimaginative but cost-effective policy of encouraging the Indians to come to the bay to trade. But with French competitors pushing inland from Montreal as far as the Saskatchewan River forks by the early 1750s, fewer Indians were bringing fewer furs to the bay posts. It did not take much foresight to conclude that once the French were able to resolve the challenge of supplying their distant western posts on a regular basis, trading trips to the bay would become unnecessary. And as long as the company clung to its defensive posture, hunkered down along the rim of the Bay, the French were likely to emerge triumphant. Something had to be done—and soon—if the HBC was to have a future in the beaver skin trade.

James Isham, the astute governor of York Factory, had argued as early as 1743 that an inland post would be the most forceful response to the escalating French threat. But the company, despite operating in North America for decades and dealing with the local peoples on a continuous basis, did not really "know the interior, and clothed it with difficulties and even terrors."[4] Nor did the HBC, for that matter, have any true appreciation of the nature and extent of the French presence in the North-West, especially since its vague and incomplete understanding of the inland geography made it difficult to assess what Indian informants were reporting about French activities. All the company servants understood was that the Montreal pedlars were there and undercutting English trade in apparent defiance of the 1670 royal charter. It made more sense under the circumstances, then, to send someone inland on a kind of reconnaissance—to learn exactly where the French were and what they were doing. More importantly, a servant could try to convince western Indians who were not involved in the trade, collectively known as the Archithinue ("strange" Indians), to visit York Factory or Churchill. Such an initiative was not intended to be a departure from long-established company policy but rather serve to rescue, perhaps even bolster, bay trade by increasing the number of Indian customers.[5]

The servant hand-picked by Isham to tackle this mission—in his words, to "Enlarge and Encrease the Said Company's trade &c with unknown Ind"[6]—was twenty-nine-year-old net-maker and labourer Anthony Henday (sometimes spelled Hendey or Hendry). Isham considered Henday a "Very Serviceable man,"[7] an assessment that may have been based in part on his career as a smuggler before joining the HBC in 1750. His fitness for the expedition was compromised, however, by his limited understanding of Cree, the lingua franca of the trade. Perhaps that is why he was accompanied by Connawappaw, one of the local or "homeguard" Cree who earned a living supplying York Factory with country provisions and performing other duties in and around the post. It is more than likely, though, that Henday learned to speak some Cree during the trip because he had a female partner or "bedfellow," a companion who unfortunately is never named. Without her help and that of other Cree, like Attickasish and Connawappaw, the English trader would not have survived the arduous trip inland and back to the bay, let alone carried out his assignment.[8] He learned from them how the interior fur trade was conducted and was introduced to Indian groups who had neither desire nor interest in going to the distant English posts.

Henday—comparable to the modern-day hitchhiker[9]—travelled inland with the Pegogamaw by way of the Middle Track to the Saskatchewan River. His route over the next several months is more certain than that of his predecessor Kelsey, but only because he kept a more complete daily journal.[10] Henday was terrible at estimating distances, particularly by canoe. His landscape entries were also spare—what one fur trade specialist has forgivingly described as "nose-to-the-ground," while another has declared "oddly uninformative."[11]

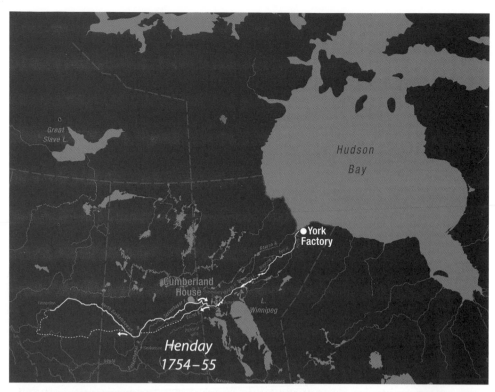

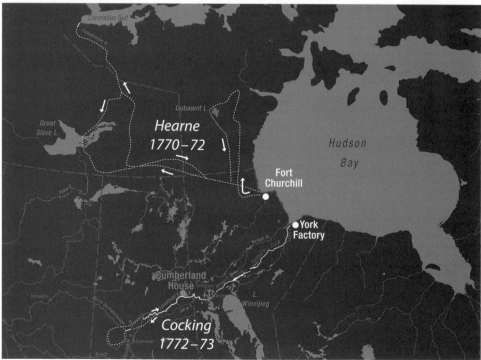

Inland trips by HBC servants Anthony Henday, Samuel Hearne, and Matthew Cocking

There are four distinct versions of Henday's journal—one submitted by Isham to London in 1755 and another three among the papers of his successor Andrew Graham—which only adds to the puzzle. Those who have written about his epic travels have not helped matters. Because Henday was a guest of the Pegogamaw, he went where they went, and their course and direction were determined by the availability of resources and structured by traditional practices. Some authors, however, have deliberately straightened out his "wanderings" to make for a neater route, as well as attributed to him the first sighting of the Rocky Mountains by a European in the western interior.[12] But Henday never mentioned seeing the mountains in the many versions of his journal, raising the legitimate question about how far west he reached. Then, there was the second-guessing whether the trip should have even been undertaken. Less than two months after Henday had set off with Attickasish, Ferdinand Jacobs, Isham's counterpart at Churchill, wondered whether anything would be accomplished by the trip, especially whether the Archithinue could be brought directly into the trade through hearty encouragement and a few presents.[13] Making sense of Henday's celebrated trip is consequently not without its challenges.[14]

Within days of reaching the Saskatchewan River and paddling westward, the Pegogamaw came upon the French fort Basquia (or Paskoya 2 at *opaskweyaw* [narrows between woods]) at present-day site of The Pas, Manitoba, on 22 July 1754. By this point, less than a month into the expedition, Henday had secured the distinction of being the second HBC emissary (after Kelsey) to travel along the mighty river and the only Englishman to visit any of the French posts west of Lake Superior before the Seven Years' War (1756–63).[15] His more immediate concern, though, was whether the French would follow through on their threat to detain him at the post—something that a smiling Attickasish told him "they dared not."[16] They then continued along the Saskatchewan for several miles before portaging into the river delta and up the Carrot River until the water became too shallow and they abandoned their canoes. Somewhere near Red Earth (Saskatchewan) on 27 July, the Pegogamaw met the families they had

HBC servant Anthony Henday's visit to the Blackfoot as portrayed today in a Royal Alberta Museum diorama.

ROYAL ALBERTA MUSEUM

left behind weeks earlier. "In a starving condition, for want of food," Henday glumly noted, "and we are in the same condition."[17] The group, as many as four hundred in number, spent several difficult and hungry days walking southwest along the ancient Ayisiyiniw–Meskanaw trail to the aspen parkland somewhere around the Melfort–Tisdale area.[18] Here, they filled their stomachs on nuts, berries, moose, and elk—in Henday's words, "a pleasant and plentiful country."[19]

By 20 August, the Pegogamaw had reached the South Saskatchewan River (somewhere north of Saskatoon) and then the elbow of the North Saskatchewan River four days later. But there was no sign of the Archithinue, only occasional camps of Assinipoets (Assiniboine or Nakota) who at the time probably outnumbered the Cree in central Saskatchewan.[20] Henday discovered that many of these people had no interest in trading at the bay because they were able to secure goods at the French forts or from the Pegogamaw. Others had never traded directly with any European trader.

From the North Saskatchewan River in the Battlefords region, the Pegogamaw headed mostly southwest across the "Muscuty" plains (from the Cree word, *muskotao*, for prairie) in search of the Archithinue (either the Blackfoot [Siksika], Blood [Kainai], Peigan [Piikani], or Gros Ventre of the Blackfoot Alliance—also known as the Niitsitapi). Henday killed his first bison, an old scrawny bull, on 10 September. Soon the animals were "so numerous [we were] obliged to make them sheer out of way."[21] Using bows and arrows instead of expending their scarce ammunition, the Pegogamaw found it easy sport to kills dozens of bison. They took from the carcasses only what they could carry—mostly the tongues—and left the rest to the large packs of wolves that followed them. On 20 September, after probably crossing the Battle River a few days earlier, Henday met another small group of Assinipoet and traded a gun for a horse to carry his provisions. Horses were still scarce among the Cree and to a lesser extent the Assiniboine in the 1750s, and most were put to work as pack animals. The Indian groups to the west, on the other hand, had already made the transition to a mounted hunting society. This disparity was driven home to Henday over the next few weeks as the pedestrian Pegogamaw, still using dogs as pack animals, regularly encountered Archithinue on horseback as they made their way westward over the open plains for their rendezvous with the Archithinue leader. At that meeting near Red Deer, Alberta, on 14 October—more than four and a half months after leaving York Factory— Henday and his Pegogamaw guides entered an impressive camp of over two hundred tents, arranged in two neat rows like a street. Grazing nearby was a large herd of fine horses, with their feet fettered to discourage theft. Once pipes had been solemnly smoked to establish the proper atmosphere, the English emissary explained through his interpreter why he had been sent and asked that some of the young Archithinue men be allowed to return with him to the bay. But the leader politely dismissed the request, indicating that his people lived by the bison hunt and did not canoe or eat fish.[22] Besides, he had heard that those who made the arduous trip to the bay regularly faced starvation.

After a few days, the Archithinue broke camp and headed west, evidently intent on going to war against their enemy, the Snake, also confusingly known in Cree as Archithinue. Both Attickasish and Connawappaw, along with some other men in Henday's party, joined the campaign. Henday, for his part, spent the winter in present-day central Alberta, probably somewhere south of Edmonton, with a small group of Cree, mostly women and children. They moved camp every few days, never too far, and fed on bison, elk, or moose. Wherever they went, he was surprised that his companions killed only a few beaver for food and clothing when the wetlands and waterways would have provided a wealth of skins. He also chastised them for not taking wolf pelts, preferring instead to spend the cold winter days smoking, feasting, drumming, and dancing. But he was bluntly informed "that the Archithinue Natives would kill them, if they trapped in their country." When Henday persisted, wondering where they were going to get their furs to trade at the bay, "they made no answer; but laughed to one another." Later, his bedfellow cautioned him to "say no more about it [trapping], for they would get more Wolves, Beaver &c. from the Archithinue Natives in the spring, than they can carry." Henday came to this realization in the early new year when none of the Indians had made any effort to commence trapping even though conditions were ideal. "I plainly observe," he noted in his journal, "all our Traders must be supplied with Furs from the Archithinue & Asinepoet Natives."[23]

By mid-March 1755, Henday's companions had taken him to a canoe-building site along the North Saskatchewan River, probably beyond the mouth of the Battle River, where there were white or paper birch trees on the north side of the valley. Although white birch does not grow in pure stands, large trees grow in the moister areas of the river valley, where they are less susceptible to fire. The other essential tree for canoe-making was spruce, white (*Picea glauca*) and black (*Picea mariana*), scattered throughout the parklands, mostly in river valleys, and along the southern edge of the boreal forest. Spruce roots provided cordage (for sewing together birch bark sections), while the pitch sealed and waterproofed the canoe. Framing and paddles could also be made from the wood.[24] The Pegogamaw worked the better part of a month constructing boats for the trip to York Factory, all the while being joined up and down along the river, wherever there were stands of white birch, by Indian groups with the same purpose in mind. The two-to-four-person birchbark canoe, known for its lightweight, streamlined design and load-carrying capacity, was truly an engineering marvel—and has not been improved upon to this day.[25]

Once the ice had broken up, Henday set off downriver on 28 April in a flotilla that included twenty canoes paddled by Assinipoets. Two days later, he was reunited with Attickasish and a large number of Pegogamaw at another boat-building encampment. Henday probably expected the push to the bay to begin in earnest. But around mid-May, they came upon one hundred tents of Archithinue, camped atop the steep banks of the wide river, apparently waiting their arrival. Despite Henday's protestations that the Indians should take their trade to York Factory, the Pegogamaw exchanged old axes and any other used European items for Archithinue wolf pelts and beaver skins. An even larger trade was conducted a few days later farther downriver, only this time it was the Pegogamaw who reached the rendezvous place first before the Archithinue.

For many Indian groups, bison hunting took precedence over trading trips to Hudson Bay.

Henday's companions used the delay to hunt bison found grazing along the river. Women and children then processed and dried the meat in preparation for the demanding trip to the bay. None of the Archithinue, however, could be persuaded to join them. "I talked with them," Henday alluded to his mission, "but all to no purpose."[26] And why would they? Not only were the Archithinue able to trade most of their furs to the Pegogamaw, but they were also a mounted society who lived by the bison hunt. Henday himself marvelled at their fine horses, especially in comparison to his sickly beast that he had nursed through the winter and eventually given away at the canoe-building site.

By the time the Pegogamaw resumed their trip downriver, having nearly exhausted their supply of trade goods, the flotilla now numbered about sixty canoes and was heavily laden with furs. It was exactly the kind of cargo that was needed to help revive York Factory's flagging fortunes. But on 23 May, the Pegogamaw reached Fort à la Corne, the French trading post below the Saskatchewan River forks. Henday could only watch helplessly as his companions accepted watered-down brandy for their furs—in his estimation, over one thousand of their best skins. A few days later at Basquia, the other

French establishment on the Saskatchewan that had been visited on the way inland, the Pegogamaw once again freely dealt furs for brandy. In fact, Henday was convinced that the Pegogamaw would have paddled no farther than Basquia "if they could persuade the French to take their heavy furs." He also feared that French access to Brazil tobacco would effectively have the same effect—if the interior posts were ever able to carry this favoured Indian luxury item, it "would entirely cut off our [English] trade."[27] As it was, the Pegogamaw spent four raucous days at Basquia, intoxicated for much of their stay, before a frustrated Henday was able to cajole them to resume their trip to York Factory. They were joined by several Basquia Cree, who lived in the area and travelled annually to the bay to trade. Several Assinipoet, however, decided against continuing, preferring to assign their leftover furs to the Cree canoes with trade instructions. Some three weeks later, on 20 June, and nearly twelve months after his departure, Henday returned to his bay home with a crude map and journal in hand but more importantly, an unprecedented understanding of the interior workings of the fur trade.

Anthony Henday's 1754–55 journey has been heralded for laying the basis for the English claim to the western interior. By travelling through the future provinces of Manitoba, Saskatchewan, and Alberta, the HBC servant helped ensure this region became part of Canadian confederation.[28] But what this interpretation ignores is that Henday was not really an explorer and discoverer; at best, he was a visitor on a trade mission organized and led by the Pegogamaw. A less charitable assessment, on the other hand, suggests that Henday is only noteworthy for being the first European to spend a winter inland, beyond the French posts on the Saskatchewan.[29] But in downplaying, even belittling, his achievement—living with the Pegogamaw in the upper Saskatchewan River country for almost a year—the larger significance of his trip is missed. During his time inland, Henday learned that the Pegogamaw served as trade brokers between Europeans and other Indian groups and that they did not trap the furs and pelts they brought to the bay. He also found that the Archithinue were not necessarily opposed to trading with Europeans but rather reluctant to trade at

LIBRARY AND ARCHIVES CANADA C-000403, A. J. MILLER

The bison jump took advantage of the terrain but required careful execution to be successful.

the distant bay posts. They had readily adopted the horse into their culture to become a proud mounted hunting society that largely depended on the great bison herds—and not European goods—for their subsistence. The Pegogamaw, by comparison, were still relatively horse-poor and used the animals for hauling purposes, much like oversized dogs. But it seemed only a matter of time, with more and more horses becoming available, before they migrated out onto the grasslands to become plains hunters and challenge others already there. Until then, the Pegogamaw, situated along the Saskatchewan River, were ideally positioned to dominate the fur trade, exchanging recycled or cast-off European items for furs collected by other Indian groups, trading the furs for luxury goods, like rum, at the French posts, and then taking poorer or leftover furs to the bay to secure more heavier English items that the French could not bring into the interior. The Pegogamaw moved goods and furs between buyers and sellers, much like a modern-day commercial clearing house. And they were always looking for ways to maximize their benefit with minimum effort.[30] If the French traders had been able to satisfy all their trade needs, the Pegogamaw would have stopped going to York Factory.

What Governor Isham did with Henday's findings has been decried as a "deliberate suppression and distortion."[31] In forwarding the journal to the London Committee in 1755, Isham altered the document to suggest that Henday's trip was an unqualified success—that the Archithinue could be expected to make trading trips to the bay. This falsification of Henday's journal is somewhat baffling, in that Isham had been an early proponent of establishing a HBC post inland to meet French competition head-on. But he had also come to realize that the company was in no position to challenge directly its French rivals on the Saskatchewan for the simple reason that it could not man or equip a post there. Indeed, the irony is that the Archithinue were not the only ones in the North-West not to use canoes—neither did the English on the bay. Nor did they have the building materials at hand to build canoes even if they knew how. The compromise position, then, and one that Isham put forward in sending the doctored Henday journal to London, was that the company adopt a policy of sending a few trusted men inland every year to discourage Indians from dealing with the French, while bringing more bands into the orbit of York Factory's trade hinterland. This wintering program, as it became known, was certainly attractive, in that it was not only a relatively cheap way to deal with the French presence in the interior but, equally important, did not require the company to make any changes to the way it ran its operations in North America. Indians would still come to the bay to trade. But the London Committee had serious reservations about the reliability of Henday's journal, questioning the distances he covered and griping about his vague geographical descriptions.[32] In the end, though, the HBC endorsed Isham's new policy because it held out the real prospect of maintaining, perhaps even expanding, company trade: "bringing down Indian strangers at the Fort to Trade ... we judge to be the only means of enlarging the York Fort Cargoes."[33]

Anthony Henday's journey inland consequently became the first of fifty-six wintering trips by HBC servants between 1754 and 1775.[34] These trips provided some of the few accounts of life in central Saskatchewan in the mid-eighteenth century, as well as improved the company's understanding of the interior geography. But it was still a narrow or skewed snapshot. The winterers' primary concern was the beaver trade, and even though they were newcomers to the western interior, they rarely commented on what it looked, sounded, or smelled like during their travels. They also spent their time mostly with those Indians directly involved in the English fur trade, and as Henday learned, some inland groups, like the Archithinue of the Red Deer region, did not necessarily need European goods to live quite comfortably as mounted bison hunters. The HBC men were also never inland in summer, because they were either travelling from or back to York Factory with their Indian hosts, and gained limited insight into the lives of those groups who made up the canoe brigades to the bay. How—and if—they recorded their experiences and findings was another problem. Many of the winterers were poorly educated and were capable of writing only semi-literate accounts whose value greatly varied, if they could be deciphered.[35]

Not surprisingly, Henday was one among the first of the new company winterers, heading back inland with another servant, William Grover, only a week after his return to York Factory. But Grover found the rigours of travelling to be too much, and the pair returned to the bay after only a few weeks. Henday was given a new assignment in 1756, this time to select a site for a possible settlement that Isham proposed to build upriver at some time in the future. But ill health chased him home and kept him at the bay until 1759 when he and Joseph Smith apparently wintered in Archithinue country; no account of the trip has been found. Henday left company service in 1762, coincidentally a year after the death of Isham at York Factory, and promptly disappeared from the historical record. He thought he deserved a promotion and better pay. He also likely chafed at the ridicule he endured from fellow servants who refused to believe his stories, especially about horse-riding Indians.[36] But in sailing back to England, he left behind a Pegogamaw partner and possibly a child.

Even though Henday had severed his ties with the HBC, there were other servants who followed in the wake of his 1754–55 initiative. One was Joseph Smith, a labourer who spent five winters inland, including one with Henday.

Another was Joseph Waggoner, the mixed-descent son of a HBC worker at Fort Albany. Together in August 1756, the two Josephs, as Isham nicknamed the pair, accompanied a Sturgeon Cree trading captain inland beyond Cedar Lake and the Porcupine Hills to the upper Assiniboine River in present-day east-central Manitoba and west-central Saskatchewan. It was their job to revive the Sturgeon trade at York Factory, which had dropped off quite sharply because of the heavy French presence in the region. The Sturgeon answer was for the English to establish a post in their territory, even recommending where it should be located.[37] A French trader, meanwhile, deliberately followed the two winterers with a supply of goods in the late winter of 1757, trying to ensure that the Sturgeon were not won over with HBC promises and take their trade to the bay. He even threatened at one point to kill both men. But the Indians countered with their own threat. "If they [French] did or offered to do any harm to us," Smith recounted, "they would kill them all."[38] The Sturgeon were determined to uphold and enforce their sovereignty in their home territory and welcomed, even cultivated, the rivalry between the French and English for their trade.

Smith and Waggoner returned to Sturgeon country the following year. In the late summer of 1757, the Sturgeon traders rejoined their families at Mossy Portage at the south end of Cedar Lake and then continued west to Red Deer Lake, where they abandoned their canoes and struck southwest for the open parklands. Henry Kelsey had likely visited this same area in the early 1690s. Reaching modern Good Spirit Lake, the group continued on to the Touchwood Hills, where Smith and Waggoner observed several small Assiniboine camps pounding bison—one of the first European records of this procurement strategy. The Sturgeon, in contrast to their plains neighbours, had not yet adopted pounding but broke up into small groups for the winter to hunt bison and trap wolves. Come early spring, they came together at a canoe-building site on possibly the Woody or Swan Rivers in the Porcupine Hills in preparation for the trip to the bay.[39]

These and other wintering trips appeared to bring about the much-needed turnaround in York Factory's trade. When Smith and Waggoner

Fires regularly swept across the northern plains.

returned to the bay in the late spring of 1757, they were escorted by thirty-nine canoes (compared to only thirteen in 1755). That number rose to fifty-seven in 1758 after their second winter with the Sturgeon. The following year, another pair of HBC winterers, Isaac Batt and George Potts, came down to York Factory with sixty-four Sturgeon canoes. That was slightly more than the sixty-one canoes that Henday and Smith returned with in the spring of 1760 after spending the winter with the Pegogamaw in the Saskatchewan country.[40] But this "great advance in the trade,"[41] as Isham crowed about the success of his wintering policy, was deceptive. More canoes coming to the bay did not necessarily mean higher profits as long as the French interior posts continued to siphon off the prime beaver skins, leaving the English with the unwanted, heavier pelts and less valuable non-beaver pelts. The good news, though, and the real reason for the increased canoe traffic, was that the French had been forced to withdraw from the North-West when they could no longer be provisioned from Montreal because of the Seven Years' War. Without supplies to carry on business, the French quietly abandoned Fort à la Corne in 1757. That same problem may have been the reason that local Indians plundered and burned Fort Bourbon on Cedar Lake the following

173

year.[42] Basquia managed to hold out until 1759—the year Quebec City fell to the British— when it too shut down operations, bringing an end to the French trade in the North-West that the La Vérendrye family had initiated.

The capture of New France probably seemed like a godsend to the HBC. By knocking Montreal out of the interior fur trade, British forces had done the company a great favour removing a festering trade irritant. Indeed, any argument in favour of establishing inland posts had now been negated, as evidenced by the dramatic rise in York Factory's returns. Trade in Made Beaver steadily climbed from 21,000 in 1754 to 27,000 in 1756 and then 33,642 in 1760, the same year that Montreal surrendered to the British.[43] There was also no continuing need to send HBC men inland to winter with the Indians because any European trade was only possible now at the bayside posts. Perhaps that is why, for the first time since Henday's initial trip, there were no winterers in Indian country in 1762–63. The following year, though, Joseph Smith and Isaac Batt travelled inland, probably with a group of returning Pegogamaw, in another effort to bring the Archithinue into the English trade. They wintered somewhere near the Eagle Hills of west-central Saskatchewan, feeding on bison, sometimes in cooperation with the local Assiniboine, before moving to the South Saskatchewan River in the early spring to build canoes at Birch Hills. As they paddled back to the bay, the pair did not find any sign of competitors, only the ruins of French posts along the way.[44]

This monopoly situation—something the HBC insisted it enjoyed by charter but was unable to enforce on the ground—was remarkably shortlived. In fact, the company might be excused for thinking it had imagined that it finally had the rich fur hinterland of the North-West to itself. For as Smith and Batt returned to York Factory in 1764, Canadian traders began pushing into the interior again from Montreal. Their arrival so quickly on the scene should not have been unexpected—nor was it really that surprising. Even though France ceded its North American colony to the British by the 1763 Treaty of Paris and thereby ceased to be an imperial power on the continent, the decades-long trade connections between Montreal and the interior were not ended with the stroke of a pen. In what was known as the old North-West, the upper Mississippi region south of the Great Lakes, French-Canadian merchants, traders, and voyageurs remained part of an informal transnational community—a French "river world"—that included Montreal, Detroit, and St. Louis (established in 1764 on the west side of the Mississippi River opposite the old Indian village of Cohokia). Commerce, kinship, and religion held these French communities together until the early nineteenth century.[45] Above the Great Lakes, to the North-West, the old canoe routes and trading spots remained in place after the British conquest. All that was needed were people to plug into the Montreal network and reactivate it. That void was quickly filled by Canadian traders who never left the interior, and later by Anglo-American and British (especially Scottish) merchants, who not only hired experienced traders and trippers but also had access to British markets and capital. It was a sure formula for success. The Hudson's Bay Company was about to face its most formidable adversary, especially after 1768 when the British government deregulated trade in the North-West.

The first indicator that something was amiss in the interior was the drop in trade volume at York Factory. The MB returns had bounced back in the early 1760s but began to fall off again around mid-decade. Smith and Batt were sent back inland with trading captains in 1763 with specific instructions "to make Inquiry & get what Intelligence you Can of the approaches of the People of Canada, how far they have Penetrated into the Country."[46] Smith wintered with the Pegogamaw somewhere west of the Saskatchewan River forks, while Batt lived with the Basquia around the Upper Assiniboine River—both obvious places to try to re-establish the Montreal trade. But neither servant encountered any pedlars, the contemptuous name that the HBC assigned its new competitors. They were there the next winter, though, when Batt returned to the same region, and many of the Basquia that he brought down to the bay in the spring of 1766 had traded first with the Montreal men—as they had done before the French withdrawal. Henceforth, news of the pedlars and their activities, both real and imagined, infused post journals and official correspondence.

These traders included Charles Chaboillez, Jean-Baptiste Cadot (Cadotte), Maurice-Régis and Joseph-Barthélemy Blondeau, and Nicholas Montour—all of whom cut their fur trade teeth in the Superior country before moving west to trade directly with the Indians as *marchands-voyageurs* (or *bourgeois* as called by their canoemen).[47] The most frequently mentioned trader on the lower Saskatchewan was François Jérôme (*dit* Latour), also known as François Le Blanc, Franceway, Saswe, Shash, or Shashree. Born in New France in 1706, Jérôme signed a voyageur contract in 1727 to work in the *pays d'en haut*. Sixteen years later, he was employed by the famous La Vérendrye family and may have been involved in the establishment of the French posts west of Lake Winnipeg. Jérôme remained in the North-West during the Seven Years' War and emerged as a trader in his own right by this time. In 1767, he was issued a fur trade licence at Michilimackinac and used this supply base to support his operations on the lower Saskatchewan. Those who encountered him for the first time were struck by his easygoing manner, gentlemanly ways, and immersion in the Indian world: speaking Cree effortlessly, adopting Cree dress, and taking a Cree partner. But the trader, known up and down the river by one of his many nicknames, was a keen competitor who used his familiarity with the local Indians and their ways to carry on a lucrative trade.[48]

The company answer to this new challenge was to send even more winterers inland in 1766—six separate trips[49]—in a desperate bid to get more Indians coming to the bay. But this policy would work only if these servants had the Indian trade to themselves—something that they actually faced losing to the Montreal traders. "The Pedlars had goods to offer," one fur trade historian weighed the contest, "the English had no more than persuasions and promises."[50]

By 1768, Montreal trader James Finlay had opened a post at Basquia, while Saswe (François Jérôme) had now set up shop farther west up the Saskatchewan River at the Indian aggregating centre, *nīpowwinihk* (a standing place) near present-day Nipawin.[51] HBC winterer William Pink came across Finlay at Saswe's fort in the spring of 1769 on his way back to the bay with a

Pegogamaw canoe flotilla. The meeting was politely cool, if not a little testy. When Pink handed Finlay a printed warning that interlopers were to stay out of company territory, he shot back that the HBC charter applied only to the land around the rim of the bay. Finlay later claimed that Pink was "collecting the Indians and driving them like slaves down to York Fort" to prevent them from dealing with him.[52] What really mattered, though, in the unfolding commercial struggle was whether these Montreal pedlars could supply the Indian needs, something they still had not mastered. Many of the Canadian posts were consequently understaffed or abandoned for periods of time during the late 1760s.

The news that Pink and other HBC winterers were bringing back to York Factory was disturbing in its own right. Even more unsettling was what Andrew Graham, the chief factor there, learned when a solitary Archithinue appeared at the fort in June 1766. The visitor, probably a member of the Blackfoot Alliance, had heard about the English trading place and to satisfy his own curiosity made the trip to the bay with a Cree party.[53] The Archithinue confirmed that the Pegogamaw were middlemen—he called them "the Trading Indians"—and that they depended on furs trapped by other Indians. "They were more obliged to Him & his Country men," he maintained, "than he was to them." He also expressed shock over what the Trading Indians were getting for furs at the post, especially when the Archithinue had to "give them 40 or 50 Wolves for an old Gun or Kettle," but confessed that his people accepted this lopsided trading arrangement because they would never visit the bay because they did not use canoes.[54] This information was really old news—something that Henday had uncovered during his trip inland a decade earlier—but it still had grave implications. If the Montreal pedlars were able to extend the reach of their trade to Archithinue country and displace the Indian middlemen, York Factory was likely doomed.

Ferdinand Jacobs, who had replaced Isham as governor at York Factory in 1762, was never a supporter of the wintering program, but since the company had come to embrace it as the best way to shore up the bay trade, he had no choice but to send servants inland. By 1768, though, it had become painfully apparent to Jacobs that the policy was failing, and miserably so. And that was because trade at York Factory that year dropped by almost half from the average of the previous ten years (from thirty thousand to eighteen thousand MB).[55] This abrupt downturn, Jacobs told the London Committee, was directly attributable to the "Canadian Pedlars ... all over the Heart of the Trading Indians Country." He also warned that continued losses should be expected because there was no guarantee that the winterers, no matter how experienced, would have any "Influence in promoting Your Honours Trade." Jacobs respectfully suggested that the answer for the HBC was to expand to "the most Convenient Places to stop the Pedlars robbing you of your Trade."[56] His proposal even included the kind of boats that would be needed—light, flat-bottomed vessels that drew little water.

Jacob's call for inland posts was sensible and timely. The longer the company hesitated, the more time the Montreal traders had to solidify and expand their hold on the interior trade. Still, the idea represented a sea change in the trade strategy that had been the backbone of HBC operations for almost a full century. Servants had become accustomed to the routine and ritual of the annual canoe brigades to the bay posts. Even if the company decided to take the commercial battle to the pedlars, establishing a settlement on or near the Saskatchewan River represented a formidable undertaking. Bay men were only able to go inland as passengers and even then were at the mercy of the Indians who travelled where and particularly when it suited their interests. It was much easier for the company to persist with the wintering policy, while adjusting the trade standard—as it did in 1769—in the naive hope that the more favourable terms would prove attractive to Indians and keep them coming to York Factory.[57]

Until the HBC decided to build an inland post, "trusted" trading captains continued to ferry company servants into the interior for the winter in the expectation that they would be handsomely rewarded for bringing them back to the bay the following spring. Jacobs, in turn, defended this arrangement as the only way to maintain allegiance of these Cree leaders, given the lure of the Montreal competitors, and thereby ensure that they and their followers continued to trade at York Factory.[58] Many winterers lived several years with a particular trading group, such as the Basquia, Pegogamaw, or Sturgeon, in a single-minded effort to keep a close watch on local pedlars and try to counteract their influence. Their journals, however, also documented how the Cree along the Saskatchewan River were extending their range from the edge of the boreal forest into the grasslands. William Pink, for example, who spent the better part of four consecutive winters inland (1766–70) in present-day central Saskatchewan and may have travelled as far west as the area Henday reached in 1769–70,[59] found that his returning party went directly to the grasslands where they divided into small hunting groups for the long North-West winter. These camps were never large—a few families at most—and were counted in tents. Only when the weather became too severe did they follow the bison and seek shelter in the nearby parklands.[60] Come late winter, they moved to canoe-building sites along the edge of the boreal forest, before congregating in larger bands at traditional aggregation centres, such as *Pasquatinow* (downstream from Tobin Rapids on the Saskatchewan River), where the families usually remained while the canoe brigades journeyed to and from the bay.[61]

Cree participation in trade in the mid-eighteenth century did not evolve into dependence on European goods. Certainly, they had a reputation as "militant consumers"[62] who demanded particular products, especially metal items, but these new tools were adapted to traditional tasks. Nor did better prices encourage more individuals to trade more furs. The Cree had fairly consistent needs, and what newcomers usually dismissed as laziness was actually an ability to make do with surprisingly very little. The winterers also observed how the Cree easily reverted to the use of bows and arrows, saving their scarce shot and powder, and how indigenous weapons were better suited than guns in particular hunting scenarios.[63]

This ability to continue to pursue varied subsistence practices allowed the Cree to withdraw from the fur trade whenever it suited their interests or when resource availability changed. Newcomer reliance on Indians, in turn, enabled the Cree to control, even dictate, the trade relationship. They had no qualms in dealing with the Montreal pedlars over winterers' protests, even if they received less for their furs, because it saved them the near-starvation trip to and from the bay. They also expected special treatment for delivering a company servant back to York Factory. Some trading captains had even started to threaten to go over to the pedlars. "The Leading Indians were unreasonable in their demands of Presents," Jacobs said of the 1768 spring trading session at York Factory, "which I was obliged to comply with."[64] The Cree generally looked down upon the traders—they were helpless foreigners in Indian country—and resorted to threats and other brutish behaviour to see that their wishes were met.[65]

HBC winterers also found that the mounted bison hunt was working against greater Indian engagement with the fur trade. During his first trip inland in 1766–67, for example, William Pink encountered an Assiniboine group who had never journeyed to the bay.[66] Instead, they prospered on the grassland by hunting the great bison herds on horseback. Other groups on the northern plains, in particular the Cree, were striving to follow the same route to food security and material wealth that came with mounted nomadism, albeit at a much slower rate. The sticking point was the availability of horses—and keeping them alive. Because the northern plains fell on the wrong side of what has been called "the ecological fault line of Plains Indian equestrianism,"[67] the first horses in the Saskatchewan country regularly fell victim to the severe winter weather, especially if they were worked hard in the fall hunt. It required equal amounts of perseverance and hands-on knowledge to successfully start and maintain a herd. Being horse-poor meant that those Cree who wintered on the grasslands were effectively delayed in making the transition to mounted hunting. They had to rely more on the traditional method of bison hunting by pounding.[68] But even then, the Cree lack of practical experience with this labour-intensive procurement activity, including bringing the bison to the hunters, often resulted in failure. The Assiniboine were much more adept at pounding.

Being on foot on the grasslands made the Cree feel vulnerable. There was a perpetual fear of the Snake, who had used their access to horses to launch a mounted military expansion into the northern plains in the early eighteenth century. The Pegogamaw were consequently ever watchful, seemingly expecting the Snake to appear over the horizon at any moment on a raiding trip. But the Snake did not really have the numerical strength to occupy all of the territory and were being forced to retreat southward by the now mounted Archithinue, intent on reclaiming their traditional lands.[69] The Cree not only joined these warring expeditions against a common foe but gave the Archithinue the fighting edge by trading guns that they themselves had secured from the HBC. This support did not really translate into an explicit military alliance; the relationship between the two groups was more informal, purposely flexible, and always in flux. The Cree would never have been allowed into Archithinue territory, let alone be able to hunt or trap there, unless the two groups got along. During the winter of 1769–70, William Pink documented how his Cree party and some "Black Footed" people (the Siksika), later to be joined by a few Assiniboine, camped together in the present-day Manito Lake region west of the Eagle Hills and cooperatively worked a bison pound and snared wolves.[70] Friends one day, however, could be enemies the next, and the dealings between northern plains groups were marked by wariness. Conflict could erupt at any time and then give way to a period of peaceful co-existence. Pink reported that there were many reasons for "going to war." Death or sickness, for example, could be assuaged only by striking out against other Indian groups to make up for the loss. These skirmishes might appear reckless, even senseless, but they were nonetheless unavoidable, as different peoples migrated into the region and jostled for position and access to the same resources.[71]

Winterers' journals were largely silent about Indian partners—and probably for good reason. At first, the London Committee officially forbade its servants from having sex with the indigenous population. But such a prohibition was simply unrealistic in the all-male world of the HBC, especially if the company did not want its servants to engage in homosexual activity.[72] Many Indian bands also sought to establish friendship ties with newcomers by lending wives or daughters, provided the practice was approved by the husband or father. It was not long, then, before senior company officials had Indian wives, sometimes more than one.[73] Governor James Isham justified the practice on trade grounds. Marital alliances, in his words, were "a great help in Engaging them [Indians] to trade."[74] Chief Factor Andrew Graham, who also married according to the "custom of the country" (*mariage à la façon du pays*), was more philosophical. "The intercourse that is carried between the Indian ladies and the Englishmen," he remarked, "is not allowed, but winked at."[75]

When newcomers entered a "country marriage," they became part of a kin relationship that might have included connections across several bands over a wide region. As trader George Nelson once remarked about his unexpected encounters with his partner's relatives, "There is no end to relationship among the Indians."[76] As a relative, a HBC servant was expected to provide trade favours and gifts to his wife's family, as well as assistance to the band in times of future need. Prestige also came with a trader as a son-in-law. His partner's family, in return, was expected to patronize the post, encourage other band members to do so, and supply provisions. By taking his wife into the post, the trader was seen to be affirming these reciprocal obligations. It was much more than a matter of living together.[77] The company grudgingly accepted the existence of these relationships, and the children that they produced, but sought to avoid supporting the families, especially when servants retired or died. Some mixed-descent sons did, however, find employment at the bay posts.[78]

Winterers were held to a different standard. They were under strict instructions to live and behave as Englishmen in the interior and keep their distance from their Indian hosts,[79] which apparently included taking a wife. When Isham consequently prepared Anthony Henday's journal for submission to the London Committee in 1755, he judiciously removed the few references to his "bedfellow." But having a female companion was an absolute must if HBC men were going to survive a winter inland. Women were not just sexual partners. They performed any number of everyday domestic duties, including the making of moccasins and snowshoes, and generally kept the HBC traders

LIBRARY AND ARCHIVES CANADA C-000412 A.J. MILLER

Mounted hunting bands skirmished over access to territory and bison.

fed, clothed, and sheltered. One of their special jobs was collecting *wattappe* or spruce tree roots that were carefully separated into fine thread and then used in the stitching of birchbark canoes.[80] The significance of this female care and support was plainly evident when Henry Kelsey returned to York Factory in 1692 after two winters inland and refused to enter the post unless his partner accompanied him. In fact, all winterers likely had a wife and family. Perhaps the saddest episode was when Joseph Smith's "canoe and tent mate" showed up at York Factory in the spring of 1765 with the news that her husband had died enroute. She and her child were sent away with goods equal to the value of Smith's personal effects.[81]

Women were largely responsible for the success of HBC servant Samuel Hearne's third attempt to reach the Coppermine River in 1771–72. Even though the company did not admit it, their participation in the expedition made all the difference. The London Committee had always been concerned about the trade west of Fort Churchill, but 1758 had been a particularly bad year when no Chipewyan came to trade at the post. The governor at Churchill tried to remedy this situation by copying the wintering policy being employed by York Factory. But the servant sent inland in 1759 turned back before his party had gone far.[82] The need to visit the region became only more urgent over the next decade when Indians reported the existence of several copper deposits along a great river. A sample of ore backed up their claim.

The person tagged for the investigation of the Coppermine area was Samuel Hearne, who had served in the Royal Navy during the Seven Years' War before joining the HBC in 1766 as a twenty-one-year-old mate on company ships in Hudson Bay. (He has left graffiti behind at Sloops Cove, near Prince of Wales Fort, where he carved his name and date on a rock.) Hearne had been working at Churchill in 1769 during the transit of Venus observations there and had learned from the scientific team how to take astronomical readings with a quadrant.[83] It was his youthful tenacity, though, that enabled him to stare down defeat, even at the bleakest of times, that made him a perfect choice for the assignment. Hearne had no sooner left Churchill in November 1769 when his guides abandoned him in the Seal River Valley. He set off again in February 1770 and made it to the Dubawnt River country (north of present-day northeastern Saskatchewan) only to get lost in the barrens and break his quadrant. Somehow he made it back to Churchill but not before being robbed by local Cree.

It fell to Matonabbee, a Chipewyan middleman trader, to rescue the twice-aborted Hearne expedition. He knew the territory in question—had once brokered a truce between the peoples of the region—and understood that the availability of resources, and not the destination, should dictate the direction and pace of travel. But what made his "gangs" so functional in the harsh environment, shuttling trade goods and furs across the barren lands, were women packers. Women, Matonabbee claimed with rhetorical flourish, "were made for labour; one of them can carry, or haul, as much as two men can do … [and] though they do everything, are maintained at a trifling expence … the very licking of their fingers in scarce times, is sufficient for their subsistence."[84]

The ruins of Prince of Wales Fort (Fort Churchill) photographed in the early 1900s.

When Hearne left Churchill for the third time in December 1770, Matonabbee and his six wives led the way. They took a more southerly route, skirting the top of present-day Manitoba and Saskatchewan, before turning north for the Coppermine. The days were marked by "all feasting, or all famine."[85] When Hearne and his companions finally reached their objective in July 1771, it was immediately apparent that the "great" river was not suitable for larger ships. The reported copper mines were a disappointment, too.. But what was most disturbing for Hearne was watching helplessly as Matonabbee and his gang massacred a camp of Inuit—a nightmarish event commemorated by the name, Bloody Falls.[86] Hearne surveyed down the Coppermine to where the river emptied into the Arctic Ocean (the first European to reach it overland), before being taken south and across Great Slave Lake (again, the first European to do so). Here, in the new year, he met Chipewyan who were still using bone and stone tools because the Cree blocked access to the English traders to the east. The party then made for the Hudson Bay coast and reached Churchill in June 1772.

It was a remarkable trip, but as Hearne himself confessed," not likely to

RCMP MUSEUM 34.6.41

LIBRARY AND ARCHIVES CANADA R9266-3032

A Chipewyan trading party took HBC servant Samuel Hearne inland from Prince of Wales Fort to the Coppermine River.

prove of any material advantage."[87] In the past, the HBC had jealously guarded information about Rupert's Land—somewhat ironic, because company shareholders included members of the prestigious British Royal Society. In fact, maps of that part of North America were largely based on information coaxed out of sea captains sailing to and from the bay. But the London Committee had been enlivened by the HBC's participation in the transit of Venus observations at bayside and chose to share Hearne's manuscript with British naturalists and geographers. These journals and maps created quite a stir in scientific circles since that part of northern North America was still mostly unknown.[88] Hearne was flattered by the attention and prepared an enlarged, popular version of the manuscript, with additional material on the peoples and animal life of the region, that was published to great acclaim in 1795, three years after his death.

Hearne's field notes were not the only materials that the HBC made available to British scientists in the early 1770s. With encouragement from the London Committee, servants began collecting and sending natural history specimens to London; the first shipment in 1771 included a species new to science, the Eskimo curlew (*Scolopax borealis*). Several of these items were

GEOLOGICAL SURVEY OF CANADA 199525

Hearne carved his name and date on a rock at Sloops Cove near Prince of Wales Fort.

supplied by Indian people.[89] It is not known, however, whether the HBC winterers had gathered any of the specimens. In fact, Hearne's return from the interior coincided with the long-in-coming admission that the wintering policy was not working. One hundred fewer canoes came to York Factory in 1771 than the previous trading season and what they carried was of little value—"refuse" or damaged furs that the Montreal pedlars would not take.[90] Even Cree trading captains were deserting the HBC. *Wapinesiw* (White Bird), who had been recruited by Anthony Henday and going to the bay since 1755, was lured away by the Canadians.[91] But before suspending the program completely, Andrew Graham, chief factor at York Factory, argued that the company did not really have an accurate picture of what was happening inland because past winterers' reports were generally "incoherent & unintelligible." What was needed was "a sensible Person" who would "make many observations that may be of utility … [and] give a rational Account of things."[92]

That sensible person was Matthew Cocking. Initially hired as a post writer in 1765 and rising to deputy governor at York Factory, the twenty-nine-year-old Cocking was literate, trained in practical astronomy, and could speak Cree. But like other HBC servants who worked at bayside, he was not a canoeist. Cocking headed inland with a group of Pegogamaw on 27 June 1772, but because many of the Indians were "sickly," there were days when the brigade was simply not able to travel. That was one of the unexpected hazards of visiting York Factory, being exposed to unfamiliar diseases carried by the Englishmen. What normally took twenty days to return to their waiting families consequently stretched into forty-five. The party reached Basquia (*opāskweyāw*) on the Saskatchewan River at the end of July. "Many Natives had been here lately," Cocking said of the spiritual significance of the site. "This is a long frequented place where the Canadians rendezvous & trade with the Natives: Many of their Superstitious & Fanciful marks are seen here."[93] Over the next ten days, they paddled past the remains of two trading posts before meeting their families at another former French settlement, Fort à la Corne, near the Saskatchewan forks on 11 August. There were nearly 150 people camped here, probably members of a regional band whose seasonal round was oriented to this site.[94]

Leaving behind their canoes, Cocking's party followed a major Pegogamaw trail southwest through the Birch and Minachinas Hills and across the South Saskatchewan River (somewhere around present-day Batoche). Here, they met another regional band, with about fifteen to twenty tents, using the site as a gathering place. Proceeding west to the north branch of the river, they picked up another trail that ran southwest to the elbow, where it was joined by Eagle Creek. Another, much larger group—perhaps three or four regional bands—were camped at the mouth of the creek.[95] Entering the Eagle Hills on 6 September, Cocking spotted stone cairns atop several hills, a remnant of past hunting societies. The group soon broke up for

A WINTER VIEW IN THE ATHAPUSCOW LAKE, BY SAMUEL HEARNE, 1771

Face p. 188

BURPEE, THE SEARCH FOR THE WESTERN SEA

Samuel Hearne's sketch of Athapuscow Lake (Great Slave Lake) during his 1770–72 trip inland

the winter, many securing tent poles to take with them.[96] Cocking remained in the area—what he described as "a plentiful Country of provisions"[97]—never venturing too far from the Asquith and Biggar districts. To ensure a good winter, the leaders of his party held a ceremony in early October during which *wippetanassowin* (offerings to the spirits) were "prescnted ... to be given to the ground to induce it to favour them with plenty of furs & provisions."[98] The next day, the men sang their bison pound songs.

Cocking did his best to encourage every Indian group he encountered to avoid trading with the pedlars and travel to the bay instead. But he knew that they had no intention of keeping their promises—"they are such notorious liars"—and that they frequented the Canadian posts because of the ready availability of rum. And if the Indians had their way, the HBC men would have traded with them on their home ground. "I find they consider an Englishman's going with them," he explained, "as a person sent to collect Furs."[99] Cocking also met several mounted, bison-hunting bands, considerably more people on horseback than Henday had come across two decades earlier. The Cree, on the other hand, were still using horses as pack animals and still resigned to losing them, especially during the cold winter months when feed was scarce. "They say [it] is the case at this season of the year," Cocking reported.[100] What may have raised the mortality rate that winter was the decidedly colder climate. Whereas Henday wore only moccasins because of the relatively mild January temperatures, Cocking talked about how the new year ushered in a prolonged spell of cold and snowy weather: eighteen inches of snow on the ground by early January and twenty-six inches of ice on the North Saskatchewan. The colder winter made for more difficult hunting conditions for the pedestrian Pegogamaw, and there were days when Cocking and his companions were "hard pinched for want of food."[101]

Chief Factor Graham had deliberately selected Cocking for this investigative trip because he wanted a more complete understanding of the inland situation. He was not to be disappointed. Whereas other winterers usually provided a myopic perspective, often in cryptic prose, Cocking opened the lens for a wider or panoramic view. He used Cree names for many geographical features, especially in Pegogamaw territory, and therein captured the affinity between the people and the landscape. The "Younger Brothers" southwest of the Birch Hills, for example, were probably the Minachinas Hills.[102] Cocking also made a number of significant ethnographical observations. In October 1772, at an old Archithinue campsite, he found part of a discarded "vessel … in the form of an earthen pan."[103] Two months later, while camped in the Bear Hills near present-day Ruthilda, his party was joined by several tents of White Clay people (Gros Ventre), whose "Victuals are dressed in earthen pots, of their own Manufacturing."[104] These two comments constitute the only historic references to indigenous pottery in Saskatchewan.[105] The Pegogamaw also took Cocking to an Archithinue "tobacco plantation," a long, narrow strip of plants, sheltered from the north wind by a row of poplars. His journal reference to the plot is the only mention of Indian horticulture in the province.[106] He also examined a sample of leather armour that had been taken from the Snake as war booty: a vest, six-fold-thick and quilted. Cocking noted that the horse-riding Gros Ventre wore similar leather jackets to protect them from arrows and lances.

190

BILL WAISER

Many HBC winterers and Canadian traders passed through the Saskatchewan Forks region.

The English trader was so struck by their fine appearance, atop their "Sprightly Animals," that he claimed that they were "more like Europeans."[107] But what made the Gros Ventre seem so different, especially from his travel companions, was their successful transition to a mounted hunting lifestyle. The Pegogamaw laboured for days, trying to repair an old Archithinue bison pound and then seeking out animals to drive into it, all without success. It was not until the Gros Ventre arrived on the scene in early December that several small herds of bison were quickly rounded up. "In all their actions," an impressed Cocking noted, "they far excell the other Natives."[108] He probably knew, even before he extended the invitation, not once but twice, that they had no reason to travel to the bay.

The Pegogamaw and Gros Ventre lived together for about two weeks— on friendly terms—before going their separate ways because of the scarcity of bison in the Bear Hills. The Gros Ventre headed southwest, apparently to war with the Snake, while the Pegogamaw walked northeast through the Eagle Hills and later across the frozen North Saskatchewan River to the eastern edge of the Thickwood Hills. At Red Deer Hill (*waskesew-wachee*), south of present-day Prince Albert, Cocking's party, along with several tents of Assinipoet, cooperatively worked several bison pounds through the late winter. Following one of the kills, he watched a leader with a lighted pipe ceremoniously blow several puffs of smoke at each individual animal before the meat was divided among the hunters and their families; spirit offerings that had been presented to each of the fallen bison were also buried near the pound or tied to it. Cocking's account of this ritual stands alone in the historical literature.[109]

By early April 1773, the Pegogamaw had moved to the river, somewhere near the future South Branch House, and built canoes and gathered provisions for the return trip to the bay. Once on the water, the flotilla visited several Montreal pedlars along the Saskatchewan, where the richest furs were exchanged for rum. It would be a mistake to simply regard the Cree here as hapless victims. They were the ones, according to Cocking, who demanded liquor from the Canadians and threatened to take their furs and supplies, even kill them, if they were not given what they wanted, including presents. Cocking got his own taste of this treatment when the Pegogamaw, tired of him stopping to take readings or write in his journal, refused to let him do so on the trip back. And when they reached York Factory on 18 June 1773, the Cree demanded that brandy be dispensed as a gift for safely returning the Englishman.[110]

Cocking had no sooner returned to the bay than he prepared his "Thoughts on Making a Settlement Inland." He could see no other alternative for the HBC, especially when the wintering policy, in his opinion, "will Answer no end."[111] His findings, however, had been pre-empted by Andrew Graham, who made the same recommendation in August 1772, ironically while Cocking was still making his way inland. Graham's call for inland posts represented quite a change of mind. When Ferdinand Jacobs had put the idea forward in 1769, it was Graham who pooh-poohed the "wild" scheme, arguing that the company should not concern itself with a handful of "poor pedlars from Canada" who led "a wretched vagabond life after a few furs." It would be far better for the company to "look sharp after the fur trade in all its branches" than to stoop to the "pitiful game" of the "Canadian pilferers."[112] But then, after Cocking had left for the interior in 1772, a deserter from the Canadian side had come down to York Factory with a group of Indians and told Graham about the mercantile muscle behind the new Montreal-based traders. Quite simply, the HBC faced a "far deadlier commercial menace" than the French had ever represented.[113] If the company continued to dawdle at bayside, then all would assuredly be lost.

DISORDER FLYING THROUGH THE COUNTRY

THE HUDSON'S BAY COMPANY PROBABLY NEVER IMAGINED THAT CUMBERLAND House would become the oldest continuously occupied settlement in the future province of Saskatchewan. It was just glad to have its first foothold in the interior. But no sooner had Cumberland House been established in 1774 than it was challenged by a series of competing posts[1] that intensified the commercial struggle and led directly to the formation of the North West Company. The struggle for the beaver skin trade was now to be fought primarily in Indian country as Canadian and English traders moved up the Saskatchewan River in the late eighteenth century, battling one another at every opportunity to gain the advantage and the spoils. Indians were not bystanders to this development. The Basquia and Pegogamaw Cree sought to affirm control over their traditional territory by exploiting the commercial rivalry to their advantage. They also assumed a new role as trade provisioners by spending more time on the northern plains to hunt the great bison herds. But they could not escape a devastating smallpox epidemic in 1781–82 that literally remade the map of the region by wiping out one-half to two-thirds of some band populations.

York Factory Chief Factor Andrew Graham's 1772 petition for an inland post was straightforward, if not surprisingly frank. He told the London Committee that Canadian competition had to be answered by a settlement on the

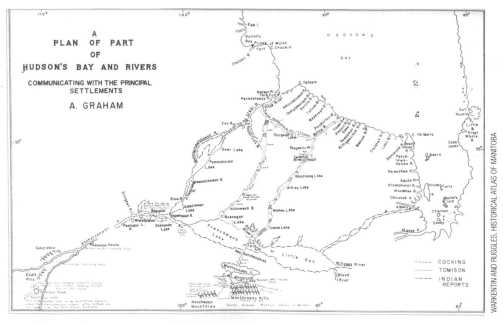

The map that accompanied HBC Chief Factor Andrew Graham's 1772 petition for an inland settlement on the Saskatchewan River

Saskatchewan River. Because Indians enjoyed the convenience of getting their trade goods from Montreal traders positioned inland, "every inducement to visit the Company's Factorys is forgot … & unless Your Honours exert your selves speedily, the trade at York Fort will be ruined."[2] Graham included a sketch map of the interior, showing the location of the Canadian posts and where a new HBC post should be located. He also reproduced a far more negative version of the Anthony Henday journal in his letter; this time, the expedition was a failure, with the Archithinue refusing to come to trade at the bay.[3] In London, Graham's memorandum was backstopped by Isaac Batt, a long-time HBC winterer who, by lucky coincidence, was on leave in England and spoke to the company officers about his experience in the interior, including one particular case in which a large body of Indians travelling to the bay abruptly abandoned him when they learned that the pedlars were nearby with liquor and other trade goods.[4]

On 18 May 1773, the London Committee officially decided to establish a post on the lower Saskatchewan River. The company plan was to supply and dispatch a small party from York Factory that summer, but ironically, the supply ship with the directive arrived too late to get started that year.[5] The delay made little difference. The Montreal pedlars were already established on the Saskatchewan, already carrying on a substantial trade, and already threatening to win the commercial battle as their numbers and reach grew. Even the Indians looked upon the English as being "to late in comeing."[6] But in deciding to move inland, however late, the HBC had taken a momentous step.

HBC servant Samuel Hearne is credited with founding Cumberland House on the northern edge of the Saskatchewan River delta. That is a generous interpretation. Fresh from his impressive trip across the barren lands from Fort Churchill to Lake Athabasca, Hearne was asked in August 1773 to head the expedition to establish the company's first inland post. But he could not convince any Indians to help undertake the task because of exceedingly low water levels and lateness of the season. August 1773 to July 1774 is the driest twelve-month period in a three-hundred-year tree ring record from the Cypress Hills area.[7] And when Hearne and a handful of HBC servants finally did set off early the following summer, they travelled as passengers in Indian canoes— but only because they had paid for their transportation with presents. Even then, they could not travel together but left for the lower Saskatchewan River with separate trading parties on different days. On 23 June 1774, Hearne set off with Cree trading captain Me-sin-e-kish-ac, while Matthew Cocking followed ten days later with another Cree group that was returning inland via Lake Winnipeg. Along the way, Cocking encountered two other expedition members, Isaac Batt and Moses Norton, who had left York Factory before him but had been unceremoniously abandoned by their Indian guides. Another servant, Robert Flett, had to be rescued by pedlars after his goods and most of his clothes were stolen. Few of these men, and the supplies that had been entrusted to them, reached Hearne. The Sturgeon Cree, for example, wanted any new HBC post to be sited in their territory, not farther north on the Saskatchewan River. They consequently took Cocking to the Upper Assiniboine country and forced him to winter around Good Spirit Lake (west of present-day Canora).[8]

The HBC contemplated two possible locations for its inland initiative, both in present-day Manitoba: Grand Rapids at the mouth of the Saskatchewan River and the site of the old French Fort Bourbon, and Basquia (The Pas).[9] But after consulting at length with local Indian leaders and seeing first-hand what they were suggesting, Hearne settled on a bay on Pine Island (Cumberland) Lake, sixty miles beyond Basquia and just north of the Saskatchewan River. Although not a traditional gathering centre, the site had been recommended to Hearne because it was across from the portage mouth at the nexus of several major trade routes: northeast to the HBC posts on the west side of the bay, northwest to the Churchill River and Athabasca country, and west along the Saskatchewan towards the Rocky Mountains. In other words, the location of the HBC's first inland post in western Canada, like French and then Canadian settlements before it, was determined by existing Indian social geography.[10] But unlike a century earlier, when the HBC first began operations on the bay, Hearne apparently did not hold any special ceremony or enter into any solemn pact with local Indians to secure their trade allegiance. His journal only describes meeting a group of Basquia "who seem'd very Courtious, ask'd me how I lik'd their Country and said they approv'd of my settleing in their Quarter."[11]

Hearne began supervising the building of Cumberland House on 3 September 1774 on a "fine and Levle" spot with "a Commanding view … for several miles Each way."[12] The significance of the moment was not lost on him. The simple log structure may not have been much, but as Hearne later noted, it was much closer to York Factory—only seven hundred miles by canoe—than to Canada and promised to give the HBC an immediate advantage over its Montreal-based competitors. But he also admitted that the ability of the company to go on the offensive, now that it finally had a foothold in the western interior, was thwarted by "the want of Proper Cannoes" and men able to use them.[13]

It was trading Indians, for example, who brought news to York Factory that Cumberland House had been established, and it was these same trading

PRINCE ALBERT HISTORICAL SOCIETY T-15

One of the first photographs of Cumberland House

Indians who were hired to carry supplies back to the new post. In the end, Hearne glumly estimated that it cost more in Indian presents to transport the trade goods inland than they were actually worth.[14]

Cumberland House (*wâskahikanihk* or "house") was beset with problems. One was the incredible mosquito population during summer, which made working outside, let alone in the nearby woods, miserable, if not impossible at times.[15] Another was the frequent flooding. Servants wore "duck trousers" made from Russian duck (hemp sheeting with a glazed waterproof finish) in an effort to keep dry.[16] Hearne also expected to live off the land, as he had done during his Coppermine expedition, and deliberately brought along more trade goods than food. But he was soon complaining "tho the men went ahunting each Day they did not kill any thing."[17] Cumberland House was situated in "a conspicuously empty game region,"[18] and although there may have been plenty of fish to live on, there was little meat available for Hearne and his men that first winter. The Basquia knew all about this deficiency and moved throughout the region to exploit food resources on a seasonal basis according to wildlife population cycles. The HBC men, on the other hand, were hunkered down in a fixed spot and could not look to York Factory to feed them because of the distance and costs involved. Instead, they came to depend on country provisions that Indians brought to the post, increasingly as trade items. It could be said that "wild game circulated as the first currency of the northwest."[19] But this supply was never consistent nor reliable because local Indians did not want to jeopardize their own survival. Most refused to become post provisioners, settling nearby on what was known in fur-trade parlance as the "plantation," but chose to scatter to their winter hunting grounds. The men at Cumberland House consequently had to be put on reduced rations and constantly griped about the scarcity of food.[20] If there was one consolation, several Cree women remained behind at Cumberland House over the first winter to prepare clothing and snowshoes so that company servants could at least travel outside in search of small game and firewood.[21]

Just like the bay posts, then, the very survival and success of Cumberland House depended on Indian goodwill. The movement of HBC traders inland may have ended the Indian role as trade intermediaries between the English and interior bands, but the convenience of having goods delivered to their doorstep did not mean that the Cree were prepared to forfeit control over their home territory or access to it. Rather, they continued to hold the upper hand in the HBC trade. Goods, furs, and servants going to and from Cumberland House could be transported only in Indian canoes. The Basquia Cree pressed this advantage by demanding presents, usually brandy, and then regularly stopped to extract another "payment" before proceeding. And if they were not accommodated, they usually took what they wanted. Other Cree tripmen simply quit, sometimes at the most inconvenient place, only to be rehired in the future because the HBC had no choice.[22]

Indian control also extended to provisions. Because of Cumberland House's precarious food situation, traders were at the mercy of Indian hunters who expected special treats in exchange for supplying meat, either green (fresh), beat (dried and then pounded into a fine "flour"), or dried. If traders refused to cooperate, they faced the prospect of starvation. This "provisioning challenge," one scholar has argued, "tested … the commercial viability of the fur trade itself."[23] The failure to have certain trade items in stock could also prove disastrous. Matthew Cocking, who took over from Hearne as Cumberland House master, was almost attacked in August 1776 when his liquor supply ran out. "The Indians left off trading [dried moose flesh] and were ready to have torn me to Pieces," he recounted. "If it was not for the Liquor and Tobacco We should not get a bit of Victuals to put in Our Mouths, but what We would have caught ourselves."[24]

The Cree welcomed the increased trade competition that came with the HBC moving inland, and deftly manipulated it to serve their interests. Up to then, as Cocking observed during his wintering trip in 1772–73, the Cree had willingly paid the higher prices demanded by Montreal pedlars if it saved them from making the arduous trip to the bay to secure English goods.[25] But as Hearne headed inland in the late summer of 1774 to find a place to put Cumberland House, his Basquia travelling companions refused to divulge the trade terms being offered by Canadian competition, only that they were well treated. A skeptical Hearne noted in his journal, "The Pedlors genorosity is much talk'd of, and are say'd to give away great quanies of goods for nothing." At the same time, he was troubled to encounter so many Cree families outfitted in Canadian clothing and "furnish'd with every other Necessary artical." Maybe the Basquia were not exaggerating because they "seem'd not to be in want of any thing."[26] At the very least, the Cree created the impression that the HBC would have to be equally generous to win them over.

Once Cumberland House had been constructed, Hearne discovered to his chagrin that the Cree were not prepared to trade their furs on the spot but waited to see what the Canadians were offering. Invariably, pedlars captured the lion's share of this business because they lavishly distributed alcohol both as a gift and a trade item. That they were able to operate in Basquia territory, however, was at the pleasure of the regional bands—something that was driven home to a large party of Montreal traders, including Alexander Henry the Elder, headed up the Saskatchewan River in October 1775. At Basquia, Chief Chatique (also known as the Pelican), backed by armed followers, confronted the men when they pulled ashore in their canoes and demanded a toll. "We must be well aware of his power to prevent our going further," a humbled Henry later recalled, "that if we passed now, he could put us all to death on our return." Chatique consequently "expected us to be exceedingly liberal in our presents; adding, that to avoid misunderstandings, he would inform us of what it was that he must have."[27] The Canadians wisely complied. Then and only then did Chatique share his pipe with them. But after the traders had pushed on, the headman chased after them in a canoe and extracted another tribute.

Montreal traders had been moving upriver for almost a decade. As early as 1768, HBC winterer William Tomison claimed that there were "a vast Number of Pedlars" in present-day southern Manitoba.[28] The remark might have been an overstatement but not when measured against the undeniable truth that the company had no employees based in the Saskatchewan country at the time. It also proved prescient. From their foothold on the lower Saskatchewan River at Basquia and Nipawin (*nīpowwinihk*), pedlars had established Fort aux Trembles (also known as Isaac's House) halfway between Nipawin and the Saskatchewan forks (*pêhonân*) and then three years later, moved up to the mouth of the Sturgeon River (also known as Net Setting or Setting River) on the North Saskatchewan just west of present-day Prince Albert.[29] These early posts were crude structures, little more than wood shanties, usually with a trading room, living quarters, and storage place.

The driving force behind this expansion was an assortment of independent entrepreneurs—William Holmes, Alexander Henry, Charles Paterson, Patrick Small, Robert Grant, Thomas Corry (or Curry), Joseph and Thomas Frobisher, Peter Pangman, and Peter Pond—who brought their experience from the Great Lakes and upper Mississippi trade in search of new, more lucrative business opportunities in the North-West. They were some of dozens of pedlars vying for the beaver trade by the time the HBC finally responded with its first inland settlement in 1774. And their numbers continued to grow. The thirty-canoe brigade that Chatique intercepted just a year later was made up of several rival interests, 130 men in total, who stopped briefly at Cumberland House before dispersing to their respective winter quarters.

The Frobishers were headed back towards Frog Portage (*Portage du Traite*) in the fall of 1775. Two years earlier, instead of going west, they had wintered on Namew Lake, immediately north of Cumberland House (just inside the eastern boundary of present-day Saskatchewan). And in the spring of 1774, they boldly moved up the Sturgeon–Weir River to Frog Portage on the Churchill River (*missinipi* to the Cree, English to the pedlars) and triumphantly intercepted several Indian trading parties headed to Fort Churchill with their furs. The returns were so rewarding that they set up a post on Beaver (Amisk) Lake during the winter of 1775–76, determined to use it as a springboard into the Churchill River country and choke off the flow of furs to the bay. To this end, Thomas Frobisher proceeded almost two hundred miles up the Churchill in the summer of 1776 and founded a settlement on Lac Île-à-la-Crosse (known to the Cree as *sākitawāhk*).

For Robert Longmoor, a HBC servant stationed inland, the pedlars "set the pace ... in every way."[30] But they too were stymied by provision problems. In moving into the Churchill watershed, the Frobishers had made the mistake of spending the winter of 1774–75 at Frog Portage and suffered extreme privation because of the want of food. One, possibly two, members of the party starved to death, while Indians evidently shot another man for resorting to cannibalism.[31] This food shortage temporarily held back the westward advance of the Montreal traders along the Churchill River. It also forced the pedlars in the Saskatchewan River delta area to extend their operations upriver in the mid-1770s, even though the lower section still had plenty of furs and a limited HBC presence.[32] There was just not enough meat available to support their growing numbers, especially when they set up large camps to winter over in a particular district. Such was the case at Beaver Lake in 1775–76, where the Frobishers, smarting from their experience the previous winter, divided their forty men into three gangs: one to build the post, the other two to catch fish. Other pedlar posts practised what was called *cawway*. The company divided into two parties and then decided by lot which group would be given nets, powder, and shot, and sent into the woods for the winter.[33]

Alexander Henry, who had entered into a loose partnership with the Frobishers, found out first-hand the difference between wintering in the forested lake region and on the northern edge of the Great Plains. On New Year's Day 1776, he set off on foot from Beaver Lake for the HBC post at Cumberland House. There, he was welcomed by Matthew Cocking, "making us partake of all he had which however was but little ... fish." Henry then continued west through deep snow and bitter cold, using the Saskatchewan River as his guide, and reached the pedlar post at Fort des Prairies in a starving condition three weeks later. This time, though, he was treated to a table covered with the spoils of the bison hunt. "The quantity of provisions which I found collected here," Henry testified, "exceeded everything of which I had previously formed a notion."[34] This bounty from the plains not only came to sustain the growing number of pedlar posts, but feed the canoe brigades on their way in and out of the North-West. Without dried bison meat in the form of pemmican, the Montreal traders would not have been able to extend their reach deep into the region at such an aggressive pace.

Cumberland House, by contrast, limped along as best it could. Samuel Hearne took the first trade season of furs back to York Factory in May 1775 but again had to rely on Indian canoes to transport both himself and the cargo. When he returned inland with more post supplies two months later, he was frustrated to discover that "the villins of Indians that accompd me embezzeld at least 100 galns of the Brandy besides a Bag containing 43 lbs of Brazil Tobaco."[35] Hearne's solution was for the company to have its own fleet of canoes. But when Charles Isham and Robert Longmoor, the two best canoemen in HBC service, were sent inland with a band of Cree in the winter of 1775–76 to learn how to build boats at a site on the South Saskatchewan River, pedlars ruined the plan by buying the finished canoes.[36] Matthew Cocking, in the meantime, tried to lessen Cumberland House's overreliance on fish (mostly sturgeon) by accumulating a meat surplus in the fall to try to carry the servants through the winter. The trade for provisions was consequently just as important as that for furs. Moose meat and fat became a common trade commodity but was

Alexander Henry was one of several Canadian wintering partners who expanded the Montreal-based fur trade up the Saskatchewan and Churchill Rivers.

replaced by bison in the late 1770s. The traders also consumed whatever the local Indians delivered to their "victualing shed" at whatever the cost. Geese traded for 1 Made Beaver in 1775.[37] These famine prices prompted Cocking to send some servants to winter with local Indian groups and thereby lessen the demand for food at Cumberland House. But these men placed a burden on their hosts and often returned to the post grumbling about "their having been almost Starved at times."[38]

The Montreal traders benefitted from Cumberland House's precarious existence, all the while intent on driving the HBC competition from the field. The post was little more than "a lone blockhouse besieged by the foe on every side."[39] Neither Hearne nor Cocking backed away from the commercial struggle but went on the offensive, regularly dispatching company servants into the same areas where pedlars operated. Robert Longmoor, for example, gamely took on the Frobisher brothers and Alexander Henry in the area north of Cumberland House, while William Walker took up temporary residence near the pedlar settlement at the Saskatchewan forks. "If the desired end [securing the Indian trade] is not effectually obtained by this proceeding," Matthew Cocking reasoned, "it will at least increase the Pedlers Expences by causing the Native to rise in their demands upon them."[40] But these combative efforts were simply no match for the Canadian use of rum, especially as a trade inducement. It was not only easy to transport in kegs, but could be watered down, making the supply last longer. "The Indians cannot come past a place where Liquor is without stopping," it was reported, "and when they are intoxicated few of them have discretion to keep their furrs."[41]

The HBC tried to counter pedlar influence by allowing alcohol to become an actual trade item at Cumberland House in May 1777. Whereas there was a limited market for heavy or bulky goods, liquor was consumed at the post and could be diluted. The London Committee even sent a still to York Factory to produce spirits that could be shipped inland.[42] It was a significant departure from past practice. Up until the 1740s, the company provided little alcohol to the trading Indians at York Factory.[43] But as Cocking grudgingly admitted, with the establishment of Cumberland House, if the company expected a share of the interior beaver trade, then Indians "must either have Liquor traded with them or else must have it given to them Gratis."[44] This policy change ironically led to the situation where liquor was actively traded for provisions to keep Cumberland House operational—a far cry from the reason for moving inland. It also made little difference to the battle with the pedlars. In 1778, William Tomison, Cocking's successor as Cumberland House master, gave presents to some Basquia Cree to take the season's furs to York Factory, only to have the local pedlars offer more presents if they stopped helping the bay men. Those Indians willing to serve as company tripmen only did so if they received special treatment, especially because it was no longer necessary to go to the bay. Even then, Tomison had to lavish presents on Basquia leader Catabobinow to ensure that both furs and trade goods reached their destination.[45]

A sketch of Île-à-la-Crosse drawn by Sister Sara Riel, the sister of
Métis leader Louis Riel

The provision question forced the HBC to reconsider its inland strategy. Cumberland House was supposed to help the company revive its sagging trade in the western interior. Instead, the constant search for food raised doubts about the commercial viability of the initiative. That provisions increasingly came from an ever-widening hinterland, including the great plains to the southwest, suggested that another post, closer to the bison grounds, was needed.[46] Those who spent any time at Cumberland House certainly believed so. "This Place," Cocking conceded in January 1777, "will not be able to maintain above Ten or Twelve men well … [and] enforces the necessity of the Company's making an early Settlement up above towards the Buffalo Country." Moving upriver, Cocking argued, would enable the HBC to break out of the Basquia region "so incumbered with the Canadians" and away from Indian groups who had come to expect alcohol in their dealings. It also allowed the company to copy the pedlar practice of collecting provisions along the northern edge of the plains for its settlements in the forest, in this case, Cumberland House.[47]

The governor at York Factory looked upon the recommendation as an opportunity to strike a blow at the Montreal traders, and in July 1777 called for the immediate establishment of a temporary post beyond the last pedlar establishment on the Saskatchewan.[48] But it was more than a year, not until September 1778, before Robert Longmoor led a small HBC party up the Saskatchewan River just beyond the forks. By then, pedlars Peter Pangman and Joseph-Barthélemy Blondeau had already pushed the North Saskatchewan River trade well beyond the Sturgeon River (Upper Settlement) to the Eagle Hills and the Battle River. The late start, combined with unseasonably cold weather, forced Longmoor to overwinter at one of the new Canadian settlements, Fort du Milieu or Middle Settlement (near present-day Silver Grove, Saskatchewan), midway between Hudson House and the Crossing Place (where a trail ran from the north to the south branch of the river).

Not wanting to operate in the shadow of their competitors, Longmoor and Cumberland House master William Tomison resumed the search for a post site the following summer and settled on a location about fourteen miles downriver from the wintering site and next to an Indian trail running from the Thickwood Hills to the Sturgeon River (around Brightholme, Saskatchewan). Named Hudson House, the new HBC settlement was ideally placed to procure both furs and bison. But the company's second inland post had a difficult first few years, not unlike the experience at Cumberland House. In the fall of 1780, the Assiniboine deliberately burned the prairie to drive off the bison and push up the prices in the provisioning trade. The tactic backfired. Not only did HBC men go hungry that winter but Indians also had little to hunt and faced outright starvation. A plaintive letter from Longmoor in February 1781 described "a very bad Situation."[49] Within a few years, though, there were several Cree hunters keeping the post supplied, while a garden produced greens, cabbage, turnips, and barley.

The Montreal pedlars remained on the offensive during these years. In

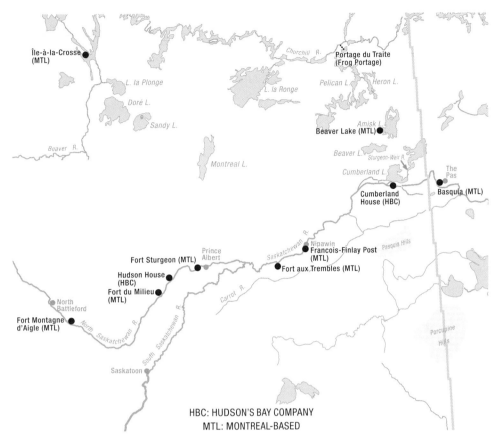

Selected fur trade posts in Saskatchewan, circa late 1770

the late spring of 1776, Alexander Henry confirmed the great promise of the Churchill River country when he travelled north from Beaver Lake and collected thousands of furs from Indian parties headed to the bay. But even greater riches seemed within reach if the trade could be expanded to the northwest beyond the new pedlar settlement on Lac Île-à-la-Crosse to Lake Athabasca. That task fell to Peter Pond, an irascible American who left the army to become a trader in the Detroit region after the capture of New France. Pond's nose for opportunity soon pointed him northwest and he entered the Canadian fur trade at Dauphin Lake in 1775. Within a year, he decided to ascend the Saskatchewan River but first moved his supply base forward from Michilimackinac to Grand Portage on the north shore of Lake Superior. He also went into partnership with Montreal merchant Thomas Williams. Pond's two seasons (1776–78) at the junction of

211

the Sturgeon River, near present-day Prince Albert, secured his reputation as a scrappy trader. It was his superb organizing skills, though, that thrust him forward as the best person to try to reach the Athabasca country.

Given the remaining pedlar stock at Cumberland Lake in the spring of 1778, Pond headed west along the Churchill to Lac Île-à-la-Crosse, where he tackled Methye Portage (Portage la Loche), the twelve-mile height of land between the Hudson Bay drainage system and the Arctic watershed. That winter, from his base on the Athabasca River, Pond traded for over eight thousand furs (140 packs)—more than his canoes could carry. But the enormous haul that his trip men managed to bring out was proof enough that the thickest, darkest furs were found in the Athabasca country and that the Montreal pedlars would secure an enormous advantage if they could maintain a settlement there and save the Indians from having to travel to Fort Churchill on the bay.[50] The added bonus was that the region fell outside the Hudson Bay watershed and therefore beyond the region claimed by the HBC as its charter area. Methye Portage, though, stood in the way. The first eight miles may have been relatively level, but there was no drinking water. Then, beyond Rendezvous Lake, the trail became steeper and wetter on the Clearwater River side. It took on average six days to travel the portage—a gruelling pace when men were expected to make five separate load-carrying trips over two-mile intervals each day.[51]

The pooling of goods for Pond's Athabasca initiative convinced several veteran winterers and Montreal entrepreneurs of the merits of working together and dividing the returns each trade season. Up to then, most partnerships were short-term, profit-driven arrangements because of the uncertainties associated with the trade. But the great distances involved in carrying on the trade in the western interior was an expensive handicap without the additional liability of pedlars competing among themselves. And even when independent traders did form temporary winter partnerships at some of the settlements, they still had to contend with arranging supplies and credit. It made better business sense to form a kind of cooperative to maximize trade and the potential profit,

The Churchill River is actually a maze of lakes that can be confusing
for the inexperienced canoeist.

while bringing regularity to the movement of goods and furs. This "general concern" as it was first called, the forerunner to the North West Company (NWC), came into existence in 1779, probably during the annual rendezvous at Grand Portage. It brought together several separate interests, both inland traders and Montreal merchants, into a sixteen-share partnership for a five-year period. Among them were the Frobisher brothers, the McGill family, and Simon McTavish. Many had Scottish kinship ties.[52] But it was almost another decade before this consortium ruled the Montreal fur trade and displaced the once dominant Canadian participation in the *pays d'en haut*. There were still too many independent traders, fiercely struggling against one another, trying to capture a share of the lucrative fur market.

This cutthroat competition sometimes led to violence. Peter Pond spent the winter of 1781–82 alongside rival trader Jean-Étienne Waddens on Lac la Ronge on the Churchill River system. The two men, although affiliated with different Montreal firms, were expected to cooperate. But Pond apparently resented that Waddens had followed up his lead in the Athabasca country

LIBRARY AND ARCHIVES CANADA C-5746

A *coureur de bois*

by bringing out furs from the region that he considered his own private trading ground. Operating side-by-side that winter only aggravated their differences, and in March 1782, Waddens died of a gunshot wound during an altercation. Pond never answered for the murder.[53]

There were also several deadly incidents involving Indians. To outmaneuvre their rivals, pedlars sent their assistants out into the field with alcohol. This practice, known as *en dérouine*, was considered nothing less than "dangerous" by HBC servant Robert Longmoor.[54] The Canadians cajoled, intimidated, and even beat their Indian customers—anything they could do to get their furs—when not plying them with rum. Demeaned, when not angered by this ill-treatment, some Indians finally retaliated by murdering three traders in the Sturgeon River area in 1777. Further trouble erupted at the uppermost pedlar settlement in the Eagle Hills. In the fall of 1778, traders there gave a troublesome Indian an overdose of laudanum during a drinking episode. The Cree returned for vengeance the following spring and killed pedlar John Cole and another man before taking over the post and chasing its occupants downriver.[55] Nor was the HBC immune to this strife even though it genuinely believed "we have more friends than enemies among the Indians."[56] In early March 1781, a party of Cree got drunk at Hudson House and then tried to break down the gate and the stockades when the alcohol was gone. The Indians were easily subdued because of their condi-

Bison meat became a food staple of the fur trade.

tion and, once sober, quietly slipped away with "no bad words."[57]

HBC men attributed these violent incidents to the reckless behaviour of the pedlars who seemed willing to use any tactic or press any advantage to gain the upper hand in the trade. In April 1779, for example, William Holmes imprisoned some Indians at the Middle Settlement to force them to trade their furs. When HBC servant Magnus Twatt tried to intervene, Holmes beat him "in a cruel manner."[58] Later that year, upon learning of the establishment of Hudson House, Holmes set up a rival post on the opposite side of the river and then told the HBC men, in a bald-faced lie, that Indians had destroyed Cumberland House. No wonder William Tomison branded the Montreal-based traders "a parcle of great villains."[59]

These tensions were aggravated by demographic change in the region. Not only were more and more newcomers present inland, steadily extending their reach deep into the interior up the Saskatchewan and Churchill Rivers, but Indians were also on the move. The Sturgeon, Basquia, and Pegogamaw Cree, having been released from the necessity of making annual trips to the bay if they wanted to participate in the European trade, spent more time on the northern plains, especially beyond the Eagle Hills and along the South Saskatchewan River country (the west and southwest). This shift to specialized

215

UNIVERSITY OF SASKATCHEWAN ARCHIVES AND SPECIAL COLLECTIONS 2.2-22A-P01

The acquisition of the horse enabled Cree bands to spend more time on the northern plains.

bison hunters had been slowly underway for the past few decades, especially with the acquisition of the horse. It now picked up momentum as the Cree and others groups, such as the Assiniboine, embraced their new role as provision hunters for both the Montreal and bay trading systems. Indeed, the demand for foodstuffs seemed insatiable once Canadian traders began to exploit the fur riches of the Athabasca country.[60]

The Cree transition to the northern grasslands was not without its challenges. They faced the persistent problem of keeping their horses alive through the winter. Nor were the Cree at first particularly adept at pounding. It was not something that they initially practised on the northern prairies, in part because of their smaller camp size. Bison pounding was labour-intensive and required many people to build the pound, drive the animals, and slaughter the kill. "Four Sturgeon River Indians ... say they have had but little Success," Tomison reported in January 1780 about their failure to bring meat to Hudson House, "by reason they are ... not thoroughly acquainted with the method of driving Buffalo into the pound."[61] But once Cree numbers increased on the plains and they learned how to build and maintain large pounds, they were able to supply the newcomer market with bison meat.[62]

SASKATCHEWAN ARCHIVES BOARD S-B776

Fur trade historian A. S. Morton stands on the site of a fur trade post in a
ploughed field in the 1940s.

The Cree presence on the northern plains brought them into increasing
contact with members of the Blackfoot Alliance, especially the Gros Ventre who
occupied present-day southwestern Saskatchewan. These relations remained
generally amicable, as they continued to exchange trade goods and horses and
collectively fight their enemies. But then, an invisible invader turned the Indian
world upside down. It was during the summer of 1781 that a joint Cree–Peigan
party attacked a Snake village in the Red Deer River area, only to find, in the
words of one participant, "no one to fight with but the dead and the dying."[63]
Not knowing that they had stumbled upon smallpox, carried north from New
Spain, the warriors took a few war trophies and then retreated to their home
communities with devastating consequences.

Smallpox first appeared on the North Saskatchewan in the early fall of 1781. HBC servant Mitchell Oman, who had been sent to winter among the Indians of the Eagle Hills region, came across a camp of Assiniboine decimated by the disease; a few weak survivors bore the telltale pox marks on their bodies and faces. Soon, stricken Indians—suffering from debilitating headache, painful backache, intense fever, and violent vomiting—began straggling into the Company's two inland posts in search of relief. A thoroughly shaken William Walker, master at Hudson House, was so taken aback by the "disorder flying though the Country" that he predicted "that in a short time I do not suppose that there will be a staid Indian Living."[64] Tomison at Cumberland House was astounded by how quickly the Indians succumbed to the disease, many of them dying within only a few days, before the blister-like rash developed. "There is something very malignant," he pondered, "either in the Constitution of the Natives or in the Disorder."[65]

What made the suffering worse was the widespread starvation that accompanied the disease. Survivors were likely too incapacitated to hunt. But healthy people could also not locate game, at least in areas where animals were normally found. And climate may have been the culprit. The winters leading up to and during the epidemic were notoriously cold, so much so that wine actually froze at Hudson House in early January 1782. These conditions seem to have altered game migration patterns, making the usually plentiful bison, in the words of one observer, "vagrant."[66]

Inoculation against smallpox was still in the experimental stage in the late eighteenth century, and it was not until the mid-nineteenth century that vaccination against the disease became widespread. But because European populations had developed a general resistance to smallpox from past exposure, only one inland trader evidently contracted and died from the disease. Mixed-descent peoples were not so fortunate, but those who fell ill during the epidemic usually survived. Charles Isham, the mixed-descent son of a former chief factor, was among them.[67] The Indians took the full brunt of the epidemic. They had no immunity against the virus and did not realize how

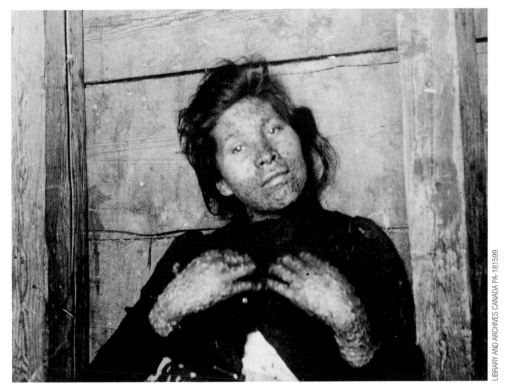

Smallpox had a devastating impact on the indigenous population
of the western interior.

LIBRARY AND ARCHIVES CANADA PA-181599

contagious it could be—that the disease was easily transmitted from person to person. Those stricken seemed at first to have flu-like symptoms, but after about ten days to two weeks, small reddish spots broke out, first inside the mouth and throat, and then all over the body. The rash then erupted into pus-filled lesions (macules) that left the face permanently scarred—if the infected person survived.

HBC servants, according to post journals, attended to sick Indians as best they could, but could not really do much given the ruthless virulence of the *Variola* strain. "It cuts me to the Heart," Tomison acknowledged, "to see the Miserable condition they are in."[68] But there were limits to this sympathy. Servants, ostensibly sent out in March 1782 to bury the dead, confiscated any beaver skins if the victims were known to be company debtors.[69] These furs, along with the few others that had been collected at the two inland settlements over the trade season, were transported to York Factory late that spring. As the

219

Cumberland House brigade paddled to the bay, the reach of the epidemic could be seen in the sick Indians encountered along the way. But it was not until the inland traders arrived at the coast that smallpox first had made its appearance among the Indians. From there, the disease jumped to Fort Churchill up the western coast of Hudson Bay and soon spread to the Cree and Chipewyan who patronized that post. Smallpox, one historian has argued, "had unwittingly become an article of trade."[70]

The 1781–82 pandemic has been called "the most momentous event in the indigenous history of the Great Plains."[71] But it was overshadowed at the time by the American Revolutionary War and remains relatively unknown to this day. Nor is it possible to state with any certainty how many Indian people perished, especially given where the deaths took place. Based on information that the Cumberland House brigade brought to York Factory, Matthew Cocking concluded that "the many different Tribes ... are all almost wholly extinct ... not one in fifty of those Tribes are now living."[72] And it is easy to understand why Tomison and other inland servants believed that the Indians were probably all dead because both Hudson House and Cumberland House were epidemic epicentres, places of unrelenting death for several months. Samuel Hearne, meanwhile, suspected that the disease "carried off nine-tenths" of the northern Indians, a catastrophe remembered in the name, Portage des Morts, along the Churchill River trade route.[73]

These mind-boggling mortality rates have since been adjusted downward to a range between one-half to two-thirds of the Indian population.[74] It is still an unbelievable measure of human loss, possibly more than the Black Death in Europe in the mid-fourteenth century, which has been estimated to have carried away from one-third to half the affected population. Not a single Indian group in the western interior—except for small, isolated hunting camps-—escaped the scourge, and those who were left came together to form new societies. Some of the hardest hit were the Assiniboine, rarely mentioned thereafter in HBC journals, and the Basquia and Pegogamaw Cree, who ceased to be identified as a distinct people, thereby shrouding their pivotal role in the first century of the fur trade. In their place, there emerged new regional bands based around Cumberland House and the Saskatchewan River forks. The epidemic also decided several territorial struggles. The Snake were effectively vanquished from the northern plains, while the Mandan–Hidatsas villages of present-day North Dakota were so weakened that the Sioux were finally able to push westward onto the plains. Congregating centres that once brought together bands in large annual gatherings, meanwhile, fell into disuse.[75] Smallpox was clearing the North-West of its indigenous population. It "killed a larger proportion of the region's population than any disaster before or since."[76]

Saukamappee, one of the Peigan raiders on the Snake camp, described the post-epidemic world to trader David Thompson. "When at length it left us, and we moved about to find our people," he recalled in apocalyptic terms, "it was no longer with the song and the dance; but with tears, shrieks, and howlings of despair for those who would never return to us." He grimly conceded, "We shall never be again the same people. To hunt for our families was our sole occupation and kill Beavers, Wolves, and Foxes to trade our necessaries; and we thought of War no more."[77]

Traders, by contrast, reduced the impact of the smallpox epidemic to an accounting column. Canadian returns declined by almost 70 per cent the year of the epidemic (from 330 fur packets to 84), while the English intake at York Factory had been cut in half (29,901 MB to 12,837).[78] As late as September 1785, the governor at York Factory was warning the London Committee to expect a much-reduced trade for the foreseeable future because there were "few, very few, Indians being left."[79] The pedlars, on the other hand, seemed to take some consolation in the fact that the epidemic had saved them from possible further Indian hostility in response to their heavy-handed tactics. Indians had destroyed two Canadian settlements on the Assiniboine River in the fall of 1781 and were preparing to ransack a third when they were stricken with smallpox.[80] The stricken bands now faced bigger problems. How many had survived? And would they ever recover what they had lost in the epidemic?

Several rival fur trade posts occupied Pine Island in the North Saskatchewan River.

CHAPTER SEVEN

A CAULDRON OF CONFLICT

INDIAN BANDS WERE STILL ABSORBING THE ENORMITY OF THEIR LOSSES TO THE 1781–82 smallpox epidemic when Canadian traders resumed their relentless offensive to remain at the forefront of the beaver skin trade. The building of posts had been stalled in the late 1770s by the increasing incidence of Indian-newcomer violence. Now, a growing number of pedlars, brandishing alcohol as a trade inducement, aggressively moved farther up the North Saskatchewan River, as well as along the Churchill River into the Athabasca region. The Hudson's Bay Company seemed to be always one step behind the competition, always trying to catch up. The driving force behind the newcomer push into the North-West was the continuing rivalry between Montreal-based companies. Even though the North West Company concluded a new five-year partnership agreement in 1784, two years after the devastating smallpox epidemic, several Canadian firms were excluded from the reorganization. The scramble for furs consequently only worsened: multiple posts on the same site all vying for the same Indian trade. This intensification of the fur trade rivalry in west-central Saskatchewan was tolerated by the Blackfoot Alliance, which up to then had remained relatively aloof from European and Canadian newcomers. But the demand for provisions to support the new inland posts rivalled the demand for beaver pelts, placing a new stress on local ecosystems. The transition of some Cree and Assiniboine bands to mounted bison-hunting societies was also frustrated by the loss of their horses to several harsh winters in the 1780s and 1790s. In the ensuing struggle over access to guns and horses, Indian groups on the northern plains became embroiled in a vicious cycle of skirmishing and retaliation. Even traders did not escape being drawn into the vortex of violence and death.

In 1785, North West Company partner William Holmes re-established a post in the Eagle Hills, this time near the mouth of the Battle River. He then moved to meet a new competitive threat from Peter Pangman on the upper South Saskatchewan River. Left out of the new NWC partnership, a disgruntled Pangman had turned to the firm of Gregory and MacLeod and convinced the Montreal company to focus on the Canadian North-West to make up for its lost business in the Detroit and Michilimakinac areas following the American Revolutionary War and the 1783 Paris peace agreement. This "new concern" (to differentiate it from the NWC "general concern") enabled Pangman— and not the Hudson's Bay Company—to emerge as the most serious threat to the North West Company's Saskatchewan operations in the mid-1780s. He not only challenged the partnership at the Battle River post but also took the unprecedented step of setting up operations on the south branch of the river, some forty miles from the forks, at a place named Fort des Iles (near a group of treed islands just above the Fenton Ferry). He also moved up the North Saskatchewan when a third Montreal company, spearheaded by Donald MacKay, reached beyond the Battle River to place a fort on the half-mile-long Pine Island near Gully Creek (north of present-day Standard Hill). In response, the NWC tried to outdistance its rivals by leapfrogging even farther upriver, some fifty miles from the last post on the North Saskatchewan. It also positioned traders at the same sites, usually right next to the competition. This side-by-side location was as much for defensive purposes as it was to keep an eye on trade rivals. Traders sought to make their inland settlements as secure as possible by deliberately building close to the water on the north side of the Saskatchewan and adding a wooden palisade. Large equestrian bands, arriving from the south, would have to cross the river to trade.[1]

These pedlar posts in west-central Saskatchewan offered direct access to

226

members of the Blackfoot Alliance and effectively ended a limited trade with the English at Hudson House. The Gros Ventre had first visited the HBC post in November 1779. Before then, they secured any trade goods through Cree and Assiniboine intermediaries. Almost three years later in August 1782, a group of Siksika or "blackfooted" Indians arrived with some Assiniboine. They were followed that fall by more Gros Ventre. These face-to-face encounters were constrained by the company servants' complete ignorance of the Niitsitapi language. Nor could they rely on the Assiniboine to serve as translators because the HBC men did not understand much of that language either—even though Hudson House was in Assiniboine territory.[2]

The other impediment to regular contact was an embarrassing lack of trade goods. In the late summer of 1782, a small French war fleet had travelled north from its base in Haiti into Hudson Bay in support of their American revolutionary allies. There, they razed Fort Churchill and then York Factory. The loss of the two bayside posts meant there were no supplies for inland operations, a situation made worse when HBC ships failed to appear the following summer. The men at both Cumberland House and Hudson House consequently had to rely on pedlar generosity to get through the winter of 1783–84. They were also more dependent on Indian provisioners than ever before and had to ensure that they had a supply of alcohol and other presents for this trade. "You are not to let the Men have any Brandy upon any Account whatever," Tomison threatened a servant at Cumberland House, "when that Articles is gone we may Starve."[3] But he still expected the Cree to continue to bring in furs even when his supplies ran out. And when they stopped coming to the settlement, he lashed out at them for being "mad for Liquor."[4]

Once the bayside posts were rebuilt and resupplied, the HBC endeavoured to match the new pedlar settlements on the Saskatchewan. In 1786, Tomison went upriver from the competition on the south branch and chose a level spot at the edge of the grasslands where a trail crossed the river (later known as Gardepuy's Crossing) to build South Branch House. Both the North West Company and Gregory and MacLeod immediately located nearby. That same year up the North Saskatchewan, the HBC established Manchester House on Pine Island, a site soon to be occupied by four rival concerns. This movement westward marked a new phase in HBC operational plans on the Saskatchewan. Cumberland House now served as a company supply point, while Hudson House and the new South Branch House became the focus of company trade with the Cree and the Assiniboine. These changes dovetailed with Cree practice following the smallpox epidemic. With the population generally shifting westward in the 1780s, Cumberland House emerged as a rendezvous centre and a place of refuge for the old and infirm. No longer were the surviving local Cree considered as "troublesome" as they had been a decade earlier.[5]

Direct trade between the HBC and Montreal pedlars and all four peoples of the Blackfoot Alliance was conducted at the Pine Island posts in the latter half of the 1780s. Because these Indians were no longer "strangers," the traders stopped using the Anglicized Cree term "Archithinue," but called them "Slave Indians" (not to be confused with the Slavey of northern Canada).[6] They were the dominant people of the northern plains. And the HBC was determined to secure their trade allegiance despite the intensely competitive atmosphere on the North Saskatchewan. To this end, the company turned to its past practice of sending men to winter with small bands, so that servants could learn the language, develop friendships, but most of all, capture their business. Some of the first company men to perform this duty, beginning in 1786, were Isaac Batt and James Gaddy. They were followed by two recent recruits, Peter Fidler and David Thompson, who both enjoyed distinguished careers in the trade. Thompson helped build South Branch House, where he kept the first post journal, before being sent to live among the Peigan during the winter of 1787–88. That was the same winter that he collected Saukamappee's story.[7] Fidler spent consecutive winters with Indian bands, first with the Chipewyan (1791–92) and then the Peigan (1792–93). He later reported that he actually dreamed in Chipewyan one night.[8]

The Niitsitapi-speaking peoples preferred to patronize the Pine Island posts and later Fort George (NWC 1792) and Buckingham House (HBC

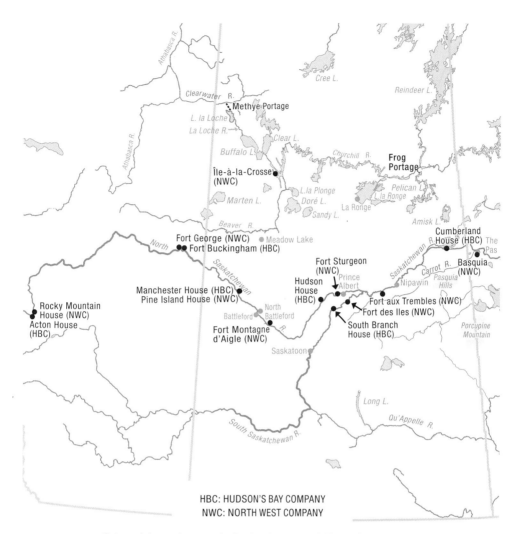

Selected fur trade posts in Saskatchewan and Alberta in late 1700s

1792) farther up the North Saskatchewan in the Moose Hills in present-day Alberta (near a former canoe-building site at Moose Creek). The bands sent runners ahead to the settlements to announce their impending arrival, and the traders in turn sent the messengers back with gifts of tobacco and some powder—similar to the old ceremonies at York Factory. Once the trading party had arrived, discharging a few guns as it approached the gate, there would be the distribution of more presents, usually rum and tobacco, the smoking of the pipe, and the relaying of news. Then and only then would exchange commence.[9]

The Blackfoot peoples were discerning consumers, just like other Indian groups who had traded earlier at the bay, and knew exactly what they wanted from the newcomers, such as good quality tobacco. No longer restricted to trading through Cree and Assiniboine intermediaries, they coveted muzzle-loading guns for their war campaigns and initially could not get enough of the weapons because of the heavy demand.[10] The other popular commodity was rum, something that both the HBC and Montreal pedlars distributed freely to each band in a reckless effort to triumph over the opposition. "Profusion is absolutely necessary to secure the trade of an Indian," is how Nor'Wester Duncan McGillivray justified the heavy drinking at Fort George.[11] Tomison of the HBC was not so resigned to the situation, especially when the Blackfoot smartly took advantage of the competitors crowded onto Pine Island. "Indians has nothing to do," he lamented, "but go from house to house, get Drunk and beg Goods on Expectation of what they are to bring."[12]

One of the reasons for traders pushing up the North Saskatchewan was to exploit new fur grounds. But even though the wetlands in the region were teeming with beaver, the Niitsitapi refused to hunt the animal for spiritual and ecological reasons. The beaver was sacred in Blackfoot culture and could not be killed for material gain. Its role in conserving and maintaining surface water, especially during dry years on the plains, was also appreciated among these Indians. Dammed sloughs and creeks provided a source of water, as well as attracted game.[13] The Niitsitapi consequently collected mostly wolf pelts for the trade even though the newcomers were primarily interested in procuring other, finer furs. This decision to pursue their own interests, and not those of the London and Montreal markets, was irksome to the traders. "These Indians are lazy and improvident," one Nor'Wester protested.[14] But the HBC and Montreal pedlars were fortunate to have any trade at all with the Blackfoot because of proximity of the great bison herds. The animals were a source of food and other materials. Nor did the Blackfoot have any urgent need for ammunition because of their continued use of the bow and arrow to kill their prey. "The Inhabitants of the Plains are so advantageously situated that they could live very happily

Montreal merchant Simon McTavish made the North West Company a marvel of efficiency, organization, flexibility, and enterprise.

independent of our assistance," McGillivray confided to his journal. "They are surrounded with innumerable herds ... of animals." It was only "our luxuries," he recognized, that attracted them to the posts.[15]

Competition was just as fierce in the Churchill district after the smallpox epidemic, but the HBC watched largely from the sidelines. In 1784, Patrick Small of the NWC (and David Thompson's future father-in-law) took up residence at Île-à-la-Crosse, only to be followed the next year by Alexander Mackenzie of Gregory and MacLeod. The two competing firms also established side-by-side operations on Lac au Serpent (known today as Pinehouse Lake) in 1786, supplemented by other small seasonal posts throughout the region. This pattern was replicated in the Athabasca country, where John Ross tenaciously challenged the NWC, beginning in 1784. But when Ross was shot in a dispute over furs, an incident that once again involved Peter Pond, the two concerns decided to unite to avoid further bloodshed and formed a new, twenty-share partnership in 1787.

This latest version of the North West Company was a marvel of efficiency, organization, flexibility, and enterprise. It had to be, given that it operated across more than half a continent from Montreal to Lake Athabasca. The reorganization handed control of eleven of twenty NWC shares to the Montreal firm of McTavish, Frobisher and Company and thereby consolidated the securing of supplies and the marketing of furs. Under Simon McTavish's steadfast leadership, the NWC was forever seeking out fresh business opportunities, such as shipping furs to China in the early 1790s in exchange for tea, porcelain, and silk. McTavish also encouraged the expansion of the fur trade hinterland into new, untapped areas, where there was no competition and hence greater profit potential. Increasing production, while limiting costs, was the company credo.[16]

McTavish's counterpart in the interior was Alexander Mackenzie, whose natural bent for exploration was matched by a stubborn determination that refused to "accept ... defeat as final."[17] Born on the Isle of Lewis, one of the Outer Hebrides to the west of mainland Scotland, Mackenzie chose the fur trade over schooling and soon found himself immersed in the fur trade war along the Churchill River in the mid-1780s. It was here that he got to know Peter Pond and his dream of breaking out west from the Athabasca country to the Pacific Ocean and getting out from "the weight of [the] handicap"[18] of trading from Montreal. But it was the restless, at times high-strung, Mackenzie who executed Pond's plan. Leaving from Fort Chipewyan, a new NWC post on the south shore of Lake Athabasca, in June 1789, the twenty-five-year-old Mackenzie headed down the mighty Mackenzie River only to find that it emptied into the Arctic Ocean—hence the nickname, the River of Disappointment. Four years later, he left Fort Chipewyan again, this time heading west, following the Peace River headwaters upstream into the northern Rockies and then descending the Fraser River to the Pacific Ocean on 22 July 1793. It was the first crossing of North America north of the Rio Grande River. Ironically, though, neither trip helped the North West Company reduce its burdensome transportation problems. Instead, both suggested that the best solution was probably a foothold in Hudson Bay. But when Simon McTavish appealed to the British government to cancel the Hudson Bay Company's monopoly, or at least allow the NWC to pay for access to Hudson Strait, he was rebuffed.[19]

Mackenzie was able to carry out these great exploratory feats in such short time–the three-thousand-mile trip to the Arctic Ocean and back took only 102 days—because of his crack canoe team. Voyageurs, or *engagés* as they were sometimes called, were usually illiterate French-Catholic men, recruited from the Montreal and Trois-Rivières areas for a fixed term or engagement contract. They numbered around five hundred in the early 1780s, but as the Montreal companies pushed to the far northwest into the next decade, their ranks swelled. Those who worked between Montreal and the provisioning depot at Grand Portage on Lake Superior, in the large *canots de maître* or Great Lakes master canoes, were known as *mangeurs du lard* or "porkeaters" because of their diet. Those, on the other hand, who manned the brigades in the interior, spending their winters in the *pays d'en haut* and negotiating the rivers and lakes in the smaller *canots du nord* (north canoes), were *hommes du nord* (northmen) or *hivernant*. A further distinction was given to those voyageurs who worked northwest of Methye Portage (Portage de la Loche). These Athabasca men were the toughest, most experienced, and most revered— qualities that set them above all others in a culture that valued manliness. Self-reliant and indomitable, they had a mystique about them. Many met only once a year on Methye Portage at the appropriately named Rendezvous Lake, where they exchanged fur packs for goods and supplies from Montreal. Mackenzie undoubtedly played upon their reputation and ambition in his push to find the way to the Pacific Ocean.[20]

Voyageurs could be an unruly lot. The Scottish and English managers (*bourgeois*) and clerks often engaged in a battle of wills with their servants, who once inland, tried to renegotiate their contracts or at least offered a different "reading" of their responsibilities, such as how many ninety-pound packs (*pièces*) they could reasonably be expected to carry at portages. But there was also a certain order to voyageur working lives; otherwise, they would not have survived the superhuman demands placed on them. They sang, for example,

LIBRARY AND ARCHIVES CANADA C-001348

North West Company partner Alexander Mackenzie reached the Arctic Ocean in 1789
and the Pacific Ocean four years later.

as they paddled, measuring mileage in pipes (the distance between smoking breaks). They also mapped their world by marking or recognizing important geographical boundaries. As they entered a new region—the shield country along the Ottawa River, the height of land beyond Lake Superior, and Methye Portage—the voyageurs insisted on performing a mock baptism of anyone who was passing that threshold into the interior for the first time. Even masters did not escape this ritual but were forced to participate and thereafter expected to be fair in their dealings with their men.[21]

Voyageurs had voracious appetites, and the fuel that kept them going was pemmican (*pimîhkân* from *pimiy* [grease or lard]), an energy-rich food that rarely spoiled, was easily transported, and delivered an incredible thirty-two hundred to thirty-five hundred calories per pound. Indians had produced pemmican—from pounded meat, fat (grease), and sometimes berries—for thousands of years. But the fur trade transformed and regularized its production

The Montreal canoe route to the Athabasca country

by providing a growing market. Metal knives and copper kettles allowed for the quicker and more efficient manufacture of pemmican and the leather bags (*parflêches*) in which it was stored.[22] It was then moved and stored strategically throughout the region, based on the seemingly incredible allowance of eight pounds of meat per person per day! The North West Company established depots at Île-à-la-Crosse (1776), Green Lake (1782), and Fort Chipewyan on Lake Athabasca (1788) to accept pemmican brought north from Fort George and other posts in bison country. It also relocated the post at Basquia to Cumberland House, right beside the existing HBC settlement, to serve this same purpose. These pemmican storage centres fed the canoe brigades going in and out of the interior, whether along the Saskatchewan or Churchill Rivers or into the Athabasca country. There was simply no time for voyageurs to fish or hunt, given the distances they had to cover daily during the open-water months. Pemmican was also distributed to the remote posts in northern Saskatchewan, including Reindeer Lake and Lac la Ronge, to ensure that company men had something to eat and did not have to rely on the vagaries of

235

LIBRARY AND ARCHIVES CANADA C-145940, GEORGE BACK

The fur-rich Athabasca country was reached by crossing the gruelling Methye Portage in present-day northwestern Saskatchewan.

local provisioning.[23] It clearly was one of the deciding factors in the success of Mackenzie's expeditions to the two coasts.

The Hudson's Bay Company, for its part, seemed willing to let the North West Company take the lead in expanding the fur trade frontier. While Peter Pond and other pedlars were moving into the promising Athabasca country, the London Committee sent surveyor Philip Turnor to Cumberland House in 1778 to determine the exact location of inland posts and to map the canoe routes from Hudson Bay. He then performed the same work at the southern end of the bay, surveying (and later mapping) the location of posts and routes in present-day northwestern Ontario, between Lake Superior and James Bay. It was not until 1789—a full decade after the formation of the North West Company—that the HBC re-engaged Turnor to determine the location of Lake Athabasca and find a possible route there from the Saskatchewan River. Turnor spent the fall of 1789 and part of the new year preparing for the trip at Cumberland House, where he trained both David Thompson and Peter Fidler in mathematics, surveying, and astronomy. Thompson had badly broken his leg in a sledding accident at Manchester House two days before Christmas in 1788. The injury was so severe that he had to be carried down to Cumberland House the following spring; he did not take his first step with crutches until August 1789. Turnor's arrival at Cumberland House that fall was a fortuitous consequence, and Thompson became his pupil. But by the following spring, Thompson was still lame and now temporarily blind in one eye. It consequently fell to Turnor's other student that winter, Peter Fidler, to serve as his assistant.

The Turnor surveying party finally reached Île-à-la-Crosse in the fall of 1790, one year after Mackenzie had touched the waters of the Arctic Ocean. Turnor devoted the following summer to measuring distances and recording longitudes and latitudes around Lake Athabasca and the south shore of Great Slave Lake.[24] Fidler, meanwhile, established the HBC's first settlement on the Churchill River at Île-à-la-Crosse in 1791. But he was so harassed by Nor'Wester Patrick Small and his band of *battailleurs* (enforcers) that he soon withdrew, leaving the abandoned post to be burned. All was not lost, though. Fidler rejoined the Turnor camp and spent the winter of 1791–92 living with the Chipewyan along the Slave River and learning their language as a prelude to securing their trade.

The plodding pace of the HBC is often attributed to its locational advantage. Its operating costs were much lower because ocean-going ships could sail to the west coast of Hudson Bay where bayside posts served as jumping-off points into the interior. It did not have to contend with the long inland water route that confronted the Montreal pedlars, forcing them to seek out new fur grounds and collect the most pelts to cover the expense of moving freight over great distances both ways. In other words, the HBC could survive in competitive areas, while the NWC looked to realize a profit in those areas where there was little or no opposition. That's why Small did everything he could to intimidate and drive away Fidler at Île-à-la-Crosse, knowing full well that there was no room for rival traders when Montreal was so far away.

But there was another explanation for the limited HBC activity along the Churchill and into the Athabasca country in the 1780s. The company was divided over where it should concentrate its energies. In 1786, William Tomison was named chief factor at York Factory but continued to live inland where he could oversee the campaign against the pedlars. Tomison ardently believed that the battle with the NWC would be won or lost on the Saskatchewan and consequently refused to contemplate any initiative to take the war to the pedlars on the Churchill and the difficult Methye Portage beyond.[25] It was a narrow, if not blinkered, assessment of the situation, in that it gave the NWC a near monopoly in northern Saskatchewan. It also threatened to undermine the commercial viability of Fort Churchill. William McGillivray of the North West Company, who was given responsibility for the English (Churchill) River department in 1790, built several new posts in the region, including one at the confluence of the Churchill and Kississing Rivers, to capture the trade of Cree and Chipewyan who travelled to the coast. HBC trade at Fort Churchill suffered as a consequence.

This sorry situation might have been avoided if the London Committee and company servants in North America had a more direct and responsive way of communicating about developments in the trade—similar to the North West Company. Every spring, the Montreal and wintering partners rendezvoused at Grand Portage to discuss policy and strategy with an overall view to what was in the best collective interests of the company and its financial bottom line. The HBC, in comparison, was feeling its way in the dark because it was administered from London by people who had never visited the field and had no real idea of the conditions. It was a classic example of colonial rule. The company also had to make decisions based on information several months old (sent from Hudson Bay in the late summer or early fall) and then hope that any new directives were the best response by the time they reached the Hudson Bay posts the following late summer on the supply ship. Then, there was the problem of different agendas between those working inland and those at York Factory. Because of Tomison's intransigence, the HBC's appearance in the Athabasca country was delayed for several years, all the more so because the resources necessary for this initiative were in demand elsewhere. The energy that was eventually put into the Athabasca project was also misdirected. In the early 1790s, David Thompson and Malcolm Ross were given the unenviable task of finding a shorter route through the so-called muskrat country, directly west from York Factory to Reindeer Lake and Lake Athabasca, in order to skirt

LIBRARY AND ARCHIVES CANADA ACC. R9266-2738 WINKWORTH COLLECTION

The North West Company had to carry freight by canoe over great distances
into and out of the western interior.

the pedlars on the Churchill. They failed miserably. "The maze of rivers and lakes" before the two surveyors, one author has observed, were "a geographic metaphor for the complex problems ... plaguing the company at this time."[26]

William Tomison was only one of the many men from the Orkney Islands of northern Scotland who found a career in the HBC in the latter half of the eighteenth century. With company ships stopping at the islands for supplies before their trip across the North Atlantic, single, young men looked to the trade as a way to escape local poverty and a dead-end future. Their ability to eke out a living from the harsh maritime environment of their homeland— something they proudly ascribed to their Norse heritage—made them valued servants. And the company increasingly turned to them to fill its labour ranks, especially after it moved inland in the 1770s. By the end of the century, they made up a remarkable 80 per cent of a workforce that numbered over five hundred men. One scholar has suggested that the HBC posts were "expatriate Orkney communities."[27] Orcadians had a reputation for being drudges: dour, solitary figures inured to hardship and deprivation. Pedlars liked to deride them as "oatmeal eaters." But they proved an extremely versatile lot who quickly developed the skills demanded by their new fur trade lives. James Gaddy, for example, became conversant in the Blackfoot language, while Malcolm Ross was considered the equal of any Indian in shooting rapids in a canoe. They were also given the opportunity for advancement, as evidenced by Tomison's promotion to inland chief, and were not restricted to the lower ranks like their French-Canadian counterparts in the North West Company.[28]

It was only natural for Orkneymen to form relationships with Indian women in the interior. After all, these were young males in their sexual prime, placed in a setting where the only female companionship was found among the trading bands. The HBC accepted this undeniable fact of life, or at least did nothing to prevent it, beyond insisting that company men assume responsibility for the maintenance of their families even though their relationship was not sanctioned by the church. When Matthew Cocking retired to England in 1782, eight years after his wintering trip to west-central Saskatchewan, he sent his three mixed-descent daughters, who were known by their Indian names, an annual allowance. This support continued after his 1799 death—as specified in his will—and included "Ginger Bread, Nuts &tc, as they have no other means of obtaining these little luxuries."[29] Several Orkney servants stationed inland also took country (Indian) wives and fathered mixed-descent offspring. William Annal lived with his Assiniboine spouse and two children at South Branch House, while Malcolm Ross was accompanied by his wife and children during the 1790–91 Turnor expedition to the Athabasca country. The presence of the Ross woman was greatly appreciated by fellow traveller Peter Fidler because of her skill in making moccasins and snowshoes and performing other chores "that the Europeans are not acquainted with." But despite being "particularly useful," she was never identified by name.[30]

The Nor'Westers also pursued liaisons with Indian women. Here, they were following a practice established by their French predecessors before the Seven Years' War. As the Montreal pedlars moved deeper into the interior, they turned to Indian women to help them survive, as well as using them as a means of forming alliances with the local population. Their role in facilitating trade should not be underestimated. When Alexander Mackenzie, then of

Voyageurs were crack canoe men who performed superhuman feats of endurance.

Gregory and MacLeod, took on the North West Company in the Churchill River country in the mid-1780s, he bemoaned the fact that his rivals had already established connections with the local Indian communities. "See what it is to have no wives," he groused. "I find none of my men speak Cree."[31] Montreal pedlars tended to look upon their relationships with Indian women as casual, if not transient, affairs, in part, because they were constantly on the move, rolling back the fur trade frontier. Unlike the HBC servants, they were also under no obligation to look after their partners and families during their time of service. Lasting alliances were not that common. The Nor'Westers were also shamelessly involved in the trading of women, especially by voyageurs in search of female company.[32] Their renowned appetite for food was exceeded only by that for sex.

The presence of Montreal pedlars along the Churchill and Athabasca Rivers led to the emergence of Métis communities, particularly at Île-à-la-Crosse, in the late eighteenth century. Incoming traders sought Indian wives from among the local Cree and Chipewyan (who had relocated south into the region following the smallpox epidemic). And when the men moved on, they left behind their offspring to be raised and nurtured by their maternal relatives. In the English River district, a trader called Belanger entered into a relationship with a Chipewyan woman, and their daughter, known simply as the Belanger woman, married another outsider, Antoine Laliberte, and together had a son named Pierriche Laliberte. Over time, these children, and their children, formed the basis of the Métis people in present-day northwest Saskatchewan.[33]

There were also several small "Freemen" (*hommes libres*) settlements scattered throughout the interior, generally on the margins of HBC and pedlar settlements. These individuals were former *commis* (clerks) or *coureurs de drouine* (itinerant traders) who had completed their term of service and opted to remain in the North-West with their Indian wives and families rather than return to Canada. The first recorded instance of a Freeman was at Manchester House in 1789.[34] Living apart from the local trading post and Indian band made these men free or independent. But it was their connections that gave them status, power, and a certain degree of wealth. Because they were married *à la façon du pays*, Freemen were no longer considered "outsiders" but accepted by their male Indian relatives and allowed to live, hunt, and trap in band territory. They also maintained ties with the local post by supplying provisions, performing temporary work, but most importantly, facilitating trade with the local band. This ability to straddle both worlds—to serve as cultural brokers—made Freemen respected leaders who dominated the local trade. Over time, their communities were the progenitor of distinct mixed-descent or proto-Métis hunting bands in the North-West.[35]

The movement and interplay of peoples, as they jostled for position in the region, sparked tensions over territory and access to food resources and trade goods. This friction was more pronounced on the northern plains and was exacerbated by some dramatic climate fluctuations in the closing decades of the eighteenth century. Up until around 1770, the western interior had experienced a reprieve from the cooler temperatures associated with the Little Ice Age.[36] This warm interval, lasting more than half a century, had aided the spread of horses to the northern plains. But then, a series of particularly severe winters battered the region. Climatic variability had always been a feature of local weather conditions, but the variability during these decades was more intense, more acute—a response, in part, to a protracted La Niña event over the Pacific Ocean in the late 1770s, followed by the eruption of the Laki volcano in Iceland in 1783. The snow was so deep during the winter of 1783–84 that dogs could not be used at Cumberland House for several months, while William Wishart of Hudson House got lost and perished during a storm. The winters of 1788–89 and 1789–90 were even worse, arriving in the early fall and lasting into the late spring. "In the whole of this winter," Mitchell Oman at South Branch House complained in early April 1790, "there has been the most Snow that has been seen Inland this 15 years past."[37] Before the month was over, another foot of snow fell. Malcolm Ross at Cumberland House was just as exasperated. "I never knew the spring to be so backward before," he observed on 4 May, "nor the ice to stay so long."[38] The annual canoe brigade never left for York Factory so late.

These were also exceptionally arid years, despite the heavy snow cover, on the northern prairies. Tree-ring data, covering much of the last four hundred years, point to two prolonged droughts, including twenty-four years of below median June-July precipitation for the Medicine Hat area during the interval from 1768 to 1802.[39] The drier conditions enlarged the area of the Great Sand Hills of southwestern Saskatchewan. They also drastically reduced the stream flow of the North Saskatchewan River. When the HBC established Manchester House in 1786, canoes could carry only half their regular cargo that fall because the water was so low. It was no better the following spring, forcing the company to abandon the use of boats completely. The grip of the drought tightened in the 1790s. The period from 1792 to 1802 has been recognized as the most arid decade in the past five hundred years. Imagine walking across the riverbed of the North Saskatchewan! That was possible in places in 1793, the lowest inferred single-year stream flow in the past millennium. These extraordinarily low water levels were probably not just a consequence of the reduced rainfall. Colder summer temperatures, brought on by another bout of volcanic activity in the first part of the 1790s, meant there was less runoff from the mountains in the spring.[40] There was no shortage, though, of smoke in the air from the fires that raged across the prairies because of tinder-dry conditions. South Branch House was constantly under threat during the spring and summer of 1792. A trader at the post gloomily reported, "the ground on fire all around us," in September of that year.[41]

Indians were accustomed to these climatic fluctuations. But their horses were not, and they died in great numbers. The toll among Cree and Assiniboine bands on the northeastern plains was particularly high in the 1780s. These bands had no interest in winter herding, preferring to turn their horses loose near the woods to fend for themselves over the winter. More animals might have made it through had they not been worked so hard during the fall bison hunt. But the decidedly colder weather during these years hastened the almost complete collapse of their horse herds except for a few pathetic survivors rounded up in the spring. Those losses prevented these Indian groups from completing their transition to mounted hunting societies. Many were forced to continue to procure bison through the traditional method of pounding.[42]

The Cree and Assiniboine expected to replace their lost horses through trade with the Blackfoot Alliance. But once trading posts had been established on the North Saskatchewan River in present-day west-central Saskatchewan, the Cree and Assiniboine lost their role as intermediaries and with it, the gun-for-horse trade that had been the basis for amicable relations between northern plains groups. The Blackfoot Alliance could now secure newcomer goods, in particular firearms, directly from the Canadians and Europeans and consequently stopped trading horses, especially because they too were losing animals to the colder winters and summer droughts. As mounted bison hunters, they needed to maintain their horse stock to meet their subsistence needs.

It had also been the horse, in combination with the gun, that had enabled the Blackfoot in mid-century to begin to reoccupy their traditional territory to the south and push back the Snake. These skirmishes continued through the 1780s and into the 1790s, but they were not so much over territory as they were

244

over horses. The Blackfoot sought to replenish their diminished herds through lightning-quick, guerilla-like raids on enemy camps, which in turn provoked counter-raids by the Snake and their allies, the Flathead and Crow. These "horse wars" were fought almost continuously because of the warrior culture of these equestrian societies and the prestige and status that came with each successful raid. But the growing availability of guns ramped up the danger, and those who lost their lives had to be avenged, leading to even deadlier raids. The fallout was a gender imbalance in many camps, where there were three males to every four females.[43]

The Cree and Assiniboine also became inveterate horse thieves. Desperate to replace the animals they had lost to the cold and the snow, they began to raid trading posts, spiriting away horses that had been carefully tended through the harsh winter months. In April 1788, the Assiniboine stole thirteen animals from Manchester House. They came back two months later to take several more. Nor did the Cree and Assiniboine care where they got the stock to rebuild their herds. Because the Blackfoot no longer exchanged horses, their former trading partners simply took them through raiding. Indians from the Swan Hills region travelled several hundred miles across the northern plains to steal horses from other Indian bands and traders.[44] What had started out as raiding, however, escalated into warfare between the Cree in eastern Saskatchewan and the Gros Ventre. It was as if the trading posts were sitting on the northern edge of "a cauldron of conflict."[45]

The trouble erupted in the spring of 1788 when a large band of Cree attacked and murdered a small party of Gros Ventre near the Battle River posts. Special attention was reserved for the leading man: "they cut off his arms, head, Private Parts and took out his bowels."[46] The Cree then traded the furs they had stolen from their victims at a Canadian House. This unprovoked incident marked a decisive change in the relations between the two groups. When the Cree and the Assiniboine first began moving into the region west of the South Saskatchewan River in the early eighteenth century, they co-occupied the territory with the Gros Ventre. Their interactions were generally peaceful, if not congenial, as evidenced by their cooperative effort to repair a bison pound in the Bear Hills during Matthew Cocking's 1772–73 wintering trip. But after the smallpox epidemic, the Cree sought to consolidate and expand their place on the northern plains and their role in the bison-provisioning trade. That the Gros Ventre were the most easterly group of the Blackfoot Alliance placed them directly in the path of this Cree invasion. William Tomison became so uneasy about the deteriorating situation that he feared for the safety of Manchester House and temporarily shut down the post in the summer of 1788.[47] The view from South Branch House was equally bleak. "The whole Country is in a Stur," warned William Walker.[48]

The HBC did not help matters. The company had sought direct trade with the Blackfoot Alliance but soon found that the market was glutted with wolf pelts. It responded in 1789 by downgrading the trade value of the furs; one wolf pelt was now worth one Made Beaver, instead of two. This loss of purchasing power became a source of grievance to the Blackfoot, who were already resentful of the better treatment given by the HBC to the Cree and Assiniboine for providing beaver skins.[49] They had also been forced to cope with the loss of most of their horses to starvation in the deep snow of the winter of 1788–89. It is understandable, then, why the Blackfoot people might have felt under threat and why they became increasingly difficult, at times quarrelsome, in their dealings with the HBC and Montreal pedlars. When Tomison re-opened Manchester House in 1789, he did so in the realization that the local Indians had become "much more daring then they used to be."[50] This observation came tragically true in the summer of 1791 when Isaac Batt, an "almost worn out" servant, agreed to go hunting with two Blood men. They killed him at the first opportunity—shot in the head as he smoked—and took his horses, guns, and other possessions. Batt was the first HBC employee killed by members of the Blackfoot Alliance.[51]

Cree–Gros Ventre hostilities, meanwhile, seem to have subsided. While the Cree had temporarily retreated down the Saskatchewan to avoid retaliation after the 1788 incident, the Gros Ventre stayed away from the North

Because of the short open water season, voyageurs rose at dawn and put in long days in the canoe.

Saskatchewan posts for two years. The winter of 1791–92 was also unusually warm, resulting in the loss of fewer horses and perhaps easing the tension between the northern plain bands.[52] That appeared to be the case when Peter Fidler spent the following winter with the Peigan in present-day southern Alberta. Near the Vermilion River, they were joined by a party of Cree, on their way west to hunt beaver, who traded medicines.[53] Fidler also saw first-hand how the worsening drought of the 1790s was leaving its imprint on the open grasslands. Fresh water was not only difficult to locate, necessitating an erratic travel pattern, but large sections of land had been burned over, leaving nothing for their thirsty horses to feed on. What he found most bewildering, though, was the size of the bison herd that had gathered near the Red Deer River in the new year. "The ground is entirely covered by them & appears quite black," he recorded. "I never saw such amazing numbers together before. I am sure there was some millions in sight."[54] Fidler surmised that the bison were congregating near water to escape the worst ravages of the drought on the northern prairies. He later learned that a group of Assiniboine to the east could not find any bison that winter and were reduced to eating some of their horses to avoid starvation.[55]

This intense and persistent drought may have triggered the renewal of hostilities between the Cree and Gros Ventre in the summer of 1793, coincidentally the same year that the North Saskatchewan River ran dry in places. A large party of Cree and Assiniboine chanced upon a camp of sixteen Gros Ventre tents beside the South Saskatchewan River and "fell upon them like hungry Wolves and with remorseless fury butchered them all in cold blood except a few children whom they preserved for Slaves."[56] The Cree and Assiniboine then fled to the cover of the nearby woods, safe in the knowledge that the Gros Ventre were reluctant to pursue them into unfamiliar territory and sustain further losses. The brutal attack demanded retaliation. But the Gros Ventre knew they would be badly outgunned in any war against the Cree and Assiniboine because of the superior weapons they secured through the fur trade.

That left only one other option—besides retreat—and that was to strike at the source of Cree and Assiniboine support. As Nor'Wester Duncan McGillivray later explained: "The Gros Ventres ... formed the design of attacking us, whom they considered as the allies of their enemies."[57] Whereas the traders enjoyed kinship ties with the Cree and Assiniboine, they found the Gros Ventre language difficult to master. And whereas the traders offered firearms and other newcomer goods for beaver skins, they grudgingly accepted wolf pelts but at a lowered price. From the Gros Ventre perspective, then, directing their frustration and anger against the Montreal pedlars and HBC men was the next best way of securing vengeance for Cree and Assiniboine aggression and expansionism.[58]

The Gros Ventre "war of survival in the Saskatchewan area"[59] got underway in the early fall. In October 1793, a Cree man killed a Blood man during a quarrel at the HBC's new Buckingham House. Traders along the Saskatchewan immediately realized that the incident would lead to further violence but were not sure when. Nor did they expect to be drawn into any future trouble, because they naively regarded themselves as neutral in these struggles between bands.[60] Several days later, a combined Gros Ventre–Blackfoot party of about forty men arrived at the Pine Island posts seemingly intent on trading.

Portages provided a break from the hours of paddling but were equally demanding.

Once across the river, though, they attacked the HBC's Manchester House, roughing up the only two men there, before moving on to plunder the NWC's Pine Island House. Driven off by armed resistance, the attackers regrouped and relaunched their assault on Manchester House, ransacking the post for anything of value. They made a point of carrying the liquor supply to the front gate and destroying it without one drop being consumed. They then returned to their pillaging of the NWC fort, before being once again repulsed by gunfire and forced to retreat with their wounded and dying.

The attack on the Pine Island posts was a warning, one that could have been much worse. The Gros Ventre and Blood could have killed some, if not all, of the traders but spared their lives. They could also have laid siege to the posts and forced the occupants into submission. While they were not necessarily opposed to the posts in their territory, they wanted better trade terms and were prepared to use force to get their way. But the traders did not appreciate the danger they faced. The HBC's William Tomison blithely believed that his men were unfortunate victims of circumstance, robbed because the Gros Ventre were unable to strike back at the Cree and Assiniboine for the summer massacre.

"What they have done," he reasoned, "I judge to be out of spite."[61]

The harassment of the upper Saskatchewan trading posts continued into the new year. In early January 1794, a party of about 150 Blood, led by O-mok-apee (Big Man or Gros Blanc), descended on the NWC's Fort George and the HBC's Buckingham House, spoiling to avenge the warriors they had lost in the attack on the Pine Island posts. But because the posts were too secure, they ended up stealing about sixty horses. They also took the goods and clothes of Nor'Wester Duncan McGillivray and two other men, who had been confronted on the open prairie on their way back to Fort George after a trading trip. The trio were lucky that their lives had been spared.[62] A month later, another large group of Gros Ventre and Blood appeared at Manchester House and, after trading several hundred wolf skins, spirited away more than fifty horses that night. A now wary Tomison reported, "its not known what lengths they would have gone to" if there had not been so many armed men at the nearby Canadian post.[63]

Either incident that winter could have led to bloodshed. But the Indians chose restraint because the posts were too well-guarded. That was not the situation in the early summer when traders returned to Grand Portage or York Factory for trade goods. Most interior forts were reduced to a skeletal staff, and therefore vulnerable. The North West Company was worried about this situation, especially given the recent troubles on the North Saskatchewan, and suggested that the settlements be co-occupied for mutual security. But Tomison distrusted the Montreal pedlars and insisted on keeping a few men at each of the HBC posts.[64] It was a fateful decision. The Gros Ventre would have been aware of the traders' annual routine, known that most of the men would have left with the canoe brigades for the bay. And they would strike with pent-up ferocity.

That day came on 24 June 1794 at South Branch House. While James Gaddy was collecting birchbark several miles distant from the post, Magnus Annel and Hugh Brough were rounding up stray horses with help from a Cree man, the Flute. Their search was interrupted by the sound of pounding horse

Dogs teams were used for travel in winter.

hooves. A panicked Flute shouted that it was the Gros Ventre and pleaded with his two HBC companions to hide with him in the bush. But Annel and Brough insisted that the riders must be Assiniboine and waited to greet them. They were soon surrounded by a large party of Gros Ventre; estimates vary from 100 to 250. Several warriors dismounted and killed and scalped the two servants. They then made for the post.[65]

South Branch House afforded little protection to its inhabitants. It was surrounded, in the words of Cornelius Van Driel, one of only two company men there that morning, "with stockades that the 1st gale of wind ... would level with the ground."[66] Van Driel heard the approach of the galloping horses and instinctively closed the gates. He then climbed atop the house for a better view—initially he assumed that the horsemen were Assiniboine—and spied warriors skulking about the fort, looking for a breach in the stockade. The Gros Ventre would have met little resistance. Besides Van Driel, there was only one other servant at the post, William Fea, along with Magnus Annel's Assiniboine wife (now widow) and their two children, and three other Indian women whose partners had gone to York Factory. Fea became the first casualty when a

251

shot fired through a gap in the stockade broke his arm.

Although well-armed, Van Driel decided to wait to see what the assailants would do. "The number of Indians being so great," he recounted, "I dared not fire, knowing it to be impossible for us to escape." One of the Gros Ventre warriors walked up to the front gate, kicked it, and then launched into a short harangue "which none of us understood." Several other men then set fire to the stockade. A frantic Van Driel and Fea, "not well knowing what to do," first retreated to their rooms, but hearing "the frightful noise" of the warriors breaking through the stockade, jumped out windows and hid in a pair of old cellars near the post garden. The Gros Ventres easily found Fea by following his trail of blood and murdered him. But Van Driel had covered his body with refuse at the bottom of his cellar and escaped detection. As he lay there, he heard crying followed by the sound of the house on fire. He later learned that the three Indian women had been taken captive. Magnus Annel's wife, with her two children placed astride her stomach, was found stabbed and hacked to death.[67]

The war party then turned its attention to the nearby Canadian post, about two hundred yards away on the same side of the river. Like the HBC settlement, the residents had not been taken completely by surprise and managed to secure the gates before the Gros Ventre arrived. But any similarities ended there. The NWC fort was built to withstand attack and featured heavily reinforced, elevated blockhouses. The handful of men in the post poured a withering fire on the attacking warriors and forced them to take cover behind a small rise of ground. After half an hour of futile shooting, the war chief, L'Homme de Calumet, led a second advance on the gates but was shot dead as he urged his fighters forward. His death brought the assault to an abrupt end, and the Gros Ventre gathered up their dead and wounded and rode off.[68]

The horrific incident at South Branch House sent shockwaves through the fur trade community of the North-West, compelling everyone involved to pull back. Both HBC and NWC traders retreated down the Saskatchewan River to below the forks, while other posts in Blackfoot Alliance country were either closed or fortified. The Gros Ventre fled south, abandoning the region that they had fought to maintain. Even the Cree withdrew from the contested territory in present-day east-central Alberta. But this pause was short-lived. The North West Company was not ready to give up on the trade in the northern prairies. Nor was the HBC, especially since it had lost an estimated ten thousand MB in the ransacking of Manchester House and razing of South Branch House. The company was anxious to make up for the losses by downplaying, if not ignoring, what had happened in the larger interests of profit. The "circumstances ... gave Us much pain," the London Committee soberly observed the following spring, "tho' We are happy no worse consequences ensued." It then urged a quick resolution to the matter: "let no means be lost in trying to Reconcile those Natives with our Servants."[69] It was as if the deaths of more than a dozen people—the "circumstances" as they were clinically called—were an aberration.

CHAPTER EIGHT

No Allies, Only Interests

THE SOUTH BRANCH HOUSE KILLINGS WERE NOT EASILY FORGOTTEN. ELEVEN YEARS later, while travelling up the South Saskatchewan River for the first time, North West Company clerk Daniel Harmon made special mention of the Gros Ventre attack in his journal and how the bloody incident had forced the traders to abandon their forts.[1] If Harmon was somewhat uneasy about his new posting, about six miles from the site of the killings, he had good reason. Despite the presence of Hudson's Bay Company and Montreal traders inland for half a century, the Saskatchewan country remained Indian territory. The posts were only allowed to operate in the region because of Indian consent, only allowed to collect furs and other local resources because Indians wanted newcomer goods, in particular guns, tobacco, and alcohol. This exchange was mostly peaceful, even cooperative at times, but there was always a charged undercurrent of tension. Indians on the northern plains fought one another over territory, bison, horses, and trade goods and were not going to let outsiders decide their future. This friction has been largely downplayed in favour of highlighting the bitter commercial struggle between the Montreal and bay traders in the Churchill and especially the Athabasca country.[2] But just as two newcomer frontiers developed almost simultaneously in the Saskatchewan and Churchill–Athabasca districts,[3] there were essentially two fur trades in the late eighteenth and early nineteenth centuries. Rival companies along the Saskatchewan River system generally coexisted on civil terms, while trying to secure the trade of local Indian bands who had their own interests and ambitions. And even though the number of posts in the region proliferated during this period, traders were still essentially interlopers. Their very presence and activities generated a range of Indian responses—from allegiance to toleration to avoidance to retaliation—depending on the circumstances at the time.[4]

It was beaver skins that first brought traders inland from Hudson Bay and Montreal in the second half of the eighteenth century, and it was the lack of beaver skins that forced a reorganization of the interior Saskatchewan trade by the end of that century. "The Country arround Fort George is now entirely ruined," Duncan McGillivray of the North West Company conceded in the spring of 1795. "The Natives have already killed all of the Beavers, to such a distance that they lose much time in coming to the House during the Hunting Season."[5] The obvious solution was to extend the NWC trade farther up the North Saskatchewan River, beyond the reach of the Hudson's Bay Company at nearby Buckingham House and into an area where beaver-hunting Cree and Assiniboine bands could collect pelts.

Nor'Wester Angus Shaw chose a site near the Beaver Hills, about five days' travel upriver, where the open prairies gave way to the parkland, for the new Fort Augustus. Not to be outmanoeuvred, the HBC under William Tomison followed the NWC lead and built Edmonton House there the next fall. This new trade centre became the respective administrative headquarters for both the NWC (Fort des Prairies department) and HBC (Saskatchewan district) for a vast trade region that stretched from the Saskatchewan River forks west to the Rocky Mountain foothills and between the Athabasca River to the north and the Missouri River to the south. It was also from Fort Augustus that the NWC planned to push to the Pacific coast, while initiating trade with trans-mountain Indian groups, such as the Kutenai. A senior NWC officer came to reside there, and, as if in lock-step, so too did Tomison, the inland governor for the HBC.[6]

The expansion towards better beaver grounds farther up the North Saskatchewan did not spell the end of the Fort George–Buckingham House complex in present-day east-central Alberta. These posts, like Cumberland

The Hudson's Bay Company established Edmonton House to keep pace with the North West Company as it moved farther up the North Saskatchewan River.

House before them, became provisioning centres for the interior trade until they were eventually replaced by Fort Vermilion (NWC) and Paint River House (HBC) farther down the North Saskatchewan at the Vermilion River in 1802. Nor did the abandonment of the South Branch House site after the Gros Ventre raid mean that traders withdrew from the area. One year after the killings, new fortified settlements were established just below the Saskatchewan Forks at Peonan Creek: Fort St. Louis (NWC) on one bank and Carlton House (HBC)[7] on the opposite bank.

During the next decade, the number of posts on the northern plains grew exponentially as both the NWC and HBC sought out fresh fur grounds or food sources. They were joined by dozens of traders from Quebec firms who had operated south of the Great Lakes in the Upper Mississippi country during the American Revolutionary period but were forced to retreat to British territory under the provisions of Jay's Treaty in 1794. Some of these new posts were built at the margins of the fur trade frontier, such as Rocky Mountain House (NWC) and Acton House (HBC) near the headwaters of the North Saskatchewan River in 1799. But the vast majority were part of a general "in-filling" along the

Both the North West Company and Hudson's Bay Company had to respect and accommodate Indian dominance on the northern plains.

BURPEE, THE SEARCH FOR THE WESTERN SEA

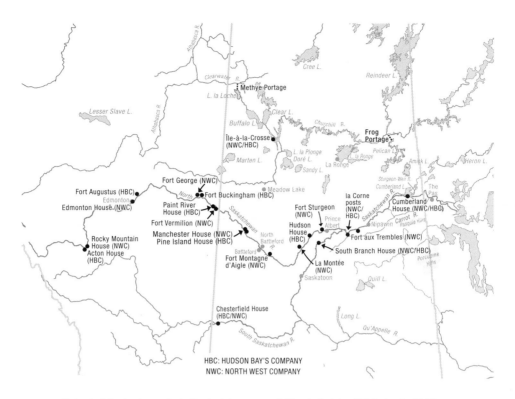

Selected fur trade posts in Saskatchewan and Alberta in late 1700s/early 1800s

Saskatchewan River watershed and other major rivers of the northern plains and parklands.[8] In the search for new beaver grounds, for example, posts were constructed near Turtle and Meadow Lakes and along the Root (Carrot), Red Deer, and Swan Rivers. Only the cellars of a few survive today because of the wood construction; some abandoned posts also fell victim to erosion along the riverbanks.

The seemingly insatiable demand for food, meanwhile, led to the establishment of houses, in the first instance by the NWC, along the Assiniboine and Qu'Appelle[9] Rivers (Forts Alexandria and Espérance [near Welby, Saskatchewan], respectively) in present-day southeastern Saskatchewan and southern Manitoba. Here, within sight of the great bison herds, newcomers secured pemmican, fat, and fresh meat produced by local Indian pounds. These provisions became so crucial to the viability of the larger fur trade— for both the canoe brigades and the growing number of newcomers working and living inland—that the seven NWC settlements in this region (including along the Red River) were soon opposed by fourteen rival posts, many of them independent traders. Indeed, 1790–1804 marked the greatest period of post construction in western Canadian fur trade history. A whopping 323 posts were built throughout the North-West during these fifteen years, compared to fewer than ninety in the preceding fifteen.[10] Many of these forts, small ramshackle structures at the best of time, were short-lived and a winnowing process in subsequent years ensured that only the most optimally located survived.

The NWC spearheaded this flurry of post construction in a calculated attempt to drive any competitors out of business by forcing rivals to try to keep pace with them. The HBC resolutely tried to respond, matching the Montreal-based company wherever and whenever possible post for post—often side-by-side or "cheek-by-jowl." But the London company was hard-pressed to find enough new servants to take up the NWC challenge because of the manpower demands of the Napoleonic wars in Europe. "We are ... distressed here for men," an apologetic James Bird wrote from Edmonton House in November 1799, "the number of houses ... under the necessity of settling have so scattered us that there is scarcely a sufficient number of men ... to oppose our new opponents."[11] The other embarrassing complication was the lack of goods at some of the new HBC posts. Bird had spent the winter of 1798–99 at the Net Setting (Sturgeon) River on the North Saskatchewan and had no sooner arrived at the site than he was begging for cloth, blankets, powder, spirits, and other trade articles. It is not surprising, then, that Joseph Howse at Carleton House spoke of "our own enfeebled situation" when measured against "the still increasing strength of our opponents."[12]

The great leveller in this rivalry was the climate. A series of severe winters in the latter half of the 1790s, precipitated by volcanic eruptions and low solar activity (known as the Dalton Minimum),[13] disrupted the trade and played havoc with travel through the region. Cold, snowy conditions around Fort George delayed trading until early April 1795 when a small band of Blackfoot and Blood finally arrived on foot—"their horses," according to Duncan

McGillivray, "being too much exhausted by hunger to undergo the fatigues of the Journey."[14] Later that same year at Fort Augustus–Edmonton House, it was possible to ride on horseback across the frozen North Saskatchewan River by mid-November.

These colder temperatures drastically reduced glacier melt the following spring, and the annual brigades could not depart on time because "there was no water in the river for canoes."[15] They were delayed again the following year, not because of low water but because of the late spring. "The Country around has the appearance of Winter," James Bird gloomily reported on 2 May 1797, "the Snow being still deep on the ground."[16] The HBC brigade somehow managed to reach Cumberland House on 4 June only to find "the [Cedar] lake is still frozen over apparently as solid as it was in the middle of winter." The HBC men hunkered down with the stranded North West brigade before they were able to break their way through the ice-choked waters to Lake Winnipeg some two weeks later. Once again, though, they were "brought up by the ice ... the lake frozen over ... a circumstance never known before," at least by them.[17] The next two trading seasons were just as difficult, even more so when the early onset of winter prevented the restocking of many of the posts. "I have never experienced so miserable a time ... inland," William Tomison bemoaned his provisions shortfall in November 1798, "and no prospect of its mending."[18]

Indian groups had to contend with the same harsh climate conditions. They struggled to meet their own subsistence needs during the severe winters and rarely visited the Saskatchewan posts. George Sutherland at Buckingham House, for example, did not see any Indians during the winter of 1797–98 until early March when four young Blackfoot men "came to beg tobacco; they say the snow is too deep for horses or dogs to travel."[19] And when the cold temperatures finally abated, as they did during the winter of 1799–1800, Indian bands stayed out on the plains to hunt the bison herds that continued to graze well south of their usual winter range because of the unseasonably mild weather. The Blackfoot trading parties that visited Edmonton House that February consequently brought few furs and even fewer provisions. Traders

LIBRARY AND ARCHIVES CANADA C-0˙1743, W. ARMSTRONG

Fort William was the North West Company's major transhipment depot and rendezvous centre at the head of Lake Superior.

went hungry again because of the shortage of food.

The unusually cold weather also chilled relations between different equestrian bands. Horse herds were decimated by the cruel winters, setting off an inevitable round of raiding and counter-raiding. The Assiniboine search for replacement stock in the upper Missouri country earned the enmity of the Sioux, who retaliated with ferocity. As many as 450 Assiniboine may have perished in battles with the Sioux in the mid-1790s.[20] The Assiniboine also looked west to the neighbouring Blackfoot Alliance and tried to spirit away whatever animals they could. These persistent raids so angered the Blackfoot that they told an Edmonton House trader in December 1796 that they were preparing to go to war against the Assiniboine the following spring. Intertribal relations had clearly reached a breaking point.[21]

The traders tried to put a damper on any talk of war, counselling peace at every turn in the interests of trade. But the Indians were their own masters and did what they wanted, not what was expected of them, to the chagrin of the newcomers. The Blackfoot bands, for example, were supposed to

265

continue to patronize only the Fort George–Buckingham House posts, on the understanding that the Edmonton-area posts were for beaver-hunters. But they blithely ignored these wishes and supplied most of the trade at the new settlements. The Peigan (known as Muddy River Indians in fur trade documents) also subverted trader attempts to engage the Kutenai in order to protect their middleman role and prevent the arming of their rivals. They regularly blockaded the mountain passes, preventing the Kutenai from travelling to the posts. Even the Cree actively resisted a NWC attempt in 1799 to build a new post at "the Stonney Mountain" and forced the construction party to abandon the project, not once but twice.[22]

Perhaps the best example of Indian dominance was the return of the Gros Ventre to the Saskatchewan country a year and a half after the South Branch House killings. The perpetrators of the crime, admitting "they have been lately like wolves,"[23] came seeking peace at Fort Augustus–Edmonton House on 25 November 1795. HBC inland chief Tomison refused to deal with them, insisting to his NWC counterparts that the culprits should surrender and submit themselves to British justice. But Nor'Wester John McDonald of Garth, known as *Le Bras Croche* because of his withered right arm, questioned whether such punishment would have the desired effect on the Indians. He chose instead to trade with them after receiving assurances that they would behave themselves.[24]

The Gros Ventre were back just over a year later, this time in a group numbering four hundred, visiting during a brief spell of remarkably warm, rainy weather in mid-December 1796. Both companies took the precaution of guarding their gates and buildings before inviting the principal men into a room to be addressed through an interpreter. There, the traders told them that their past conduct was unacceptable, that they had every right to punish them, "but that we would forgive them this time." This leniency delighted the Gros Ventre, who responded with gifts of wolf skins and horses to affirm their peaceful intentions. But it did not sit well with George Sutherland, who noted in the HBC post journal: "It's well known to all those who understand the customs and manners of Indians that the oftener they escape with impunity the more daring they grow."[25] It is easy to conclude that the traders were more concerned with restoring trade relations than provoking further trouble. Or that they were following established diplomatic practices among Indian bands in resolving such disputes. The simple truth, though, is that the newcomers were in no position to confront the Gros Ventre. They had to accept intimidation and aggression as a cost of doing business in Indian territory.[26]

The most powerful Indian group during this period—in terms of military power and territorial reach—was the Blackfoot Alliance. With horses and guns, they not only dominated the northern plains but aggressively pushed southward beyond the South Saskatchewan to the Missouri River. These campaigns against their regional enemies were often launched from HBC and NWC posts, which doubled as staging grounds for arming and assembling the warriors.[27] Other equestrian peoples, like the Crow, who did not have access to the same weaponry, were hopelessly disadvantaged. And they remained so until American traders arrived in the trans-Mississippi West in the early nineteenth century. Even then, the Blackfoot tried to prevent the arming of the Crow and other enemies by attacking the traders.

The Blackfoot might be expected to be beholden or at least deferential to their arms dealers, the English and Canadian traders. But as fiercely independent, bison-hunting bands, they visited the posts infrequently and only when it suited their purposes. Their relationship with the traders was consequently a limited one, best described as distant, if not strained. (David Thompson's and Peter Fidler's overwintering with the Peigan in 1787–88 and 1792–93, respectively, were rare exceptions.) Few came to be known by name, while any conversation was constrained because there were few interpreters who could understand Niitsitapi. The Blackfoot also rarely intermarried with the newcomers. Nor did they receive goods in advance on credit.[28] What they were, though, were grudging customers—one trader likened them to "blackguards"[29]—who carried on their business at the forts in a spirit of defiance and superiority when not complaining about their treatment or the

SASATCHEWAN ARCHIVES BOARD R-A24811

"Fur bales" were easier to handle and transport.

escalating price of trade goods relative to the value of their wolf pelts.[30]

It has been said that the Blackfoot were much like the British and Americans in their foreign relations at this time: "they had no allies, only interests."[31] This strategy can be seen in their decision to accept the fur traders and their posts as they moved up the North Saskatchewan. No longer did they have to deal through Cree and Assiniboine middlemen to secure guns and luxury goods. It can also be seen in their decision to maintain generally peaceful relations with the Cree and Assiniboine to the east and north at a time when they were fighting their enemies to the south and trying to prevent the traders from expanding into the trans-mountain west. These diplomatic efforts were the work of moderate leaders, especially the Peigan Young Man and Blackfoot Old Swan, who used their considerable influence to try to keep tensions in check in the early 1790s. Working against them were more warlike leaders, like the Blackfoot Big Man. He resented the arming of the Cree and Assiniboine, especially when these weapons were used to terrorize the Gros Ventre, and had taken part in the attack on the Pine Island posts in 1793. The persistent horse-raiding by the Assiniboine only served to validate his claims and push the competing bands closer to outright confrontation. Until that time, both the Blackfoot and the traders remained wary, if not suspicious, of one another.[32]

By contrast, the Cree and Assiniboine enjoyed a much closer relationship with the traders, who sought to smooth over difficulties with the various bands in order to avoid disruptions to the fur trade and provisioning system. But the Cree and Assiniboine were neither docile nor duty-bound to the traders and could be just as intransigent in their dealings with the HBC and NWC. In the Cumberland area, for example, even though the posts there had evolved into major provisions-transshipment centres by the end of the eighteenth century, the local Cree continued to be needed as a source of labour, furs, and country produce. And they used this dependence to extort presents, mostly liquor, sometimes rudely demanding more than the traders were prepared to provide. There were also times when they simply refused to do any trapping.[33] "They despise us in their hearts," bitterly complained Nor'Wester Alexander Henry the Younger, insisting that "their outward professions of respect and friendship" were feigned "to procure their necessaries."[34] Daniel Harmon formed the same impression during his dealings with the Cree and Assiniboine in the Swan River district in 1802: "friendship seldom goes farther than *their* fondness for our property and *our* eagerness to obtain their Furs."[35] In essence, both traders and Indians were involved in a mutually exploitive relationship.

Traders also courted retribution if they punished Indians. That was the worrying outcome of a horse-raiding incident at Netting River on the North Saskatchewan in May 1799. Three Assiniboine were caught stealing horses and held prisoner at the NWC post. When one of the men escaped during the night, the Canadians butchered the other two and dumped their bodies in the North Saskatchewan. This cold-blooded brutality may have been tolerated in the rough-and-tumble Athabasca district, but it rankled HBC servant James Bird. "What may be the consequences of so rash an action time only can determine," he predicted, "but I am afraid it will occasion the loss of lives of some poor Men, if ever they should be met by the Indians."[36] Bird knew from experience that the Assiniboine did not differentiate between companies in seeking vengeance. Travelling alone was potentially dangerous for traders at any time and was something to be avoided.

Most fur trade histories point to the bitter Athabasca rivalry between the HBC and the NWC as the impetus for the eventual merger of the companies in 1821. But traders in the Saskatchewan country in the 1790s had a different, equally revealing, perspective on the situation: the need for collective security or what one author referred to as "the necessity of union ... in the face of the great tribes of the plains."[37] Nor'Wester Duncan McGillivray was certainly won over to the idea after only a winter at Fort George and came to believe that "this consideration alone might have some influence with the Hudsons Bay Company."[38] One might even wonder whether the Blackfoot Alliance served as an example to McGillivray of how union facilitated survival on the northern plains, especially when there were so many competing bands vying for the same territory.

But if merger was not possible at this time, the fur trade records show how traders in the Saskatchewan country were already working together to a surprising extent. Certainly, the commercial rivals had their fractious moments, especially when the NWC insisted on using a mixture of alcohol and intimidation to divert the Indian trade away from the HBC. But generally, their dealings with one another were "strictly correct."[39] A good example of this cooperation was the building of competing posts—sometimes within the same palisades—together on the north side of the Saskatchewan River for safety. Another lesser-known example was the carrying of mail between posts. Both William Tomison and Daniel Harmon received correspondence brought by their rivals in the trade. Harmon described the HBC letter-carriers as "obliging" and added, "when one can with propriety render a service to the other, it is done with cheerfulness."[40] That was the case when the Nor'Westers helped put out a fire at Buckingham House and, in return, were invited to a dance at the HBC post. The residents of Fort George also drew their water from a HBC well, and when Tomison tried to stop this practice during a drought, the dispute was peaceably resolved when Nor'Wester John McDonald of Garth suggested to the Orkneyman that he might find himself at the bottom of the well.[41] The HBC and NWC brigades also travelled together at times for security

Voyageurs often suffered from debilitating injuries later in life because of the loads they carried over portages.

purposes. One might even suspect that the football game played at Edmonton House on Boxing Day in December 1796 featured players from both forts who welcomed the chance to get in a good lick.

The relatively settled nature of the Saskatchewan trade enabled both companies to focus on improving their interior operations. Post gardens became more common and more prolific. The HBC had initially tried sending out seeds to lessen servant dependence on imported food, but the Hudson Bay lowlands stymied these early agricultural efforts. Now, in the late eighteenth and early nineteenth centuries, rich prairie soils and a longer growing season encouraged traders to plant extensive gardens at the Saskatchewan forts. The list of vegetables—cold-climate root crops typically grown in the poor soils of the Orkney Islands—was quite impressive: radishes, carrots, beets, onions, parsnips, turnips, and potatoes. Cumberland House was also renowned for its barley fields and livestock, including pigs. (The first documented cultivation of wheat in Saskatchewan, however, was not until 1815.[42]) Traders grew vegetables to add some variety to their otherwise steady, monotonous diet of meat and fish. And some of the harvests could be quite bountiful, both in volume and size, especially once newcomers became familiar with the local growing conditions. But climatic variability, such as an early frost or prolonged drought, played havoc with crop production.[43] The busy time of year for traders—spring and fall—also conflicted with planting and harvesting. Then there were the insects. At Fort Alexandria in July 1802, Daniel Harmon's garden fell victim to a horde of grasshoppers "in such astonishing numbers ... that they almost [hid] the Sun from our sight."[44] More often than not, then, posts had to turn to country provisions when gardens failed.[45]

Both companies also tinkered with their transportation system. In order to do away with the need for canoe brigades to travel from the Saskatchewan district all the way to and from York Factory, the HBC established an inland depot in 1793, about one hundred miles up the Hayes River, at the "Painted Stone" (echomamis in Cree), more popularly known as "the Rock" (Gordon House). Company men travelling to and from the interior, bringing in supplies or taking out furs, now only had to travel to the Rock depot, which was serviced by other crews based at York Factory. The chances of canoes being stopped by an early fall freeze-up were now lessened, while goods reached their inland destinations sooner so that HBC posts were better able to meet NWC competition.[46]

The HBC had also been searching for a larger capacity, more durable boat in place of the canoe, and in 1795 at Fort Edmonton, George Sutherland launched an experimental vessel on the North Saskatchewan. The clinker-

The HBC adopted the more durable York boat in the 1790s. It carried heavier loads
than the canoe and used sail power whenever possible.

built, flat-bottomed craft, pointed at both bow and stern, appeared heavy and
sluggish when compared to the graceful, sleek canoes of their Montreal rivals:
the proverbial HBC tortoise pitted against NWC hare. But the York boat,[47] as it
became known, could carry more cargo with half the crew, withstand storms
and floating ice, and be powered by sail. In the spring of 1797, Sutherland
took "2 fine large Batteaux ... thirty feet Keel each" down the Saskatchewan

River and was able to force a passage through the ice-choked waters in several places—something that was not possible with canoes.[48] Thereafter, the York boat became the mainstay of the run between the Rock and Edmonton House.

Transportation improvements were a constant obsession of the Montreal-based NWC as it tried to keep costs down in order to maximize profits. But despite its popular image as a restless group of independent-minded traders, what enabled the Nor'Westers to continue to meet the challenges of its overland route and prosper in the fur trade was its highly centralized and regulated structure. William McGillivray suggested in 1800 that "the tentacles of the Company's control reached everywhere along the waterways of the trade."[49] Partners were not only mostly Scots, but usually related, if not close family friends. Many had begun their career in the trade as apprentice clerks because of the sponsorship of an influential patron. This support demanded enduring loyalty. But it was no guarantee that clerks would be offered a share in the company at the end of their contract (five to seven years). That, too, depended on a patron.[50] This means of recruitment and promotion ensured that the company remained a closed, tightly knit group. Partnership also came with benefits—from a scheduled year's leave from the business (known as "rotation") to retirement in wealth in Quebec, Great Britain, or the United States. It was only natural, then, that Montreal agents and wintering partners actively worked to improve the efficiency and extend the reach of the trade, for it increased the company's profitability and hence the value of their shares.

The most vexing transportation problem for the NWC in the late eighteenth century was a direct consequence of Jay's Treaty, which formally determined the boundary between the United States and British North America following the American Revolutionary War. The great inland entrepôt at Grand Portage on Lake Superior was now in American territory. This new border was a major headache for the company. Not only was the annual rendezvous held here, but Grand Portage had mushroomed into an impressive complex of warehouses, offices, housing, and canoe-building yards. And it had to be abandoned in favour of a site north of the new border. Fortunately, in 1798,

Roderick McKenzie consulted with the local Indians and was directed to the Kaministiqua River and the old French route over the height of land. The move there took several years, in part because the NWC insisted on building a much bigger facility in keeping with the company's stature and ambition. But by the time it was completed, the new wilderness headquarters—bringing together around three thousand people during the busy, boisterous rendezvous—was the largest settlement between Montreal and Russian America in the far northwest. It was officially named Fort William, after head partner William McGillivray, in 1807.[51]

The relocation to Fort William was accompanied by other changes to the eastern half of the NWC transportation system. The company employed a handful of larger tonnage ships on the Great Lakes, as well as built the first lock between Lakes Superior and Huron in 1799. It could not, however, do as much west of Lake Superior because of its reliance on the canoe, except for finding efficiencies. Beyond Fort William, major provisioning depots were established along the route (Lac La Pluie, Bas de la Riviere, Winnipeg River, and Cumberland House) to provide regular, specified amounts of food for the brigades headed in and out of the interior. One estimate suggests that nearly 50 per cent of the cargo space was devoted to provisions.[52] The size of the load and number of occupants in each canoe were also standardized, and carefully scrutinized by the partnership. At the 1809 rendezvous, Alexander Henry the Younger was called upon to explain why he had left Fort Vermilion in a light canoe in violation of established travel regulations. He luckily escaped with only a reprimand.[53]

One other way the NWC overcame the limitations of its western transport system was to place seemingly unrealistic expectations on the voyageurs who manned the three-hundred-pound, twenty-five-foot North canoe. To maintain any speed, especially since the canoe carried about two tons of cargo, the crew paddled at a continuous rate of forty strokes per minute for up to twelve hours. These long working days were intended to take advantage of the equally long hours of daylight and the fact that the wind was often down during the early

The high-wheeled wooden Red River cart became a popular conveyance
on the northern plains by the early nineteenth century.

morning. And the brigades covered great distances in remarkable time. But
the pace and load, week after week, placed an incredible strain on the health
of the voyageurs; the caloric deficit alone resulted in small, undernourished
bodies. Portaging was an added burden. Two men carried the canoe *upright* on
their shoulders, while the others were loaded down with two ninety-pound
packs—more than their own body weight. Because the stress often led to
skeletal damage and odd bone spurs, some voyageurs must have lived with
painful chronic injuries.[54]

One of the most "dreaded" stretches along the North Saskatchewan
was just beyond the forks, around Garden River, where the current was so
strong that the men had to place themselves in harness and drag the canoes
upriver along the narrow, muddy north shore. These efforts were rewarded
at La Montée (the Mount-up), about forty miles southwest of present-day
Prince Albert, where the boreal forest opened up to the prairie and the NWC
maintained a small herd of horses (hence the name). The clerks rode off in
search of bison to provide the first fresh meat in weeks for their appreciative

crews. This hunt became such a tradition that the incoming brigades were given only enough provisions at Cumberland House to take them to La Montée.[55]

The other transportation innovation during this period—to go along with the HBC adoption of the York boat—was the NWC reintroduction of the cart to the North-West. The French had first used carts at their Saskatchewan forts in the mid-eighteenth century; several traders visiting the sites of the former posts years later reported finding the remains of carriage wheels and rutted trails. But they fell into disuse after the French withdrew from the North-West, and it was not until 1801 that the first reference to carts is found in Alexander Henry the Younger's journal for Pembina River post.[56] The carts were extremely crude and featured wheels made from the sawed-off ends of tree trunks; but they were quickly refined to be able to carry heavier loads, perhaps as much as nine hundred pounds in ten bags. And because this load could be hauled by a single horse, the carts represented a considerable saving. They were also perfectly suited for the relatively flat terrain of the eastern prairies and, consequently, were quickly incorporated in the NWC regional transport system as a complement to the canoe brigades.[57] Within time, they became known as Red River carts.

The carts were mostly used to haul food: bison meat and fat, or the finished product, pemmican. As the fur trade extended its reach into the interior, especially the Athabasca country, and more and more newcomers entered the region, bison flesh from the northern plains became ever more important to the commercial struggle for beaver skins. "Want of Provisions," John McDonald of Garth bluntly summed up the situation in 1793, "would prevent progress & stop the Trade."[58] But even though posts along the Saskatchewan increasingly traded for food, or in some cases, became mainly provisioning centres, Indians in the region never supplied enough bison meat to meet the demands of the trade. The NWC and HBC consequently established posts on the northeastern plains in present-day southern Manitoba and southeastern Saskatchewan (Souris Basin) to be closer to the bison on their winter range and the Indians who exploited them. Alexander Henry the Younger even built an observation platform atop an oak tree near his post at Park River so that he could track the movement of the great herds. In mid-September 1800, he looked out upon "more Buffalo at one view then I had seen at any other time ... the meadow seemed as if in motion as there was scarcely a vacant spot where the grass could be seen."[59]

Henry hoped these bison and others would find their way into the NWC pantry for future consumption. The cooler temperatures of the northern plains were ideal for assembling the ingredients for the mass production of pemmican, particularly the harvesting and handling of fat. But getting the local Indians along the Red, Assiniboine, and Qu'Appelle Rivers to become fully involved in supplying bison meat—in the quantity increasingly required by the fur trade—was neither easy nor straightforward. Food for the Assiniboine and Cree was a reciprocal trade item, something not only to be shared with competing traders but also sometimes given on credit in the expectation that they might need help in the future. From the Indian perspective, it made more sense to hedge their bets and deal with both companies. But both the NWC and HBC wanted monopoly access to the bison of the region to the exclusion of the other. The Indians of the region, much like the Blackfoot Alliance to the west, also secured most of their subsistence requirements from the bison hunt and had little need for newcomer goods, except for luxury items. What provisions they were willing and prepared to provide were therefore limited.[60]

Rivals tried to win over the allegiance of local bands to the bison meat trade by bestowing gifts and special honours, much as the HBC used to do when trading captains came to the bay with their followers. Many became known by name and were collectively called "our hunters." The Cree and Assiniboine, in return, steadily demanded more in trade for their business, and the traders had no choice but to raise the prices they were willing to pay from one season to the next.[61] "A great hurt" is how Robert Goodwin described the inflated costs at Brandon House in 1798.[62] Most of the provision trade involved the exchange of bison meat and fat for alcohol, tobacco, ammunition, and knives. Indians also expected certain courtesies, such as the right to drink inside the post. Daniel

GLENBOW ARCHIVES NA-1344-2

Pounding was a widespread bison procurement method on the northern plains.

Harmon regularly complained of sleepless nights at Fort Alexandria because of drunken Indians: "both Men & Women .... make an intolerable noise, for they talk, Sing & cry all at the same time."[63] But he and others had no one to blame but themselves for making alcohol so readily available and in such great quantities. After an Assiniboine party left Brandon House after a drinking spree, the local trader quipped, "I really believe their horses and dogs were drunk also."[64]

By the beginning of the nineteenth century, the production of pemmican on the northeastern plains had become almost an industrial-scale operation. In response to the steady demand for bison meat, Assiniboine and Cree hunters worked their pounds more intensively, re-using the same successful site two or more times over the fall and winter months. They sometimes fired the grasslands to influence the movement of the herds, including driving them away from rival pounds, so that the fall skies were often choked with billowing clouds of smoke that obscured the sun. The NWC and HBC also sent men to visit the pounds to buy up whatever meat and fat was available before it could fall into the hands of a rival post, and then haul it back by sled. Winter pounds could produce only so much, and these limitations were reflected in the escalating prices and the poorer condition of meat being purchased. Posts enlarged their storage facilities, adding meat sheds, ice houses, and log-walled cellars, to prevent provisions from spoiling. One author has even claimed that these provisioning forts were more like abattoirs.[65]

The pemmican manufactured at the posts, known as "trade pemmican," had a different composition from the sweeter, traditional Indian product. Because of market demand, Indian hunters rarely harvested the softer exterior fats and bone marrow grease from the bison carcass. Instead, they used the more easily accessible back fat or *depouillé* and interior core fat of the animal. These unsaturated fats created a distinctively waxy pemmican that could last for years and yet still provide a caloric punch. And the amounts that were shipped out of the region were truly astounding: five hundred bags annually from just the NWC Qu'Appelle post.[66] Indian women would cut the meat into thin strips for drying and then pound it to a rhythmic beat: "the endless lub-dub, lub-dub, lub-dub ... went on for day after day, sometimes for weeks."[67] They also broke down and melted the *depouillé* together with other fat and then mixed it with the pounded meat. Sometimes pounded berries, such as choke cherries (*Prunus virginiana*) or saskatoons (*Amelanchier alnifolia*), were added.[68] The finished pemmican was closely packed in hide bags or *taureaux* that had been cut, folded, and sewn together from bull skins, again by women. Their pillow-like shape (about 30 inches by 20 by 4) made the bags ideal for transport and storage, but they were still heavy at around ninety pounds, the typical or standard amount that could be stuffed into a bull skin.[69] To accommodate the production, both the NWC and HBC built huge warehouses at their provisioning centres. A surplus was always maintained. If needed, the hundreds of pemmican bags stored at Cumberland House, for example, could supply the food needs of the entire district in the event of famine and not just the local traders and canoe brigades.

Increased pemmican production coincided with the reinvigoration of the beaver skin trade along the Saskatchewan. In the 1770s, Ojibwa from the east side of Lake Winnipeg, on friendly terms with the Cree and Assiniboine, began moving westward up the Saskatchewan River to Cumberland House and beyond. The pace of this migration quickened in the 1780s because of the Indian losses during the 1781–82 smallpox epidemic. By the end of the 1790s, large bands of Ojibwa (known to the traders as Bungee and later called Saulteaux) were found west of the Red River along the Assiniboine and Qu'Appelle Rivers, and all the way up the Saskatchewan to Fort Augustus/Edmonton House and Rocky Mountain House— even as far north as Lac la Biche.

As skilled beaver hunters, the Ojibwa soon emerged as the primary supplier of pelts at several Saskatchewan posts, replacing the Cree and Assiniboine, who had taken up bison hunting on the northern plains. Both the NWC and HBC actively courted the Ojibwa, seeking to secure their trade allegiance through gifts and bribes, but the trapping bands generally resisted allying themselves with any particular company or fort. Instead, the Ojibwa used their position in the trade to fully exploit the English-Canadian rivalry. They were not above toying with the traders, such as when they asked men from the competing Brandon House posts to run to their camp during the night to see who would be first to collect their furs. The Ojibwa wanted and expected alcohol but also had a penchant for silver jewellery, cloth and beads, and blankets.[70]

A favourite trade item was the HBC "point blanket," brightly coloured (scarlet, empire blue, or green) with a black stripe at each end. Short indigo lines woven below the stripes indicated the weight and size of the blanket, and these "points" determined the value of the blanket in Made Beaver. It was not until the early nineteenth century that the distinctive HBC "chief's blanket," off-white with stripes of indigo, yellow, red, and green at both ends, was introduced.[71] Contrary to popular belief, the famous trade blanket was not English in origin. "Pointed" blankets (listed as *canadast* on shipping invoices) were part of the French North American Indian trade as early as the 1730s. The points on the edge of the blanket (usually stored folded and piled) made it easy for the trader to sort and the buyer to select. Indian tastes varied. The Iroquois preferred deep colours like red and especially blue. In 1779, Montreal trader Germain Maugenest advised the HBC on what new items should be incorporated into the company's interior trade. The following year, the first HBC point blankets were shipped to Fort Albany. They quickly became a trade staple.[72]

The Ojibwa were not the only Aboriginal group to move into the region during this period. Beginning in the late eighteenth century, Iroquois from the Montreal area (also known as *domiciliés*) signed on with the North West Company to work in the western interior as voyageurs, labourers, and trappers. Many of these Iroquois *engagés* fulfilled only one contract but, instead of returning to Quebec at the end of their service, remained in the west and joined the ranks of Canadian Freemen living in small communities throughout the region. Their employment has been called a "subsidized relocation venture."[73] The first reported presence of Iroquois trappers in the western interior was at the NWC post near Netting River in 1794. Several also came to trade at the HBC's Buckingham House three years later. But it was in 1801 that the NWC brought in more than three hundred Iroquois, under three-year contracts, to the Fort Augustus–Edmonton House district to collect beaver skins that the local Cree no longer provided.[74] Other large contingents were recruited over the next two decades, including among them *Tête Jaune* or Yellowhead, whose name is memorialized today in a pass and major highway. Supplied with steel traps and castoreum (scent marking) to attract the animals, the Iroquois cleared entire areas of beaver. William Tomison called them "Robbers and despoilers."[75] But the HBC soon began hiring Iroquois and Algonquin from Quebec to keep pace with the NWC.

Some of these Iroquois *engagés*, who left contracted service, worked for the fur trade settlements in the Saskatchewan country. These forts were not lonely outposts, where English and Canadian men battled boredom and isolation as much as their rivals. Given the different peoples involved in the trade, settlements were racially diverse, inter-ethnic communities, where many languages could be heard when not drowned out by the clatter of children's

HUDSON'S BAY COMPANY ARCHIVES E12.5 FO.7

The Ojibwa (also known as the Saulteaux) moved west in the late eighteenth century to trap for the NWC and HBC.

voices.[76] They were also severely crowded. Alexander Henry the Younger took a census at his Fort Vermilion post in 1809 and counted thirty-six men, twenty-seven women, and sixty-seven children within the confines of the small, walled settlement. This higher proportion of women and children to men was typical at most posts. Most traders had taken Indian wives and enjoyed little family privacy in their cramped quarters unless they were a company officer and accorded separate accommodation. Indian war parties also sometimes left women and children behind at the posts in the expectation that they be protected and cared for. Women's presence at the posts came with the understanding that they would perform any number of menial but essential tasks for the trade, such as manufacturing bales of *watapiy* from spruce and pine roots to stitch everything made from birchbark (canoes, baskets, moose-calling bugles). Their role in pemmican production also meant they were found in even greater numbers at the provisioning posts.[77] When the HBC Committee complained about the cost of supporting these women and children in 1802, the response could not have been more forthright. "Women are deserving of some encouragement and indulgence," the York Factory Council insisted, "they are Virtually your Honors Servants."[78]

Native-newcomer marriages, known as the "custom of the country," have been recognized as a respected institution, equivalent to a formal or church-sanctioned union. But the phrase assumes a uniformity of understanding and purpose when there was actually a "range of diversity ... across time and space... [and in] the degree of internal complexity."[79] William McGillivray of the NWC, for example, took Susan, a mixed-descent woman, for his partner, probably at Île-à-la-Crosse in the late 1780s. And even though they had four children together, he later married the sister of another company partner in 1800. But Susan was not completely abandoned. Upon her death on 28 August 1814, she was buried in Mountainview Cemetery in Thunder Bay (near Grand Portage). Her grave marker reads, "Susan, A Wife of William, A Daughter of the Land, A Mother of the Country."[80] James Bird of the HBC, on the other hand, had an Indian wife at every posting he held along the Saskatchewan and several children through these different liaisons. What is also evident from the surviving historical record is that fur trade couples were never certain what would become of their relationship in the long run. "Indeterminacy," a specialist on the topic has concluded, "was the order of the day."[81] The deeply religious Nor'Wester Daniel Harmon repeatedly resisted accepting a country bride but finally relented in October 1805 when he shared his bed with the fourteen-year-old daughter of a French-Canadian *engagé*. Even then, he intended to live with Lisette only until it came time to leave the North-West, when he would "place her into the hands of some good honest Man"; what was known in the fur trade world as "turning off."[82] But in 1819, Harmon balked at the abandonment of "this woman ... my wife" and his "equally dear" children and took them back (called "taking down") to his New England home.[83] Other traders, such as George Nelson and John Macdonnell, experienced similar periods of doubts and uncertainty "before admitting their unions as marriages."[84]

The headstone of Susan McGillivray, the wife of a North West Company partner

Harmon's marriage to a mixed-descent woman was the harbinger of an 1806 NWC rendezvous decision that henceforth forbade all company men from taking Indian wives and living with them within the posts at company expense. This ruling was intended to rein in the costs of maintaining families. But it was also designed to help mixed-descent daughters find husbands among new company personnel. Winterers, like most fathers, were worried about what would become of their girls and, through this measure, hoped to ensure a more secure future for them. These daughters of the fur trade, knowing only life in the interior, were portrayed as ideal wives. Their marriages to incoming traders would also bolster company solidarity. At the same time, though, they were expected to leave behind their Indian identity and heritage for a more "civilized" life, even though the skills that made them so valuable to the trade had been learned from their mothers.[85] The HBC was no different in this regard. Successive waves of new English servants who came through the bay provided marriage partners for locally born mixed-descent daughters. The alternative was for these girls of company fathers to join their Indian relatives.

The fate of mixed-descent boys was a different challenge. Fathers in positions of authority tried to find work for their sons at the posts, but without any formal education or training, their opportunities were extremely limited. They either returned with their mothers to their Indian families or more likely eked out an existence beyond the forts, providing whatever services they could. This fate did not sit well with some partners and bourgeois, and by the late eighteenth century, they began putting their sons in canoes to be educated back in Montreal. HBC fathers did not have this option, but a few servants managed to find a way around company policy and sent offspring home to England. One of them was HBC officer Ferdinand Jacobs. His son Samuel was educated in England and joined the British East India Company. His daughter Thu'cotch married a local Cree.[86]

Better prospects, at least for HBC boys, appeared at the beginning of the nineteenth century. After blithely ignoring the existence of mixed-descent children for over a century, the company now looked upon the young male population at the posts as an untapped source for apprentices and consequently did away with its decades-long practice of securing teenaged recruits in England. The filling of these apprentice roles by local youths was formalized in 1806 when the HBC Committee announced that it was prepared to educate servants' children at the posts in an effort to "attach them to our Service" and create "a Colony of very useful Hands."[87] These "native" boys, as they were called, played an increasingly important role in trade operations. But their mixed race sentenced many of them to a labouring life with little prospect of advancement.[88]

The other significant HBC policy decision around this time was the dispatch of Peter Fidler to establish a new post, named Chesterfield House, at the junction of the Red Deer and South Saskatchewan Rivers in 1800. This move out onto the northern Great Plains, deep into Blackfoot Alliance territory, has been interpreted as an English effort to generate new trade to make up for the poor returns along the North Saskatchewan. The same year that Chesterfield House was founded, James Bird complained, "There is very little appearance of any trade at this place [Edmonton House] ... there being nothing ... to kill."[89] A decade later, he was even more pessimistic about the fur resources of the region: "I know not how the trade of this River can be supported."[90] The other difficulty for the HBC was that many of its traditional Cree and Assiniboine trading partners had made the transition to mounted hunting societies and were more interested in pursuing bison. One trader bitterly complained that this new lifestyle had made them "a useless sett of lazy indolent fellows a mear nuisance to us."[91]

But if the HBC expected Chesterfield House to make up for this lost trade, then it was deluded. The bulk of the Blackfoot Alliance trade was in wolf pelts, something that the English company devalued once again in 1800—to one-half Made Beaver per pelt—and then ceased collecting in 1809. The other item that plains bands increasingly brought to the posts were bison hides. Here again, though, the HBC was not interested in developing a robe trade because they were difficult to transport to York Factory and there was no market for the bulky skins in Europe. The more likely explanation for the establishment of Chesterfield House was that the HBC and NWC were looking for a major navigable river that would enable them to reach the Pacific. Neither the North Saskatchewan nor Athabasca Rivers appeared to offer a practical transportation route to the west side of the continent, while the South Saskatchewan was still a largely unknown river to the newcomers.[92]

Chesterfield House was located on the advice of the Blackfoot, who in turn assumed the role as post provisioners. They also welcomed the NWC, which followed close on the heels of the HBC to the site. Despite recent troubles, especially with the Gros Ventre, Indian-newcomer relations were generally amicable because trade goods were now more readily available. An estimated fourteen hundred Blackfoot men, women, and children converged on the post in the fall of 1801. Several Indian men even drew maps for Fidler, sharing their knowledge of the geography of the northwestern plains, in particular the South Saskatchewan and Missouri River basins.[93] The situation turned threatening, though, when the Gros Ventres suffered a firestorm of calamities: heavy casualties in two lopsided skirmishes with the Cree and Assiniboine in the summer of 1801; then one hundred deaths, mostly children, in a localized smallpox epidemic that same year; and finally, the loss of more than 250 horses to cold weather and theft during the winter of 1801–02.[94] Reeling from their misfortunes, the Gros Ventre once again sought revenge against the traders who were supplying their enemies. They "appears desperate," is how Fidler described their demeanour, "and ... nearly ready to fall on anyone they can."[95] Such was the fate of a small group of Iroquois and Canadian Freemen, who had been killed and mutilated after being caught out on the open plains in March 1802. But before the Gros Ventre could assemble a war party to attack the palisaded Chesterfield House, both English and Canadian traders fled at the first opportunity under the protection of the Blackfoot.

Relations between the Cree and Assiniboine and their supposed Blackfoot Alliance allies were little better at the time. Since the late 1790s, the two groups—with the Gros Ventre thrown into the mix—had regularly skirmished each summer in an ongoing contest over territory, bison, and horses. Daniel Harmon in the Swan River department noted that the Cree and Assiniboine usually returned from these clashes with enemy women and children as slaves. But by August 1803, "both parties," according to Harmon, had become "weary of such a bloody War ... for such a length of time ... and are therefore much inclined to patch up a Peace on almost any terms whatever."[96] This truce could not withstand, however, the unremitting demand and competition for horses. With the Mandan–Hidatsas villages of the Upper Missouri now able to secure goods from HBC, NWC, and increasingly American traders in the early nineteenth century, the Cree and Assiniboine had to look westward for replacement stock. In fact, they were the ones who had taken the Gros Ventre horses during their winter of discontent in 1801–02. They also continued to raid Blackfoot herds, despite the general desire for peace, and effectively brought about a realignment in tribal affiliations. The tenuous cooperation between the Blackfoot Alliance and Cree and Assiniboine bands, which dated back to the mid-eighteenth century on the northern plains, came to an end. In its place, the Blackfoot Alliance sought to assert its independence as the dominant bison-hunting peoples on the north-central plains, picking allies and fighting

This graffiti (F.B. Porteous July 26,1810) on a sandstone outcrop along the Souris River, near the present-day Roche Percee, was probably left by a trader who worked at one of the pemmican posts in the area.

enemies in keeping with its interests.

What finally triggered the collapse in relations was a heated squabble, ironically, over a horse. While travelling together in July 1806, Blackfoot and Cree/Assiniboine bands came to blows over who owned the animal. After a pitched battle, in which many more Blackfoot were killed, the Cree and Assiniboine hastily dispersed to the shelter of the nearby woods. But there was no hiding from the repercussions. "Indiscriminate Vengeance," is what James Bird expected upon learning the news as he travelled inland to Edmonton House that August. "How far the effects of this quarrel may extend its impossible to foresee."[97] The HBC brigade that Bird was leading soon caught up to its NWC counterpart on the North Saskatchewan and found the Montreal men stricken with fear. They had been fired on by a large group of mounted Assiniboine. The two groups warily pushed on in tandem and eventually came upon the same Assiniboine, camped along the river and themselves afraid of being attacked by the Blackfoot. Bird found the mood equally dark on reaching Fort Augustus– Edmonton House, where the residents were worried for their safety.[98]

No Blackfoot came to trade at the North Saskatchewan posts during the winter of 1806–07. Nor did many Cree and Assiniboine venture out onto the northwestern plains south of the river. These developments alarmed the traders, who were not simply concerned about the securing of country provisions in the short term but also worried about the larger implications, especially if the intertribal feud continued for several trade seasons. Blackfoot bands finally appeared at Fort Edmonton in the late spring of 1807, and after a quiet summer of little unrest, a peace seemed to have taken hold. But then fighting erupted again, transforming the region into a combat zone.[99] Indian leaders, in particular the Blackfoot Old Swan and Peigan Young Man, who might have had a moderating influence on the situation, as they had done in the past, were now dead.[100] Nor could traders simply remove themselves from the unfolding conflict but faced constant danger as the warring parties railed against them for arming their enemies. In the fall of 1807, an Assiniboine group abruptly shot dead HBC servant William Walker when he balked at surrendering his horses. The perpetrators of the killing told the Indian women accompanying Walker, "all white Men were equally satisfactory Objects for their Vengeance."[101]

By the end of the first decade of the nineteenth century, both the HBC and NWC were on the defensive. It was even rumoured that the Cree and Assiniboine planned to launch an offensive against the newcomers and drive them from the Saskatchewan country. The traders deliberately avoided any provocation, often resorting to alcohol in an effort to maintain cordial relations with the various bands. But they also consolidated some of their operations. Their houses (St. Louis [NWC] and Carlton [HBC]) on the South Saskatchewan River were abandoned in 1810 in favour of building new forts together, for a short period of time, on the north branch. They were helpless, however, in curtailing the incessant horse raiding, a seeming prelude to an eventual attack. That is certainly what Alexander Henry at Fort Vermilion had come to expect: "the Indians ... were in general badly inclined towards us, and fully determined to do us mischief, if they could find an opportunity."[102] The days of accommodation had evidently come to an end, and trade might have to withdraw from the northern edge of the great plains in favour of confining its activities to the boreal forest. But there, too, a fierce battle raged, only this contest was fought between the traders over control of the Athabasca country.

The Hudson's Bay Company spent several years searching for a feasible trade route from Reindeer Lake (pictured here) to the Athabasca country.

BILL WAISER

CHAPTER NINE

HOW VERY DIFFERENT

ON 21 MAY 1797, DAVID THOMPSON LEFT BEDFORD HOUSE AT VERMILION POINT on the remote western shore of Reindeer Lake and headed south about sixty miles to the rival North West Company post at the bottom of the huge lake. His contract as "Surveyor to the Northward" with the Hudson's Bay Company had ended that day and he wanted to join the opposition. Thompson's defection was yet another indication of how the Montreal merchants were winning the fur trade war in the North-West. Even though the young Welsh-born apprentice had been specially trained in astronomy over the winter of 1789–90—the Indians knew him as the man who gazed at stars—Thompson felt no allegiance to the company. In fact, the York Factory governor claimed that the Nor'Westers had secretly promoted the surveyor's departure. Thompson certainly did not need much encouragement. He saw only a dead-end future with the English company and made his move once winter had released its grip on Bedford House. "How very different," he later wrote, "the liberal and public spirit of this North West Company ... from the mean selfish policy of the Hudson's Bay Company styled Honourable."[1]

The short, stocky Thompson, with his mixed-descent partner Charlotte[2] at his side, surveyed several thousand miles for the North West Company. He crossed the prairies to visit the Mandan–Hidatsa villages in North Dakota and push the fur trade over the Rocky Mountains. And in 1814, two years after his retirement to Quebec, he produced his master work, a great map of northwestern North America that hung in the Great Hall at the NWC rendezvous headquarters at Fort William at the northwestern end of Lake

Superior.[3] But ironically, even though Thompson decided to throw in his lot with the Nor'Westers, it was a reinvigorated Hudson's Bay Company that emerged triumphant in 1821.

HBC servant David Thompson may have wanted to work for a company with imagination and drive, but it was the balance sheet that revealed how much the Nor'Westers were dominating the fur trade. As of 1795, the North West Company controlled 11/14ths or nearly 80 per cent, while the HBC had a paltry 2/14ths (less than 15 per cent). Independents fought over the remainder. These "magnificent returns" were necessary—no, required—if the NWC was going to "make the system pay" and overcome the costs of its inland transportation route from Montreal.[4] But they also underscored how the rival HBC was effectively absent from the fur-rich Athabasca country. Because the company sought to avoid the Canadian presence on the Churchill River, Thompson had devoted four dispiriting years (1792–96) to finding an alternative trade route west through present-day northern Saskatchewan, from Reindeer Lake

Charlotte Small and David Thompson statue at Invermere, British Columbia

349-TRACKING UP ATHABASCA RIVER,

UNIVERSITY OF SASKATCHEWAN ARCHIVES AND SPECIAL COLLECTIONS MSS C550/1/24.1

Tracking up the Athabasca River

to Lake Athabasca. He finally accomplished the task in the summer of 1796, only to quit the HBC a year later in frustration. Thompson believed that if the company had taken a more expansive view of its opportunities, he "might have had the northern part of this continent surveyed to the Pacific Ocean, and greatly extended their trading posts!"[5]

The NWC, by contrast, had a much better appreciation of Thompson's talents and immediately put him to work locating the new international boundary established by Jay's Treaty. From Grand Portage in the late summer of 1797, Thompson surveyed westward to the Red and Assiniboine Rivers, then cut south to the Missouri and the headwaters of the Mississippi, before returning eastward along the south shore of Lake Superior and around to his starting point. The year-long exercise determined which NWC posts were in American territory. It also forced the Montreal fur merchants to question their continued operation in the United States—no small matter when the southwest trade constituted almost half the value of their business. Many like Simon McTavish were ready to withdraw north of the border, reasoning that "losses to the south should be replaced by expansion in the north and west." But by "turn[ing] with full purpose" to the vast hinterland beyond Lake Superior, the Nor'Westers not only intensified their struggle with the HBC but also made the fur-rich Athabasca country all the more important to their commercial supremacy.[6]

The North West Company went virtually unchallenged above the Churchill River until the end of the eighteenth century. There had been competitors nosing into the region in the 1780s and 1790s, but all had been "crushed," in the words of an early fur trade scholar, "with ruthless efficiency."[7] And with the Montreal traders firmly in control, travel to and from the region assumed a regularity that seemed nothing short of miraculous given the great distances involved. The canoe route from Grand Portage at the western end of Lake Superior followed a series of lakes and rivers west to the mouth of Lake Winnipeg, then northwest across Lake Winnipeg to Cedar Lake and the entrance to the Saskatchewan River. At Cumberland House, the route continued north through the Sturgeon–Weir River to the Churchill River, turned west along the Churchill to Buffalo Narrows (Île-à-la-Crosse), and then north to Methye Portage. On the other side of the watershed, the route went down the Clearwater and then Athabasca River to Lake Athabasca (straddling present-day northwestern Saskatchewan and northeastern Alberta). Nor'Wester Alexander Mackenzie reckoned that it was 2,750 miles from Montreal to the far northwest—and that did not include the rivers and lakes beyond Lake Athabasca. To deal with this great distance, a second transhipment point, specifically for the Athabasca brigades, was developed at Portage Lac la Pluie (Rainy Lake) in present-day northwestern Ontario; here, they exchanged furs in mid-July for goods that had been brought up from Grand Portage and took on or left behind any personnel.[8] Speed was also an essential feature of the trade traffic, as Peter Fidler witnessed from his HBC posting at Cumberland House in 1796. On 29 June, he reported that a NWC brigade, carrying one hundred bundles of fur in four canoes, had required only six weeks to reach there from Great Slave Lake. Then, on 19 August, he greeted

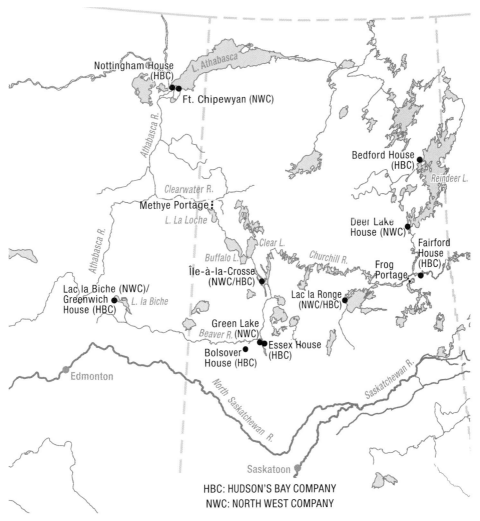

Selected fur trade posts in northern Saskatchewan and Alberta, circa late 1700s

another brigade, this one headed inland in a race against freeze-up, which had covered the distance from Lac la Pluie in just seventeen days.[9]

These travel speeds were, in part, made possible by the unrelenting search for efficiencies. No detail was too trivial if it gave the NWC an advantage, especially given the short open water season on northern lakes. At Methye Portage, for example, voyageurs sometimes hired Indian packers to help move goods and furs along the formidable trail. They also used tar, found oozing from the banks of the Athabasca, to gum the bottom of their canoes to increase their resiliency.[10] But what really placed the Nor'Westers in a commanding position in Athabasca, and enabled them to move between there with such authority, was the location of another interior depot—known as Fort Chipewyan—along the southwestern shore of the lake in 1788. This rendezvous centre, second only to the one at Grand Portage, was called the "Grand Magazine" of the north because its storehouses contained two years' worth of goods. Philip Turnor of the rival HBC called it "the compleatist inland House I have seen in the country."[11] Fort Chipewyan gave the NWC a secure supply base that allowed for and promoted a regularity of travel to and from the region. It also facilitated direct trade with the Chipewyan, while supporting expansion into the Peace and Mackenzie districts. Even the perennial food problem was resolved through the development of a provision trade with Indian bands along the Peace River. But any pemmican produced at the fort was usually reserved for the brigades, leaving the residents to subsist largely on fish, at a daily allowance of eight pounds per man![12]

The local Chipewyan welcomed the establishment of Fort Chipewyan because it saved them from making the perilous overland trip to Fort Churchill to trade with the HBC. Up to then, they could not count on a reliable source of goods from the Canadians. In 1786, for example, a NWC attempt to establish a post on Great Slave Lake ended in failure, and the Chipewyan were forced to take their furs to the English the following spring. Now, with a major NWC entrepot on Lake Athabasca, the Chipewyan used their emerging position as "home" Indians to prevent other northern bands from dealing directly with the NWC. They also employed the same tactics as the Montreal traders and bargained fiercely for their furs and provisions. At times, not even free-flowing liquor or a beating could get them to lessen their demands. The Nor'Westers retaliated by taking women and children as hostages in order to force the Chipewyan men to cooperate or at least be more compliant. Some decided to take their business to Fort Churchill, even if the journey to the Hudson Bay coast brought them to the brink of starvation.[13]

NWC operations along the Churchill River corridor, or what was known as the English River district, ran more smoothly. A growing mixed-descent

Fort Chipewyan served as the North West Company supply base on Lake Athabasca.

population served as the local labour force, particularly at the administrative depot at Île-à-la-Crosse and the provisioning post on Lac Vert (Green Lake), which collected pemmican from the forts on the North Saskatchewan for the northern brigades. These children of the fur trade included Charlotte Small, David Thompson's partner, and Louis Riel, Sr., both born at Île-à-la-Crosse. There were times, though, when the Nor'Westers in the region doled out "rough justice" to anyone who came between them and the trade. Such was the case in June 1796 when two Cree men, Beardy and Little Gut, accused of murdering a trader near Île-à-la-Crosse, were pursued to Cumberland House by several Canadians. Little Gut was shot dead, and Beardy summarily hanged, but only after he had been forced to confess to the crime with the rope about his neck. Both bodies were left to rot, but Peter Fidler, shocked by the incident, saw to it that they were buried.[14] The message was brutally clear: NWC men would take whatever revenge was necessary to impose their will in what they regarded as their territory.

Violence became the norm once a new rival entered the western Canadian fur trade at the end of the eighteenth century. The Montreal firms of Forsyth,

Richardson and Company and Parker, Gerald, and Olgivy wanted to become partners in the NWC when Jay's Treaty brought an end to their commercial operations south of the new international border. But they were offered only a piddling share in the North-West trade. They consequently launched, in 1798, a rival amalgamation of merchants and winterers, appropriately called the New North West Company. (It was later known as Sir Alexander Mackenzie and Company, when the disaffected trader and explorer became a leading partner in 1802.) To differentiate its fur bales from the "N" and "W" used by the NWC, the new company marked its goods with "X" and "Y." This simple measure resulted in the popular alternative name, the XY Company.

The Nor'Westers mockingly referred to the new competition as the "Little Company," or less charitably, as the "Potties" (probably from the French words, *les petits*). Daniel Harmon's declaration—"we would wish to crush them at once"—captured the attitude of many in the trade anxious to put this new challenger in its place.[15] The XY Company, though, was no pushover. It brought to the western trade the same strength, determination, and methods as its older Montreal rival and was ready to resort to whatever means were necessary to capture the spoils, including, if necessary, meeting violence with violence. What embittered this contest, made it more of a war in all but name, was the hatred that one-time partners Alexander Mackenzie and Simon McTavish held for each other. There was no reconciliation as long as these two men dominated their respective companies. And why should there be? Both sides paid lip service to the belief that whatever company emerged triumphant would easily subdue the weaker and vulnerable HBC, as if it were some kind of consolation prize for the losses that had to borne in winning the battle.[16]

Booze has been called "the corner-stone" of the pedlar trade.[17] That observation took on new meaning during the protracted struggle between the NWC and the upstart XYC. In the mid-1790s, the NWC brought into the western interior on average about ninety-six hundred gallons of alcohol per trading season. But by 1803, five years after the launch of the XYC, the new and old companies were annually importing five thousand and sixteen thousand

A provisioning depot at Green Lake collected pemmican from the northern plains
to feed canoe brigades.

gallons, respectively. In other words, the volume of spirits—*before* they were diluted for the trade—had more than doubled.[18] The ready availability of booze was accompanied by a mixture of gift-giving, flattery, cajoling, bullying, or outright intimidation, all dependent on the particular situation. As a further inducement, the two Montreal-based companies also adjusted the standard of trade, offering Indians more goods for fewer furs to try to secure the loyalty of local bands, especially in highly competitive areas. But this tactic actually worked against the rival trading firms, in that they often ended up with diminishing fur returns relative to the amount of goods demanded in exchange. The NWC and XYC responded to this problem by hiring an ever-increasing number of Indian trappers, mostly Iroquois, but also Nipissings and Algonquins, from central Canada in the first few years of the nineteenth century. This spike in "paid" hunters led to over-trapping in several districts, all the more so because the quality of the beaver skin no longer mattered because of advances in the making of hat felt by mechanized combing. Any beaver at any time of year was now valued and taken in the trade.[19]

The XY Company entered the NWC stronghold in Athabasca in 1799. It built competing posts near Fort Chipewyan and outlying areas and drew provisions from the Peace River country. The Nor'Westers regarded these actions as a direct threat to their fur trade empire and were determined to expel the intruders, if not neutralize their operations. They watched their opponents' movements constantly and, when not verbally and physically harassing them, scooped up any available furs and provisions. "Preventing the opposition from making returns is the Great Point," declared one trader, "and nothing must stand in its way."[20] The NWC was able to overwhelm the competition by sheer force of numbers. Because the Athabasca trade was so profitable, over one-third of all company personnel, provisions, and goods were concentrated there. The NWC consequently had at least twice as many men in the field (more than one thousand) to the XYC's four hundred.[21] And what the Nor'Westers could not achieve by numerical strength, they did so with deadly force. But unlike the HBC, which recoiled from any violent confrontation with the NWC, the XYC gamely struck back. As one historian noted, the fur trade had been carried on "within the limits of the legitimate" to the end of the eighteenth century. The NWC/XYC feud changed that. "Men in ordinary circumstances inclined to be honourable," he observed, "became steeped in dishonour."[22]

The HBC stepped into the middle of this struggle in 1802 when it returned to the Athabasca country after a ten-year absence. The company's reappearance on the shores of Lake Athabasca had been delayed because of William Tomison's insistence on focusing on the Saskatchewan country and later infighting between Fort Churchill and York Factory over which post should spearhead the expansion. It had also experienced difficulty in finding men willing to take part in the initiative. And when the HBC finally embarked on the campaign, it took a "purposeful approach" from the Saskatchewan country to the south, not the "hard and bitter route" that David Thompson had plotted west from Reindeer Lake. Under surveyor Peter Fidler's leadership and directed by an Indian guide (simply identified as White Boy), posts were first established in 1799 at Green Lake (Essex House), Meadow Lake (Bolsover House, named after Fidler's birthplace in England), Île-à-la-Crosse, and Lac la Biche (Greenwich House). Surveys were also conducted in the region, especially

Nor'Wester Peter Skene Ogden (left) did all he could to drive the HBC from
the Athabasca and Churchill regions.

the river routes. Three years later, Fidler crossed Methye Portage and built
Nottingham House, not far from the fabled NWC Fort Chipewyan.[23] William
Auld, stationed at Green Lake, documented in his journal the many problems
that the HBC had faced in gaining this claim to a share of the Athabasca trade:
from an inadequate supply of provisions, especially brandy, to the difficulty of
travelling with heavy York boats to the need for company servants "who can
talk with the Natives or who understand them."[24]

The HBC entry into the Athabasca trade presented local Indians
with an alternative trading partner. But the XYC and especially the NWC
men forcibly prevented the Indians—by beatings and other forms of
brutality if necessary—from dealing with their English counterparts. They
also substantially increased their use of alcohol and other inducements to
reinforce their trade loyalty.[25] "We are so very few," Fidler lamented at one
point," they so numerous."[26] The HBC servants had good reason to stay out
of the fray, because they were salaried employees and were paid regardless
of how much trade was conducted. The company had also instructed its men
to "avoid all occasion of violent conflict [and] any act of aggression," but

practice "forbearance."[27] The other problem was their lack of experience in this kind of angry trade atmosphere. Among the recent company recruits in the late eighteenth century were boys, aged twelve to fourteen years old. The Nor'Westers delighted in ridiculing them "not because they were slow to take offence but because they could not fire a gun."[28]

The Cree and Chipewyan, on the other hand, used the heightened competition to insist on even higher prices for even fewer of their furs and provisions. Returns actually declined in some areas as the consumption of alcohol became rampant among local Indians. The NWC and XYC consequently increasingly turned to Iroquois trappers, maintaining, for example, seventy-six and ninety-three men, respectively, in the Peace River district in 1804.[29] The efficiency of these imported hunters further alienated the Chipewyan, many of whom decided to abandon the trade and return to their traditional caribou-hunting lifestyle on the barrens. Some of the more aggrieved, though, retaliated against the traders. In 1804, four Canadians were murdered outside Fort Chipewyan, while the seasonal NWC Fond du Lac post at the extreme easterly end of Lake Athabasca (in Saskatchewan) was destroyed and the inhabitants, including women and children, killed.[30]

These incidents were accompanied that same year by a major development in the Canadian fur trade—the folding of the XYC into the NWC. The July 1804 death of Simon McTavish opened the way to negotiations between the two Montreal companies, and a deal was reached in November to bring the firms and wintering partners of the XYC into an enlarged NWC. Interestingly, one of the key features of the agreement was an article anticipating the future takeover of the HBC. This provision reflected the thinking of Sir Alexander Mackenzie during his time at the head of the XYC. Looking at the distance problem from a continental perspective, Mackenzie had come to believe that the best way to carry on trade to the Pacific coast (via the Columbia River) and eventually China was through Hudson Bay and not Montreal. He first tried to convince the British government to grant him access to the bay, and when that failed, he tried unsuccessfully to buy enough controlling stock in the HBC. Now, with the

The NWC sought to deal directly with the trapping Indians and prevent them from
trading with the HBC.

two Canadian companies united, the NWC could use its commercial prowess
to force the HBC into negotiations.[31]

The battleground for this new contest remained the Athabasca country.
It was here that the NWC secured the profits that allowed it to underwrite the
otherwise prohibitive costs of its overland route, and it was here that the NWC
decided to strike at HBC operations and drive the English company from the
region and all the way back down the Churchill River. Fidler at Nottingham
House bore the brunt of the Nor'Wester abuse. No sooner had news of the
merger reached the district than his opponents warned him that they would

"act with the greatest of rigor toward us."[32] This threat was executed by Samuel Black, a former XYC clerk who was little more than a ruffian. He built a blockhouse to keep Indians and their furs and provisions away from the HBC post. He stole the firewood and pulled up the vegetable garden. He destroyed the fishing nets and chased away any game. He broke their canoes. And he skulked about the fort, shouting and discharging his pistols at all hours.

The bullying and harassment extended to the English River district. In August 1804, HBC chief trader William Linklater at Île-à-la-Crosse had to squelch the rumour, roundly circulated by the Canadians, that Fort Churchill and its garrison had been wiped out. Then, in October 1805, a NWC gang kidnapped HBC servant Magnus Johnston near Green Lake because he was wintering with the local Cree. Dragged away from the settlement, he was informed that he was to have no dealings with "their" Indians and then abandoned on an island with no canoe. When Linklater learned what had happened to Johnston, he demanded an explanation from his NWC counterpart for their "Villainous Action." The answer came in the form of a warning: "they could do us a deal more mischief if they pleased."[33] The Cree certainly understood the local fur trade dynamics. Linklater reported that the Indians had been browbeaten to the point where they refused to trade with the English out of fear of being punished by the NWC.[34] This kind of intimidation was unthinkable in the Saskatchewan country, where pre-trade ceremonies remained essential to securing the allegiance of local bands.

In 1806, a beleaguered Fidler abandoned Nottingham House and retreated south of Methye Portage and the height of land to Île-à-la-Crosse. It was an ignominious end to the HBC presence in the Athabasca country. But even the Chipewyan were withdrawing from the NWC trade. Despite the difficulties of the trip across the barrens, a large party arrived at Fort Churchill in August 1807 and another one the following spring, both intent on maximizing their trade with the English.[35] Fidler, meanwhile, spent the summer of 1807 looking for an alternative water route to Lake Athabasca through present-day northern Saskatchewan. David Thompson had performed the same search in

The NWC and HBC had a tumultuous relationship at Île-à-la-Crosse, shown here.

1795–96, and a decade later under Fidler, the result was no different: Methye Portage remained the most practical way to get to the Athabasca country. During his survey, Fidler named Wollaston Lake, a huge lake immediately west of Reindeer Lake, in honour of George Hyde Wollaston, a member of the HBC London Committee. Thompson had earlier noticed that Wollaston Lake (known to the local Chipewyan as Hatchet or Axe) was "perhaps without a parallel in the world" because it straddled two watersheds; water from the lake flowed to the Arctic Ocean through both the Mackenzie River and Hudson Bay drainage basins.[36]

Fidler's withdrawal from Lake Athabasca and the disappointing results of his subsequent survey in northern Saskatchewan were symptomatic of a general malaise that gripped the HBC in the early nineteenth century. "Laughably weak" is how the NWC regarded the English company's recent attempt to wrest away some of the Athabasca trade, and certain to result in a "succession of repeated indignities" if it continued along the same lines. Nor were HBC servants much more charitable about company operations. One who spent the winter of 1808–09 in "the most miserable hovel that imagination can conceive" on Reindeer Lake, suggested that his experience evoked "the glimmering dying lights of an expiring Commerce."[37] Back in England, the mood of the London Committee was equally bleak, so much so that there was talk of withdrawing

LIBRARY AND ARCHIVES CANADA C-001916, PETER RINDISBACHER

The NWC tried to secure access to Hudson Bay to overcome the disadvantages of the Montreal route.

from the fur trade. Shareholder dividends that had once averaged around 8 per cent had declined by half in the new century and then ceased being paid in 1809. Company stock prices reflected this downturn in company fortunes. And there appeared to be little likelihood of the situation turning around as long as Europe was engulfed in the Napoleonic wars. The company had not been able to export furs to the continental market since 1806. Union with the rival NWC offered a possible way out of the financial quagmire. But instead, at Wollaston's urging, the HBC contemplated going into the timber trade.[38]

This defeatist attitude did not sit well with some of the men who had done battle with the North West Company. William Auld, who commanded Churchill, was frustrated by the activities of the Montreal pedlars in the HBC's own backyard. "Good God!" he bemoaned. "See the Canadians come thousands of miles beyond us to monopolise the most valuable part of our Territories."[39] Auld bluntly told the London Committee during a visit to England in 1809 that the company had to make a stand in Athabasca and that it had to start by reconsidering how it engaged its rival in the trade. His voice was joined by Colin Robertson, a NWC defector who travelled to London to present his views on the trade. Robertson suggested that the HBC effectively had to go to "war" in the Athabasca country, turning the NWC's advantage there into a liability by challenging its monopoly position in the region.

Until that challenge was forthcoming, the HBC presence even along the Churchill River was tenuous at best. Having driven its English competitor from Lake Athabasca, the NWC set its sights on undermining the HBC post at Île-à-la-Crosse under the command of Robert Sutherland. Fidler was there that winter, and his 1810–11 journal is an account of unrelenting NWC abuse and intimidation, largely at the hands of his nemesis Samuel Black and his thuggish partner Peter Skene Ogden. The two brutes, brandishing daggers and pistols, did everything they could to make life miserable for the HBC servants, all the while daring anyone to stand up to them. When Fidler finally confronted them one day in late October and protested their presence inside the settlement stockade, Ogden slashed his coat with his dagger, while Black broke his left thumb with a blow from a stick. Later that winter, the pair threatened to break the legs of any HBC man who left the post, saying that they would watch for footprints in the snow to see that they were obeyed.

This confinement might have been tolerable if local Indians had visited the settlement, but Black and Ogden chased them away, often resorting to physical force. Even worse, HBC fisherman Andrew Kirkness and his Indian partner had an argument that sent her scurrying over to the NWC post in anger. When Kirkness tried to retrieve her the next day, the Nor'Westers vowed to cut off her ears if she left. Kirkness consequently went to live with her, leaving the HBC settlement without the services of the couple. Fidler's wife Mary, a Swampy Cree woman from York Factory, had to do the fishing for the post. And when Kirkness later tried to rejoin his HBC colleagues, Black told him that "they would make every Canadian in their House ravish his woman before his Eyes."[40] This terrorization campaign—and that is exactly what it was—steadily ate away at any remaining HBC resolve. By late January 1811, Fidler confided to his journal that "every man of ours here say they would not remain here again for any thing whatever."[41] The entire garrison glumly abandoned the post on 4 June for the bay and had travelled only a few hours before smoke was seen coming from the evacuated structures.

This retreat was not repeated. Instead of withdrawing from the fur trade, the HBC found a new purpose and vitality under the steadying hand of Andrew Wedderburn, also known as Colvile, who joined the London Committee at its nadir. Colvile pushed for a reorganization of company operations based on the principles of efficiency and initiative, what he called his "retrenching" or "new system." He imposed a new administrative framework on North America, dividing Rupert's Land into Northern and Southern departments, each with their own districts and posts, in an effort to bring greater order to company operations. (All posts above Cumberland House were part of a new Saskatchewan district in the Northern department.) Post masters, meanwhile, were to be granted greater discretion in how they handled the trade in their particular region, including the setting of exchange standards or prices, without having to look to London all the time for direction and approval. And taking a page from the NWC business plan, employees were promised improved compensation, including a possible share of HBC profits. These changes were announced in a company circular in 1810, which called on servants to replace the "abject submission" of the past with a "determined firmness" in the future. "Weakness or timidity" could not offer a "defence of the Company's just Rights."[42]

Colvile's retrenching plan was regarded as a necessary first step in the eventual HBC assault on the NWC Athabascan stronghold. It was only after company business affairs were in better shape and servants better attuned to the new company philosophy that a campaign there would have any hope of success. But the decision to remain in the fur trade and update and revise company practices also reflected the new realities of North American geopolitics and trade dynamics. In 1803, the United States acquired France's claim to the Louisiana Territory, a parcel of land over eight hundred thousand square miles from the Mississippi River west to the Rocky Mountains The

The NWC viewed the establishment of the Red River colony as a threat to the
bison hunt in the region—and its pemmican supply.

following year, Meriwether Lewis and William Clark left St. Louis on their now
famous reconnaissance expedition and ascended the Missouri River before
continuing overland to the Pacific coast. They carried with them Alexander
Mackenzie's *Voyages from Montreal ... to the Frozen and Pacific Oceans*, as well
as copies of some of David Thompson's and Peter Fidler's maps. Although the
expedition had fact-finding purposes—to acquire knowledge about the region,
its peoples, and resources—the Thomas Jefferson administration was wary of
the activities of Canadian traders in the upper Missouri region and sought to
assert American sovereignty and promote American commerce.[43]

John Jacob Astor's American Fur Company, founded in 1808, was one of
the beneficiaries of this new aggressive expansion policy. By the end of the first
decade of the nineteenth century, then, the HBC and NWC had to contend
with an upstart, increasingly powerful competitor in the North American
fur trade. And if the HBC vacated the field, even temporarily, it would allow
the NWC to consolidate and enlarge its trade empire northwest of the Great

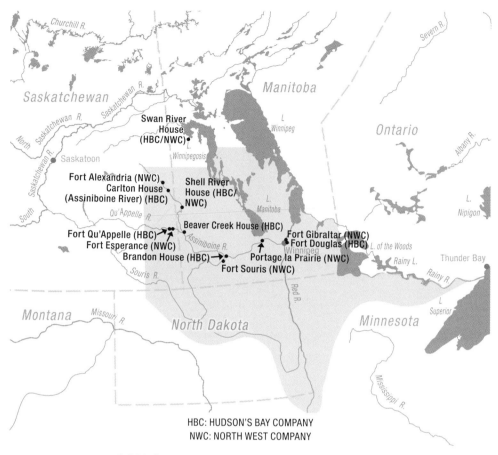

HBC: HUDSON'S BAY COMPANY
NWC: NORTH WEST COMPANY

Selkirk Grant and selected fur trade posts in early 1800s

Lakes, and equally important, make it difficult to get back in. The HBC really had no choice but to gird itself and go on the offensive, or be pushed aside by the continent-wide contest for territory and trade.

One of the key elements of the HBC's revitalization scheme was the establishment of an agricultural settlement in company territory. The idea for the Red River Colony originated with Thomas Douglas, the Fifth Earl of Selkirk and a major HBC stockholder. Douglas was deeply troubled by how changes in agricultural practices were displacing Scottish crofters and had initially conceived of the settlement as the new home for these sturdy farmers. But with the HBC looking for a way out of its difficulties, the scheme was expanded to include retired company servants and their families in order to relieve posts of the burden of supporting those who chose not to return to the British Isles at the end of their term of service. It also dovetailed nicely with Colvile's retrenching system in that the colony was expected to provide agricultural foodstuffs and thereby save the company the expense of importing provisions—a perennial problem since the establishment of the HBC. And as a bonus, the settlement served as a future labour pool for the fur trade, providing a steady supply of native-born servants whose ready familiarity with the environment would probably enable them to step more easily into various positions.

The Red River Colony, later known as Assiniboia, was formally established in June 1811 when the London Committee granted Selkirk 116,000 square miles of land in present-day southern Manitoba.[44] It was situated squarely in the region that was the source for much of the trade pemmican, and the NWC immediately charged that the settlement was a thinly disguised attempt to undermine its operations in the Athabasca country. "They are striking at the very root of the Fur trade," ominously warned one Nor'Wester.[45] This apparent linkage between the colony and the HBC's wider ambitions was not difficult to make. Food was the limiting factor in the expansion of the fur trade. Without access to a steady and ample supply of bison pemmican, newcomers were not able to push their activities from the rim of the great plains and the Saskatchewan country into the boreal forest and beyond. It was the energy source that not only fuelled the competitive fur trade in the western interior in the late eighteenth and early nineteenth centuries, but also propelled the NWC to the distant northwest despite its long supply line from Montreal. Pemmican was also essential to the financial viability of the NWC. Without the constant production of pemmican, the NWC would not have been able to reap the great rewards of the Athabasca trade. That is why, then, the production of bison meat and fat became such an industry in the Red, Assiniboine, and Qu'Appelle districts. It is also why a summer hunt was introduced when winter pounding could not meet the demand. To facilitate this new activity, the Canadians traded for horses from the Mandan–Hidatsa villages on the upper Missouri. Many of these animals ended up in the hands of Freemen or Métis who took up mounted hunting to provide the NWC with pemmican.[46]

CANADA BEFORE CONFEDERATION

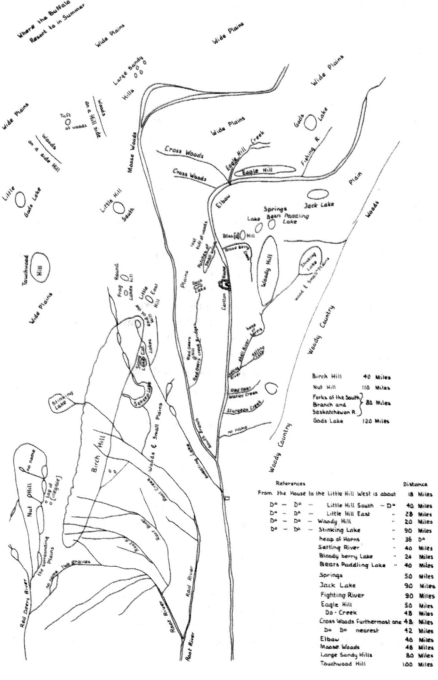

HBC servant James Bird's sketch of the Carlton district (redrawn)

The NWC first tried to derail the Selkirk scheme by proposing a partition of the fur country. Just days after the land grant was approved, senior Nor'Westers in London put forward a plan that confined the HBC to the land east of Reindeer Lake. The Athabasca country (including Lac Île-à-la-Crosse) and the region beyond the Rockies were to be closed to the English company. Nor did the proposal mention HBC control of the Red River area. That was open to negotiation but only if the Athabasca district was recognized as NWC territory. The Nor'Westers maintained that they were acting in the interests of avoiding conflict and possible bloodshed. But the London Committee flatly rejected any partition of the country, insisting instead that the NWC was obligated to respect its charter rights.[47]

When the Selkirk Settlement consequently went ahead, it was seen as an attack on its provisioning system and, hence, its Athabasca operations. The early years of the settlement seemed to confirm this interpretation. Because of poor harvests, the settlers had to take refuge during their first few winters at the HBC post at Pembina and subsist largely on pemmican. In fact, the acute shortage of food prompted the colony's governor in January 1814 to impose a one-year ban on the export of pemmican from the region. Drought compounded the problem. The exceedingly hot, dry summers of 1812 and 1813 spawned immense fires across the northern prairies that consumed large swaths of grassland and drove the bison herds south.[48] Hunters scrambled to find meat supplies for the provisioning posts. It was not until 1815, when the bison returned in great numbers to the northern plains, that the posts were flush with pemmican again. This surplus, though, did nothing to dissuade the NWC from its determination to destroy the fledgling colony. The Nor'Westers told local Métis hunters that Selkirk's scheme was a threat to their provisioning activities and encouraged them to harass the settlers to force them to abandon the project. These hit-and-run raids became deadly when the two groups unintentionally clashed at Seven Oaks in June 1816. Twenty-two settlers were felled by the skilled Métis horsemen. The horrific incident gave "a new edge"[49] to the rivalry between the rival companies and promised to make the battle over the Athabasca country all the more bitter and vicious. Colin Robertson, the former Nor'Wester turned HBC man, certainly had no delusions about what lay ahead. "Opposition as these men understand it," he wrote of the forthcoming campaign in his diary.[50]

But what neither side expected was a dramatic change in the climate. The late 1810s were decidedly colder, part of a long interval of below average temperatures from the late eighteenth to the mid-nineteenth century. Based on tree ring records from the Canadian Rockies, the 1810s stand out as one of the coldest four decades in the past nine hundred years.[51] But it was not just the winters that were frigid; the summers were cold, too, especially 1816, popularly known as the year without summer. The culprit was a volcanic eruption—the largest in fifteen hundred years—on Sumbawa Island in present-day Indonesia. In April 1815, Mount Tambora literally blew up, spewing a massive volume of ash into the earth's atmosphere. By the following spring, cool weather descended on parts of northeastern North America and western Europe, precipitating widespread crop failures for one, sometimes two or three consecutive seasons. Nor was the North-West spared. By 1819, Peter Fidler at Red River was complaining, "Within the last 3 years the climate seems to be greatly changed the summers being so backward."[52] These cooler temperatures proved a frustrating irritant to the two rivals and their operations. At the very least, the open water season was shorter, thereby lessening the time frame to move goods and supplies into the "war" zone. There was also less water in the rivers because of reduced spring runoff. And there was an even greater reliance on pemmican because of the failure of post gardens and field crops.

The NWC struck first in 1816 by seizing the HBC pemmican supplies at Brandon House and its Qu'Appelle River posts. This action was intended to monopolize control of dried provisions in order to delay, if not prevent, the English company from challenging the NWC's exclusive control of the Athabasca country. But "the drawback to North West methods was that both sides could use them," and the HBC was ready.[53] As a complement to its Cumberland House depot, it now maintained a second major supply base,

UNIVERSITY OF SASKATCHEWAN ARCHIVES AND SPECIAL COLLECTION MSS C525/1/6_17 NO 2

With the 1821 merger of the NWC and the HBC, all trade was henceforth conducted through York Factory on Hudson Bay.

Norway House, at the north end of Lake Winnipeg. It had also embarked on an aggressive bison trade at Carlton House on the North Saskatchewan River. Over a two-month period during the winter of 1814–15, the post master recorded the receipt of almost forty-five thousand pounds of meat (from 107 bison). The intake for November 1815 was even higher. In one month alone, Carlton House filled its sheds with the meat from two hundred bison, all destined to be dried and pounded into pemmican. Under Colvile's retrenching system, the company had also discontinued its practice of securing servants in the Orkney Islands in favour of "more spirited" men from the west coast of Scotland, including the Hebrides. But what really signalled the HBC's intention of taking on the NWC at its own game was the arrival of a force of Irish recruits. They were to be called upon wherever a show of muscle was required, and in particular, helped re-establish the HBC presence at Île-à-la-Crosse in 1815.[54]

Despite these preparations, the HBC's return to the Athabasca country was a disaster. And once again, as in the case of the Red River settlement, the issue was food. At Cumberland House in the late summer of 1815, expedition leader John Clarke foolishly set off without enough provisions in the misguided belief that Indian hunters could secure fresh game along the way. By the time his party reached Methye Portage, it was out of pemmican. But Clarke doggedly pushed on to Lake Athabasca, establishing Fort Wedderburn there in early October before heading off for the Peace River and the NWC's Fort Vermilion. The Nor'Westers knew of the expedition's predicament, how Clarke and his men were desperately short of supplies, and might have been expected to share food as had happened in the past between the two companies. Instead, game along the river was chased away in advance of the expedition, while local Indians were warned against providing any assistance. The cold, unrelenting winter only added to the misery. By the time the HBC party managed to straggle back to Lake Athabasca, eighteen people, including a clerk with a woman and child, had perished. The survivors, meanwhile, had been starved into submission. They turned over all their trade goods for some food, and also signed an agreement not to work against the NWC for one year. An angry Colin Robertson called the tragedy "the most deliberate and wanton acts of cruelty towards the Company's servants." The NWC, by contrast, greeted the outcome with "exultation" and rewarded the local clerk who had orchestrated the starvation with promotion to partner.[55]

Such NWC "cruelty" kept the HBC away from the Athabasca country in the past. But Clarke returned to Fort Wedderburn with another contingent of men for the winter of 1816–17. This time, the Nor'Westers decided to forcibly prevent the local Chipewyan from providing provisions or trading with the English fort; being placed in irons was the cost of disobedience. They also interfered with the HBC fishery on the lake and generally tried to keep the HBC men confined to the post. Their boldest move, though, and one that was intended to assert their dominance in the eyes of the local Indians, was taking Clarke prisoner and seizing the fort in the early new year. This action was followed by the capture of the HBC posts at Île-à-la-Crosse, Green Lake, and Reindeer Lake in the early spring of 1817. It was even rumoured that the forts on the North Saskatchewan were next. If there were any doubts about NWC control of the Athabasca–Churchill trade, clerk Peter Skene Odgen put them to rest. When a hapless Indian was caught visiting the HBC post at Green Lake in 1816, Ogden forcibly dragged him out on the ice and murdered him on the spot. Sadly, this kind of brutality had its rewards. Even though the HBC sent another batch of servants to the region for the 1817–18 season, it was completely shut out of the Athabasca trade. The NWC, on the other hand, brought out 430 fur packs in the spring.[56]

These repeated setbacks did not deflect the HBC from its Athabasca campaign. The company had finally realized that the NWC was at its most vulnerable in the same region that made the Canadian trade so profitable. That is where the blow had to be inflicted if the commercial damage to its Montreal rivals was going to be fatal. To do so, though, Robertson assembled a formidable force of over 180 men in twenty-seven canoes; the new reinforcements included voyageurs and Iroquois ironically hired in Montreal. He then personally led the expedition into the NWC stronghold in the late summer of 1818 and proceeded to battle for every available fur, pushing the trade beyond Athabasca into other promising districts. The encouraging results from that winter's trade marked a turning point in the Athabascan fur trade war, and although it took a few more seasons, the HBC had delivered a mortal wound to its Canadian counterpart. The NWC had been forced to hire extra personnel and extend its operations into other areas to deal with the trade competition. But the costs quickly proved ruinous. The Montreal company also lost many of its Indian customers. Given the presence of the HBC in force, the Chipewyan could no longer be intimidated and consciously chose to trade with the English company because of its less aggressive practices. A telltale sign of the possible breakup of the NWC coalition was the rift between winterers and Montreal traders at the 1820 annual rendezvous meeting at Fort William.[57] Unless these differences were resolved, the existing partnership might dissolve once the current agreement expired in 1822.

Negotiations between company representatives took place in London over the winter of 1820–21. The British government, cognizant of the deaths and depredations of the past few years in northwestern North America, wanted the fur trade war ended and a compromise reached. So too did the two commercial rivals. The HBC was not sure how long it could sustain losses in the Athabasca country, while the NWC was uncertain how long it could hold out there. What was really remarkable, though, was that the English company was still in the beaver skin business in 1820, given its pitiful share of the trade at the beginning of the nineteenth century. "Drawn by a dead Horse" is how the Canadians once likened their rival's operations.[58] But the HBC, despite its smug sense of moral superiority, had survived by becoming more like the NWC. Colvile's retrenching plan smacked of the same efficiencies and organizational rigour that characterized the trade out of Montreal. And although servants may have lacked the famous NWC *esprit de corps*, they did not shrink from standing up to their Canadian rivals once it was decided to enter the Athabasca trade—and stay there, going back with fresh reinforcements if necessary year after year. One fur trade scholar has argued that a settlement was possible in 1821 only because "the Hudson's Bay Company had become an organization the North Westers could join."[59]

The agreement, to take effect 1 June 1821, embraced the strengths of both companies. There was to be no small mindedness, pettiness, or retribution, or the coalition would be fatally flawed. Henceforth, all trade was to be conducted through Hudson Bay. Nor'Wester Alexander Mackenzie had once extolled this shorter, ocean-going route as the best way to prosecute trade in the northern half of the continent, but he did not live to see its realization. This focus on London and Hudson Bay effectively ended the century-long connection between Montreal and the northwestern interior. Fort William was allowed to languish, while the west-east canoe routes were abandoned except for express traffic. The reach of the new HBC, however, would now be larger, more ambitious, than ever in the past. Not only did it retain exclusive charter trade rights in Rupert's Land, but it also secured a twenty-one-year monopoly licence over the fur trade in all the remaining territory of British North America (except for Upper and Lower Canada). To help the London Committee map out policy for this three-million-square-mile empire, chief factors in North America met face-to-face on an annual basis, as had been done during NWC days. Senior company personnel also received a percentage share of the annual profits of the trade. Nor'Westers filled many of these new positions. Clearly, the longer strategic view took precedence over deciding winners and losers.[60]

But there were losers, what might more accurately be called "the wreckage of battle."[61] Entire districts had been stripped of fur-bearing animals with a single-minded efficiency, while bison had been reduced to tens of thousands of bags of pemmican at factory-like provisioning posts. Indians had been demeaned, abused, beaten, and debauched by alcohol. As if this treatment at the hands of the traders was not enough, they were visited by another round of disease—measles followed by whooping cough in 1819 and 1820—at the very moment the struggle between the NWC and HBC had reached its climax. This one-two punch may have killed up to 25 per cent of the Indians along the canoe route between Rainy River and Lake Athabasca.[62] Then there were the NWC voyageurs and other contracted employees—an estimated thirteen hundred men—who lost their jobs through redundancy and faced the prospect of returning to Quebec and an uncertain future. Several, including Iroquois hunters, chose to remain in the West as Freemen, drawing on their fur trade skills to carve out an existence as best they could with their Indian or mixed-descent wives and children. It was not the first time. When the NWC and XYC merged in 1804, some of the displaced men found work supplying pemmican for the brigades, acting as post provisioners, serving as guides and interpreters, maintaining the Lac la Pluie–Athabasca canoe route, or collecting furs for the trade.[63] These Freemen and their growing families may have been an unexpected consequence of the fur trade rivalry but, collectively, they constituted a new and distinctive people in the region. They and their children and children's children would figure prominently in the history of Native-newcomer relations in the region throughout the nineteenth century.

Hudson's Bay Company Governor George Simpson was nicknamed the "little emperor."

CHAPTER TEN

AN ASPIRATION RATHER THAN
A REALITY

A "STATE OF THE MOST PERFECT TRANQUILITY" IS HOW GEORGE SIMPSON DESCRIBED
the mood in the western Canadian fur trade to his London superiors in 1837.[1]
It was a characteristic boast from the man who ran the Hudson's Bay Company
territory as if it was his own fiefdom and he was the English lord who presided
over every detail of its operations, no matter how trivial. Indeed, the "little
emperor," as the diminutive Simpson was known, has been widely hailed for
"leav[ing] a mark upon the Canadian fur trade such as no other man has ever
equalled."[2] He was the one who oversaw the coalition period, the so-called
"halcyon era of the Great Monopoly,"[3] when the HBC dominated more than
half the land area of present-day Canada and enjoyed the most rewarding
period of prosperity in its corporate history. But the reality on the ground was
far from Simpson's "most perfect tranquility." No amount of heavy-handed
regulation or number of rigorous efficiencies, imposed from above and outside,
were going to completely undo the way that the fur trade had evolved and
been pursued in Rupert's Land. Nor could the HBC, even under Simpson's
obdurate management style, control and direct the lives of Indian bands and
the growing number of Freemen or Métis people as if it had a monopoly over
their activities, too. Rather, the inhabitants of the region responded to the
changed circumstances after 1821 by doing what was in their best interests
and not necessarily what the HBC expected, sometimes demanded, of them.
They practised an opportunity-based subsistence lifestyle during the mid-

nineteenth century in a determined effort to maintain their independence in the newly reorganized fur trade world.[4]

It was one of the most thrilling sections of the canoe route between the Saskatchewan River and Lake Winnipeg. In the early summer of 1821, George Simpson, a fur trade novice with one inland winter under his belt, and his pregnant, mixed-descent partner Betsy Sinclair, shot the Grand Rapids—a drop of 125 feet over twelve miles—in a light canoe that had been specially made for the trip out from the Athabasca country. The descent that day was heavy with meaning both for Simpson and his employer, the Hudson's Bay Company. At the end of the run, a North West Company party met Simpson with the news that the two rival fur trade companies had reached a coalition agreement. Union gave Simpson "his opportunity." While the HBC had "at last achieved mastery" in the Canadian fur trade, it found in the former London sugar clerk "its master."[5] Simpson's finely honed business skills counted more than his limited experience in the trade, and in 1821 at age twenty-nine, he was placed in charge of the sprawling Northern department. Five years later, he was promoted to North American governor, a position that was not formalized until 1839 (governor in chief of Rupert's Land). Knighted in 1841 by a young Queen Victoria, he immediately set off on a round-the-world trip via British North America and Russia. The tour resulted in a book and confirmed Sir George's reputation as an indefatigable overland traveller. It was apparently part of a carefully contrived plan to cover up the stain of his illegitimate birth, a plan that included living in the grandest mansion in Lachine, Quebec, from which he presided over the HBC fur trade empire until his death in 1860.[6] It's been said that Simpson blurred the line between his life and that of the company. That's why he worked so tirelessly for the HBC. And he personally profited. But what mattered most to Simpson was status—what one historian has called "that sense of unchallenged supremacy he so dearly loved."[7]

Simpson found that feeling of supremacy in the new Hudson's Bay

Company, which effectively became "an imperial state" after union with the North West Company.[8] The Northern and Southern departments, created under Colvile's earlier retrenching system, were joined by two other departments: one west of the Rocky Mountains to the Pacific Coast, known as the Columbia department; the other, the Montreal department, which included Upper and Lower Canada and Labrador. As of 1821, the HBC operated from coast to coast to coast. Those lands that fell within the company charter area (the Hudson Bay drainage basin) continued to be called Rupert's Land, while the remaining districts were designated the Indian Territories. Within a short time, though, the great land mass was alternatively known as HBC Territory, and understandably so. In exchange for exclusive trading rights, the company was charged with the administration of justice in the vast territory in the absence of any formal government. This standing-in for British sovereign interests has been characterized as "a sort of imperialism on the cheap."[9] But Simpson seemed to relish the responsibility because he regarded the HBC as representing the British government and he as its emissary. Besides, this arrangement essentially gave him free rein as long as he retained the support and confidence of the governing London Committee.

Simpson's major task in taking charge of the Northern department in 1821 was quite simple: to improve the profitability of the new HBC. Even though the fur trade was the only newcomer activity in the North-West and produced tens of thousands of skins for export, it never generated great wealth, especially when compared to other British commercial activities at the time. Nor did it account for much of British North America's export trade by the early nineteenth century but had been eclipsed in particular by timber. Only a handful of Montreal merchants profited from the fur trade, not Canadians in general.[10] The cutthroat competition between the NWC and HBC in the late 1810s had also severely reduced any profits, and if not for the fur resources of the Athabasca country and beyond, it would have been a losing enterprise. Union probably saved the trade from collapse because the costs of the HBC–NWC war were unsustainable. But it was Simpson who righted the listing HBC financial

LOUIS COCHIN

A Métis elder from the Île-à-la-Crosse region

ship and put it on a course of sustained profit. By 1825, and as long as Simpson was at the North American helm, the annual dividend never sank below 10 per cent and, in some years, even floated above 15 per cent. Commissioned officers, in the meantime, whether chief factors or chief traders, shared in the largesse and were well-compensated by income standards at the time.[11]

It is easy to suggest that the HBC enjoyed financial success after 1821 because it finally enjoyed monopoly trading privileges. Up to then, it really had what might be termed a "counterfeit" monopoly because, first the French, and then the NWC from Canada, ignored HBC charter claims by trading in Rupert's Land. It was only with coalition that the company finally had the opportunity, technically, to operate without rivals in the field and introduce a measure of uniformity and regulation to the trade.[12] And that was one of Simpson's many talents. He was the first HBC employee with a background in business, and his "'counting-house' approach to the fur trade," as one author put it, ensured that every pound and penny was painstakingly tallied.[13]

But Simpson was much more than a meticulous bookkeeper. He took great interest in the everyday nuts-and-bolts of the trade and preferred to investigate any problem or issue personally to have a better, more complete understanding of the situation. He was notorious for his impromptu post visits, dropping in unannounced and asking questions of the inhabitants, no matter their position. These fact-finding trips took him across the North-West on a regular basis and gave him insight into the trade that would have been impossible to acquire if he simply spent his working days at York Factory, the Red River settlement, or later Lachine, Lower Canada. It also meant that the annual council meeting of governors and chief factors, held at Norway House or Red River to make arrangements or adjustments for the next trading season, were generally "subdued affairs."[14] Simpson had either made an on-the-spot decision during his inspection tours or had a resolution drafted for council consideration. And there was no shortage of resolutions in the first few years after coalition. One trader privately griped that "more attention is paid to these miserable trifles than to matters of far greater moment to the concern."[15] Simpson would have strenuously disagreed, insisting that waste, disorder, and inefficiencies were the downfall of the trade.

Simpson began by closing posts and dismissing personnel in the Northern department (from Hudson Bay to the Rocky Moutains). With amalgamation, there were too many surplus establishments.[16] Many HBC and NWC settlements were located next or near to one another. They had also been hurriedly built and could only charitably be called forts. Simpson decided to carry on the trade from a few strategic and more permanent locations, while ensuring that all traffic to and from the interior was channelled through Hudson Bay; the old Montreal canoe route was to be used only for express business. The HBC Fort Carlton on the North Saskatchewan River, for example, superseded the NWC Fort La Montée and remained a major provisioning post. Because of its location between warring Cree, Assiniboine, and Blackfoot Alliance bands, the rectangular-shaped post was reconstructed and given tall stockade walls with fortified bastions and small cannon in each corner. The HBC post at Cumberland House was also chosen over the NWC post of the same name. But unlike Carlton, even though Cumberland remained a storage/provisioning depot, it soon ceased to be a key post on the route to the Athabasca country and began a slow, steady decline. Along the Churchill River, NWC forts were retained over those of the HBC, largely because the region had been a Nor'Wester stronghold for decades. The Lac la Ronge post, one of the oldest settlements on the lake of the same name, replaced the nearby HBC establishment, while Île-à-la-Crosse and Green Lake House took over from the HBC Fort Superior and Essex House, respectively. Île-à-la-Crosse remained as headquarters for the English River district after 1821 and doubled as a provisioning centre, supplied by pemmican brought north from Carlton via the Green Lake track.[17]

Simpson also realized that the HBC was in the freighting business and "that time and space were the Company's worst enemies."[18] He consequently ordered the rebuilding of York Factory and Norway House in keeping with their roles as major supply and transportation hubs. Much of this reconstruction work was done in the early 1830s but, in the case of York Factory, carried on until 1847 when the last of the old structures at the venerable post was replaced. Work also resumed on the cutting of a winter road from York Factory to Lake Winnipeg—first started in the early nineteenth century—but the project was abandoned in the 1830s. At Methye Portage, meanwhile, only cargo was carried over the watershed while separate crews waited on either side of the divide. Even then, the volume of freight hauled over the fearsome

BURPEE, *THE SEARCH FOR THE WESTERN SEA*

The York boat served as the backbone of the HBC transportation system.

portage was reduced when Simpson decided in 1824 to supply the region by an overland horse trail from Fort Edmonton to Fort Assiniboine on the upper Athabasca River. This change made Edmonton (chosen over the NWC Fort Augustus in 1821) the most important post on the Saskatchewan River, and it was completely rebuilt in the early 1830s to reflect this status and to provide better protection in the event of a possible Indian attack. One of the most remarkable features of the post, one that Chief Factor John Rowand delighted in showing visitors, was the so-called Indian Hall that was garishly painted in bold colours.[19]

The nucleus of the HBC transportation system was the York boat. Simpson wanted to do away with the use of canoes wherever possible and replace them with the sturdier flat-bottomed York boat with an average carrying capacity of about four thousand pounds in the 1820s (higher in later decades). He estimated that shipping costs could be shaved by at least one-third.[20] To do so, though, the company had to find reliable sources of good timber and start using water routes better suited for the bigger boats. Portages were also widened and upgraded, in some instances by putting down a bed of logs to serve as rollers.

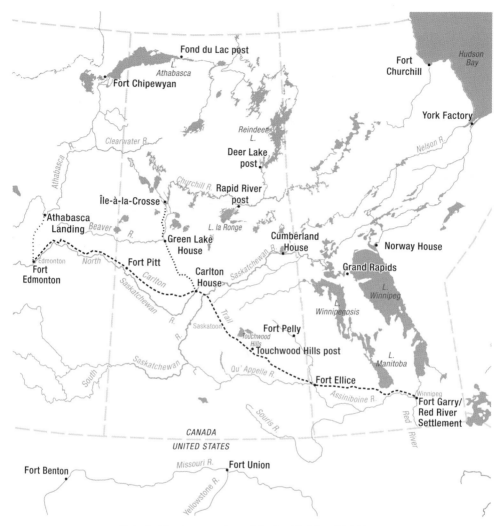

Selected fur trade posts and Carlton Trail in mid-1800s

And in keeping with Simpson's penchant for exactness, the dimensions of the boat, up to then built at the posts in a variety of sizes, were standardized at the 1826 Northern Council meeting.[21] Each York boat was manned by a crew of six to eight, featuring a steersman, bowsman, and middlemen or rowers, collectively known as tripmen. Every June, brigades, made up of several boats and dozens of men, toiled their way up the Saskatchewan and Churchill Rivers, taking in the annual outfit from Norway House and returning laden with fur bales for York Factory; sometimes, a separate brigade travelled the Red River–Norway House–York Factory route. Even though the season lasted only five months, the sweeping of the oars, carrying of ninety-pound "pieces" over portages, and dragging at rapids or low water points made for heavy, demanding work, especially for those who worked the La Loche brigades under guides Aléxis Espérence and Baptiste Bruce. Boats lasted only three, maybe four years, and it was said that tripmen were never the same again.[22]

Because of the switch from canoes to York boats, Simpson dismissed hundreds of voyageurs in the wake of the fur trade union. But dealing with the larger personnel question was potentially more complicated because the merger brought bitter enemies together under one roof. Simpson, however, showed a decided preference for former NWC officers, especially in filling senior ranks in the new HBC, because of their "superior enterprise and efficiency."[23] This emphasis on commercial skills did not mean, though, that there was a greater chance for promotion for those who demonstrated initiative and drive. Unlike the pre-coalition HBC, where it was possible for meritorious servants to assume management positions, the HBC after 1821 was a stratified company where class divisions were quite pronounced and rigidly enforced, as they were in British society in general at the time. Chief factors and traders, known as commissioned gentlemen, lived a gentrified existence at the posts and actively cultivated the distance between themselves and company servants. Admission to this officer class depended largely on connections and patronage, in much the same way that the former NWC awarded partnerships to clerks.[24] Those at the bottom of the company hierarchy, on the other hand, were hired on term, increasingly casual contracts, and had no prospect of promotion. They either worked as tradespeople in and around the posts, acted as interpreters, manned boats, or performed general labour.

It was these workers, numbering about two thousand in 1821, that Simpson targeted for dismissal. Many, such as French-Canadian *engagés*, had been hurriedly hired during the final few years of the Athabasca trade war and had now been made redundant by union. Others had served the companies longer in various capacities but, because of their perceived slovenly habits, were considered expendable in the new fur trade climate. Most had families, and large ones at that. Beginning in the early nineteenth century, more frequent pregnancies resulted in a dramatic increase in the number of mixed-descent births, on average from seven to nine children, or a doubling of the late eighteenth-century family size.[25] Even senior managers were almost "all Family men" who insisted that their wives and children accompany them on the brigades.[26] Simpson regarded support of these dependents as a drain on company resources and probably used their presence at the posts as extra incentive to slash the number of employees to about seven hundred by the middle of the 1820s. In the Saskatchewan district, for example, the 171 personnel were reduced to eighty by 1824.[27] Those who kept their jobs were expected to purchase what the company had once provided as part of their employment contract—namely, their food, clothing, and equipment—as well as pay for the support of their families. But there was such a backlash against these regulations that Simpson had to back down. There were also new rules about family life. Fathers were expected to provide their children with some basic educational and religious instruction, such as the alphabet and simple prayers. The use of Indian languages was to end as well. Only English or French were to be spoken. Even dancing was forbidden except during the Christmas holiday season.[28]

Simpson also wanted the post-1821 labour force to work for less and looked to the Orkney Islands once again to serve as the source for cheap and steady recruits. But the company could never sign up enough men, in part because the low wages paled in comparison to what the Orcadians could make in the North Atlantic fisheries. The HBC consequently had to turn to Lower Canada and other parts of Great Britain, in particular some of the other Scottish Islands, to find men willing to enter into contracts for limited compensation. Even then, it still had difficulty meeting its labour needs after Simpson's excessive job-slashing and, with great reluctance, began to hire a few Métis. Rupert's Land would seem to have been an obvious source to fill the company's manpower vacancies. But Simpson regarded Métis peoples as "indolent" and was only willing to risk hiring a few young men every year.

LIBRARY AND ARCHIVES CANADA C-020286

Boat brigades headed up the Saskatchewan and Churchill rivers with the annual outfit every June and returned laden with fur bales.

What emerged by default and not design, then, was an ethnically diverse labour force. Simpson accepted this situation and tried to regulate company hiring through the 1820s to maintain a "judicious mix of men." Servants of different origins and backgrounds were less likely to challenge company authority and its employment conditions, especially given the constant turnover of workers. Outside recruitment, though, began to falter and by 1830, the company grudgingly began to hire more and more Métis to keep its labour force up to full complement. Some as young as fourteen, hired as apprentices on seven-year contracts, were the sons of fur trade workers but could not be employed in the same districts as their fathers.[29]

Simpson and the company, meanwhile, had to deal with the problem of what to do with the hundreds of discharged employees and their families— and the growing number of abandoned women and children, left behind when dismissed servants returned to Great Britain or moved to Canada. Leaving them to fend for themselves, argued the London Committee, posed too much of a

An increasing volume of freight was hauled by the two-wheeled Red River cart.

threat to the stability of the trade. "These people form a burden which cannot be got rid of without expence," it observed, "[and] it would be impolitic and inexpedient to encourage or allow them to Collect together in different parts of the Country where they could not be under any proper superintendence."[30] The solution was to move retired servants and their mixed-descent families to the Red River settlement where they could settle on the land and take up farming in an organized community.

Concentrating this mixed-descent population in one particular location served to give expression to their identity as a separate people. Up until the early nineteenth century, people of mixed ancestry were generally associated with one of the trading companies and either called Native English, (bois) brulé, Indian, or Native, depending on their cultural affiliations and familial ties. Around the time of the merger, though, the NWC had begun to differentiate the steadily growing mixed-descent population from both newcomer and Indian by using new terms: halfbreed and Métis (from the French word métissage, for mixed).[31] This sense of being a distinct people was accelerated by their experience at Red River. Agriculture was supposed to provide a quiet livelihood for the Métis, while at the same time keep them from becoming involved in illicit trade or other activities that challenged the company monopoly. But crops frequently failed in the 1820s and 1830s,[32] forcing the Métis at Red River to seek out other opportunities in the region that over time not only gave expression to their identity, but their rights to the land and its resources, something that was completely at odds with HBC official policy for these people and their offspring. The Métis search for other livelihoods was also made necessary because Simpson was determined to shut them out of the fur trade—except for the lower rungs—because of their race. He even went so far as to create the new position of post master for better educated fur-trade sons who were otherwise prevented from entering company service as apprentice clerks, and therefore eligible for advancement. Several served a "paper bondage" for years, if not decades, under the new regime. A good many more could not find work in the trade and, as the Métis population continued to boom at Red River, they were forced to find other pursuits.[33] As early as 1824, Simpson was warning the London Committee that "the half-breed population ... required great good management if it was not to become dangerous."[34]

Several Red River Métis did become farmers, but experienced more failure than success because of climatic conditions in the 1820s and had to find other ways to supplement their uneven harvests. Some took steady, seasonal employment as tripmen. They served on the York boats during the open water season and then spent their winters hunting in the settlement area. A few worked the fisheries, along the Red and Assiniboine Rivers and on Lakes Winnipeg (Grand Marais) and Manitoba (Oak Point). Still others served as freighters for the HBC. Low seasonal water levels in the fall, for example, meant that goods could be hauled at the driest time of year along a trail running up the Assiniboine River to Fort Pelly, and later to outposts to the south and west. The vehicle used for this overland transportation was the two-wheeled Red River cart, first introduced for the pemmican trade in the area in the early nineteenth century and, like the York boat, assuming a standard form by the time of union. The box of the cart was six feet long, two feet nine inches wide, and two feet four inches deep, with a narrow railing to keep the load in place.[35] One of its most distinctive features was its huge wheels, five feet high, and ideally suited for travel over the tough prairie sod or marshy ground. It was also made entirely of wood—except for the green bison hide that was wrapped around the wheels for durability—and therefore could be relatively easily repaired from local trees whenever there was a breakdown. But its most unforgettable characteristic was the constant screeching when it was in motion, a simply "hellish" noise caused by the friction of the wheels against the dry axle.[36]

The main Métis occupation at Red River—and the only really viable economic activity for the growing population—was the annual bison hunt. The company had to feed hundreds of transportation workers at the standard daily ration of eight pounds of pemmican per man; it is estimated that more than a million pounds of pemmican were consumed annually.[37] To meet this demand for bison meat, Métis families travelled out onto the plains in large caravans, both to ensure the success of the hunt and to provide security against the Sioux who exploited the same herds. In June 1826, 680 carts left Red River for the summer hunt; a decade later, the number had climbed to 970. The original rendezvous point for the hunt was Pembina, south of the Red River settlement at the present-day international boundary. But as the number of participating families increased and the herds contracted southwestward, separate hunts were organized from the Pembina Valley near Turtle Mountain and from near the junction of the Souris and Assiniboine Rivers. This longer reach of the hunt was only possible because of the cart. Once the herds were located, the Métis killed as many animals as they could, butchered their kill on the spot, and then processed the meat into pemmican for transport back to Red River by late July or early August.[38] They were sometimes joined on the hunt by the Ojibwa, later the Cree and Assiniboine, who appreciated the protection afforded by the large parties and came to intermarry with both Métis men and women. These kinship ties with plains Indian groups suggests that there was no fixed or single identity for Métis people at the time, but one that was fluid and situational.

BRIAN CHENOWYTH

A freighter's winter dress

Some Métis centred their world on the Red River settlement, others gravitated towards an armed and mobile bison-hunting society on the Souris plains.[39]

The annual "dried meat hunt" gave the Red River Métis a promising foothold in the new HBC economic order. Perhaps that is why Simpson considered them "dangerous" and in need of "great good management." What he had in mind was to "take that part of the business [pemmican trade] into our hands ... we can dictate our own terms ... I expect there will be a very considerable saving."[40] The HBC began to assume monopoly control of pemmican production by driving down the price and coordinating post purchases so that by 1827, it traded for one-quarter of what it had been worth in 1821. Métis hunters had to accept these rates of return because the HBC was the only buyer and had financed their hunting expeditions by extending goods to them on credit. But the lower prices meant that hunters had to slaughter more bison if they were to pay off their debts. The company also bought all the available pemmican, following a shortage of provisions during the harsh winter of 1825–26, and stored the surplus at Norway House. By the end of the 1820s, then, the cheap and plentiful food source fuelled HBC operations. It was even used for such discretionary purposes as supporting Indian trappers. Métis hunting had to respond to keep pace, while searching for other markets for their hunting activities beyond the HBC.[41]

Another so-called "dangerous" group were the Freemen, former Canadian and Iroquois *engagés* who had served as independent brokers between the companies and Indians at the height of the Athabasca trade war. Because of their connections with local bands, they had effectively controlled the trade at the post level. Simpson wanted to stamp out their influence. He ordered an immediate end to their special status by refusing to recognize them as trading captains, dispensing with ceremonies and denying them gifts. He also introduced a resolution at the 1825 Northern department council that prevented them from securing goods on credit at reduced prices. Freemen were given few options. They could either assume menial roles in the trade, settle at Red River, or leave Rupert's Land. Some took on jobs as post provisioners, freighters, or tripmen, especially on the La Loche brigade. But rather than accept the humiliation of a demotion and working for the new HBC, several other Freeman and their families either joined Indian bands or moved to other areas in the North-West, such as portages where they could maintain their connection with the trade.[42] Simpson responded by refusing to provide them with land or allowing them to cultivate the soil anywhere else but at Red River. He also proposed to remove, by force if necessary, those Freemen settlements that had taken shape at such places as Swan River, Basquia, or Rivière du Pas (later the Paw, and finally The Pas), Cedar Lake, Cumberland House, and Grand Rapids on the Saskatchewan River. What really bothered Simpson was that these Freemen groups were competing with the HBC in violation of the company's monopoly. His threats, though, were never followed up, and Freemen communities took root across the North-West.

In response to these new policies, members of the Desjarlais family, headed by the old Canadian Freeman Joseph and his Ojibwa partner Okimaskwew, gradually drifted eastward from the Athabasca country towards the Red River region. Leaving Lesser Slave Lake in 1823, they were reported trapping along the Carrot River and trading at Cumberland House in present-day east-central Saskatchewan four years later. They then hunted north of Swan River before breaking into two groups in 1829: one son took up residence near Fort Carlton, another headed southwest from Swan River to the Fishing Lakes on the Qu'Appelle River. Another relative settled his family at Baie St. Paul at Red River. By the mid-1830s, many of the Desjarlais hunted and trapped with other Freemen families in a territory bounded by the Swan River to the Turtle Mountains, and the Qu'Appelle Lakes to Lake Winnipeg. Any remaining connection with relatives in Lower Canada had been lost by this time. It had been replaced by strong familial bonds between Freemen groups over hundreds of miles. But these mixed-descent people, unlike the Métis at Red River, did not yet identify themselves as a distinct and separate community because of their constant movement and relative isolation in family units for most of the year. Many Freemen groups also maintained their affinity with local Indian bands through intermarriage.[43]

Simpson also wanted to bring Indian people under his thumb: dictate to them how they could best serve the company's interests and profitability. There were to be no more gifts, limited credit, and a reduction and an eventual ban in the trading of alcohol except in areas where it was necessary to secure and maintain Indian allegiance to the new HBC. As Simpson told a member of the London Committee, Indians were to be "ruled with a rod of iron."[44] This paternalistic, if not intrusive, policy probably found its fullest expression in Simpson's conservation program. Anxious to restore the beaver population after years of indiscriminate and wasteful trapping, the HBC refused to accept both beaver taken out of season (summer beaver) and cub beaver. To reinforce this new policy, it stopped providing steel traps. It also encouraged Indians to trap and hunt other animals for trade. And in an ironic twist from past practice during the competitive era, beaver skin quotas were established for each district in 1826, based on a percentage of the returns for each post for the past three years. This "rest and recuperation" program has been hailed as "one of the earliest attempts in North America to put a primary resource industry on a sustained yield basis." But it is questionable whether the company "chang[ed] the Indian's way of life in some fundamental ways."[45] More often than not, they challenged the sudden change in decades-long practices.

Without doubt, Indians began to procure different species for trade; one author has concluded that the company "gathered the skins of as many as forty-two animals and birds" in addition to grease, feathers, and bone.[46] The trade for swan skins and quills, for example, led to the near extirpation of the trumpeter swan in North America.[47] The most popular alternative to beaver was muskrat, whose skin was in demand at the time for the fashion trade in the eastern United States and Canada. But the population was subject to periodic crashes because of low water levels, such as 1824 on the lower Saskatchewan River, and was never a reliable substitute. Indians continued to hunt beaver whenever they needed trade goods, and traders in turn took the pelts rather than follow the Simpson 1822 directive and lose a future customer. The company was still complaining into the 1830s that too many substandard beaver skins were being shipped from York Factory.[48] Traders were also supposed to turn away Indians from another district in order to force bands to confine their hunting and trapping to fixed territories. But that regulation was ignored, too. Chief Factor John Rowand of Fort Edmonton was criticized for taking furs from Indians who had travelled there from the upper Churchill River area. "It is more than I am able to do," he said in defence of his decision to go against company policy. "I could not do it to a dog, much less a human being."[49] And even though alcohol was no longer available in the Churchill district by 1827, the plan to eliminate liquor entirely in other districts by 1836 had to be aborted because of its potential impact on HBC trade. As the company historian observed: "The policy was less as an aspiration rather than as a reality."[50]

One of the other ways that Simpson sought to nurse back the beaver population was to close posts and open new ones in the same district and thereby reorientate Indian procurement activities. In present-day northeastern Saskatchewan, the Reindeer Lake post operated until 1824, was abandoned until 1831 when it was temporarily re-opened for one season, and then finally re-occupied in 1839. The Lac la Ronge post, by contrast, was closed in 1830 because "the surrounding country has been much impoverished."[51] It was to be superseded by the post on Reindeer Lake, but the local fur-bearing population had still not recovered. Instead, a new settlement was established on the Churchill River near the mouth of the Rapid River in 1831. On the northwestern side of the province, the returns were so bad—a legacy of the Athabasca fur-trade war—that Harrison's House at the eastern end of Lake Athabasca (near the Oldman River) was abandoned in 1821. It was another three decades before another post, Fond du Lac, was established there. That these three regions north of the Churchill River had to be rested after the HBC merger, to allow the beaver population to recover, is truly remarkable given the vastness of the territory and the predominance of water. But even York Factory and Fort Churchill were collecting a total of only three hundred Made Beaver from local trappers in the early 1830s.[52]

Île-à-la-Crosse, as district headquarters for the English River district, took on a permanence in the region as a distinctive fur-trade/Métis community. With union in 1821, NWC and HBC employees who lost their jobs, along with local Freemen, were expected to leave northwest Saskatchewan. But many chose to remain there with their wives and children. These "outsider" males enjoyed access to the land and its resources through their Métis partners and their maternal connections to the local Indian population. And within a few years, specific families with either French, English, or Indian surnames (such as Morin and Laliberte) came to be associated with particular localities in Cree and Chipewyan territory. These men, at the same time, continued to find employment in the fur trade and fulfilled a variety of contractual and temporary roles in and around the post and at Methye Portage to supplement their subsistence lifestyle. Women and sometimes children also worked the post fishery or tended the gardens. Local HBC men tried to maintain the loyalty of these labourers by supporting them in time of need; they, in turn, asked the traders for favours, such as jobs for their children. Despite Simpson's many regulations, then, the fur trade in the Île-à-la-Crosse district was "more than just an occupation."[53] The HBC and local Métis communities were bound together like family. This reciprocal relationship was quite different, moreover, from the experience of the Métis at Red River and suggests that mixed-descent people in the early nineteenth century were "moving in varied cultural and ethnic directions."[54]

The day-to-day operations at Cumberland House on the Saskatchewan River also seemed little affected by the Simpson post-1821 reforms. Because of the post's chronic need for country provisions, the local Cree continued to receive goods on credit. And when they had furs to trade, they insisted that traders visit their camps to fetch them, a practice (*en dérouine*) that evidently continued into the late 1830s. The Cree also refused to trap furs whenever they faced a food shortage and often put their traditional hunting and gathering activities first, frustrating the traders, who accused them of being "indolent." Repeated requests, meanwhile, to stop killing beaver elicited "cool replies." The animal, the Cree defiantly claimed, was a favourite food and essential to their survival.[55]

Mixed-descent people also figured prominently in the Cumberland House journals for the period. Two of the most frequently mentioned individuals were Mansack and Willock Twatt, the sons of HBC servant Magnus Twatt, who died at Carrot River in 1801. The two Twatt boys were raised by their mother's Cree family but were known to the post as being of mixed descent. By the 1820s, they were heading their own Cree group, known as the Twatts band, and although based at Nipawin, pursued a subsistence cycle that took them to the Pasquia Hills, Candle Lake, the Torch River, and The Pas. They were also recognized as leading "Indians" at Cumberland House, a designation that earned them liberal credit and gifts, including rum, which had to be provided if fur returns, according to Mansack, were not to suffer. Other mixed-descent connections with the post included the growing Freemen community at The Pas, as well as the families of company servants. George Sutherland, Thomas

GEOLOGICAL SURVEY OF CANADA 199728

Fort Pelly on the Assiniboine River in present-day east-central Saskatchewan

Isbister, George Flett, and Alex Kennedy, among others, all had families but lived apart from them during the winter because they could not be supported at the post. This temporary separation masked the fact that Cumberland House had a deepening relationship with the local Indian and Métis peoples and was not in any sense an isolated outpost of British commerce.[56]

Perhaps the best example of how Simpson's reforms proved impractical was the experience at Fort Pelly (southwest of the village of Pelly near the present-day Manitoba–Saskatchewan border). By 1824, the HBC had abandoned all of the posts along the Assiniboine, Swan, Red Deer, and upper Red Rivers in favour of a single new settlement for the Swan River district. Named Pelly, after the governor of the company, the post was ideally located on the elbow of the Assiniboine River at the west end of the portage between the Swan and Assiniboine Rivers; packages could be sent in and out of the region either by York Factory or the Red River settlement. There was also a good supply of wood for building boats. Pelly's establishment was part of a concerted company effort to draw Indians away from other areas so that the local beaver populations could recover.[57] And trade thrived there in the latter part of the 1820s because the local Cree shifted from beaver to muskrat hunting. But then

347

the "rat" population plummeted, reducing returns from £7,000 in 1830 to less than £100 the following year.[58] Other furs were just as scarce. So, too, were fresh provisions except for fish from local lakes and rivers. Simpson consequently toyed with closing the post—a notice was sent to that effect in February 1832—but backed away from the decision in order to maintain the Indian trade. "Tell me ... why the Houses are So often changed," one of the leaders complained, "we no Sooner become attached to one than we are ordered to be removed to Some other." Another wondered, "What have we done that our post is to be thrown away?"[59] Pelly not only remained in operation, being rebuilt in 1842–43 when it was destroyed by fire, but Indian visitors continued to be recognized with a musketry salute, the hoisting of the flag, and chiefs' outfits whenever they came to trade. Alcohol was an integral part of these sessions. After a raucous drinking spree by a large Cree trading party at the post in the spring of 1844, the chief trader likened their departure to the "perfect calm after a hurricane."[60]

Simpson's closure of posts in present-day southwestern Manitoba and southeastern Saskatchewan in the early 1820s also ironically encouraged some Indian bands to abandon trapping or take up the bison hunt. That was certainly the case of the Ojibwa in the Pelly region. Ojibwa leaders were insulted by the unilateral changes to the trade policy and responded in ways not expected by the HBC. As one trader noted: "These people know well how to take advantage of the times."[61] Some Ojibwa trapped for the new fort—four men, for example, brought in eight thousand muskrats in 1829—but then abandoned the trade when the rat population collapsed, to resume a more traditional lifestyle. They also grew potatoes, from seed obtained at the post, as well as tried to use their relationship with the HBC to ask the traders for provisions. Their use of the term "starvation" was intended to elicit generosity and did not mean that they had become dependent on the post for their survival.

Other Ojibwa, faced with the declining fur and game resources in the parklands, abandoned trapping to move out onto the plains to hunt bison. Their migration westward towards the Qu'Appelle Lakes and the Touchwood Hills did not represent a complete break from their seasonal rounds, such

The bison hunt was the mainstay of the Red River settlement economy in the mid-nineteenth century.

as fishing, just a desire to broaden their subsistence base.[62] But some were becoming increasingly plains-oriented as confirmed by the use of the term "plains Saulteaux" in the Pelly journal for the first time in 1833. Their transition to a mounted bison-hunting group was facilitated by their peaceful association with the Cree and Assiniboine. They lived and travelled together in large mixed camps and shared the same enemies in the region. They also intermarried. The future Cree leader, Big Bear or *mistahai maskwa*, born in 1825 at Jackfish Lake, was the son of Black Powder and a Cree woman. Even though his father was Ojibwa, Big Bear learned Cree first and observed Cree cultural traditions because of the predominance of Cree in these multi-ethnic camps.[63]

One of the reasons that the Cree, Assiniboine, and Ojibwa increasingly hunted together in large inter-ethnic parties on the plains was for protection against the Blackfoot Alliance. The 1821 fur trade merger had made no difference to the war footing between the two groups. "The word with them is still war & war," John Rowand reported in 1825, "a thing so Common now that it is not worth mentioning."[64] Because Fort Carlton largely traded with the Cree and Assiniboine, any Blackfoot presence in the area was viewed by the post's inhabitants with unease. Fort Pitt, a new provision post on the North Saskatchewan, near the Red Deer Hills between Carlton and Edmonton House, was in an equally precarious position when it was established in 1829. A watch was kept there around the clock.[65] Tensions between the warring parties abated somewhat in the late 1820s when a tenuous peace was agreed upon. Climate may have been a factor. Deep snow during the winter of 1830–31 led to starvation. Then, during the following two winters, in particular 1832–33, the temperatures were so mild that the bison stayed out on the plains instead of moving north to their winter range. During these difficult times, the Cree, Assiniboine, and Blackfoot brokered temporary peace accords that enabled them to camp close to one another along the North Saskatchewan River and concentrate on winter pounding.[66] War erupted again, though, in the spring of 1832 and was so fierce that Pitt closed that summer and stayed closed over the following winter. One of the casualties was the Assiniboine leader The Man That Holds The Knife. His death sparked retributive raids that engulfed the entire northern plains in seemingly unrelenting warfare during the summer of 1833. The HBC responded by putting extra crew on the York boats travelling between Edmonton House and Fort Carlton.[67]

The Blackfoot Alliance, in particular the Peigan, were able to fight these battles because of guns they secured through trade. It represented a dramatic change in their fortunes and their relationship with newcomers. Up until the 1821 coalition, the Blackfoot remained generally aloof from the beaver trade and usually supplied food to secure goods to supplement their subsistence needs.[68] But Simpson looked to take the trade into Blackfoot territory—to the Bow and South Saskatchewan Rivers in present-day southern Alberta. This idea had first been raised by James Bird in the 1810s in response to the exhausted beaver returns along the North Saskatchewan River. It assumed greater urgency under Simpson's command; he even recommended to the London Committee that company operations along the North Saskatchewan be shut down and moved south. But the one hundred-man-strong expedition to the

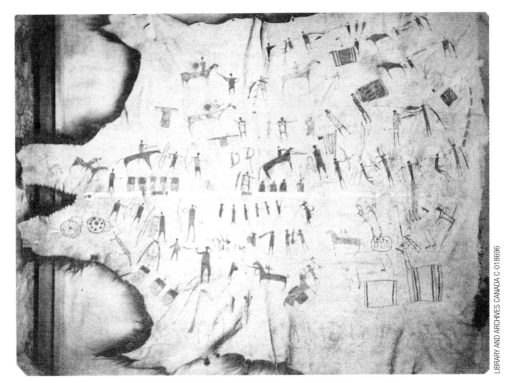

A Blackfoot warrior's robe

region in 1822–23 found few furs, and the plan was dropped. Disappointed, the Blackfoot still wanted to engage in the beaver trade because they now faced enemies on three fronts: the Flathead to the west, the Crow to the south, and the Cree and Assiniboine to the east. And to survive this difficult position and maintain control over their hunting grounds, especially after the losses from the 1819 measles epidemic (up to a third of the population),[69] they set aside their earlier prohibitions against trapping beaver and began collecting pelts to trade for weapons at the North Saskatchewan posts.[70]

The major players in this new Blackfoot Alliance trade were the Peigan, whose southern territory included the beaver-filled headwaters of the Missouri River. That the furs were trapped south of the forty-ninth parallel suited Simpson's conservation policy. It also meant there was a buffer zone between where the Peigan secured their furs and where they traded them. Simpson did all he could to promote this trade, even if it meant violating some of his new policies. The Saskatchewan district had the smallest returns in 1821 and the

GLENBOW ARCHIVES NA-2021-6

A Peigan encampment near Fort McKenzie on the Missouri River

new Peigan business held out the prospect of reversing this situation. The HBC traders consequently supplied steel traps and promised to take all the Peigan beaver skins; the 1826 quota system was not applied here. Alcohol also infused the trading sessions and remained a standard gift. As one trader confessed, "Liquor we must have or we might as well give up."[71] The turnaround in the Saskatchewan trade was nothing less than remarkable. By the end of the 1820s, the district had become the most profitable in the HBC system, not because of provisions, but because of the furs obtained in the United States.

This lucrative beaver source soon slipped away from the HBC. In the 1820s, American trappers moved up the Missouri River, only to be driven out, if not killed, for trespassing on Peigan territory. It was only when American traders sought permission to establish posts—first, Fort Union, above the mouth of the Yellowstone River in 1829, and then, Fort Peigan (later McKenzie, then Benton), near the mouth of the Marias River (and the highest navigable point on the Missouri River) in 1831—that the Blackfoot Alliance accepted their presence. These posts dramatically altered trade patterns on the northern plains. The Peigan could now get the same items they secured at the Saskatchewan posts but at lower prices and within their own territory, because of the navigational advantages of the Missouri River.[72] Even though Fort Union was nearly two thousand miles from St. Louis, the boats that travelled upriver had greater carrying capacity and a longer working season than those in place on the Saskatchewan River. It was only logical, then, that the Peigan took their trade to the Americans at the expense of their HBC suppliers to the north. Nor would they be won back. "It is hoped," a company official ruminated on the defection, "things will yet come round to what they were."[73] But by 1835, Fort Edmonton was losing an estimated three thousand beaver skins to the Missouri posts.[74]

Other Indian groups in the North-West took advantage of the new competition as well. Both the Cree and Assiniboine let it be known that they had visited the Americans posts and used the threat of taking their business there to extract concessions from the HBC posts. The ban on alcohol, for example, was unenforceable as long as it was available five days' travel from Fort Pelly. Simpson, for his part, initially downplayed these developments but soon found himself in the unexpected position of trying to protect the company's Indian trade. To that end, he opened a new post, Fort Ellice, at the junction of the Beaver Creek and the Assiniboine River (just inside the Manitoba border). Starting in 1833, he also paid the American Fur Company £300 per year not to trade with Indians in the British North-West.

These measures did not stop the growing trade with the Americans. The Missouri posts had not only ended the HBC monopoly—ironically, after less than a decade—but also threatened to take an even larger share of the trade when they started collecting bison robes. The leather made ideal machinery belting, and as the United States industrialized in the mid-nineteenth century, a market developed for the heavy, bulky robes. This new demand meant new opportunities for Indians. The Blackfoot Alliance and other Indian groups had participated in the pemmican trade, but grudgingly on the margins and only because they needed guns, ammunition, and other goods. They resented the lower prices, which were a far cry from the competitive days of the trade, and looked to their own subsistence needs first before trading any excess meat from their pounding activities.[75] The new bison robe market offered a welcome alternative.

Indians had tried trading robes in the late eighteenth and early nineteenth century, but few were accepted by the HBC and NWC, and only because the rival concerns wanted to maintain their business. Now the American forts were happy to take as many robes as the Indians could supply. This trade reoriented many Indian bands away from the crowded winter pounding grounds along the Saskatchewan. They did not forsake their bison-subsistence lifestyle; only incorporated the robe trade into their seasonal rounds. It also meant less travel for them. "Finding a market for their Skins or robes on the Spot," Simpson bemoaned the consequences for HBC trade, "instead of being at the trouble of dragging them overland a distance of several hundred miles."[76] But the robe trade made little difference to the domestic lives of Indian women. They went from the smoke and the heat of the fires, sweating over kettles as they prepared pemmican, to scraping by hand the inside of the bison skins.

The robe trade boomed along the upper Missouri River in the 1830s. The hide was so ubiquitous that the American Fur Company made it the standard of trade at its posts. The HBC Northern Council tried to counter the American competition by passing resolutions at its 1832, 1833, and 1836 meetings, imploring its traders to accept more bison robes. But the company received on average only one robe for every eight traded in the United States. In 1832, seventy-two hundred robes were shipped from Fort Union. Two years later, nine thousand robes left Fort McKenzie, the new post at the Marias River. Despite the bulkiness of the cargo, steamboats now working the Missouri River easily handled the steadily growing volume. The HBC simply could not compete; probably 50 per cent of the robes traded south of the border came from British territory.[77]

One of the major trading groups at the American posts was the Assiniboine. They traded robes, meat, and fat for weapons in their push to extend their territory southward, closer to the bison herds. The repercussions were felt throughout the region. After a particularly hard winter in 1833–34,

UNIVERSITY OF SASKATCHEWAN ARCHIVES AND SPECIAL COLLECTIONS 28540

The sanctity of country marriages was undermined by HBC Governor George Simpson.

the Assiniboine conducted their trade at Fort Union and then attacked nearby Hidatsa villages. "War, war, war is their constant cry," declared one trader.[78] The Blackfoot Alliance also increasingly patronized the American posts. The Peigan, in particular, abandoned beaver trapping for the robe trade, something more in keeping with their bison-hunting skills, and now rarely came north to the HBC posts. A sure sign of how things had changed, from when the Peigan had once made Fort Edmonton one of the most profitable posts in the system, is that Simpson thought it was fruitless to try to recover their trade and began to regard them as "American" Indians.[79]

George Simpson would not have admitted it, but practice did not always

355

follow policy in the post-merger HBC world and the situation on the ground could not be so easily changed, let alone controlled. There was one fur trade practice, though, that Simpson appeared to accept. After his relationship with Betsy Sinclair in the early 1820s ended, he had two sons with his new mixed-descent companion Margaret (Peggy) Taylor: George in 1827 and John in 1829. And although Simpson, renowned for his overactive libido, had several liaisons and fathered at least half a dozen children (the exact number is unknown), he seemed to have formed a stable relationship with Peggy. But then, that changed in 1830 when Simpson returned from a trip to England, married to his first cousin Frances. Peggy and her children were quickly and quietly shuffled away, while Mrs. Simpson took up residence as the governor's wife, "always terrified to look about her," she said, "in case of seeing something disagreeable."[80]

Frances was not the first white woman in Rupert's Land. There were at least two before her, including Marie Anne Lagimodière, the maternal grandmother of Louis Riel, who came west in 1806 with her Nor'Wester husband and eventually settled at Red River.[81] Fur trade men, moreover, often had "double" or two families, one in the North-West, the other in Canada or England. But Frances's physical presence in Rupert's Land, as the British bride of Simpson, represented a break with fur-trade tradition and sent shockwaves through the fur-trade community, especially when most other company officers had country marriages. Simpson's behaviour has been castigated as racist, that his marriage was just another indication of his discriminatory attitude towards Métis peoples—except when it came to satisfying his lust. But the governor was also obsessed with status and sought to elevate himself above others. That is why he always had a crack canoe team and dramatically swept into a post during his visits. It is also why he retained a piper, starting in 1827, to announce his arrival. And it is also why he married Frances. A British wife added an "aura of respectability," and to maintain that respectability she had to be kept apart from other women who were beneath her standing.[82] Many officers were upset when their wives could not be introduced to Frances, but as far as Simpson was concerned, "the greater the distance at which they are kept apart the better."[83]

Other HBC officers followed Simpson's example and secured British-born wives. James Hargrave at York Factory, for example, found it regrettable that fur traders had become entangled in country marriages and thereafter could not go back to the "civilized world" but "buried themselves alive in the forests of the country."[84] That would not do for him, and in 1840, he wed Letitia Mactavish in Scotland. These "genteel" marriages symbolized how the isolation of the North-West was ending. Certainly, the fur trade had intruded on the region and its peoples. But for a century and a half, it operated without much interference. It was the only newcomer activity that had dealings with the Indian population in the western interior. Now, other peoples and other forces began to move into the region in the early to mid-nineteenth century. The social stratification of fur trade society introduced and promoted by Simpson was just the beginning.

The Red River settlement in 1860

WE THINK IT THE BEST

HIS MISSIONARY ACTIVITIES WERE NOT WANTED THERE. IN THE LATE SPRING OF **1840,** Reverend Henry Budd, along with his wife and family, headed to Cumberland House on the Saskatchewan River to establish a Church Missionary Society station. It was the first time that any religious organization had moved out beyond the Red River basin to minister to the people of the western interior and establish schools for their children. CMS officials realized that, in dealing with Indians, Budd would need "a proper sense of God's love... to exercise... patience... in encountering barbarism and its attendant evils apathy, obstinacy, and indolence."[1] It was the traders at Cumberland House, however, who proved inhospitable, if not hostile, to Budd's presence and forced him to move the proposed mission station downriver to The Pas. The Hudson's Bay Company under Governor George Simpson was not necessarily opposed to the presence of missionaries in Rupert's Land but deliberately chose to keep their numbers down and limit their proselytizing to areas where they could not harm the fur trade. "An enlightened Indian," a dismissive Simpson observed, "is good for nothing."[2] But neither the HBC nor its overseas governor could hold back a mid-nineteenth century imperialist movement bent on "civilizing" Rupert's Land and its peoples. "That vast territory," Royal Engineer M. H. Synge confidently predicted in *Great Britain, One Empire,* "would be rescued from the condition of a wilderness scarcely trodden by civilized man, and be transformed into an empire teeming with activity and life."[3]

It did not matter that the inhabitants of the region may not have wanted to be "rescued" or that they already had their own distinctive society "teeming with activity and life." The civilizers—whether missionaries, adventurers, or scientists—were going to remake the region. It was not a question of why, or even how, but only when.

Rupert's Land had never been immune to outside forces. One of the most devastating up until the nineteenth century was disease, appearing both without warning and with deadly regularity. Indeed, sickness in one form or another had stalked the land ever since newcomers had arrived but, thankfully, seldom reached epidemic proportions. That changed in 1837 when another smallpox outbreak, equal in mortality to the 1781–82 scourge, raged across the northern grasslands. The contagion came from the south. An annual supply boat from St. Louis carried the disease up the Missouri River to Fort Union in June 1837. Indians frequenting the post were immediately infected, culminating weeks later in what one eyewitness described as "the greatest destruction possible."[4] The virulence of the disease was made worse by the unusually cold wet spring, which had left many Indian families vulnerable. The mortality rate among the Assiniboine and Blackfoot reportedly ranged from one-half to two-thirds. Some bands were effectively "shattered into tiny, starving remnants."[5] The Mandan population dropped below the genetic survival threshold.

The disease reached the Saskatchewan country by the early autumn of 1837. William Todd, chief factor of the Swan River district and, fortunately, a physician by training, was not sure from Indian reports whether he was dealing with smallpox but decided to vaccinate any Indians in the Fort Pelly area through the fall and into the winter. Todd also taught Indian headmen the procedure so that they could treat their followers, as well as sent fresh cow vaccine to other HBC posts to the west and north. These preventative measures constituted "the first extensive vaccination program among the Indians of western Canada."[6] And they saved hundreds, perhaps thousands, of lives, especially since the disease was stopped from spreading beyond the Saskatchewan River. But the death toll on the northern plains was nonetheless staggering. The Assiniboine

Swampy Cree Henry Budd (Sakacewescam), the grandson of HBC servant Matthew Cocking, trained as an Anglican priest for the Church Missionary Society.

and Blackfoot, because they were not vaccinated, suffered population losses from 50 to 75 per cent. "It seems as if the very genius of desolation," one observer lamented, "had ... wreaked his vengeance on everything bearing the shape of humanity."[7] The Cree, and the Saulteaux, by contrast, were largely spared and

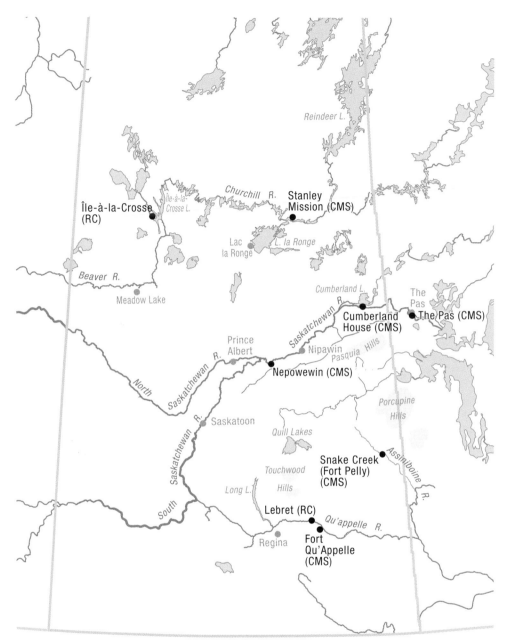

RC: OBLATES OF MARY IMMACULATE (ROMAN CATHOLIC)
CMS: CHURCH MISSIONARY SOCIETY (ANGLICAN)
Missions in Rupert's Land

moved farther south and west in mixed bands into lands that had been emptied by the disease. Ironically, the Cree emerged from the epidemic as a dominant tribe, whose numbers continued to grow into the mid-nineteenth century.[8]

It was in the aftermath of the 1837–38 epidemic that the Church Missionary Society decided to expand its evangelical efforts into the Saskatchewan country. And just as smallpox was an unwelcome intruder, so too was the proposed mission station at Cumberland House. Missionaries had been active in the Red River settlement since 1818, when two Roman Catholic priests arrived at the invitation of Lord Selkirk. Two years later, John West, a Church of England priest, was named chaplain to the HBC and agent for the Church Missionary Society at Red River. These missionary endeavours were endorsed by several members of the HBC London Committee for the positive benefits they would bring to HBC employees and Aboriginal peoples in Rupert's Land and were to be supported through financial and other aid, such as the free transporting of personnel and supplies.[9] But they were also to be carefully circumscribed.

George Simpson, upon assuming direction of the Northern department, questioned the value of religious instruction, maintaining that Indians would be "rear[ed] ... in habits of indolence."[10] Nor was he alone in his racist views. James Hargrave, writing from York Factory in 1827, wondered whether "darkened minds" could be opened to Christianity.[11] But what mattered more to Simpson and other traders was how missionaries could interfere with the company's business. Reverend West, for example, complained about HBC men working on Sundays. He also railed against the importation and use of alcohol in the trade. Most worrisome, though, was West's ambitious plan for a series of mission stations at every HBC post throughout the North-West. At these places, Indians would not only be introduced to Christianity, but actively encouraged to abandon the hunt and settle down permanently to a farming life, centred on the church and the school.[12] These "civilizing" initiatives represented a clear threat to the conduct of HBC operations. And the best way to prevent them, in Simpson's words, from "do[ing] harm instead of good to the Fur Trade"[13] was to require any new mission in Rupert's Land to be authorized by the Northern department. "Every mission if successful," Simpson reasoned, "must be considered the germ of a future village."[14]

One of the ways that the CMS, and Reverend West in particular, sought to extend the reach of Christianity into Rupert's Land was to recruit and train a "Native" ministry that could work among their own people—to indigenize the church in Indian territory. To this end, on his way to Red River in 1819, West brought a fatherless seven-year-old Swampy Cree boy from York Factory, named Sakacewescam (Going-up-the-Hill), to be educated under his guidance at a school he opened in the settlement. It was a common belief at the time— and into the twentieth century—that Indian children could best be converted and assimilated if separated from their family influence and indigenous culture. In Sakacewescam's case, he was inducted into the English world of his maternal grandfather, mid-eighteenth-century HBC servant Matthew Cocking, and renamed Henry Budd at his baptism in 1822.[15] By the time he left school in 1827, his disciplined training, often in the form of memorization and recitation, had instilled in him the principal beliefs and teachings of the Anglican Church. That he was able to preach in both English and Cree was also considered a bonus. But toleration and acceptance of any other aspects of Indian culture beyond language was considered contrary to his role as a civilizer.[16]

Henry Budd got the opportunity to serve the CMS in the interior in 1840 when he was dispatched to establish an Indian mission at Cumberland House, the HBC's first inland post and an ideal location for the Anglican's initial foothold in the interior. Governor Simpson had initially looked positively upon the proposal because he wanted to discourage the continuing migration of inland groups and families to the Red River settlement. But, in clear defiance of Simpson's authority, the CMS never asked permission and quickly learned how uncooperative the HBC could be, even though the mission was funded in part by the estate of James Leith, who had once commanded Cumberland House.[17] Budd had to relocate instead to The Pas, a traditional Cree gathering place and a winter outpost on the Saskatchewan River (just on the Manitoba side of the present-day interprovincial boundary). His arrival there was equally tense, as many of the Cree spiritual leaders regarded him with suspicion, if not contempt. But Budd and his spouse, Betsy Work, the mixed-descent daughter of a HBC trader, accepted the challenge and began clearing land on the south

HIND, NARRATIVE, V. 1

The Upper Nepowewin mission (left) on the north side of the Saskatchewan River
and directly across the river from Fort à la Corne.

side of the river for the new Christ Church station, later known as Devon.[18]

By 1842, only two years into his mission, Budd's proselytization activities had recruited thirty-one pupils for the school and nineteen adults on average attending Sunday services. These numbers, however heartening, masked several difficulties. Even though the site at The Pas was better suited for agriculture than Cumberland House, Budd struggled to establish a successful farm in the face of early frosts and the frequent flooding of the river. Supplies had to be imported from York Factory or Red River to ensure the continued survival of the village.[19] The arrival of Reverend James Hunter in 1845 to take over the mission also relegated Budd to a secondary role; manual labour was given precedence over his teaching duties. The CMS may have wanted a Native ministry but assumed that graduates like Budd required a heavy supervisory hand because of their race and the feared prospect of them deviating from Anglican doctrine.[20] Hunter also believed that the local Indians had been ruined by the fur trade—he initially derided them for being "lazy and impudent"—while Budd held out some real hope that they could be changed for the better.[21] Nor were traditional Indian practices to be respected. After Hunter had taken charge, a sacred rock, known as the Painted Stone or *ka mik wa pisa sik,* was dumped into the river in order to ensure that converts did not fall back on their traditional beliefs. He also tried to induce local Cree leaders to abandon the hunt and settle down and build houses in the village by offering material gifts, much like the trading companies had been doing for decades.[22]

Christ Church station tended to have a fluid population, a reflection of the seasonal nature of the local subsistence economy. In the spring, entire families would forsake the village for the annual muskrat hunt and the tapping of birch sap. Men would also serve as HBC tripmen for the summer, leaving behind their families to tend to their few stock and small garden plots, seeded mostly with potatoes. In the fall, reunited families would participate in the annual goose and duck hunt, and then the men would be off again, outfitted at Cumberland House for winter trapping, while woman and children worked the local fishery in nearby lakes and rivers.[23] The mission school population consequently greatly fluctuated, especially if starvation was to be avoided. "We cannot keep the children together for a long time," Budd confided to his journal, "and just the time when they would be getting on and beginning to understand what they are doing they always leave the School."[24] One wonders, though, how much they actually learned by memorizing English passages. Attendance was encouraged through the distribution of clothing, blankets, and food to pupils. But even here, Budd ran into trouble with parents for his decision to ration food and instill in his charges a sense of discipline, something that went against Indian cultural practice.[25] Despite this kind of misunderstanding, the mission became a place of refuge where the infirm, the sick, the elderly, the banished, and the hungry gathered to survive on Christian charity.

The Church Missionary Society used The Pas station as a springboard for other proselytizing activity in the region. With HBC approval, Budd founded a new mission at "Upper Nepowewin" on the north side of the Saskatchewan River in August 1852. The site was directly across the river from Fort à la Corne (*nicawakihcikanisihk* or Little Garden), occupied by the HBC from 1850–85, and a traditional gathering place known as the "Waiting Place" (*pehonān*), where

SASKATCHEWAN ARCHIVES BOARD R-A7512

Cree catechist James Settee (centre rear) spearheaded Anglican proselytizing efforts in the English River district.

Indians waited for the arrival of the canoe brigades.[26] Much like the traders before them, the missionaries chose places where Indians tended to congregate for spiritual and other purposes.

Budd was welcomed at first, on the mistaken assumption that he was there as a trader. But when the Indians learned of his true purpose, he was told to leave.[27] Mansack, leader of the Twatts band, complained that "wherever religion came, it drove the animals away."[28] Budd persisted but found that as a Swampy Cree he had difficulty relating to the Assiniboine, Saulteaux, and even the Plains Cree, who sometimes visited the site. "They are *truly heathen*, and *truly barbarous*," he described the bison-hunting Cree. "They are more independent, and therefore more haughty."[29] Budd maintained that they would never "learn the civilized life" unless he travelled and camped with them, but his CMS superiors were more interested in a successful mission at Nepowewin than itinerant preaching among strange and distant bands. He therefore concentrated his energies on converting the Woodland Cree, in particular the mixed-descent Twatt brothers, probably in the belief that they would be more accepting of Christianity because of their HBC Orkney father Magnus Twatt. Budd's journal details the many conversations that he had with Willock Twatt about "white" religion and how the medicine man steadfastly resisted abandoning traditional practices for an uncertain way of life. "Each one," Willock pronounced, "should keep the Religion God has given them."[30] Like The Pas station, then, Nepowewin came to serve largely as a sanctuary, but one that never had a secure food supply despite its agricultural pretensions. Indeed, the difficulties of farming were often used in CMS fundraising campaigns. It also provided employment to those willing to work in and around the mission, including hunting for provisions, something that "civilized" Indians were supposed to give up. The few converts, meanwhile, were either ostracized by fellow Cree or tempted by rum to rejoin their band.[31]

Anglican activity also extended south, west, and north across present-day Saskatchewan in the 1850s. In 1851, Charles Pratt (born Askenootow), a Cree–Assiniboine catechist trained at Red River, established a mission house on Snake Creek, a short distance from Fort Pelly in the Swan River district. He was chosen for the task, in part, because he and his wife had relatives in the area and these kinship ties could often break down barriers.[32] The HBC, however, was upset by the move because it was done without Simpson's authorization. But the larger problem in getting established proved to be a shortage of food, which often forced the closure of the school; the local resources could not sustain a larger, semi-sedentary population. The garrison at Pelly was also not the best role model for Euro–North American civilization. A missionary described the traders as "perfectly honest, their chief sins seem to be drunkenness, idleness and unbelief."[33]

Pratt founded another mission farther west in the fall of 1852 near the HBC post between the second and third of the Qu'Appelle (Fishing) Lakes. But the station was forcibly closed in 1859, albeit temporarily, by warriors from Young Dog's band who objected to a settlement in their hunting territory. This incident did not prevent Pratt from building a new Anglican mission that same year in the Touchwood Hills near the HBC post of the same

SASKATCHEWAN ARCHIVES BOARD S-B2822

An Anglican service at Lac La Ronge

name. And when the HBC relocated its fort to the Little Touchwood Hills the following year, the mission followed.[34] While searching for a suitable site for the buildings, Pratt came across a stone image, painted in ochre, atop one of the highest hills, and rolled it away. "My heart mourned within me," he recounted in his journal, "to think of the Kingdom of darkness reigning over this vast empire."[35] This attitude towards traditional spirituality is challenged by family oral history, which remembers Pratt as someone caught between Indian and newcomer worlds.[36]

The CMS also set its sights again on Cumberland House and its resident population and sent Budd there in 1859 to ascertain the prospects for a mission. This time, the HBC traders and their families welcomed his presence, and within two years, a church and school were established near the post on the understanding that they would be self-supporting. Budd also visited Fort Carlton on the South Saskatchewan in 1853 and distributed books to the children and Bibles to the adults. But it would be another four years before he returned, this time finding almost fifty children living in the fort. Budd baptized and married some of the post's occupants but could do little more, given his other responsibilities, than institute a schedule of quarterly visits over the next few years. This itinerant work ended in 1867 when Budd was placed in charge of The Pas parish, the first in Rupert's Land under a Native pastor, with oversight of the Nepowewin and Cumberland House missions. He remained, though, under the direct supervision of an English church official. This brake on his independence was probably accepted in the knowledge that converts were becoming the majority in the three communities. He had not only convinced Mansack to convert but had developed a friendship with Plains Cree chief Mistawasis (Big Child).[37]

The CMS also looked north to the sprawling English River district. In 1846, Cree catechist James Settee and his mixed-descent wife, Sally, the daughter of HBC officer Joseph Cook, headed to the HBC Lac la Ronge post to lay the groundwork for a mission. It was the second time that the couple had taken on such a task; the first time among a mixed Cree–Assiniboine band in the Moose Mountain region in 1841–42 had ended in failure. Settee's Swampy Cree background, however, proved helpful in his proselytizing efforts at Lac la Ronge, and when Reverend Hunter from The Pas station visited a year later, he baptized over one hundred adults and children. This encouraging beginning may have been an Indian response to the ready availability of a new source of European goods. But it nonetheless prompted the CMS in 1849—the same year the Anglican diocese of Rupert's Land was created—to send English priest Robert Hunt to oversee the establishment of a permanent mission. With Settee's help in 1851, Hunt chose a favourite Cree gathering place on the north side of the Churchill River, known as âmaciwispimowinihk (shooting arrows uphill place). The Church of England had grand ambitions for what became known as Stanley Mission. By the end of the decade, the graceful Gothic

ALAN STURLEY NUNN

Holy Trinity Church at Stanley Mission is Saskatchewan's oldest extant structure.

Revival Holy Trinity Church, with its towering spire, anchored a large mission complex, including a school, parsonage, barn, storeroom, warehouse, and grist mill. But farming was an uncertain enterprise because of the thin layer of soil and short growing season, and the mission had to rely on the HBC and local Indians for provisions. Settee, meanwhile, chafed at his second-class treatment at the hands of Hunt, but his loyalty and devotion to the church never faltered. And even though he is remembered today as the founder of Stanley Mission, he was transferred before work started on Holy Trinity Church and spent most of his career as Rupert Land's second ordained Native minister in the Swan River district.[38]

Anglican expansion across Rupert's Land was motivated by a keen rivalry with the Roman Catholic Church. In the race for Indian souls, the CMS wanted to get there first. But if George Simpson had had his way, Catholic priests would not have been allowed into the region as "a measure of policy ... every measure should be used to check the Roman Catholic influence."[39] This stance was countered by Eden Colvile, the new HBC representative in the Red River colony, who questioned why there was "so much prejudice" against Catholic missionaries, especially when "they are much better fitted" to this role because of "the way they accommodate themselves to the circumstances of the country."

373

Colvile submitted to Simpson, "I suppose everyone ... will admit that it is better for people to be Roman Catholics, than not to be Christian at all."[40] But neither the Anglicans nor the Catholics were so open-minded about faith and conversion. Just as the old Hudson's Bay Company and North West Company had once fiercely competed for fur trade supremacy, so too did the two religious denominations in the mid-nineteenth century—only this time, the battleground was largely restricted to the Saskatchewan and English River districts.

In 1840, the same year that the CMS had sent Henry Budd to Cumberland House, Father George-Antoine Bellecourt started Catholic missions on Lakes Winnipegosis (St. Norbert at Baie-des-Canards [Duck Bay]) and Manitoba (Notre Dame du Lac). These first steps were followed up by Jean-Baptiste Thibault, who at the request of Bishop Joseph-Norbert Provencher of Saint-Boniface, rode west on horseback from Red River to Edmonton House in the summer of 1842 to bring the gospel to the region's residents. Thibault was the first Catholic priest to visit many of the HBC posts in the Swan River and Saskatchewan districts. And even though the priest's trip went against Simpson's wishes, he encountered no animosity and conducted over three hundred baptisms, most likely for the mixed-descent children of French-Canadian Freemen. He later established Lac Sainte Anne mission at a popular Cree gathering place, known as Lake Manitou, west of Edmonton House.[41] Thibault was under no illusions about the task ahead of the church in ministering to a migratory people. "Only when the last buffalo is dead," he confessed, "shall we be able to do something for [the Indians]."[42]

Thibault's reception contrasted sharply with that of his confrère Jean-Édouard Darveau. Already hassled by the Anglicans at his Baie-des-Canards mission, Darveau decided to take the battle directly to the CMS at The Pas mission in 1843. Here, he was met with threats and intimidation from the Protestant community, including Henry Budd, which evidently claimed that the priest was a windigo or cannibalistic half-beast. Darveau's presence also sowed confusion among the Indians. As long as the Anglicans operated in isolation from their Catholic counterparts, the newcomer world revolved around the

Oblate Alexandre-Antonin Taché helped establish the Sainte-Jean-Baptiste mission at Île-à-la-Crosse.

fur trade and the mission—two clearly different options for Indian peoples. Now, with denominational rivalry being played out before them, the Cree faced a more complicated, if not bewildering, situation.[43] One Indian leader at Baie-des-Canards told rival missionaries that his band would keep their own religion until their disagreements were resolved. "When you both agree, and travel the same road, we will travel with you," he promised, "till then, however, we will adhere to our own religion; we think it the best."[44]

Sadly, one of the casualties of this religious competition was Darveau, who died under mysterious circumstances in 1844. Initially assumed to have drowned, he was probably murdered by Indians who believed that he was an evil spirit and the source of an epidemic.[45] His death served as an exclamation mark for the general failure of these early Catholic missions among the Saulteaux in the Manitoba Lake region. Not only was the church hard-pressed to find enough resources, but the Indians also proved indifferent to the efforts of the priests. "I think God does not want the Saulteaux," Father François-Xavier Bermond wrote in frustration, "since they want so little of Him and his priest."[46]

Catholic missionaries enjoyed their greatest success at Île-à-la-Crosse in present-day northwestern Saskatchewan—a development that caused an alarmed CMS to dispatch James Settee to Lac la Ronge as a countermove. Father Thibault had visited the area in the spring of 1845 as part of his search for possible mission sites and held mass and performed several hundred baptisms, particularly among the Chipewyan, during his stay at the HBC post. He also found a receptive host in Chief Factor Roderick McKenzie, who was being pestered by the local populace to secure the services of a priest. McKenzie readily appreciated the benefits of a mission to the largely Métis population of the region, many of whom worked for the company, and had already written Bishop Provencher at Red River about the matter. This request, along with Thibault's report about the encouraging prospects in the English River district, convinced Provencher to give his blessing to the project. Simpson did, too, even though he reprimanded McKenzie for inviting a priest there on his own initiative. Whereas other missions in Rupert's Land sometimes clashed with fur trade interests, he hoped that the presence of clergy would stabilize the regional population and ensure its continued involvement in HBC activities. Simpson consequently offered to provide free transportation to any priest, maintain them at the post until the mission was completed, and if necessary, help with the construction of the mission if the workers' wages and food were paid for by the church. As one scholar has commented, the establishment of a permanent Catholic mission at Île-à-la-Crosse was "neither accidental nor unexpected."[47]

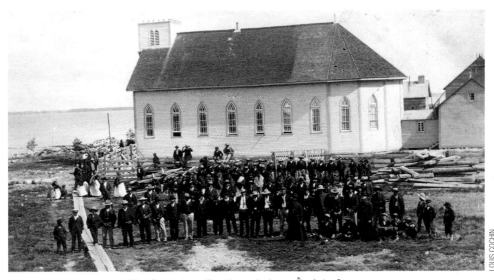

LOUIS COCHIN

The Saint-Jean-Baptiste mission at Île-à-la-Crosse

The two priests chosen to establish the Saint-Jean-Baptiste mission were Louis-François Laflèche and Alexandre-Antonin Taché, both from the order Oblates of Mary Immaculate (OMI), otherwise known as the Oblates. Both fathers would quickly rise to prominence in the church: Laflèche as bishop of Trois-Rivières, Quebec, and Taché, at just twenty-nine, as bishop of the new diocese of Saint Boniface. The two missionaries left for Île-à-la-Crosse in July 1846 and travelled with McKenzie from Norway House westward with the annual brigade. They lived at the post over the following winter as guests of McKenzie and used the time to learn to speak both Cree and Chipewyan, something they began on their canoe trip inland. Taché also slipped away for several months to visit outlying areas where the HBC operated posts and potential missions might be started. These trips over the next year took him first to Green and Reindeer Lakes and then Portage la Loche and Lake Athabasca; he deliberately avoided Lac la Ronge, which had just been claimed by Settee for the Anglicans. In the spring of 1847, work started on the presbytery and chapel, about a mile from the HBC post and at the edge of the peninsula where the NWC had first located in the 1770s. The priests also put in a garden and purchased a cow to provide fresh milk and butter. The main staple, though, was fish, sometimes complemented with potatoes. Facilities were enlarged over the next few years in keeping with Île-à-la-Crosse's role as administrative centre for pastoral activities throughout the vast region. The mission population also steadily grew, and soon included two other Oblates, Henri Faraud and Vital-Justin Grandin, who both served at the isolated La Nativité mission near Fort Chipewyan on Lake Athbasca. That Faraud and Grandin also became bishops led to the nickname, nursery of bishops, for Île-à-la-Crosse. It was also sometimes called the Bethlehem of the North.[48]

The Île-à-la-Crosse clergy quickly learned that one of the most effective ways to initiate contact and religious instruction with the Cree and Chipewyan population was to hold regular proselytizing missions when they gathered at the post in the spring and fall either to trade furs or secure supplies. These sessions could last several days, if not a week or more, and were designed to introduce the Indians to the basic tenets and practices of Catholicism. The local Métis people, on the other hand, were much more receptive to the mission, an attitude usually attributed to their French-Canadian heritage and predilection to Catholicism. After all, nearby Portage la Loche was the final "baptismal" site on the voyageur route inland from Montreal before crossing over into the Athabasca watershed. This ritual, along with other Catholic ceremonies and rites, was part of a local folk tradition that had been incorporated into the lives of the Métis of the English River district well before priests arrived. But the social foundations of the community were female and Indian, not male and Francophone, and consequently, "the acceptance of Christianity in any form" was not necessarily "natural." Instead, Catholicism was embraced and integrated into the Métis worldview because of its emphasis on home and family. The mission, in particular the clergy, became part of the larger community family and were looked to and relied upon in the same way that family members were expected to help one another. In turn, Catholic traditions and events were incorporated into the Métis identity, providing another means for community, family, and individual expression, while the church set standards of responsibility, morality, and obligation.[49]

This relationship between the local Métis community and the church

LOUIS COCHIN

The Grey Nuns operated a hospital, school, and orphanage in this building at Île-à-la-Crosse.

was best exemplified when the Sisters of Charity, more popularly called the Grey Nuns because of their habits (grey cassocks), arrived at Île-à-la-Crosse in October 1860 to assist with the mission. The sisters' headquarters, named Hôpital Saint-Bruno, was an impressive two-storey building, featuring a classroom and the region's (and province's) first hospital. The day they arrived, a sick young boy became their first patient, while just weeks later, they began operating a residential school in the building (École Sainte Famille) and enrolled their first pupils. The nuns also operated an orphanage. These church-run institutions were accepted by the Métis for the support and benefits they provided to the region's families and thereby strengthened the spiritual bond between the mission and the community. This connection was further reinforced when Métis parents asked members of the religious orders to serve as godparents to their children. Sister Sara (Marguerite Marie) Riel, for example, whose father was born at Île-à-la-Crosse and whose brother was the famous Métis leader, acted in this capacity for several families. To be accepted into the local community, moreover, outsider Protestant men, mostly HBC servants, had to convert to Catholicism before they could marry local women and become part of large extended families. Protestant HBC personnel did not enjoy the same relationship with the community but remained socially apart.[50]

The other Catholic beachhead in present-day Saskatchewan was the Qu'Appelle Valley. Bishop Provencher had visited there in 1819, as did Father Bellecourt in the early 1840s, but these probes were never followed up in a serious way. Father Taché, now bishop of Saint Boniface, changed that in 1864 when he passed through the region and encountered Métis families living in the scenic river valley. Taché's strategy in dealing with the North-West's vastness and the Protestant menace, was to establish a few key administrative centres at strategic points that would then support a collection of smaller missions at fur trade posts from which priests could undertake itinerant evangelizing trips among Indian bands, much like the fur trade companies had organized their operations. To this end, the bishop returned to the valley the next year and selected a site for a mission (Saint Florent) south of the HBC Fort Qu'Appelle at a place that became known as Lebret. That the CMS had been making regular visits to the area since 1842 did not matter to the priest. A "sadly grieved" James Settee, now working there, begged to differ: "the papist Bishop of these parts, had availed himself of the vacancy of this place ... this place belongs to the C.M. Society."[51] Taché sent Father Noël-Joseph Richot to the valley in 1866 and 1867 before naming a resident priest, Jules DeCorby, who spent part of each year accompanying the Indians and Métis on their hunting rounds. Thereafter, the Lebret mission became the headquarters of the western district of the Saint Boniface diocese.

Missionaries were not the only "outsiders" who became interested in Rupert's Land in the mid-nineteenth century. At the end of the Napoleonic wars in Europe, British attention once again turned to the search for the North-West passage, something that would occupy an otherwise mothballed British Navy. Between 1819 and 1822, John Franklin headed an overland expedition to map the arctic coastline east of the Coppermine River. Because the fur trade war between the HBC and NWC was still in full swing, Franklin received only minimal support as his party made its way to Fort Chipewyan. This chronic shortage of provisions—the men were reduced to boiling their moccasins—

"Passing from Touchwood Hills to Level Prairie" from Overlander William Hind's sketchbook

was one of the reasons that the expedition failed.

The second Franklin overland expedition (1825–27) had learned from this sorry experience and was better prepared for its exploration of the arctic coast east and west of the Mackenzie River delta. The HBC was also in a better position to provide assistance now that the feud with the NWC had been resolved. George Simpson believed that the promotion of science would not only boost the company's public image, but that exploration and mapping might possibly open up new fields of trade.[52] The HBC consequently provided logistical support during the expedition, including accommodation at posts, as well as ensured that it was well supplied with pemmican.[53] It was during this second expedition that Franklin reported in November 1825 that he and his men were playing hockey on the frozen ice along the southwest shore of Great Bear Lake, one of the earliest references to the game. "Till the snow fell," he wrote a scientific friend in England, "the game of hockey played on ice was the morning's sport."[54] And when Franklin went missing two decades later during his third arctic expedition, an 1848 search party, wintering at Cumberland House, volunteered their labour to build the manse at The Pas mission.[55]

The HBC also cooperated in the search for the magnetic north pole. Leaving Lachine, Quebec, with a company brigade in May 1843, J. H. Lefroy and his assistant conducted magnetic surveys in Rupert's Land during a five-thousand-mile, eighteen-month trek. Even though the bulk of the readings were conducted at Forts Chipewyan and Simpson, the pair made observations at more than three hundred stations across the North-West.[56]

Lefroy's other secondary task was to collect samples of flora and fauna from the region, but his rigorous routine—taking observations every hour, then every two minutes during high magnetic activity—left no time for this task. One of the first systematic natural history surveys in Rupert's Land was made by John Richardson during the first Franklin overland expedition and resulted in the identification and naming of several new species, such as Richardson's ground squirrel or flickertail, often colloquially called a gopher. Richardson and Thomas Drummond continued this field research during the second overland expedition, with Drummond remaining behind at Cumberland House in June 1825 and spending the next two years securing specimens, mostly botanical, up and down the Saskatchewan River, through the Rockies to the Columbia River, and north of present-day Jasper to the Athabasca River. This collecting complemented that of botanist David Douglas who gathered seeds from across western North America, including near Carlton House. Some of the plants from these seeds came to flourish in ornamental gardens in England.[57]

The quest for unusual specimens brought other collectors to the northern plains: big-game hunters. Men of fortune and title from the United Kingdom and to a lesser extent continental Europe headed to Rupert's Land for adventure and sport, especially the chance to shoot bison. The first aristocrats to venture into the region, as Simpson's guests, were the Earls of Caledon and Musgrave in 1841.[58] Outfitted with Métis guides, they went in search of bison southwest of the Red River settlement.

Others followed in their wake, a steady succession of wealthy young sportsmen through the 1840s and 1850s, as news of the great herds and the "wild" Indians that lived upon them spread among elite hunting circles. Many

"Upset Cart, Touchwood Hills" from Overlander William Hind's sketchbook

of these well-heeled interlopers vilified Indian procurement methods—the use of pounds and jumps and the killing of females and calves—as barbaric and wasteful, a violation of the accepted gentlemanly hunting code that separated man from beast.[59] But the large shaggy bulls that white sportsmen triumphantly brought down as trophies dressed out tough and musty, and probably elicited knowing smiles from their guides. Some Indian bands looked upon the hunting parties with curiosity and demanded presents; others saw them as trespassers. In 1862, the Lord Dunsmore group decided not to go to the Cypress Hills when their Métis guide James McKay could not guarantee their safety. And when it was returning from the Souris plains, the Young Dogs, the mixed Assiniboine–Cree band that had forced the temporary abandonment of the CMS Fort Qu'Appelle mission a few years earlier, insisted on payment for game taken in its hunting territory. Dunsmore sensed that the band was uneasy about their presence but even more so about their intentions.[60]

What the Young Dogs and other peoples of the region could not prevent the strangers from doing was giving British names to places in Rupert's Land. Granted, fur traders had applied newcomer names to rivers leading to Hudson Bay and to their settlements, often at traditional gathering places. But hunters and adventurers were at the forefront in assigning names to geographical features: after themselves, nobility, their friends, their homes, and anything else with British Empire connections. They took satisfaction in being the "first" European to visit a particular location, regardless of who might have come before them. Two of the most ambitious were Viscount W. F. Milton and Dr. Francis Cheadle who crossed Rupert's Land in 1862–63 and commemorated their trip in the jointly authored *The North-West Passage by Land*—and the names they left behind. By this act, repeated over and over again, outsiders took symbolic possession of the land and effectively erased its past history. Nameless space had been transformed into a particular place on a map and was one step closer to being civilized.[61] One scholar, though, has likened the process to leaving graffiti on the landscape, "saying, 'I was here.'"[62]

Travellers also recast Rupert's Land in their published accounts as something distinctly familiar and British. Streams, for example, morphed into highland rivers, while the open plains were reminiscent of English estates. James Carnegie, the Earl of Southesk, could not have been more rhapsodic in *Saskatchewan and the Rocky Mountains* as he crossed the prairie beyond Fort Qu'Appelle in 1859. "Flowers of the gayest colour enlivened the landscape," he gushed as if transported to an English garden. "Sometimes acres and acres were covered with intermingled masses of the orange [tiger] lily and the pendulous blue-bells ... a vast oriental carpet had been thrown upon the plain." And when an approaching thunderstorm chased his party into a coulee for shelter, Carnegie found in the "secluded glen" three young wolves who "kept up a chorus all night ... with mewing whines, like a family of peevish kittens."[63] It was also quite common to make comparisons with home. The Baronet of Netherby equated his crossing of the North Saskatchewan River in 1847 to the Thames River at Westminister.[64] Nor was this picturesque landscape confined to writing. Artist Paul Kane, with Simpson's sponsorship, spent more than two years on an oil painting trip from Toronto across Rupert's Land to the Pacific Coast and back between 1846 and 1848. Kane is lauded today for his vibrant portrayal of the peoples and their activities. His sketches of that particular time and place have no equal. But some of his paintings show classical European influences.[65] And when he published a book about his experience more than a decade later, *Wanderings of an Artist among the Indians of North America* (1859), Kane portrayed the region in highly romantic terms.[66]

There was nothing romantic about the experience of the "Overlanders" who headed to the Fraser River goldfields in British Columbia by crossing the northern plains in 1858 and 1859. Seemingly oblivious to the distance and risks involved, several hundred prospective miners from the eastern United States and Canada, some with partners and families, set off by cart from Red River for Edmonton House and the mountains beyond. Most were forestalled by winter and forced to wait it out at fur trade posts along the North Saskatchewan, while others, driven by gold fever, pushed on. Some turned back, defeated by the enormity of the undertaking.[67] Their journals make for lively reading, what with the hardships and misadventures. One American overlander nearly lost his party's horses when he started a fire on the open prairie one night to drive off the mosquitoes.[68]

Mishaps aside, what these accounts and those of other travellers provided was another source of information about Rupert's Land. It may not have been completely accurate. It may not have been comprehensive and broad-ranging. And it may not have captured the complexities or defining features. But their stories and writing offered a perspective on the region and its future that was different from the fur trader and even the missionary. That the overlanders crossed the continent via British territory revived Alexander Mackenzie's idea of a northern route to the Pacific. British adventurers, meanwhile, dismissed Indian peoples as relics of an uncivilized past who were doomed to disappear. In their place, they held out the prospect of an agricultural eden where the best features of British civilization would take root and flourish in the largely "empty"—more correctly, emptied—landscape. "From Red River to the Rocky Mountains," Milton and Cheadle trumpeted, "at least sixty millions of acres of the richest soil lie ready for the farmer *when he shall be allowed to enter in and possess it.*"[69] The question, though, was when.

The HBC began the process of finding an answer when it requested a renewal of its exclusive trading licence in 1857. The first twenty-one-year licence had been renewed four years early in 1838 and the company now sought another extension. The request could not have been made at a worse time for the company. For the past decade, there had been a growing volume of criticism of the HBC's management of its vast domain and its trade monopoly. In 1846, Alexander Kennedy Isbister, a former mixed-descent employee born at Cumberland House but educated in Edinburgh, published a blistering attack in *A Few Words on the Hudson's Bay Company*. British parliamentarian and future prime minister William Gladstone, in the meantime, hammered away at company privileges in the House of Commons at a time when Great Britain was moving in the direction of ending its preferential trade policies in favour of open markets and fewer colonial responsibilities; what has been called the imperialism of free trade.

There was also some question about the HBC's ability to protect and maintain British interests against an aggressive United States, especially after the 1846 Oregon crisis had ended in the loss of the territory, known as the Columbia district, to the Americans. That outcome had nearly resulted in a British House of Commons investigation into the company's operations.[70] Now, with the HBC licence renewal request before it, the Commons took advantage of the opening it had been handed and passed a resolution on 5 February 1857 establishing a Select Committee "to consider the state of those British Possessions in North America ... under the Administration of the Hudson's Bay Company."[71] The open-ended nature of the resolution was troubling for the company, but even more ominous was that another older monopoly concern, the East India Company, seemed headed for the dustbin.

In deciding whether the HBC monopoly should be renewed, the British government also had to consider whether Rupert's Land should be opened to agricultural settlement. And since these interrelated questions necessarily involved the interests of the United Province of Canada (Canada East [Quebec] and Canada West [Ontario]), the British Colonial secretary asked Governor

General Sir Edmund Head whether the Canadian government wanted to be represented at the Select Committee hearings. The Reform (later Liberal) members of the Canadian Parliament, headed by Toronto *Globe* publisher George Brown, jumped at the opportunity. Since the late 1840s, Brown had derided the HBC and its ancient charter for standing in the way of westward expansion from the confines of the lower Great Lakes. "It is unpardonable," he declared in one of his fiery editorials, "that civilization should be excluded from half a continent on at best a doubtful right of ownership."[72] What lay behind this malicious campaign against the company was the urgent need for Canada West to expand. The province, hemmed in by the Canadian Shield to the north, was running out of agricultural land and if it was not going to stagnate and see its booming population siphoned off by the United States, then its boundaries would have to expand westward beyond Lake Superior. That the northern plains were believed to be fertile was all that mattered, especially for a Toronto business community entranced by the great profits to be made from a large western market populated by thousands, maybe even hundreds of thousands, of farmers. In an 1856 dispatch to the colonial office, an amused Head reported, "All sorts of dreams and speculations are floating in the public mind here, even among sober and good men ... it seems to be assumed ... that there is an inherent right on the part of Canada to some of the spoils of the Hudson's Bay Company."[73]

The British invitation to be represented at the Select Committee inquiry prompted the Canadian Legislature to hold its own parallel investigation in the late spring of 1857 into the rights of the HBC and the agricultural potential of Rupert's Land. It was a cursory hearing. Only three witnesses were questioned—only one of whom had been employed in the region, mostly around James Bay. George Brown's participation as one of the commissioners also ensured that its findings would support the Canadian position that the HBC monopoly should end. That was the same argument that the Canadian government advanced in its brief to the British Select Committee, drawn up before its own hearings on the matter got underway. The memorandum insisted that Canada was the rightful heir to Rupert's Land because of French and then North West Company activities in the western interior and that this claim had not been extinguished in 1821 when the Montreal-based traders joined with the HBC.

As for the HBC charter, Canada maintained that it was completely invalid and that even if the company had claim to any land, it was confined to the shores of Hudson Bay. Interestingly, the British government was prepared to ask the Judicial Committee of the Privy Council to determine the boundary between Canada and the HBC, something the company did not oppose. But when Canada countered that the validity of the charter should really be tested, both the British government and the HBC balked. Having recognized the charter for generations, the British Crown was not about to question past practice. Nor did the company want the validity of its claim subjected to legal scrutiny. The charter was consequently never tested in British courts.[74]

Because the Canadian position revolved around the legality of the HBC charter, Chief Justice William Draper of Canada West represented Canada before the British Select Committee. His was a limited mandate, probably because his instructions came from John A. Macdonald, the attorney general West and future Canadian prime minister, who at the time was not an advocate of westward expansion. Sent there as only an observer, Draper was not to enter into any negotiations nor agree to any plan—just ensure that Canada's interests were not sacrificed by a renewal of the company's licence. The hearings themselves were ambitious and thorough when compared to Canada's middling counterpart. Nineteen members of the British House of Commons heard evidence from twenty-four witnesses, including Draper, over forty days. Even though only one of the questioners—Edward "Bear" Ellice, a HBC shareholder—had any direct experience with Rupert's Land, a concerted effort was made to hear from people who had lived, worked, or travelled there. A premium was placed on the opinions of scientific explorers John Richardson and J. H. Lefroy.

One of the most vexing issues was what would become of the Indians if the region was opened to agricultural settlement or even competitive trade.

All of the witnesses were unanimous in questioning whether Indians would be able to cope with dramatic change. Nor did any of them expect Indians to decide their own future, let alone retain their identity. David Anderson, who had served as Anglican bishop of Rupert's Land since 1849, naturally argued for the continued support of western missions and their special role in preparing Indians for civilization. Here, he was voicing the ambivalent role of missionaries as agents of deliberate cultural change and protectors against outside forces. But others, such as arctic explorer and former HBC man Dr. John Rae, were not as positive or hopeful about Indian hunters settling down and becoming agriculturalists. It might work for certain bands in certain locations, but it was unrealistic to expect all tribes to make the transition to "civilization."[75] One of the few dissenting voices—and one that was not widely heard—was former Nor'Wester John McDonald of Garth, now in his mid-eighties, who took it upon himself to craft his own response to the British Select Committee. Writing forcefully to both Draper and Ellice, he called for a separate, self-supporting Indian reserve, west of the Mississippi River, where all tribes would be part of a federation under one central chief. "Is it not better," he asked Draper, "to make it last forever as it is."[76]

The other major question, this one more contentious, was the suitability of the region for agriculture. And at the centre of the firestorm sat George Simpson. Speaking on behalf of the company, he decreed: "I do not think any part of the Hudson's Bay Company's territories is well adapted for settlement; the crops are very uncertain."[77] This statement flatly contradicted what he had said ten years earlier in his book, *Narrative of a Journey Round the World*, and led to some aggressive questioning by members of the committee. But the alternative view voiced at the hearings that the region had the potential to become an agricultural wonderland was "ignorant optimism" at its best.[78] Simpson, when reorganizing the trade in the 1820s, had certainly encouraged the tending of gardens and crops, where it was practical, to cut back on the costs of imported food. He had also required chief factors, as of 1830, to provide a list of livestock at the posts, the acres under cultivation, and the size of each harvest. These efforts, though, were designed to "diversify a monotonous meat diet; or, more basically still, ... raise something to eat."[79] Any pretense that farming represented a new purpose for Rupert's Land was undermined by the dramatic fluctuations between good and bad years at the Red River settlement and the posts and the subsistence nature of these efforts. The defining feature of fur trade agriculture was unpredictability, not certainty—and not necessarily because of the soil, but the climate. Simpson, for his part, may have offered a pessimistic assessment given his fur trade leanings, but his testimony "came nearest to the realities as they were experienced at that time."[80]

The Select Committee report, released at the end of July 1857, might have been an attempt at compromise, but there was a clear winner and a loser. During the hearings, Judge Draper chose not to raise the validity of the charter, but asked that Canadian interests be accommodated. His request was rewarded with the recommendation that "it is essential to meet the just and reasonable wishes of Canada" to provide for the annexation of territory in the southern reaches of Rupert's Land.[81] At the same time, the HBC would be allowed to retain its exclusive trading privileges, but only in the more northerly regions (the Athabasca and Mackenzie districts) where there was little immediate prospect for British settlement. George Simpson took the outcome in stride and advised against the company spending any money to defend its charter rights. With or without a trade monopoly, he asserted, "we could carry on our business just as well as at present."[82] Ever the astute businessman, he also recognized that the HBC's dominance was on the wane and that it would be best to secure financial compensation for the surrender of its charter rights before Canada simply took what it wanted. Those future negotiations, however, would take place without the little emperor, who died in 1860 after four decades' service to the HBC.

The Select Committee report, together with the HBC's acquiescence to the coming changes, seemed to suggest that the way was clear for Canada to take over the western interior. After all, the British government could have created a Crown colony there, as it had done on the Pacific Coast with

Vancouver Island in 1846, but it was more practical—and cheaper—to have Canada assume responsibility for the territory.[83] That transaction, though, was still more than a decade away and required Canada to deal first with internal issues.

This delay left the HBC standing fast and effectively alone against possible American incursions. The border between the United States and central British North America had been set by treaty in 1818 at the forty-ninth parallel but never been officially marked, and existed more on maps than on the ground. The flip side of the delay was that Canada gained some much-needed time to secure new and reliable information about the region and its peoples. Since the union of the HBC and NWC in 1821, the North-West had become "a foreign country" to Canada.[84] Expansionists may have thought they knew the region's true value and purpose, but their creative re-imagining of the western interior had little basis in reality and left little room for the way things actually were. These real and potential difficulties did nothing, however, to dull the starry-eyed outlook of those who believed that civilization would soon march westward. "I hope you will not laugh at me as very visionary," the normally circumspect Draper told the Select Committee in an expansive moment, "but I hope to see the time, or that my children may live to see the time when there is a railway going all across that country and ending at the Pacific ... I entertain no doubt that the time will arrive when that will be accomplished."[85]

The English River district was relatively immune from the changes in southern Saskatchewan in the mid-nineteenth century.

CHAPTER TWELVE

IF SOMETHING IS NOT DONE

IT WAS A "MOST REMARKABLE MILITARY FEAT."[1] IN MID-JUNE 1851, A MÉTIS HUNTING party from the Red River settlement encountered a large Sioux encampment on the Grand Coteau or Missouri Plateau, southeast of present-day Minot, North Dakota. These plains people regularly skirmished over access to bison, especially when herd numbers began to decline in the 1830s and 1840s and the Métis had to push farther southwest each summer into Sioux territory. Little did they expect that June, though, to face an enemy force numbering over two thousand. Circling their carts into a defensive barricade and concealing themselves in rifle pits, fewer than one hundred Métis hunters, including a young Gabriel Dumont, repelled repeated Sioux attacks throughout the day and into the night. The next morning, the men and their families chose to retreat a seemingly foolhardy decision and a difficult military manoeuvre given the size of their camp. The Métis travelled only a few miles before they were once again forced to take up a defensive position and once again successfully held off the Sioux. When the gunfire finally subsided, a Sioux chief rode up to the corral, gesturing that he approached in peace, and said that the warriors would never again fight the Métis. The entire war party then madly galloped around the Métis camp, discharging guns and shooting arrows at the carts in one last defiant act. As the Sioux rode off, a thunderstorm rumbled over the battleground and unleashed a torrential rainfall. It was as if the heavens were applauding the decisiveness of the Métis victory: they had lost only one scout.

The Battle at the Grand Coteau is a classic example of Métis military prowess—how bison hunters had become disciplined soldiers of the plains who were not averse to abandoning the horse in favour of an entrenched position.[2] But the incident also underscored how many Indian and Métis peoples in the mid-nineteenth century were on the move throughout the region, entering lands they had never exploited nor occupied before and sometimes fighting over resources. Politicians in Canada and the United States also eyed the territory, looking towards the future, not the present. In the end, the fate of Rupert's Land was determined not by battles like Grand Coteau but by decisions at the negotiation table and in legislatures thousands of miles away.

Governor George Simpson sought to reform the western Canadian fur trade in the post-1821 merger period to guarantee consistent and strong returns. And he certainly made the Hudson's Bay Company a financial success story—all the more remarkable when the beaver felt hat began to be replaced by the so-called silk topper at the end of the 1830s. But even though the company was never more prosperous, Simpson was less successful in bringing about a total makeover of the trade. He was never able, for example, to recruit enough outside labourers from Europe and Canada to meet the demand for servants and increasingly had to hire Métis and Indians. By the 1850s, Aboriginal peoples dominated the company labour force, especially in the more remote areas of the Northern department.[3] Simpson also sought to direct, if not control, the participation of indigenous groups in the fur trade in order to put the HBC on a more stable footing. But he was forced to concede shortly after the merger with the North West Company: "The Plains Tribes ... continue as insolent and independent if not more so than ever; they conceive that we are dependent on them for the means of subsistence."[4] Simpson's frustration with the mounted, bison-hunting bands of the northern great plains was a consequence of larger forces at play in the region in the mid-nineteenth century. Indeed, the situation in the two fur-trade frontiers had reversed itself. Whereas the boreal forest of the Athabasca–English River districts was once the scene of reckless

BURPEE, *THE SEARCH FOR THE WESTERN SEA*

Fond du Lac at the eastern end of Lake Athabasca was both a HBC provision post and Roman Catholic mission.

competition and frequent violence before 1821, it now supported a peaceful, if not "sleepy" trade. The interior plains and by extension the Saskatchewan country, by contrast, were a place of tension, relocation, convergence, and conflict. It is understandable, then, why Simpson was prepared to forgo the company claim to the southern reaches of Rupert's Land by the time of the 1857 British Select Committee on the understanding that it would be business as usual in the northern subarctic and arctic regions.[5]

The English River district, located around Île-à-la-Crosse in present-day northwestern Saskatchewan, was one of the most stable zones of HBC activity in the mid-nineteenth century. Once swept up in the bitter rivalry between the HBC and NWC, the community entered a period of relative tranquility after the 1821 merger, thanks in large part to a close and reciprocal relationship between Native and newcomer societies. Métis, and to a lesser extent Cree and Chipewyan, came to work for the HBC in different capacities in various locations, from interpreters and guides to woodcutters and provisioners. Because Île-à-la-Crosse served as the district hub, with trails leading to a series of posts and outposts in all directions, the HBC also began to employ local Métis as "runners" who were responsible for the trade in a particular outlying district; this arrangement was similar to the *la dérouine* practice from pre-merger days.[6] Employment opportunities also expanded with the establishment of the Saint-Jean-Baptiste mission. And when steady work was not available at the post or mission, local HBC officials often offered part-time or seasonal contracts to unemployed or underemployed men so that they could support their families. "The role of the HBC locally," one Métis scholar has written, "was to ensure that it had a contented and satisfied workforce to ensure the larger entity's economic success."[7]

One of the most critical elements in sustaining the Île-à-la-Crosse fur trade economy was the labour of women and children, what has been called "useful hands."[8] They tended the local fisheries year-round, using their catch to feed the post population, those working in the transportation system, and the winter dog teams. They also gathered traditional plants and picked berries, depending on the season. Their busiest time of year, though, was May to October when they planted and maintained huge gardens that produced an incredible volume of root crops. In 1850, for example, 870 kegs of potatoes were harvested in a single day. Because these women were not contracted employees, they tended not to be identified by name in company records. But over time, their names came to be listed—a sure sign of the significance of their activities and, equally important, an indication of how local families and the HBC came to be interwoven together.[9]

Much of the work in the district, and the success of the company's operations, revolved around the regional transportation network. The annual La Loche brigade was headed by Métis Alexis Bonami(s) *dit L'Esperence*, with Baptiste Bruce responsible for the second flotilla. These two men were renowned for their ability to get their valuable cargo, estimated at fifty thousand dollars in the 1860s, safely up and down the Churchill River in a timely manner. A large resident labour force, meanwhile, maintained Methye Portage to ensure that packages moved efficiently over the arduous height of land. When oxen and carts were introduced in the 1840s, the trail was first widened and then later reshaped to allow for switchbacks on the steep descent to the Clearwater River Valley. A similar arrangement was in place at the Green Lake post on the lake of the same name (also called Lac Vert). Here, another resident labour pool made constant repairs and upgrades to the bog-riddled Green Lake trail to Fort Carlton so that pemmican from the southern provisioning posts was available for the northern brigades.[10]

Ironically, the Métis role in the HBC transportation system in the mid-nineteenth century made them carriers of disease. Influenza, measles, and dysentery all struck the Red River settlement in succession in 1846 and were soon spread by the brigades throughout the English River and Athabasca districts with devastating consequences. Governor Simpson, no stranger to past epidemics, including smallpox in 1837, claimed that sickness that year "led to a greater mortality than at any former period within my recollection."[11] He could have added that the HBC was culpable. Even though disease was widespread in the settlement that spring and likely infected outbound crews, company officials at Red River and later Norway House blithely dispatched the brigades. As one commentator remarked about the decision: "Financial interests took precedence over public health."[12] And it backfired on the company. The northern transportation system collapsed as crews were crippled by sickness and those men who might have replaced them fell ill as well. "Almost all of the Outfits for the Northern Districts next year ... are still in our stores," a solemn James Hargrave reported from York Factory, "boats are still on the beach, many of the crews are dead, and as such as remain are either in the last stages of disease or are so enfeebled as to be totally incapable of even the slightest labour this season."[13] It was a year or more before the system recovered, in part because some labourers came to associate the brigades with sickness and were reluctant to work on the boats.

Nor were northern posts spared. Measles intruded on the otherwise "quiet" trade around Lac la Ronge, killing at least twenty-nine people.[14] The HBC had operated a post at the mouth of the Rapid River (near Nistowiak Falls) from 1831 to 1853 when it was relocated across from the new Stanley mission on the Churchill River. It too produced a steady, reliable trade now that the region had recovered from the over-trapping engendered by the HBC–NWC war. Trade on the far northwest and northeast side of the future province, on the other hand, remained largely undeveloped. The Fond du Lac post at the eastern end of Lake Athabasca was closed at the time of the merger and remained closed as long as the Chipewyan, could trade at nearby Fort Chipewyan. The HBC was more active around Reindeer Lake (sometimes called Caribou Lake). Here, it had operated a post since 1839 at the head of the Reindeer River at the southern end of the huge lake; hence the alternative name, Southend. Some local Chipewyan were involved in the freighting of goods up from the Churchill River, but it was generally inconvenient for bands to travel to the bottom of the lake when they largely hunted caribou to the north. And if they wanted to trade, they could still make the overland trip to Churchill (Fort Prince of Wales) on Hudson Bay.

This limited HBC activity in the more northern reaches of Saskatchewan came to an end in the 1850s when the company determined that caribou could be an alternative food source to pemmican. It consequently re-opened Fond du Lac as a provisioning post in 1853, as well as granted permission to the Oblates to establish a mission (Our Lady of Seven Sorrows) under Father Pierre-Henri Grollier.[15] Six years, later, another provisioning post, Lac du Brochet, was founded at the top end of Reindeer Lake, just inside the Manitoba border. Soon, the Chipewyan (*idthen-eldeli*) were producing caribou meat and trapping furs in exchange for goods and supplies at Brochet. Nor was the Roman Catholic church far behind. Bishop Alexandre-Antonin Taché followed up his March 1847 visit to Reindeer Lake during his days as a priest at Île-à-la-Crosse and, in keeping with his word to the Chipewyan of the region, founded St. Pierre's Mission at Brochet in 1861.[16]

The combination of post and mission attracted Chipewyan, Cree, Métis,

Lac du Brochet post at the top of Reindeer Lake, just inside the present-day Manitoba border

and even Inuit to Lac du Brochet. The HBC records for 1881 list 386 Chipewyan, 29 Cree, and 217 Inuit "belonging" to the post.[17] Relations were strained at first, in part because Chipewyan hunters insisted that traders come to their camps to retrieve any meat. In January 1866, for example, a handful of Chipewyan from Wollaston (Lac la Hache) and Brochet (Lac de Brochet) Lakes arrived at the post with little to trade but reported they had plenty of caribou where they had come from. "The Chip. are a hard set of miserly beggars to deal with," trader William Whiteway expressed his displeasure, "but they will find themselves in the wrong box if they think to get their own way with me."[18] These difficulties prompted the HBC to withdraw its personnel temporarily from the post to the bottom of the lake in 1870. But the move served only to antagonize the Chipewyan.

The other potential difficulty at Lac du Brochet was the past enmity between the Cree and Chipewyan, and the Chipewyan and the Inuit in particular. But much had changed in the past one hundred years. When HBC servant Samuel Hearne crossed the country north of present-day Manitoba and Saskatchewan in 1770, he found Chipewyan, or "Northern Indians" in his words, occupying the southern barren lands and the northern reaches of the subarctic

401

boreal forest; there were no Inuit present and if they dared enter the region, they would have been killed. Father Alphone Gasté from the St. Pierre mission entered the same region in 1868, taking "the old way north" with a group of Chipewyan who knew the traditional route from Reindeer Lake to the Kazan River and on to Dabawnt Lake in today's Nunavut Territory. Gasté's Chipewyan companions regarded the territory as essentially "Eskimo land," a legacy of the 1782 smallpox epidemic. With the contraction of the Chipewyan population to the south and west because of the death toll from the disease, Inuit gradually moved inland to take advantage of the security offered by the caribou herds and occupied what was once Chipewyan traditional territory, including around Nuetlin Lake. Over time, the two groups learned to live together, sometimes even hunt together, and it was because of these generally peaceful relations that the Inuit became frequent visitors to Lac du Brochet.[19] A few even resided there with the Chipewyan and the growing number of Cree and Métis who came from the south to work at the post. This reorientation of the Chipewyan and the Inuit away from Churchill did not sit well with HBC operations there. But putting aside the sometimes-testy relationship between the company and the missions, if it were not for the presence and activities of the Oblates, these northern provisioning posts would probably not have survived long.

George Simpson attributed the stability and dependability of the northern trade—stretching from Hudson Bay to the Athabasca country and down the Mackenzie River—to his twin reform policies of economy and efficiency. They were certainly a factor. But so too was the vast region's relative isolation from outside forces that might have interfered with, if not challenged, HBC operations. Missionaries like Father Gasté took the seclusion in stride, secure in the knowledge that the Catholic church largely had the field to itself as priests devoted decades to converting Indian and Inuit peoples to Christianity. Their writings suggest that the only real test was the physical strain that came with the deprivation and hardship, both at their primitive missions and during their long proselytizing trips.

Working in remote places, by contrast, weighed heavily on HBC servants,

SASKATCHEWAN ARCHIVES BOARD R-A980-1

St. Pierre's Roman Catholic mission at Brochet

all the more so when their lives were measured against the remarkable technological advancements and innovations outside Rupert's Land. The distance from Grand Rapids on the Saskatchewan River to Lac du Brochet, for example, was roughly 650 miles by canoe. Mail came once a year in the spring when the annual brigades began their arduous journey inland. And then there were the months when there was little to do except try to stay warm and fed. Some officers in the field, especially in more northern regions, were recruited as lay collectors for the Smithsonian Institution in Washington, D.C., and submitted specimens, field notes, and ethnological material, often in exchange for books or other favours.[20] Others, though, seemed close to losing their sanity. "The only advantage I have here over what a prisoner has in the civilized World," observed a despondent Richard Grant at Oxford House on the route between Hudson Bay and Lake Winnipeg, "is that besides being a prisoner I am also the Gaoler."[21] John Bell was just as lonely in "this miserable and distant part" of the country. "The World might have been at an end," he bemoaned from the Mackenzie River, "without my hearing of it!"[22] Jon Tod even claimed that the isolation of his posting on the Peace River came at the cost of his ability to speak in his own tongue.

BRIAN CHENOWYTH

Métis hunting parties, described as "movable armies," entered the plains in force in search of bison herds.

Isolation was not the problem in the northern plains portion of Rupert's Land. According to the 1818 Convention between the United States and Great Britain, designed to settle any outstanding issues from the 1783 Treaty of Paris, the international boundary west of the Lake of the Woods was to be set at the forty-ninth parallel. This line effectively meant that the southern tip of the 1811 land grant secured by Lord Selkirk for the Red River settlement (which dipped below the parallel because the headwaters of the Red are part of the Hudson Bay watershed) fell in American territory. It also put the community of Pembina, a gathering place for Métis hunting parties before they headed out on the plains in search of bison, just south of the international boundary (in North Dakota). Although an unwelcome complication for the HBC, the location of the boundary was not a pressing issue for the company in the 1820s and 1830s.[23] In fact, Governor Simpson quietly tolerated private trading by Métis individuals in the border region, even though it went against the company's exclusive trade in furs. He did not want an open clash with his American competitors, especially when there was not much profit to be gained. Besides, any furs secured there ended up in HBC hands.

Then, in 1844, Norman Kittson of the American Fur Company set up shop at Pembina. Métis private traders rejoiced at the competition because they now had an alternative market for their "illicit" furs. The HBC, however, decided to enforce its monopoly by legal means and brought charges against four men, including Guillaume Sayer, in May 1849. The largely Métis population at Red River wanted free trade, which offered a chance to break out of the limited opportunities imposed by the HBC. And when the court found Sayer guilty but did not sentence or fine him and dropped the charges against the other three, there was only one possible conclusion: "*La Commerce est libre!*"[24] This outcome was only a glancing blow for the powerful HBC as it continued to rely on its economic clout to hold off any trade contenders. But it foreshadowed how things were changing and continued to change. Within a decade of the Sayer decision, the cart traffic that shuttled up and down the Red River Valley was joined by the first sternwheelers from St. Paul, Minnesota. Boats such as the *Anson Northup* carried with them the ambitions of American markets and suppliers and were poised to undermine York Factory's centuries-old role as the trade gateway to Rupert's Land.

The opening of Rupert's Land to American markets profoundly affected the annual Métis bison hunt by providing a second or alternative buyer for meat and especially robes. Up to then, the Métis were locked into the HBC provision trade, and because the company monopolized the market for pemmican, it was able to buy all that it wanted at cheap prices. The St. Paul trade now offered not only more competition for the products of the hunt but more demand. The value of beaver, at the same time, began to stagnate because of the introduction of the cheaper silk hat. Simpson bullishly pooh-poohed the development as a temporary fad, but by the mid-1840s, the beaver skin had lost its place as the staple of the trade because of reduced demand.[25] This development further encouraged Métis involvement in the robe and meat trade over a wider area and at a more intensified rate. It was not what George Simpson and the HBC had planned for the Métis. They had hoped that they would stay put at Red River and become sedentary farmers, not carve out a separate niche into

Rupert's Land economy as the main supplier to the American robe market.

The Métis were already well positioned to intensify the bison hunt. By the end of the third decade of the nineteenth century, these "movable armies," as HBC Red River clerk Alexander Ross described them, were entering the plains in force. In 1840 alone, 620 men, 650 women, and 360 children left Pembina as part of a 1200-cart caravan. This number of participants was not simply a reflection of the growing population at Red River but an indication of how many people were involved in the summer or dried meat hunt, including priests, who regularly held mass and performed other Roman Catholic rites on the trail.[26] Ross, who tagged along with the Métis in 1840, provided one of the best accounts of the organization and operation of the hunt. At the rendezvous, the assembled hunters elected a president or chief and twelve councillors, usually senior, experienced men. They, in turn, decided the rules that were to be followed out on the open plains, particularly during the hunt. Captains were also chosen by ten hunters voluntarily lining up behind prospective leaders. Where these procedures came from is not known; they could be either Indian or French in origin.

Led by a guide carrying a flag on a staff, the cart caravan, sometimes several miles long, slowly worked its way southwest across the plains. Advance scouts searched for bison, as well as kept a careful watch for the Sioux. There is no record of any Métis camp being routed; never more than a few scouts were ever lost. Once a herd was located, camp was immediately set up nearby and everything readied. The chief led the hunters out to the herd, and it was only on his shout that they charged the startled bison. Each hunter guided his horse towards a particular animal, dropped the reins once close enough, and then fired across the saddle into the beast. He then rode after another animal and kept shooting and killing until any remaining bison were too scattered to pursue. The sounds of the slaughter saturated the air: the high-pitched cries of the hunters, the rapid pounding of the hooves of the bison and horses, the constant blasts of gunfire, the whinnying of the horses with each kill and redirection, and the bleating of the bison and the heavy, throaty

A Métis hunting camp (with ruts in the prairie left by their carts)

breathing of those dying on the blood-soaked plains. Dust rose and enveloped the scene, adding a surreal quality to the killing field. It filled the eyes, nostrils, and mouths of the hunters, mixed with the taste and smell of blood and shit.

The Métis were precision marksmen. But what made them so efficient during the hunt was their specially trained horses, known as buffalo runners. They had also perfected the reloading of their muzzle-loaders on the fly. With a few balls of shot in his mouth and his front coat pockets filled with powder and more shot, each hunter frantically poured a handful of powder down the barrel of the gun after it was discharged, spit in a ball, and then whacked the stock of the gun against his hip. The rapidity with which they were able to fire caused their gun barrels to overheat, sometimes with unfortunate consequences. Spills, bruises, and sprains were also quite common.

The dead bison were butchered on the spot. Working quickly because of the hot summer temperatures, the hunters and their families removed the skin, tongue, back fat or *depouillé*, meat, tendons, and any other serviceable body parts, before abandoning the carcass to the wolves, coyotes, and birds. Back at camp, the less glamorous but real work began. Women, sometimes with help from children, meticulously scraped the robes to ensure that any flesh was removed. Dressing and tanning the skin, to make it soft and marketable, took several days of painstaking labour. They also dried meat in long strips in the sun and either tied it up in bales or pounded and mixed it with fat to produce pemmican that was then poured into bison leather bags. At night, there was feasting, storytelling, and singing to the accompaniment of the fiddle. After several successful hunts, the heavily loaded carts, each carrying the meat and robes of eight-to-ten bison, trundled back to Red River, usually in late summer, where the Métis sold or traded the products of the hunt and paid off their debts.[27] Their absence meant they had less time to devote to their subsistence farms. But it did provide a dependable living, something that eluded those who suffered through repeated crop failures at Red River. The time spent together on the hunt on the open plains, moreover, instilled in the Red River Métis a strong sense of identity, of being a nation with its own distinctive culture and traditions. With this identity came a feeling of independence, that they were no longer beholden to the HBC but could decide what was in their best interests. This confidence as a separate people was further boosted by their successful skirmishes with the Sioux. They had come to see themselves as "masters of the plains wherever they might choose to march."[28]

By the end of the 1840s, several Métis Red River traders "eagerly responded" to the opening of the American market, particularly at St. Paul, "by transforming their household economies into 'factories'" for bison products.[29] Acquiring large outfits on credit, they hired others to work for them, usually people related through kinship ties. They also promoted a second or smaller hunt in the fall, usually from September to early November, to secure robes and fresh meat.

This metamorphosis of the bison trade into a commercial operation caused some Métis families to abandon any pretension of farming at Red River. It also expanded the hunt deeper into the interior. By the 1830s, bison herds were rarely found east of Brandon House on the Assiniboine River. Two decades later, the same northern herds had contracted westward to the Touchwood Hills. To carry on the hunt, then, Métis parties had to travel greater distances from

Red River, increasingly into Sioux territory. It was if the international border did not exist. The 1840 hunt that Alexander Ross accompanied, for example, was almost three weeks from Red River before finding its first large bison herds near the Cheyenne River in present-day South Dakota. And because these longer journeys were costly, they had to secure as many robes and as much meat as possible to ensure that traders' credit advances were covered. Nor were these parties only hunting to fill their carts. The large caravans also had to eat on the way there and back.[30] Tens of thousands of bison were consequently slaughtered to meet the demand of this new industry, in addition to those taken to meet the continuing pemmican needs of the HBC and feed the Red River settlement. The toll on the herds can be read in the St. Paul trade statistics. The value of the bison trade, consisting mostly of robes but also meat and leather products, jumped from fourteen hundred dollars (eight carts) in 1844 to three hundred thousand dollars (fourteen hundred carts) in 1865.[31]

Summer hunts were also organized by the Freemen living around Forts Edmonton, Pitt, and Carlton on the North Saskatchewan River. These expeditions were not as large as the Red River caravans—generally only about one-quarter the size—but they did provide the HBC provisioning posts with a supply of pemmican. And that became an issue in the mid-nineteenth century as herds contracted southward and the Americans provided an alternative market for bison products. Whereas the HBC had once dominated the pemmican trade, even collecting a surplus for discretionary purposes, the company now had to scramble to accumulate enough bison meat for its northern operations. At Fort Edmonton in the 1860s, interpreter Abraham Salois, a prominent local Freeman, was re-engaged as a trader and, with an assortment of goods secured on credit, travelled to the camps of distant Cree bands to retrieve bison meat for the post. These forays sometimes took Salois and his hired Freemen more than two weeks' travel one way. And he no sooner returned to the post than he was off again a few days later in search of more bison meat. Sometimes, Salois's freighting parties were harassed by the Blackfoot, but more often the bigger problem was that the food collected was also needed by the Freemen and some of it was traded to them before it ever reached the post.[32]

The HBC took steps to deal directly with Cree and Saulteaux hunters in present-day east-central Saskatchewan, south of the Saskatchewan River, by establishing outposts. Egg Lake (evidently on the east shore of Nut Lake north of Kelvington) was the satellite of the Touchwood Hills post, while Last Mountain (on the lake of the same name) served Fort Qu'Appelle. But the company, to its frustration, could not evade Freemen competition for the bison trade in these areas. The HBC responded with "flying" posts, temporary winter encampments that were moved around to trade with Indian hunting parties.[33] One of HBC servant Willie Traill's first postings in 1866 was a crude shack in the Moose Mountains, sarcastically dubbed Fort Defiance, where he was expected to do battle with free traders. In the end, it proved more effective for Isaac Cowie at Fort Qu'Appelle and Archibald Macdonald at Fort Ellice either to travel out on the plains with horses and carts to trade for meat from Indian bands in their camps, or to send some of the post's employees to travel with them on their hunts, sometimes as far as American territory. It was a complete reversal of how the pemmican trade was conducted in the late eighteenth and early nineteenth centuries. But it was the surest way for the HBC to get its needed food supplies. One such expedition from Fort Ellice in 1865 netted almost fifty thousand pounds of pemmican and dried meat, most of which was forwarded to Fort Pelly for eventual shipping north.[34]

Many of the independent traders who cut into the HBC bison trade on the northern plains in the 1850s and 1860s were either Freemen or their descendants who had been displaced by the 1821 fur trade merger and forced to find new opportunities. They and their mixed-descent families had taken up residence near the Saskatchewan posts and pursued subsistence activities, supplemented by temporary work for the company, until the American bison trade opened up to them. There were those, though, such as Antoine Desjarlais who flouted the HBC monopoly before the decisive 1849 Sayer trial and established two private trading posts in the Souris River basin. The larger of the two, Fort Desjarlais, a substantial stockade housing his extended family, was

BRIAN CHENOWYTH

A Métis home at Wood Mountain

built near present-day Lauder, Manitoba, in 1836. Desjarlais, his brothers, and his brothers-in-law continually faced the shutting down of their operations and the confiscation of their furs, goods, and provisions by the HBC. But they survived and persisted because of their kinship relations in the region.[35] And by the 1840s and 1850s, other Métis families were copying their example, only this time as legitimate HBC competitors.

What induced many Red River Métis to winter inland were the progressively longer distances they had to travel from the settlement to reach the herds. It was far more practical to live closer to the bison in *hivernant* communities. These wintering settlements took root wherever there was sufficient shelter, wood, water, but most importantly, proximity to bison. That's why they constantly shifted. One was at Grosse-Butte near present-day Humboldt, another at Prairie Ronde south of present-day Saskatoon, and still another at Petite-Ville on the west bank of the South Saskatchewan at Gros Ventres Fork (in the vicinity of Fish Creek).[36] A good many were located on the tributaries of the Missouri River—the Big Muddy, Poplar, and Whitemud (Frenchman)—often built into the sides of the treed coulees. Others were established on lakes, where they might have access to fish and waterfowl. Their

411

size varied from only a few families to larger camps that sometimes attracted visits from itinerant priests. Some were no more than a few crude log buildings; others had workshops for processing bison products and even small gardens. Norbert Welsh, sometimes referred to as "the last buffalo hunter," claimed in his memoirs that he built more than a dozen houses on the plains. One of the more sizeable settlements was at Lac Qu'Appelle, the home to Métis from Red River, Turtle Mountain, and even Antoine Desjarlais and his extended family.

By wintering near the herds, fewer and fewer Métis participated in the summer hunt from Red River; only 150 carts left the settlement in 1866. Those inland, meanwhile, were now able to hunt bison from the late fall into the early winter, what was known as the third hunt. It was actually the best time to take females. Not only were they pregnant and hence rich in fat, but their coats were also at their prime. With the robes from this hunt and any other bison products and furs, many winterers returned to Red River in the spring, trying to arrive there for Queen Victoria's birthday celebrations in May. That connection to the settlement, though, diminished over time because it was more convenient to take their trade to Forts Union and Benton in the United States.[37]

Among the wintering families were Edouard Pelletier, born in the Red River parish of St. François-Xavier in 1834, and his partner Madeleine Morand (also spelled Morin). The birth places of their children reflect how they were continually on the move: François (1865) at Portage la Prairie; Marie Rose (1869) at Wood Mountain; Napoleon (1870) on the Souris River; Edouard (1872) at South Branch, near the Cypress Hills; Jean Marie (1875) at Long Lake; Thérèse (1877) and William (1878) in the Cypress Hills; and Joseph (1880), Samuel (1882), and Louise (1884) at Pheasant Forks (near present-day Neudorf). This constant movement would not have been documented had the parents not returned to St. François-Xavier for the baptism of their children. A similar pattern can be discerned in the birth records for the John Wells (born 1847) and Julia Tanner (born 1849) family: from the Dirt Hills (near present-day Moose Jaw) to Wascana Creek (near Regina) to the South Saskatchewan River (near Saskatoon) to the Cypress Hills. One of their daughters, Marie Athalia,

Touchwood Hills post collected pemmican from Indian hunters in the region.

was born on the trail when John was working as a freighter and the family did not resume travel until Julia had recovered. Even those Métis who found steady work with the HBC, such as Pierre Lapierre in the Swan River district from 1846–69, did not remain in one place. Pierre and his spouse Adelaide Boyer had fourteen children, born here and there throughout the region, depending on his job that particular year. But unlike other Métis families who tried to maintain their connection with Red River, the Lapierre family gravitated towards the Lebret Catholic mission near Fort Qu'Appelle.

Métis living inland also turned to farming. When mixed-descent postmaster James Isbister retired from service at Fort Carlton in 1862, he started a farm about fifty miles downriver on the south side of the North Saskatchewan River—not far from Peter Pond's Sturgeon River post (1776)—at a site known as "the good wintering place." He was soon joined by several other local men and their families who laid out their farms in traditional river lot style (one-eighth of a mile wide and two miles deep). These long rectangular strips were based on the old New France seigneurial system and gave each landowner access to the river and its resources and a share of the fertile lands back from the river. In 1866, the early agricultural success of the Isbister settlement convinced James Nisbette to establish a new Anglican mission there instead of Fort Pitt. One of

413

Nisbette's first acts was to rename the community Prince Albert in honour of Queen Victoria's late consort. The HBC endorsed the name change by naming its new post here, Fort Albert. The remaking of the site continued in 1882 when the old Indian graveyard was divided into town lots.[38]

Indians were also adjusting to changed circumstances during these same years. In the Saskatchewan delta area, in present day east-central Saskatchewan, members of the Shoal Lake and Red Earth Cree bands moved south to their wintering grounds in the Pasquia Hills to live together there year-round. It appeared that they believed they could no longer sustain themselves around Fort à la Corne, Cumberland House, and The Pas but chose to "retreat" to a more isolated area as a new regional band.[39] Cree living farther south in the Swan River district, meanwhile, vainly searched for food wherever they could. Anglican catechist James Settee tried three times in the 1850s to preach among Spreadwing's people but gave up because the Cree band was constantly on the move.[40] This scarcity of game led many local Cree and Saulteaux to turn to the HBC for support. While these pleas for help were quite common—if not expected—over the winter, Robert Campbell noted in the Fort Pelly journal for November 1863 that "it is rather early to complain of starvation on the part of our Indians." A month later, he added, "it appears to be the cry all over."[41] To the west at Fort Edmonton, John Rowand reported that some bands had abandoned the boreal forest entirely. "The whole of the strong wood Indians are out in the plains," he observed, "not only those connected with this district but from many other parts of the Country ... [they] are afraid of starving to death with their families if they are made to return to their land."[42]

Cree bands living along the Saskatchewan River were not much better off. By the mid-nineteenth century, these Indians were known to the HBC as downstream (*mâmihkiyiniwak*) and upstream (*natimîwiyiniwak*) people and their names were associated with their home territories. The downstream included Calling River (Qu'Appelle Valley), Rabbit Skin (between the Qu'Appelle and Assiniboine Rivers), and Touchwood Hills (Touchwood Hills–Long Lake) peoples; while upstream were the Parkland or Prairie Willow (south

SASKATCHEWAN ARCHIVES BOARD S-B7E32

In their search for bison, the Assiniboine spent more time in Wood Mountain, Cypress Hills, and present-day northern Montana by the 1850s.

and east of Fort Carlton), House or Fort (Carlton), River (between the North Saskatchewan and Battle Rivers), and Beaver Hills (west of the Battle River to the foothills) peoples.[43]

Each group faced resource challenges, but the Beaver Hills Cree found themselves in a particularly awkward situation. The winter of 1847–48 was one of the harshest in recent years—the height of the period known as the Little Ice Age[44]—and led to widespread starvation among the Cree around Fort Edmonton, especially because bison rarely came that far north anymore. Maskepetoon (Broken Arm), leader of the Rocky Mountain Cree, responded by taking his band downriver in order to have better access to the herds. But there were not many bison to the east and it consequently fell to Maskepetoon to broker peace agreements with the Blackfoot if his Cree followers were going to travel south into enemy territory to reach the dwindling herds. Maskepetoon often undertook these diplomatic initiatives alone and on foot and regularly reached deals with the Blackfoot to share winter pounding sites. But as the herds contracted southward and hunger became a growing threat, any spirit

415

A Cree man

of cooperation gave way to steadily escalating tensions that undermined the peace. One of the casualties in 1869 was Maskepetoon, murdered when Siksika Chief Many Swans ordered the killing of an unarmed Cree party.[45]

This Cree–Blackfoot warfare had been one of the defining features of intertribal relations on the northern plains since the early nineteenth century. But whereas it had once been over access to horses and trade goods—and the prestige and honour that went with raiding—the fighting by mid-century was increasingly over the steadily diminishing bison herds. The Fort or House Cree, for example, had been able to meet most of their subsistence needs in the Carlton area by following a seasonal hunting round that took them from present-day Rosetown to the southwest, the Eagle Hills and the Battle River to the west, and Redberry Lake to the northwest. Their nutritional edge, though, came from bison meat, a protein-rich diet that produced the tallest humans in the world at that time.[46] Among them was Ahtahkakoop, a future leader who stood six feet, three inches in height with a muscular frame. He was sometimes called *misi-minahik* (tall pine).[47] Young Ahtahkakoop and his brothers earned reputations as warriors through their frequent skirmishes with the Blackfoot, but any large-scale battles were discouraged by the existence of neutral territory southwest of the Battle River, a kind of buffer zone between the warring groups. The Cree and Blackfoot sometimes exchanged children, or leaders adopted young men from the other tribe in an effort to promote peace. Saukamappee, David Thompson's informant, was born Cree but grew up Peigan.[48] The two groups even camped together one time at Stopping Hill (*nakiwaciy*) on the present-day Sweetgrass reserve in the Battlefords area to talk about their differences.

The steady contraction of the northern range of the bison made this kind of meeting between the Cree and Blackfoot impossible by the 1850s and 1860s. The only time the two groups came together thereafter was to fight, usually over dwindling resources. It has been estimated that the northern plains of the western interior likely supported from five to six million bison in the early nineteenth century. But by the 1860s, two-thirds of the animals

417

were gone.[49] Or, as Methodist missionary George McDougall gloomily summed up the situation along the upper North Saskatchewan River: "A time of starvation. No buffalo."[50]

The Fort People and other Cree bands responded to this worsening crisis by becoming more protective of their hunting territories. No longer were the northern plains a bison commons, open to all, but increasingly claimed by particular bands to ensure access to the depleted herds.[51] Perhaps the most vigilant group were the Young Dogs, a mixed Cree–Assiniboine band that patrolled the area from the Qu'Appelle Lakes to the elbow of the South Saskatchewan River as if it had proprietary rights over the region and its increasingly scarce food resources. HBC trader Isaac Cowie recounted a run-in during his first meeting with one of their headmen, Yellow Head, who demanded a tribute for his warriors, offering nothing in return. When a small amount of tea and tobacco was placed on a dressed bison skin before a sitting Yellow Head, the headman angrily swept the tea into the fire, stood up and threw the roll of tobacco, and then slapped Cowie on his cheek.[52]

Staking out territory as their exclusive hunting grounds only worked for the various Indian bands as long as bison continued to come north with any regularity to the Saskatchewan River. But by the 1860s, few herds were to be found north of Wood Mountain and the Cypress Hills. Just as the Métis hunting caravans from Red River, then, had to travel greater distances to the south and west, so did the Cree, Assiniboine, and Saulteaux (Plains Ojibwa) to find enough animals to meet their needs. This migration was facilitated by disease. The 1839 smallpox and 1846 measles epidemics opened up areas to mixed bands of Cree, Assiniboine, and Saulteaux who steadily pushed southwestward from the Qu'Appelle region to Wood Mountain, the Cypress Hills, and present-day northern Montana and the Poplar and Milk Rivers. The ethnic composition of these hybrid bands greatly varied. Some included Métis, while others were made up of only two tribes. But what brought these peoples together was the collective need for survival in the wake of disease.[53] Cree from the Saskatchewan country also travelled south to camp alongside Assiniboine bands in the Cypress Hills and beyond. These gatherings intensified the strong kinship ties between these traditional allies. They were also necessary for defensive purposes because the hunt increasingly took them into Blackfoot territory. "Given their numbers," one author has observed, "they were [both] war parties that hunted buffalo and buffalo hunters traveling as armies."[54] It was not uncommon to have camps of two hundred or more tents in contested territory. Even the nature of warfare changed to large, pitched battles involving several hundred fighters.

One of most violent war zones was west of present-day Moose Jaw to the Cypress Hills and south of the South Saskatchewan River, especially where the river bends like an elbow. It was here that the Battle of the Red Ochre Hills took place in March 1866. A Blackfoot war party, travelling east through the present-day Vermilion Hills of the Missouri Coteau, came to a hilltop overlooking the river valley and saw a small Assiniboine camp on the other side at the entrance to Snakebite Coulee (north of Demaine, Saskatchewan). A much larger Cree–Saulteaux camp was hidden from view farther up the coulee. The Blackfoot slipped across the frozen river on foot, planning to take the Assiniboine camp by surprise. But several women raised the alarm and alerted the main camp. The Cree and Saulteaux drove the Blackfoot back down to the river. Other defenders hurried over the ice to the other side to prevent the enemy from escaping.[55] No mercy was shown to the Blackfoot. Isaac Cowie visited the site of the battle five years later and came across the remains of the dead. "I followed, from the mouth of that death trap of the Blackfeet, for miles up the flat bottom lands of the South Saskatchewan valley," he recounted, "a trail of bleached bones of the Blackfeet who had fallen, in the panic-stricken retreat, to the fury of the pursuing Crees."[56] Today, the battle is commemorated by a stone cairn near the ninth green of the Harbour golf course at Elbow, several miles northeast of the actual site. And that is because the battleground was submerged when the south branch of the river was dammed in 1959 to create Lake Diefenbaker. All that remains above water is probably the hill on which the Blackfoot made their grievous miscalculation.

Indian groups also tangled with the Métis over access to the diminishing bison herds. Even though many of the multi-ethnic bands included mixed-descent people, they resented the increasing reach of large Métis hunting parties into the western interior and considered their encroachment as both an invasion and a threat to their livelihood. The Indians were particularly annoyed with Métis procurement practices. "The manner of his hunt is such not only to kill," complained Plains Saulteaux leader Green Setting Feather, "but also to drive away the few he leaves, and to waste even those he kills."[57] Indians responded by threatening small Métis parties and harassing the larger caravans by starting fires to drive away the herds. By the early 1850s, some Cree leaders began advocating the closure of the hunt to outsiders, including the Métis.[58]

This tension between Aboriginal groups over access to the bison was perhaps best illustrated by the strained relationship between Métis leader Gabriel Dumont and Cree headman Big Bear. Big Bear's father Black Powder, the leader of a mixed Cree–Ojibwa band, had made the transition to a plains bison hunter and was probably among the first Ojibwa to pound bison south of the Saskatchewan River. When Big Bear, whose face bore the marks of the 1839 smallpox epidemic, succeeded his father as chief in 1865, he became a resolute leader for the interests and rights of the Plains Cree. On one occasion, when Big Bear and Dumont were stalking the same herd, the chief tried to take some of the animals for his hungry band. Dumont intervened, driving the bison back toward the Métis camp and then humiliating an unrepentant Big Bear by hitting him in the stomach with the butt of a gun as a warning. The incident made for hard feelings between the two men.[59]

Hunting competition for the remaining northern bison herds intensified in 1862–63 when Dakota from Minnesota sought asylum in British territory following their unsuccessful uprising against United States government control. The Dakota leaders claimed the right to settle in Rupert's Land because of their role as military allies of the British during the War of 1812 and the promises that the Crown had been made them for this support. The exact number of Dakota that fled north is uncertain—at least more than one thousand. None were welcomed at first because of the added stress they placed on ever-diminishing resources, and they regularly clashed with local Indian groups and the Métis until peace agreements were reached. Many Dakota came to live west of the Red River settlement along or near the Assiniboine River. The Tatankanaje and Wapahaska bands crossed the border at the Souris River and then made their way westward towards the Qu'Appelle Lakes. Both bands probably spent time together but generally occupied separate territories to be able to eke out an existence. Tatankanaje ranged from Fort Ellice south to the Missouri River, while Wapahaska remained farther north, between Moose Mountain and the South Saskatchewan River. Hunting, trapping, trading, even working for the HBC, enabled the Dakota to survive their first few years in their new homeland, but the refugees could not escape the deprivation, hunger, and sickness that was the misfortune of other Indian tribes.[60]

While the declining bison herds threatened the livelihood of Indian and Métis peoples and the viability of the HBC trade, a new future for the region was being investigated by scientific exploring parties—one British, the other Canadian—in the late 1850s. The British expedition, organized in March 1857, was a response to conflicting testimony before the HBC Select Committee about the agricultural potential of Rupert's Land. During the hearings into the future of the HBC, the colonial secretary had recognized the need for reliable information about the resources of the western interior and asked Captain John Palliser to report on the country between the North Saskatchewan River and the international boundary with the United States and between Red River and the Rocky Mountains. Palliser's qualifications to lead such an important expedition might have been suspect—he was an Irish country gentleman who had hunted on the great plains ten years earlier—but the Royal Geographical Society ensured that he was surrounded by an impressive scientific team, including geologist James Hector and botanist Eugène Bourgeau.[61]

The Canadian expedition, by contrast, was dispatched to substantiate the expansionist claim that Rupert's Land had unlimited potential and rightfully belonged to Canada. This insistence that the HBC charter was invalid meant that the expedition did not seek the assistance of the company. Nor did the Canadian government even bother to inform the HBC that it was sending an exploratory party into the territory. The Canadians quickly learned, however, as did previous outsiders to the region, going as far back to Henry Kelsey over 150 years earlier, that travel through the region for the uninitiated was difficult at the best of times. The Palliser expedition, for its part, engaged a large number of local people from guides and interpreters to hunters and teamsters who knew the region. It also spent two winters inland as guests of the company. There was good reason for the HBC to provide assistance; a favourable report about the resources of Rupert's Land might increase the eventual price that Canada would have to pay if it wanted to acquire the territory.[62]

The Palliser expedition took to the field in July 1857, travelling south from the Red River settlement to Pembina at the international border, turning west to Turtle Mountain and then on to Fort Ellice on the Assiniboine River. Here, as pre-arranged, the renowned Métis guide James McKay joined the party. Palliser also hired Maskepetoon, the Cree peacemaker who just happened to be at the Qu'Appelle Lakes post when the expedition arrived there in early September. In the last few weeks of summer, they headed into the open prairie country: southwest towards the boundary again near present-day Roche Percée, Saskatchewan, then northwest across the Regina plains (and the future site of the Saskatchewan capital on Wascana Creek) to the South Saskatchewan River near the Elbow, and finally northeast to their winter quarters at Fort Carlton. Palliser had wanted to follow the South Saskatchewan as far as the Red Deer forks before retreating to Carlton, but the hired men, including McKay, were reluctant—despite Maskepetoon's presence—to venture too far into Blackfoot territory.

The following spring, with Métis Peter Erasmus hired as interpreter, the expedition headed west from Carlton to evaluate the country between the north and south branches of the Saskatchewan River before splitting up near present-day Irricana, Alberta, to assess the suitability of several mountain passes for a transcontinental railway. Geologist James Hector was

Fort Carlton on the North Saskatchewan River hosted the Palliser expedition in the late 1850s.

almost left for dead when he was knocked unconsciousness near the summit of one of the mountain valleys. The accident resulted in the name, Kicking Horse Pass. After wintering at Edmonton House, the party crossed the open prairies southeast to the forks of the Red Deer and the South Saskatchewan Rivers and then south to the Cypress Hills. The expedition members also resumed the probing of the mountain passes before returning home. Captain Palliser, for example, crossed the Rockies through the Kootenay Pass and reached the Pacific coast via the Columbia River. The detailed observations and findings from the three field seasons (1857–59) were published in British parliamentary "blue books." Expedition records were also used to create a finely detailed map (1865) of the western interior, between the North Saskatchewan River and the international border, one that came to be the standard reference source over the next few decades.[63]

The Canadian expedition was really two expeditions over successive field seasons. In late July 1857, George Gladman, a former HBC officer, headed the Red River Exploring Expedition. Civil engineer and surveyor Simon J. Dawson was responsible for finding the best possible route between Lake Superior and the Red River settlement, while Henry Youle Hind, a professor of chemistry at Toronto's Trinity College, made geological and natural history observations along the Red and Assiniboine River valleys. The "hastily mounted and poorly organized" expedition made for "a number of misadventures," but the Dawson and Hind reports convinced the Canadian government to extend the exploratory work for another field season.[64] In 1858, though, both Hind and Dawson headed separate parties with their own instructions. Dawson resumed his examination of the district between Lake of the Woods and Red River before travelling by canoe through the Manitoba interlake region to Grand Rapids on the Saskatchewan River and then up the Swan River and down the Assiniboine River. Hind, on the other hand, was to assess the farming and mining prospects of the country west of Red River. Before he left for the field again, he secured permission to hire photographer Henry Lloyd Hime to accompany his expedition. It was the first time that the prairies were photographed.[65] In fact, the use of the camera came to be a hallmark of scientific work in the region in subsequent decades. But Hind was more interested in the promotional value of photographs and how they could be used to support the agricultural colonization of the region, and more importantly, his ambition as a "frontier publicist."[66]

Hind's 1858 Assiniboine and Saskatchewan exploring expedition lasted six months, June to November, and covered an estimated four thousand miles through Rupert's Land.[67] Surprisingly, even though the Palliser party was in the same general area at the time, it was as if the two expeditions existed and operated in parallel worlds. No mention was ever made of one another. Hind worked his way westward along the Assiniboine and Souris River valleys to the international border and then set off overland to Forts Ellice and Qu'Appelle. He devoted considerable time to investigating the Qu'Appelle Valley, apparently because of its beauty, and even came up with the idea of diverting water from

The Hind expedition

the South Saskatchewan River, near the Elbow, into the Qu'Appelle River for
navigation purposes. Hind then paddled down the South Saskatchewan River
as far as Fort à la Corne and then made his way along the Carlton Trail back
to Fort Ellice. His last few months in the West were spent in the Manitoba
interlake region. This duplication of Dawson's fieldwork stemmed from Hind's
"tendency to place himself in the spotlight."[68] It was a trait, according to his
biographer, that also led Hind to produce a two-volume, popular account of his
western adventures, widely known by its short-form name, *Narrative* (1860).
Based on "the Victorian formula of explore and publish," the work was a tour
de force that captured the land and its life in vivid prose, while evoking a future
for the region that fit perfectly with the ambitions of Canadian expansionists.[69]
But Hind's quest for fame hurt his reputation in the scientific community, and
though he longed to return to the North-West, his desire to head another
expedition was never realized.

Both the Palliser and Hind expeditions commented on the relationship between plains Indian cultures and the bison. Hind documented procurement patterns in present-day southeastern Saskatchewan, as well as carefully studied Cree pounding operations. In one memorable scene from *Narrative*, in a small valley in the sand hills between the Qu'Appelle and South Saskatchewan Rivers, a guide took Hind "through a lane of branches of trees, which are called 'dead men' to the gate or trap of the pound" where "lay tossed in every conceivable position over two hundred dead buffalo."[70] Concern was also expressed about what would become of the Indians if bison numbers continued their steady decline and migration patterns became increasingly unpredictable and erratic north of the border. "These herds are the last means of maintaining their resistance," Palliser predicted.[71] Indians were equally uneasy about their possible fate. One man told expedition member Thomas Blakiston: "If this continues our children cannot live."[72]

The most significant—and since then, controversial—finding of the British and Canadian expeditions was what they had to say about the western interior's climate and the region's fitness for agricultural settlement. It is generally accepted that both parties visited the prairies during a period of drought. The proxy data collected at several locations in the Great Plains indicate that there was a severe drought around 1860. But the climate story for the region at that time is more nuanced, more variable. It was only after the winter of 1857–58 and during the summer of Palliser's second year in the region that precipitation was below the expected normal for the western prairies, a situation that became even more pronounced in 1859. The eastern prairies, by comparison, where Hind was active in 1858, experienced above the expected average precipitation. It was not until the latter part of 1859 that the extreme drought in present-day Alberta extended its reach eastward.[73] The other contributing factor to their perception of the region was a huge fire— probably one of the largest in the history of Rupert's Land—that roared across the prairies for at least one thousand miles south of the North Saskatchewan River in the early fall of 1857. The sky was so thick with smoke at Fort Carlton that it made Palliser's men "all black as [chimney] sweeps."[74] For outsiders unfamiliar with the peculiar plains environment, the fire served to underscore the aridity of the open plains. The "awful splendour," as Hind described it, reduced a wide swath of the grasslands to a desolate, blackened landscape.[75]

Neither Palliser nor Hind was the first visitor to comment on the flatness and treelessness of the prairie landscape. HBC servant Henry Kelsey was struck by the lack of relief on seeing the grasslands for the first time, while Nor'Wester Daniel Harmon claimed that the plains were "level as a House floor."[76] Nor were the expedition members the first outsiders to use the term "barren" to describe the terrain. But barren had a different connotation for the HBC men who increasingly lived and worked on the edge of the northern plains in the latter part of the eighteenth century. For them, barren grounds meant grasslands, a completely different environment from the more familiar boreal forest to the north. Fur traders knew that the plains were a vital source of bison provisions and not in any sense a wasteland. Nor, for that matter, did other inhabitants of the northern plains at the time consider "any part of the area in which they lived a desert."[77] Following the Louisiana Purchase in the early nineteenth century, though, explorers began to investigate the vast region west of the Mississippi River (the trans-Mississippi West) and determined that the semi-arid, seemingly sterile plains constituted a Great American Desert, a condemnatory term that found its way onto the maps of the western United States. This desert idea contradicted the view north of the international border, but the concept nonetheless had to be taken into account by those assessing the potential of the British North American plains. And that is exactly what Hind did in *Narrative* when trying to make sense of the interior geography. Aware of the concept from his reading of American sources and having consulted Palliser's initial report on the "dry" region in present-day western Saskatchewan and all of southern Alberta, Hind introduced the idea of a desert into his discussion of the vegetation zones. "A model was simply plucked from the south," a historical geographer has argued, "and applied to a seemingly similar area in British North America, where it took on a new life of its own."[78]

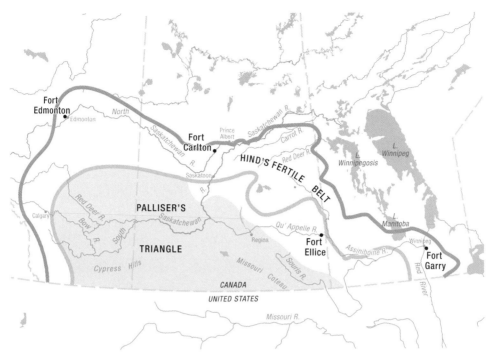

Palliser's arid triangle and Hind's fertile belt, 1860

When the Palliser expedition members subsequently read Hind's book, they followed his lead in their final 1863 report, eschewing any earlier caution, and spoke forcefully of a central triangle-shaped desert radiating southeast and southwest from a point (apex) near Moose Woods (south of present-day Saskatoon). Today, it is known as Palliser's triangle.[79]

Hind did not just introduce the idea of a desert in the northern plains. In his *Narrative*, he also coined the phrase "Fertile Belt" to describe "a broad strip of fertile country" along the Assiniboine and North Saskatchewan Rivers. "No other part of the American continent," he enthusiastically declared, "possesses an approach even to this singular disposition of soil and climate."[80] This claim—coming from a scientist—that the best land for agricultural settlement in North America lay within reach of Canada, and not the United States, made Hind the darling of expansionists, as well as won over a number of new converts. It was the kind of pronouncement that suggested that a transcontinental nation, reaching to the Pacific coast, was not idle speculation but a realizable dream.[81] The problem, though, is that these sweeping resource generalizations were just that: too sweeping, too general. They were based on limited experience in the region and consequently failed to capture the marked year-to-year variation in moisture conditions so characteristic of the northern plains. What got lost in assessing the region's overall potential was that the Palliser expedition also distinguished three successive steppes or prairie levels, rising in elevation from Lake Manitoba to the foothills, and that these relief features had different soils, vegetation, and climate. Instead, Canadian propagandists latched onto the simpler idea of great sections of good and bad land, when, in fact, farming success would vary from place to place and from year to year.[82]

The expansionist search for positive information about the North-West was also bolstered by the work of American climatologist Lorin Blodget. In his provocative 1857 book, *The Climatology of North America*, Blodget had taken limited meteorological data to produce summer isothermal lines that bent northwestward into Rupert's Land. These lines of equal temperature suggested that the climate at more northerly locations supported agriculture and that latitude was not a true determinant. The potential for settlement and development, according to Blodgett, was "gigantic," and if not for the fur trade, the region "would long since have been opened to colonization."[83] Blodgett's findings provided the scientific explanation for the wonderful crops that were routinely reported by visitors to HBC posts. They also served to counter the negative farming reports emanating from missionaries intent on securing greater charitable assistance for their missions.[84] But his work also found a disciple in James Wilkes Taylor, a St. Paul lawyer and writer who had fervently been pushing for the expansion of the frontier state of Minnesota (1858) into HBC territory. "Saskatchewan" Taylor, as he was nicknamed, demanded that the United States take over the British North American plains, while Canada and Great Britain dithered on the future of the region.[85] After all, Blodgett's northward sweeping isothermal lines seemed to support American manifest destiny.

The suggestion that the North-West could be an agricultural wonderland, combined with the American annexationist threat, should have pushed Canada towards acquisition of Rupert's Land in the early 1860s, even if it meant accepting the HBC charter rights and negotiating with the company. But a constitutional obstacle stood in the way. Annexing the North-West necessarily meant a new political arrangement that would undermine the current equal balance between Canada West (Ontario) and East (Quebec) representation in the united Parliament. Confederation of the Provinces of Canada or the colonies of British North America consequently had to be achieved first, with adequate protections for the future province of Quebec, before expansion westward could become a reality. Even then, some Canadian political leaders were uneasy about assuming responsibility for so much territory, estimated at almost three million square miles. It was the kind of empire that belonged to other, older nations—not a new dominion that would not have control over its external affairs.

Conservative leader John A. Macdonald, one of the architects of Canadian confederation and the country's first prime minister, was himself a reluctant expansionist. "It seems to me that that country [Rupert's Land] is of no present value to Canada," he observed on the eve of a trip to London to discuss the confederation agreement. "I would be quite willing, personally, to leave that whole country a wilderness for the next half century, but I fear if Englishmen do not go there, Yankees will."[86] These words nicely captured Macdonald's quandary—how he was essentially bound by political necessity, and not personal enthusiasm, to Canadian acquisition of the North-West. He and his largely Montreal-based supporters subscribed to the old commercial empire of the St. Lawrence, while the drive to settle the British North-West was a Reform plan, spearheaded by George Brown, to satisfy Toronto's economic ambitions.[87] But if the Great Coalition of 1864 was to bring about constitutional renewal in place of deadlock, then territorial expansion into the western prairies had to be a planned feature of the confederation deal (section 146 of the BNA Act). Overall, though, Macdonald was preoccupied, if not overwhelmed, with the problems of the United Province of Canada, and according to his most recent biographer, his interest in territorial expansion "varied from negligible to non-existent."[88]

Conservative leader and Canada's first prime minister, John A. Macdonald, was a reluctant expansionist.

What changed Macdonald's reluctance and that of others was the apparent threat of American encirclement. On 30 March 1867, only one day after Queen Victoria had signed the British North America Act (effective 1 July 1867), the United States and Russia reached an agreement for the purchase of Russian Alaska. Even before confederation became a reality, then, the United States seemed to have been manoeuvring to outflank the new dominion and threaten its future takeover of the North-West. Chief Justice Draper of Upper Canada had raised this prospect in 1857 when the future of the region was being debated in Canadian political circles. "If something is not done," he warned about American intentions, "that territory will in some way or another cease to be British Territory."[89] The American purchase of Alaska now seemed to confirm Draper's prediction. "If the United States desire to outflank us on the West," Quebec East politician Alexander Galt thundered in 1867, "we must ... lay our hand on British Columbia and the Pacific Ocean. This country cannot be surrounded by the United States—we are gone if we allow it ... We must have our back to the North."[90] In other words, since the United States was transcontinental, then Canada had to be transcontinental and expand, sooner rather than later, to the Pacific Ocean.[91]

Just how realistic was this American threat is debatable. Certainly, it became a constant refrain in Macdonald's verbal political arsenal once he embraced the idea of a sea-to-sea nation. "The Hudson's Bay question must soon be settled," he said during the negotiations to secure the North-West. "The rapid march of events and the increase of population on this continent, will compel England and Canada to come to some arrangement respecting that immense country."[92] But even though American Secretary of State William Seward had continental ambitions, he believed that his dream could be achieved without the resort to arms, that British North America would fall into the American lap.[93] This view was shared by many American officials at the time, and was perhaps best elucidated by a July 1867 *New York Times* editorial marking the creation of Canada: "when the experiment of the 'dominion' shall have failed, as fail it must, a process of peaceful absorption will give Canada her proper place in the Great North American Republic."[94] In retrospect, then, the threat alone was what really mattered. As one scholar observed, "the confederation movement badly needed some unifying sentiment," and the threat of American aggression underlying the Alaskan purchase was "shrewdly used... as a political lever to harmonize the various prejudices and local interests which stood in the way of a Canadian union."[95] The anxiety over what the United States might do consequently helped bring the colonies together and led to the eventual Canadian takeover of the North-West.

The HBC, for its part, was ready to embrace a new future. In 1863, Edward Watkin, president of the Grand Trunk Railway, had bought the company with financial backing from some of the largest banks in London.

432

Watkin thought in terms of settlement, not trade, and how the HBC could benefit from the sale and development of its charter lands. But it was not until the confederation agreement was reached that Canadian negotiators finally sat down with the HBC directorship in London over the winter of 1868–69. No representatives from Rupert's Land were invited to participate, let alone even consulted. Discussions soon reached a stalemate, largely over Canadian questioning whether the company actually owned the disputed territory. At this point, British Colonial Secretary Lord Granville, acting as an intermediary, proposed a settlement that was effectively forced on the two parties. The HBC agreed to surrender its charter rights to Rupert's Land in exchange for £300,000 compensation from the Canadian government. The company also kept its posts and surrounding land and would be entitled to a land grant of one-twentieth of the Fertile Belt. Canada, in return, secured title to Rupert's Land and the British North American mainland that was not drained by Hudson Bay, officially known as the North-Western Territory (literally northwest of Rupert's Land).[96] The transfer, to take effect 1 December 1869, increased the size of the dominion by seven times.

Canadian takeover of the North-West did not bring an end to the fur trade. The HBC not only continued its traditional operations north of the new settlement frontier but also created a Land department to handle its new real estate interests. And these interests proved quite substantial. In the British order-in-council sanctioning the land transfer, clause six extended the southern boundary of the Fertile Belt, once confined to the North Saskatchewan country, to the forty-ninth parallel.[97] It is not known how and why this expansive interpretation came about. There had been no other scientific surveys of the western interior since the Palliser and Hind expeditions. There is no doubt, though, that the new boundaries substantially increased the HBC's land grant over the next few decades; one estimate has placed the windfall at close to five million acres.[98]

The enlarged Fertile Belt also mirrored Canada's great ambitions for the region. Once dismissed as a frozen wilderness, the North-West had been transformed into an agricultural eden that would provide the means to empire for the young dominion. And because the region was deemed so essential to Canada's future prosperity and well-being, the land had to be settled and developed as quickly as possible, even if that process conflicted with the interests of the local population. The transfer marked a new beginning in the history of the western interior. And as Aboriginal peoples of the region rudely learned, they were part of a past that had no place in the imagined future of the region.

435

Constable David Cowan upon enlisting in the North-West Mounted Police

CHAPTER THIRTEEN

A GREAT SOURCE OF STRENGTH

THE FRESH-FACED RECRUIT IN THE TIN-TYPE PHOTOGRAPH LOOKED MORE LIKE A CHILD
playing at soldiering than a constable in the North-West Mounted Police. But
as eighteen-year-old David Cowan told his mother in January 1883 in one
of his first letters home from Fort Walsh in the Cypress Hills, "As for being
a man I am big enough to be one ... it is time to stop calling [me] a boy."
Cowan's youthful bravado mirrored the great hopes and expectations for
Canada's North-West. Here was a land of unlimited opportunity where hard-
working Anglo-Canadian settlers would easily convert the prairie wilderness
into farms that would feed the world. It did not matter that Cowan's tunic,
especially the sleeves, was a few sizes too big for him. That was the nature
of the region: there was plenty of room to grow and prosper. Nor would any
obstacles threaten its potential. "We got our buffalo coats this afternoon,"
Cowan proudly wrote his mom in another letter, "so I don't care how cold
it gets." The West's new future, though, did not include Aboriginal peoples,
dismissed by Cowan as "the very worst sort." They were to be pushed to the
sidelines and left behind, if not exorcized from the region's history. Cowan
triumphantly boasted to his family back in Ottawa that, even though slight
in build, he could "put a pair of bracelets [handcuffs] on any half breed or
Indian that I ever seen yet and that alone." Anything seemed possible at the
time, and the word, destiny, seemed to be on every newcomer's lips. "The
boys got a blanket the other night," Cowan happily recounted the Dominion

Day celebrations at Walsh, "and tossed every body they could lay their hands on. I had to take my turn."[1]

Despite all the talk and plans for Canada's new western empire, the Conservative government of John A. Macdonald did the minimum possible to incorporate the region into confederation. Under the terms of the Rupert's Land Act—passed by both houses of Parliament without a single word of debate—Canada planned to assume control of the three-million-square-mile territory on 1 December 1869 by means of a temporary government based in Red River.[2] All existing laws were to remain in force, unless revised or rescinded by a lieutenant-government and appointed council, until the federal government had a chance to evaluate the situation and make more permanent arrangements. But the Red River Métis, led by Louis Riel, resented the lack of consultation and forced Ottawa to negotiate the entry of the region into Confederation. The Red River Resistance, as it became known, foiled the Canadian plan to treat the vast land transfer as little more than a simple real estate transaction. It did not prevent the federal government, though, from directing western settlement and development over the next few decades. Manitoba may have joined the dominion as Canada's fifth province on 1 July 1870, but it was kept deliberately small. At 13,500 square miles, it was less than one-eighth the size of the original 1811 Selkirk land grant, giving rise to its nickname, the postage-stamp province. It also did not exercise control over its public lands and resources, a provincial right that was enshrined in the 1867 British North America Act and enjoyed by all other provinces at the time. The North-West Territories, meanwhile, were treated like a colonial appendage. The temporary government that Ottawa had intended for the territories was quietly made operative through sections 35 and 36 of the Manitoba Act. The North-West Territories became a legal entity in 1870, but beyond that, "effective government remained almost completely unknown."[3] Some might reasonably have wondered whether the imperialism of the HBC had simply been superseded by that of the government of Canada.

THE CANADIAN GARGANTUA
This youngster has absorbed the whole of British North America to the wonder of all nations.

CANADIAN ILLUSTRATED NEWS, OCTOBER 1880

Expansion westward turned the young Canadian dominion into a "gargantua."

Ottawa was only interested in the agricultural settlement of the southern North-West Territories, the area south of a line from present-day Winnipeg northwest to Prince Albert and Edmonton. The great remainder of what was sometimes called the unorganized territories—to the north, west, and east—continued to be the exclusive domain of the fur trade. In fact, it is one of the great myths of western Canadian history that the two-century-old fur trade ended with the acquisition of the region by Canada. It did not. But even HBC shareholders at the time wondered whether the company should continue in the fur trade—what many regarded as an outdated, anti-modern enterprise—and become involved instead in several promising new business ventures in the region. After all, under the terms of the agreement with the government

LOUIS COCHIN

A Métis family at Île-à-la-Crosse

of Canada, the HBC received title to forty-five thousand acres of land around its existing posts and the right to claim one-twentieth of "any township or district within the fertile belt in which land is set out for settlements."[4] A study commissioned for the shareholders concluded, however, that large-scale agricultural settlement of the territories was still several years away without a transcontinental railway and that the company could still profit from its "monopoly" position in the fur trade. There were changes, though.[5]

Beaver skins had once been the staple of the HBC trade. But over-hunting of the animal and the switch to silk hats in the mid-nineteenth century greatly lessened its importance to the HBC balance sheet. Muskrat emerged as the dominant fur in the post-1870 period, representing as much as 50 per cent of the company returns in some years, followed by beaver (20 per cent), and marten (10 per cent). Bison robes from the prairie parkland were still traded but were only a small percentage of company business. The heavy reliance on muskrat pelts reflected the realities of the ecology of the subarctic, especially in "muskrat country," the marshy lowlands extending west from Hudson Bay to the Saskatchewan and Churchill Rivers. But muskrat was a low-value fur subject to extreme population swings. It consequently offered marginal and erratic returns to Indian and Métis trappers, even when fur prices in general started to climb in the 1880s. Nor did all pelts find their way into company hands. The late-nineteenth-century European and American demand for fur products sent scores of competitors into the territories who tried to wrest trade away from the HBC by offering better prices and alcohol. Far from fading away, then, the fur trade industry enjoyed something of a renaissance as garment manufacturers turned to Canadian sources.[6]

Two brothers who tried their hand at trading were Donald and John Finlayson. In late September 1888, after being outfitted with goods at Cumberland House, they arrived at Reindeer Lake and spent the fall building a cabin about thirty miles north of the south end of the lake. Local HBC officials knew they had entered the district and why they were there. On 8 December, the pair set off over the ice with a sled and two dogs to visit Lac du Brochet at the extreme northeast end of the lake. But a little more than a week into the trip, they were out of food and had collected no furs. Turning back in the face of a snowstorm instead of continuing on to the HBC post, they lived on the few fish they were able to catch but, by Christmas, were reduced to eating fish tails and bones. On 2 January, around midday, they stopped to make some tea. One of the brothers passed out near the campfire, probably from hunger and exhaustion. The other apparently collapsed in coming to his aid. When their frozen bodies were found three weeks later, the brothers were only eight miles from their cabin. The story of their brief career as traders, right up until the fateful tea break, was documented by Donald in a small diary that he carried in his pocket. A search of their belongings turned up ten cents.[7]

Itinerant traders like the Finlaysons were able to compete with the HBC on its own turf because of improvements that the company made to its transportation system. The old way of moving goods and furs by cart, canoe, and York boat was too labour-intensive and thereby too inefficient. In its place, the HBC decided to introduce steamboat service on the major lakes and rivers in the region, not only to ship its own freight but also capture any new business and passenger traffic.[8] But it was a difficult transition. In 1871, the last York boat brigade arrived at York Factory. Thereafter, the HBC used steamers on Lake Winnipeg and the Red River, working between the transhipment point at Grand Rapids in the northwest corner of the lake and the burgeoning provincial capital and future railroad hub at Winnipeg. The first two attempts to get a boat beyond Grand Rapids into the Saskatchewan River system, however, ended in failure. It was not until August 1874 that the *Northcote,* a low-draft sternwheeler built at Grand Rapids and specially equipped to deal with the challenges of prairie rivers, made its maiden voyage to Fort Carlton in just twelve days.[9]

Three years later, a second vessel, the smaller, steel-hulled *Lily,* began working the Saskatchewan as far west as Fort Edmonton. Other steamboats soon followed. The *Marquette* managed to ascend the Assiniboine River to Fort Pelly in 1881, "a hard-won victory" because of "the innumerable loops and curves on [the] winding river."[10]

These "fire canoes," as they were called by the Indians because of their belching smoke stacks, certainly accelerated the movement of HBC freight. But shipping schedules and length of season were dictated by fluctuating water levels, which not only grounded boats but also increased the number of hazards, such as sandbars and boulders, that lay in wait. Even deep, open water could be treacherous for the shallow-draft, flat-bottomed boats. "A very little breeze," one deck hand remembered, "and they would get going like a snake in the grass."[11] The HBC adoption of steamships displaced hundreds of labourers who manned the carts and York boats. Some found employment cutting cordwood, usually scrub timber, that was hauled and stacked at fuelling stations along the river to supply the steamships. Others came to work on northern lakes and rivers. And even though the brigades no longer made their annual pilgrimage between York Factory and the interior, York boats continued

PRINCE ALBERT HISTORICAL SOCIETY J168

The HBC steamer, *Saskatchewan*, on the river of the same name

to be used in present-day northern Saskatchewan into the twentieth century. A visitor to Pelican Narrows in 1912 learned that the boats were the backbone of the transhipment centre.[12] With steamers able to deliver goods and supplies to communities along the North Saskatchewan River, the HBC pioneered new north-south cart trails. The old Green Lake trail that ran north from Fort Carlton, for example, was eventually replaced by one from Prince Albert to Montreal Lake. Freight was hauled in the winter months when low-lying, water-logged sections were frozen and snow-covered.

Senior HBC officials also moved after 1870 to discontinue the support of families of company men. It was a reform that Governor George Simpson first tried to implement almost half a century earlier, with limited success. HBC men in the field knew that if they were going to maintain the loyalty of their labour force, they had to lend assistance, especially during lean times.[13] Feeding families in and around the northern posts was also a necessity. The northern fur trade communities placed a heavy strain on game and fish resources, and food shortages were the norm. Sometimes, the HBC acted almost like a family member. In the English River district, for example, local traders were part of the larger community, from hosting dances and holiday feasts to assisting widows and arranging for funerals. The Métis population, in return, was not necessarily beholden to the company, despite the HBC's economic dominance, but acted according to its best interests and needs.

As long as the HBC served as a provider to men and their families, the local workforce was supportive and cooperative, such as when three generations of women weeded the potato plot at Île-à-la-Crosse in 1889. But when senior management attempted to reduce operating costs by hiring men, preferably single, on a strictly payment-for-service basis, some Métis turned to independent trading and tried to use their family connections to divert business away from the HBC. Green Lake was a particular trouble spot for this activity, and traders there and elsewhere in present-day northwestern Saskatchewan worked hard to ensure or win back Métis allegiance to the company. Even the discontinuance of a company pension or shedding of other expected obligations could have far-reaching consequences.[14] The Métis population had grown in size over the nineteenth century, expanding throughout the region and maintaining connections with Cree and Chipewyan communities. And if an individual had a grievance against the company, then the extended family felt alienated, too. Because Métis "familial loyalty" came first over all other considerations, "the HBC was never really secure in the region."[15]

HBC shareholders thought about getting out of the fur trade and into land development because of the wonderful things that were being said about the western interior and its enormous potential. And who could blame them? In an 1859 essay, Alexander Morris, a future lieutenant-governor of Manitoba and treaty commissioner, had declared that Canada would inherit the British position as head of the English-speaking world by claiming the North-West. "There are noble provinces in these territories well adapted for settlement," he predicted, "provinces which will yet become important members of the New

GLENBOW ARCHIVES NA-1408-11

Agricultural colonization of the Saskatchewan country was expected to proceed
smoothly, if not quickly.

Britannic Empire which is quickly being built-up on these Northern shores."[16]
George Denison of Toronto, a member of the Canada First group, was equally
effusive about the North-West on the eve of the Canadian takeover. "I have
every confidence ... it will prove a great source of strength to the Dominion,"
he crowed, "[and] teach the Yankees that we will be ... a dominant race."[17]

What these and other expansionists were saying was that the region
guaranteed Canada's future existence by offering the very real prospect of
greatness. By occupying and developing the North-West, Canada would
become stronger, more powerful, but most of all, more secure on a continent
now dominated by the aggressive United States. It was therefore imperative
that the West be settled as quickly as possible.[18] Nor could this task, given
the singular importance of the region to Canada's success, be handed over
to any territorial or provincial government. Federal oversight, particularly the
administration of western lands and resources, was a "national necessity."[19]
At the same time, though, the North-West would have to pay for its own
development because of the opposition that had been voiced in the Canadian
House of Commons to the acquisition of the vast territory. Expansion might

447

BRIAN CHENOWYTH

A marker along the international border with the United States

have offered the prospect of empire, but some parliamentarians, like Nova Scotian Joseph Howe, charged that acquisition of the North-West was a lavish, if not reckless, expenditure that served only to increase the national debt.[20] That seemed unlikely, though, to the advocates of westward expansion. Not only was the region rich in resource wealth, but also its transformation from a subarctic wilderness to an agricultural eden was considered inevitable.

Much like the Hudson's Bay Company under George Simpson in the first half of the nineteenth century, Canada's control over its new western frontier in the second half of the century was based on the desire for order and stability. Ottawa wanted to avoid a replica of the wild and woolly American West by creating the conditions whereby the best features of British civilization would take root and flourish on the northern plains. The ideal West was conservative, agricultural, and Anglo-Canadian. This vision could only be realized, though, if the defining values and principles of the new society were imposed from outside. There was no allowance for local or democratic initiatives, no recognition that the indigenous peoples of the region might foresee a different future. Backing this Canadian plan, moreover, was a supreme

PRINCE ALBERT HISTORICAL SOCIETY H-122

Dominion Lands Survey teams imposed order on the North-West landscape.

confidence—bordering on arrogance—that the re-making of the region would proceed smoothly, if not quickly. Ottawa did not expect to encounter any major challenges or difficulties, and if it did, they would be largely insignificant. Nor did the Red River Resistance offer a corrective to Canadian plans. There could be no deviation from the ideal or the ideal would be compromised, even lost.[21]

One of the first tasks to be undertaken following the land transfer was the surveying of the international boundary line from the Lake of the Woods to the Rocky Mountains. Although the forty-ninth parallel had been formally established by treaty in 1818, the only step taken in the interim was the determination of the so-called northwest angle at the Lake of the Woods in 1826. Both sides supported the initiative, as did the British Foreign Office, which continued to represent Canadian interests in international matters. The United States was worried that an ill-defined boundary could lead to a possible future international incident. Canada, on the other hand, wanted to put an end to American expansionist ambitions by formally defining the territorial extent of its new Western empire. Indeed, some American newspapers editorialized at the time that the northward bend of isothermal lines not only made possible agriculture at northern latitudes, but "was the cartographic representation of the directional flow of the American frontier."[22] Ottawa also considered the marking of the boundary as a necessary step in establishing Canadian authority over the region. No longer would the northern plains be regarded as one large ecological zone, but divided into separate jurisdictions. No longer would people be able to travel freely throughout the region but be forced to

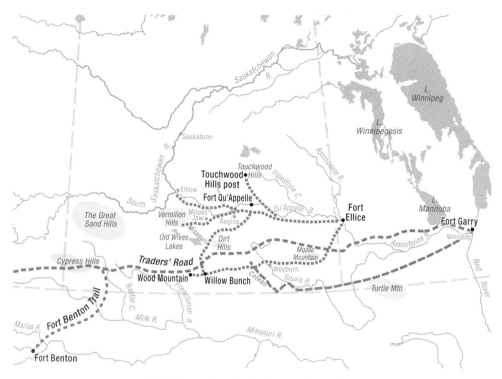

Trails in southern Saskatchewan, circa 1860

declare themselves Canadian or American. The once-great open commons was coming to an abrupt end. One author has likened the process to building "the first fence ... on the great western grasslands."[23]

After determining the position of the forty-ninth parallel at the Red River in September 1872, the fixing of the boundary west from the base camp at Pembina (renamed Dufferin in honour of the Canadian governor general) began in earnest in June 1873. To the unsuspecting observer, it must have looked like an invasion. The British Commission alone numbered over 250 men, along with wagons, carts, horses, oxen, equipment, and supplies. There were local teamsters, axemen, and general labourers, in addition to thirty armed and mounted Métis scouts, known as the Forty-Ninth Rangers, who had been recruited to serve as an advance reconnaissance party and provide possible protection. A majority of the personnel served in a support capacity. It had also been decided to use the boundary survey to gather scientific information and, consequently, the commission personnel included geologists and naturalists.

Two sappers with the Royal Engineers received special training in photography before leaving for the field. It was the first time that the country and the people in the international border region were captured on glass plate.[24]

During its first season, the commission marked, without incident, four hundred miles of boundary as far west as the Missouri Couteau (near present-day Killdeer and the eastern block of Grasslands National Park). British and American astronomical parties, using the zenith telescope, located the boundary at alternate observation stations spaced twenty miles apart. It was exacting work, requiring almost a week to determine the latitude at each station.[25] Surveying parties then followed, chaining, marking, and mapping a narrow belt of land along the border, while teamsters brought forward wagonloads of supplies. Some of the pyramid-shaped sod mounds that served as original boundary markers (every three miles) fell victim to bison who liked to rub against them. But surveying technology today has found that the difference between the boundary, as marked on the ground almost a century-and-a-half ago, and a computer-imposed perfect parallel is less than four inches.[26]

The British Commission used the same operational plan for the 1874 field season. Before work began, a new base camp was established near the Métis wintering camp in the Wood Mountain uplands. Chief Astronomer Samuel Anderson named it Wood End depot, a nod to the fact that the treeless badlands lay just to the west. Resuming their work in June, the various work parties were soon exasperated by the lengthy detours they were forced to make around wide, deep ravines and high, conical hills. Stone cairns now replaced earthen mounds to mark the border. Beyond the Whitemud River, the broken country eventually gave way to an arid plain, but it was considered little better. "It was something terrible," Assistant Surgeon Dr. Thomas Millman scribbled in his diary, "when you consider the heat, dust, barrenness—cacti over the whole ground, no water! and the monotony of the scene!"[27] The country resumed its rugged character near the Milk River, making travel difficult once more, but the commission, anxious to complete its assignment, laboured on and managed to push the boundary up into the foothills by the end of August.

Several commission members voiced opinions about the region's settlement potential. Geologist George Mercer Dawson offered the most judicious assessment. During the 1873 and 1874 field seasons, the diminutive Dawson had wandered widely—as much as fifty miles from the boundary—investigating any interesting phenomena. He paid particular attention to the geology, especially any lignite exposures and their possible use as fuel for the Pacific Railway. He also worked up the natural history, keeping his collecting net, plant press, and can of preserving alcohol close at hand. From his diary, however, it appears that he shot at birds more out of a desire for something new to eat than to secure specimens.[28] Dawson's report, published as a thick monograph complete with a coloured map and several appendices, did much to foster his reputation as one of Canada's foremost scientists. He stated that the second and third prairie steppes—with their light soils, scanty precipitation, lack of wood, and high incidence of frosts—did not compare favourably with the fertile belt, "which must form the basis of settlement." But he was equally determined to correct the false impression about the short-grass prairie district that had been generated by the Palliser and Hind expeditions. Whereas Dawson had expected to find a desert landscape, he announced that "a part of it may be of future importance agriculturally, and that a great area is well suited for pastoral occupation and stock farming." Unlike earlier investigators, then, who imposed their own values on the grasslands and so naturally concluded that the region was deficient, Dawson urged that the progress of settlement should be "a natural growth taking advantage of the capabilities of the country."[29]

While the North American Boundary Commission Survey was marking the southern territorial limit of Canada's new western empire, teams of dominion land surveyors were dividing up the western terrain into homesteads for the anticipated rush of settlers. Ottawa, in fact, had been so anxious to get agriculturalists on the land that actual surveying began several months before the official land transfer. During the summer of 1869, a survey team was sent to Red River and established the prime or first meridian approximately ten miles west of the settlement (97°27'28.4"). The plan was to ignore the traditional river-lot system that had been in use along the Red and Assiniboine Rivers for over half a century and impose a grid system based on nine-mile-square townships of sixty-four equal sections (810 acres). But while the surveyors were marking off the major grid lines, the Métis abruptly halted the work—they stood on the chain—in order to get the Canadian government to deal with their concerns, including their land holdings. The ensuing Red River Resistance not only delayed the entry of the region into confederation for several months but led to a review of the proposed survey system. Ottawa still refused to recognize the river-lot system, deciding instead to reduce the size of the proposed townships to six square miles (or thirty-six sections) so that the homestead available to the farmer in either the American or Canadian West was identical in size (160 acres). The slightly revised system came into force on 25 April 1871.[30]

The first dominion surveyors who took to the field in the summer of 1871 faced a formidable challenge. Given the size of the area to be surveyed (roughly 1.4 billion acres in the North-West) and the urgency attached to the task, the surveying system needed to be applied swiftly yet accurately. Federal control of public lands helped this process. Because all of the western interior was subject to the same grid system, work could proceed at a fairly steady pace, a particularly important consideration because homesteads could be filed for occupation only after the land had been surveyed. The system was also precise not simply because it was based on astronomical observation but because it was applied uniformly throughout the region and therefore less subject to error. Any natural features—be it a valley, moraine, or slough—were completely ignored in favour of an artificial checkerboard ordering that can be seen from an airplane today. The only major adjustments were "correction lines" that were necessary to take into account the gradual northern convergence of meridians.[31]

As for the actual surveying of the land, the federal government initially assumed that settlement would be confined to the fertile belt that had been identified by the Palliser and Hind expeditions in the late 1850s. The Dominion Lands Survey (DLS) was consequently organized to begin in Manitoba and then proceed northwestward along the North Saskatchewan River through present-day central Saskatchewan and Alberta—what was regarded at the time as the "settlement belt." Surveyors and their gangs suffered through a host of difficulties in the field, as evidenced by the daily journal kept by Otto J. Klotz. In 1879, for example, he described how they battled prairie fires, how the ponies kept wandering off at night, and how his men suffered severe bouts of diarrhea because of brackish water. Then there were the mosquitoes. "When writing the word mosquito," Klotz mused, "I am tempted to indulge in some of my 'sacred' profanity ... the numbers we encountered here defied mathematicians to express by finite numbers."[32] Despite such irritations, the DLS managed to survey 10.5 million acres in its first four years. Thereafter, the pace actually quickened. By the end of 1887, the total number of subdivided acres topped seventy million. And when survey teams reached the foothills, they used the camera to take a series of panoramic views from several stations that were predetermined by triangulation; the photographs were then used to plot the maps back in Ottawa. Phototopography, as it became known, represented a quantum leap in Canadian surveying history.[33]

Surveyors associated with the Special Survey (created in February 1874) were also involved in evaluating the country and its potential. This work included a reappraisal of the region that the Palliser and Hind expeditions had ruled out for settlement. The person largely responsible for this reassessment was plant geographer John Macoun, professor of natural history at Albert College, Belleville, Ontario. Macoun was no stranger to the North-West. He had extolled the Peace River country in 1872 and 1875 for its ability to support plant species that grew where agriculture was already being practised in Ontario. He had also told a House of Commons committee in 1876 that the assessment of the Palliser and Hind expeditions was a hasty conclusion and that portions of the arid southern plains were suited for stock raising and possibly grain production, even though he had never personally seen the southern grasslands. Now, as the newly appointed explorer for the Canadian government in the North-West Territories, he was asked in 1879 and 1880 to examine the prairie district south of the Qu'Appelle and South Saskatchewan

Rivers, especially those areas that had been condemned as sterile. Macoun's findings supported his earlier assertion. Travelling during several consecutive exceptionally wet summers—he often complained about the rain[34]—he came across thick swards of luxuriant grasses and standing water where there was supposed to be a desert environment. Macoun consequently concluded that the shallow, light soils would become productive once the ground had been broken and cultivated. He even went so far as to challenge the long-standing assumption that settlement should be initially restricted to North Saskatchewan country and trumpeted the virtues of the treeless plain. At one of his many public talks about the North-West over the winter of 1880–81, the botanist declared: "There [is] no such thing as the fertile belt at all—it [is] all equally good land."[35]

Macoun's pronouncements about western Canada's agricultural potential were certainly exaggerated. In a stinging rebuke, *Manitoba and the North-West Frauds*, H.Y. Hind flatly dismissed Macoun's findings as "nothing less than the concoctions of a scientific rogue."[36] Charles Horetzky, who had photographed western Canada in the 1870s, was just as damning in his denunciation. "It cannot ... be doubted," he sarcastically predicted in *Some Startling Facts*, "that much of the arid, cactus region north of the boundary line will be forever obliterated" by a future expedition.[37] What mattered more at the time, though, was that Macoun's statements perfectly matched Canadian expectations. Ottawa had acquired the North-West in 1870 in the belief that the region would soon become home to countless millions and wanted these great expansionist hopes to be substantiated. Macoun, in a sense, then, was a programmed observer: he saw not necessarily what there was to see, but what he wanted and should see. Nor was he alone in his findings. As the survey progressed along the North Saskatchewan in the late 1870s, surveyors' field reports indicated that the amount of arable land was much greater than had been previously estimated. Similarly, the southern district "has turned out to be specially fitted, both by fertility of soil and by the nature of its surface, for agricultural production."[38] But sweeping generalizations about the potential of the western interior were no substitute for reality. They were misleading and potentially harmful in the long run, especially because they suggested that the standard 160-acre homestead was appropriate throughout the region because of the presumed uniform fertility and that the settler would require little assistance at the pioneering stage. "All that is needed," Macoun assuredly advised, "is a mere scratching of the soil."[39]

Marking the international boundary and surveying western lands helped integrate the region with Canada. But until the new territory was linked with the young dominion, it would remain isolated no matter how many homesteads were measured for occupation. Providing dependable communication and transportation within and through the region was therefore just as important as getting the land ready for settlement, and getting the future crops of hundreds of thousands of prospective farmers to market. The existing system of trails, largely developed in the first half of the nineteenth century, simply would not do. The most famous at the time— and the most heavily used—was the nine-hundred-mile Carlton Trail, which ran from the Red River settlement northwest to Fort Edmonton. Known by a number of names depending on the district, the broad trail entered present-day Saskatchewan (from Fort Ellice) near Welby/Spy Hill, continued northwest (just south of Melville) through Ituna to Touchwood Post (near Lestock south of the Quill Lakes) and then continued (passing near Lanigan and Humboldt) on to Batoche, where it crossed the South Saskatchewan River before reaching Fort Carlton; from Carlton, the trail ran north of the North Saskatchewan River (just south of Edam and Turtleford) to Fort Pitt and ended at Fort Edmonton.[40] It took on average twenty-two days to travel its length at a rate of about forty miles per day, certainly not at a speed that matched Canada's great ambitions for the region. The trail was also deeply rutted in places from the constant freight traffic and presented something of a nightmare during wet weather because of the mudholes.[41] It functioned for several decades, nonetheless, as the major transportation artery through the western interior and was intersected by several other trails in the southern

RUSSELL, THE CARLTON TRAIL

A section of the nine-hundred-mile Carlton Trail from the Red River settlement to Fort Edmonton

half of the province. Any visitor to the region in the mid-nineteenth century, including explorers and surveyors who ironically had been sent West to help inaugurate a new future for the region, invariably travelled part of the Carlton Trail.

Victorian Canadians looked to railroad technology to make sea-to-sea nationhood a reality. Any rail link between the original Canada and the Pacific coast had to be an all-Canadian line, pushed through the rugged, rock-and-muskeg-riddled shield country instead of running across American territory south of the Great Lakes. The steam engine promised to fulfill this national requirement by effectively shrinking distance, while instilling a confidence that the intervening wilderness could be tamed. The vast North-West land mass would "dissolve ... into insignificance."[42] It was all a relatively simple matter, according to Canadian expansionists, of plotting a route and then noting and overcoming any engineering problems. Canadian Pacific Railway Chief Engineer Sandford Fleming, however, was not so certain, or at least, not to be rushed. He was given the job in 1871 of fulfilling the Canadian pledge to the new province of British Columbia to build a transcontinental railway—the so-called national dream—to the Pacific within ten years. Fleming, best remembered today as the inventor of standard time, was notoriously meticulous, to the point where *all* possible routes for a transcontinental rail line had to be thoroughly investigated. No less than twenty-one field parties (eight hundred men) were consequently dispatched in the summer of 1871, many to perform costly instrument surveys (measurement of the land by chain, transit, and level). He also insisted that a telegraph line erected along the proposed railway route precede the railroad. It would serve as a kind of "spinal cord" in the eventual communication and transportation network. Canadian expansionists were much more pragmatic. They regarded an overland telegraph as vital to Anglo-Asian commerce.[43]

What western Canada got by the end of the decade was an unreliable telegraph and no railway across the western interior. Like the Dominion Lands Survey work, it was initially assumed in the early 1870s that the railway would travel along the North Saskatchewan country (the fertile or settlement belt) and then through the mountains by the Yellowhead Pass. And that was the route where the telegraph was erected between Winnipeg and Edmonton by the end of 1876, with the exception of the Lake Winnipeg section (from Selkirk on the Red River [north of Winnipeg] across the Lake Manitoba Narrows and then north of the Duck Mountains to the Swan River district along the present-day Manitoba-Saskatchewan border). This "pioneer" telegraph lived up to its name. Because of the speed with which the line was located, the routing was based less on settlement potential and more on ease of grades and the availability of construction materials. Several miles passed through wet, unstable ground, and the poles kept falling over and damaging the wire, throwing sections of the line out of commission for days, if not weeks. Service could be expected with any certainty only during the winter months. Even then, an official government assessment of the line in 1879 concluded that the project was nothing short of a fiasco. It was not until almost a decade later, in January 1887, that a reliable transcontinental telegraph was in operation.[44]

Fleming, in the meantime, could not decide on a route for the Canadian Pacific Railway—even though it was supposed to follow the same general course as the telegraph—and continued to send out field parties every season,

SASKATCHEWAN ARCHIVES BOARD S-B10299

Maintaining and repairing the dominion telegraph line during the winter

especially to the mountains and the shield country north of the Great Lakes. In an 1877 recap of CPR Survey operations, he reported that his crews had logged forty-six thousand miles over the past six years at a cost of over three million dollars. But even though a "practicable" route had been established between Lake Superior to the Rocky Mountains, he still dithered on the route to be followed through the mountains. The seven possibilities in 1874 had now expanded to eleven! Fleming was obsessed that the railway serve the best interests of the country and believed that it was best to err on the side of caution. "The way," he lamely justified his indecision, "must be felt little by little."[45] A subsequent royal commission investigation into the CPR project was not so understanding. The chief engineer's handling of the CPR Survey was declared "a sacrifice of money, time, and efficiency."[46]

As for the delay, it did little to hurt the CPR project because the federal government was still waiting for a private builder to take on the project. The first attempt to find a consortium in the early 1870s had ended in failure when it was learned that the Montreal competitor for the contract had provided secret financial donations to the ruling Conservative Party. The resulting

BILL WAISER

The arrival of the North-West Mounted Police is commemorated by a sculpture
outside the rebuilt Fort Walsh.

Pacific Scandal cast a pall over the project, made worse by the recession that
hobbled the Canadian economy in the mid-1870s. The Liberal government
of Alexander Mackenzie (1873–78) continued to support Fleming's surveys—
even though it believed that Ottawa's railway promise to British Columbia was
unrealistic—but could do little more, given the prevailing economic climate.
In fact, one of the first things that the new Macdonald government did after
returning to office in 1878 was to try to settle the route question, but only after
field parties were dispatched for the ninth consecutive summer. In October
1879, the Cabinet formally endorsed the Yellowhead-Burrard Inlet route for the
railway.[47] There was still no builder, though, for the Pacific main line. And until
then, passenger and freight traffic through the western interior continued to
use the trails or the new steamboat service.

The 1874 arrival of the North-West Mounted Police, by comparison, was
a success story. But their establishment almost did not happen. And they were
successful, not because as generations of authors have suggested that the force
brought law and order where chaos reigned,[48] but because they survived their

EASTEND HISTORICAL MUSEUM

The Eastend North-West Mounted Police post in 1879

"long march" across the southern prairies and set up operations in the region. The idea for a mounted police force, which performed both military and civil roles, originated with Prime Minister John A. Macdonald in 1869 and was modelled after the Royal Irish Constabulary. Macdonald wanted a federal force, directed from Ottawa, to be on the scene in advance of settlement to ensure peaceful relations between Indians and immigrants and, at the same time, demonstrate to the United States that Canada exercised effective sovereignty over the North-West Territories. As one military historian observed, it was the absence of a Canadian presence in the western interior that raised the prospect of future trouble.[49] Such a force, according to the prime minister's original plan, was also to reflect the multiracial character of the region and include both white and Métis members. The 1869–70 Red River Resistance, however, temporarily derailed Macdonald's scheme. And it was not until May 1873, in response to disturbing reports coming from the West about the violent whisky trade along the border in present-day Alberta and Saskatchewan, that the Conservative government passed enabling legislation to create a mounted police force at some future date. There was no requirement or mention, though, that the force be multiracial.[50]

One of the reasons that the recruitment of the mounted police was put on hold was that Prime Minister Macdonald did not believe that the situation in Whoop-Up country was "sufficiently grave."[51] News of a terrible massacre, though, forced his hand. In the 1850s, American traders from Fort Benton, Montana, began to travel north with bull trains loaded with supplies to trade with Indians and Métis in HBC territory. They set up for the winter wherever they could find a sheltered place with wood and water and then exchanged goods for robes and furs before returning with their haul to Benton in the spring. One of the most popular trade items was alcohol, which was often laced with tobacco, pepper, molasses, and ink to produce powerful and debilitating concoctions. The most notorious of the whisky posts was Fort Whoop-Up at the St. Mary and Belly Rivers, whose vile "firewater" had condemned the Blackfoot people to a wretched existence.[52] But it was on Battle Creek in the Cypress Hills on 1 June 1873 that violence erupted. American wolfers and a nearby band of Assiniboine had been drinking heavily that morning, supplied booze by two rival stores on the creek. When the wolfers heard that a horse had gone missing (actually just wandered off), and already spoiling for a fight because of past horse thefts, they headed to the Assiniboine camp, intent on retribution. Armed with repeating rifles, they fired indiscriminately at the helpless Indians who scattered for their lives. The exact number of Assiniboine dead is uncertain—the toll ranges from twenty to fifty—but only one wolfer died. When the shooting was over, the wolfers stuck the head of one of the chiefs on a lodge pole and raped those Assiniboine women who had been taken captive. The next day, once the traders had packed up their stores, the wolfers set fire to the two posts and the Assiniboine camp before skulking back across the border.[53]

Word of the atrocity reached Ottawa from Washington in the late summer of 1873. Dire warnings of a possible Indian war were also received—repeatedly—from the lieutenant-governor of Manitoba, who served in the same capacity for the territories. Macdonald decided to recruit half the planned police force of three hundred men and send them immediately to Winnipeg

THE SCOTSMAN, 16 SEPTEMBER 1881

An Indian dance at Fort Qu'Appelle, the site of Treaty 4 agreement

before winter set in. This decision was no sooner taken than the Conservative government fell because of the Pacific Scandal. At first, Macdonald's successor, Liberal Alexander Mackenzie, wanted to ask the United States government to send a military expedition to deal with the whisky traders, even if it meant operating in Canadian territory. But in March 1874, the new prime minister decided to follow through with Macdonald's soldier-policeman model and complete the force's organization in time for a summer expedition. Recruits had to be fit, of good character, able to ride, and read and write in either English or French. The pay for a constable was a dollar a day and the prospect of 160 acres of homestead land at the end of three years of service.[54]

Nearly three hundred North-West Mounted Police, under the command of Commissioner George A. French, set off from Dufferin, Manitoba, on 8 July 1874 for Whoop-Up country. Wearing red serge tunics and white helmets and divided into six troops (A to F), each with its own distinctive troop horse colour, the mounted officers and men rode westward into near disaster. Many of the difficulties were the first commissioner's doing. Instead of accepting advice

Blackfoot Kyi-otan (Bear Shield) photographed at Fort Walsh by T. George N. Anderton

from boundary commission leaders who had already spent a year in the field and had a good understanding of the challenges of travelling along the border, French insisted on using Canadian horses that were not really suited for the prairies, did not bring along enough feed, made no provision for carrying water, and dragged along two field guns and two mortars that encumbered the march. He also preferred his own advice over that of his few Métis scouts. These shortcomings were complicated by the Mackenzie government's instructions to take a more northerly route, paralleling the border, instead of following the entire boundary commission trail. By the time the police reached Roche Percée (near present-day Estevan) a little more than two weeks into the march, French realized that he could only reach his objective if he divided his troop and sent the ailing men and faltering horses north to Fort Ellice and then on to Edmonton. Continuing westward, the commissioner committed another gaffe when he decided against taking Traders' Road, which ran through a gap in the Missouri Coteau to Wood Mountain and the Cypress Hills. Instead, he inexplicably headed northwest across an unforgiving, trackless stretch of the coteau to Old Wives Lakes.

Unlike the boundary commission, there was no photographer to document the bumblings and calamities of the great trek westward, only an artist with the *Canadian Illustrated News,* who captured the mounties as they strained with their artillery through the Dirt Hills. By 20 August, the police were just north of present-day Gravelbourg on the Wood River, headed for the Cypress Hills. Early September found them in the vicinity of Medicine Hat and practically lost. The police made for the safety of the Sweet Grass Hills and found temporary refuge there at a camp they fittingly nicknamed Dead Horse Coulee. As for the whisky traders in the vicinity, there were none to be found, only abandoned posts. And that was a good thing because the police were not able to mount much resistance. French left Assistant Commissioner James Macleod behind to deal with Fort Whoop-Up, while he returned eastward, this time following established trails. He and his men rode to Wood Mountain, where he purchased the depot for police purposes, and then struck north to

Fort Qu'Appelle and Fort Ellice before returning to Dufferin for the winter. It was a miraculous outcome to what could have been a tragedy, and the beginning of the mountie legend.[55]

Assistant Commissioner Macleod arranged for the construction of the first NWMP post in the interior (Fort Macleod) on the Belly (Oldman) River in present-day southern Alberta in the fall of 1874. Ironically, it was built and supplied by the same Fort Benton merchant who did business with the whisky traders. The following year, it was decided that the temporary police post at Wood Mountain was not well positioned to suppress the local whisky traffic and, consequently, it was closed in favour of a second major post (Fort Walsh) in the Cypress Hills, not far from the site of the massacre. Both posts took a turn serving as police headquarters. Constable David Cowan was assigned first to Fort Macleod before being sent to Walsh.

Many of the first police recruits signed up for adventure or to escape an unhappy situation in eastern Canada. And there was no shortage of shake-outs during the first few years of the force's existence, including at the start of the long march. Cowan himself was thinking of getting out at the end of his three-year service. Because Ottawa wanted the police to serve as government handymen, enlisted men were called upon to perform a wide range of civil duties when not drilling or on guard duty. Cowan quickly realized that there was little chance of advancement unless one had connections.[56] Officers, on the other hand, were a social class unto themselves—with servants—and had a clear sense of their position and authority. They expected to impose the same respectability and civic virtue on the western frontier that shaped and informed their own lives. The gulf between the ranks was evident in Police Surgeon J. G. Kittson's records for Fort Walsh. Because the men lived in two single-storey barracks built directly on the ground and with leaky roofs, they faced "a tide of illness" that had almost one-quarter of the garrison reporting sick at times. Sanitary practices were also negligent. Personal hygiene was "disgustingly poor in many cases," while syphilis was rampant. Archaeological work at the site has also revealed that the troops handled the boredom and loneliness by turning to drink: what they had been sent to suppress. Hundreds of empty bottles were left behind when the fort was closed.[57] It was not the romantic life portrayed in pulp fiction and movies.

Through messengers, the lieutenant-governor of Manitoba had warned the Blackfoot and Cree beforehand of the entry of the mounted police and boundary commission into their territory. Gifts had also been distributed.[58] These precautions were considered necessary because these were anxious times for the Indians. Bison numbers were already in steep decline by the mid-nineteenth century, but the drier climate of the 1850s had not only reduced the carrying capacity of the northern plains but also kept herds from coming north for winter shelter. A decade later, bison were generally to be found only in Blackfoot country beyond the Battle River and out of reach of bands along the North Saskatchewan. The Cree, Assiniboine, Saulteaux, and even some Métis responded by joining together into cooperative hunting parties that entered enemy country in force. In 1869, for example, a large, multi-ethnic group from the Edmonton district slaughtered five thousand bison around Nose Hill, about two hundred miles to the southeast.[59] These armed invasions put an end to diplomacy, as evidenced by the 1869 killing of the Cree peacemaker Maskepetoon, and led to outright war. The fighting even continued during yet another smallpox epidemic in 1869–70 when the disease once again spread north from the Missouri country, first to the Blackfoot and then the Cree. Ironically, the Cree became infected when a raiding party overran a stricken Blackfoot camp.

The death toll from this latest smallpox epidemic may have ranged from 15 to 40 per cent.[60] The Blackfoot were hit hard. The Cree suffered as well, especially those living along the North Saskatchewan, including Fort Carlton. But the disease never spread east beyond the Touchwood Hills and the Qu'Appelle Lakes because of the quick thinking of HBC servant Isaac Cowie. The son of a doctor, he used a piece of window glass to draw some lymph from the arm of a child who had been recently vaccinated at Red River and created his own serum to administer to the local population.[61] That smallpox never reached the Red River settlement was a blessing. But because much of Canada's attention was focused on the Métis resistance and the delay in the land transfer, the epidemic was largely ignored, even if it was known about at the time.

So too was one of the largest battles in plains Indian warfare. In October 1870, the Cree decided to launch a major attack against the Blackfoot, convinced that their foe had been so weakened by smallpox that they would easily be vanquished. Some six to eight hundred warriors, led by chiefs Big Bear, Little Mountain, Little Pine, and Piapot, advanced west towards the junction of the Belly and St. Mary Rivers (near present-day Lethbridge). Here, they fell upon a small group of Peigan, not realizing that a much larger Peigan and Blood encampment was nearby. When the alarm was raised, a fierce counterattack was launched. Armed with repeating rifles secured through trade in Montana, the Peigan and Blood drove their assailants down to the river and into the surrounding coulees. The retreating Cree, with only muzzle loaders and bows and arrows, were mowed down like targets in a shooting gallery. The Belly ran red with blood. An estimated two hundred to three hundred Cree warriors died that day, while the Peigan and Black lost some forty people.[62]

The following spring, the Cree sent the Blackfoot tobacco, and a peace agreement was later reached at a meeting at the Red Deer River. The "buffalo wars," as they are sometimes called, had come to an end but only after terrible losses on both sides. When the smallpox dead were added to the death toll from the wars, it is easy to understand why the Cree and Blackfoot felt under siege. Some bands lashed out at the white population for bringing disease into the country and tried to spread the infection to the Methodist mission at Victoria and Fort Pitt on the North Saskatchewan River.[63] Nor did the coming of peace between the tribes alleviate the suffering. The rotgut peddled by whisky traders made murder commonplace, while weakening the resistance of individuals to a new disease threat—scrofula, a form of tuberculosis that affects the lymphatic system.[64] There was also widespread starvation in the wake of the smallpox epidemic. In 1869, William Christie at Fort Edmonton had warned, "Buffalo are fast decreasing." Four years later, he spoke of famine conditions along the North Saskatchewan, later confirmed in a report that the Cree who had wintered on the plains in search of bison had "suffered frightfully" and been reduced to eating their horses. Even the pet dog of the Anglican missionary at Touchwood Hills became a meal.[65]

The Cree who lived along the North Saskatchewan west of Fort Carlton had come together in the Hand Hills over the winter of 1870–71 to discuss their plight and the unsettling news that the Canadian government had bought their lands from the Hudson's Bay Company. Newcomers meant more competition for the dwindling bison resource. When Methodist missionary John McDougall visited the camp and was unable to assuage many of the concerns, it was decided that Sweetgrass, the leading chief in the Pitt district and successor to Maskepetoon, would send a message from Edmonton to the lieutenant-governor. "Great Father,—I shake hands with you, and bid you welcome. We heard our lands were sold and we did not like it," the petition began. "We want cattle, tools, agricultural implements, and assistance in everything when we come to settle—our country is no longer able to support us." It continued, "We invite you to come and see us and speak to us. If you can't come yourself, send some one in your place."[66] But no one came. Whereas Ottawa was preparing the land for agricultural settlement, it had no immediate plans to negotiate treaties with those bands living west of the new province of Manitoba. And so the Cree took matters into their own hands. They stopped a construction crew from building a telegraph line near Fort Carlton. They also turned back a Geological Survey of Canada party near the elbow of the South Saskatchewan River in 1873. Geologist Robert Bell reported that he was treated as an intruder who had no business being in the area. "In their interview with me," he reported, "they talked of nothing else."[67] The Cree were determined, in the words of one white observer, "to oppose the running of lines, or the making of roads through their country, until a settlement between the Government and them had been effected."[68] Canada had no choice. If it wanted to guarantee the peaceful, orderly settlement of the region, Ottawa had to reach an agreement with the Cree for their lands sooner rather than later. But it drew the line at negotiating with bands from the boreal forest region whose lands were considered unsuited for agriculture.[69]

In making treaties with the western Indians, Canada was following a British tradition that had been established by the Royal Proclamation of 1763. In recognition of the important role that First Nations had played as allies in the military struggle between Great Britain and France, the British promised not to allow agricultural settlement of Indian territory until title had been surrendered to the Crown by means of treaties. This policy of negotiating through the Crown for Indian lands had been followed, albeit imperfectly, in the late eighteenth and early nineteenth centuries and had become well-entrenched by the time Canada acquired its North-West empire in 1870.[70] The motives underlying the process, though, had changed. Whereas British military officials had been anxious to secure and maintain Indian allies in their struggle with an aggressive, expansionist United States, Canadian civil authorities now wanted to avoid costly Indian wars over western lands. In other words, negotiation was the cheaper course of action. The merits of this policy were clearly borne out by the experience south of the border, where the United States spent more money fighting Indian wars in 1870 than the entire Canadian budget for the year.[71] The young dominion feared that the First Nations, as "savage" races, could explode with violence if not handled delicately. Ottawa did not want a repeat of the troubles at Red River in 1869–70. "I am very anxious, indeed, that we should be able to deal with the Indians upon satisfactory terms," Prime Minister Macdonald told the HBC governor in 1871. "They are the great difficulty in these newly civilized countries."[72]

The treaty process was also imbued by an imperialist ideology that held that Indians would inevitably vanish as a distinct race in the face of the white man's "superior" civilization and that it was Canada's duty to remake them into loyal subjects of the Crown.

This notion that the Cree and other groups faced certain extinction unless saved by Canadian humanitarian efforts did not jibe with reality. Although the

A Métis family at the Prairie-Ronde settlement (near present-day Dundurn)

Cree faced a number of difficulties in the early 1870s, they were not a defeated or doomed people. They not only practised an opportunity-based economy but were also an extremely dynamic, resilient people who had faced similar challenges in the past and adapted accordingly. The Cree saw themselves as equals in their dealings with Canada and were prepared to negotiate in order to guarantee their future security and well-being in the region as an independent nation. They had no interest in or need for a Canadian crutch. They recognized, though, that the rapid decline of the bison forced them to convert to agriculture in order to compete with newcomers. Indeed, they regarded an alliance with the Crown—similar to the relationship that they had enjoyed with the HBC in the past—as the best hope of restructuring their economy.[73]

The agreement to be negotiated at Fort Carlton in August 1876 was the sixth of seven western treaties that were signed between 1871 and 1877. The deliberations proved to be a long, at times protracted, process because Indian

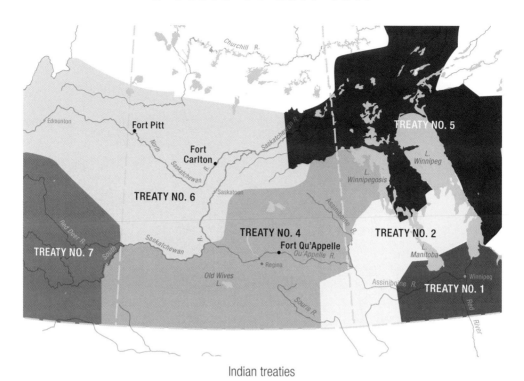

Indian treaties

negotiators insisted on better terms than those offered in the formal treaty. They also tried to build on the concessions that had been won in previous agreements. The treaty commissioners, in turn, were under strict orders to concede as little as possible to the Indians and not make any additional or "outside" promises to the original terms. In his later account of the Treaty Six proceedings, Métis interpreter Peter Erasmus compared the dominion government stance to "a boxer sent into the ring with his hands tied."[74] But like a prize fight, there was much at stake. The proposed treaty area covered some 120,000 square miles in present-day central Saskatchewan and Alberta—lands crucial to Canada's westward expansion. Securing Indian agreement would not be straightforward. Just two years earlier at Fort Qu'Appelle, the Saulteaux had angrily refused to begin Treaty Four talks (which included much of southern Saskatchewan) because they resented the sale of their lands and demanded that HBC compensation be paid to them instead. They also challenged the meeting location, insisting that negotiations be held away from the fort, on their territory. And when the meeting finally got underway under protest, they did not hold a pipe ceremony. This sense of Indian proprietorship evidently prompted the Crown representatives to insert a "blanket extinguishment" clause—for the first time in the numbered treaties—that specifically stated that the Indians agreed to surrender "their rights, titles and privileges whatsoever *to all other lands wheresoever situated within Her Majesty's North-West Territories.*"[75]

Treaty Six negotiations got underway in mid-August 1876 at a traditional camping area, known to the Cree as pêhonânihk or the waiting place, about a mile from Fort Carlton. There were no photographers present for this momentous event; in fact, despite the widespread use of the camera during this period, no photographs exist of any of the treaty meetings in the 1870s. From the start, Indian Commissioner Alexander Morris, accompanied by a North-West Mounted Police escort, assured the assembled Cree that the Queen, the so-called "Great Mother," was genuinely concerned about their welfare and future well-being. "My Indian brothers," he began, "I have shaken hands with a few of you, I shake hands with all of you in my heart." He also implored the Indians to take his words seriously and to think of the future: "What I will promise, and what I believe and hope you will take, is to last as long as that sun shines and yonder river flows."[76]

Commissioner Morris told the Cree that the Queen had no intention of interfering with their traditional form of making a living by hunting, fishing, and gathering. Such activities were guaranteed for future generations. He pointed out, however, that the wild game was disappearing and that the Indians had to learn how to grow food from the soil if they were to provide for their children and their children's children. To facilitate this transition to farming, the Canadian government would set aside reserve lands for each band based on the formula of one square mile for every family of five. This suggestion that land would be given to the Cree sparked a stinging rebuke from Poundmaker, one of the bolder young men. "This is our land!" he protested loudly. "It isn't a piece of pemmican to be cut off and given in little pieces back to us. It is ours and we will take what we want."[77] Momentarily stunned by the outburst, Morris advised the Indians that thousands of prospective homesteaders would

473

soon invade the country and that the reserves would be held in trust by the Queen. "[I]t is your own," he counselled them, "and no one will interfere with you ... no one can take [your] homes." He then listed the specific agricultural items—from tools and implements to animals and seed—that would be given to the bands to help them become farmers. He also emphasized the cash payment that every man, woman, and child could expect to receive for the life of the treaty. And he promised special gifts for the chiefs and headmen; these presents included symbols of the new order: treaty uniforms, silver medals, and a British flag. "I hold out my hand to you full of the Queen's bounty," Morris concluded, "act for the good of your people."[78]

Mistawasis and Ahtahkakoop, the two leading Carlton chiefs, responded that they needed time to discuss the treaty among themselves. The detractors, who were given the opportunity to speak first in the Indians' private council, acknowledged the hardship caused by the disappearance of the bison but placed little faith in agriculture: to trade their land for an uncertain future was an admission of defeat. Mistawasis, on the other hand, could see no other future for his people. "Have you anything better to offer our people?" he directly challenged those who opposed the treaty. "I ask, again, can you suggest anything that will bring these things back for tomorrow and all the tomorrows that face our people?" He went on to argue that the bison would soon disappear and that the treaty offered the best protection against future uncertainty. "I for one will take the hand that is offered," he concluded. Ahtahkakoop also voiced his support. "Let us not think of ourselves but of our children's children," he argued. "Let us show our wisdom by choosing the right path now while we yet have a choice."[79] This right path, according to the Cree leader, was the adoption of agriculture. There was no reason that the Indians could not make a living from the soil, especially when the Queen's representatives promised assistance and instruction. There was also the example of bands already engaged in farming, such as the William Twatt or Sturgeon Lake band, which was cultivating a small parcel of land on the north side of the North Saskatchewan River near the Sturgeon (Net-Setting) River.[80]

When the negotiations resumed, Commissioner Governor Morris warned the Indians that his time was limited. Poundmaker then stepped forward and stated that while his people were anxious to make a living for themselves, he wanted assurances that they would receive adequate help when needed. This request clearly went against what the government was prepared to do at the time. It was also generally assumed that Indians would be able to learn how to farm fairly rapidly and that the bison would be around long enough to smooth the transition to agriculture. Morris consequently refused, insinuating that the real problem was Indians' laziness. "I cannot promise ... that the Government will feed and support all the Indians," he replied. "You are many, and if we were to try to do it, it would take a great deal of money, and some of you would never do anything for yourselves." The Badger then attempted to clarify their motives: "We want to think of our children; we do not want to be too greedy; when we commence to settle down on the reserves that we select, it is there we want your aid, when we cannot help ourselves and in case of troubles seen and unforeseen in the future." When Morris countered that the Cree had to trust the Queen's generosity, Mistawasis responded: "It is in case of any extremity ... this is not a trivial matter for us."[81]

This request for famine relief was one of several counter-demands presented to Morris. The list also included additional tools, implements, and livestock; a supply of medicines free of charge; exemption from war service; the banning of alcohol; and schools and teachers on the reserve. Realizing that the negotiations were in danger of collapse, Morris granted most of the new demands. He agreed, for example, that a medicine chest (medical supplies) would be kept at the house of each Indian agent. He also promised, albeit reluctantly, to add a clause to the treaty providing famine assistance. The Alexander Mackenzie administration later criticized these terms for being too generous. But it is difficult to deny that the treaty, which settled Indian claims to several thousand square miles of rich agricultural land, was a good bargain for Ottawa. The majority of the Cree chiefs and headmen, on the other hand, realized they had to adjust to new circumstances and affixed their mark to the revised treaty on the understanding that the Great Mother and her representatives would keep a "watchful eye and sympathetic hand."[82] The references that Morris made to family and kin, then, were not just empty rhetoric to the Cree participants who valued the spoken word. They fully expected and looked forward to a beneficial and meaningful relationship with the Crown.[83]

The treaty commission's next pre-arranged stop was at Fort Pitt in early September. Even though several local bands were away hunting, the meeting with the Cree still went ahead. After the sacred pipe-stem ceremony,[84] Morris told the assembly that he had come at the Indians' request—an obvious reference to Sweetgrass's earlier message that he wanted a treaty. He then explained that the Queen was prepared to take them under her protective care. "I see the Queen's councillors taking the Indian by the hand saying we are brothers." Morris forecast, "We will lift you up, we will teach you ... the cunning of the white man." The Indians at Pitt were offered the same terms agreed upon at Carlton. And to Morris's surprise—and probably relief—there was not a single word of dissent. Sweetgrass acknowledged that the days of the bison hunt were numbered and that he was prepared to turn to farming. "Let us be one," he said in reference to the treaty. "Use your utmost to help me and help my children, so that they may prosper." The other chiefs shared this sentiment. Seekaskootch admitted that what he "once dreaded most [treaty] ... is coming to my aid and doing for me what I could not do for myself."[85]

Treaty Commissioner Morris was preparing to leave Pitt when Big Bear, one of the leading local chiefs, finally arrived from the hunt. The fact that an agreement had already been reached, and that several of the chiefs were urging acceptance, placed Big Bear in an awkward situation. But he was worried that Indians might lose their freedom under treaty, and using a metaphor, pleaded with Morris to "save me from what I most dread, that is: the rope to be about my neck." Unfortunately, the statement was incorrectly translated to suggest that Big Bear feared hanging as a punishment when he was actually making reference to a tethered animal. This apparent request that Indians not be punished for serious crimes shocked Morris, and he replied, "No good Indian has the rope about his neck."[86] Big Bear, somewhat confused by the response, raised the need for further talks and chose not to sign the treaty. But the damage had been done. Those bands who remained outside treaty acquired a reputation as potentially troublesome when, actually, leaders like Big Bear not only believed that the treaty provisions were inadequate but also wanted to see if the government kept its sweet promises.[87]

During the Treaty Six meeting, Mistawasis asked that the local Métis population be admitted to treaty and allowed to live on reserves with the Cree. A similar request was made twice at the Treaty Four negotiations at Fort Qu'Appelle in 1874. It was not a surprising proposal, given that the Saulteaux, Assiniboine, and Cree had intermarried with the Métis and at one time formed large bison-hunting expeditions southwest into Blackfoot territory. Commissioner Morris was non-committal, though, simply stating that the Queen would "deal justly, fairly and generously with all her children."[88] But the Canadian government was not averse to using the Métis as intermediaries between Ottawa and the Indian peoples, in much the same way that the HBC had employed mixed-descent servants at its posts. In the immediate pre-treaty period, Métis emissaries travelled regularly to Indian camps, assuring the bands about Canadian intentions and distributing gifts. These actions may help explain why there was no violence between Indians and newcomers after Canada had acquired the territory. And once the treaty process was underway, the Métis served as interpreters, brokers, and witnesses to the agreements. Commissioner Alexander Morris singled out James McKay for his diplomatic efforts on behalf of Treaty Six. He camped near the Cree during the Carlton meeting and used his influence to help ease any concerns. Then there was Peter Erasmus, who was hired by Mistawasis and Ahtahkakoop to translate for them and ended up being employed by the government because of his linguistic abilities.[89] Erasmus later provided an "insider" account of the Treaty Six negotiations, documenting the arguments for and against the treaty, especially the dramatic speeches of Mistawasis and Ahtahkakoop and how their moving words had influenced the assembly to take the Queen's hand.

The Métis were also adjusting to the rapid decline in bison numbers by relocating or turning to other activities. Families used to spend their summers in present-day North Dakota and Montana before retreating to Wood Mountain or the Cypress Hills for the winter. Geologist George Dawson encountered hunting camps along the Milk and Whitemud Rivers during his work for the boundary commission. But with herds no longer coming as far north, the Métis increasingly moved into American territory—the border was meaningless to them—and remained there. One of the more popular destinations was the Spring Creek settlement in the Judith Basin of central Montana, where descendants of the emigrants still live today (Lewistown).[90]

Some of the Métis families who took up residence in the United States were replaced in the Canadian North-West by families from the Red River settlement. This movement westward in the 1860s and increasingly into the 1870s might appear puzzling, given the decline of bison hunting in the same period. But there were limited opportunities in Manitoba for Métis who remained committed to the bison robe trade, especially when the market there was monopolized by the HBC, and cross-border commerce at Pembina was now subject to tariffs. Poorer Métis who practised subsistence farming were also out of place in the new province, a feeling confirmed by their treatment at the hands of intolerant Protestant settlers from Ontario. They consequently left for Willow Bunch, Wood Mountain, and the Cypress Hills by following Traders' Road, which ran directly west from Red River to the wintering communities. Others moved to the Carlton, Pitt, and Edmonton districts along the North Saskatchewan River or to the South Branch communities, a string of settlements between the North and South Saskatchewan Rivers from Prince Albert to the north and Moose Woods to the south. Here, in places such as Prairie Ronde, Petite Ville, St. Laurent, and Batoche, Métis families were involved in trapping, trading, freighting, and farming.[91] As these villages grew, they attracted resident priests, supported a range of businesses and services, and developed rules for governing themselves; but most of all, fostered and encouraged a sense of

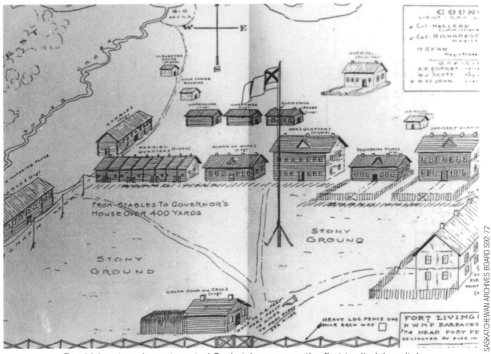

Fort Livingstone in east-central Saskatchewan was the first territorial capital.

identity among the Métis as a distinct people.

The North-West Territories government was also on the move in the mid-1870s. At the time of the transfer, the first territorial government was based at lower Fort Garry (just north of Winnipeg on the Red River) and headed by an appointed lieutenant-governor who served in the same capacity for the territories. The legislation also allowed for an appointed council (with executive and legislative duties) of not less than seven members and no more than fifteen. But when Lieutenant-Governor A. G. Archibald named the first councillor in October 1870, Ottawa overturned the appointment. Any and all decisions made by the lieutenant-governor required the approval of the Canadian government, and the Macdonald Conservatives preferred a policy of administrative economy. In other words, do nothing and save money until action was absolutely necessary. There was not even any provision for territorial government staff.[92]

In 1872, Alexander Morris replaced Archibald and took on the additional

duties as Indian commissioner for Manitoba and the North-West Territories—
again, a cost-saving measure. Morris made the first appointments to council
in December of that year—eleven in total—and convened the first legislative
session the following March. It was a short session, lasting only two days,
but the councillors, with Morris serving as speaker, began to institute laws to
govern the vast territories. At the second meeting in March 1874, for example,
the council recommended the creation of the North-West Mounted Police in
response to the Cypress Hills massacre. But any council ordinances still needed
Ottawa's blessing. And several members of council also sat as members of the
federal House of Commons or the Manitoba Legislature. Perhaps worst of all,
it was a "foreign" government, physically situated outside the territories.

The Alexander Mackenzie Liberal government tried to correct some of
these deficiencies in the 1875 North-West Territories Act (approved 8 April 1875;
effective 7 October 1876). The act provided for a separate government for the
territories, as well as brought together in a single statute all previous legislation
concerning the governance of the region. Although the government structure
remained the same—an appointed lieutenant-governor and council of no
more than five—the lieutenant-governor now had to reside in the territories
and hold council meetings there. Allowance was also made for elected council
members as the newcomer population increased. The significance of a resident
government was negated, however, by the location of the first territorial capital.
Instead of choosing Edmonton, Pitt, Carlton, Prince Albert, or any number of
places along the North Saskatchewan and the so-called settlement belt, the
Mackenzie government originally designated Fort Ellice, an HBC post farther
south, as capital in May 1874. But then it changed its mind only weeks later
and settled on a site at the junction of Swan River and Snake Creek (north of
present-day Kamsack just inside the Saskatchewan border).

The selection of Fort Livingstone, named for the famous British African
explorer, as headquarters for the North-West Territories government and the
North-West Mounted Police is one of the great mysteries of western Canadian
history. The site, located on a small rocky ridge in a heavily timbered area, had

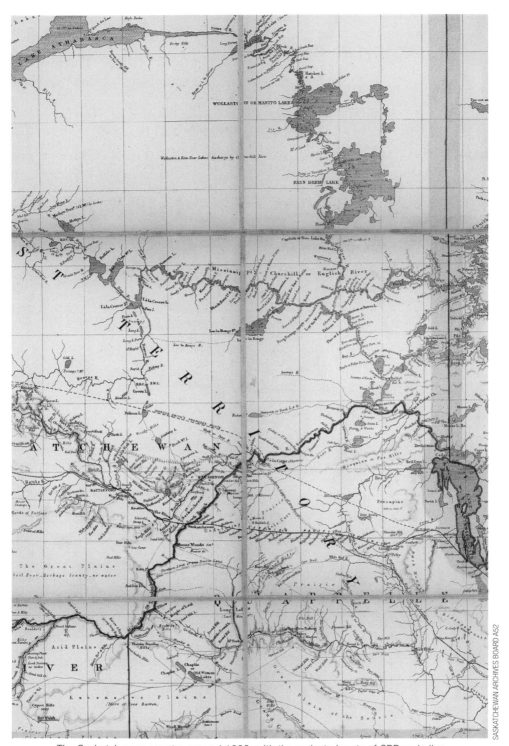

The Saskatchewan country around 1880, with the projected route of CPR main line

few redeeming features, except that it was near Fort Pelly, a Hudson's Bay Company post, and three Indian reserves (Keeseekoose, the Key, and Cote) that were part of Treaty 4. It was probably chosen because it was on the route of the dominion telegraph line; the transcontinental railway was supposed to follow. Sam Steele, one of the most famous mounties of the nineteenth century, wondered, "How on earth any person ... could have selected such a situation it is difficult to imagine." Commissioner George French was especially disgruntled because of Livingstone's distance from the illegal whisky trade in the southwest: the very reason for the police march. He reported that a group of local Métis "laughed outright when I asked opinions as to its suitability."[93] An unexpected bonus was a nearby garter snake hibernaculum. The snakes were everywhere, making the grass writhe with their numbers.

Livingstone, and the legislation that enabled its establishment, were symptomatic of all that was wrong-headed or contradictory about federal plans for Canada's new western empire. Settlement of the region was "a complex and challenging process," but Ottawa had "both compressed the time frame expected for its accomplishment and minimized the difficulties involved."[94] The federal government naively assumed that all the land was of equal quality and that once the western wilderness was marked out into orderly, uniform homesteads, the region would be turned almost overnight into the world's granary. There was no attempt to follow George Dawson's advice that western settlement should be "a natural growth taking advantage of the capabilities of the country."[95] Nor was there any attempt to listen and learn from those who lived and worked in the North-West Territories, including Alexander Morris who, despite his experience, was replaced by the Mackenzie government before his term was up. The federal government believed that it knew what was best for the region; that it could determine and shape its future. And the consequences of this attitude and the policies that went hand in hand with it were encapsulated in the misguided selection of Livingstone as the first territorial capital. The other peculiar aspect of federal development plans is that the region that was supposed to be the means to empire was administered by Ottawa like a colony. The 1875 North-West Territories Act did allow for the eventual election of council members, but it was conspicuously silent about when a greater measure of responsible government would be forthcoming. It also did not say anything about future provincial status.[96] This subordinate treatment at the hands of the federal government was just one of many issues and problems that bedevilled the region as it struggled to fulfill Canadian expectations in the late 1870s and 1880s. The unfortunate result was disillusionment, alienation, grievance, and resistance.

When the Canadian Pacific Railway was re-routed across the southern prairies, Swift Current was made a divisional centre.

CHAPTER FOURTEEN

NEED EXPECT NOTHING

IT WAS KNOWN AS THE "RIDGE."[1] LOCATED JUST OUTSIDE THE SOUTHERN BOUNDARY
of the Prince Albert settlement, the name came from a low ridge of pine trees
that ran northeastward between the branches of the Saskatchewan River
towards the forks. The trails from Fort Carlton, Batoche, and Duck Lake also
came together here before turning north to Prince Albert. Thomas Scott settled
at the Ridge in the late 1870s. The seventeen-year-old had been recruited in
the Orkney Islands by the Hudson's Bay Company in 1870. But he left the
service to work for a local trading firm before starting a farm at the Ridge and
later marrying Mary Jane Isbister, the mixed-descent daughter of the founder
of Prince Albert. Scott's three-hundred-acre farm—at almost twice the size
of a standard homestead grant—was renowned for its harvests. In fact, the
agricultural promise of the area attracted a number of settlers to the area—white,
French Métis, and English Métis[2]—who established farms and businesses in
anticipation of the coming of the Canadian Pacific Railway through the region.
Among them were the mixed-descent sons of HBC servant Peter Fidler (buried
today with their partners in the St. Catharine church cemetery in the old
Lindsay district). For these people, racial divisions were often blurred as they
interacted and intermarried, as they had done for almost two hundred years.
They also came together in the early 1880s in an effort to get a distant federal
government to deal with their grievances, especially the feeling of political
impotence. But when protest crossed the line to open rebellion, sides had to be
taken, and ties between families and friends came undone.

According to the development plan for western Canada, agricultural settlement and the transcontinental railroad were to proceed apace. But with immigration to the region more a trickle than a flood, and with not a single mile of track laid beyond Winnipeg by 1879, the building of the Canadian Pacific Railway became a prerequisite to settlement. To facilitate the project, the federal government offered a whopping one-hundred-million-acre land grant. But even that failed to attract a private builder. It was not until the winter of 1880–81 that Ottawa finally reached an agreement with the Canadian Pacific Railway Syndicate, an international consortium, including Donald Smith of the HBC and George Stephen, president of the Bank of Montreal, to build and operate a transcontinental line by the end of the decade. The deal came with a federal grant of twenty-five-million dollars and twenty-five-million acres of western land. There were also several generous concessions because of government insistence on an all-Canadian line and the consequent costs of building north of the Great Lakes and through the Rocky Mountains. The most controversial—and most criticized—clause was a twenty-year monopoly over western traffic. No railway was to be built south of the main line unless it ran southwest and thereby served as a feeder or branch line. George Stephen justified this privileged treatment on the grounds that "the interests of the country and the company are identical."[3] But there were those who questioned the wisdom of placing the national railway in the hands of a private builder. George Munro Grant, the principal of Queen's University, said of the agreement: "It looks as if now there would be no check on the plunderers."[4]

The ink on the CPR contract was barely dry when the syndicate announced a dramatic route change across the North-West Territories. Throughout the 1870s, it had been assumed that the line would travel through the North Saskatchewan country, the so-called "fertile belt," to the Yellowhead Pass. But in the spring of 1881, the Syndicate boldly decided to build directly west from Winnipeg across the southern prairies and through a more southerly mountain pass. This decision profoundly altered the region's development by focusing settlement activity for the next two decades along a thin line through

SCOTT FAMILY

English Métis James Isbister was largely forgotten as the founder
of the Prince Albert settlement.

the grasslands. "The 'North-West,' for practical purposes," noted one scholar,
"became replaced by the 'West.'"[5] Many reasons have been advanced for the
abandonment of the more popular and more certain Yellowhead route, in
particular the re-evaluation of the dry mixed-prairie district by botanist John
Macoun and others in the 1870s. But the location of the railway had more to
do with strategic business decisions than the quality of the land. The main line
was to be constructed as close to the international border as possible—even if it
was not the best quality farmland—in order to keep out American competition.
A more southerly route was also necessary if the railway was going to capture

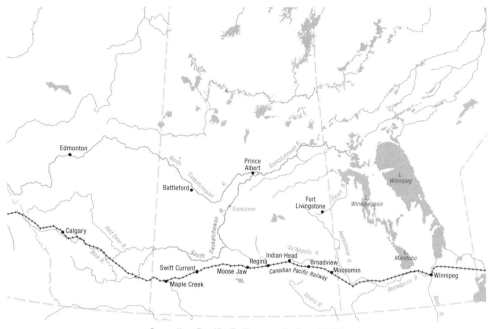

Canadian Pacific Railway main line, 1885

all the traffic of the North-West and offset the costs of operating the otherwise "useless" section north of Lake Superior. The CPR Syndicate initially wanted to send the railway through the Crow's Nest Pass, but when the Macdonald government objected for security reasons, it settled on Kicking Horse Pass.[6] The CPR builders also ensured that the company did not get saddled with marginal land by insisting in the contract that its twenty-five-million-acre grant not only had to be "fairly fit for settlement" but also could be selected anywhere in the territories. Nearly half the acreage was taken in the future province of Saskatchewan and included compensation for railway mileage in northern Ontario and British Columbia. The speed at which land surveying was carried out may have been a consequence of pressure from the new CPR Syndicate.[7]

The re-routing of the CPR main line was a severe blow to the hopes and ambitions of the people of the North Saskatchewan country. By the mid-1870s, the Prince Albert area boasted a population of three hundred, the majority of them English Métis (Anglican or Scot Presbyterian) from Red River. They settled not only in the townsite (the original Isbister settlement), but to the

490

west at Pocha's settlement (also known as the Lindsay district), at the Ridge and Red Deer Hill between the north and south branches of the Saskatchewan River, and at Halcro and Adam's Crossing (today's Fenton) along the south branch. Just in Prince Albert alone, river lots (one-eighth of a mile wide and two miles deep) stretched for fourteen miles along the south bank of the North Saskatchewan River in 1874.[8] Other English Métis river-lot holdings were laid out at Pocha and Halcro (and are still discernible today).

What initially drew these English Métis to the Saskatchewan valley was familiarity with the region (some were born in or worked in the area), family ties, and the desire for a new beginning, especially after the 1869–70 Red River Resistance. Some of the first settlers hunted bison or carried freight for the HBC. But by the end of the 1870s, it was the great agricultural promise of the region and the anticipated arrival of the transcontinental railway that proved so alluring.[9] By the time of the 1881 national census, 2,161 people were counted in Prince Albert area, a number that more than doubled to an estimated five thousand the following year. Among the new residents were several merchants, tradesmen, and professionals from Ontario and Great Britain, including D. H. Macdowall, Alexander Sproat, the brothers T. O. and J. O. Davis, and Hayter Reed. These immigrants dominated local commerce and eventually transformed the townsite into a white community. But the English Métis remained the majority group in the outlying area; their population was even larger than the neighbouring French Métis communities along the south branch of the river (south of Halcro). Even in Prince Albert, their river-lot system (formally surveyed in 1878) prevailed. Poet and postmaster Charles Mair had to swallow his contempt for Métis peoples, going back to his days in Manitoba during the Red River Resistance, and purchased lot 68 in the townsite.[10]

Agriculture boomed during these years. Local farmers harvested sixty-two thousand bushels of wheat in 1881, more than half the production for the entire territories. That volume shot up to two hundred thousand bushels the following year as more land was broken by the plough, especially to the southwest, including the Ridge. The wheat kept three Prince Albert mills busy day and night, supplying flour to other communities throughout the West, as well as to Indian reserves, because it was cheaper than shipping it from Winnipeg. Nor was the economy restricted to agriculture. Over the winter of 1878–79, the lumber industry got underway when the first white spruce logs were taken out of the nearby forest. Stobart, Eden and Company sought to cash in on the expected bonanza by transferring its trade headquarters there from Duck Lake, while the rival Hudson's Bay Company moved its regional offices and supply operations from Fort Carlton. All that was needed was the railway to ensure that Prince Albert, with a commercial hinterland the size of Nova Scotia, realized its destiny.[11] "Already in imagination," the local newspaper confidently predicted, "we hear the whistle and see the white smoke of the locomotive speeding on its way to the Pacific."[12]

Battleford, more than a hundred miles upriver at the junction of the North Saskatchewan and Battle Rivers, shared the same expectations. In 1874, surveyors and other government workers had chosen a popular Cree camping place on a ford near the mouth of the Battle River as their headquarters in the area. Two years later, on 6 April 1876, telegraph communication had been established between Winnipeg and Telegraph Flat. The Canadian Pacific Railway was supposed to follow. In fact, in an order-in-council dated 7 October 1876, the same day that the new North-West Territories Act finally came into effect, the federal government admitted its mistake in placing the capital at Livingstone and declared that the seat of the territorial government would henceforth be based in the newly named Battleford. That the non-descript telegraph crossing was to become an administrative and transportation centre meant that the North-West Mounted Police should be headquartered there, too, and a fort (now a national historic site) was constructed on the height of land between the two rivers. Commissioner George French suggested that the force would now be better situated to respond quickly to any unrest. A substantial Government House, one of the finest buildings west of Winnipeg, was also erected in remarkably little time, especially given the location and lack of heavy timber.[13] The new lieutenant-governor, David Laird, a former Prince Edward Island journalist and member

Government House, the new territorial capital building at Battleford, was lost to fire in 2003.

of Parliament, privately complained to the prime minister about the hardship his family endured during their first winter in the building. "When the high winds and cold come together," he reported in January 1878, "we are all nearly perished."[14] The lure of the capital, though, attracted a steady stream of settlers, including French and English Métis families from Manitoba, including some former HBC employees like the Pambruns. Among them was Patrick Gammie Laurie, who hauled his printing press by ox-cart from Red River in the summer of 1878 and began publication of the *Saskatchewan Herald*, the first newspaper between Red River and the Rocky Mountains. By the time the census was taken in 1881, Battleford, with 852 people, was the second-largest community in the territories after Prince Albert.

James Clinkskill, a Scottish merchant, looked to these flourishing communities to rescue him from a dead-end life in Glasgow. Arriving in Winnipeg in 1882, Clinkskill heard about booming Prince Albert and decided to open a general store there, even though the railway main line no longer passed through the region. He sent the bulk of his goods by steamboat up the

North Saskatchewan, while he travelled overland by cart with the remainder of his stock. Clinkskill faced stiff competition in Prince Albert from already established businesses and chose to relocate in May 1883 to Battleford, where there seemed to be even greater potential. He never doubted his decision to ply his trade away from the railway. He quickly learned, though, that freighting was his lifeline and became quite adept at managing that side of his business. His memoirs are full of stories about dealing with the challenges of distance and isolation. Mail service left Winnipeg for Edmonton every three weeks, and Clinkskill would sometimes travel with the outfit. The fare from Winnipeg to Battleford was seventy-five dollars.[15] But passengers had to feed themselves and be prepared for "a spell" every four hours when the animals were rested and fed and a great kettle of tea was made. When the mail reached Battleford, the telegraph operator would hoist the Union Jack during the day or put a lantern out at night. Clinkskill also had vivid memories of winter social events, especially his first bachelors' ball. The largest storeroom in Battleford was cleared for the fiddler and people would dance reels and jigs until the next morning.[16]

Clinkskill's business costs were reduced when the new Canadian Pacific Railway reached Swift Current and carts could now carry goods directly north by trail to Battleford. But the pushing of the railway across the southern prairies—reaching Calgary in 1883—introduced a new metropolitan pattern in the future province of Saskatchewan. The North Saskatchewan communities were soon superseded by new urban centres along the main line, from Moosomin on the east to Maple Creek on the west. Some of the new places, like Troy (Qu'Appelle) near Fort Qu'Appelle, became important transshipment points north and south of the main line. The CPR-named Whitewood, for example, served the new community of Yorkton (York Farmers' Colonization Company) in present-day east-central Saskatchewan. This focus on the open prairies was accelerated when the territorial capital was moved yet again, this time, to Pile of Bones on Wascana Creek on 27 March 1883. Like Battleford before it, the new capital needed a more uplifting name, all the more so because it sat on a flat, treeless plain, and when the first CPR train arrived that August,

LIBRARY AND ARCHIVES CANADA PA118776

The *Leader* newspaper office in Regina

the townsite was christened Regina after Queen Victoria.[17]

Almost overnight, settlement and development reflected the realities of a southern rail line and a southern territorial capital. A special 1884–85 census of the region found that the population of the Assiniboia district was twice as large as that of the Saskatchewan district (22,083 to 10,746). In particular, the Qu'Appelle and Regina sub-district had 9,540 people, while the more easterly Broadview sub-district had 8,367. Prince Albert, by contrast, had 5,373 people, and Battleford 3,603.[18] These numbers—in the thousands—did not come close to the hundreds of thousands predicted by Canadian expansionists. Immigrants preferred to settle in the American West during these years. Still, in the words of one historian, "there was optimism in the Territories—an optimism based more on potential than real development."[19] The emerging demographic pattern on the prairies also represented a distinct break from the fur trade past when rivers and lakes determined settlement location. It heralded a new future where access to the railroad was paramount, especially in getting crops to market.

The head-counting in the special 1884–85 census did not extend much beyond Prince Albert. This northern territory had no immediate value in the

LOUIS COCHIN

Kids playing in the water at Île-à-la-Crosse

new agricultural West, apart from a source of lumber, and was simply left to the fur trade. The old ways consequently persisted and were not lost to the new settler society. Cree and Chipewyan bands continued to follow their seasonal rounds, including visits to local posts for ammunition, twine, tobacco, and other trade goods. Some found temporary employment with the HBC, but it was the Métis who remained the core of the labour force, even when senior company officials wanted to limit, if not stop, the support of servant families. Local post managers knew that their operations stood to benefit by providing for the Métis and their families, and sometimes went out of their way to see that such assistance was there. In 1885, for example, HBC clerk James Sinclair at Green Lake warned his counterpart at Île-à-la-Crosse that he would probably need any surplus fish that year to feed the local Métis population. Such support served to affirm Métis cultural values and identity in the region.[20]

There were other ways, though, that the HBC chose to streamline and modernize its activities in the North-West, while securing other sources of business. In 1883, the *Grahame* steamed up the Clearwater River from the present-day site of Fort McMurray to the northern end of Methye Portage

496

and ended the need for canoes, scows, and York boats on that section of the historic route to the Athasbasca country. This change was preceded a few years earlier by the relocation of the Northern department depot from York Factory to Winnipeg to take advantage of the coming of the railway. The HBC also negotiated a preferential freight rate with the CPR syndicate. But the company never realized the volume of retail trade that it expected. Nor did the anticipated sales from its land grant materialize. Settlement was not only sluggish, but HBC dominance was largely confined to the northern half of the province. Fortunately, there were lucrative government contracts—an estimated five hundred thousand to one million dollars per year—and by the early 1880s, the HBC was one of two major suppliers for the Indian department and the North-West Mounted Police. Only I.G. Baker and Company, based in Fort Benton, Montana, secured more dominion business in the North-West because of its more reliable transportation system.[21]

The HBC was initially able to fulfill these government contracts because of its monopoly of the pemmican market. But by 1879, the bison were gone from the northern plains. There had been warning signs during the previous decade that all was not well with the herds. In 1870, when Oblate Jean-Joseph Lestanc arrived at the Saint Florent mission, he found the outlying *hivernant* camps barely subsisting on a few skinny bulls and wondered how long the Métis would remain in the Wood Mountain uplands before they followed the herds into Montana. The situation was just as bad to the north. The HBC posts on the upper North Saskatchewan (Edmonton, Pitt, and Carlton) could not meet their 1874 pemmican quota: they collected only 148 of 250 bags. This scarcity made for desperate times. Winnipeg resident Charles Bell reported that the Cree who had wintered on the plains had "suffered frightfully" and been reduced to eating "their horses, dogs, buffalo skins and in some cases their snowshoe laces & moccasins and then died."[22] And whenever the herds returned—as they unexpectedly did to the plains southeast of Fort Qu'Appelle in 1875—hunters killed as many animals as they possibly could because they might never have the opportunity again. The HBC purchased an incredible six thousand bags of pemmican from the hunt that season. This abundance, though, could not be sustained, especially when hunters relentlessly pursued the remnants of the once-great herds in the few remaining areas of their northern range. Nor did the 1871 Blackfoot–Cree peace help matters. Instead of Indians coming together in large cooperative hunting parties for protective purposes, small groups and individuals now hunted the bison indiscriminately wherever and whenever they could be found. Cows were preferred. Their lighter robes were easier to process, while their meat had a higher fat content.[23] The removal of the breeding stock further reduced the sustainability of the herds.

The dwindling bison herds made the Indians extremely protective of their hunting rights and extremely wary of competition from the incoming settler society.[24] Treaty 4 Agent M. G. Dickieson reported that when treaty payments were being disbursed at Fort Qu'Appelle in 1876, every chief and headman made the same request: "that something should be done to prevent the entire extermination of the buffalo." Normally, they would have had one spokesperson, but "adopted this method," according to Dickieson, "to impress the gravity of their position upon me."[25] This hunting pressure on the herds would get only worse over the next year when thousands of refugee Sioux crossed the "medicine line" into Canadian territory after the Battle of the Little Big Horn in June 1876.

It was not the first time that the Lakota had ventured north. The Sioux had regularly traded at Métis wintering communities along the borderlands for at least a decade, perhaps longer. Hunkpapa Chief Sitting Bull, for example, was reported to be in the Wood Mountain region during the winter of 1870–71, while another leader, Little Knife, appeared at Fort Qu'Appelle in 1872. HBC trader Isaac Cowie had counted seven hundred Lakota lodges in the Cypress Hills in December 1873.[26] It should have been expected, then, that the Lakota would have sought the security of Canada after the defeat of General George Armstrong Custer and the American 7th Cavalry. Advance scouts appeared outside Jean-Louis Légaré's Wood Mountain trading post on a bitterly cold 17 December 1876. "We left the American side because we could not sleep," explained their leader. "We heard that the Big Woman [the Queen] was very good to her children and we came to this country to sleep quietly."[27] When NWMP Inspector James Walsh arrived four days later, there were nearly three thousand Lakota camped at the mountain. And more would soon follow. In March and May 1877, Chief Four Horns and then Sitting Bull led their followers up the Frenchman River valley, east of the Cypress Hills, into Canada. One estimate has suggested that the refugee Sioux represented more than one-third of the Canadian Indian population of all the numbered western treaties (1–7). But the number of Indians is difficult to determine with any precision because census numbers for the population are generally unreliable.[28]

The Lakota Sioux presence added to the urgency that something be done to save the bison from possible extirpation. Action was not forthcoming, however, until March 1877 when the newly constituted North-West Territories Council held its first and only meeting at Livingstone. Lieutenant-Governor Laird proclaimed ten ordinances at the end of the two-week session, including No. 5, "An Ordinance for the Protection of the Buffalo" (to take effect 1 June 1877). The legislation has been hailed as one of Canada's first pieces of environmental legislation: an attempt to save one of the iconic creatures of the northern plains. But the regulations upset the Indian population, the very people who had been asking for protective measures, because of the restrictions that were to be placed on bison procurement activities. Indians had wanted the bison protected for their exclusive benefit. They were not expecting to have their hunting activities controlled, nor their use of pounds and jumps banned. There was also some question if and how the regulations were going to be enforced, let alone obeyed, and whether the legislative action was actually too late to save the rapidly declining bison herds. Within a year, then, the ordinance was quietly rescinded and the bison no longer came under any protection.[29]

While bison protection remained a moot question, several leading Cree chiefs, among them Big Bear, Piapot, and Little Pine, met with the Blackfoot and the Sioux during the summer of 1878 to talk about regulating the hunt. But simmering animosities and a general mistrust between the groups stood in the way of any agreement.[30] There were also bison in the region that summer. Because of spring fires to the south, following the snow-free or "black" winter of 1877–78, the bison congregated on the prairies between the North and South Saskatchewan Rivers, where they were heavily hunted by hungry bands. It was the last time that bison would be so plentiful.[31] The lifting of the bison protection regulations late that summer ironically coincided with the disappearance of the animal from the northern plains. Except for a few small herds that occasionally wandered north into Canadian territory, they were essentially gone by 1879.

Many in the West believed that the bison would be lost one day, but that was supposed to be at least a decade away. Assistant North-West Mounted Police Commissioner James Macleod was personally shocked by how suddenly it happened.[32] So too was the new Indian Commissioner Edgar Dewdney, who claimed in his first annual report that the "disappearance of the buffalo had taken the Government as much by surprise as the Indians."[33] It was quite an understatement. Dewdney toured the North-West during the summer of 1879, and according to his diary account, he was forever encountering Indians who were anxious about how they were going to survive the coming winter.[34] Henriette Forget, the wife of Lieutenant-Governor Laird's clerk, also kept a record of how the disappearance of the bison was playing out at the new territorial capital at Battleford. "Rumours of starvation, from different parts of the country," she wrote in late April 1879, "the buffalo having disappeared rendered the condition of the Indians most deplorable, what a question to solve."[35] Then, in early May, two hundred starving Cree arrived, soon followed by hundreds of others, including Blackfoot, all wanting to see the lieutenant-governor (who doubled as Indian commissioner) to beg for government assistance. An uneasy Forget nervously prepared meals in her home with the windows closed and the blinds down, even covering the key hole to keep cooking smells from escaping. But the weeks passed without incident. "Altogether their [Indian] conduct, considering their destitute condition," Laird reported to Ottawa at the end of June, "is more creditable than would be displayed by most men in civilized communities if suffering want to a like extent."[36]

Indian bands responded to the looming famine crisis by travelling south across the international border in search of bison. Canadian government officials knew about this movement and did nothing to discourage it. When Dewdney met with a large party of treaty Cree at Sounding Lake in August 1879, for example, he hurriedly distributed their annuity payments so that they could get away to the remaining hunting grounds to the south. This gesture was not really done in the interest of the Indians; rather, it was intended to reduce the number of Indian mouths that Ottawa might have to feed. And feeding them was the only other option. At a special emergency meeting later that same month at Battleford, which included both the outgoing (Laird) and incoming (Dewdney) Indian commissioners, it was resolved that "the fears entertained of an approaching famine are only too well grounded ... unless a very large supply of provisions is furnished by the government."[37] This motion capped two days of official discussion during which letters and telegrams were read aloud and entered into the record, minutes carefully recorded, and regular adjournments held. The contrast between the formality of the meeting and the dire situation on the northern plains was surreal. It was abundantly clear, though, that extra food supplies had to be secured. What was on hand, Dewdney estimated, would last no more than a month.[38] The unfolding tragedy was made worse, moreover, by the fact that the Indian commissioners and other officials were caught completely flatfooted by the sudden disappearance of the bison.

The Canadian government grudgingly fed the Indians over the winter of 1879–80 but did not want to make it an ongoing commitment. By the end of the 1870s, Ottawa was already regretting the financial commitment it had assumed in the western numbered treaties. Eleven per cent of all territorial expenditures went to meet treaty obligations, an amount that alarmed federal parliamentarians.[39] It is undoubtedly why Dewdney had been instructed upon assuming his duties as Indian commissioner to exercise "the strictest possible economy."[40] This penny-pinching ran contrary to the Indian understanding of the treaty relationship. During the negotiations, both Crown representatives and Indian leaders had talked about the treaties as the beginning of a long-term, reciprocal relationship rooted in the concepts of family and kin. Indians were prepared to accept the Queen's hand because of the repeated assurances that assistance during the difficult days ahead would not only be forthcoming but generous—in much the same way that Indians had been generous in sharing their territory.[41]

The federal government's attitude towards its treaty obligations also contrasted sharply with how the HBC had provided assistance during hard times—albeit, motivated to maintain allegiance to the company. When in 1874, for example, the trader at Fort Pitt reported that "buffalo are nowhere near us," he added, "we are in a manner bound to maintain them [Indians]."[42] The Canadian state, for its part, had no interest or desire in continuing these fur trade practices, even if they had been an integral part of the Native-newcomer relationship for decades. Lawrence Vankoughnet, deputy superintendent general of Indians Affairs for nearly two decades, particularly deplored the age-old custom of food and gift exchanges as "most irrational"—not simply because of the cost but also because Indians had come to expect this kind of treatment. For Vankoughnet and others who shared his Victorian thinking, government assistance had to be kept to an absolute minimum and, when relief was necessary, extended only to "deserving" Indians. Otherwise, if the state provided help to "every man, woman, and child," then it would become addictive and promote laziness.[43] If there was one consistent criticism of government Indian policy during this period, it was that the federal treasury was spending too much to keep a dying race alive. For many non-natives, Indians were deadbeats, standing in the way of progress and a greater future.[44]

The architect behind late-nineteenth century federal Indian policy was Sir John A. Macdonald. The Conservative leader believed that it was "necessary" for the prime minister to have Indian matters "in his own hands" and he consequently assumed the portfolio upon returning to power in 1878.[45] But his involvement in Indian policy actually dated from his pre-confederation political career. It is tempting to characterize Macdonald as racist and his term as Canada's longest-serving Indian Affairs minister (October 1878–October 1887) as one of "outright malevolence."[46] But if Macdonald believed that

LOUIS COCHIN

Scrubbing floors at the Île-à-la-Crosse mission

Indians were a hopelessly doomed people, to be cast aside by the advance of civilization, then he would not have wasted time dealing with them. Instead, he regarded Indians as culturally inferior but capable of being uplifted to embrace Euro-Canadian ways. If Indians were to take their place in the new emerging West, they had to be educated, Christianized, and enfranchised. And this transformation was possible only if they gave up their nomadic ways and tribal system and became self-reliant farmers.[47] That is why the Macdonald government decided to devote greater attention to the development of on-reserve agriculture—what was known as the "home farm" system—so that Indians could feed themselves. The prime minister later told the House of Commons that he was "not at all sorry" that the bison had disappeared. "So long as there was a hope that buffalo would come into the country," Macdonald reflected, "there was no means of inducing the Indians to settle down on their reserves."[48] In other words, the bison hunt was incompatible with civilizing the

SASKATCHEWAN ARCHIVES BOARD R-A5044 AND R-A5045

The (presumed) daughter of the Sioux Chief Sitting Bull photographed at
Fort Walsh by T. George N. Anderton

Indian and had no place in the new, modern society destined to take shape and
flourish on the northern plains.[49]

Several Indian bands certainly wanted to make the transition to
agriculture. But those who tried to begin farming after taking treaty, such
as Cree chiefs Mistawasis and Ahtahkakoop, found that there were lengthy
delays in getting their reserves surveyed (at Snake Plains and Sandy Lake,

respectively) and that equipment and supplies were not only defective or insufficient but arrived too late in the season to begin cultivation. Others, including Poundmaker's group in the Battleford area, worked incredibly hard to break rolling, heavily wooded reserve land that was better suited for traditional pursuits such as hunting and gathering. When their first crops failed, they came to face to face with the harsh reality that large-scale farming in the North-West was anything but certain in the late nineteenth century. It would take several years of experimentation and failure, both by Natives and newcomers alike, before the northern prairies could be turned into anything close to the agricultural eden prophesied by Canadian expansionists.

The 1879 home farm program was supposed to be the remedy. Resident farm instructors were to teach bands how to raise grain and vegetables and thereby end any further need for government assistance. But the patronage appointees were generally unsuited for the task—there was a high turnover rate—and had little understanding or sympathy for the Indians and the adjustments they faced. Many acquired a reputation for laziness, incompetence, but most of all, brutality; as one senior HBC trader observed, "answering [the Indians] with kicks and blows, accompanied with showers of profanity."[50] Farm instructors quickly learned that, until reserve lands could be successfully cultivated, their most important duty was to distribute food from on-reserve supply depots. These relief provisions were not given freely. Some form of labour, no matter how demeaning or degrading, had to be performed before hungry Indians were fed. This "work for rations" policy clearly violated the spirit and intent of the treaties. But government authorities countered that easy access to food would only encourage Indian idleness.[51] What was sadly ironic, though, was that the Liberal Opposition constantly rebuked the Macdonald Conservatives for doing too much, forcing the prime minister to admit at one point that his officials "are doing all they can, by refusing food until the Indians are on the verge of starvation, to reduce expenses."[52] Even that was too much for one Conservative backbencher. Dr. John Christian Schultz insisted that Indians be rounded up, shipped north, and forced to subsist on fish.[53]

Treaty Indians, on the other hand, tried to loosen the government's grip on their lives by adopting more assertive tactics. In 1880, the Willow Cree chiefs were rounded up for destroying government property—they had sent men to slaughter reserve cattle—and spent several weeks in North-West Mounted Police custody before being acquitted.[54]

Another hunger-provoked incident on the Sakimay reserve, east of Regina, nearly resulted in bloodshed if not for Indian restraint. In February 1884, Yellow Calf and several armed men knocked the uncooperative farm instructor aside and raided the government storehouse for food. When the mounted police arrived to apprehend the culprits, Yellow Calf claimed that his band was starving and that they had only taken what rightfully belonged to them. "If the provisions were not intended to be eaten by Indians," Yellow Calf pointedly asked, "why were they stored on our reserve?"[55] These incidents served to drive a wedge between the Indians and the mounties.

Indian officials faced even bigger challenges in dealing with bands who remained outside treaty or had entered treaty but not taken up land or had left their reserves. Here, they applied the provisions of the 1876 Indian Act, which effectively defined Indians as dependants, not equals, and essentially gave the federal government the authority to regulate their lives. Not a word had been said about the passage of this legislation at the Treaty 6 negotiations with the Cree that same year. And if the act proved inadequate, Indian Commissioner Edgar Dewdney was prepared to implement several coercive and interfering measures—in his words, "sheer compulsion"—for the government's purposes.[56] It was quite the change on Dewdney's part. In the spring of 1881, after only two years as Indian commissioner, he had wanted to step down because of the onerous workload and the criticism of how he was performing his duties. His predecessor, Lieutenant-Governor David Laird, had abruptly resigned the position for similar reasons in 1879. But Prime Minister Macdonald offered Dewdney the lieutenant-governorship and an increase in salary if his good friend stayed on as Indian commissioner and helped implement the Conservative government's Indian policies. In December 1881,

SASKATCHEWAN ARCHIVES BOARD R-A7621

Henriette, the wife of Lieutenant-Governor Laird's clerk A. E. Forget, kept a diary during
the starvation spring of 1879.

Dewdney replaced Laird and would occupy the two positions until 1888. Three
years later, when Macdonald died at his Ottawa residence, Dewdney was at his
bedside.[57]

When Dewdney had first toured the North-West during the summer
of 1879, he had readily agreed that several Cree and Assiniboine chiefs could
settle their bands on reserves in the Cypress Hills in the expectation that they
would make a start at agriculture while continuing to hunt the remaining bison
in the area. But by 1881, the hills had become the last refuge of more than three
thousand Indians camped in the vicinity of Fort Walsh, many of whom had
defiantly abandoned their reserves to the north rather than starve there. The
implications were disturbing to Canadian authorities. How could such a large
gathering be controlled? And if Canadian Indians continued to pursue bison
south of the border, there was the real possibility of an international incident.
Their long absences were also now regarded as an impediment to the successful
settlement of their home reserves and making headway in farming. The matter
was further complicated by the re-routing of the Canadian Pacific mainline
across the prairies. The vital national transportation link would have skirted a

ADRIAN PATON

The bison had disappeared from the northern plains by 1879.

possible concentration of reserves in present-day southwestern Saskatchewan and thereby been vulnerable to any future unrest in the area.

Dewdney responded to the "problem" with calculated coolness. He withheld rations from Indians who had refused to take treaty or had left their reserves. This hard-hearted policy starved Big Bear and his followers into submission, and after holding out for six years, the chief reluctantly entered treaty at Fort Walsh in December 1882. Dewdney also broke his promise to Cree and Assiniboine leaders and told them that reserves had been selected for them along the North Saskatchewan and in the Qu'Appelle Valley. If they wanted rations, they had to take up residence there. To enforce this eviction order, Fort Walsh was closed, thereby eliminating the only source of provisions and one of the last inducements for remaining in the hills now that local game resources were exhausted. Hundreds of Indians forcibly left for their new homes under police escort. Whereas there had been almost 8,500 Indians not on reserves in 1882, the number dropped to 1,307 the following year.[58]

The dispersal of the Fort Walsh refugees to different parts of the North-West was supposed to make Indian bands more manageable. By isolating them

SASKATCHEWAN ARCHIVES BOARD, G.F. SHEPHERD FONDS

Indian Commissioner Edgar Dewdney took on the additional duties of lieutenant-governor for the North-West Territories in 1881.

on reserves, government officials could exercise greater control. But the Indian sense of grievance and alienation only festered as the situation worsened. Rations rarely met daily caloric needs and were generally unfit for human consumption, especially the salted pork that was shipped by barrel. Over one hundred members of Piapot's band reportedly died from rancid bacon during the winter of 1883–84. The malnutrition, in turn, suppressed immune systems and made band populations extremely vulnerable to disease, especially a relatively new killer—tuberculosis.[59]

Indian leaders and their followers might have been expected to lash out against their oppressors. But they were determined to bring about change by

509

peaceful means. One of the first opportunities to voice their frustration came in August 1881 when several Cree chiefs met the Canadian governor general, the Marquis of Lorne, at the territorial capital at Battleford. The Indians keenly appreciated Lorne's stature, because he was also the Queen's son-in-law, and used their own relationship with the Crown to speak with candour. "At the time of the Treaties," Mistawasis complained about government neglect, "it was mentioned that while the sun rose and set and the water ran the faith in the treaties was to be kept."[60] Mistawasis's comments were surprising, if not worrisome, for Indian officials, particularly because he had always been highly regarded for his cooperative and accommodating nature. But a growing number of chiefs were now coming together to lobby for better support and assistance. To that end, Beardy called a council meeting at Duck Lake in July 1884 to discuss a range of grievances, from the lack of schools and health care to poor farming equipment, clothing, and rations. "[I]t is almost too hard for them," reported subagent J. A. Macrae, "to bear the treatment received at the hands of the Government after its 'sweet promises' made in order to get the country from them."[61] That senior Indian officials chose to downplay the growing sea of disillusionment and resentment was confirmed in a subsequent investigation by Hayter Reed, Commissioner Dewdney's assistant, who dismissed the Duck Lake complainants as "ill-disposed and lazy ... looking for extra aid."[62] Prime Minister Macdonald, meanwhile, was anxious for any positive news and demanded that Dewdney deliver "a full *and favourable*" report on Indian settlement and agriculture—and the "prospect of *diminishing* expenditures."[63]

The Métis, especially those south of Prince Albert, shared the Cree sense of alienation and grievance. The first settlers at Petite-Ville (in the Fish Creek vicinity) on the west side of the South Saskatchewan River were plains people who sought to continue their traditional lifestyle from a more permanent base in the Fort Carlton district in the 1860s. But the disappearance of the bison from the region forced a turn to subsistence farming. It also necessitated a move to better agricultural land and, in 1871, a new community was founded

SASKATCHEWAN ARCHIVES BOARD R-A461

Indian Commissioner Dewdney closed Fort Walsh in 1882 in order to force Indians to move
to their new reserves.

to the north around the future St. Laurent de Grandin mission. The 322 people counted there in a HBC census were supplemented by two major migrations during the next decade: one in 1877–78 and the other 1882–83. Most of these families were from the Red River settlement, but some also came from the Qu'Appelle Valley, Wood Mountain, and the Cypress Hills to join relatives already there. This influx of settlers brought the population to about fifteen hundred, distributed on both sides of the river from Fish Creek in the south to Duck Lake on the west and St. Louis (Boucher) to the north. Within this triangle of lands, known collectively as the South Branch settlement, were four parishes: St. Laurent de Grandin, St. Antoine de Padoue (Batoche), Sacré Coeur (Duck Lake), and St. Louis de Langevin. Batoche, named after merchant François-Xavier Letendre, *dit* Batoche, who operated both a store and ferry there, served as administrative centre for the district and was sometimes known as the Métis capital.[64]

What brought the Métis together to the South Branch community was the overriding desire to find their own place—a new home—in the North-West. That is why entire families, sometimes three generations, settled together along the South Saskatchewan. And over the years, well into the mid-twentieth century, they intermarried with other migrants, even close relatives, to create "a society that could be called a 'family' in the wide[st] sense."[65] This practice— called endogamy—fostered and encouraged a sense of Métis identity peculiar to the South Branch. But the developing community also had close ties with the local Indian population. The Willow Cree of the neighbouring reserves (Beardy, Okemasis, and One Arrow) were not only generally of mixed-descent but in a few instances directly related to the original Métis settlers because of their time together on the plains before the treaties. Some hunters and freighters married Cree women. Others moved back and forth between the two groups, while a few lived on reserve as treaty Indians and collected annuities. This fluid boundary was attributable to their cultural affinity. Despite surnames being predominantly French, the mother tongue of the Plains Métis was Cree. In fact, many steadfastly remained unilingual Cree speakers—to the frustration of the Roman Catholic priests who served them. The local Métis language, Michif, reflected this Cree heritage.[66]

There were also social or class divisions within the South Branch community. Letendre, for example, exploited the commercial opportunities of the district—the location of his business on the Carlton Trail was no coincidence—to become a wealthy man at the head of a lucrative trading operation between Winnipeg and HBC posts along the North Saskatchewan River. He prided himself on being the owner of one of the finest houses in the North-West. There were also several intellectuals, such as Louis Schmidt, whose education and political activism during the Red River Resistance made him a respected community leader. The plains-bred Gabriel Dumont, by contrast, might have settled permanently in the area in 1870, even applying for a ferry licence two years later, but he continued to lead hunting parties to the south in search of bison. His last organized trip to the Cypress Hills and into the United States was the summer of 1880. Other community members worked as freighters and made the most of the limited opportunities afforded by the coming of the Canadian Pacific Railway. But these hunting and freighting activities took people away from their river lot holdings, and farming consequently remained small-scale, if not neglected, and was mostly restricted to kitchen gardens. Those from Red River, meanwhile, who brought their agricultural experience, occupied all of the better land along the east bank of the South Saskatchewan. Despite their persistence, success was elusive because of poor growing conditions, especially after the August 1883 cataclysmic eruption of the Krakatoa volcano in Indonesia and the lowering of interior North America temperatures for 1884–85. The cultivated portion of the South Branch river lots averaged a meagre ten acres.[67] While some like Letendre prospered, then, a good many, in the words of one HBC official in 1884, were "getting poorer by the year."[68]

When the Métis began to settle at St. Laurent in the early 1870s, there was no government presence. The North-West Territories lieutenant-governor and appointed council were still based outside the region in Winnipeg, while the North-West Mounted Police were just being formed. The Métis consequently decided to establish their own government for the community in the absence of Canadian authority.[69] On 10 December 1874, with priest Alexis André serving as recorder, the assembled Métis elected Gabriel Dumont as president of an eight-person council and then proceeded to debate and approve a local constitution, better known as the "laws of St. Laurent." The twenty-eight articles dealt with all aspects of community life. A further set of twenty-five rules, based on past practice, were adopted "for the Prairie and Hunting." These measures were never intended to challenge Canadian sovereignty. But a storm of controversy brewed up in the spring of 1875 when a handful of independent hunters left early for the bison herds in violation of the regulations and were forcibly stopped and later fined by Dumont for their indiscretion. Their treatment prompted Chief Factor Lawrence Clarke at Carlton to wildly complain to Lieutenant-Governor Alexander Morris that a Métis "insurrection" was afoot. A subsequent mounted police investigation determined that Clarke's charges were a gross exaggeration: the Métis were simply following traditional custom in the absence of any territorial regulations.[70] Governor General Lord Dufferin

The Prince Albert district, 1885

even suggested after reading the official police report that the "community ... appears to have honestly endeavoured to maintain order by the best means in its power."[71] But the incident served to underscore how the Canadian government presence was a tenuous one, and more importantly, how the Métis attempt to provide a form of local government could be misinterpreted as a form of resistance.

The South Branch Métis next directed their energies to securing title to their river lot holdings in the district. The issue was a sensitive one because of the lingering feeling of betrayal over the Manitoba settlement (1869–70 Red River Resistance), but it acquired a particular urgency after the Cree of the region negotiated Treaty Six with the Crown in 1876. What would become of their land rights? Some of the Plains Métis living in the community had already unsuccessfully tried petitioning the federal government to secure their own "special reserve" in the Cypress Hills.[72] Now the campaign shifted to the South Saskatchewan. Here, the problem was that the Métis had settled in informally demarcated river lots before the land had been surveyed. And they wanted title to their holdings officially recognized, especially because river lots were an integral part of their cultural identity. But when two surveyors arrived at the settlement to do some preliminary work in 1878 and 1879, around the time that hunters and freighters were away, they concluded that most of the land was largely unoccupied. Only a few individual river lots were recorded on the east bank, while the township system (with its quarter sections for homesteads) was applied to the west bank even though it was evident that people were living there.[73] As James Clinkskill recounted in his memoirs, "There was confusion as a man's house would be on one quarter-section and his fields on another."[74]

The Métis position might have been helped if the community had had a voice on the North-West Territories Council. But both the old (pre-1875) and new (post-1875) councils did not include an appointed representative from the South Branch even though it was becoming one of the largest settlements in the territories. Lieutenant-Governor David Laird questioned Ottawa's myopia. "I find there is a feeling here," he advised Prime Minister Mackenzie," that ... all members of Council are outsiders." His predecessor, Alexander Morris, was blunter. "It is a crying shame," he lamented, "that the half-breeds have been ignored. It will result in trouble and is most unjust."[75] This feeling of political impotence added to the Métis frustration as they prepared—with the support and encouragement of the local clergy—petition after petition to the territorial and federal governments seeking a re-survey of their lands into river lots in keeping with their cultural practices. But the requests were either ignored or turned down, despite repeated promises that the matter would be addressed. All that Ottawa was willing to do was to suggest that Métis subdivide the surveyed quarter sections into something resembling river lots, but only after they had secured title to the land in question. The Métis, however, refused to register for the quarter sections, insisting that they would only apply to occupy

THE GLOBE, 7 OCTOBER 1881

Cree Chief Poundmaker accompanied the Canadian governor general during his tour of the West in 1881.

river lots.[76] This stalemate over the re-survey question made the Métis even more apprehensive about the Canadian government, while doing nothing to lessen their fears over losing their land. For many, it appeared that the Manitoba experience was being repeated.

The white population, especially people living in Prince Albert, was also increasingly disillusioned, if not thoroughly frustrated, with the federal government. Those Anglo-Canadians who emigrated west in the 1870s and early 1880s had come from a tradition where they enjoyed a popular interest in political affairs and exercised a voice in governing themselves. That was one of the reasons why a lively regional press—in the form of newspapers—appeared in several communities in the North Saskatchewan country and along the CPR main line. But the new North-West Territories Council after 1875 consisted initially of only three appointees (two magistrates, the other the NWMP commissioner) who were not even paid for their duties because they were already salaried government employees. The lieutenant-governor, meanwhile, not only had sole control over the territorial budget, limited as it was, but exercised wide discretionary power over many other territorial matters.[77] The 1875 NWT Act did allow for elected representation on the council, but not until there were one thousand people in a district. It was consequently not until 1880 that Lorne, the first electoral constituency in the future province of Saskatchewan, was created in the Prince Albert area.[78]

This delay in securing elected representation might have been palatable if not for the puzzling requirement that there could be no municipal organization (and local taxation) nor the creation of school districts until an electoral district had first been established. The linking of the three meant that schools in many areas had to depend on voluntary funding, while much-needed public works were delayed by the general parsimony of the territorial government.[79] It could actually have been worse. In 1880, Ottawa floated the idea of removing the capital to Winnipeg. Even though it never happened because of the storm of regional protest, the proposal underscored the federal government's obvious contempt for territorial government. Liberal Prime Minister Alexander Mackenzie had suggested as much when he told the House of Commons that the administration of the region would effectively "be in the hands of the Government here in Ottawa."[80] His Conservative successor thought the same way. Prime Minister Macdonald believed that the lieutenant-governor had so little to do—in his words, the position was a "useless expense"—that Indian Commissioner Edgar Dewdney could easily handle both jobs.[81]

This government by executive order and proclamation spawned a spirited protest movement, spearheaded by some of the first elected territorial councillors but powered by the full force of the Anglo-Canadian community. Many westerners complained that federal promotion of immigration and settlement—spoken in terms of the region's importance to the future prosperity of the dominion—was not being materially supported by the building of

UNIVERSITY OF SASKATCHEWAN ARCHIVES AND SPECIAL COLLECTIONS MSS C550/1/24.1

Newspaper editor Frank Oliver continually railed against the colonial treatment of the region.

infrastructure or the provision of government services. The more disaffected blamed eastern indifference. It appeared that Ontario was intent on exploiting the region for its own benefit, treating it as little more than a colony rather than helping fulfill the great expansionist dreams for the North-West. A bitter Charles Mair chose a formal tribute to the lieutenant-governor to charge that the West was being deliberately held back "through circumstances over which we have had no control and which we have fought in vain."[82] Newspaperman Frank Oliver, the elected council representative for Edmonton, went much further. "If history is to be taken as a guide," he lectured in an *Edmonton Bulletin* editorial, "what could be plainer than without rebellion the people of the North West need expect nothing, while with rebellion successful or otherwise they may reasonably expect to get their rights."[83] Lieutenant-Governor Dewdney dismissed Oliver's remarks, both in his newspaper and the Regina territorial council chamber, as "wild talk."[84] But the Prince Albert *Times* was just as fierce in denouncing Ottawa, warning that "the present state of things will

518

The home of merchant Xavier Letendre at Batoche

[not] much longer be endured."[85] That western patience was quickly running out was confirmed by the 1883 launch of a second Prince Albert news sheet appropriately titled, "The Voice of the People." The answer for many was parliamentary representation. Because it was the federal government that formulated policies for the region, then it only made sense for the territories to seek accountability in the House of Commons. But when the matter was formally raised in 1884, the minister of the Interior said the idea needed study first.[86] That something might be done someday—the same thing Ottawa repeatedly told the Métis—did nothing to dampen western ambitions, and soon there were calls for North-West control over lands and resources and the granting of provincehood.

What exacerbated this growing sense of grievance was a widespread recession that discouraged settlement and hurt commercial trade. From 1883 onwards, all key economic indicators, such as the number of homesteads and

River Street in Prince Albert

acreage occupied, were down for Manitoba and the North-West Territories. Mair told a friend, "The bottom seems to have fallen out."[87] This downturn compounded the stagnation being experienced by those communities that had expected the CPR mainline to pass through the North Saskatchewan country. In Prince Albert, unbridled optimism gave way to unrelenting gloom, especially when it became painfully apparent that no railway company was prepared to build a line to the community given the depressed conditions. Several businesses could not stay afloat and shuttered their doors. Even agriculture suffered. The severe cold of the 1883–84 winter was followed by a summer drought and then heavy frost at harvest time. The 1884 crop in the district was a total failure. Interestingly, no one blamed the land or the region for not meeting immigrant expectations.[88] Instead, the answer was neglect. The territorial capital in Regina seemed a world away. Situated on the CPR mainline, it could never have a true appreciation of the woes that Prince Albert faced. The federal Department of Interior, meanwhile, should have been known as the department of indifference. Why else would it take until 1883 for a telegraph line to reach the community? And why else did the number of outstanding court cases have to become so overwhelming before a court house was finally built there?[89]

Perhaps the biggest irritant, and a surprising one at that, was the question of land title. The South Branch Métis were not the only ones frustrated with federal dilatoriness. Ottawa may have wanted the land settled and producing

The Métis wanted to secure their future in the new West by ensuring that their
land holdings were respected and recognized.

crops, but it moved at glacial speed in granting title to land holdings. Even
though Battleford was made capital in 1876, it took six years before the townsite
was surveyed. By then, there were many overlapping claims. The situation
was no better in the countryside. Delay in measuring out homesteads until
1884 resulted in a number of clashes over title. The story in the Prince Albert
district was much the same. Despite the surveying of the river lots in the old
Prince Albert settlement in 1878, it was another three years before the local
Dominion Lands office began accepting applications for any land. And those
English Métis and whites who applied for a river lot or regular homestead in

1881 had to meet the residency requirements (six months per year for three years) from that point forward before they got their patent; there was no credit for prior occupation, even though a family may have already lived on the parcel of land for several years. Some settlers outside the community discovered that they had squatted on sections of land in the 1870s that under the survey system would be made available for sale and not open to homesteading. This unfortunate situation led first to confusion, then anger, and finally wrangling with federal authorities. The English Métis were especially adamant that, as a mixed-descent people, they had an Aboriginal right to land in the North-West and that they should not be governed by the same requirements as immigrants. Ottawa chose not to deal with the sorry mess but threatened in July 1883 to put all the land in the Prince Albert area back on the market.[90]

Townspeople and farmers pushed back. On 7 October 1883, at a mass meeting in Prince Albert, about 150 whites and English Métis came together to form the Settlers' Rights Association. A set of resolutions was drafted for submission to the Macdonald government, while a committee was deputized to hold similar meetings in outlying communities. It might have appeared a tame beginning to what became known as the "agitation," but in the coming months, whites and Métis peoples would come together to confront "a complacent common enemy."[91] It was not simply a French Métis movement involving Gabriel Dumont, Louis Schmidt, Charles Nolin, Maxime Lépine, and others from the South Branch communities. Nor was it led and directed by disaffected whites, although both Will Jackson of Prince Albert and Thomas Scott from the Ridge played prominent roles. The English Métis were also deeply and vitally involved in the agitation, often pushing for more aggressive action, especially on the land question. James Isbister, the founder of Prince Albert, took a lead role. So too did Andrew Spence, a local Scottish-Métis farmer from Red Deer Hill whose contribution to the agitation has been largely forgotten, if not ignored. What was particularly noteworthy—and troubling for Ottawa—is that racial, cultural, and social differences between the groups, especially religion, were temporarily set aside in favour of pursuing their collective interests.[92]

Thomas Scott, one of the leaders of the English Métis, and his wife, Mary,
the daughter of James Isbister

"They will not shrink," the Prince Albert *Times* thundered, "from taking any steps absolutely necessary for the vindication of their rights."[93]

The winter of 1883–84 saw a series of community meetings, the mood probably made worse by the harsh weather. While the French Métis held "secret assemblies" in local homes, the English Métis met in schools and churches in Lindsay, Halcro, Colleston, and Red Deer Hill from January through to April. The two groups eventually decided to form a general Métis council and named Spence as its president. Cree was most likely the language of their deliberations. At a meeting at the Lindsay school on 6 May 1884, to which neither the white Prince Albert community nor Roman Catholic clergy were invited, it was agreed to submit a joint petition to Ottawa that sought redress of their many grievances. The second and more controversial decision—an idea put forward by Spence[94]—was to invite exiled Métis leader Louis Riel, quietly working as a school teacher in Montana, to take up their cause. When a four-person delegation, including Dumont and Isbister, reached St. Peter's mission the following month, the forty-year-old Riel said that he had been expecting them. He observed that there were four of them and that they had arrived on the fourth of June.

Louis Riel's return to Canada marked a new phase in the agitation. As the successful leader of the 1869–70 Red River Resistance, Riel was regarded as someone who could influence events and get results. But the Riel who welcomed the joint Métis delegation was not the same Riel of Red River days. Although still a charismatic leader, he had suffered a mental breakdown in the mid-1870s and assumed the mantle of God's personal emissary. In his new role as the prophet "David," he hoped to relocate the papacy to Canada—first to Montreal and then St. Vital, Manitoba—and create a homeland in the North-West for the Métis, Indians, and other oppressed peoples of the world in preparation for the Day of Judgement. This religious mission, not his past experience as a political leader, prompted Riel to lead the agitation. The invitation was the sign he had been waiting for. The melding of Métis political dissatisfaction with Riel's messianic fervour was to prove a potent combination.[95]

Riel was welcomed among both the French and English Métis communities and lost no time in taking steps to advance the grievances of the North Saskatchewan country. At a speech in Red Deer Hill on 11 July 1884, he emphasized the need to bring about change by constitutional means and expressed a willingness to work alongside the leadership of the Settlers' Rights Association in drafting a bill of rights. The same moderate tone was carried over to a meeting at Treston Hall in Prince Albert eight days later. But many of those white business people and settlers who had come to see Riel probably did so more out of curiosity, not necessarily from a desire to join forces with him. Many English Protestant Canadians believed that he still had to answer for the earlier resistance and did not trust him. Frank Oliver, for example, cautioned one of Riel's white supporters that the Métis leader was "political dynamite" and that any endorsement would be "the best possible weapon they [opponents] can have against you."[96] Riel's presence in the Prince Albert district accelerated the breaking down of the alliance between Métis peoples and whites that was already starting to dissolve.

The family of Saskatoon storekeeper George Willoughby share a light-hearted
moment with some Sioux men from the nearby Whitecap reserve at Moose Woods.

In January 1884, Surveys Inspector William Pearce had investigated land
claims complaints and subsequently sided with the settlers in his report to
the federal government. This resolution removed a major irritant. But Pearce
could not speak French and did not visit the South Branch communities.
It would not be until several months later that Ottawa finally pledged to
look into the long-standing Métis claims. This delay only hardened the Métis
sense of grievance and strengthened Riel's hand.

English and French Métis cooperation continued through the summer of
1884. In August, for example, Andrew Spence headed a welcoming committee
for Minister of Public Works Hector Langevin. But the presentation of their
joint grievances never materialized because the Conservative politician chose
not to visit the North Saskatchewan country. Cracks soon emerged on the Métis
council over how best to proceed with the agitation. In September 1885, James

Isbister chided Riel for not doing more to "have that ministry [government] awakened to our interests," but at the same time reminded him, "we want no trouble." The Roman Catholic clergy had similar concerns. Although local priests complained about federal lethargy and incompetence, they too were worried about Riel's intentions, especially given his public criticisms of the church, and refused to countenance any radical action. Even the territorial government wanted to know about Riel's plans. Hayter Reed and Judge Charles Rouleau, two members of the North-West Territorial Council, were dispatched to St. Laurent early that fall and concluded that Riel "can do a great deal of harm" if Métis grievances were not addressed.[97] A. E. Forget, clerk of the North-West Council, offered a more circumspect assessment, suggesting that the agitation was bigger than Riel and must be taken seriously.

Armed with this information, Lieutenant-Governor Edgar Dewdney recommended to Prime Minister Macdonald that Riel could be effectively neutralized if government work was given to the Métis unemployed for the coming winter: "the want of it [money] is the secret of their uneasiness."[98] It was a simple remedy, one that betrayed his limited grasp of what lay behind the agitation. A more meaningful gesture would have been the establishment of a second seat in the Lorne electoral district (because it easily exceeded two thousand people) and the awarding of that seat to the St. Laurent Métis. That also never happened. Dewdney could also have done more to see that the memorials on political reform sent to Ottawa were at least considered instead of quietly pigeon-holed. That too never happened. Nor was Macdonald prepared to do much beyond approving a *future* investigation of Métis land claims. He had other larger concerns, such as shepherding his new franchise bill through Parliament, and was generally dismissive of the reports coming out of the North-West. "No amount of concession," he told Dewdney, "will prevent ... people from grumbling and agitating."[99] If need be, Macdonald reasoned, the mounted police force could be strengthened to discourage any possible unrest. But western grievances were not law-enforcement problems.

One of the last acts of cooperation between the French and English Métis communities was the submission of a petition to Ottawa on 16 December 1884 that enumerated all the various reforms that had been advocated over the past few years. Thereafter, the continuing federal delay and resultant frustration encouraged Riel to champion more forceful measures, culminating in the declaration of a provisional government on 19 March 1885. When the English Métis learned about this unilateral action, they found themselves in a difficult position because of their shared grievances with the South Branch communities. At a meeting on 20 March at Lindsay school, with the Ridge's Thomas Scott taking a leading role, it was decided to challenge Riel's call to arms and his wooing of the Indians. A small delegation went to Batoche the next day to deliver this message to the Métis leader. Riel, in turn, tried to win over the English Métis representatives by appealing to common interests. But in a series of meetings in schools and churches over the next two days, the English Métis confirmed their determination to remain neutral. Resolutions, addressed to the new Métis governing body (called the Exovedate) and discussed at a meeting at Lindsay school on the evening of 23 March, blamed Ottawa for provoking the trouble but stressed the absolute need for a constitutional solution. Riel made a last-ditch effort to win over the English Métis when he attended a tense meeting at Lindsay school with an armed escort on 24 March. But he was publicly rebuffed when, at Scott's urging, all present signed the petition that had been prepared the night before.[100] "We cannot endorse the present attitude in taking up arms for that purpose," the document maintained, "and we hereby beg of them not to shed blood."[101] It was a naive hope.

Métis leader Louis Riel (without either moustache or beard) on the cover of the
Canadian Illustrated News during the 1869-70 Red River Resistance

CHAPTER FIFTEEN

WITHIN A BREATH

THEY HAD BEEN TRAMPING THROUGH THE DENSE BUSH FOR DAYS. THE PLAINS CREE war chief Wandering Spirit and his soldiers kept the camp moving, deliberately avoiding trails and waterways, trying to put as much distance as possible between themselves and the pursuing Canadian troops. They did not want to fight General T. B. Strange and his military column again, even though their May 1885 engagement at Red Deer Creek, popularly known as the Battle of Frenchman's Butte, had been a draw. The Indians had chosen their position well, digging two rows of defensive pits (still visible today) on the north side of the yawning, muskeg-filled creek valley. Stranded on the other side with his force, the general responded with his nine-pound cannon, known to the Cree as the "gun that speaks twice,"[1] and inflicted a punishing bombardment before the warriors pulled back to rejoin the women, children, and elderly hiding safely to the north with the white and Métis hostages. The camp had been steadily on the move ever since. But there were fewer of them. Where there had once been as many as one thousand people in the Frog Lake camp before the skirmish, small groups of prisoners, even some Cree, had begun to quietly slip away at first opportunity. The Indians had also left behind most of their provisions at the battle site in their frantic scramble to get away. A steady, at times heavy, rain now added to their misery. Weeks earlier, when Kitty McLean, the young daughter of a HBC trader, had been taken into the camp with her family and had little to eat, a Woods Cree girl had told her "to drink [water] until it comes back in your nose and mouth ... it will stop the feeling of hunger."[2]

But there was no getting over the disheartening feeling that Big Bear's band had become fugitives in their own land, unable to go home and unsure of what the future held. And there could be no rest until they either surrendered or found a way to elude capture.

One of the great fears at the start of the North-West Rebellion was that Canada would have an Indian war on its hands. Indeed, the news from the region in the spring of 1885 could not have been more disturbing. On 13 March, just days before Louis Riel declared his provisional government at Batoche, a frantic Superintendent Lief Crozier in Prince Albert had telegraphed the commissioner of the North-West Mounted Police in Regina: "If half-breeds rise, Indians will join them."[3] Farther up the North Saskatchewan River at Battleford, where more than two thousand Cree and Assiniboine lived on nine outlying reserves, Judge J. B. Rouleau, a member of the North-West Territories Council, did not wait to see what happened but hurriedly gathered up his family and fled south to the safety of Swift Current.

The mood in communities along the Canadian Pacific Railway main line was just as anxious. A steam engine stood at the ready in Moose Jaw to evacuate women and children should the small population of neighbouring Sioux raid the town. And in Broadview, just south of the Crooked Lake reserves, an armed volunteer militia patrolled the village, while local farmers made plans to form barricades with their implements.[4] This behaviour—and there are many other examples, including the erection of Fort Watson just outside Yorkton—sadly demonstrated that the immigrant white population was afraid of Indian peoples and the terrible things they might do. For many newcomers, they were "savages" who could never be trusted. This unease was partly the consequence of the size of the Indian population. Indians far outnumbered the settler population, especially in the North Saskatchewan country, and put the dream of a white West out of reach, while reinforcing the wildness of the region. But a more important factor was the ingrained racism of the period. On the eve of the rebellion, P. G. Laurie, the publisher of the *Saskatchewan*

THE GRIP, 11 APRIL 1885

TOO LATE!

Political cartoonist J. W. Bengough blamed federal negligence for driving the Métis and Indians to rebellion.

Herald, was not alone in viewing Indians as "a bloodthirsty race."[5] In the new Saskatoon temperance colony, Bessie Trounce confessed to her mother, "the Indians we are not so sure about," while Patience Caswell later remarked, "we did fear the Indians."[6] Even Anglican missionary John Hines, who had lived and worked with Ahtahkakoop's band since the mid-1870s, refused to let his daughter play with or go to school with the Cree children on the reserve.[7]

This belief that Indians would join the Métis seemed confirmed by the Battle of Duck Lake, the opening salvo in Canada's first and only civil war. Some fifteen years earlier, Louis Riel and his Métis followers had seized control of the Red River settlement and forced the Canadian government to bring the region into Confederation as the province of Manitoba, complete with guarantees for the Métis population. He now seemed intent on following the same strategy. In the first few days after the formation of the provisional government on 19 March 1885, he and his men had taken hostages and tried to bring about the surrender of nearby Fort Carlton in order to bargain from a position of strength. But in an attempt to neutralize the fledgling movement while it was still in its infancy, NWMP Superintendent Crozier, with nearly one hundred police and Prince Albert civilian volunteers, set off for Duck Lake by sleigh the morning of 26 March to prevent a batch of guns and ammunition from falling into the hands of Riel's supporters. As the combined force headed southeast from the fort along the Carlton trail, they entered Beardy's reserve and were immediately intercepted by a small mounted Métis party under Riel's adjutant general Gabriel Dumont. The tense standoff quickly dissolved into shooting, with the Métis holding the upper hand, especially after dozens of fighters arrived from Batoche.

Facing capture or possible annihilation, Crozier ordered a general retreat and then led his badly mauled force back to the relative safety of Fort Carlton. He left behind twelve dead, including nine civilians, in the blood-stained snow. The Métis lost four men. Two days later, the mounted police abandoned the fort and sought refuge in Prince Albert, where they joined Commissioner A. G. Irvine and ninety reinforcements who had arrived from Regina too late to take part in the Duck Lake operation. The police would remain hunkered down in Prince Albert for the next six weeks, leaving the Métis effectively in control of the surrounding territory.

PRINCE ALBERT HISTORICAL SOCIETY H-401

A sentry stands guard on the outskirts of Prince Albert during the rebellion.

The clash at Duck Lake made a negotiated settlement impossible and forced Riel and his followers to fight a rebellion they could not win. And the reason they could not win was that the Macdonald government, upon learning of Crozier's defeat and the evacuation of Carlton, quickly mobilized a large militia force to put down the insurrection. The prime minister, or "Old Tomorrow" as he was known, may have neglected western grievances, but war was another matter. The swiftness of Ottawa's response was also motivated in part by the misguided belief that the Cree had joined forces with Riel in a combined Indian–Métis insurgency that could sweep across the western interior like a prairie fire. Had not the battle taken place on Beardy's reserve? And had not a handful of Willow Cree men been spotted among the Métis fighters? Newspapers of the day certainly offered up this interpretation. On 30 April 1885, Sir Charles Tupper, the Canadian high commissioner to the United

Kingdom, frantically cabled Prime Minister Macdonald about a London report claiming there had been an "indian uprising" in western Canada.[8]

What was not appreciated, though, was that Riel's plan to recruit Indians to his cause had actually been a miserable failure. Over the winter of 1884–85, messengers had been sent among the local Cree bands with presents and an invitation to take up arms alongside the Métis. This behind-the-scenes intrigue was no secret to government authorities. Just the day before the declaration of the Métis provisional government, Superintendent Crozier had wired Lieutenant-Governor and Indian Commissioner Edgar Dewdney that the local Indians were "being tampered with." Dewdney personally relayed this message to the prime minister a week later.[9] Cree leaders, however, had repeatedly rebuffed Riel's overtures because of their own ongoing diplomatic efforts to bring about a workable alliance with the Blackfoot the following summer.[10] They knew that any violence would lead to retribution and thereby wreck their plans to get Ottawa to honour the treaties. Riel, however, desperately needed Indian reinforcements. When he jettisoned peaceful agitation for open rebellion, he had the active support of only a minority of South Branch Métis (about 250), and of these, only a third, mostly older Plains Métis, were "firmly committed."[11] He consequently had to look to neighbouring reserves in the expectation he would find willing recruits because of the connections between the two communities. Not only were many of the treaty Cree in the Duck Lake area of mixed ancestry, but also some Métis men had married Cree women and become part of their extended families. But only a handful of individuals answered the call.[12]

That left only one option: forcibly gathering up supporters. Michel Dumas, the farm instructor at the nearby One Arrow reserve and one of the four delegates sent to retrieve Riel from the United States in June 1884, ordered the Willow Cree band to slaughter their cattle and join the Métis camp at Batoche. Dumont's presence with a contingent of armed horsemen ensured that the Indians complied.[13] Exactly how many One Arrow men took part in the Duck Lake battle is not certain, but their presence there, even under duress, seemed convincing evidence of their participation in the rebellion.

In reality, most of the Indians of the Carlton Agency preferred to watch the struggle between the Métis and the government from the sidelines. Beardy, for example, had refused Riel's entreaties and counselled his followers to remain aloof from the unfolding drama. But Métis armed patrols regularly swept through the district, prompting band members to hide along the banks of the South Saskatchewan River or the surrounding woods to evade being pressed into service.[14] Chiefs Mistawasis and Ahtahkakoop also sought to avoid involvement by abandoning their reserves after the Duck Lake battle and relocating their people to a "neutral" camp just east of present-day Shellbrook. Riel sought to take advantage of the Duck Lake victory by sending out emissaries with a special appeal to Cree bands throughout the region to join him at Batoche: "Do what you can ... And without delay, come this way; as many as is possible."[15] But Indians on both the Touchwood Hills and Crooked Lake reserves balked at violating their treaty promises. "I said that I and my young men's fighting days were over," Chief Kahkewistahaw informed the local Indian agent. "I stick to those words no matter what may be done up north."[16] But even though the Cree vowed to remain loyal, they were just as unnerved as the white settler population by the descent into war and the possible ramifications. One of the most immediate—even before blood was spilled—was the government's apparent distrust of them. In responding to the Métis unrest in late March 1885, NWMP Commissioner Irvine and his punitive force had deliberately camped on or near reserves as it marched north to Carlton.[17] This uneasiness would give way to panic in several instances once the Canadian militia arrived on the scene.

The coming of the rebellion also had a decisive impact on the mixed-descent population and its place in the new West. Up until 1885, settlements in the western interior, in particular in the Saskatchewan country, were characterized by racial integration, today called hybridity. No one racial group dominated—except in some of the newer immigrant communities created by the building of the CPR main line across the southern prairies—and there

RACIAL COMPOSTION OF SASKATCHEWAN, 1881 CENSUS

Racial Group	% of Population
Indian	37
Mixed-descent	34
White	23
Unknown	6

Before the 1885 North-West Rebellion, three of every four people in Saskatchewan were Aboriginal

was significant intermingling between Indian, Métis, and white peoples. Work led to interracial contact, as did the search for partners. There were more men than women in the North-West, and Euro-Canadian immigrant males, like fur traders before them, formed relationships with Indian and Métis females. According to the 1881 census, 70 per cent of the formal marriages in the region were interracial. This ratio was even higher—at least four mixed marriages for every five unions—if informal unions are also considered.[18] Prince Albert sheriff Owen Hughes, for example, was married to English Métis Mary Inkster, while Poundmaker farm instructor Robert Jefferson was married to one of the chief's sisters. Indians and Métis peoples also continued to intermarry over several generations to develop extensive and complex kinship ties. Big Bear may have been one of the most prominent Plains Cree leaders of his generation, but he was related to the Desjarlais and Cardinal families, descendants of Canadian Freemen. In fact, because his father Black Powder had several children with several wives, many of the Cree bands living east of Edmonton were related through blood or marriage and included several mixed-descent members.[19] Then, there was Poundmaker, the son of an Assiniboine man and a mixed-descent Cree woman, and the adopted son of Blackfoot Chief Crowfoot.

Canada did not understand that the majority of people in the North-West had fluid, complicated identities. And with the signing of the western numbered treaties, individuals were forced to separate into Indian and Métis categories—an arbitrary distinction that ignored an individual's biological origins and cultural background.[20] Some mixed-descent peoples opted to become Indian because of the apparent benefits of entering treaty. Other individuals moved back and forth between identities, appearing on pay lists one year and not the next. Family members sometimes went different ways. When the children of brothers Antoine and Baptiste Desjarlais, who had settled in the Qu'Appelle Lakes region in the 1860s, had the option of entering Treaty Four in 1874, some did, while others chose farming.[21] This remaking of the identity of the people of the North-West was now accelerated by the rebellion. But it was now a choice between loyal and rebel. It proved terribly divisive, all the more so when families and communities found themselves on opposite sides of the divide. "The animosity created was hard to forget," one resident of Battleford recalled, "and often lasted for years."[22]

These divisions were most pronounced in the Prince Albert region. Where French and English Métis had collaborated during the heady days of the agitation, the two groups essentially followed different paths with the outbreak of the rebellion. There were a few, though, who broke ranks. Prominent Métis Charles Nolin and Louis Schmidt wanted nothing to do with Riel's gambit and fled to Prince Albert after the Duck Lake skirmish. Albert Monkman and Andrew Tate, on the other hand, chose not to remain neutral, as advocated by the English Métis leadership, and fought at Batoche. Most English Métis abandoned their farms for the crowded safety of Prince Albert, an exodus that became a retreat when Riel threatened settlers who refused to join his cause. Any remaining goodwill between the two groups was gone by the time farmers returned home to find that foraging parties had seized food and supplies for Dumont's army at Batoche.[23] Prince Albert, which had doubled in size in less than a week, anxiously waited for an attack. A crude stockade had been erected, a home guard formed, and pickets posted at the Ridge to sound the alarm in the event of an attack. "The days were literally spent in vain wondering ... what was coming next," recounted NWMP Constable John Donkin.[24] As a precaution, Commissioner Irvine imposed martial law on the settlement, even preventing local farmers from putting in their crop. He also detained English Métis leader James Isbister, as well as Thomas Scott, who had

Alexander Campbell sketches of the 7th Fusiliers on their way westward to suppress the rebellion

played a prominent role in the settler agitation. The NWMP commissioner was convinced that the besieged Prince Albert was infested with traitors, waiting for the right moment to strike from within.[25] But that moment never came. When Riel failed to get the support he had expected, he gave up any thought of an offensive campaign and chose to make his stand at Batoche.

Fort Battleford also came under an *imagined* seige during April and May 1885. Upon hearing of the Duck Lake battle, Cree Chiefs Little Pine and Poundmaker made for the fort, at the junction of the Battle and North Saskatchewan Rivers, to declare their allegiance to the Queen and secure rations for their hungry bands. But by the time the Indian delegation, about one hundred-strong, reached Battleford on 30 March, all of the town's five hundred residents had taken refuge inside the mounted police barracks in the belief that the approaching Cree were acting in concert with Riel and had warlike intentions. Little Pine and Poundmaker patiently waited all day for the local Indian agent to meet with them. It was only when it became apparent that their mission to Battleford had been in vain that some of the Indians helped themselves to provisions and other items in the abandoned stores and homes before heading back to their reserves late that night. This "pilfering like rats,"[26] as it would later be described, was an impromptu act. But from the vantage of the stockade, it appeared to the frightened residents that an attack could be "expected hourly."[27] How else would one explain the pillaging of stores and homes if Cree intentions were peaceful? The Cree, however, made no attempt to sack the fort even though the palisade was so spindly that one of the refugees joked that he could have shaken hands between the spaces. Nor did they prevent the townspeople from leaving the fort to get water from the nearby Battle River. Nor did they cut the telegraph line. Yet this same telegraph line would be used by the beleaguered residents of the stockade to plead with Canadian authorities to send a rescue party before it was too late.

The horrifying news of a massacre at the tiny hamlet of Frog Lake, along the North Saskatchewan River near the present-day Saskatchewan–Alberta border, made things even worse. Chafing at the hands of a mean-spirited Indian agent and tired of Big Bear's non-aggression tactics, several of the more aggressive band members decided to take advantage of the police defeat at Duck Lake by erecting a soldiers' lodge and taking the residents of Frog Lake prisoner in order to help themselves to some much-needed rations. But the plan turned into a murderous rampage on the morning of 2 April 1885 when Wandering Spirit and his warriors found alcohol during their looting spree and turned their guns on their hostages. By the time Big Bear, who had been pushed aside by the warrior society, could stop the carnage, nine men lay dead, including Indian Agent Thomas Quinn, the farm instructor John Delaney, and two Catholic priests, fathers Marchand and Fafard from the Notre Dame de Bon Conseil mission. Those whites and Métis peoples who survived the slaughter were taken prisoner. Among them was HBC clerk W. B. Cameron, who managed to elude certain death by being disguised as a woman.[28] He

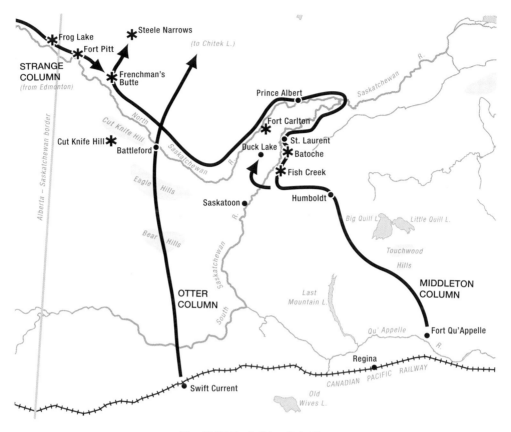

The 1885 North-West Rebellion

and the other captives joined a growing Frog Lake camp that included several Woods Cree bands who were conscripted into joining the Plains Cree in the aftermath of the murders.

The other victim that tragic morning was the Cree diplomatic initiative. Even though Beardy had remained calmly on his reserve during the hostilities and counselled his band against involvement in the Métis rebellion, the Duck Lake battle ended any hope of the Willow Cree leader hosting a larger treaty rights meeting that summer. And at Battleford, even though Poundmaker and Little Pine had peaceful intentions, the so-called siege of the fort suggested that they had broken their treaty promise to remain loyal. Now at Frog Lake, even though Big Bear exercised limited authority over his followers, he was held personally responsible for the killings. There was no attempt, for example, to see Quinn's murder as an act of retribution against a government official who

ADRIAN PATON

The North-West Field Force believed its military superiority would easily
overwhelm any rebel resistance.

was widely reviled for his "shameful brutality."[29] Nor did it occur to government
officials that the carnage across the North Saskatchewan country could have
been much, much worse if the Indians had truly decided to go to war against
the white population that spring. For the Macdonald government, the three
events provided indisputable evidence that the Cree had joined the rebel cause,
that they had fallen victim to Riel's siren call and were blindly prepared to
do anything to satisfy their primitive thirst for blood and lust, including the
rumoured defiling of the wives, now widows, of two of the Frog Lake victims.

Major General Frederick Middleton, the sixty-year-old commander
of the Canadian militia, was handed the task of organizing and leading the
North-West Field Force against Riel.[30] There was no shortage of volunteers.
From Halifax to Peterborough to Winnipeg, hundreds of citizen-soldiers
answered the call to serve their country upon hearing the news that Métis
villain Louis Riel was at it again, stirring up more trouble in the North-West.
It probably did not occur to them that they were going to war against fellow
Canadians—certainly not their fellow Canadians. Newspapers like the Toronto
Globe portrayed the enemy as non-British and therefore inferior.[31] Community
send-offs for the men reinforced this message: the torchbearers of British

543

BILL WAISER

Bill Epp's sculpture of Métis general Gabriel Dumont on the west bank of the South Saskatchewan River in downtown Saskatoon

civilization would easily triumph on the battlefield and order would be quickly restored.

Volunteers soaked up this confidence and were anxious to head west; the stories about the atrocities committed against white women gave them special purpose. Many also looked upon their mission as the adventure of a lifetime. Fifty years later, reunions would be held across the country to remember how the militia had put down the Métis and Indian insurgency. The Halifax contingent produced a burlesque show, "Halifax to the Saskatchewan: 'Our Boys' in the Riel Rebellion," that featured short skits interspersed with patriotic songs from the period.[32] Those who served, including members of the NWMP and the Prince Albert volunteers, were eligible for the North-West Canada medal. They were also offered a special homestead grant.[33] Who better to settle the land than those prepared to come to the defence of the nation?

Getting the recruits from eastern and central Canada to the western

544

prairies in good time was a formidable challenge, not simply because of the numbers involved but because sections of the CPR mainline north of Lake Superior had still not been completed. Muskeg made for a poor road base and construction delays were inevitable, and costly. The CPR builders had turned to the Macdonald government for financial assistance in late 1883 and received $22.5 million in emergency loans. They were back, hat in hand, the following year, but this time the prime minister was reluctant to ask Parliament for further aid. There is some speculation that Macdonald deliberately provoked the rebellion in order to rescue his so-called national dream: the CPR would get the necessary aid thanks to its pivotal role in getting troops quickly to the region.[34] But this conspiracy theory neglects the fact that Canada was already experiencing considerable difficulty attracting settlers to the western interior, and a frontier war, however minor or restricted, would have made the southern plains only more unattractive to prospective homesteaders—even if the railway was completed.

George Stephen, president of the CPR Syndicate, certainly did not see the outbreak of the rebellion as a good thing for the railroad. In April 1885, he complained to his business associate J. J. Hill that "this half-breed outbreak has been a nuisance ... more or less damaging to us" because it "interfered sadly with the progress of our work."[35] CPR General Manager William Cornelius Van Horne, in contrast, was quick to make the link between the railway and the rebellion and told the Macdonald government that he could get the first troops to Fort Qu'Appelle in ten days. He did it in nine, but only because the men managed to keep up with the demanding schedule. "C"Company of the Toronto Infantry School Corps left Toronto on 30 March and reached the end of rail two days later at Dog Fish Lake just beyond Biscotasing. The men then took to sleighs until they reached iron again and rode flat cars that had been boarded around to provide some protection from the cold. "[A] beautifully ventilated sleeping apartment," is how it was remembered, "the canopy of heaven for a roof, the soft side of a plank for a mattress, and a blanket two inches thick made of ice."[36]

At the next break in steel, somewhere along the north shore of Lake Superior, there were no sleighs and so the troops had to march miles through deep snow along the right of way. They were lucky, though. The train carrying Lieutenant Colonel W. D. Otter and the Queen's Own Rifles went off the track.[37] "C" Company reached Fort Qu'Appelle on 7 April. Weeks later, the CPR was rewarded with another loan of five million dollars. But the railway was not the only beneficiary. Local teamsters, businessmen, and others all profited from the arrival of the North-West Field Force. As one author quipped, "Riel brought some commerce into the Territories, even if it came via a rebellion."[38]

Old Fred, as General Middleton was mockingly called by his men, decided from the outset to concentrate his army's energies on the Métis stronghold at Batoche, believing that a quick knock-out blow there would effectively end the rebellion. He consequently started north from Fort Qu'Appelle on 6 April with the first troops in the field, confident that any resistance would melt away like the spring snow once his force arrived in rebel territory. Any concern about the fighting ability of his inexperienced men, especially on "foreign" terrain, was somewhat eased by their superior numbers and firepower. But events at Battleford and Frog Lake forced Middleton to amend his attack plan. On 11 April, he instructed Otter and his five hundred men to relieve Battleford, by proceeding north from Swift Current, instead of descending the South Saskatchewan River to Batoche as originally planned. Another assault force, headed by retired General S. B. Strange, would march north from Calgary to Edmonton and then east along the North Saskatchewan River to deal with Big Bear's band. Middleton largely regarded these secondary columns as a security measure. His sights remained firmly fixed on Batoche.

The Métis, in the meantime, made no attempt to draw on their familiarity with the countryside and conduct a guerilla campaign but calmly prepared to meet the Canadian response by building an elaborate system of defensive trenches at Batoche.[39] This decision to lie in wait on Métis home ground was made at the urging of Riel. As a prophet with a divine mission, he believed that God was on his side and that there was nothing to fear from the approaching army. The only action that Riel approved in the first few weeks of the rebellion was the dispatch of agents to outlying Indian bands to convince, cajole, or in some cases, coerce them into joining his Batoche army. Some came willingly, such as Kangi Tamaheca (Lean Crow) and other Lakota men from Wood Mountain, because of their connections with the Métis.[40] Others were pressed into service. The Petequakey band were "taken," according to an HBC labourer, "not of their own accord."[41] So too were the Dakota Sioux from Moose Woods. On their way through Saskatoon, Chief Whitecap informed his good friend, storekeeper George Willoughby, that his people were being forcibly taken north—by Charles Trottier from Prairie Ronde—but he did not want to ask for help out of fear that the Métis would attack the hamlet.[42]

By 23 April 1885, Middleton and two hundred men, now divided into columns on both sides of the South Saskatchewan River, was only two days from Métis headquarters. The proximity of the Canadian troops alarmed Gabriel Dumont and he successfully convinced the Métis council to launch a pre-emptive attack. In the early morning hours of 24 April, Dumont and about 150 men prepared to ambush one of Middleton's columns at Fish Creek, where the Batoche trail swung inland from the river and down through a wide ravine. But before the trap could be sprung, Middleton's advance scouts discovered the Métis in hiding and a fierce fire fight ensued. After an hour, the fight degenerated into a stalemate that lasted until the early evening when both sides withdrew from the battlefield. Although the ambush had failed, the battle of Fish Creek was a victory for the Métis. Not only had Middleton's inexperienced troops been badly mauled—the force suffered fifty casualties, including twelve dead—but the once-confident general was left wary and cautious. He decided to postpone his date with Riel until his column was rested and reinforced and he had a new battle plan in place.

On 7 May 1885, more than two weeks after the Fish Creek fiasco, Middleton resumed his march northward with almost nine hundred men, heavy artillery, and a fortified river steamer, the *Northcote*. He planned to surround Métis headquarters: a small force on the sternwheeler would attack the village from the river, while the main party would move overland from the east. The Batoche army, in comparison, probably numbered no more than four hundred men, including about sixty Indians from various bands. How much military support the Indians offered Riel is debatable. Not only were many aged and even more poorly armed than the Métis, but most were there reluctantly. Indian Commissioner Dewdney had also tried to limit any Indian involvement through a mixture of kindness and intimidation. Whereas several bands had been on the brink of starvation that past winter, large amounts of food and supplies now miraculously appeared.[43] This open hand was counterbalanced by a clenched fist. Troops pouring into the West during the first weeks of the campaign were trained or stationed on or near Cree reserves throughout the Qu'Appelle region in order to keep the Indians in check. But these bullying tactics only alarmed the bands. Chiefs Pasquah and Muscowpetung telegraphed the prime minister three days before Fish Creek: "Surprised to see soldiers coming here, don't know reason why ... don't think anything disloyal of us, it hurts us."[44] Many Indians chose not to wait to find out why the troops were there but fled their reserves, even though it meant certain privation and possible starvation. This turn of events left Dewdney scrambling to regain control of the Cree. And when General Middleton, in the aftermath of Fish Creek, asked that something be done to keep Indians on their reserves so that they were not mistaken as rebels, the Indian commissioner immediately issued a notice on 6 May "that all loyal and good Indians should remain quietly on their Reserves where they will be perfectly safe."[45] Several bands would subsequently be labelled disloyal—only because they were in violation of this notice.

The Canadian troops finally swooped down on Batoche on the morning of Saturday, 9 May. Middleton's plan collapsed, however, when the Métis fighters lowered a ferry cable across the South Saskatchewan and knocked over the smokestacks of the *Northcote*, sending the steamer drifting helplessly downriver. The land forces, meanwhile, did not get not much beyond the church and rectory before being forced to draw back uphill under heavy fire

PRINCE ALBERT HISTORICAL SOCIETY H-399

Shell fire during the first day of the battle of Batoche, 9 May 1885

from well-concealed rifle pits that lined the fields down to the village. The troops took refuge that night in a large fortified earthen enclosure or zareba that they hurriedly constructed just to the south. Over the next two days, while the two sides engaged in general skirmishing, Middleton developed a new plan of attack, which he tried to implement the morning of 12 May. He sent a small diversionary force to the open prairie region to the east of the village in an effort to draw the Métis away from their trenches along the riverbank and the church and rectory. But because of a strong wind that day, the main body did not hear the guns of the feinting action and failed to advance. An enraged Middleton berated the officers in charge of the infantry before storming back to camp for lunch. This stinging rebuke, coming after days of growing restlessness, sparked an impromptu advance on the village that quickly gained momentum and easily overran the defenders who were anticipating an attack from the east. The final assault in the battle of Batoche was over in minutes, largely because the remaining defenders had all but exhausted their ammunition and were unable to offer much resistance. Many paid with their lives. Whereas Middleton lost eight men during the four-day battle, the Batoche dead may have numbered as

PRINCE ALBERT HISTORICAL SOCIETY H-390

The steamer *North West* provided military transport to Battleford and Fort Pitt during the rebellion.

high as two dozen—many of them buried together as comrades in arms. Riel was much luckier. He had prayed throughout the siege and initially escaped, but decided to surrender three days later in a bid to take his cause to the courts.

The fall of Batoche was the first Canadian victory of the North-West campaign and did much to restore the swagger to Middleton's step. It also marked the end of the Métis provisional government, and with it, Riel's brief reign as prophet of the new world. His unshakeable faith in his divine cause had pushed his followers towards open rebellion but failed to save them in the end. The other losers at Batoche that May were the Indians, many of whom were in the trenches against their will. Although Chiefs Whitecap and One Arrow claimed to have taken no part in the actual fighting, they and several of their men were immediately taken into custody at Carlton as rebels. Gabriel Dumont, on the other hand, managed to elude the troops and slipped away to the United States, while several of his soldiers were simply disarmed and told to return home. Even Indians who refused to take part in the fighting were suspect. When Chief Beardy travelled to Prince Albert on 24 May to meet with Middleton and ask for rations for his hungry people, he was singled out for his band's apparent role in the start of the troubles and its collusion with the Métis.

Beardy tried to answer the accusations by insisting he had remained neutral. But the general countered that he was not fit to be chief and demanded that he and his headmen "give up your medals; they are meant for good men only."[46] They have never been returned to this day.

The other two military columns that had been sent north from Swift Current and Calgary were not as successful. Following their failed pilgrimage to Battleford, the Cree had anxiously gathered on the Poundmaker reserve in early April 1885 along a creek not far from the base of Cut Knife Hill. Far from joining the rebel cause, as events in late March had implied, the local bands were just as frightened and confused by events as the townspeople cowering inside the fort. And like their white counterparts, they had essentially come together for defensive reasons. This uneasy calm was shattered following the arrival of Colonel Otter's relief column at Battleford on 24 April. Disappointed at not seeing action on the trail north from Swift Current and determined to punish the Indians for their apparent siege of Fort Battleford, Otter assembled an attack force of about 325 men, complete with cannons and a gatling gun, and stormed the sleeping Cut Knife camp in the early hours of 2 May. But the Indians had been alerted to the coming of the troops and mounted an effective counter-attack. Otter's retreating force might have been wiped out if not for Poundmaker's restraint of the warriors.

Two days after Otter's attack, the Cut Knife camp was visited again—this time by a group of Métis emissaries who had been sent by Riel to bring the Indians to Batoche in preparation for the showdown with the North-West Field Force. Poundmaker had steadfastly avoided any such commitment since the Métis leader's return to Canada the previous summer—the two had never even met—but he was forced to go with them. The Cut Knife party, however, was soon abandoned at the east end of the Eagle Hills, just south of Battleford, when the Métis agents learned of the fall of Batoche and Riel's subsequent surrender. It now fell to Poundmaker, the diplomat, to reach a settlement with Canadian authorities and, on the morning of 26 May, exactly two months after the Duck Lake skirmish, he proudly led his people into Battleford.

The surrender of Cree Chief Poundmaker to General Middleton at Battleford, 26 May 1885

Middleton, fresh from his victory at Batoche and sitting imperiously in a chair before the seated Indians, was in no mood to be generous. After refusing to exchange greetings with Poundmaker—because he did not shake hands with rebels—the general accused the Indians of being "on the warpath since the troubles began." Poundmaker replied that the Indians were only defending themselves when they were attacked at Cut Knife: "My people made war gently."[47] One of the other Cree leaders then asked that his mother be allowed to speak on behalf of the women and children. When Middleton curtly replied that women did not address war councils, Poundmaker wondered aloud why the Queen, the Great Mother, always presided at their supreme councils. This response brought an approving shout from the Indians and even sent a ripple of laughter through the officers and men when it was translated. The meeting ended with Poundmaker being taken into custody.

That left Big Bear, who had been busy adding to his list of supposed rebellion crimes. Less than two weeks after the brutal Frog Lake slayings, Wandering Spirit and his warriors moved against nearby Fort Pitt and its mounted police detachment. Had the Plains Cree been truly hostile and intent on waging war, they would have attacked the fort almost immediately and not given the police any time to try to fortify their position. That they waited several days confirmed that the murders were unpremeditated and that this new action was largely motivated by the need for food and provisions for their large camp. The mood among the occupants of the fort, however, was one of pending doom. And when the Indians failed to appear after the Frog Lake killings, an overwrought Inspector Francis Dickens, the son of the famous British novelist, sent out a three-person search party, including David Cowan, now a corporal, and Constable Lawrence Loasby, to determine their whereabouts. The scouts had been gone for only a few hours when a large Cree party rode over the hill overlooking the fort. Although Big Bear's influence was still in abeyance, he had accompanied the warriors to prevent further bloodshed and called on the mounted police to surrender the post on the understanding that they would be allowed to slip away. While Dickens weighed the police options, the local HBC factor, W. J. McLean, went to meet with the Indian leaders. But the parley was interrupted when the scouts who had been sent to find the Cree galloped through the Indian camp in a mad dash for the fort. Their sudden appearance caught the warriors completely by surprise and, fearing an attack, they instinctively fired on the men, killing Cowan and wounding Loasby. In one of his last letters to his mother in Ottawa, Cowan had complained that Pitt was a "dull place" and that he was thinking of leaving the force once his term of service was completed for a better-paying job.[48] It appears that he volunteered for scout duty out of a desire to do something. The death of Cowan served notice that the Cree were not to be provoked and forced an agreement upon the mounted police. That evening, 15 April, while Dickens and his men retreated in a scow down the ice-filled North Saskatchewan River, the rest of the occupants of the fort, mostly families with children, walked through the gate and into captivity. The Cree took whatever they could from Pitt and headed back to

A studio portrait of the triumphant General Frederick Middleton, complete with a beaded buckskin outfit, ice skates, and ironically, a Métis sash

SASKATOON PUBLIC LIBRARY, LOCAL HISTORY DEPARTMENT PH-91-156

The "North West 1885 Canada" medal for service during the rebellion

Frog Lake. Nothing more was done. They made no attempt to leave the area or prepare for an eventual Canadian response. As in the case of the Cut Knife camp, they waited peacefully to see how the rebellion would unfold.

The answer was soon forthcoming in the form of the Alberta Field Force. On 20 April 1885, the one-thousand-man column had left Calgary for the North Saskatchewan country, and despite encountering not a hint of resistance along the trail, marched into Edmonton like liberating heroes. Not until 26 May, however, did the force finally arrive in the Fort Pitt district, just in time to interrupt a thirst dance that the Cree were holding for spiritual guidance at the base of Frenchman Butte. The arrival of the troops threw the camp into turmoil, and under Wandering Spirit's guidance, the Cree moved a few miles north to a more defensible position along the valley of Red Deer Creek. Even though the Indians successfully stopped Strange's advance on the morning of 28 May—he called the battleground, Stand-off Coulee—they were thoroughly shaken by the intensity of the attack and fled north through the muskeg-riddled forest. They eventually reached Loon or Makwa Lake on 2 June. But any hope of safe haven was dashed when NWMP Inspector Sam Steele and an advance party of police and soldiers swooped down—guns blazing—on the unsuspecting

A somewhat repentant Prime Minister John A. Macdonald caught "between justice and mercy" in deciding the fate of Louis Riel

Indians and their prisoners as they forded the lake narrows. The firefight lasted little more than half an hour: five warriors, including Woods Cree leader Seekaskootch, were killed, while the McLean children narrowly escaped injury. But the Indians could not stop, and like hunted animals, they plunged into a still-frozen muskeg—what Kitty McLean called the "big swamp" in a desperate attempt to get away.[49] Days later, with any remaining Indian resistance gone, the camp broke into smaller groups and the last of the prisoners were released.

The flight of the Indians kept the Canadian troops busy for most of June. With the capture of Riel and surrender of Poundmaker, General Middleton was determined to apprehend Big Bear and bring the campaign to a successful conclusion, even if it meant tying up his troops for several weeks in a seemingly futile chase. He consequently took a large force from Prince Albert to Fort Pitt by steamer and then overland to Loon Lake, while dispatching three other columns north: NWMP Commissioner Irvine marched north from Prince Albert to Green Lake, Colonel Otter from Battleford to Loon Lake, and General Strange from Frog Lake to Cold Lake. But the largest manhunt in Canadian history came up empty-handed. As one of Otter's men noted in his diary on 12 June: "Tramped up hill and down hill but no BB [Big Bear]."[50] In the end, it was only because the fugitive Indians decided they could not wander the northern wilderness for much longer that they either turned themselves over to one of the military columns, wandered into the nearest community, or sought asylum in the United States. These defections meant that Big Bear—by then the most wanted man in the North-West—was effectively abandoned by the time he surrendered to a surprised HBC employee near Fort Carlton on 4 July. By that point, the old chief had been reduced to a shell of his former self, while his treaty rights movement lay in total ruin.

Edgar Dewdney began to deal with the fallout from the rebellion well before hostilities had officially come to an end. In a long, reflective letter to Prime Minister Macdonald in early June 1885, he maintained that the "break[ing] loose" of a few bands had turned "a Half-breed revolt of small magnitude into an uprising of large dimensions." According to the Indian commissioner, the country had come perilously close to "an Indian war from one end of the Territories to the other."[51] This assessment was totally unrealistic and dangerously misleading. There had been murders, but as Dewdney later suggested in his annual Indian Affairs report, most bands had used the rebellion unrest "to gain the necessities of life."[52] That certainly was the case at Green Lake when about thirty Woods Cree from the Island Lake and Waterhen bands arrived at the HBC post, a major transhipment depot, on 26 May. Clerk J. N. Sinclair offered food and ammunition, but the Indians, excited by the news from the Fort Pitt area, rushed into the store when he unlocked the door.

Throughout the incident, none of the Bay employees were harmed; they were allowed to depart safely that same day for Île-à-la-Crosse, leaving the Cree to help themselves to the holdings of the abandoned warehouses.[53]

A crisis, though, could not be wasted. And with the rebellion, the Canadian government had been handed an unprecedented opportunity to rid itself of troublesome Indian leaders and their nagging call for revision of the treaties. Though privately he knew better, Dewdney deliberately portrayed the Indians as reckless allies of Riel who would cause trouble in the future unless reined in.[54] Hayter Reed, his ambitious assistant, readily agreed and was ready to act. "One of the great faults of our [military] leaders," Reed told Dewdney in a letter from Fort Pitt, "is that they do not understand the Indian character, and do not know when he is defeated, and when to follow up an advantage."[55] Even the prime minister shared his official's reading of the situation. In an exchange with Governor General Lansdowne, he had referred to the uprising as a form of domestic trouble that did not deserve to be elevated to the rank of rebellion. The governor general bristled at the comment and chastised Macdonald: "We cannot now reduce it to the rank of a common riot. If the movement had been at once stamped out by the NWM Police the case would have been different, but we were within a breath of an Indian war." A somewhat unrepentant Sir John replied in his defence, "We have certainly made it assume large proportions in the public eye. This has been done however for our own purposes, and I think wisely done."[56]

While this covert campaign against the Indians took shape, a series of trials got underway in the territorial capital. The first and most famous—both then and now—was that of Louis Riel who appeared in a Regina courtroom on 20 July 1885 charged with high treason. Believing himself guided by the hand of God, Riel used his testimony, especially his closing remarks to the jury, to affirm the rights of the Métis people while castigating the federal government for its complete disregard of the region and its interests. But rebellion was not the way to achieve justice for his people or the West, and he was found guilty and sentenced to hang. Despite a jury recommendation for mercy, several appeals, and continuing doubts about his mental fitness, Riel was hanged at Regina on 16 November—coincidentally, nine days after the driving of the last spike of the CPR in Craigellachie, British Columbia. His body lies today in the cathedral cemetery in St. Boniface, Manitoba, after being secretly moved there a few days after his execution.[57]

Much has been written about the fairness of Riel's trial and whether justice was served. It has been suggested, for example, that the charge was invalid, the trial venue inappropriate, the judge not qualified, and the jury biased. But cases of this nature could quite legitimately be held in the territories before a stipendiary magistrate and six-man jury.[58] The other complicating factor was Riel's mental state. Clearly, his messianic mission raised questions about his sanity. But Riel refused to support the defence of his own lawyers—that he was insane—fearing that his whole purpose would be compromised, if not undermined. Besides, according to the standards of the day (the McNaughton Rules), the Métis leader was considered legally sane because he knew the difference between right and wrong. Lieutenant-Governor Dewdney, for his part, believed that Riel deserved to hang because he was "a consumate vilain (sic)... too dangerous [to be] let loose on society."[59] One of the most persistent myths associated with Riel's death is that it marked the death of the federal Conservative Party in Quebec because it was the Macdonald government that allowed the sentence to proceed. But even though a protest party was elected in the province in 1886, the federal Tories continued to govern with significant Quebec support for another decade. It would take another western issue, the Manitoba Schools Question, and a Quebec francophone leader, Wilfrid Laurier, to swing Quebec to the Liberal Party.

The mass exodus of lawyers, journalists, and other interested parties from Regina following Riel's conviction did not mean that the court docket was empty. Twenty-six Métis soldiers had been rounded up in the weeks after the rebellion and charged with treason-felony. At their trials, conducted in Cree at their request, they were portrayed as a poor, ignorant lot who were not responsible for their actions. Father Alexis André, who had verbally wrangled with Riel, for example, declared that, except for a few hard-nosed disciples who had fled the country, "not one of the other half-breeds had the least idea or suspicion that there was any probability or danger of rebellion."[60] HBC manager Lawrence Clarke also made a lengthy, emotional appeal on behalf of the group, in which he argued that the prisoners did not understand the nature of the charge against them. "We are not dealing with cultivated intellect," Clarke observed. "We are dealing with wild men of the territories."[61] Judge Hugh Richardson sentenced eleven men to seven years, while the remainder were given much shorter prison terms or simply discharged. This "led away by evil counsels" defense,[62] as the Crown called it, was part of the Canadian government strategy of blaming Riel—and Riel alone—for causing the rebellion, while diverting attention from the Macdonald government's mishandling of western affairs. The Métis, under this scenario, did not have legitimate grievances. No mention was made, for example, of the fact that it was not until January 1885 that the government signalled its intention to finally investigate land claims.[63]

Ottawa reserved its most severe punishment for the Indians; eighty-one were prosecuted for rebellion-related crimes. This high number—more than three times the number of Métis defendants—would appear to support the contention that the Indians were willing accomplices of Riel. But the Macdonald government wanted to use the court to cow the Indian population. That is why four chiefs—One Arrow, Poundmaker, Big Bear, and Whitecap—were brought to trial. Convicting them of treason and sending them to their death, however, was going too far and would likely serve to poison government-Indian relations for years, if not decades. The desired effect could be achieved just as effectively through a treason-felony conviction and a prison sentence. It would send a clear message that chiefs would be personally held responsible for the actions of their followers and would be removed from their bands. Indians who had committed murder and other alleged crimes were not to be treated so leniently. The image of a wild, lawless West was one of the last things that the Canada government needed as it struggled to attract settlers to the region in the 1880s, and Macdonald sought to undo the damage by demonstrating that those who

SASKATOON PUBLIC LIBRARY, LOCAL HISTORY ROOM LH–4852

Sioux Chief Whitecap was the only Indian leader to be acquitted at trial.

had committed murder would be punished accordingly.[64]

The first major Indian trial was that of One Arrow, the Willow Cree chief who had been forced to go to Batoche, along with several of his men, after the declaration of Riel's provisional government. The elderly chief found the proceedings thoroughly confusing, even more so when the treason-felony indictment was translated as "knocking off the Queen's bonnet and stabbing her in the behind with the sword." There was no Cree equivalent for words such as conspiracy, traitor, or rebellion. "Are you drunk?" a perplexed One Arrow reportedly asked the court interpreter.[65] Not one prosecution witness was able to say that the Willow Cree leader had actually fired a shot or was even directing his band at Duck Lake and Batoche. It did not matter though. One Arrow's mere presence in the rebel camp made him guilty of breaching his treaty "allegiance to the Government, the country, and the Queen."[66] He was found guilty and sentenced to three years in the Manitoba penitentiary. So too

561

were chiefs Poundmaker and Big Bear, even though their trials demonstrated that they had done everything possible to restrain their followers and avoid bloodshed. Only Whitecap was acquitted, because he had a white witness who testified that the Dakota Sioux chief had been abducted by the Métis and that the citizens of Saskatoon were helpless to stop it. All three convicted chiefs would be released early from jail, but would be dead in less than a year.[67]

Some of the Regina Indian trials were a farce. On 16 September, nine members of Big Bear's band were tried for treason-felony. It was not the first time that the court had dealt with more than one defendant, but because of the difficulty in pronouncing the Cree names, the men were each assigned a number. In the resulting chaos, the lawyers and witnesses were never sure if they were talking about the same person.[68] In the end, all nine were sentenced to two years. An almost identical scene took place the next day and, despite the confusion, all five defendants were found guilty. No allowance was made for the fact that the Canadian system of determining guilt and assigning punishment was completely foreign to the Indians. Ottawa wanted prosecutions, and speedy ones at that. Why else would the federal minister of Justice, Alexander Campbell, tell his deputy that "the object of the Government" would be realized by "a certain number of convictions."[69] And why else would that deputy then recommend, before the Indian trials started, that Manitoba's Stony Mountain Penitentiary be enlarged to accommodate all the new prisoners.[70]

The Macdonald government had planned to hold all the rebellion trials in Regina. But once it weighed the costs of transporting all the prisoners and witnesses to the territorial capital, it decided that it would be more expedient to schedule the last set of hearings in Battleford, where some sixty Indians were in custody by early August. This change of venue made a mockery of the remaining trials. Still smarting from the so-called siege, Battleford residents expected—even demanded—the severest possible punishment.[71] And the person called upon to dispense this crude justice was Judge Rouleau, who had fled his home, fearing for his life, during the early days of the rebellion. The first prisoner, led in irons into his court on the morning of 22 September, was

GLENBOW ARCHIVES NA-363-79

The wife of Miserable Man at Battleford. Her husband was sentenced to death
for his role in the Frog Lake murders.

Wandering Spirit, who had taken over leadership of Big Bear's camp and been involved in the Frog Lake murders. He pleaded guilty once the indictment had been read and translated. The other murder trials were just as speedy, even when the defendants pleaded not guilty. There was no attempt to understand why or how the slayings had occurred: how in some circumstances, they were revenge killings to settle personal grudges. Rouleau's treatment of the other Indian prisoners, especially those from Big Bear's band, was equally ruthless. He seemed to believe that no punishment was too severe for the Cree. Ridiculously long sentences were doled out for stealing a horse or burning a building.[72] One can only wonder how Poundmaker, Big Bear, or One Arrow might have fared if all of the trials had been held at Battleford.

On the morning of 27 November 1885, just weeks after the last Indian trial, eight warriors went to their death on an immense wooden gallows erected inside the walls of Fort Battleford. Surprisingly, there are no known photographs of the scene, let alone the eight together: Wandering Spirit, Round the Sky, Bad Arrow, Miserable Man, Itka, Man Without Blood, Iron Body, and Little Bear. Dewdney wanted the hangings to be a spectacle—a contravention of the 1868 federal statute that ended public executions—and arranged for a large number of Indian families, mostly from the Moosomin, Thunderchild, and Sweetgrass reserves, to occupy the square in front of the gallows. Ottawa fully supported this handling of the condemned. One week before the largest mass hanging in post-confederation history, Prime Minister Macdonald mused in a confidential letter to Dewdney, "The executions ... ought to convince the Red Man that the White Man governs."[73] The bodies were buried in a common grave behind the fort at the base of a sandy ravine on the North Saskatchewan River. Over the years, because of erosion, some of the bones of the dead became exposed, and officials decided in late 1954 to cap the mass burial site with a concrete slab. Today, the site is marked by a marble headstone below teepee poles.

The Indian trials and executions were only the *public* part of a concerted campaign by the Indian Affairs department to crush any remaining vestiges of Indian autonomy in the aftermath of the rebellion. Indian Affairs officials were also quietly putting in place a number of repressive measures that went well beyond retribution for any Indian part, real or imagined, in the rebellion. Assistant Indian Commissioner Reed began by identifying twenty-eight bands as disloyal—not surprisingly, the bulk of them in the Carlton, Battleford, and Pitt agencies.[74] Curiously, he described Beardy's band as "all disloyal," even though the chief had not been arraigned on charges. Other bands were accused of disloyalty only because they had been reported "absent" during the fighting and therefore in violation of Dewdney's 6 May 1885 order that all Indians remain on their reserves. The arbitrary nature of Reed's list is best demonstrated by the designation of the Ahtahkakoop and Mistawasis bands as loyal even though they too were off-reserve during the troubles. But to suggest that the leading proponents of Treaty Six had been rebellious would have exposed the bankruptcy of Canadian Indian policy. Disloyal bands had annuities suspended for a few years, even though the withholding of such payments was a violation of the treaty agreement. But their punishment did not end there.[75] In order to assert its absolute control, the Indian Affairs department secretly adopted a series of measures for the future "management" of all Indians, disloyal or otherwise, including the requirement that Indians could not leave their reserve without first securing permission. That these actions against the Indians after the rebellion have been largely forgotten prompted one scholar to claim that "a great amnesia [has] descended on Canadians."[76]

The Canadian government was also determined to prosecute any whites who advocated rebellion. Indeed, federal Justice Minister Campbell told the prosecution team that this matter deserved its "special attention."[77] Finding white rebels proved difficult, though, and only two men from the Prince Albert area—William Jackson and Thomas Scott—were brought to trial. Jackson had played a leading role in the Prince Albert agitation, later serving as Riel's secretary at Batoche. But he had become unhinged during the rebellion, and with the agreement of both the prosecution and defence, he was found not guilty by reason of insanity. Jackson was committed to the Selkirk Lunatic Asylum in Manitoba, a stay that lasted only until 2 November when he quietly walked away from the facility and embarked on a new career in the United States as labour organizer Honoré Jaxon.[78]

The Crown's case against the other supposed white rebel, Thomas Scott from the Ridge, was also shaky. Scott had been nowhere near the fighting at Duck Lake or Batoche but rather held without charge by the NWMP in Prince Albert under deplorable conditions for over six weeks. It was the prosecution's contention that Scott had contributed to war through his dealings with Riel as representative of the English Métis community in March 1885. This line of argument offered little traction. A Prince Albert lawyer, asked to comment on the file before the case went to trial, suggested that Scott's only crime was "[speaking] in a tone somewhat louder than his fellows."[79] But the Crown ploughed ahead, intent on trying to prove that Scott shared some of the responsibility for the outbreak of the rebellion. Whereas Jackson's hearing was over in minutes, the Scott trial featured a procession of witnesses and heated legal sparring over two tumultuous days (the second-longest trial after that for Riel). Even though it was established that Scott had first promoted neutrality and then offered to raise a force to help put down the rebellion after the Duck Lake clash, Judge Richardson sent the matter to the jury. A not-guilty verdict, returned in thirty minutes, was greeted with cheers from the gallery.

In prosecuting Scott, the Macdonald government had unintentionally allowed its western policies to come under scrutiny, and his lawyer defended his client by taking repeated swipes at federal neglect and incompetence. Many westerners supported this line of questioning. Riel may have gone too far in defying government authority and declaring a provisional government, but there was sympathy for the Métis position. "It [the rising] is the growth of years," a newspaper correspondent reported from the region in April 1885. "The whole country sympathizes with the rebels."[80] Retired NWMP Major James Walsh certainly did, in spite of the mountie role in suppressing the rebellion and the losses sustained by the force. In an interview with the Toronto *Globe*, he asserted: "These people are not rebels, they are but demanding justice."[81] The Opposition also went on the offensive in the House of Commons. In reviewing the causes of the rebellion, Liberal leader Edward Blake placed the blame squarely on the Macdonald government and methodically went through a list of failed policies. Malcolm Cameron, meanwhile, provided a devastating critique of the Indian Affairs department, its officers, and its methods. He charged that a deliberate policy of neglect, dishonesty, and starvation had driven the Indians to fight alongside the Métis. An annoyed Macdonald countered that it was Riel who had roused the Indians and that they had no legitimate reason to revolt. In what had become a standard defence of federal policy, the prime minister laid the blame squarely on the Indians themselves by depicting the complainants as chronic whiners who would rather be fed at government expense than work. "The Indians will always grumble," he had once remarked in the House, as if it were some natural trait, "they will never profess to be satisfied." Sir John also denied that Ottawa had ignored its treaty commitments. "We have kept faith with them," he maintained adamantly, "and they have received large supplies ... if there is an error, it is in an excessive supply being furnished to the Indians."[82]

In shifting the focus away from its handling of western affairs, Ottawa made Indian peoples the scapegoat. The Canadian West had failed to attract the great number of immigrants that had enthusiastically been predicted only a decade-and-a-half earlier, and in laying the blame for this stalled development,

ADRIAN PATON

Members of the North-West Field Force washing their clothes

it was easy to target Indians. They were the ones standing in the way of progress and prosperity, resisting the transition to a settled way of life but choosing instead to complain at every opportunity. And now because of the rebellion, Indians were to be confined to their reserves and kept separate from the white settler population. This pass policy, as it came to be called, went against more than two centuries of Native-newcomer interaction. But it was a popular idea after the troubles of 1885 and was advocated by others who had experience in the region. Former Dominion Lands Surveyor and Superintendent of Mines William Pearce bluntly told the deputy minister of the Interior that Indians should have their horses and guns confiscated and be forced to remain on their reserves. Failing that, Pearce believed that all Indians should be rounded up and deposited on one large northern reserve.[83] Oblate priest Albert Lacombe also wanted to limit, if not completely prevent, Indian independence and movement. "Consider the Indians ... for many years as real minors," he observed, "they are not at liberty and under the tutelage of the Government."[84] It was assumed that Indians had actively and willingly participated in the uprising.

This forced isolation of Indian peoples could not have come at a worse time. Several bands had fled to the bush during the rebellion out of fear of being dragged into the conflict and remained hidden—and starving—for several weeks. In mid-June 1885, soldiers searching for Big Bear were shocked to come across the Beaver River band "stripped of everything, their clothes in tatters ... their tents worn and rotten."[85] Then there were those, such as Ahtahkakoop's people, who returned to their reserves only to find their homes looted and possessions stolen. The hardest hit were so-called rebel bands left to fend for themselves. "Their state ... would be impossible to exaggerate," a police inspector wrote his supervisor in mid-January 1886 about the disturbing situation he found on One Arrow. "They are miserable beyond description ... poorly clothed and huddled in their huts like sheep in a pen. ... Last summer they lived on gophers and this winter on rabbits. ... they can't go far because they have no clothes because of the severe weather." He also reported how a few old horse blankets had been welcomed like priceless gifts. This act of kindness elicited a stern reprimand from Indian Commissioner Dewdney, who wanted to limit provisions and supplies in order to assert government control. A. B. Perry, the commander of NWMP F Division, strongly took issue with this policy, suggesting that Indian Affairs should "treat them in a humane manner ... it now behooves us to shew them that we will not relentlessly pursue our advantage over them."[86] But that is exactly what Indian Affairs was determined to do in the aftermath of the rebellion, starting by effectively keeping Indians "quarantined" on their reserves and away from the white settler population.

This need to keep the races separate was not only being advocated by the federal government. When Theresa Gowanlock and Theresa Delaney were taken captive after the Frog Lake murders, it was widely speculated that a "fate worse than death" awaited them at the hands of their Indian captors and that they would have been better off perishing alongside their husbands. But when the Frog Lakes widows emerged from the bush north of Fort Pitt, they initially reported that they suffered no indignities. They had been protected by several Métis men, and the federal Indian department shouldered much of the blame for the troubles. Other white captives, especially the McLean sisters, said much the same thing. General Middleton was greatly relieved by "this good news" about the white women and mused that the incident "only shows what infamous lies are concocted in this North-West."[87] But in the published version of their experience, *Two Months in the Camp of Big Bear*, Gowanlock and Delaney described their days in captivity as one of constant fear and torment, of helplessly clinging to the precipice of barbarism. This depiction was deliberate. The contrived experiences of the two widows reinforced the need for artificial boundaries between white and Indian peoples in order to guarantee that the best features of British civilization would flourish on the Canadian plains.[88]

The emphasis on race—on whiteness—also applied to Métis peoples. Individual and community relations were irrevocably changed in the region as Aboriginal ancestry was now regarded as a liability: something to be hidden, if not purged. After all, it was the Métis who had taken up arms against the Crown and challenged the authority of the Canadian state. But it was more than a matter of mistrust. Mixed-descent people, regardless of their racial makeup, had neither place nor future in the new agricultural West. Even mixed relationships were now scorned; they threatened to destroy the honour of white men and the sanctity of the white family. That British civilization had triumphed was driven home by the North-West Field Force following its victory at Batoche in May 1885. It was not enough that the fighting had destroyed Métis homes and farms. Canadian revenge had to be complete. And in their search for souvenirs, soldiers took whatever they could. Lewis Ord's booty included a towel and some bars of soap. "[T]ook the opportunity of having a good bath in the Saskatchewan," Ord enthused, "and felt like civilized men once more."[89] It was as if he and his companions were washing away the old order.

Bison bones are loaded into a Canadian Pacific Railway boxcar.

CHAPTER SIXTEEN

A CONTINENT ON THE MOON

BISON HAD DISAPPEARED FROM THE NORTHERN PLAINS FOR LESS THAN A DECADE before a lucrative market developed for their dried bleached bones. There was no shortage of American buyers. The North-West Fertilizer Company of Chicago, Illinois, offered nineteen dollars per ton in the fall of 1888, a price that Janesville Carbon Chemical Works of Wisconsin gladly matched. John and Chester Dixon folded this business into their expanding wholesale and retail trade in the Maple Creek district. The brothers had turned every local opportunity to their advantage since their arrival at the end of the rail in April 1883, and supplying bison bones to fertilizer manufacturers was easy money. Skeletons littered the short-grass prairie north of the Cypress Hills. It was a simple matter of stockpiling the bones at sidings along the Canadian Pacific Railway—collected at ancient procurement sites near such places as Gull Lake, Colley, Crane Lake, Kincarth, and Forres—and loading them in boxcars that carried on average from ten to twelve tons. Dixon Brothers shipped sixteen boxcars of bones in 1889. They doubled that number the following year but only after asking the CPR for more cars.[1]

There was a certain irony to the business. The bones of the once great bison herds had fed people for generations and were now being cleared away for a new agricultural industry that was supposed to turn the western interior into Canada's breadbasket. But getting settlers on the land in the predicted numbers, let alone engaged in commercial farming, was not a success story by the 1880s. That naturally led to questions about whether all the federal attention and expenditure was worth it. Westerners, though, continued to believe that the region had great potential but was being prevented from realizing its destiny. The struggle for the North-West to assume its rightful place in confederation would eventually result in two provinces in the southern territories in 1905. But it was provincehood with a difference.

No sooner was the North-West Rebellion over than the Canadian government refocused its energies on developing and settling the region. Indeed, the swiftness of the trials and the severe punishment of those found guilty served to reaffirm the peaceful, orderly nature of the frontier for both immigrants and investors. But many Westerners had sustained damage to their property or lost income and business during the rebellion and needed emergency assistance—or the already anemic western economy might take a turn for the worse. The Department of the Interior consequently dispensed $132,000 in response to requests for help during the summer and fall of 1885. But so many claims continued to be submitted—some of them quite large or in need of supporting evidence—that in February 1886 the Macdonald government appointed a royal commission, headed by Montreal lawyer J. Alphonse Ouimet, to formally investigate and recommend what compensation should be paid. By the time the commission reported in July 1887, it had held sittings at Qu'Appelle, Prince Albert, Battleford, and Swift Current and considered 925 claims from whites, Métis, and Indians—almost two-thirds (577) from the Prince Albert district, the centre of the unrest. The total request for compensation was $1.2 million dollars, but only $483,000 (40 per cent) was approved, mostly for what the commission termed "unavoidable direct losses." A reading of the awards list suggests that loyalty carried financial benefit. Métis merchant Xavier Letendre, who had absented himself from Batoche during the troubles, for example, submitted a claim for $32,917 for damage to his stores and home and was granted almost $20,000. Chief Mistawasis applied for and received $210. Those applicants, on the other hand, who were considered "parties to their own losses," even if involuntarily drawn into the conflict, were rejected, while Thomas Scott of

SASKATCHEWAN ARCHIVES BOARD S-B9723

The North-West Half-Breed commission visits Duck Lake.

the Ridge had his request passed on to another department for consideration. Not surprisingly, one of the largest claims—in the amount of $165,137—was paid to the Hudson's Bay Company.[2] One case that the commission could not resolve, though, was that of Charles Bremner who maintained that General Middleton had robbed him of nearly $20,000 in furs as war booty. In 1890, a select committee of the House of Commons found the general's behaviour to be "unwarrantable and illegal" and ordered him to pay restitution.[3]

The Rebellion Losses commission was not the only federally appointed body collecting statements in the North-West in the latter half of the 1880s. For three years (1885, 1886, and 1887), the North-West Half-Breed commission travelled throughout the region adjudicating the claims of Métis residents for scrip. This process was more than a decade late. When Canada acquired the North-West Territories in 1870, it did nothing to recognize the Aboriginal title of mixed-descent peoples living west of Manitoba. Indian and Métis representatives raised the matter at both Treaty 4 and 6 negotiations. So too did Indian Commissioner Alexander Morris. "I think a census of the numbers of these [Métis] should be procured," he advised Ottawa in December 1876, "[and] suggest that land should be assigned to them."[4] But the parsimonious Mackenzie government could not be stirred to action, prompting many Métis to enter treaty for the security that it promised, especially at a time when bison numbers were in steep decline.[5]

The Métis continued to petition the federal and territorial governments for recognition of their Aboriginal land rights into the early 1880s. It was one of the grievances that led to the recall of Louis Riel from Montana in June 1884 in the belief that he could shake the John A. Macdonald government from its lethargy. And the Métis leader did get Ottawa's attention but only after adopting more aggressive tactics. As one scholar noted, the issuance of scrip was "initiated as a response to the *threat* of violence and was executed as an antidote to the actual outbreak of the North-West Rebellion."[6] In January 1885, a federal order-in-council approved the appointment of a three-person commission to enumerate—and enumerate only—the number of Métis eligible to participate in a future land grant policy. But by March and the Duck Lake skirmish, the Macdonald government hurriedly expanded the commission's mandate to include the issuance of scrip, beginning with its first scheduled sitting at Fort Qu'Appelle in early April. While the rebellion was still underway, then, Commissioners Street, Goulet, and Forget were busy questioning scrip applicants and issuing certificates—something that has generally been overlooked. The actual policy, though, was solely determined by Ottawa, including several subsequent amendments about how applicants were to be compensated. The Métis were never consulted at any stage. According to the regulations, the head of a family, living in the North-West Territories on or before 15 July 1870, was entitled to 160 acres in scrip or $160 to be used towards the purchase of land. The children of these family heads had the choice between a scrip coupon for 240 acres or $240.[7] By such means, Ottawa intended to extinguish Métis title to the land once and for all and remove a potential impediment to settlement. But unlike the treaties, which dealt with Indians collectively, Métis entitlement was handled on an individual basis.[8]

The North-West Half-Breed commission initially focused on the claims of those Métis living near the CPR main line (from Winnipeg to Calgary) and south of the North Saskatchewan River. It was only after the rebellion was over that it ventured north to Prince Albert (including Fort à la Corne and the Saskatchewan Forks), St. Laurent, Battleford, Fort Pitt, and Edmonton. In an effort to ensure that no one was missed, the commissioners could also deal "on the spot" with anyone they met on their travels between official sittings. Always lurking in the background were the representatives of banks, real estate firms, and other businesses, cash in hand, ready to buy scrip for usually half its face value. These speculators, travelling in step with the commission schedule, did a brisk business because the Métis were generally poor and in need of money or had doubts about the validity of the coupon. Fourteen Métis who lived along the Qu'Appelle River at Pheasant Creek and on the lakes, for example, opted for money scrip in 1885.[9] A land certificate also necessitated a trip to the nearest Dominion Lands office for processing, and it was often easier for the claimant to exchange the coupon for cash.

The commission visited most Western communities once, sometimes twice, but held three sittings in both Fort Qu'Appelle and Prince Albert because of the local Treaty 4 and 6 Indian populations. By the mid-1880s, federal Indian officials looked to reduce the cost of treaty obligations by culling the number of people on treaty pay lists. People of mixed-ancestry who had been accepted as Indians in the 1870s were consequently encouraged to withdraw from treaty—without having to refund their annuities—and apply for scrip before the commission.[10]

The repressive policies of the Indian department in the immediate post-rebellion period made such an identity "switch" attractive. In the end, of the estimated 3,248 Métis who qualified for scrip under the North-West Half-Breed Commission, it is quite likely that as many as eleven hundred were former treaty Indians.[11] The Canadian policy of separating western peoples into distinct categories was not so clear-cut after all.

During the commission's visit to St. Laurent, anyone known to be associated with the rebellion was disqualified from making a claim.[12] All other eligible Métis chose money over land scrip and the promise of a quick cash transaction with speculators. Their decision was a clear indication of how the South Branch communities were hurting in the aftermath of the rebellion, especially when crops failed in 1886 and debts could not be paid. The local clergy even suggested that a special reserve be created so that the Métis were not driven from their land by the widespread poverty. But the resiliency of the settlers prevailed. Letendre re-established his store at Batoche, as well as his extensive trade operations between Kinistino and Frog Lake. Other businesses thrived as well in the last years of the nineteenth century. Local farmers, meanwhile, made homestead entry for their holdings, especially after 1888 when four townships were re-surveyed into river lots. Although it took many of them more than a decade, well beyond the official "proving up" period, four of every five applicants secured patent to their land—putting to rest "the allegation that the Métis were unwilling and incapable farmers."[13] It was only when the railway bypassed Batoche that the district again fell on hard times.

The scrip commission accepted Métis claims at Cumberland House in 1885 but did not return to present-day northern Saskatchewan for another two years when it held sittings at Green Lake (in addition to traditional gathering places at Norway House, Grand Rapids, Moose Lake, The Pas, and Lac la Biche). That scrip was closely tied to western settlement was confirmed by the fact that no meeting was held at Île-à-la-Crosse, even though the Hudson's Bay Company's regional headquarters had been a Métis-dominated community for over a century. The northern half of the future province was still largely fur trade country, an economy reinforced by the booming American fur garment industry and the resultant sharp rise in fur prices. It also remained relatively isolated. While the HBC sought to modernize and streamline operations in the 1880s and 1890s, the English River district had the singular distinction of having the slowest inventory turnover rate. Most of its sales, moreover, were conducted by barter, not cash, and continued to rely on credit advances at a time when the company wanted to end the practice.[14] If anything, the distribution of scrip at

UNIVERSITY OF SASKATCHEWAN ARCHIVES AND SPECIAL COLLECTIONS 37633

The Angus McKay family at Green Lake

Green Lake in 1887 challenged this world and its distinctive culture. Whereas the people of the northwest were linked together by family, community, language, and livelihood, scrip began the process of putting up boundaries by emphasizing the differences, not the commonalities, between Indian, Métis, and white.[15]

The dividing of northern Aboriginal peoples into treaty and non-treaty continued in 1889 when two Woodland Cree bands signed an adhesion to Treaty 6. These Indians had been asking for treaty for a decade because of the depletion of fur and game resources; they believed that annuities and other treaty benefits enjoyed by their Cree neighbours to the south would help them deal with the scarcity and hardship. But not even a special appeal from a local missionary in 1887 that the Indians had been "loyal during the rebellion" secured any government sympathy. Ottawa did not want the extra expense of new treaties, especially when it considered its existing commitments a

579

PRINCE ALBERT HISTORICAL SOCIETY F-49

Loading logs at Camp 4, Prince Albert Lumber Company

financial headache. But then it was realized that the federal Department of the Interior was issuing permits to cut lumber in areas north of Prince Albert that had never been ceded through treaty. To avoid "complications," in the words of the Indian department, over access to the lucrative timber resources of the region, arrangements were immediately made to extend the boundary of Treaty 6 northward by having the affected Indians sign an adhesion during the winter trapping season.[16]

It was a bitterly cold day in February 1889 when the Montreal Lake and Lac la Ronge bands met with Crown representatives on the northeast shore of Montreal Lake (known today as Molanosa [*Montreal Lake Northern Saskatchewan*]). After greeting the commissioners with a ceremonial rifle salute, the Indians spent the first day listening to translator and Anglican archdeacon, J. A. Mackay, explain the treaty. Ottawa expected the Cree to simply accept the same terms agreed upon in 1876. But Chiefs William Charles and James Roberts questioned the need for some of the agricultural items, preferring more ammunition and twine instead, as well as insisted on annuity arrears going back to the date of the original treaty. The commissioners agreed to make the necessary adjustments to the provisions list to better reflect Indian needs in a boreal landscape, and the chiefs and their headman signed the treaty adhesion— but were not paid past annuities.[17] It was the Cree understanding, though, that they were giving access only to the "dry" land and not the waterways and that they would be able to continue to pursue their traditional practices without interference.[18] With the adhesion approved, one of the commissioners then dealt with any claims for Métis scrip. It was the first time in western treaty history that the issuance of scrip was handled at the same time, and it would become a feature of future agreements.[19]

The signing of the Treaty 6 adhesion was followed two years later by the arrival of the Qu'Appelle, Long Lake, and Saskatchewan Railway in Prince Albert. The timing, albeit coincidental, could not have been better for the frontier town. In 1888, homestead entries had dropped to just eight, while local businesses cut back on their merchandise by a third. Only the construction of government buildings kept the economy afloat.[20] The long-awaited rail link lifted the community out of its economic doldrums and invigorated the region's fledgling resource-based economy. The HBC was one of the first to take advantage of the rail connection. In 1891, instead of using Cumberland House and the Churchill River system to supply posts in northern Saskatchewan, the company shipped the district's annual outfit from railhead at Prince Albert along an overland trail to the south end of Montreal Lake and a new large depot there. This north-south cart road and the winter freighting it facilitated reoriented the regional transportation network. It also, less fortunately, displaced Indian and Métis peoples who worked seasonally on the northern waterways. And it made it easier for competitors to take on the HBC on its home ground. In 1901, Revillon Frères, a Paris-based fur company, opened a district office in Prince Albert and soon established a number of rival posts throughout the north, including one at Île-à-la-Crosse.

Fishing received an immediate boost from the coming of the railway. By 1893 so many fishermen were vying for the whitefish, trout, pickerel, and pike of the northern lakes that the federal Fisheries department took steps to limit by permit the number of fishermen and ensure that regulations were being observed. Ottawa was concerned that the northern lakes could not support a commercial fishery, as well as continue to meet the subsistence needs of the local treaty Indian population. But even though a fishing license allowed for one gill-net on one water body for a fixed season (December to March), a third of a million pounds of fish were being pulled from the large lakes in or near present-day Prince Albert National Park by the end of the century. Starting at dawn each day, the fishermen would haul in their nets and immediately gut their catch, and then pack the fish frozen in small knock-down wooden crates that would be freighted by sleigh to Prince Albert for shipment by train to American markets.[21] The nets would then be re-set under the ice for the next night's catch.

Lumbering also experienced phenomenal growth during these years. Situated on the southern edge of the boreal forest, with its virtually untouched stands of white spruce that measured three feet in diameter and one hundred feet in height, Prince Albert lumber companies harvested the nearby stands with brutal efficiency. They would sweep into an area, cut the best trees, and then move on without thought about the possible long-term environmental consequences. They also altered waterways—clearing along riverbanks and building dams—to help float the logs downriver in the spring. The 3.6 million board feet (1"x1'x1') cut by Prince Albert mills in 1900 increased an incredible four times over the next four years to fifteen million board feet or 16 per cent of western Canadian production. The two major players were the locally owned Saskatchewan Lumber Company (later the Big River Lumber Company) and the American-controlled Prince Albert Lumber Company. Between them, they leased the majority of the federal timber berths and were constantly pushing the cutting frontier steadily northward in a battle for supremacy.[22] This booming lumber business, together with the northern fishery and the HBC provisions trade, turned the crude Prince Albert–Montreal Lake trail into a major winter freight route that rivalled the traffic on the northern rivers during the heyday of the fur trade.[23]

No group was probably more pleased by the coming of the railway than Prince Albert district farmers. The line provided a much-needed outlet for agricultural products—up to then limited to the local market—and

UNIVERSITY OF SASKATCHEWAN ARCHIVES AND SPECIAL COLLECTIONS FC.3204.2 C21P76

Canadian government advertising portrayed western Canada as a veritable agricultural Eden.

rekindled some of the earlier expectations for the "fertile belt" along the North Saskatchewan River. The Lorne Agricultural Society marked the turning point by publishing a twenty-page pamphlet, plainly titled, "Prince Albert and the North Saskatchewan," that maintained that "no country under the sun offers greater natural advantages" for mixed farming.[24] This boosterism fed on the widespread belief that there were millions of acres of land *north* of the North Saskatchewan whose idle richness was just waiting to be exploited. In June 1887, for example, a Senate select committee investigation into the natural food products of the North-West determined that crop yields were greater near the northern limit of successful growth. The Senate went through a similar exercise the following year when it examined the commercial and agricultural resources of Canada's "Great Reserve" north of the Saskatchewan watershed, west of Hudson Bay and east of the Rocky Mountains. Traders, missionaries, scientists, and politicians who had either lived in or visited the region were

UNIVERSITY OF SASKATCHEWAN ARCHIVES AND SPECIAL COLLECTIONS C555/2/14.17

Settlers brought new sporting activities to the North-West. This curling rink is in Moosomin.

called upon to give evidence, while a fifty-question survey was sent to 150 respondents. The image that emerged from the Senate hearings was one of a super land that would one day be the home of super men and women. But in tabling the committee's final report, Conservative Senator John Christian Schultz reluctantly admitted that agricultural colonization of the region would have to wait until the southern prairies were settled.[25] That was certainly the case around Prince Albert. By 1904, even with the railroad, none of the land on the northern side of the river had been surveyed for homesteading.[26]

Agricultural settlement along the Canadian Pacific Railway through present-day southern Saskatchewan was highly anticipated once the line had been completed across the prairies in 1883, and the first passenger train made the transcontinental run from Montreal to the Pacific Coast in June 1886. The CPR also built a grain terminal at Port Arthur at the head of Lake Superior in 1884 to handle the expected wheat shipments from the Prairies. With the infrastructure now in place, the government's promotion machine went into high gear. "Nature has done her share, and done it well and generously," the Department of Agriculture trumpeted, "man's labour and industry are alone required to turn these broad rolling prairies to good account."[27] What was different from past efforts, though, was the championing of the open plains. Once condemned as too arid and sterile, the treeless prairie was now presented as ready for the plough. There was no need for time-consuming, backbreaking clearing: just break the land, seed, and watch the crop grow. It was all so simple, seemingly effortless, especially when the rains came at the right time of year—late spring and early summer—for the growing crop. And the crop that was best suited for these conditions was hard spring wheat. It was not only easy to grow in volume and hence financially rewarding for the farmer but also a staple on the world markets and always in demand.[28]

Dominion Lands regulations also allowed for the development of larger wheat farms. Because alternate sections in every township were set aside for railway grants, homesteaders could enlarge their original quarter-section holding by acquiring neighbouring acreages. Homesteaders could also take out a "pre-emption" on an adjacent quarter-section at the time of entry and pay a fixed price for this land after receiving patent for their original homestead. Or they could even apply for a second homestead.[29] American farmers, by contrast, did not have the same opportunity for expansion.

People did follow the rail line west. The laying of steel from Winnipeg to Calgary in 1882–83 sparked a town-building frenzy, especially in southeastern Saskatchewan. Places like Moosomin, Whitewood, Broadview, Sintaluta, and Indian Head appeared on the map, seemingly overnight. Because of the scarcity of lumber, wood had to be scavenged from nearby valleys and coulees and gave the early towns and villages a crude appearance. A mounted policemen suggested they were "more depressing ... than a burnt forest."[30] But they provided all the services that settlers would need. That demand was expected to be great because of the land rush that accompanied the railway. The year 1883 was notable for the large number of homestead entries along both sides of the main line. Many found their way to their new homes by following the old trails, which soon fell victim to the plough.[31] But before farmers could get established, the Canadian economy went into recession and languished for the better part of the next decade. Homestead applications stalled. In fact, there were fewer applications for homesteads for Manitoba and the North-West Territories in 1884 (3,333) than there had been in 1879 (3,470) and that was *after* the construction of the main line across the prairies. The price of wheat slipped as well, falling from 1883 to 1887, rallying in 1891, and then continuing its slide to 1895.[32] These dismal statistics led to the conclusion that the expansionist dream was just "a fictitious Garden of Eden" and that the difficulties of opening and developing the region had been glossed over by overzealous rhetoric. "We have annexed a continent on the moon," bemoaned the Toronto *Week*.[33]

Ottawa was reluctant to spend more money on the region, especially given the depressed conditions. It consequently tried first to end land speculation. In 1881, in order to accelerate western settlement, the Canadian government sold colonization companies large parcels of land north of the CPR line on the understanding that they would get a purchase rebate for every bona fide settler placed on their tract within five years. There was no shortage of interest—from religious and philanthropic organizations to business and real estate interests. But of the 260 applications, only 106 were accepted, and of these, only 27 secured land, including the York Farmers' Colonization Company and the Temperance Colonization Company (the forerunners of Yorkton and Saskatoon, respectively). Ottawa had wanted to sell ten million acres, in part, to help recoup the cost of the CPR twenty-five-million-dollar cash subsidy. But the colonization companies only paid the first instalment on 1.4 million acres and then had trouble finding settlers. By 1886, with sponsored settlement a failure, the contracts began to be cancelled and the land returned to the

SASKATCHEWAN ARCHIVES BOARD R-B574

A threshing unit during harvest

Crown. That was the same year that the Macdonald government ended the pre-emption privilege (later extended to 1890). Dominion officials evidently believed that the problem was the shortage of available free homestead land and too much speculation.[34]

Those who had settled the land, though, had a much different perspective on the pioneer experience. In the summer of 1884, Baroness Angela Burdett-Coutts, patron of the London Colonization Aid Society, helped send nineteen families—ninety-nine people in total—from the slums of East London's East End to Moosomin, North-West Territories. There, they would leave behind their former working class life for a new one as sturdy, independent farmers. But the families found that even if they worked cooperatively to build homes and plant crops, their success was limited by the challenges of farming in a semi-arid environment and their lack of agricultural experience. Within a decade, most had left to ply their trades in urban centres.[35] The experience in the Abernethy district, north of the Qu'Appelle River on the Pheasant Plains,

A Métis family in the Willow Bunch district

was comparable. By the fall of 1886, settlers had experienced three successive crop failures. Things seemed so bleak that there were no homestead entries in the district for 1887; cancellations mushroomed instead. These poor returns were partly attributable to marginal land. The Dominion Lands Act may have assumed that all the land was of equal value—hence the standard 160-acre homestead allotment—but stony, scrubby, and/or marshy sections were not suited for wheat cultivation. The other, more significant, factor was the colder, drier climate. Drought was a regular occurrence. The summer growing season was also short and Red Fife red wheat (requiring a growing season of more than 120 days) usually did not mature before the first frost. Abernethy farmer Samuel Chipperfield harvested a trifling two bushels per acre in 1886; only one neighbour reaped a crop in the double digits, and that was just ten bushels per acre. Crops were little better over the next two years. In 1888, W. R. Motherwell, a future Saskatchewan minister of Agriculture, sowed sixty-five acres in wheat and took off three hundred bushels, which was about five bushels per acre.[36] As one historian has aptly observed, "the agricultural potential and limitations of the physical environment were not yet understood." Until that time, homesteaders "groped toward a viable agricultural technology" based on their experience from season to season.[37]

To help struggling and future settlers come to terms with farming the semi-arid plains environment, the federal government established an experimental farm at Indian Head, in present-day southeastern Saskatchewan, in 1886. It was one of five regional centres (the others being Agassiz, British Columbia; Brandon, Manitoba; Ottawa, Ontario; and Nappan, Nova Scotia).[38] Angus Mackay, who had settled in the district in 1882, was named the first superintendent. It was a fortuitous hiring because he brought his practical experience to the position. Mackay had learned—by accident in 1885 because of the rebellion—that his land produced better crops if rested for a year. This summer fallowing technique became standard advice for farmers well into the twentieth century. Mackay also sought to limit the damage caused by drying winds by embarking on an ambitious tree-planting program to demonstrate the value of windbreaks or shelterbelts.[39] This work was just underway, though, when severe winds in the spring of 1889 destroyed most of the farm's planting; even the seeds in the vegetable garden were blown out of the soil. The lessons learned at Indian Head, especially the prohibition against continuous cropping, were adopted by local farmers. But agricultural success in the early years also depended largely on individual circumstances: time of arrival, choice of land, available capital, previous farming experience, and ability to adjust. Motherwell, whose home today is a national historic site, sold livestock and other farm produce to the local market when harvests failed, while experimenting to ensure the quality and size of his wheat crop when growing conditions were ideal.[40] Those, on the other hand, who struggled to farm a small parcel of marginal land often became "the attrition between entry and patent ... ominous gaps in the [homestead] registers."[41]

One of the chronic complaints of early homesteaders was the lack of rail service. If they were going to become commercial farmers, then they required ready access to grain handling and shipping facilities. But by the closing decades of the nineteenth century, most pioneer farms were at least a day's travel from a railway delivery point. Those living in the Abernethy district, for example, had to haul their crop thirty miles—one way![42] Freight rates at the time only worsened the pioneer struggle. Once construction was complete, the CPR had to devise a way to cover its operational expenses. It was not easily done because some sections of the line ran through regions (northern Ontario and the Rocky Mountains) where there was little traffic or difficult road conditions and other regions (southern Ontario and Quebec) where there was stiff competition from cheaper water transport. Nor could the national railway expect federal subsidies, even though Ottawa had insisted that the main line follow an "unnatural" route north of the Great Lakes. To survive, then, let alone make a modest profit during its early years, the CPR took advantage of its western monopoly and set dizzying rates that put many farms in jeopardy. The 1883 prairie schedule charged 30.6 cents to carry a bushel of wheat from Moose Jaw to Thunder Bay. That was almost half the sale price of a bushel of wheat at the time. Frost-damaged wheat fetched much less—about forty cents per bushel. Outraged farmers demanded a competitive line. But even though the CPR monopoly clause was rescinded in 1888, no American railway was prepared to move into western Canada because of the limited opportunities. At the same time, the idea of using the old Hudson Bay trade route to reach European markets never amounted to more than talk. Freight rates remained high until the negotiation of the Crow's Nest Pass agreement in 1897, while not a mile of new track was laid in western Canada in the early 1890s because of another recession.[43] Perhaps there is some truth to the story that when it hailed, farmers would shake their fist defiantly at the heavens and shout, "Goddamn the CPR."

Settlement along the CPR mainline became increasingly sparse west of Moose Jaw. Farmers deliberately avoided the dry southwest, especially the uplands, where the soils were thin, the precipitation scanty, the growing season shorter, and the isolation more pronounced. It was not until the early twentieth century, when there was a seemingly insatiable demand for homestead land, that quarter-sections were marked out—and cattle operations displaced. Ranching in the region began as a response to the need to feed the Indians and supply the North-West Mounted Police. In the mid-1870s, the I.G. Baker Company of Fort Benton, Montana, used its dominant position at the head of the regional trade and transportation network to secure Canadian government contracts to provide beef and other provisions. The business proved so lucrative—one-third of total police expenditures—that Baker devolved its ranching operations to the new Benton and St. Louis Cattle Company, known in Canada as the Circle Outfit because of its brand. The company, in turn, supplied some of the first stock to local ranchers, including former mounties who had left the force and Métis families who had to replace the bison hunt.[44] Other Métis, like Alexandre "Catchou" McGillis, Antoine Gosselin, and Harry Hourie, began adding cattle to their already established horse ranches in the Willow Bunch and Big Muddy valleys.[45] These were small operations, largely based in the high country around Wood Mountain and the Cypress Hills. It was a perfect pastoral setting, with grass, water, and shelter for the herds. But the distance to markets limited stock-raising to local demand.

The CPR, together with an amendment to the Dominion Lands Act, changed the ranching dynamic in the southwest. The coming of the railway now provided access to international markets—a boon for Canadian producers, since Great Britain had banned the import of live cattle from the United States in 1879 because of concerns about disease. Determined to take advantage of this preferred status in the British beef market, Ottawa abandoned any pretense of settling the short-grass prairie district and introduced new grazing regulations in December 1881, coincidentally just months after the rerouting of the transcontinental railway across the southern prairies. For the ridiculously low sum of one cent per acre per year, prospective ranchers could lease up to one hundred thousand acres for a twenty-one year period, provided they had one head of cattle on every ten acres within three years. These closed leases (homesteading was not permitted on the land) initiated a beef bonanza in the southwest, or what might more appropriately be called, a "Big Man's Frontier."[46]

Most of the British and Canadian investment in the western range went to present-day southern Alberta, where in a few short years, ten large companies controlled two-thirds of all stocked land. Southwestern Saskatchewan, by contrast, was passed over at first, except for the adventuresome: among them, French-Canadian Pascal Bonneau, a Regina storekeeper who was attracted to the promise of the open range. It was not until after the rebellion that large lease holdings were set aside in the region. The first in the Wood Mountain area—one hundred thousand acres—was obtained in 1885 by Samuel Chapleau, the new sheriff of Regina and brother of the federal minister of Justice in the Macdonald cabinet. The following year, because the Montana range was overstocked and overgrazed, the American-owned Home Land and Cattle Company, secured a lease near the NWMP post at Wood Mountain and started the N Bar N Ranch (N–N) with six thousand cattle. The only British-controlled operation in the area—the Canadian Agricultural, Coal, and Colonization Company—was that of Englishman Sir John Lister-Kaye who in 1887 bought up land at ten sites along the CPR main line west of Moose Jaw (including Rush Lake, Swift Current, Gull Lake, Crane Lake, and Kincorth), as well as purchased existing cattle operations, to create the 76 Ranch.[47]

All of these companies, including many of the smaller outfits in the region, benefitted from practices brought north by American range managers and cowhands. It was not just cattle that were driven across the border into Canada. Barbed wire fences, corrals, and chutes were adopted, one ranching historian has argued, "because they worked and because they could be constructed cheaply and efficiently."[48] But American experience could not tame the weather, and in 1886–87, one of the worst winters blanketed the western range in deep, hard-packed snow with disastrous consequences for newly stocked leases. The "big die-up," as it was known locally, killed tens of thousands of cattle—at least two-thirds of the N Bar N herd—and chased the big American ranchers out of Canada for a brief period. Those who ran smaller operations and better able to help their wintering herds were not as hard hit.[49]

By the early 1890s, as soon as they had rebuilt their stock, American

Cattle roundup camp in the Cypress Hills

ranchers were back in Canada. This time, though, they did not bother with federal leases. Their herds were simply allowed to roam at will, grazing back and forth across the line as if it did not exist. In 1896, thousands of American cattle were found north of the border, including herds belonging to the Bloom Cattle Company, based in Malta, Montana, along the east end of the Cypress Hills. It fell to the NWMP to drive them back to protect Canadian ranchers and the feed they put up for their own animals. But the task was never-ending. Nor was the problem ever resolved. American cowboys would go through the motions of rounding up stray cattle in the fall, "but as soon as the vicinity of the line is reached," the police reported, "those fit for shipment are carefully picked out and the balance are let go when they promptly return to their accustomed haunts on our side."[50] In frustration, it was suggested the boundary be fenced.

The mounted police did a better job putting an end to cross-border Indian horse stealing. It was quite an accomplishment given the porous boundary—what author Wallace Stegner likened to "a hair in butter."[51] Although the first

The Moose Jaw baseball team, winner of the 1895 territorial championship

contingent had symbolically marched west along the international border in 1874, the police thereafter leaned on American help. When Edgar Dewdney assumed his new duties as Indian Commissioner in 1879, for example, he travelled with eighty-three new troopers by rail to Bismarck, Dakota Territory, and then by steamboat up to the Missouri River to Fort Benton.[52] All of the NWMP posts strung along the forty-ninth parallel, meanwhile, were supplied by United States traders. Even the outgoing mail was carried south and required American stamps. This flow of people and supplies between countries was threatened when the Lakota Sioux sought refuge at Wood Mountain after the Battle of the Little Big Horn. But what could have resulted in an ugly international incident never materialized because of the sensitive handling of the matter by NWMP Major James Walsh—and the desire of the refugee Sioux to avoid trouble on Canadian soil.

By the end of the 1870s and the disappearance of the bison from the northern plains, Canadian authorities wanted to limit Indian movement, especially to the United States. In the past, Cree and Assiniboine bands regularly crossed the border in their search for food without too much notice or comment. "Cold as H. Killed chicken. A party of Indians passed nearly frozen," wrote one policeman nonchalantly about his encounter with a party of Cree headed south one winter.[53] American settlers and ranchers, however, started to complain about foreign Indians in their backyard, especially Big Bear, whose reputation as a troublesome Indian made his band unwelcome. There was also the potential for a cross-border tribal war. One of the few remaining ways for warriors to secure prestige and honour was to steal horses from American enemies, and it was feared that these raiding expeditions might provoke a violent counter-response. The NWMP consequently decided to bring an end to this activity and the "wild ways" it represented. Those caught horse-stealing or bringing stolen property into Canada were arrested, convicted, and sentenced to time in Stony Mountain Penitentiary. And with the cooperation of American authorities, a concerted effort was made to locate and return the stolen horses. This crackdown had the desired effect and by the mid-1880s cross-border horse raiding was no longer considered a serious problem.[54]

What greatly aided mounted police monitoring of the international boundary was a 175-mile trail running east-west from Wood Mountain post to Fort Walsh in the Cypress Hills.[55] Troops would conduct weekly patrols in summer, while smaller detachments would be stationed at outposts along the route during the winter. In fact, the centrality of the trail to police operations in the southwest did not diminish after Walsh was closed and police headquarters relocated to the new territorial capital at Regina in 1882. NWMP Commissioner Lawrence Herchmer was stung by criticism about the force's performance during the rebellion and implemented a network of interconnected patrols throughout the western interior to reinforce the police presence, especially in the border region. To facilitate communication with Regina's depot division, a telegraph line (known as "Pole Trail") was run between Wood Mountain post and Moose Jaw. Wood Mountain also served as a customs agency and collected duty on items entering Canada. It was impossible, though, for the mounties to be everywhere at once, despite the legendary reputation of the force. Local Métis were consequently hired as police auxiliaries in addition to their more traditional duties as guides, translators, and intermediaries. In the spring of 1885, for example, trader Jean-Louis Légaré assembled a group of Métis scouts from Willow Bunch to help patrol the boundary during the rebellion. This work assumed greater importance with the introduction of Herchmer's patrol network the following year. Métis and Lakota men, who had their own small ranch operations, also worked around Wood Mountain post, helped build and maintain the telegraph line, and herded stray cattle back across the border. Their equestrian skills were put to the test when police and local residents came together to celebrate Dominion Day in 1890 to compete in horse racing and other events. Today, the Wood Mountain Stampede is one of the oldest annual rodeos in Canada. The renowned NWMP Musical Ride may also have originated here. "B" troop, which first performed the ride in Regina over the winter of 1886–87, may have perfected the drills during their summer posting at Wood Mountain.[56]

The mounted police patrol system was part of an overarching strategy to end Indian autonomy and coerce the Cree to embrace a new, government-directed way of life in the post-1885 world. Traditions and practices were to be stamped out in the interests of forced assimilation and civilization. Patrols might not appear to be related to other, more commonly known, policies—such as residential schools or the ban on religious ceremonies—but they were nonetheless essential to maintaining a watchful eye on Indian peoples and their whereabouts. There was a real fear that the hundreds of Cree and Assiniboine who had fled to northern Montana after the rebellion were organizing war parties to strike back at Canada. But these rumours proved groundless, and the refugee Indians spent the next decade trying to secure asylum in the United States while evading deportation.[57]

Police patrols also sought to remove the potential for trouble by keeping Indian peoples separate and apart from white settlers so that agricultural

ADRIAN PATON

Andrew Littlechief of the White Bear band holding a red ensign flag

development of the region could proceed in an orderly and timely fashion, something that the Canadian government desperately desired. This hardening of police-Indian relations did not mean, though, that the force became simple enforcers of state policy after the rebellion. Although the new pass system was intended by the Indian Affairs department to control, if not stop, off-reserve movement, the mounted police regularly questioned its legality and were reluctant to wield it, especially when they claimed they were upholding "a rational system of laws that operated to the benefit of all."[58] At the same time, it is shortsighted to claim that the peaceful transformation of the region— in comparison to the wild and wooly American frontier—was largely the consequence of the "benevolent despotism" of the mounted police.[59] Indians chose to co-operate with the newcomers—in this case, the police—and without their acquiescence, the history of the settlement of the North-West might have been written in blood.

Indian Affairs officials also wanted to use the courts to "criminalize" Indian behaviour and help bring them under department control. And it is understandable how Indian peoples might run afoul of the law. Before 1870, the HBC generally accepted Indian concepts of justice, especially their ways for resolving internal disputes. Then, a new legal regime was unilaterally imposed on the region with fundamentally different rules on what constituted a crime and how it should be punished. The Indian Affairs department confidently assumed that the new criminal court would quickly bring Indian defendants to heel. But as a new study has suggested, Indians themselves used the courts to secure justice and occasionally succeeded. Nor did the courts always do the government's bidding and their rulings and sentences sometimes frustrated officials.[60] What would have better served Ottawa's purposes was a separate judicial system for Indian defendants. Failing that, Indians often appeared in court for violating the Indian Act—not necessarily as criminals—and were prosecuted for "not conforming to the new forms of relations and behaviour required ... by the legislation."[61] Julia Coté and Alex Bone discovered this sorry truth when they ran away from the Indian Industrial School in Regina in September 1894 and were subsequently charged with stealing Indian department property: ironically, the school clothes they were wearing at the time of their escape. Held in custody for over three weeks, Coté was discharged when the case went to trail, while Bone pleaded guilty and was taken back by the school.[62]

SASAKTCHEWAN ARCHIVES BOARD R-A5129

The federal Indian department offices in Regina

A much harsher fate awaited Almighty Voice when he openly defied the heavy hand of the Indian Affairs bureaucracy and then resisted police attempts to bring him to justice. By the mid-1890s, the One Arrow band, considered disloyal for its apparent part in the rebellion, was leaderless and dependent on rations for its survival. Almighty Voice killed a stray cow to feed his family in October 1895 and was arrested and held in the Duck Lake jail for taking government property. But the Willow Cree man escaped from custody and later shot a mounted policeman who had pursued him east to the Kinistino district. For the next eighteen months, Almighty Voice was Canada's most wanted fugitive. But he managed to elude capture because of help from band members. He was finally sighted in May 1897 east of the reserve in the Minichinas Hills, where he holed up in a poplar bluff rather than surrender. An ill-considered attempt to overrun his hiding place resulted in two more mountie deaths and the call for a nine-pound cannon to be hurriedly shipped north by rail from Regina. While band members watched from a nearby hill the next day, the mounted police shelled Almighty Voice's position. The tragic

599

A Cree woman and her child at Maple Creek

incident was uncommon for the time. Few Indians committed serious crimes; the only other similar case was that of Charcoal, a Blood Indian who had also murdered a mounted policeman and was hanged in 1897.[63] But one newspaper questioned why it did not happen more often. "A.V. was the champion of a race that is up against it in civilization," commented the *Toronto Evening Telegram*. "The wonder is that not an occasional brave cuts loose, but that all the braves do not prefer the sudden death to the slow extinction of their race."[64]

The reach of the Indian Affairs department even extended to marriage. But here, government officials were assisted by middle-class reformers and politicians in their quest to end what they perceived as "primitive" and "dangerous" Indian customs, especially polygamy. For them, the ideal nineteenth-century marriage was monogamous and heterosexual. That was the foundation upon which the new West was to be built: a civilized society informed by Christian doctrine, the Anglo-Saxon race, and British institutions. Indian practices that allowed for multiple spouses and divorce, by contrast, were identified with promiscuity and deviance and had to be eradicated. Indian authorities sought to impose monogamous marriage by withholding rations or removing "illegitimate" children from treaty pay lists. The department also established a showcase colony in the File Hills in 1901 where young couples were united in arranged marriages and kept separate from the undermining influences of "older Indians." This need for boundaries also applied to interracial unions and Indian-settler relations. Even though mixed-race relationships continued to be the norm in fur trade country or the southwest where several mounties found partners among the Lakota or Métis, they were increasingly denounced as inconsistent with the Anglo-Canadian ideal for the region. Those whites who married Indian women were derided as "squaw men," a label that challenged their respectability. Meanwhile, Indian peoples, because of the threat they posed, were to be deliberately isolated from white settlements. There was a popular belief at the time that Indian men were licentious, women little better than prostitutes. In reporting on the "squaw nuisance" in April 1887, for example, the Regina *Leader* suggested that if Indian women were to be allowed off-reserve, then they should be prohibited from the community after dark.[65]

That western society was to be British in sentiment and character became more pronounced after the rebellion. Prince Albert, for example, turned its back on its Métis beginnings and became an Anglo-Canadian stronghold, a process the city historian aptly termed, "discarding the old ways."[66] This new outlook found expression in a flourishing choral society that performed the latest Gilbert and Sullivan musical, such as "Iolanthe," in the town's magnificent opera house.[67] Not to be outdone, Captain Burton Dean of the NWMP built a stage in the quartermaster's warehouse at the Regina barracks and cast officers and their wives in public productions. Regina might have had "its cow dung and vacant vistas," but the "plays kept ... new elites in frontier Prairie towns in touch with the culture of the English metropolis."[68] Similiar cultural events were held at the Battleford barracks, where the mounties often gathered around an old piano—with the buffers repaired from an old felt hat—for an evening of song.[69] The North-West Territories Council also passed legislation in 1890 to encourage the creation of mechanics' institutes. First developed in Scotland and then England, these bodies housed technical libraries and hosted lectures. One of the first institutes to be established in present-day Saskatchewan was at Grenfell in 1892, where sixty-seven inaugural members paid an annual fee of one dollar.[70] Britishness also found expression in architecture. At the Battleford police barracks, even though construction had to adjust to local conditions and available building materials, the elaborate Victorian style of the buildings went hand-in-hand with the kind of society that would be the foundation of the region.[71] Successful farmers in the southeast embraced this vision. Their first crude log dwellings were replaced by substantial stone, brick, and frame houses that included separate rooms for different activities—a feature of middle-class Victorian homes in England and Ontario.[72]

This Anglo-Canadian emphasis also led territorial politicians to try to do away with French language and separate school guarantees. French had been employed in territorial government business as early as 1874 when the

LIBRARY AND ARCHIVES CANADA PA118754

The North-West Mounted Police Regina barracks

NWT Council published a consolidation of its ordinances in both French and English. But it was not given official recognition in the 1875 North-West Territories Act. Nor did the Alexander Mackenzie government plan to include French language rights in the 1877 modifications to the act until francophone Marc-Amable Girard, a former Conservative premier of Manitoba, introduced an amendment during the third reading of the bill in the Senate that called for the use of either French or English in territorial debates, council publications, and territorial courts. This last-minute amendment passed without division, but not before Interior Minister David Mills sarcastically observed that since "almost everyone in that part of the country spoke Cree ... [it] should be chosen for that purpose."[73] Separate schools, by contrast, were part of the 1875 NWT Act. The religious minority in any district (Catholic or Protestant) could establish a separate school and support it through self-assessment. This system was formalized by the territorial council in 1884 through the establishment of a board of education with distinct Roman Catholic and Protestant sections responsible for the supervision of their own schools. An unusual feature of the ordinance was that the public school in a school district could be either Catholic or Protestant, depending on the religious majority, and that the separate school was formed by the minority.

These aspects of territorial life had generated little controversy—hardly any comment—up until 1885. But any toleration quickly evaporated after the rebellion as the Anglo-Canadian majority moved to affirm the British character of the North-West. The general mood was that separate schools and the use of French had been foisted on the region by Ottawa and were not representative of the wishes and interests of the dominant society. There was also a widespread belief that French Canadians had failed the country because of their sympathetic support of the Métis traitor Riel, while Roman Catholics could not be trusted because they owed their allegiance to Rome and the pope.[74] The territorial government in Regina was expected to set things right. "One nation, one language" should be the territorial motto, urged the Qu'Appelle *Vidette* in 1888, and the surest way to promote a unity of purpose and a true national identity

"I STAND FOR JUSTICE; ANSWER, SHALL I HAVE IT?"

THE N. W. T:—I M GOING TO BE REPRESENTED HERE LIKE MY SISTER PROVINCES, OR KNOW THE REASON WHY!

Westerners regularly complained about the delay in securing federal representation in the House of Commons.

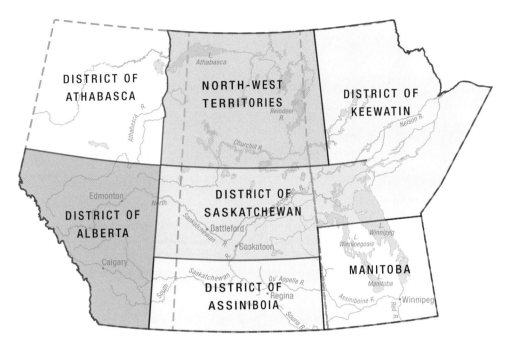

North-West Territories provisional districts

was to abolish the use of French in the government, the courts, and schools. Legislators responded in 1889 by preparing two petitions to Parliament, one calling for the repeal of French as an official territorial language and the other for the repeal of separate schools. During the debate over the resolutions, the vocal majority questioned the legitimacy of official bilingualism and separate schools, repeatedly pointing out that local opinion had never been taken into consideration. Those few brave enough to oppose the measures countered that French had been a distinctive feature of the North-West since fur trade days.

Nothing was done at the federal level, though, because politicians in Ottawa were already grappling with the thorny Manitoba schools question and did not want more controversy. The simmering issues were simply dropped back in the lap of the territorial government, effectively leaving it up to Regina to take action. That it did in early 1892, when the territorial government passed resolutions abolishing the official use of French and discontinuing the religious control of schools in favour of a single government-run Council of Public Instruction.[75] But the region's future as an Anglo-Canadian stronghold was already in doubt. According to the 1891 census, the non-British population of the territories already stood at 6 per cent—because of Scandinavian, Austro-Hungarian, French, German, Danish, Romanian, Icelandic, and Jewish immigrants—and would reach one in five by the decade's end.[76]

What the language and school controversy demonstrated to westerners was that the Regina government lacked political independence in keeping with the British parliamentary system. In fact, it had reached the point by the late 1880s, in the words of a Qu'Appelle merchant, where the region was "not prepared to accept dictation from Ottawa."[77] There had been several steps towards responsible government since the 1877 North-West Territories Act. But westerners objected to the glacial pace and the fact that Ottawa had to be repeatedly prodded. What was granted, moreover, seemed purposely designed to delay more meaningful reform. In 1880, when the first electoral district (Lorne) was created, other more populous parts of the territories in the southeast were added to the province of Manitoba. Then, in 1882, the federal government created four provisional districts (Assiniboia, Saskatchewan, Alberta, and Athabasca) in the southern territories for administrative (primarily postal) purposes. These districts became neither separate jurisdictions nor provinces, even though "provisional" implied that they were temporary. And when, after repeated delays and excuses, the territories finally secured parliamentary representation in 1886—coincidentally after the rebellion—it was given a magnanimous four seats in the 215-seat House of Commons and two Senate members. There were also more elected members on the territorial council—fourteen in 1885—but the lieutenant-governor still administered the federal appropriation.[78] It was not the kind of rule that Canadian expansionists had promised. "The North-West ... will be satisfied," the *Regina Journal* declared, "with nothing short of an administration responsible to the people in the fullest sense of the word."[79]

A new relationship between the territories and Ottawa seemed to be in the offing when Thomas White became the first minister of the Interior to tour the North-West in the fall of 1885. His visit was greeted by official delegations

SASKATCHEWAN ARCHIVES BOARD R-A7744(1)

The territorial government offices in Regina

wherever he went, all with their shopping lists. The Prince Albert petition recommended the conversion of the provisional districts into provinces with control over public lands and resources. It also called for the northward extension of the district of Saskatchewan to Hudson Bay and the naming of Prince Albert as capital of the new province.[80] White's speeches tried to lift the gloom left by the rebellion, but the jaundiced Prince Albert *Times* warned that the minister "did all a government official could do without committing himself."[81] It was another three years—punctuated by wrangling between council members, the lieutenant-governor, and the federal government—before the North-West Territories Act was amended in 1888 to create a legislative assembly of twenty-two elected members. Even then, it was a half-measure. There was to be no executive government drawn from the assembly and no assembly control of the annual federal grant. In justifying the minor amendments in the House of Commons, Prime Minister Macdonald explained that demands for responsible government did not "represent the feelings of the people" and that any further changes should be left to the new assembly "to ascertain what their own ideas are on the subject."[82]

Taking the prime minister at his word, the new North-West assembly continued the push for constitutional reform. It was a long, at times bitter, struggle because of federal intransigence. When the matter came up during a debate in the Senate in 1890, J. J. C. Abbott, the elderly Conservative leader in the red chamber, summarily dismissed the proposal as premature, given the sparse population, and then suggested that a name change—to the Western Territories of Canada—was necessary to create a more positive image of the region.[83] This kind of insensitivity exasperated Frederick Haultain, the Ontario-born Fort Macleod lawyer who had entered territorial politics in 1887 and quickly emerged as the leader in the assembly. "We [have] been dealt with like a parcel of political children," he railed against the denial of responsible government in 1888.[84] Thereafter, Haultain took up the cause with a singleness of purpose. A confidential assessment for the federal government concluded that he could be "rather inclined to pigheadedness."[85] But Haultain knew from experience that persistence, not accommodation, was needed in the struggle. That was readily apparent in 1894 in response to the latest Ottawa roadblock when he had to carefully but firmly explain to the minister of the Interior how it *was* possible for the territories to be granted responsible government without being given provincial status at the same time.

What brought the campaign to a successful conclusion was the election of the Wilfrid Laurier Liberals in 1896. Sir Wilfrid enjoyed a special attachment to the region. Elected to the House of Commons in 1874 and named leader of the opposition in 1887, Laurier had embarked on a campaign-style western tour in 1894 in order to raise his national profile. Two years later in the election that made him Canada's first French Catholic prime minister, he won in Quebec East and Saskatchewan (Prince Albert) at a time when it was possible to run in more than one riding at the same time. Although Laurier decided to represent the Quebec seat, his determination to settle the prairies and thereby complete one of the last great tasks of confederation had made him one of the West's favourite sons. Now, at Moosomin in December 1896, a representative of the new government signalled that "the swaddling clothes plan of treating

Frederick Haultain, the territories first and only premier, during a candid moment

the North-West had come to an end."[86]

When self-government took effect 1 October 1897, Frederick Haultain had the distinction of being appointed the territories' first and only premier. It might never have happened: he had entered territorial politics in 1887 only because the first elected representative for the Macleod district had resigned the seat after two years. Now, as head of the territorial government, he found that having control over government spending did not mean much if the legislature did not have much to spend. It was not a new problem. One of the persistent complaints of the territorial council and then assembly was that Parliament never voted sufficient funds for territorial needs. This revenue shortfall was particularly acute in the early 1890s when a recession forced Ottawa to slash its spending. Because of "the general cutting down" in the annual appropriation, Haultain bemoaned, the territories "were practically ground down to an amount that was not sufficient for bare necessities."[87] Responsible government would only make the situation worse because the territories were not financially equipped to handle the new demands, especially since any revenue from North-West lands and resources went to the federal treasury. Haultain was attuned to this shortcoming when the Laurier Liberals introduced the legislation for responsible government and chose not to include an annual federal subsidy. Even before territorial self-government was realized, then, he was already thinking of the next move: provincial autonomy. "[We] will go in for full provincial establishment in order to get financial recognition," he told the assembly.[88]

This financial necessity became more acute with the immigration and settlement boom of the late 1890s. The great agricultural promise of the region was finally being realized—albeit, almost three decades late—and the territorial government simply did not have enough money to meet the growing service and infrastructure demands. "We are confronted with impossible conditions," Haultain informed Clifford Sifton, the federal minister of the Interior.[89] There appeared to be only one solution. In May 1900, the territorial government submitted a memorial to the Laurier government, reviewing the constitutional evolution of the region and calling for the next logical step of drafting the terms for provincehood. A conference was subsequently arranged between territorial and federal representatives the following fall in Ottawa. It did not go well for Haultain. The Cabinet executive argued that provincehood was premature, an assessment repeated by Sifton in March 1902 in response to yet another Haultain letter on the matter. Undeterred, the territorial government re-submitted the request for provincehood, again with the unanimous support of the assembly, in April 1903. Prime Minister Laurier replied that the territories should be satisfied with the increased number of seats they were being given in the House of Commons through redistribution. By this point, Haultain had lost any remaining patience and, in a fiery letter in June 1903, insisted that negotiations be entered upon immediately to bring the territories into confederation as a province.[90]

One of the stumbling blocks to finding common ground was Premier Haultain's demand for one large western province between Manitoba and British Columbia. Haultain first voiced this vision in November 1896 when the question of future provinces was raised in the territorial assembly. "A dream of one large province holding its own in confederation, the most powerful province in confederation" he rhapsodized, "would be a much more desirable thing ... than a number of small areas confined in their powers and their influence."[91] It was a dream of the region as a whole, in its entirety: the physical expression of a territorial identity. It also perfectly fit with the concept of the North-West as a Britannic empire. Haultain likely adopted this one-province idea because of his position at the centre of territorial administration in Regina.[92] The legislative building on Dewdney Avenue was certainly modest and the local civil service relatively small, but the territorial capital was also headquarters for the NWMP and the Indian office. He may also have been influenced by the spectacular territorial exhibition a year earlier. During the first week of August 1895, Regina transformed the bald prairie west of town into a world showcase of the best of North-West agriculture, with an exhaustive slate of competitive and demonstration events vying for nearly twenty thousand dollars in prizes. If the exhibition seemed a North-West version of the World's Columbian Exposition in Chicago in 1893, Haultain might have been the reason. He visited the fair on territorial business and might have convinced Lieutenant-Governor Charles MacIntosh, who was always looking for ways to uplift North-West society, to take on the extravaganza as his own project. There was also a connection between exhibition publicity and Haultain's one-province vision. The exhibition theme, "It is a Good All-Round Country," nicely matched the premier's later statements that he wanted a province "with unlimited resources ... able to do things no province in Canada has ever been able to do."[93]

Haultain had put his vision to the public when he debated Manitoba Premier Rodmond Roblin at Indian Head on a cold December night in 1901. One thousand spectators witnessed the five-hour heavyweight match. Roblin tried to land repeated blows about the benefits of Assiniboia joining Manitoba, while a resolute Haultain intoned, "Let us stand together ... let us face the future together."[94] The audience awarded the bout to Haultain, but he was already facing a rearguard action from within the assembly. In 1898, Dr. T. A. Patrick of Yorkton had challenged Haultain's "craze for things big" and argued that the southern territories should be divided into two roughly equal provinces between the international boundary and the sixtieth parallel. What prompted Patrick to break ranks was his worry that any new province that reached "to the north pole" would always be vulnerable to some part being envied, if not annexed, by Manitoba. He also reasoned that it was in the interests of Canadian confederation not to have "one big preponderating province" and that the number of future western provinces was really a national government decision.[95]

The other challenge to Haultain's vision came from R. B. Bennett from Alberta. A successful corporate lawyer and future Conservative prime minister, Bennett spoke for the interests of Calgary and its ambitions as capital of a future province. But instead of putting Alberta first during an assembly debate in 1902, Bennett echoed Patrick's sentiments and declared that Haultain's one-province plan "would make it impossible for the provinces to work together in harmony." Pointing for special effect at the table used by the fathers of Confederation at the Quebec Conference in 1864, the same table that now served as the house table of the legislative assembly, he took Haultain's Indian Head plea and turned it on its head: "Let us not be influenced by considerations of a great overwhelming, overshadowing province. Let us be national in our aspirations and not sectional

Indian Commissioner A. E. Forget with Indian chiefs at the 1895 Regina Territorial Exhibition

in our ambitions."[96] These were noble words but behind them was the belief that the provisional districts should be provincial material.

This internal disagreement over the number of provinces hurt Haultain's bargaining strength. Then, the premier further weakened his position by actively campaigning on behalf of the federal Conservative Party in the 1904 general election. It was a serious lapse in judgement—one that crippled his future political career.[97] From his first days in territorial government, Haultain's strategy for securing concessions from the federal government was to adopt a non-partisan approach. Although a Conservative in spirit, he believed that the region could deal most effectively with Ottawa and at the same time avoid alienating the federal party in power if it spoke with a single, territorial voice. But he had become so disillusioned with the Liberal government's intransigence that he cozied up to federal Conservative leader Robert Borden, who not only promised provincehood for the West but local control of lands and resources.

These actions turned the autonomy question into a party issue—ironically, something that went against Haultain's own philosophy of putting territorial interests before political considerations. But the territorial premier was so blindly focused on achieving provincehood that he failed to see the political repercussions of his partisan actions.[98]

By January 1905, the prime minister could no longer hold off autonomy because of the unparalleled success of federal immigration policy and invited Haultain to Ottawa to discuss the entry of the region into confederation. The territorial leader outlined his vision of a single province with full constitutional powers. But the federal government had other plans and was confident of western support, especially given the strong Liberal showing in the November 1904 general election (seven of the nine territorial seats in the House of Commons were held by Liberals). On 21 February 1905, Prime Minister Laurier personally introduced two autonomy bills. That was probably Haultain's first clue that his worst fears were about to be realized. There was to be not one, but two roughly equal, north-south provinces, Saskatchewan and Alberta. The legislation also gave the federal government continued control over western lands and resources. Even more controversial, though, were the educational clauses, which seemed to call for the restoration of separate school privileges dating back to 1875.

The tabling of the autonomy bills precipitated the longest debate in Canadian parliamentary history. It was so acrimonious that the date of entry for the new provinces had to pushed back two months—to 1 September 1905— because the legislation did not receive royal assent until after the original entry date had passed. The source of the furore were the educational clauses. In the draft bills, the ambiguous phrase, "existing system," suggested that Laurier wanted to revive the old territorial dual school system and thereby secure legislative protection for Catholic minority rights. Members of the House on both the government and opposition benches reacted angrily to this seemingly blatant attempt to turn back the clock on educational matters when the largely Protestant population of the territories had been moving to secular education and public schools. Faced with a spiralling crisis—including the abrupt

Prime Minister Laurier (bottom right, greeting twins) personally introduced the legislation creating the new provinces of Saskatchewan and Alberta.

resignation of his Interior minister Clifford Sifton—that threatened to tear apart the administration and arouse latent Ontario–Quebec animosities, Laurier unceremoniously backed down and allowed a re-drafting of the offending clauses to bring them in line with current practice in the territories.[99]

The heated controversy over the educational clauses deflected attention away from the fact that Saskatchewan and Alberta were not to become full partners in Confederation. They, along with neighbouring Manitoba, were treated differently, unequally. Under the terms of the 1867 British North America Act, provinces exercised control over the public lands and resources within their boundaries. But that right was denied Manitoba in 1870, and it was denied Saskatchewan and Alberta in the autonomy bills. Clifford Sifton justified federal retention of western lands on the grounds that they were needed to promote immigration and settlement and that provincial control "would be ruinous ... disastrous" to this national endeavour. "Do not yield," he admonished Laurier.[100] The prime minister, for his part, took a different

615

tack in defending his government's policy. "Those lands were bought by the Dominion government," he reminded the House of Commons about the HBC deal in 1870, "and they have remained ever since the property of the Dominion government and have been administered by the Dominion government."[101] Ottawa attempted to make up for the loss of revenue by awarding the new provinces generous subsidies based on population. Haultain, however, wanted no part of the compensation package—it was "a matter of expediency"—and demanded the same right as other provinces in Canada.[102] He would be gamely supported by the *Calgary Herald*, which decried federal control of lands and resources as "Autonomy that Insults the West."[103]

Once the autonomy bills became law, the Liberal Party turned its attention to consolidating its position in the West and displacing Haultain, who naively expected that the premiership of Saskatchewan was his for the taking. This behind-the-scenes manoeuvring was hardball politics at its worst, especially given the territorial premier's defining role in the struggle for provincehood. Haultain was, in effect, a father of confederation, much like Métis leader Louis Riel in Manitoba. But his spirited opposition to the legislation—even though he was defending the interests of western Canada—had made him the enemy of the Liberal Party. Prime Minister Laurier, who was extremely wary of his political adversary, gladly shunted Haultain to the sidelines when he threatened to challenge the constitutionality of the autonomy terms in the courts.[104] A. E. Forget, a lifelong Liberal who had first come West in 1876 as clerk for the North-West Territories Council, was retained as lieutenant-governor, while Walter Scott, a Liberal backbencher in the House of Commons and owner of several western newspapers, was asked to become premier. That Haultain's fall from power and influence was so complete and so precipitous was clear when he was not asked to speak at the Regina inauguration ceremonies. Perhaps the most telling comment on his fate was an editorial cartoon that featured the former territorial premier up against a wall before a Liberal firing squad. Haultain, a smoker and drinker, should have at least been offered a last cigarette and toasted with his favourite whisky.

THE SASKATCHEWAN MUSKETEERS

LAURIEYAY
FORGHAYE
SCOTTAYE } "If our old friend, Riel, could
have seen us yesterday."

WINNIPEG TRIBUNE, 14 DECEMBER 1905.

The Saskatchewan Musketeers (from bottom right: Liberals Walter Scott, A. E. Forget, and Wilfrid Laurier) execute Frederick Haultain—and with him, his dream of a large western province and serving as the new province's first premier.

Breaking the prairie sod

A GOOD THING AHEAD OF US

"HAD A SLOW TRIP OWING TO SO MUCH TRAFFIC."[1] PERCE TURNER OF BEALTON IN southwestern Ontario had expected to be in Winnipeg sooner. But it had taken six days by railway from Toronto in mid-March 1906. He might have made better time if his train had not crashed into the rear of another one, sending the engine and several cars off the track. As it was, Perce was lucky. None of the "settlers' effects" he was bringing West in a freight car were damaged: four horses, one cow, one pig, sixteen chickens, and a dog. By 23 March 1906, Perce was in Regina, making plans to go north to Saskatoon and then out the Goose Lake Trail with other Ontario men he had met along the way. He had selected a homestead in the Eagle Hills (just north of present-day Herschel) at a place named Glenallen (township 32, range 16, west of the 3rd). Lillian, Perce's twenty-two-year-old wife, followed almost a month later. "I have not heard anything but N.W. since I boarded the train," she wrote her mother from northwestern Ontario. "Nearly everyone is going there." Perce was waiting at the Saskatoon station when Lillian arrived on 13 April 1906. They were fortunate to get a room for the night—"the hotels are so full"—and left as soon as they could on the three-day trip to their homestead. Along the trail, their wagon got stuck in a deep mud hole. Perce unloaded as much as he could to lighten the load and then yelled at the horses to draw. "What did Frank do," Lillian recounted in frustration, "but lay down." They were eventually rescued by two men who hitched their oxen up to the stranded wagon and easily pulled it out. That was their only mishap before reaching their new home, a 16' by 18', one-room, wooden shanty, flying a flag. Perce had a sense of the moment.

Perce and Lillian Turner were two of the tens of thousands of settlers who made Saskatchewan the fastest-growing province in Canada. A mere six years after entering confederation in 1905, Saskatchewan's population had almost doubled to 492,432. It was larger than Alberta in population, even larger than Manitoba, which had a thirty-five-year advantage over the upstart Saskatchewan. And the province's population was expected to continue to grow exponentially. More settlers applied for homesteads in western Canada in the first decade of the twentieth century than during the entire previous century. In fact, for the years 1906 to 1911, three of every five homestead entries in the three prairie provinces were in Saskatchewan. That's why the Turners encountered so many people heading West in the spring of 1906, providing more traffic than the Canadian Pacific Railway could handle and creating delays in getting to the land of promise. But the story of Perce and Lillian is more than one homesteading couple's experience. What they saw and what they thought—what Lillian in particular wrote about in her letters during their first year on the land—provides insight into the Saskatchewan of the time.

The Turner homestead was in the Eagle Hills, part of the Missouri Coteau plateau running from the Battle River near the Battlefords southeast to present-day Highway 14 between Purdue and Wilkie. A "roller coaster" landscape, often described as hummocky or undulating, it does not look anything like the Saskatchewan of the national imagination today. Great vistas alternate with deep, at times heavily wooded, ravines. The hills have been known for generations by a Cree name, *mikisiw waciy* (eagle hills), in recognition of the eagles that nested in the area. They were a popular camping place for the Blackfoot, Gros Ventres, Assiniboine, and Cree who spent several months each year, hunting and trapping in the area, especially during the winter.

Newcomers followed in the eighteenth century. Anthony Henday (1754) and Matthew Cocking (1772), both Hudson's Bay Company servants, travelled through the uplands with their Indian escorts as part of their investigations

LASHBURN CENTENNIAL MUSEUM

The Gully Post Office

to determine how and where the interior trade was being siphoned away by Montreal-based competitors. Part of the answer was Fort Montagne d'Aigle, also known as the Eagle Hills Fort, along the northern edge of the hills. By the nineteenth century, Indians and Métis groups increasingly turned to the plentiful resources of the hills as the great bison herds slid towards near extinction. Black Powder, the father of Cree chief Big Bear, often pitched his skin lodge in the area. In the 1870s, three Assiniboine (Grizzly Bear's Head, Lean Man, and Mosquito) and one Cree (Red Pheasant) bands were deposited on reserves in the northwest part of the hills so that they would not interfere with agricultural settlement to the south. The rolling, timbered landscape suited traditional pursuits like hunting and gathering, but it proved poor farmland at a time when the federal government expected Indians to begin to raise crops to feed themselves.

Perce and Lillian were probably not aware of this history. Nor should they have been expected to know it. They had come West to start a new life, and for them and thousands of other settlers, the past was irrelevant. It was the future that mattered. Even though the bison herds had been gone for only a quarter-century, there is no mention in any of Lillian's letters of coming across the remnants of bison pounds or even finding bison bones in the area. Nor does she give any indication that other people might have been there before she and Perce took out their homestead. That the land had never been broken suggested that it had never been occupied. It was empty, waiting for homesteaders like them.

When an Indian did make an appearance there—only once in a one-year period—there was near-panic. In early June 1906, Perce went to Battleford, leaving Lillian alone for several days. Within hours, an Indian on a pony arrived at her doorstep with a note that he was looking for some stray horses. "You can imagine how I felt," she wrote her mother, "one often reads of them and sees them pictured ... my best safety was in bravery." Lillian pointed towards the lake where they drew their water, thinking that the horses might be there but became "more frightened all the time" as the Indian looked around the homestead. He finally rode off and found the horses a short time later hidden behind some hills. "I had the shotgun close at hand," she recounted, "and I think I would have used it if it had been necessary." It was not an idle boast. Lillian had waged war with gophers in the garden and mice in her house, as well as stood guard over her laying chickens from marauding hawks. An Indian was another pest, in Lillian's mind, best confined to his reserve.

One thing that Lillian could not escape was the isolation. In her first letter from the Glenallen homestead to her folks on 29 April, she reported that their milk cow was not doing well. "If we did not keep her tied, she should run away," she half-jokingly remarked. "I think she is lonesome." Lillian was little better off. "I suppose you are wanting to know what I think of the country here," she added. "I would not want to have to always live here." It was not a surprising admission. Like other newcomers before her, Lillian found it hard being cut off from the outside world, or at least the world she had known and missed. Perce had to retrieve their mail from the nearest post office, at first travelling as far east as Harris. Lillian looked forward to the letters from her mother and was disappointed when they were delayed reaching her. "News is so long getting here," she complained. And she would hurriedly dash off

SASKATCHEWAN ARCHIVES BOARD R-B1754

The Saskatoon train station

a note if she learned that someone was going to town and could take her letters. She devoured the newspapers sent from her former home, especially the *Star Weekly*, and deliberately set aside time to read them. For Lillian, it was important to maintain the connection to her former life, tenuous though it might be, believing that it would help her deal with what lay ahead. One can understand her upset, when after two weeks on the homestead, "we forgot to wind the clock last night so we have no time."

Lillian quickly came to believe, though, that the future would arrive sooner than expected. "I like it here better the longer I stay, and I haven't been homesick yet," she confessed by early July. "Lonesome sometimes, of course, but I am sure there is a good thing ahead of us." She was even more confident

ADRIAN PATON

Evelyn and Walton McNeile represented the new Saskatchewan.

a few days later in a letter home: "Everything is prospering and going ahead out here as it should." What helped lift her spirits was the taking of the census in mid-June. "The census man [George Huntley] ... said he was told he would find twenty families back here and it would take him about two days, but he had been here for a week and still there were people as far as he could see," Lillian beamed. "There is quite a settlement of us all right." The "us" were people from Ontario and "not foreigners like so many" she had encountered during her first days in the West. "We have very nice neighbours," Lillian assured her mother. "They seem to be well educated and intelligent. As soon as it is possible, they will put up nice buildings and we will have a nice country." It was still a man's world, though. "There are about six men here to one woman," she noted. "Some of them would like to get married all right but they never see a woman." But things were looking up. Lillian met a "young fellow [whose] wife is coming out in a couple of weeks. They are just a half mile from us, so you see it won't be long until I will have a woman within reach."

Lillian was silent about their first harvest the fall of 1906. It was not easy teasing a crop from the gravelly, if not sandy, terrain, especially for first-time farmers in the region, and Perce helped thresh wheat for other farmers until snowfall to supplement their meagre income. Lillian spent their separation in Saskatoon doing piece-work for a dressmaker. But there was no escape from the race to get the crop off. "The grain is wonderful and you can hardly imagine what it is like without seeing it," she enthused. "It is grand to see fields of it stretch for miles and miles. If you saw it you would understand why it takes thousands of men to harvest it." What surprised Lillian, though, were people working on Sunday: "that [the sabbath] does not count in this country." But she herself was just as busy, acknowledging at one point, "I seem[ed] to have such a little time to myself since I have been here." She looked forward to the day when the railway, being pushed west along the southern edge of the hills, would end the isolation and reduce the time to do things.

Perce and Lillian planned to spend their first western winter in Saskatoon but were back on the homestead by mid-October. They missed the place and reasoned that they could live on game in the hills, especially the deer and pronghorn; ironically, much like the Indians and Métis in past decades, who had hunted the bison that had sought shelter from winter's biting winds in the coulees. What they did not expect to face, though, was one of the most brutal winters in western Canadian history. Fierce storms swept across the northern plains in mid-November, blanketing the region in deep snow and sending temperatures to bitter lows. The wretched weather did not loosen its grip until late spring and delayed seeding by several weeks. Trains could not

LOUIS COCHIN

The faces on this Métis family suggest apprehension and uncertainty.

get through the heavy snow and settlers faced a dire fuel shortage. The Turners came through the "killing" winter of 1906–07 without too much difficulty, even though they began to wonder by mid-April "if we are ever to have warm weather here again." Perce spent more time fetching wood from the ravines, often getting back to the homestead after sunset, and the pair had to hunker down for several days when another blizzard struck. But they were surprised to find the mounted police checking on homesteaders in the district in late February and early March, following up stories that people had starved or frozen to death.

Lillian's mother circulated her daughter's letters among family and friends. But what Lillian did not know, until the local school back home in Wingham sent her a note of thanks, was that her letters were being read aloud to the students. "You could have knocked me over," Lillian blushed. When "the school [was called] to order and said they had another letter from Mrs. Turner," Lillian was told, "you could hear a pin drop everything was so quiet."

Saskatchewan was being heavily promoted as the "last best west" and people were anxious for any first-hand news about one of Canada's newest provinces. Lillian's candid letters filled that void. Her stories of starting a new life with her husband, of literally stepping back in time on their homestead but never losing hope or faith, enthralled the students. "I see people craining [sic] their necks and with their mouths open upon hearing my letter read," Lillian imagined. She was probably not far off the mark, especially when she talked about the neighbour who lived in a dugout in the hills or that she did not wash her hair for over two months because of the shortage of rain water.

But Lillian's letters were equally important for what was not in them. Saskatchewan pinned its hopes in 1905 on becoming the world's granary and wanted to put behind, if not forget, the pre-modern past and the distinctive society that had taken shape over more than two centuries of interaction between Indians and newcomers. Nothing was going to stand in the province's way of assuming its dominant place in confederation, not even environmental obstacles posed by the climate. But if Saskatchewan was going to secure

A ground view of the Moose Mountain medicine wheel today

this destiny, then Indians, like the man who visited the Turner homestead, were expected to ride off into oblivion and never be heard from again. There was also no place for the Métis unless they submerged their identity. Their marginalization was confirmed in the 1906 special western census—the same one that collected the Turners' data—when the Métis category was dropped. It was as if they had ceased to exist as a distinct people and were not worth counting. Lillian's letters give no hint of this other side of Saskatchewan history, no hint of these people and their stories. She was more concerned with better days ahead, if not for her and Perce, then for their children and their children's children. For many of the newcomers that took up homestead land or moved to booming communities along an ever-expanding network of rail lines, Saskatchewan's past had no meaningful place in their memory. All that remained in 1905 were the few physical reminders on the ground that over time were either destroyed, removed, or simply neglected and left to deteriorate and disappear. Nor did stories of an earlier time resonate with those looking to the province's future. Englishman Henry Kelsey's visit to the northern prairies two hundred years earlier had been forgotten and was not even mentioned in any of the provincial inauguration ceremonies in September 1905. Saskatchewan's rich history before provincehood had become ... a world we have lost. And the people of the province were poorer for not knowing that past or choosing to ignore it.

ACKNOWLEDGEMENTS

THE IDEA FOR *A WORLD WE HAVE LOST* ORIGINATED AT A REGINA CONFERENCE IN the fall of 2005. I had been asked to reflect on my new book, *Saskatchewan: A New History*, as part of a session on the writing of Saskatchewan history. In my remarks, I noted that the front end of the story—the period before Saskatchewan became a province—had to be re-visited and re-considered in light of new work in the area. After mulling it over, I decided to write a compendium piece to my centennial history of the province. I likened my assignment to George Lucas of *Star Wars* fame, who went back to the beginning after the movie success of episodes 4, 5, and 6.

Researching and writing the Sask prequel, as the project became known, took several years. I published other books in the interim, but continued to read and think about the early Saskatchewan story and did the chapters in fits and starts. Sometimes the thinking delayed the writing. Along the way, people would ask me about the progress of the book, and their interest and concern kept me going, especially those times when I wondered whether I would ever see the finish line. It is to them that I owe a big thank-you.

I greatly benefited from the research assistance of several graduate students: Jennie Hansen, Megan Hubert, Glenn Iceton, Brendan Kelly, Laura Larsen, Merle Massie, Dustin McNichol, Christa Nicholat, Myles Shingoose, and Scott Silver. They handled a number of research tasks in a timely and helpful manner. I was the one who could not keep up in producing the draft manuscript.

I also leaned on several colleagues and friends to read and comment on the manuscript in its various iterations: Alwynne Beaudoin, Ted Binnema, Stuart Houston, David Meyer, Jim Miller, Dale Miquelon, Dale Russell, and John Warkentin. I never hesitated to ask them for guidance and advice (even about a location, a phrase, a map, or a footnote), and they, in turn, shared their expertise selflessly and generously—and their opinions. They all wanted me to get it "right," and I have been extremely fortunate to have been saved from making questionable statements and stupid mistakes. Naturally, any errors are my responsibility.

George Colpitts kindly provided an early peek at his new book, *Pemmican Empire*, while it was still in manuscript form. Doug Chisholm and his Cessna float plane took me on two flying trips over northern Saskatchewan and enabled me to secure a better understanding and appreciation of the region's fur trade past.

Getting the manuscript to production fell to Charlene Dobmeier who approached the editing with professional care and sensitivity. She did a marvellous job and never lost sight of the larger story while dealing with the minutiae with painstaking care. Working together on this project reminded me of why she is such a good book person—and good friend.

Assembling the archival photographs was a small project in itself, and I tried to use Saskatchewan resources whenever possible. To do so, I was warmly helped by Jamie Benson, Rene Charpentier, Ted Douglas, Patrick Hayes, Tim Novak, Adrian Paton, Joel Salt, Cindy Scheer, Eric Story, and George Tosh. They made my job easier, and the photograph selection better. The real visual highlight, though, are the stunning colour images by John Perret of Light Line Photography.

Brian Smith and Mike McCoy at Articulate Eye Design prepared the maps and ensured that they conveyed a "sense of place" in an informative and engaging way. Tom Shields made the notes a model of consistency and accuracy. Penny Hozy prepared the index—no easy chore given all the names and places.

Kerry Plumley took a big manuscript, full of information, and turned it into a handsome publication that people will instinctively pick up and dip into. His creative design nicely captures the story and underscores the continued vitality of the printed book.

Sharon Fitzhenry patiently waited a long time for the manuscript—never prodded nor nagged, but knew that I would deliver … eventually. Our Toronto meetings with Tracey Dettman and Rowan DeHaan energized me to push the project through to completion.

Research funding was provided through a grant from the Social Sciences and Humanities Research Council of Canada. The Office of Research Services at the University of Saskatchewan (through its Publications Fund Committee) helped cover the cost of some of the maps. And the A.S. Morton Research Chair allowed me to "test drive" some of the book's arguments in public talks. All sources of support are gratefully acknowledged.

My bride Marley (40 years and counting) understands that this book was a tough one. She knows that the research and writing took me off to another world—and that I might be "gone" for hours, if not days. When I came "back," she always had encouraging words of support and advocated the restorative powers of malt. And, of course, she was right. Cheers everyone! Thank you for making this book a reality—one that will introduce readers to another Saskatchewan.

MAP SOURCES

Henry Kelsey's probable route, 1690–92

J.H. Richards, ed., *Atlas of Saskatchewan* (Saskatoon: University of Saskatchewan, 1969).

Wisconsinan glacier over western Canada (18,000 years BP [maximum], 9,000 years BP, and 6,000 years BP)

A. S. Dyke and V.K. Prest, "Paleogeography of northern North America, 18 000 – 5600 years ago," Geological Survey of Canada, 1987 http://geoscan.nrcan.gc.ca/starweb/geoscan/servlet. starweb?path=geoscan/fulle.web&search1=R=133927 (accessed 18 August 2015).

Major ecological zones of Saskatchewan

G.A.J. Scott, *Canada's Vegetation: A World Perspective* (Montreal: McGill–Queen's University Press, 1995).

Selected archaeological sites in Saskatchewan

K.I. Fung, ed., *Atlas of Saskatchewan* (Saskatoon: University of Saskatchewan, 1999).

Cree rendezvous sites in east-central Saskatchewan

D. Meyer and P. Thistle, "Saskatchewan River Rendezvous Centers and Trading Posts: Continuity in a Cree Social Geography," *Ethnohistory* 42, no. 3 (1995): pp. 403–15.

Major culture groups in Saskatchewan, circa 1700

D. Meyer and D.R. Russell, "Aboriginal Peoples from the Ice Age to 1870" in B.D. Thraves et al., *Saskatchewan: Geographic Perspectives* (Regina: Canadian Plains Research Center, 2007), pp. 101–18.

Rupert's Land and early Hudson's Bay Company posts

Fung, ed., *Atlas of Saskatchewan*.

Major canoe routes between York Factory and central Saskatchewan

E.W. Morse, *Fur Trade Canoe Routes of Canada: Then and Now* (Ottawa: Queen's Printer, 1969).

Hudson's Bay Company trading partners in early 1700s

D. Meyer and D. Russell, "So Fine and Pleasant, Beyond Description": The Lands and Lives of the Pegogamaw Crees," *Plains Anthropologist* 49, no. 191 (2004): pp. 217–52.

French trading posts in western Canada

D.B. Miquelon, *New France, 1701–1744: A Supplement to Europe* (Toronto: McClelland and Stewart, 1987).

Inland trips by HBC servants Anthony Henday, Samuel Hearne, and Matthew Cocking

Fung, ed., *Atlas of Saskatchewan*.

Selected fur trade posts in Saskatchewan, circa late 1770

Fung, ed., *Atlas of Saskatchewan*.

Selected fur trade posts in Saskatchewan and Alberta in late 1700s

Fung, ed., *Atlas of Saskatchewan*.

The Montreal canoe route to the Athabasca country

B. Macdougall, *One of the Family: Metis Culture in Nineteenth-Century Northwestern Saskatchewan* (Vancouver: University of British Columbia Press, 2010).

Selected fur trade posts in Saskatchewan and Alberta in late 1700s/early 1800s

Fung, ed., *Atlas of Saskatchewan*.

Selected fur trade posts in northern Saskatchewan and Alberta, circa late 1700s

Fung, ed., *Atlas of Saskatchewan*.

Selkirk Grant and selected fur trade posts in early 1800s

G. Colpitts, *Pemmican Empire: Food, Trade, and the Last Bison Hunts in the North American Plains* (New York: Cambridge University Press, 2014).

Selected fur trade posts and Carlton Trail in mid-1800s

R.C. Russell, *The Carlton Trail* (Saskatoon: Modern Press, 1955).

Missions in Rupert's Land

K. Pettipas, "A History of the Work of the Reverend Henry Budd conducted under the Auspices of the Church Missionary Society, 1840–1875," (master's thesis, University of Manitoba, 1972).

Palliser's arid triangle and Hind's fertile belt, 1860

D. Owram, *Promise of Eden: The Canadian Expansionist Movement and the Idea of the West, 1856–1900* (Toronto: University of Toronto Press, 1980).

Trails in southern Saskatchewan, circa 1860

T. Petty, "Trails of Saskatchewan," 1962, Glenbow Archives, Calgary.

Indian Treaties

B. Waiser, *Saskatchewan: A New History* (Calgary: Fifth House Publishers, 2005).

Canadian Pacific Railway main line, 1885

W.K. Lamb, *History of the Canadian Pacific Railway* (New York: Macmillan, 1977).

The Prince Albert district, 1885

P. Code, "Les Autres Métis: The English Métis of the Prince Albert Settlement, 1862–1886," (master's thesis, University of Saskatchewan, 2008).

The 1885 North-West Rebellion

B. Stonechild and B. Waiser, *Loyal till Death: Indians and the North-West Rebellion* (Saskatoon: Fifth House Publishers, 1997).

North-West Territories provisional districts

L.H. Thomas, *The Struggle for Responsible Government in the North-West Territories, 1870–97* (Toronto: University of Toronto Press, 1956).

TABLE CREDITS

Drought as recorded by tree rings

R.A. Case and G.M. MacDonald, "A Dendroclimatic Reconstruction of Annual Precipitation on the Western Canadian Prairies since A.D. 1505 from *Pinus flexilis* James," Quaternary Research 44 (1995): p. 273–75.

Archaeological periods and cultures by vegetation zone

D. Meyer and D.R. Russell, "Aboriginal Peoples from the Ice Age to 1870" in B.D. Thraves et al., *Saskatchewan: Geographic Perspectives* (Regina: Canadian Plains Research Center, 2007), p. 102.

Racial composition of Saskatchewan, 1881 census

E.J. Millions, "Ties Undone: A Gendered and Racial Analysis of the Impact of the 1885 North-West Rebellion in the Saskatchewan District," (master's thesis, University of Saskatchewan, 2004) p. 26.

ENDNOTES

INTRODUCTION NOTES

1. Quoted in C.N. Bell, "The Journal of Henry Kelsey," *Transactions of the Historical and Scientific Society of Manitoba*, n.s., 4, (1928): p. 3.

2. English-born Charles William Jefferys (1869–1951) was celebrated for his series of Canadian historical scenes, reproduced in the three-volume *The Picture Gallery of Canadian History*.

3. J.W. Whillans, *First in the West: The Story of Henry Kelsey, Discoverer of the Canadian Prairies* (Edmonton: Applied Art Products, 1955). In the early 1950s, Saskatchewan newspapers covered Whillans's efforts to revive Kelsey's memory. Whillans even suggested that Kelsey had traveled as far west as the present-day Saskatchewan–Alberta border. See, for example, the *Saskatoon Star-Phoenix,* 31 July 1952 and *Regina Leader-Post*, 5 July 1954.

4. A.S. Morton, *A History of the Canadian West to 1870–71* (Toronto: Thomas Nelson and Sons Ltd., 1939), p. 110.

5. Ibid, p. 148; Whillans, *First in the West*, p. 42.

6. Bell, "Journal of Henry Kelsey," p. 4.

7. See, for example, A. Ronaghan, "Reconstructing Kelsey's Travels" in H. Epp, ed., *Three Hundred Prairie Years: Henry Kelsey's "Inland Country of Good Report"* (Regina: Canadian Plains Research Center/ Saskatchewan Archaeological Society, 1993), pp. 89–94.

8. The matter of how the Kelsey papers came into Dobbs's possession is another mystery. K.G. Davies, "Kelsey, Henry" in D.M. Hayne, ed., *Dictionary of Canadian Biography, vol. 2, 1701–1740* (Toronto: University of Toronto Press, 1969), pp. 309, 314.

9. Ibid.

10. See D. Russell, "The Puzzle of Henry Kelsey and his Journey to the West," in Epp, ed., *Three Hundred Prairie Years*, pp. 74–88.

11. Quoted in Davies, "Kelsey, Henry," p. 308.

12. H. Kelsey, *The Kelsey Papers* (Regina: Canadian Plains Research Center, 1994), 1–2. (Note that the spelling and punctuation in the papers is per Kelsey's original text.)

13. J. Warkentin, "Introduction to the 1994 Edition" in Kelsey, *The Kelsey Papers*, p. xiii.

14. C.G. Calloway, *One Vast Winter Count: The Native American West Before Lewis and Clark* (Lincoln: University of Nebraska Press, 2003), p. 136.

15. Ibid., p. xiii–xiv.

16. Kelsey, *The Kelsey Papers*, p. 2.

17. Ibid.

18. Warkentin, "Introduction to the 1994 Edition," *The Kelsey Papers*, p. xiv.

19. Calloway, *One Vast Winter Count*, p. 11.

20. D. Meyer and D. Russell, "'Through the Woods Whare Thare Ware Now Track Ways': Kelsey, Henday and Trails in East Central Saskatchewan," *Canadian Journal of Archaeology* 31, no. 3 (2007): pp. 165–69, 181–82; D. Meyer and P. Thistle, "Saskatchewan River Rendezvous Centers and Trading Posts: Continuity in a Cree Social Geography," *Ethnohistory* 42, no. 3 (1995): pp. 403–15; J. Turnquist, "A Pilgrimage to the God Stone," *The Blue Jay* (July–Sept. 1952): p. 19.

21. Warkentin, "Introduction to the 1994 Edition," *The Kelsey Papers*," p. xxiii; J.S.H. Brown, *Strangers in Blood: Fur Trade Families in Indian Country* (Vancouver: University of British Columbia Press,1980), p. 53.

22. Quoted in Bell, "The Journal of Henry Kelsey," p. 4.

23. Ibid.

24. Kelsey, *The Kelsey Papers*, p. 3. The Cree word for Siouan-speaking people was *pwat*, which became poet to English-speakers.

25. Ibid., pp. 3–4.

26. Ibid., pp. 4–5.

27. Meyer and Russell, "'Through the Woods Whare Thare Ware Now Track Ways,'" pp. 184–85.

28. Ibid., pp. 183–84. Parts of the Greenbush Trail still cut deeply into the vegetation from heavy use.

29. Kelsey may have been referring to needle and thread grass (*Hesperostipa comata*), today the official grass of Saskatchewan.

30. Kelsey, *The Kelsey Papers*, pp. 7–8.

31. Ibid., p. 10.

32. Ibid., pp. 10–11.

33. Russell, "The Puzzle of Henry Kelsey and his Journey to the West," in Epp, ed., *Three Hundred Prairie Years*, p. 84. See also D. Russell, *Eighteenth-Century Western Cree and Their Neighbours* (Hull: Canadian Museum of Civilization, 1991), pp. 77, 210–11.

34. This document, dated 1691–1692, was found among the Kelsey papers discovered in Ireland in 1926.

35. Kelsey, *The Kelsey Papers*, pp. 11–15.

36. Quoted in Russell, *Eighteenth-Century Western Cree*, p. 63.

37. Davies, "Kelsey, Henry," p. 310.

38. G. Williams, "Highlights of the First 200 Years of the Hudson's Bay Company," The Beaver 50, no. 2, (Autumn 1970): p. 23.

39. E.E. Rich, ed., *Letters Outbound*, 1688–96, p. xlvii.

40. Warkentin, "Introduction to the 1994 Edition" in Kelsey, *The Kelsey Papers*, p. x; A.M. Carlos and F.D. Lewis, *Commerce by a Frozen Sea* (Philadelphia: University of Pennsylvania Press, 2010), p. 77.

41. Williams, "Highlights of the First 200 Years," p. 23.

42. Warkentin, "Introduction to the 1994 Edition" in Kelsey, *The Kelsey Papers*, p. vii.

43. Calloway, *One Vast Winter Count*, pp. 7–9.

CHAPTER ONE NOTES

1. D. Flores, *The Natural West: Environmental History in the Great Plains and Rocky Mountains* (Norman: University of Oklahoma Press, 2001), p. 101.

2. A.B. Beaudoin, "Climate and Landscape of the Last 2000 Years in Alberta" in J.W. Brink and J.F. Dormaar, eds, *Archaeology in Alberta: A View from the New Millennium* (Medicine Hat: Archaeological Society of Alberta, 2003), p. 10.

3. C. Savage, *Prairie: A Natural History* (Vancouver: Douglas and McIntyre, 2004), p. 14.

4. D. de Boer and L. Martz, "Topography" in K. I. Fung, ed., *Atlas of Saskatchewan* (Saskatoon: University of Saskatchewan, 1999), p. 89; L. Martz and D. de Boer, "Digital Terrain Models" in Fung, *Atlas of Saskatchewan*, p. 94.

5. A.B. Beaudoin and G.A. Oetelaar, "The Changing Ecophysical Landscape of Southern Alberta During the Late Pleistocene and Early Holocene," *Plains Anthropologist* 48, no. 187 (2003): pp. 193–201.

6. D. Flores, *Caprock Canyonlands* (Arlington: University of Texas Press, 1990), p. 16.

7. R. Gibbons, "Examining the Extinction of the Pleistocene Megafauna," *Anthropological Sciences* (Spring 2004): pp. 22–27; N. Owen-Smith, "Pleistocene Extinctions: The Pivotal Role of Megaherbivores," *Paleobiology* 13, no. 3 (1987): pp. 351–62; D. Flores, *Caprock Canyonlands*, pp. 16–17.

8. B. Shapiro et al., "Rise and Fall of Beringian Steppe Bison," *Science* 36 (2004): pp. 1561–65; M. Kornfeld et al., *Prehistoric Hunters-Gatherers of the High Plains and Rockies* (Walnut Creek CA: Left Coast Press, 2010), p. 159.

9. Flores, *The Natural West*, p. 57.

10. See A.K. Knapp et al., "The Keystone Role of Bison in North American Tallgrass Prairie," *Bioscience* 49, no. 1 (January 1999): pp. 39–50.

11. Savage, *Prairie*, p.70.

12. Ibid., p. 126.

13. Ibid., pp. 22–23, 64–68, 102–03.

14. Knapp et al., "The Keystone Role of Bison," p. 47.

15. A.B. Beaudoin, "What They Saw: The Climatic and Environmental Context for Euro-Canadian Settlement in Alberta," *Prairie Forum* 24, no. 1 (Spring 1999): p. 7; R.E. Vance et al., "The Paleoecological Record of 6 ka BP Climate in the Canadian Prairie Provinces," *Géolographie physique et Quaternaire* 49, no. 1 (1995): pp. 93–94; P.H. Carlson, *Deep Time and the Texas*

High Plains: History and Geology (Lubbock: Texas Tech University Press, 2005), pp. 59–61.

16. Vance et al., "Paleoecological Record," pp. 82–95.

17. B. Reeves, "The Concept of an Altithermal Cultural Hiatus in Northern Plains Prehistory," *American Anthropologist* 75, no. 5 (1973): pp. 1228, 1237, 1246; W.R. Hurt, "The Altithermal and the Prehistory of the Northern Plains," *Quaterneria* 8 (1966): pp. 110–11.

18. V.L. Harms, "The Characteristic and Unique Flora of the Churchill River in Saskatchewan" in P. Jonker, ed., *The Churchill: A Canadian Heritage River* (Saskatoon: University of Saskatchewan, 1995), p. 4; G.R. Bortolotti et al., "Diversity and Population Trends of the Birds of Besnard Lake" in Jonker, ed., *The Churchill*, p. 37.

19. Savage, *Prairie*, p. 194. All aspen trees in a single grove sprout from the roots of a single parent tree and are therefore genetically identical.

20. J. Thorpe, "Natural Vegetation" in Fung, ed., *Atlas of Saskatchewan*, p. 136; C.S. Houston "The Life: Bird Observations" in H. Epp, ed., *Three Hundred Prairie Years: Henry Kelsey's "Inland Country of Good Report"* (Regina: Canadian Plains Research Center/Saskatchewan Archaeological Society 1993), p. 27.

21. Beaudoin, "Climate and Landscape," p. 28.

22. Savage, *Prairie*, pp. 118–22; 140–41. The pronghorn is the only even-toed North American ungulate to shed its horns.

23. Kornfeld et al., *Prehistoric Hunters-Gatherers*, pp. 148–50.

24. See T. Herriot, *Grass, Sky, Song: Promise and Peril in the World of Grassland Birds* (Toronto: Harper Collins Publishers, 2009).

25. Savage, *Prairie*, p. 159.

26. M. Boyd et al, "Reconstructing a Prairie-Woodland Mosaic on the Northern Great Plains: Risk, Resilience, and Resource Management," *Plains Anthropologist*, 51, no. 199 (2006): pp. 235–6.

27. Savage, *Prairie*, p. 80.

28. Beaudoin, "Climate and Landscape," pp. 26–37; D.J. Sauchyn and A.B. Beaudoin, "Recent Environmental Change in the Southwestern Plains," T*he Canadian Geographer* 42, no. 4 (1998): pp. 343–44, 346–48, 350; R.A. Case and G.M. MacDonald, "A Dendroclimatic Reconstruction of Annual Precipitation on the Western Canadian Prairies since A.D. 1505 from *Pinus flexilis* James," *Quaternary Research* 44 (1995): p. 273–5; B.H. Luckman and R.J.S. Wilson, "Summer Temperatures in the Canadian Rockies during the Last Millennium," *Climate Dynamics* 24 (2005): p. 137. See also K.R. Laird et al., "Greater Drought Intensity and Frequency Before A.D. 1200 in the Northern Great Plains, U.S.A.," *Nature*, no. 384 (December 1996): pp. 552–54; S. St. George et al., "The Tree-Ring Record of Drought on the Canadian Prairies," *Journal of Climate* 22 no. 3 (February 2009): pp. 689–710; D. Bamforth, "An Empirical Perspective on the Little Ice Age Climatic Change on the Great Plains," *Plains Anthropologist* 35 (1990) pp. 359–66.

29. H. Kelsey, *The Kelsey Papers* (Regina: Canadian Plains Research Center, 1994), p. 9. (Note that the spelling and punctuation in the papers is per Kelsey's original text.)

30. Herriot, *Grass, Sky, Song*, p. 28.

CHAPTER TWO NOTES

1. J.F.V. Millar, "Mortuary Practices of the Oxbow Complex," *Canadian Journal of Archaeology* 5 (1981): pp. 103–117; L. Bryan, *The Buffalo People: Prehistoric Archaeology on the Canadian Plains* (Edmonton: University of Alberta Press 1991), pp. 72–78.

2. T. Binnema, *Common and Contested Ground: A Human and Environmental History of the Northwestern Plains* (Norman: University of Oklahoma Press, 2001), p. 55.

3. M. Kornfeld et al., *Prehistoric Hunters-Gatherers of the High Plains and Rockies* (Walnut Creek CA: Left Coast Press, 2010), p. 66.

4. Reproduced in J.S.H. Brown and R. Brightman, eds., "The Orders of the Dreamed": *George Nelson on Cree and Northern Ojibwa Religion and Myth, 1823* (Winnipeg: University of Manitoba Press,1988), p. 48. The Nelson journal is one of the best records of Cree spirituality and mythology collected before the twentieth century.

5. Ibid., pp. 47–48.

6. See E. Dewar, *Bones: Discovering the First Americans* (Toronto: Random House Canada, 2001). Knut Fladmark of Simon Fraser University first proposed that humans arrived earlier in the Americas ("Routes: Alternative Migration Corridors for Early Man in North America," *American Antiquity*, 44, no. 1 (1979): pp. 55-69. Mitochondrial DNA extracted from the skull of a teen-aged girl found in a submerged cave in Mexico's Yucatan peninsula directly links the 12,000-year-old skeleton to the same Siberian-based population that is the basis of existing indigenous groups in the New World, *Globe and Mail* (16 May 2014): pp. A6–A7. A study of Siberian and northwestern North America languages suggests that there might have been more than one migration to the New World. M. Ruhlen, "The Origin of the Na-Dene," *Proceedings of the National Academy of Sciences* 95 (November 1998): pp. 13,994–13,996.

7. Because ceramics entered the archaeological record in the late pre-contact period, projectile points have, by default, become the best way of determining and separating cultural complexes. J.S. Wilson, "Artifacts" in H.T. Epp and I. Dyck, eds., *Tracking Ancient Hunters: Prehistoric Archaeology in Saskatchewan* (Regina: Saskatchewan Archaeological Society, 1983), pp. 23–26.

8. T.R. Peck, *Light from Ancient Campfires: Archaeological Evidence for Native Lifeways on the Northern Plains* (Edmonton: Athabasca University Press, 2011), pp. 24, 35–36; T.F. Kehoe, "The Distribution and Implications of Fluted Points in Saskatchewan," *American Antiquity* 31, no. 4 (1966): pp. 530–539; J.B. Hall, "Pointing It Out: Fluted Projectile Point Distributions and Early Human Populations in Saskatchewan" (master's thesis, Department of Archaeology, Simon Fraser University, 2009). See also Muriel Carlson's 1993 report, "Collections Can Speak for Themselves," available through the Saskatchewan Heritage Branch, about paleo-Indian lithics found in west-central Saskatchewan. The standard reference work on southern Saskatchewan prehistory is I. Dyck, "Prehistory of Southern Saskatchewan" in Epp and Dyck, eds., *Tracking Ancient Hunters*, pp. 63–139.

9. D. Flores, *Caprock Canyonlands* (Arlington: University of Texas Press, 1990), p. 16.

10. R. Gibbons, "Examining the Extinction of the Pleistocene Megafauna," *Anthropological Sciences* (Spring 2004): pp. 22–27; N. Owen-Smith, "Pleistocene Extinctions: The Pivotal Role of Megaherbivores," *Paleobiology* 13, no. 3 (1987): pp. 351–62.

11. D.K. Grayson and D.J. Meltzer, "Clovis Hunting and Large Mammal Extinction: A Critical Review of the Evidence," *Journal of World Prehistory* 16, no. 4 (2002): pp. 313–59.

12. Peck, *Light from Ancient Campfires*, pp. 23, 37–38.

13. Ibid., p. 39.

14. Kornfeld et al., *Prehistoric Hunters-Gatherers*, pp. 176–77, 209, 481.

15. C.G. Calloway, *One Vast Winter Count: The American West before Lewis and Clark* (Lincoln: University of Nebraska Press, 2003), p. 36.

16. Kornfeld et al., *Prehistoric Hunters-Gatherers*, pp. 160, 178–89, 181, 184, 208.

17. Peck, *Light from Ancient Campfires*, pp. 45–47.

18. Ibid., p. 449.

19. Kornfeld et al., *Prehistoric Hunters-Gatherers*, pp. 226–47.

20. D. Meyer, "The Prehistory of Northern Saskatchewan" in Epp and Dyck, eds., *Tracking Ancient Hunters*, pp. 142–46.

21. D. Meyer and E.G. Walker, "Glacial Retreat and Population Expansion" in K. I. Fung, ed., *Atlas of Saskatchewan* (Saskatoon: University of Saskatchewan, 1999), p. 20; D. Meyer, "Precontact Archaeology of Northern Saskatchewan" in Fung, ed., *Atlas of Saskatchewan*, p. 23; D. Meyer, "Churchill River Archaeology in Saskatchewan: How Much Do We Know?" in P. Jonker, ed., *The Churchill: A Canadian Heritage River* (Saskatoon: University of Saskatchewan, 1995), pp. 54–55; J.F.V. Millar, "The Prehistory of the Upper Churchill River Basin, Saskatchewan, Canada," *BAR International Series S668* (Oxford, U.K., 1997).

22. P.H. Carlson, *Deep Time and the Texas High Plains: History and Geology* (Lubbock: Texas Tech University Press, 2005), p. 55.

23. Kornfeld et al., *Prehistoric Hunters-Gatherers*, p. 291.

24. E.G. Walker, *The Gowen Sites: Cultural Responses to Climatic Warming on the Northern Plains (7500–5000 B.P.)* (Hull: Canadian Museum of Civilization, 1992), pp. 123–45; M.S. Sheehan, "Cultural Responses to the Altithermal: The Role of Aquifer-Related Water Resources," *Geoarchaeology* 9, no. 2 (1994): pp. 113–37; D.J. Meltzer, "Human Responses to the Middle Holocene (Altithermal) Climates of the North American Great Plains," *Quaternary Research* 52 (1999): pp. 404–16; M. Boyd et al., "Reconstructing a Prairie-Woodland Mosaic on the Northern Great Plains: Risk, Resilience, and Resource Management," *Plains Anthropologist* 51, no. 199 (2006) pp. 235–52.

25. Meyer, "Precontact Archaeology of Northern Saskatchewan," p. 20; Meyer, "Prehistory of Northern Saskatchewan," pp. 148, 153–59.

26. J.W. Brink, *Imagining Head-Smashed In: Aboriginal Buffalo Hunting on the Northern Plains* (Edmonton: Athabasca University Press, 2008), pp. 8–9.

27. Peck, *Light from Ancient Campfires*, pp. 193, 450–51.

28. See C.L. Ramsay, "The Redtail Site: A McKean Habitation in South Central Saskatchewan" (master's thesis, University of Saskatchewan, 1993).

29. Peck, *Light from Ancient Campfires*, pp. 275–77.

30. L. Bryan, *Stone by Stone: Exploring Ancient Sites on the Canadian Plains* (Surrey: Heritage House, 2005), pp. 70–72.

31. Kornfeld et al., *Prehistoric Hunters-Gatherers*, p. 530.

32. T.E.H. Jones and S. L. Jones, *St. Victor Petroglyphs: the Place of the Living Stone* (Saskatoon: Houghton-Boston, 2012).

33. Bryan, *Stone by Stone*, pp. 64–65, 135–37. See also J.D. Keyser and M.A. Klassen, *Plains Indian Rock Art* (Vancouver: University of British Columbia Press, 2001).

34. Peck, *Light from Ancient Campfires*, pp. 278, 281; E.G. Walker, "The Bracken Cairn: a Late Middle Archaic Burial from Southwestern Saskatchewan," *Saskatchewan Archaeology* 3, no. 1–2 (1982): pp. 8–35.

35. J. Cruikshank, *Reading Voices* (Vancouver: Douglas and McIntyre, 1991), pp. 65, 68; D.J. Sauchyn and A.B. Beaudoin, "Recent Environmental Change in the Southwestern Canadian Prairies," *Canadian Geographer* 42, no. 2 (1998): pp. 337–53.

36. E.S. Burch and O. Blehr, "Herd Following Reconsidered," *Current Anthropology* 32, no. 2 (August–October 1991): p. 442; D. Meyer and D. Russell, "Aboriginal Cultural Groups" in K. I. Fung, ed., *Atlas of Saskatchewan* (Saskatoon: University of Saskatchewan, 1999), p. 22.

37. Meyer, "Precontact Archaeology of Northern Saskatchewan," pp. 23–24; Meyer, "Churchill River Archaeology," pp. 56–57; D. Meyer et al., "The River House Complex: Middle Woodland on the Northwestern Periphery," *Canadian Journal of Archaeology* 32 (2008): pp. 43–76; D. Meyer and T.R. Smith, "The Mudrick Site: Selkirk in the Saskatchewan Parklands," *Canadian Journal of Archaeology* 34 (2010): pp. 174–211; D. Meyer, "People Before Kelsey: An Overview of Cultural Developments" in H. Epp, ed., *Three Hundred Prairie Years: Henry* Kelsey's *"Inland Country of Good Report"* (Regina: Canadian Plains Research Center/Saskatchewan Archaeological Society, 1993), pp. 57–58, 62–63.

38. D. Meyer, "The Newly Recorded Rock Paintings of Southwestern Reindeer Lake" (unpublished paper kindly provided to author, 1996).

39. T.E.H. Jones, *The Aboriginal Rock Paintings of the Churchill River* (Saskatoon: Saskatchewan Archaeological Society, 2006).

40. Quoted in G. Marchildon and S. Robinson, *Canoeing the Churchill: A Practical Guide to the Historic Voyageur Highway* (Regina: Canadian Plains Research Center, 2002), p. 207. It is not known whether Mackenzie stopped there in 1787 on his way down the Mackenzie River or in 1792 on his way to the Pacific Coast. See also K.A. Lipsett, "Pictographs in Northern Saskatchewan: Vision Quest and Pawakan" (master's thesis, Department of Anthropology and Archaeology, University of Saskatchewan, 1990).

41. See Brown and Brightman, eds., *The Orders of the Dreamed*.

42. G.A. Oetelaar and D. Meyer, "Movement and Native American Landscapes: A Comparative Approach," *Plains Anthropologist* 51, no. 199 (2006): pp. 357–62; D. Meyer and P. Thistle, "Saskatchewan River Rendezvous Centers and Trading Posts: Continuity in a Cree Social Geography," *Ethnohistory* 42, no. 3 (1995): pp. 415–16.

43. Quoted in B. Belyea, ed., *A Year Inland: The Journal of a Hudson's Bay Company Winterer* (Waterloo: Wilfrid Laurier University Press, 2000), p. 64; P. Erasmus, *Buffalo Days and Nights*, 5th ed. (Calgary: Fifth House Publishers, 1999), p. 231.

44. N.J. Turner et al., "Living on the Edge: Ecological and Cultural Edges as Sources of Diversity for Social-Ecological Resilience," *Human Ecology* 31, no. 3 (September 2003): pp. 439–61.

45. D. Walde et al., "The Late Period on the Canadian and Adjacent Plains," *Revisita de Arquelogis Americana* 9 (1995): pp. 18–21; Peck, *Light from Ancient Campfires*, pp. 356–63.

46. There is an ongoing debate in the Canadian archaeological community whether the Besant Phase and Avonlea Horizon co-existed on the northern plains. It is worth noting that Besant components have consistently been found below Avonlea components.

47. B.J. Smith, "The Historical and Archaeological Evidence for the Use of Fish as an Alternate Subsistence Resource among Northern Plains Bison Hunters" in K. Abel and J. Friesen, eds., *Aboriginal Resource Use in Canada: Historical and Legal Aspects* (Winnipeg: University of Manitoba Press, 1991), pp. 37–40.

48. Meyer, "People Before Kelsey," pp. 69–70.

49. See T.F. Kehoe, "The Gull Lake Site: A Prehistoric Bison Drive Site in Southwestern Saskatchewan," *Publications in Anthropology and History* 1 (1973).

50. Brink, *Imagining Head-Smashed In*, pp. 110–11.

51. R.G. Morgan, "Bison Movement Patterns on the Canadian Plains: An Ecological Analysis," *Plains Anthropologist* 25, no. 8 (May 1980): pp. 145–46; R.L. Barsh and C. Marlor, "Driving Bison and Blackfoot Science," *Human Ecology* 31, no. 4, (December 2003): pp. 571–93.

52. Oetelaar and D. Meyer, "Movement and Native American Landscapes," pp. 363–67.

53. Walde et al., "Late Period on the Canadian and Adjacent Plains," pp. 14–16.

54. The "parkland convergence" model was put forward by A.J. Ray in *Indians in the Fur Trade: Their role as hunters, trappers, and middlemen in the lands southwest of Hudson Bay, 1670–1870* (Vancouver: University of British Columbia Press, 1974) and challenged by D. Meyer and H.T. Epp, "North-South Interaction in the Late Prehistory of Central Saskatchewan," *Plains Anthropologist* 35, no. 132 (1990): pp. 321–42. See also J.R. Vickers and T.R. Peck, "Islands in a Sea of Grass: The Significance of Wood in Winter Campsite Selection on the Northwestern Plains" in B. Kooyman and J. Kelley, eds., *Archaeology on the Edge: New Perspectives from the Northern Plains* (Calgary: University of Calgary Press, 2004), pp. 95–124.

55. Walde et al., "Late Period on the Canadian and Adjacent Plains," pp. 30–32.

56. Ibid., pp.40–46.

57. D. Walde, "Sedentism and pre-contact tribal organization on the northern plains: colonial imposition or indigenous development," *World Archaeology* 38, no. 2 (2006): p. 302.

58. Walde et al., "Late Period on the Canadian and Adjacent Plains," p. 40. The one and only exception was a reference by HBC servant Matthew Cocking to the growing of tobacco in west-central Saskatchewan in 1772. See Meyer, "People Before Kelsey," pp. 69–70.

59. Walde, "Sedentism and pre-contact tribal organization," p. 302.

60. Ibid., pp. 298–306.

61. Binnema, *Common and Contested Ground*, p. 68. The occupants of Cluny were probably Hidatsa.

62. See D.B. Bamforth, "Indigenous People, Indigenous Violence: Precontact Warfare on the North American Plains," *Man* 29, no. 1 (March 1994): pp. 95–115.

63. It has been estimated that there were about 189,000 people living in the Great Plains region in 1700. *Handbook of North American Indians, 13, Plains, pt. 1*, (Washington: Smithsonian Institution, 1978), p, 12

64. See D.G. Mandelbaum, *The Plains Cree: An Ethnographic, Historical, and Comparative Study* (Regina: Canadian Plains Research Center, 1979).

65. That the Cree and Assiniboine already occupied these places and were trading partners at the time of contact is suggested by the archaeological evidence. Walde et al., "The Late Period on the Canadian and Adjacent Plains," pp. 49–50, 56. See also D. Meyer and D. Russell, "The Pegogamaw Crees and Their Ancestors: History and Archaeology in the Saskatchewan Forks Region," *Plains Anthropologist* 51, no. 199 (2006): pp. 315–17.

CHAPTER THREE NOTES

1. See J.W. Whillans, *First in the West: The Story of Henry Kelsey, Discoverer of the Canadian Prairies* (Edmonton: Applied Art Products, 1955).

2. C.G. Calloway, *New Worlds for All: Indians, Europeans, and the Remaking of Early America* (Baltimore: Johns Hopkins University Press 1997), pp. 5–12; 115–17.

3. For the connection between social and political upheaval and climate history in Spanish America in the late seventeenth and early eighteenth centuries, see B. Skopyk, "Undercurrents of Conquest: The Shifting Terrain of Indigenous Agriculture in Colonial Tlaxcala, Mexico" (PhD diss., York University, 2010).

4. C.G. Calloway, *One Vast Winter Count: The American West before Lewis and Clark* (Lincoln: University of Nebraska Press, 2003), p. 254.

5. Calloway, *New Worlds for All*, p. 10.

6. Calloway, *One Vast Winter Count*, pp. 71–73.

7. T.E. Emerson and R.B. Lewis, eds., *Cahokia and the Hinterlands: Middle Mississippian Cultures of the Midwest* (Urbana: University of Chicago Press, 1991). See also R.G. Kennedy, *Hidden Cities: The Discovery and Loss of Ancient North American Civilization* (New York: Penguin, 1994); G. Hodges, "Cahokia: America's Lost City," *National Geographic*, January 2011.

8. Calloway, *New Worlds for All*, p. 143.

9. J.R. Miller, *Compact, Contract, Covenant: Aboriginal Treaty-Making in Canada* (Toronto: University of Toronto Press, 2009), p. 10.

10. Ibid., p. 5.

11. Calloway, *New Worlds for All*, p. 128.

12. Rich, *The History of the Hudson's Bay Company, 1670–1870, vol. 1* (London: Hudson's Bay Record Society, 1958–59), p. 49.

13. D.B. Miquelon, *New France, 1701–1743: A Supplement to Europe* (Toronto: McClelland and Stewart 1987), pp. 567.

14. Rich, *History of the Hudson's Bay Company, vol. 1*, p. 22.

15. A.S. Morton, *A History of the Canadian West to 1870–1871* (London: Thomas Nelson, 1939) claims that there was no ship more important than the *Nonsuch*. The ship "effected the first direct and vital contact of the North-West with hoary Europe," p. 52.

16. The HBC was set up as a joint-stock company with an initial capitalization of 10,500 pounds to minimize the risk.

17. Quoted in G. Williams, "Highlights of the First 200 Years of the Hudson's Bay Company," *The Beaver* 50, no. 2 (Autumn 1970): p. 8.

18. Charles II, Royal Charter of the Hudson's Bay Company, 2 May 1670, http://www.hbcheritage.ca/hbcheritage/collections/archival/charter/charter/asp (accessed 26 February 2015). See also K. McNeil, "Sovereignty and the Aboriginal Nations of Rupert's Land," *Manitoba History* 37 (Spring/Summer 1999): pp. 2–7.

19. P.C. Newman, *Company of Adventurers* (Markham: Viking, 1985), pp. 85–91.

20. Rich, *History of the Hudson's Bay Company, vol. 1*, p. 56.

21. Ibid., p. 57.

22. Williams, "Highlights of the First 200 Years," p. 8.

23. Newman, *Company of Adventurers*, p. 143.

24. London Committee to Henry Sargeant, 22 May 1685 in E.E. Rich, ed., *Copy-book of Letters Outward, 1679–94* (The London Committee: The Champlain Society for the Hudson's Bay Record Society, 1948), p. 142.

25. London Committee to P.E. Radisson, 20 May 1686 in Rich, ed., *Letters Outward*, 1679–94, p. 198.

26. London Committee to Governor Geyer, 21 May 1691 in E. E. Rich, ed., *Copy-book of Letters Outward*, 1688–96 (The London Committee: The Champlain Society for the Hudson's Bay Record Society, 1957), p. 114.

27. London Committee to Henry Sargeant, 27 April 1683 in Rich, ed., *Letters Outward*, 1679–94, p. 76.

28. See A.J. Ray and D.B. Freeman, *"Give Us Good Measure": An Economic Analysis of Relations between the Indians and the Hudson's Bay Company before 1763* (Toronto: University of Toronto Press, 1978).

29. Knight letter of 17 September 1716 in K.G. Davies, ed., *Letters from Hudson Bay*, 1703–40 (London: Hudson's Bay Record Society, 1965), p. 57.

30. Newman, *Company of Adventurers*, p. xix.

31. London Committee to John Bridgar, 22 May 1682 in Rich, ed., *Letters Outward*, 1679–94, p. 36.

32. Miller, *Compact, Contract, Covenant,* pp. 12–15.

33. London Committee to Governor Geyer, 2 June 1688 in Rich, ed., *Letters Outward*, 1688–96, pp. 14–15.

34. London Committee to John Nixon, 22 May 1682 in Rich, ed., *Letters Outward*, 1679–94, p. 48.

35. London Committee to John Bridgar, 15 May 1682 in Rich, ed., *Letters Outward*, 1679–94, p. 35; London Committee to Henry Sergeant, 27 April 1683 (Ibid, 76); London Committee to Henry

Sergeant, 22 May 1685 (Ibid, 141).

36. W.L. Morton, *Manitoba: A History* (Toronto: University of Toronto Press, 1967), pp. 14–15.

37. London Committee to Henry Sargeant, 27 April 1683 in Rich, ed., *Letters Outward*, 1679–94, p. 73.

38. D.B. Miquelon, "Ambiguous Concession: What Diplomatic Archives Reveal about Article 15 of the Treaty of Utrecht and France's North American Policy," *William and Mary Quarterly*, 3rd ser., 68, no. 3 (July 2010): p. 461. Miquelon argues that the Utrecht settlement did not represent a reversal of French policy to dominate the interior because no such policy existed at the time (pp. 479–80).

39. Morton, *History of the Canadian West*, p. 125.

40. Quoted in Williams, "Highlights of the First 200 Years," p. 13.

41. Morton, *History of the Canadian West*, pp. 128–29.

42. Calloway, *New Worlds for All*, pp. 116–24; 184.

43. A.J. Ray, *Indians in the Fur Trade: their role as hunters, trappers, and middlemen in the lands southwest of Hudson Bay, 1660–1870* (Toronto: University of Toronto Press, 1974), p. 13.

44. D. Russell, *Eighteenth-Century Western Cree and Their Neighbours* (Hull: Canadian Museum of Civilization, 1991), pp. 12–13, 127–28.

45. E.W. Morse, *Fur Trade Canoe Routes of Canada: Then and Now* (Toronto: University of Toronto Press, 1969), pp. 36–47.

46. Ray, *Indians in the Fur Trade*, p. 55.

47. T. Binnema, *Common and Contested Ground: A Human and Environmental History of the Northwestern Plains* (Norman: University of Oklahoma Press, 2001), pp. 96–97.

48. Ray, *Indians in the Fur Trade*, p. 55.

49. Russell, *Eighteenth-Century Western Cree*, pp. 14; 78–79.

50. Ray, *Indians in the Fur Trade*, p. 72.

51. Binnema, *Common and Contested Ground*, pp. 74–75. See also H.W. Pyszczyk, "The Use of Fur Trade Goods by Plains Indians," *Canadian Journal of Archaeology* 21, no. 1 (1997): pp. 45–84.

52. H. Kelsey, *The Kelsey Papers* (Regina: Canadian Plains Research Center, 1994), p. 2. (Note that the spelling and punctuation in the papers is per Kelsey's original text.)

53. See the 1682 letter from Governor John Nixon complaining that the Cree and Assiniboine were forcibly preventing the Dakota Sioux from traveling to the bay posts in Ray and Freeman, *"Give us Good Measure,"* p. 44.

54. Russell, *Eighteenth-Century Western Cree*, pp. 74–76. See also D. Meyer, "Time-Depth of the Western Woods Cree Occupation of Northern Ontario, Manitoba and Saskatchewan" in W. Cowan, ed., *Papers of the Eighteenth Algonquin Conference* (Ottawa: Carleton University, 1987), pp. 187–200; M. Magne, "Distributions of Native Groups in Western Canada, A.D. 1700 to A.D. 1850" in M. Magne, ed., *Archaeology in Alberta*, 1986 (Edmonton: Alberta Culture and Multiculturalism, 1987), pp. 220–32.

55. Morton, *A History of the Canadian West*, p. 113. The idea that the Cree and Assiniboine migrated from

present-day northwestern Ontario/southeastern Manitoba into east-central Saskatchewan was first put forward by David Mandelbaum in *The Plains Cree: An Ethnographic, Historical and Comparative Study* (New York: American Museum of Natural History, 1940).

56. Quoted in Morton, *A History of the Canadian West*, 147.

57. Ibid., 133.

58. Ray and Freeman, "*Give us Good Measure*", p. 241.

59. G. Williams, "Stuart (Stewart), William" in D.M. Hayne, ed., *Dictionary of Canadian Biography, vol. 2*, 1701–1740 (Toronto: University of Toronto Press, 1969), p. 615.

60. Russell, *Eighteenth-Century Western Cree*, pp. 81–82.

61. Morton, *A History of the Canadian West*, pp. 137–38

62. Ibid., pp. 138–39

63. Quoted in A.M. Johnson, "Norton, Richard," in F.G. Halpenny, ed., *Dictionary of Canadian Biography, vol. 3*, 1741–1770 (Toronto: University of Toronto Press, 1976), p. 489.

64. Williams, "Stuart (Stewart), William," in D.M. Hayne, ed., *Dictionary of Canadian Biography*, vol. 2, p. 616.

65. Ibid.

66. Johnson, "Norton, Richard," in F.G. Halpenny, ed., *Dictionary of Canadian Biography, vol. 3*, p. 489.

67. Rich, *History of the Hudson's Bay Company, vol. 1*, p. 57.

CHAPTER FOUR NOTES

1. Quoted in E.E. Rich, *The History of the Hudson's Bay Company, 1670–1870, vol. 1* (London: Hudson's Bay Record Society, 1958–59), p. 507.

2. A.S. Morton, *A History of the Canadian West to 1870–1871* (London: Thomas Nelson, 1939), p. 178; R.I. Ruggles, *A Country So Interesting: The Hudson's Bay Company and Two Centuries of Mapping, 1670–1870* (Montreal: McGill–Queens University Press, 1991), p. 32.

3. A.J. Ray, *Indians in the Fur Trade: their role as hunters, trappers, and middlemen in the lands southwest of Hudson Bay, 1660–1870* (Toronto: University of Toronto Press, 1974), p. 59.

4. D. Russell, *Eighteenth-Century Western Cree and Their Neighbours* (Hull: Canadian Museum of Civilization, 1991), pp. 9, 125.

5. Ibid., pp. 5–9, 122, 135, 172.

6. Ray, *Indians in the Fur Trade*, pp. 55–59. These Indians, mistaken as Blackfoot, were more likely Cree. See Russell, *Eighteenth-Century Western Cree*, pp. 132–33.

7. Quoted in Ray, *Indians in the Fur Trade*, p. 55.

8. Morton, *A History of the Canadian West*, pp. 127–35 ; Rich, *History of the Hudson's Bay Company*, p. 436; Ray, *Indians in the Fur Trade*, p. 57.

9. W.R. Wood and T.D. Thiessen, eds., *Early Fur Trade on the Northern Plains: Canadian Traders Among the*

Mandan and Hidatsa Indians, 1738–1818 (Norman: University of Oklahoma Press, 1985), pp. 18–21.

10. Russell, *Eighteenth-Century Western Cree*, pp. 133–36.

11. Dale Russell disputes the interpretation that the Cree and Assiniboine pushed westward across Manitoba and into Saskatchewan with the coming of the beaver trade. Using historical and archaeological evidence, in addition to linguistic work, he situates the Cree and Assiniboine in the western interior before the end of the seventeenth century. See his *Eighteenth-Century Western Cree* for a more detailed explanation.

12. Ibid., p. 186.

13. Ibid., pp. 172, 200–01, 210–16.

14. Rich, *History of the Hudson's Bay Company, vol. 1*, pp. 487–89, 530.

15. The Swan did, however, return from one of his trips with a tar sand sample from the Athabasca River.

16. A.J. Ray and D.B. Freeman, *"Give Us Good Measure": An Economic Analysis of Relations between the Indians and the Hudson's Bay Company before 1763* (Toronto: University of Toronto Press, 1978), p. 211.

17. A.J. Ray, "Higgling and Haggling at Ye Bay," *The Beaver,* Outfit 308:1 (Summer 1977): pp. 38–46; see also Ray and Freeman, *"Give Us Good Measure,"* pp. 60–62.

18. J.R. Miller, *Compact, Contract, Covenant: Aboriginal Treaty-Making in Canada* (Toronto: University of Toronto Press, 2009), pp. 15, 21.

19. G. Williams, ed., *Andrew Graham's Observations on Hudson's Bay, 1767–91* (London: Hudson's Bay Record Society, 1969), pp. 316–18.

20. Quoted in Ray and Freeman, *"Give Us Good Measure,"* p. 66.

21. P.C. Thistle, *Indian-European Trade Relations in the Lower Saskatchewan River Region to 1840* (Winnipeg: University of Manitoba Press, 1986), p. 37.

22. Williams, ed., *Andrew Graham's Observations*, p. 318.

23. James Isham to London Committee, 20 July 1739 in K.G. Davies, ed., *Letters from Hudson Bay, 1703–40* (London: Hudson's Bay Record Society, 1965), pp. 278–80.

24. Quoted in Ray and Freeman, *"Give Us Good Measure,"* p. 66.

25. Ibid., p. 170.

26. T. Binnema, *Common and Contested Ground: A Human and Environmental History of the Northwestern Plains* (Norman: University of Oklahoma Press, 2001), p. 9.

27. T. Macklish to London Committee, 8 August 1728 in Davies, ed., *Letters from Hudson Bay*, p. 136.

28. S. St. George et al., "The Tree Ring Record of Drought on the Canadian Prairies," *Journal of Climate* 22, no. 3 (February 2009): p. 700; R.A. Case and G.M. MacDonald, "Tree Ring Reconstructions of Streamflow for Three Canadian Prairie Rivers," *Journal of American Water Resources Association*, no. 39 (2003): p. 711.

29. Morton, *A History of the Canadian West*, p. 205; D.B. Miquelon, *New France, 1701–1743: A Supplement to Europe* (Toronto: McClelland and Stewart, 1987), p. 181.

30. Morton, *A History of the Canadian West*, p. 205.

31. *Pacific Historical Review* 53, no. 1 (February 1984): p. 82. There are, however, eight La Vérendrye commemoration sites in Winnipeg. See S. Berthelette, "The Making of a Manitoba Hero: Commemorating La Vérendrye in St. Boniface and Winnipeg, 1886–1938," *Manitoba History* 74 (Winter 2014): pp. 15–24.

32. Miquelon, *New France, 1701–1743*, p. 182.

33. Ibid., pp. 182–83.

34. Morton, *A History of the Canadian West*, p. 183.

35. Quoted in M.N. Crouse, *La Vérendrye: Fur Trader and Explorer* (Toronto: Ryerson, 1956), p. 98.

36. W.L. Morton, *Manitoba: A History* (Toronto: University of Toronto Press, 1967), pp. 158–62.

37. K. Sapoznik, "Where the Historiography Falls Short: La Vérendrye through the Lens of Gender, Race and Slavery in Early French Canada, 1731–1749," *Manitoba History* 62 (Winter 2009): pp. 22–32; see also M. Trudel, *L'esclavage au Canada français: histoire et conditions de l'esclavage* (Quebec City: Presses universitaires Laval, 1960), pp. 36–37.

38. Morton, *Manitoba: A History*, p. 28.

39. Ibid., pp. 24–25, 27.

40. Y.F. Zoltvany, "Gaultier de Varennes et de La Vérendrye, Pierre," in Halpenny, ed., *Dictionary of Canadian Biography, vol. 3, 1741–1770* (Toronto: University of Toronto Press, 1974), p. 252.

41. Morton, *A History of the Canadian West*, p. 197.

42. G. Wilson, *Frontier Farewell: The 1870s and the End of the Old West* (Regina: Canadian Plains Research Center, 2007), pp. 1–2.

43. Quoted in L.J. Burpee, ed., *Letters and Journals of Pierre Gaulthier de Varennes de la Vérendrye and His Sons* (Toronto: The Champlain Society, 1927), p. 250.

44. Ibid., p. 487.

45. Rich, *History of the Hudson's Bay Company, vol. 1*, p. 521.

46. Ibid., p. 528.

47. Ray and Freeman, *"Give Us Good Measure,"* p. 171.

48. Rich, *History of the Hudson's Bay Company*, vol. 1, p. 556.

49. Morton, *A History of the Canadian West*, pp. 191, 194. These posts included the two (Maurepas and La Reine) established by La Vérendrye and a temporary fort at the forks of the Red and Assiniboine rivers.

50. J. Isham to London Committee, July 27, 1740 in Davies, ed., *Letters from Hudson Bay, 1703–40* (London: Hudson's Bay Record Society, 1965), p. 311.

51. G. Williams, "Highlights of the First 200 Years of the Hudson's Bay Company," *The Beaver* 50, no. 2 (Autumn 1970): p. 16.

52. Rich, *History of the Hudson's Bay Company, vol. 1*, p. 575.

53. Quoted in Williams, "Highlights of the First 200 Years," p. 20.

54. Miquelon, *New France, 1701–1743*, p. 185.

55. K. Rasmussen, "The Myth that La Corne Grew Wheat in 1754," *Saskatchewan History* 33, no. 1 (Winter 1980): pp. 25–29; C.S. Houston, "The La Corne Farming Hoax," *Saskatchewan History* 33, no. 1 (Winter 1980): pp. 30–33.

56. D. Meyer and P. Thistle, "Saskatchewan River Rendezvous Centers and Trading Posts: Continuity in Cree Social Geography," *Ethnohistory* 42, no. 3 (Summer 1995): pp. 410–19.

57. J.C. Ewers, "Intertribal Warfare as the Precursor of Indian-White Warfare on the Northern Great Plains, *Western Historical Quarterly* 6, no. 4 (October 1975): p. 400.

58. Quoted in Sapoznik, "Where the Historiography Falls Short," p. 29.

59. Burpee, ed., *Letters and Journals*, pp. 451–52.

60. P.E. Hackett, *A Very Remarkable Sickness: Epidemics in the Petit Nord, 1670–1846* (Winnipeg: University of Manitoba Press, 2002), pp. 59-73.

61. C.G. Calloway, *One Vast Winter Count: The American West before Lewis and Clark* (Lincoln: University of Nebraska Press, 2003), p. 211.

62. The first smallpox epidemic in the Americas began in 1519–20 in Tenochtitlan (Spanish America) and then spread over the next four decades as far north as the eastern seaboard of the American colonies and as far south as Chile. It is not known whether the disease reached the northern plains.

63. D.R. Prothero, *Evolution: What the Fossils Say and Why It Matters* (New York: Columbia University Press, 2007), pp. 301–03, fig. 14.3.

64. The exact identity of the Snake Indians is at present being debated among Canadian plains archaeologists. Although many historical accounts suggest that the Snake were Shoshone (Shoshoni), D.A. Walde and G. Oetelaar of the University of Calgary challenge this interpretation in an article in preparation, tentatively titled, "Identifying the Snake: A New Look at the Anthropological, Historical, and Archaeological Evidence." Half a century ago, R.G. Forbis raised the same concerns in "The Direct Historical Approach in the Prairie Provinces of Canada," *Great Plains Journal* 3, no. 1 (1963): p. 11, saying, "Each mention [of Snakes] must be examined on its own merits, with recognition of the possibility that no identification may fit the facts." The term "Snakes" is used throughout this book.

65. Morton, *A History of the Canadian West*, p. 195.

66. Calloway, *One Vast Winter Count*, p. 267. See also P. Hämäläinen, "The Rise and Fall of Plains Indian Horse Cultures," *Journal of American History* 90, no. 3 (2003): pp. 833–62.

67. M. Liberty, "Hell Came with Horses: Plains Women in the Equestrian Era," *Montana History* 32, no. 3 (1982): pp. 10–19.

68. R. White, *The Roots of Dependency: Subsistence, Environment and Social Change Among the Choctaws, Pawnees, and Navahos* (Lincoln: Nebraska University Press, 1983), p. 183.

69. Quoted in F.R. Secoy, *Changing Military Patterns on the Great Plains* (Locust Valley, New York: J.J. Augustin Publisher, 1953), p. 35.

70. Ibid., p. 35.

71. Ibid., p. 36.

72. Ibid., p. 37; Binnema, *Common and Contested Ground*, p. 91.

73. M. Wagner, "Asleep by a Frozen Sea or a Financial Innovator?: The Hudson's Bay Company," *Canadian Journal of History* 49, no. 2 (2014): pp. 179–202.

74. Rich, *History of the Hudson's Bay Company, vol. 1*, pp. 573, 586.

75. Ibid., p. 525.

CHAPTER FIVE NOTES

1. Quoted in P.C. Thistle, *Indian-European Trade Relations in the Lower Saskatchewan River Region to 1840* (Winnipeg: University of Manitoba Press, 1986), pp. 27, 32.

2. Ibid., p. 31.

3. Other trading captains included Cockamanakisick, Miss'sin'kee'shick, Sesiwappew, and Commeseskew. Little is known about these men. See D. Meyer and D. Russell, "'So Fine and Pleasant, Beyond Description': The Lands and Lives of the Pegogamaw Crees," *Plains Anthropologist* 49, no. 191 (2004): p. 228.

4. A.S. Morton, *A History of the Canadian West to 1870–1871* (London: Thomas Nelson, 1939), p. 242.

5. E.E. Rich, *The History of the Hudson's Bay Company, 1670–1870, vol. 1* (London: Hudson's Bay Record Society, 1958–59), p. 436.

6. J. Isham, "A Copie of Orders and Instructions to Anthy Hendey" in B. Belyea, ed., *A Year Inland: The Journal of a Hudson's Bay Company Winterer* (Waterloo: Wilfrid Laurier University Press, 2000), p. 39.

7. Quoted in Belyea, ed., *A Year Inland*, p. 2.

8. Thistle, *Indian-European Trade Relations*, pp. 20–23.

9. D. Smyth, "The Niitsitapi Trade: Euroamericans and the Blackfoot-speaking Peoples to the mid-1830s," (Ph.D. thesis, Carleton University, 2001), p. 110.

10. D. Meyer and D. Russell, "'Through the Woods Whare Thare Ware Now Track Ways': Kelsey, Henday and Trails in East Central Saskatchewan," *Canadian Journal of Archaeology* 31. no. 3 (2007): p. 187.

11. G. Williams, "The Puzzle of Anthony Henday's Journal," *The Beaver,* Outfit 309:3 (Winter 1978): p. 56; Belyea, *A Year Inland*, p.1.

12. Belyea, ed., *A Year Inland*, p. 331.

13. Smyth, "The Niitsitapi Trade," p. 112.

14. For a detailed examination of Henday's trip, especially in present-day Alberta, see A.B. Beaudoin and H.W. Pyszczyk, "Where Was Anthony Henday and What Did He See?" *Alberta Archaeological Review* 28 (1998): pp. 25–31.

15. L.J. Burpee, ed., "York Factory to the Blackfeet Country: The Journal of Anthony Henday, 1754–55," *Transactions of the Royal Society of Canada, vol. 1*, sect. 2 (1907), pp. 312, 314.

16. Ibid., p. 326.

17. Ibid.

18. Meyer and Russell, "'Through the Woods," p. 188.

19. Burpee, ed., "York Factory to the Blackfeet Country," p. 327.

20. Meyer and Russell, "So Fine and Pleasant," p. 225.

21. Burpee, ed., "York Factory to the Blackfeet Country," p. 333.

22. There is no oral evidence that the Niitisitapi, a plains people, used canoes or traveled to the Bay. Smyth, "The Niitsitapi Trade," p. 92.

23. Burpee, ed., "York Factory to the Blackfeet Country," pp. 344–5.

24. R.J. Marles et al., *Aboriginal Plant Use in Canada's Northwest Boreal Forest* (Vancouver: University of British Columbia Press, 2000), pp. 92–93, 145–49.

25. For an explanation of how the Cree built canoes, see C.L. Lodge, "The Birch Bark Canoe as a Demographic Factor in the Canadian Shield," *Napao* 1, no. 1 (April 1968): pp. 3–12.

26. Burpee, ed., "York Factory to Blackfeet Country," p. 351.

27. Ibid., p. 353.

28. Morton, *A History of the Canadian West*, p. 250.

29. Belyea, ed., *A Year Inland*, p. 2.

30. Thistle, *Indian-European Trade Relations*, p. 23.

31. Williams, "Puzzle of Anthony Henday's Journal," p. 56.

32. Belyea, ed., *A Year Inland*, pp. 369–77.

33. Ibid., p. 377.

34. D. R. Russell, *Eighteenth-Century Western Cree and Their Neighbours* (Hull: Canadian Museum of Civilization, 1991), p 91.

35. Ibid., pp. 91–92.

36. C. Wilson, "Henday, Anthony" in F.G. Halpenny, ed., *Dictionary of Canadian Biography, vol. 3*, 1741–1770 (Toronto: University of Toronto Press, 1974), p. 286.

37. Smyth, "The Niitsitapi Trade," pp. 131–32.

38. Quoted in Thistle, *Indian-European Trade Relations*, p. 24.

39. Russell, *Eighteenth-Century Western Cree*, pp. 112–13.

40. Smyth, "The Niitsitapi Trade," p. 132; G.E. Thorman, "Smith, Joseph" in Halpenny, ed., *Dictionary of Canadian Biography, vol. 3*, p. 595; Brown, J.S.H., "Batt, Isaac" in F.G. Halpenny, ed., *Dictionary of Canadian Biography, vol. 4*, 1771–1800 (Toronto: University of Toronto Press, 1979), p. 47.

41. Quoted in Smyth, "The Niitsitapi Trade," p. 132.

42. Thistle, *Indian-European Trade Relations*, p. 24.

43. Rich, *History of the Hudson's Bay Company, vol. 1*, p. 644.

44. Russell, *Eighteenth-Century Western Cree*, p. 98.

45. R.Englebert, "Beyond Borders: Mental Mapping and the French River World in North America, 1763–1812" (Ph.D. diss., University of Ottawa, 2010). An attempt is being made today to save the dialect known as Missouri French. See *Ottawa Citizen*, June 25, 2014.

46. Quoted in Morton, *A History of the Canadian West*, p. 274.

47. W.S. Wallace, *The Pedlars from Quebec* (Toronto: Ryerson Press, 1954), pp. 1–18.

48. R. Swan and E.A. Jerome, "Indigenous Knowledge, Literacy, and Research on Métissage and Métis Origins on the Saskatchewan River: The Case of the Jerome Family," *Prairie Forum* 29, no. 1 (Spring 2004): pp. 1–24.

49. These men were James Allen, Isaac Batt, James Dearing, Edward Lutit, William Pink, and Louis Primeau. G. Williams, ed., *Andrew Graham's Observations on Hudson's Bay, 1767–91* (London: Hudson's Bay Record Society, 1969), p. lxvii.

50. Morton, *A History of the Canadian West*, p. 278.

51. Thistle, *Indian-European Trade Relations*, p. 26; See also D. Meyer and P. Thistle, "Saskatchewan River Rendezvous Centers and Trading Posts: Continuity in Cree Social Geography," *Ethnohistory* 42, no. 3 (Summer 1995): pp. 411–13.

52. Quoted in Morton, *A History of the Canadian West*, p. 279.

53. Smyth, "The Niitsitapi Trade," p. 138.

54. Ibid.

55. G. Williams, "Highlights of the First 200 Years of the Hudson's Bay Company," *The Beaver* 50, no. 2 (Autumn 1970): p. 28.

56. Quoted in Belyea, ed., *A Year Inland*, p. 378.

57. Williams, "Highlights of the First 200 Years," p. 28.

58. Brown, "Batt, Isaac," p. 47.

59. Belyea, ed., *A Year Inland*, p. 338.

60. See M.E. Malainey and B.L. Sherriff, "Adjusting our Perceptions: Historical and Archaeological Evidence of Winter on the Plains of Western Canada," *Plains Anthropologist* 41, no. 158 (November 1996): pp. 333–57.

61. D. Meyer and P. Thistle, "The Pegogamaw Cree and Their Ancestors: History and Archaeology in the Saskatchewan Forks Region," *Plains Anthropologist* 51, no. 199 (2006): p. 307; see also D. Meyer et al., "The Quest for Pasquatinow: An Aboriginal Gathering Centre in the Saskatchewan River Valley," *Prairie Forum* 17, no. 2, (Fall 1992): pp. 201–23.

62. Thistle, *Indian-European Trade Relations*, p. 44.

63. B.J. Given, *A Most Pernicious Thing: Gun Trading and Native Warfare in the Early Contact Period* (Ottawa: Carleton University Press, 1994), p. 107.

64. Quoted in Belyea, ed., *A Year Inland*, p. 393.

65. Ibid., pp. 44–48.

66. Smyth, "The Niitsitapi Trade," pp. 138–39.

67. P. Hämäläinen, "The Rise and Fall of Plains Indian Horse Cultures," *Journal of American History* 90, no. 3: p. 846.

68. Ibid., pp. 847–48.

69. T. Binnema, *Common and Contested Ground: A Human and Environmental History of the Northwestern Plains* (Norman: University of Oklahoma Press, 2001), p. 92.

70. Smyth, "The Niitsitapi Trade," pp. 141–43.

71. Belyea, ed., *A Year Inland*, pp. 360–63.

72. For an examination of how post governors handled incidents of homosexual activity and sexual impropriety with animals, see P.C. Nigol, "Discipline and Discretion in the Mid-Eighteenth-Century Hudson's Bay Company Private Justice System" in J.S. Swainger and L.A. Knafla, eds., *Law and Societies in the Canadian Prairie West, 1670–1940* (Vancouver: University of British Columbia Press, 2005), pp. 165–70.

73. S. Van Kirk, *"Many Tender Ties": Women in Fur-Trade Society, 1670–1870* (Winnipeg: Watson and Dwyer, 1980), pp. 38–39; J.S.H. Brown, *Strangers in Blood: Fur Trade Families in Indian Country* (Vancouver: University of British Columbia Press, 1980), pp. 60–61.

74. Quoted in Van Kirk, *"Many Tender Ties,"* p. 29.

75. H.R. Driscoll, "'A Most Important Chain of Connection': Marriage in the Hudson's Bay Company" in T. Binnema et al., eds., *From Rupert's Land to Canada* (Edmonton: University of Alberta Press, 2001), p. 91.

76. J.S.H. Brown, "Partial Truths: A Closer Look at Fur Trade Marriage" in T. Binnema et al., eds., *From Rupert's Land to Canada*, p. 72.

77. Brown, *Strangers in Blood*, p. 66.

78. D. Fuchs, "Embattled Notions: Constructions of Rupert's Land Native Sons, 1760–1860," *Manitoba History* 44 (Autumn 2002/Winter 2003): pp. 10–11.

79. Belyea, ed., *A Year Inland*, p. 345.

80. Ibid., p. 61.

81. Morton, *A History of the Canadian West*, p. 275.

82. Rich, *History of the Hudson's Bay Company, vol. 1*, p. 645.

83. T. Binnema, *Enlightened Zeal: The Hudson's Bay Company and Scientific Networks, 1670–1870* (Toronto: University of Toronto Press, 2014), p. 105.

84. S. Hearne, *A Journey from Prince of Wales's Fort in Hudson's Bay to the Northern Ocean, 1769, 1770, 1771, 1772* (Toronto: Macmillan, 1958), p. 35.

85. Quoted in C.S. Mackinnon, "Hearne, Samuel" in Halpenny, ed., *Dictionary of Canadian Biography, vol. 4*, p. 340.

86. For an examination of the Bloody Falls murders, see S.E. Roberts, "Trans-Indian Identity and Inuit

'Other': Relations between the Chipewyan and Neighbouring Aboriginal Communities in the Eighteenth Century," *Ethnohistory* 57, no. 4 (2010): pp. 597–624; I.S. MacLaren, "Samuel Hearne's Accounts of the Massacre at Bloody Fall, 17 July 1771," *Ariel: A Review of International English Literature* 22, no. 1 (January 1991): pp. 25–51.

87. MacKinnon, "Hearne, Samuel," p. 340.

88. Binnema, *Enlightened Zeal*, pp. 102–105. For the role of the French captain (who captured Fort Prince of Wales in 1782) in the eventual publication of Hearne's journal, see E.G. Allen, "American Ornithology before Audubon," *Transactions of the American Philosophical Society, vol. 3*, pt. 41 (1951), pp. 522–24.

89. Binnema, *Enlightened Zeal,* pp. 102–105. See C.S. Houston et al., *Eighteenth-Century Naturalists of Hudson Bay* (Montreal: McGill–Queen's University Press, 2003).

90. Smyth, "The Niitsitapi Trade," pp. 147–48.

91. A.J. Ray, "Wapinesiw" in Halpenny, ed., *Dictionary of Canadian Biography, vol. 4*, p. 761.

92. Quoted in Belyea, ed., *A Year Inland*, p. 341.

93. L.J. Burpee, ed., "An Adventurer from Hudson Bay: Journal of Matthew Cocking, from York Factory to the Blackfeet country, 1772–1773," *Transactions of the Royal Society of Canada, vol. 1*, sect. 2 (1907), p. 99.

94. Meyer and Russell, "So Fine and Pleasant," p. 244.

95. Ibid., p. 233, 234.

96. J.R. Vickers and T.R. Peck argue that the availability of wood was more important than the availability of game in the selection of winter campsites. "Islands in a Sea of Grass: The Significance of Wood in Winter Campsite Selection on the Northwestern Plains" in B. Kooyman and J. Kelley, *Archaeology on the Edge: New Perspectives from the Northern Plains*, eds. (Calgary: University of Calgary Press, 2004), pp. 95–124.

97. Burpee, ed., "An Adventurer from Hudson Bay," p. 107.

98. Ibid.

99. Ibid., p. 103.

100. Ibid., p. 114.

101. Ibid., p. 113.

102. Meyer and Russell, "So Fine and Pleasant," p. 229.

103. Burpee, ed., "An Adventurer from Hudson Bay," p.108.

104. Ibid., p. 111.

105. D. Meyer, "People Before Kelsey: An Overview of Cultural Developments" in H. Epp, ed., *Three Hundred Prairie Years: Henry Kelsey's "Inland Country of Good Report"* (Regina: Canadian Plains Research Center/Saskatchewan Archaeological Society,1993), p. 69. The pottery may have been from the Old Women's phase.

106. Burpee, ed., "An Adventurer from Hudson Bay," p.109; D.W. Moodie and B. Kaye, "Indian Agriculture

in the Fur Trade Northwest," *Prairie Forum* 11, no. 2 (Fall 1986): p. 172.

107. Burpee, ed., "An Adventurer from Hudson Bay," p.111.

108. Ibid.

109. Meyer and Russell, "'So Fine and Pleasant, Beyond Description': The Lands and Lives of the Pegogamaw Crees," p. 241.

110. Thistle, *Indian-European Trade Relations*, pp. 31–32.

111. Quoted in Belyea, ed., *A Year Inland*, p. 391.

112. Quoted in Williams, "Highlights of the First 200 Years," p. 28.

113. Ibid., p. 27.

CHAPTER SIX NOTES

1. There were approximately 300 documented posts in Saskatchewan alone. See D. Russell and D. Meyer, "The History of the Fur Trade ca. 1682–post-1821" in K. I. Fung, ed., *Atlas of Saskatchewan* (Saskatoon: University of Saskatchewan, 1999), pp. 34–5.

2. Quoted in B. Belyea, ed., *A Year Inland: The Journal of a Hudson's Bay Company Winterer* (Waterloo: Wilfrid Laurier University Press, 2000), pp. 388–89.

3. G. Williams, "The Puzzle of Anthony Henday's Journal," *The Beaver*, Outfit 309:3 (Winter 1978): pp. 51–52. There are actually three "failure" versions of Henday's journal in Graham's Observations.

4. A.S. Morton, *A History of the Canadian West to 1870–1871* (London: Thomas Nelson, 1939), p. 301; G. Williams, "Highlights of the First 200 Years of the Hudson's Bay Company," *The Beaver* 50, no. 2 (Autumn 1970): p. 29.

5. G. Williams, ed., *Andrew Graham's Observations on Hudson's Bay, 1767–91* (London: Hudson's Bay Record Society, 1969), p. lxiv.

6. J.B. Tyrrell, ed., *Journals of Samuel Hearne and Philip Turnor* (Toronto: Champlain Society, 1934), p. 105.

7. D.J. Sauchyn and A.B. Beaudoin, "Recent Environmental Change in the Southwestern Plains," *The Canadian Geographer* 42, no. 4 (1998): p. 348.

8. D. Smyth, "The Niitsitapi Trade: Euroamericans and the Blackfoot-speaking Peoples to the mid-1830s" (Ph.D. thesis, Carleton University, 2001), pp. 155–57; D.R. Russell, *Eighteenth-Century Western Cree and Their Neighbours* (Hull: Canadian Museum of Civilization, 1991), p. 116; P.C. Thistle *Indian-European Trade Relations in the Lower Saskatchewan River Region to 1840* (Winnipeg: University of Manitoba Press, 1986), p. 54.

9. Basquia is used interchangeably with Pasquia, a shortened form of the Cree word, opāskweyāw, and the traditional name for The Pas.

10. Tyrrell, ed., *Journals of Hearne and Turnor*, p. 113; D. Meyer and P. Thistle, "Saskatchewan River Rendezvous Centers and Trading Posts: Continuity in Cree Social Geography," *Ethnohistory* 42, no. 3 (Summer 1995): pp. 430–31.

11. Tyrrell, ed., *Journals of Hearne and Turnor*, p. 111.

12. Ibid., pp. 114–15.

13. Ibid., p. 157.

14. Smyth, "The Niitsitapi Trade," p. 156; Thistle, *Indian-European Trade Relations*, p. 55.

15. See for example in Tyrrell, ed., *Journals of Hearne and Turnor*, the Cumberland House journal entries for July 1781, in which mosquitoes are the dominant subject.

16. A.M. Johnson, ed., *Saskatchewan Journals and Correspondence* (London: Hudson's Bay Record Society, 1967), p. 118.

17. Tyrrell, ed., *Journals of Hearne and Turnor*, p. 108; A.S. Morton, *A History of the Canadian West*, p. 302.

18. G. Colpitts, "'Victuals to Put into our Mouths': Environmental Perspectives on Fur Trade Provisioning Activities at Cumberland House, 1775–1782," *Prairie Forum* 22, no. 1 (Spring 1997): p. 4.

19. G. Colpitts, *Game in the Garden: A Human History of Wildlife in Western Canada to 1940* (Vancouver: University of British Columbia Press, 2002), p. 14.

20. Colpitts, "'Victuals to Put into our Mouths,'" pp. 4, 18.

21. S. Van Kirk, *Many Tender Ties: Women in Fur-Trade Society, 1670–1870* (Winnipeg: Watson and Dwyer, 1980), p. 58.

22. Thistle, *Indian-European Trade Relations*, p. 55.

23. Colpitts, "'Victuals to Put into our Mouths,'" p. 3.

24. E.E. Rich and A.M. Johnson, eds., *Cumberland House Journals and the Inland Journals, 1775–1782*, 1st and 2nd ser. (London: Hudson's Bay Record Society, 1951), 14 August 1777, p. 80.

25. Thistle, *Indian-European Trade Relations*, p. 30; Meyer and Thistle, "Saskatchewan River Rendezvous Centers," p. 430.

26. Tyrrell, ed., *Journals of Hearne and Turnor*, p. 105.

27. Quoted in Thistle, *Indian-European Trade Relations*, p. 53.

28. Quoted in T. Binnema*, Common and Contested Ground: A Human and Environmental History of the Northwestern Plains* (Norman: University of Oklahoma Press, 2001), p. 106.

29. Meyer and Thistle, "Saskatchewan River Rendezvous Centers," p. 415; Rich and Johnson, eds., *Cumberland House Journals*, p. 76.

30. Quoted in A.S. Morton, *A History of the Canadian West*, p. 324.

31. Tyrrell, ed., *Journals of Hearne and Turnor*, p. 190.

32. H.W. Duckworth, ed., *The English River Book: A North West Company Journal and Account Book of 1786* (Montreal: McGill–Queen's University Press, 1990), p. xiv; Binnema, *Common and Contested Ground*, pp. 117–18.

33. Morton, *A History of the Canadian West*, pp. 312–13; Colpitts, *Game in the Garden*, pp. 21–22.

34. M.M. Quaife, ed., *Alexander Henry's Travels and Adventures in the Years 1760–1776* (Chicago: R.R. Donnelley and Sons Company, 1926), pp. 258, 265.

35. Tyrrell, ed., *Journals of Hearne and Turnor*, p. 175.

36. J.S.H. Brown, "Isham, Charles Thomas" in F.G. Halpenny, ed., *Dictionary of Canadian Biography, vol. 5, 1801–1820* (Toronto: University of Toronto Press, 1983), pp. 450–51.

37. Colpitts, "'Victuals to Put into our Mouths,'" p. 5; Thistle, *Indian-European Trade Relations*, p. 58.

38. Rich and Johnson, eds., *Cumberland House Journals*, 1st ser., 24 January 1777, p. 109.

39. Morton, *A History of the Canadian West*, p. 305.

40. Johnson, ed., *Saskatchewan Journals and Correspondence*, p. 45.

41. Rich and Johnson, eds., *Cumberland House Journals*, 1st ser., 18 May 1776, p. 47.

42. E.E. Rich, *The History of the Hudson's Bay Company, 1670–1870, vol. 2* (London: Hudson's Bay Record Society, 1958–59), p. 228.

43. A.M. Carlos and F.D. Lewis, *Commerce by a Frozen Sea: Native Americans and the European Fur Trade* (Philadelphia: University of Pennsylvania Press, 2010), pp. 11–12.

44. Quoted in Morton, *A History of the Canadian West*, p. 307.

45. Thistle, *Indian-European Trade Relations*, pp. 60–61.

46. Colpitts, "'Victuals to Put into our Mouths,'" pp. 3,16.

47. Rich and Johnson, eds., *Cumberland House Journals*, 1st ser., 24 January 1777, p. 112 and 2 October 1778, p. 264.

48. Ibid., September 12, 1777, p. 188.

49. Rich and Johnson, eds., *Cumberland House Journals*, 1st and 2nd ser., 1 February 1781, p. 134.

50. B.M. Gough, "Pond, Peter," in Halpenny, ed., *Dictionary of Canadian Biography, vol. 5*, pp. 681–86.

51. C.S. Mackinnon, "Some Logistics of Portage La Loche (Methy)," *Prairie Forum* 5, no. 1 (1980): pp. 51–66.

52. Morton, *A History of the Canadian West*, pp. 326–27.

53. B. Macdougall, *One of the Family: Metis Culture in Nineteenth-Century Northwestern Saskatchewan* (Vancouver: University of British Columbia Press, 2010), pp. xv–xvi.

54. Quoted in Morton, *A History of the Canadian West*, p. 324.

55. Ibid., pp. 324–25; Binnema, *Common and Contested Ground*, pp. 111–13.

56. Rich and Johnson, eds., *Cumberland House Journals*, 1st ser., 27 April 1779, p. 333.

57. Rich and Johnson, eds., *Cumberland House Journals*, 2nd ser., 4 March 1781, p. 182.

58. Quoted in A.J. Ray, "Holmes, William" in F. Halpenny, ed., *Dictionary of Canadian Biography, vol. 4, 1771–1800* (Toronto: University of Toronto Press, 1979), p. 366.

59. Rich and Johnson, eds., *Cumberland House Journals*, 2nd ser., 5 December 1779, p. 79.

60. Binnema, *Common and Contested Ground*, pp. 113–18; D. Meyer and P. Thistle, "The Pegogamaw Cree and Their Ancestors: History and Archaeology in the Saskatchewan Forks Region," *Plains Anthropologist* 51, no. 199 (2006): p. 307.

61. Rich and Johnson, eds., *Cumberland House Journals*, 2nd ser., 11 January 1780, p. 84.

62. Russell, *Eighteenth-Century Western Cree*, p. 117.

63. J.B. Tyrrell, ed., *David Thompson's Narrative of His Explorations in Western America, 1784–1812* (Toronto: Champlain Society, 1917), p. 337.

64. Rich and Johnson, eds., *Cumberland House Journals*, 2nd ser., 22 October 1781, p. 262 and 9 November 1781, p. 265.

65. Ibid., 2 February 1782, p. 234.

66. Ibid., 11 January 1782, p. 230; Sauchyn and A.B. Beaudoin, "Recent Environmental Change," p. 347; A.R. Hodge, "'In Want of Nourishment for to Keep Them Alive': Climate Fluctuations, Bison Scarcity, and the Smallpox Epidemic of 1780–82 on the Northern Great Plains," *Environmental History* 17 (April 2012): p. 388.

67. Brown, "Isham" in Halpenny, ed., *Dictionary of Canadian Biography, vol. 5*, pp. 450–51.

68. Rich and Johnson, eds., *Cumberland House Journals*, 2nd ser., 22 January 1782, p. 232. It has been suggested that Cumberland House essentially served as a field hospital during the epidemic. C.S. Houston and M. Massie, *36 Steps on the Road to Medicare* (Montreal: McGill–Queen's University Press, 2013), p. 3. See also C.S. Houston and S. Houston, "The first smallpox epidemic on the Canadian Plains: In the fur-traders' words," *Canadian Journal of Infectious Diseases* 11, no. 2 (March/April 2000): pp. 112–15.

69. See, for example, Rich and Johnson, eds., *Cumberland House Journals*, 2nd ser., 14 March 1782, p. 242, and 27 March 1782, p. 244.

70. E.A. Fenn, *Pox Americana: The Great Smallpox Epidemic of 1775–82* (New York: Hill and Wang, 2002), p. 182.

71. Binnema, *Common and Contested Ground*, p. 108.

72. Quoted in Smyth, "The Niitsitapi Trade," p. 167.

73. W.K. Lamb, ed., *The Journals and Letters of Sir Alexander Mackenzie* (Toronto: Macmillan, 1970), p. 122.

74. A recent study has lowered the mortality rate to less than twenty percent. A.M. Carlos and F.D. Lewis, "Smallpox and Native American Mortality: The 1780s Epidemic in the Hudson Bay Region," *Explorations in Economic History* 49 (2012): pp. 277–90.

75. Russell, *Eighteenth-Century Western Cree*, p. 144; Meyer and Thistle, "Saskatchewan River Rendezvous Centers," p. 422.

76. T. Binnema, "'With Tears, Shrieks, and Howlings of Despair': The Smallpox Epidemic of 1781–82" in M. Payne et al., eds., *Alberta Formed—Alberta Transformed, vol. 1* (Edmonton: University of Alberta Press, 2006), pp. 127.

77. Tyrrell, ed., *David Thompson's Narrative*, pp. 337–38.

78. Fenn, *Pox Americana*, p. 194.

79. Quoted in Smyth, "The Niitsitapi Trade," p. 186.

CHAPTER SEVEN NOTES

1. A.S. Morton, *A History of the Canadian West to 1870–1871* (London: Thomas Nelson, 1939), pp. 335–39; T. Binnema and G. Ens, eds., *The Hudson's Bay Company Edmonton House Journals, Correspondence, and Reports, 1806–1821* (Calgary: Historical Society of Alberta, 2012), pp. 23, 30.

2. D. Smyth, "The Niitsitapi Trade: Euroamericans and the Blackfoot-speaking Peoples to the mid-1830s," (Ph.D. thesis, Carleton University, 2001), pp. 159, 174–6, 188.

3. Quoted in L. Green, "'The House in Buffalo Country': Hudson House on the North Saskatchewan River, 1778–1787," *Saskatchewan History* 56, no. 1 (2004): p. 34.

4. Quoted in Smyth, "The Niitsitapi Trade," p. 184.

5. P.C. Thistle, *Indian-European Trade Relations in the Lower Saskatchewan River Region to 1840* (Winnipeg: University of Manitoba Press, 1986), pp. 62, 75–77; D. Meyer and P. Thistle, "Saskatchewan River Rendezvous Centers and Trading Posts: Continuity in Cree Social Geography," *Ethnohistory* 42, no. 3 (Summer 1995): p. 431.

6. Smyth, "The Niitsitapi Trade," p. 190.

7. Ibid., pp. 189–94.

8. Fidler loved reading and amassed a library of over 500 books. See D. Lindsay, "Peter Fidler's Library" in P.F. McNally, ed., *Readings in Canadian Library History* (Ottawa: Canadian Library Association, 1986), pp. 209–229.

9. A.S. Morton, ed., *The Journal of Duncan McGillivray of the North West Company at Fort George on the Saskatchewan, 1794–95* (Toronto: Macmillan,1929), p. 30.

10. Smyth, "The Niitsitapi Trade," pp. 201–22.

11. Morton, ed., *Journal of Duncan McGillivray*, p. 30.

12. Quoted in Smyth, "The Niitsitapi Trade," p. 193.

13. For a fuller discussion of this issue, see R.G. Morgan, "Beaver Ecology/Beaver Mythology," (Ph.D. diss., University of Alberta, 1991).

14. Ibid., p. 1.

15. Morton, *Journal of Duncan McGillivray*, p. 47.

16. F. Ouellet, "McTavish, Simon" in F.G. Halpenny, ed., *Dictionary of Canadian Biography, vol. 5, 1801–1820*, pp. 560–67.

17. Morton, *A History of the Canadian West*, p. 413.

18. Ibid., p. 409.

19. Ibid., pp. 420–22.

20. C. Podruchny, "Baptizing Novices: Ritual Moments among French Canadian Voyageurs in the Montreal Fur Trade, 1788–1821," *Canadian Historical Review* 83, no. 2 (June 2002): pp. 175–80.

21. Ibid., pp. 165, 181–83; C. Podruchny, "Unfair Masters and Rascally Servants? Labour Relations Among Bourgeois, Clerks, and Voyageurs in the Montréal Fur Trade, 1780–1821, *Labour/Le Travail* 43 (Spring 1999): pp. 47–48. This mock baptism was similar to the sailor's custom of "baptizing"

crew and passengers who "crossed the line" (the Equator) for the first time.

22. G. Colpitts, *Pemmican Empire: Food, Trade, and the Last Bison Hunts in the North American Plains, 1780–1882* (New York: Cambridge University Press, 2015), pp. 87–99.

23. Morton, *A History of the Canadian West*, pp. 349–51.

24. R.I. Ruggles, *A Country So Interesting: The Hudson's Bay Company and Two Centuries of Mapping, 1670–1870* (Montreal: McGill–Queen's University Press, 1991), p. 54. The HBC Athabasca surveying expedition was part of a larger British search for navigable inlets along the Pacific Ocean being investigated at that same time by George Vancouver.

25. Nicks, J., "Tomison, William," in F.G. Halpenny, ed., *Dictionary of Canadian Biography, vol. 6, 1821–1835* (Toronto: University of Toronto Press, 1987), pp. 775–77.

26. B. Belyea, *Dark Storm Moving West* (Calgary: University of Calgary Press, 2007), p. 28.

27. C.A. Purdey, "Orkneymen to Rupert's Landers: Orkney Workers in the Saskatchewan District, 1795–1830," (master's thesis, University of Alberta, 2010), p. 22.

28. Ibid., pp. 11, 25–27.

29. J.S.H. Brown, *Strangers in Blood: Fur Trade Families in Indian Country* (Vancouver: University of British Columbia Press, 1980), p. 71; I.M. Spry, "Cocking, Mathew" in F.G. Halpenny, ed., *Dictionary of Canadian Biography, vol. 4, 1771–1800* (Toronto: University of Toronto Press, 1979), p. 157. Two of Cocking's daughters married HBC officers.

30. J.S.H. Brown, "Ross, Malcolm" in Halpenny, ed., *Dictionary of Canadian Biography, vol. 4*, pp. 684–85.

31. Quoted in Brown, *Strangers in Blood*, p. 81.

32. Ibid., pp. 85–89.

33. B. Macdougall, *One of the Family: Métis Culture in Nineteenth-Century Northwestern Saskatchewan* (Vancouver: University of British Columbia Press, 2010), pp. 4, 43–44.

34. Smyth, "The Niitsitapi Trade," p. 318.

35. J.E. Foster, "Wintering, the Outside Adult Male and the Ethnogenesis of the Western Plains Métis," *Prairie Forum* 19, no. 1 (Spring 1994): pp. 1–14; H. Devine, *The People Who Own Themselves: Aboriginal Ethnogenesis in a Canadian Family, 1660–1900* (Calgary: University of Calgary Press, 2004), pp. 131–33.

36. A.B. Beaudoin, "What They Saw: The Climate and Environmental Context for Euro-Canadian Settlement in Alberta," *Prairie Forum* 24, no. 1 (Spring 1999): p. 32. See also S. Houston, T. Ball, and M. Houston, *Eighteenth-Century Naturalists of Hudson Bay* (Montreal: McGill–Queen's University Press, 2003), p. 115.

37. Quoted in J. Daschuk and G. Marchildon, "Climate and Aboriginal-Newcomer Adaptation in the South Saskatchewan River Basin, A.D. 800–1700," Institutional Adaptations to Climate Change Project, 2005. http://www.parc.ca/mcri/iacc007.php http://www.ca/mcri/papers.php (accessed 18 August 2015).

38. Ibid.

39. D.J. Sauchyn, J. Stroich, and A. Beriault, "A Paleoclimatic Context for the Drought of 1999–2001 in the

Northern Great Plains of North America, *The Geographical Journal* 169, no. 2 (2003): pp. 158–67. Nor was drought restricted to the northern prairies. Both the Comanche and Hopi had to contend with extremely dry conditions on the southern plains in the mid-1770s. See C.G. Calloway, *One Vast Winter Count: The Native American West before Lewis and Clark* (Lincoln: University of Nebraska Press, 2003), pp. 384, 391.

40. J.S. Nicks, "The Pine Island Posts, 1786–1794: A Study of Competition in the Fur Trade," (master's thesis, University of Alberta, 1975), pp. 101–104; R.A. Case and G.M. MacDonald, "Tree Ring Reconstructions of Streamflow for Three Canadian Rivers," *Journal of the American Water Resources Association* 39, no. 3 (June 2003): p. 711; S.A. Wolfe et al., "Late 18th Century Drought-Induced Sand Activity, Great Sand Hills, Saskatchewan," *Canadian Journal of Earth Sciences* 38, no. 1 (2001): p. 105; D.J. Sauchyn and W.R. Skinner, "A Proxy Record of Drought Severity for the Southwestern Plains," *Canadian Water Resources Journal* 26, no. 2 (2001): pp. 253–72; Daschuk and Marchildon, "Climate and Aboriginal-Newcomer Adaptation."

41. Quoted in Daschuk and Marchildon, "Climate and Aboriginal-Newcomer Adaptation."

42. T. Binnema, *Common and Contested Ground: A Human and Environmental History of the Northwestern Plains* (Norman: University of Oklahoma Press, 2001), p. 141; R. White, *The Roots of Dependency: Subsistence, Environment, and Social Change among the Choctaws, Pawnees, and Navajos* (Lincoln: University of Nebraska Press, 1983), p. 183; P. Hämäläinen, "The Rise and Fall of Indian Horse Cultures," *Journal of American History* 90. no. 3 (December 2003): pp. 847–88.

43. Hämäläinen, "The Rise and Fall of Indian Horse Cultures," pp. 351–52; Calloway, *One Vast Winter Count*, p. 114; J.C. Ewers, "Intertribal Warfare as the Precursor of Indian-White Warfare on the Northern Great Plains," *Western Historical Quarterly* 6, no. 4 (October 1975): p. 402.

44. Binnema, *Common and Contested Ground*, p. 142; Daschuk and Marchildon, "Climate and Aboriginal-Newcomer Adaptation."

45. Calloway, *One Vast Winter Count*, p. 112.

46. Quoted in Binnema, *Common and Contested Ground*, p. 149.

47. Smyth, "The Niitsitapi Trade," pp. 217–20; D. Meyer and P. Thistle, "The Pegogamaw Cree and Their Ancestors: History and Archaeology in the Saskatchewan Forks Region," *Plains Anthropologist* 51, no. 199 (2006): p. 319; Nicks, "The Pine Island Posts," p. 152; Binnema, *Common and Contested Ground*, p. 142.

48. Quoted in Smyth, "The Niitsitapi Trade," p. 217.

49. Binnema, *Common and Contested Ground*, p. 140.

50. Quoted in Ibid., p. 144.

51. J.S.H. Brown, "Batt, Isaac" in Halpenny, ed., *Dictionary of Canadian Biography, vol. 4*, pp. 46–48.

52. Binnema, *Common and Contested Ground*, pp. 143, 154.

53. D.R. Russell, *Eighteenth-Century Western Cree and Their Neighbours* (Hull: Canadian Museum of Civilization, 1991), p. 109.

54. B. Haig, ed., *Journal of a Journey Over Land from Buckingham House to the Rocky Mountains in 1792 & 3* (Lethbridge: Historical Research Centre, 1992), p. 76.

55. Ibid., pp. 80–82.

56. Morton, ed., *Journal of Duncan McGillivray*, p. 62.

57. Ibid., p. 63.

58. Binnema, *Common and Contested Ground*, pp. 144–45; Smyth, "The Niitsitapi Trade," pp. 162, 219, 223.

59. V.C. Trenholm, *The Arapahoes, Our People* (Norman: University of Oklahoma Press, 1970), p. 27.

60. Smyth, "The Niitsitapi Trade," p. 213.

61. Quoted in Binnema, *Common and Contested Ground*, p. 156.

62. Ibid.

63. Ibid., p. 157.

64. Smyth, "The Niitsitapi Trade," p. 234.

65. Ibid., p. 157.

66. The Van Driel written account is reproduced in M.A. Markowski, "Tracking Down South Branch House: A Critical Look at the Identification of the Hudson's Bay Company South Branch House," (master's thesis, University of Saskatchewan, 2009), appendix A.

67. Ibid.

68. Morton, ed., *Journal of Duncan McGillivray*, pp. 14–15.

69. Quoted in Smyth, "The Niitsitapi Trade," p. 229.

CHAPTER EIGHT NOTES

1. W.K. Lamb, ed., *Sixteen Years in the Indian Country: The Journal of Daniel Williams Harmon* (Toronto: Macmillan, 1957), p. 97.

2. G.J. Ens, "Fatal Quarrels and Fur Trade Rivalries: A Year of Living Dangerously on the North Saskatchewan, 1806–07" in M. Payne et al., eds., *Alberta Formed—Alberta Transformed, vol.1* (Edmonton: University of Alberta Press, 2005), pp. 133–34, 155–56.

3. D.W. Moodie, "The Trading Post Settlement of the Canadian Northwest, 1774–1821," *Journal of Historical Geography* 13, no. 4 (1987): p. 367.

4. David Smyth suggests that the perceived danger of the Blackfoot Alliance prevented traders from employing the same violent tactics that characterized the Churchill and Athabasca trade. D. Smyth, "The Niitsitapi Trade: Euroamericans and the Blackfoot-speaking Peoples to the mid-1830s," (Ph.D. thesis, Carleton University, 2001), p. 271.

5. A.S. Morton, ed., *The Journal of Duncan McGillivray of the North West Company at Fort George on the Saskatchewan, 1794–95* (Toronto: Macmillan, 1929), p. 77.

6. T. Binnema and G. Ens, eds., *The Hudson's Bay Company Edmonton House Journals, Correspondence, and Reports, 1806–1821* (Calgary: Historical Society of Alberta, 2012) p. 14.

7. Carlton was likely named after Carlton House in Pall Mall, London, the home of the Prince of Wales

(later King George IV). A.M. Johnson, ed., *Saskatchewan Journals and Correspondence* (London: Hudson's Bay Record Society, 1967), p. 7.

8. Moodie, "The Trading Post Settlement," p. 367. See the mapped summary of fur trade post distribution, density and duration in R.C. Harris, *Historical Atlas of Canada, vol. 1* (Toronto: University of Toronto Press, 1987), pp. 158–59, plate 62.

9. The Cree told traders that they often heard a human voice up and down the river—hence the source of the name Qu'Appelle [Qui appelle?], which translates in English to "Who Calls?" Lamb, ed., *Sixteen Years in the Indian Country*, p. 76.

10. Morton, ed., *Journal of Duncan McGillivray*, p. 58; Moodie, "The Trading Post Settlement," p. 367.

11. Johnson, ed., *Saskatchewan Journals and Correspondence*, p. 223.

12. Ibid., p. 233.

13. The late eighteenth to early nineteenth signal in tree ring and other records from the Canadian Rockies document the most severe part of the Little Ice Age. See B.H. Luckman, "The Little Ice Age in the Canadian Rockies," *Geomorphology* 32 (March 2000): pp. 357–84; B. Menounos et al., "Latest Pleistocene and Holocene glacier fluctuations in western Canada," *Quaternary Science Reviews* 28 (2009): pp. 2049–74, fig. 12 in particular.

14. Morton, ed., *Journal of Duncan McGillivray*, p. 69.

15. Johnson, ed., *Saskatchewan Journals and Correspondence*, p. 57.

16. Ibid., p. 94.

17. Ibid., pp. 94–95.

18. Ibid., p. 184.

19. Ibid., p. 131.

20. G. Doige, "Warfare Patterns of the Assiniboine to 1809," (master's thesis, University of Manitoba, 1989), p. 145.

21. Ibid., p. 143.

22. Binnema and Ens, eds., T. Binnema and G. Ens, eds., *The Hudson's Bay Company Edmonton House Journals*, pp. 3, 11; T. Binnema, *Common and Contested Ground: A Human and Environmental History of the Northwestern Plains* (Norman: University of Oklahoma Press, 2001), p. 167; Johnson, ed., *Saskatchewan Journals and Correspondence*, p. 202.

23. Smyth, "The Niitsitapi Trade," p. 230.

24. Tomison later accused McDonald of stating, "It was not for the paltry Consideration of the Loss of three Hudson's Bay Company Servants that he would lose the Trade of so valuable a Tribe of Indians." See L.G. Green, "An Analysis of the Autobiographical Notes of John McDonald of Garth,1791–1816" (master's thesis, University of Saskatchewan, 1999), p. 66.

25. Johnson, ed., *Saskatchewan Journals and Correspondence*, p. 76.

26. T. Binnema, "Old Swan, Big Man, and the Siksika Bands, 1794–1815," *Canadian Historical Review* 77, no. 1 (March 1996): p. 12.

27. Binnema, *Common and Contested Ground*, p. 180.

28. Binnema and Ens, eds., *The Hudson's Bay Company Edmonton House Journals*, pp. 22–30.

29. Johnson, ed., *Saskatchewan Journals and Correspondence*, p. 203.

30. Binnema, *Common and Contested Ground*, p. 177.

31. T. Binnema, "Allegiances and Interests: Niitsitapi (Blackfoot) Trade Diplomacy and Warfare, 1806–1831," *The Western Historical Quarterly* 37, no. 3 (Autumn 2006): p. 349.

32. Binnema, *Common and Contested Ground*, pp. 173–78. The 1806 American Lewis and Clark expedition was fearful of meeting the Blackfoot. Binnema and Ens, eds., *The Hudson's Bay Company Edmonton House Journals*, pp. 31–32.

33. P.C. Thistle, *Indian-European Trade Relations in the Lower Saskatchewan River Region to 1840* (Winnipeg: University of Manitoba Press, 1986), pp. 76–80.

34. B.M. Gough, ed., *The Journal of Alexander Henry the Younger, 1799–1814, vol. 1* (Toronto: The Champlain Society, 1988), p. 175.

35. Lamb, ed., *Sixteen Years in the Indian Country*, p. 55 [the italics are in the source].

36. Johnson, ed., *Saskatchewan Journals and Correspondence*, p. 168.

37. A.S. Morton, *A History of the Canadian West to 1870–1871* (London: Thomas Nelson, 1939), p. 461.

38. Morton, ed., *Journal of Duncan McGillivray*, p. 65.

39. Morton, *A History of the Canadian West*, p. 461.

40. Lamb, ed., *Sixteen Years in the Indian Country*, p. 103.

41. Morton, *A History of the Canadian West*, p. 461.

42. K. Rasmussen, "The Myth that La Corne Grew Wheat in 1754," *Saskatchewan History* 33, no. 1 (Winter 1980), p. 28.

43. See B. Soloway, "The Fur Traders' Garden: Horticultural Imperialism in Rupert's Land, 1670–1770" in G. Morton and D.A. Wilson, eds., *Irish and Scottish Encounters with Indigenous Peoples: Canada, the United States, New Zealand, and Australia* (Montreal: McGill-Queen's University Press, 2013), pp. 287–303.

44. Lamb, ed., *Sixteen Years in the Indian Country*, p. 61.

45. Binnema and Ens, eds., *The Hudson's Bay Company Edmonton House Journals*, pp. 71–73; Thistle, *Indian-European Trade Relations*, p. 81.

46. Binnema and Ens, eds., *The Hudson's Bay Company Edmonton House Journals*, p. 69.

47. See R. Glover, "York Boats," *The Beaver,* Outfit 279 (March 1949): pp. 19–23.

48. Johnson, ed., *Saskatchewan Journals and Correspondence*, p. xli.

49. Gough, ed., *Journal of Alexander Henry, vol. 1*, p. xxvii.

50. J.S. Hamilton, "Fur Trade Social Inequality and the Role of Non-Verbal Communication," (Ph.D. diss., Simon Fraser University, 1990), p. 45.

51. M.W. Campbell, *The North West Company* (Toronto: Macmillan, 1957), pp. 112–13, 160.

52. A.J. Ray, "The Northern Great Plains: Pantry of the Northwestern Fur Trade, 1774–1885," *Prairie Forum* 9, no. 2 (1984): p. 265.

53. Gough, ed., *Journal of Alexander Henry, vol. 1*, p. xxx.

54. E.W. Morse, *Fur Trade Routes of Canada: Then and Now* (Toronto: University of Toronto Press, 1969), pp. 5–8; N.C. Lovell and A.A. Dublenko, "Further Aspects of Fur Trade Life Depicted in the Skeleton," *International Journal of Osteoarchaeology* 9 (1999): pp. 248–56.

55. Campbell, *The North West Company*, p. 99; Morton, *A History of the Canadian West*, p. 454. A trail went from La Montée to the posts on the South Saskatchewan; it cut across the land separating the two branches of the river.

56. B. Kaye and J. Alwin, "The Beginning of Wheeled Transport in Western Canada," *Great Plains Quarterly* 4 (Spring 1984): p. 122.

57. Ibid., pp. 122–23.

58. Morton, ed., *Journal of Duncan McGillivray*, p. xlviii.

59. Gough, ed., *Journal of Alexander Henry, vol. 1*, p. 54.

60. G. Colpitts, *Pemmican Empire: Food, Trade, and the Last Bison Hunts in the North American Plains, 1780–1882* (New York: Cambridge University Press, 2015), pp. 75–76.

61. Ibid., pp. 107–10

62. Quoted in Ibid., p. 110.

63. Lamb, ed., *Sixteen Years in the Indian Country*, p. 37.

64. Quoted in Colpitts, *Pemmican Empire*, p. 111.

65. Ibid., pp. 62, 84–85.

66. Ibid., pp. 87–88, 94–97, 103–104.

67. Campbell, *The North West Company*, pp. 101–102.

68. See R.J. Marles et al., *Aboriginal Plant Use in Canada's Northwest Boreal Forest* (Vancouver: University of British Columbia Press, 2000).

69. J.B. Tyrrell, ed., *David Thompson's Narrative of his Explorations in Western America* (Toronto: The Champlain Society, 1918), p. 434.

70. L. Peers, *The Ojibwa of Western Canada, 1780 to 1870* (Winnipeg: University of Manitoba Press, 1994), pp. 30–46.

71. W.R. Swagerty, "The Blanket-Cloth Trade of North America: Four Converging Traditions" in D.G. Halaher, ed., *Selected Papers of Rupert's Land Colloquium 2002* (Winnipeg: Centre for Rupert's Land Studies, 2002), pp. 257–68. The points on the blankets today indicate their bed size (single, twin, queen, or king).

72. D.B. Miquelon, *Dugard of Rouen: French Trade to Canada and the West Indies* (Montreal: McGill–Queen's University, Press 1978), Ch. 5; Parks Canada, "Point Blankets." http://www.pc.gc.ca/lhn-nhs/ab/rockymountain/natcul/natcul2/07.aspx (accessed March 12, 2015).

73. J. Grabowski and N. St. Onge, "Montreal Iroquois *engagés* in the Western Fur Trade, 1800–1821" in T. Binnema et al., eds., *From Rupert's Land to Canada* (Edmonton: University of Alberta Press, 2001), p. 34.

74. Ibid., pp. 23–29, 38–39.

75. Quoted in Smyth, "The Niitsitapi Trade," p. 238.

76. Binnema and Ens, eds., *The Hudson's Bay Company Edmonton House Journals*, pp. 65–66.

77. Colpitts, *Pemmican Empire*, pp. 81–83.

78. Quoted in Johnson, ed., *Saskatchewan Journals and Correspondence*, pp. xcix–c.

79. J.S.H. Brown, "Partial Truths: A Closer Look at Fur Trade Marriage" in Binnema et al., eds., *From Rupert's Land to Canada*, pp. 59–60. A similar argument was made by Carol Judd about lumping the Métis experiences together as if they were all the same. See "Moose River was not Red River" in D. Cameron, ed., *Explorations in Canadian Economic History* (Ottawa: University of Ottawa Press, 1985), pp. 251–68.

80. G. McGillivray, email communication to author, May 16, 2013.

81. Ibid., p. 62.

82. Lamb, ed., *Sixteen Years in the Indian Country*, p. 98.

83. Ibid., pp. 194–95. Harmon spoke to his children in Cree.

84. Brown, "Partial Truths," p. 73; S. Van Kirk, *"Many Tender Ties": Women in Fur-Trade Society, 1670–1870* (Winnipeg: Watson and Dwyer, 1980), p. 78.

85. Van Kirk, *"Many Tender Ties,"* pp. 95, 109, 111.

86. J.S.H. Brown, *Strangers in Blood: Fur Trade Families in Indian Country* (Vancouver: University of British Columbia Press,1980), pp. 156, 170–71.

87. Quoted in Ibid., p. 77.

88. Ibid., pp. 164–65.

89. Quoted in Johnson, ed., *Saskatchewan Journals and Correspondence*, p. 282. The news from Carlton House and Cumberland House was equally discouraging around the turn of the century.

90. Quoted in Smyth, "The Niitsitapi Trade," p. 268.

91. Quoted in J.S. Milloy, *The Plains Cree: Trade, Diplomacy, and War, 1790–1870* (Winnipeg: University of Manitoba Press, 1988), p. 29.

92. T. Binnema, *Enlightened Zeal: The Hudson's Bay Company and Scientific Networks, 1670–1870* (Toronto: University of Toronto Press, 2014), p. 116.

93. See, for example, D.W. Moodie and B. Kaye, "The Ac Ko Mok Ki Map," *The Beaver*, Oufit 307:4 (Spring 1977): pp. 4–15.

94. Johnson, ed., *Saskatchewan Journals and Correspondence*, p. 317.

95. Quoted in Ibid., p. 294.

96. Lamb, ed., *Sixteen Years in the Indian Country*, p. 69.

97. Quoted in Ens, "Fatal Quarrels and Fur Trade Rivalries," p. 138.

98. Ibid., p. 143.

99. Ibid., pp. 152–55.

100. Binnema, *Common and Contested Ground*, p. 180.

101. Quoted in Ens, "Fatal Quarrels and Fur Trade Rivalries," p. 134.

102. Gough, ed., *The Journal of Alexander Henry the Younger 1799–1814, vol. 2* (Toronto: The Champlain Society, 1988), p. 428.

CHAPTER NINE NOTES

1. Quoted in V.G. Hopwood, *Travels in North America, 1784–1812* (Toronto: Macmillan, 1971), p. 150.

2. Charlotte was one of three mixed-descent children (the others being Patrick and Nancy) of Patrick Small, one of the original members of the 1779 North West Company partnership, and an unknown Cree woman from Île-à-la-Crosse. When Small retired from the fur trade in 1791, he left behind his wife and children. Thompson married the fourteen-year-old Charlotte in 1799, and together, they had thirteen children. They both died in poverty in 1857 after more than fifty years of marriage. J.S.H. Brown, "Seeking Charlotte Small Thompson: Identities in Motion," *The Rupert's Land Newsletter*, no. 24–25 (Spring/Fall 2008): pp. 14–18.

3. See D. Jenish, "The Great Map," *The Beaver* 84, no. 1 (February/March 2004), pp. 36–39.

4. E.E. Rich, *The History of the Hudson's Bay Company, 1670–1870, vol. 2* (London: Hudson's Bay Record Society, 1959), p. 186.

5. Quoted in Hopwood, *Travels in North America*, p. 150.

6. Rich, *History of the Hudson's Bay Company, vol. 2*, pp. 203, 226.

7. W.S. Wallace, ed., *Documents Relating to the North West Company* (Toronto: The Champlain Society, 1934), p. 22.

8. N. St. Onge, "Early Forefathers to the Athabasca Métis: Long Term North West Company Employees," in U. Lischke and D. McNab, eds., *The Long Journey of a Forgotten People: Métis Identities and Family Histories* (Waterloo: Wilfrid Laurier University Press, 2007), pp. 113–14.

9. A.M. Johnson, ed., *Saskatchewan Journals and Correspondence* (London: Hudson's Bay Record Society, 1967), pp. 43, 64.

10. G. Marchildon and S. Robinson, *Canoeing the Churchill: A Practical Guide to the Historic Voyageur Highway* (Regina: Canadian Plains Research Center, 2002), p. 95; W.K. Lamb, ed., *Sixteen Years in the Indian Country: The Journal of Daniel Williams Harmon* (Toronto: Macmillan, 1957), p. 99.

11. Quoted in J. Parker, *Emporium of the North: Fort Chipewyan and the Fur Trade to 1835* (Regina: Canadian Plains Research Center, 1987), p. 1.

12. Ibid., pp. 45–49, 59.

13. W.A. Sloan, "The Native Response to the Extension of the European Traders into the Athabasca and Mackenzie Basin, 1770–1814," *Canadian Historical Review* 60, no. 3 (September 1979): pp. 283, 289–91.

14. Johnson, ed., *Saskatchewan Journals and Correspondence*, pp. 40–41.

15. Lamb, ed., *Sixteen Years in the Indian Country*, p. 70.

16. See M.W. Campbell, *The North West Company* (Toronto: Macmillan, 1957), chap. 4.

17. A.S. Morton, *A History of the Canadian West to 1870–1871* (London: Thomas Nelson, 1939), p. 306.

18. T. Binnema, *Common and Contested Ground: A Human and Environmental History of the Northwestern Plains* (Norman: University of Oklahoma Press, 2001), p. 164.

19. Rich, *History of the Hudson's Bay Company, vol. 2*, pp. 189–90, 229; J. Grabowski and N. St. Onge, "Montreal Iroquois *engagés* in the Western Fur Trade, 1800–1821" in T. Binnema et al., eds., *From Rupert's Land to Canada* (Edmonton: University of Alberta Press, 2001), pp. 30, 34.

20. Quoted in D. Francis, *The Battle for the West: Fur Traders and the Birth of Western Canada* (Edmonton: Hurtig Publishers, 1982), p. 78.

21. N. St. Onge, "Early Forefathers to the Athabasca Métis," p. 119; Francis, *The Battle for the West*, p. 79.

22. Morton, *A History of the Canadian West*, pp. 508, 512.

23. G.J. Ens, "Fatal Quarrels and Fur Trade Rivalries: A Year of Living Dangerously on the North Saskatchewan, 1806–07" in M. Payne et al., eds., *Alberta Formed—Alberta Transformed, vol. 1* (Edmonton: University of Alberta Press, 2005), p. 147; Rich, *History of the Hudson's Bay Company, vol. 2*, pp. 210, 281; Johnson, ed., *Saskatchewan Journals and Correspondence*, pp. lxix, 198.

24. Johnson, ed., *Saskatchewan Journals and Correspondence*, p. 230.

25. Sloan, "The Native Response," p. 293.

26. Quoted in Morton, *A History of the Canadian West*, p. 520.

27. Ibid., p. 532.

28. Rich, *History of the Hudson's Bay Company, vol. 2*, p. 269.

29. Grabowski and St. Onge, "Montreal Iroquois *engagés*," pp. 39–40.

30. Sloan, "The Native Response," pp. 295–96.

31. Morton, *A History of the Canadian West,* p. 420; Rich, *History of the Hudson's Bay Company*, pp. 215–16, 221–62, 230, 521.

32. Quoted in Morton, *A History of the Canadian West*, p. 519.

33. Quoted in L.G. Green, "An Analysis of the Autobiographical Notes of John McDonald of Garth, 1791–1816" (master's thesis, University of Saskatchewan, 1999) p. 130.

34. B. Macdougall, *One of the Family: Métis Culture in Nineteenth-Century Northwestern Saskatchewan* (Vancouver: University of British Columbia Press, 2010), p. 36.

35. Sloan, "The Native Response," p. 296.

36. T. Binnema, *Enlightened Zeal: The Hudson's Bay Company and Scientific Networks, 1670–1870* (Toronto: University of Toronto Press, 2014), p. 140; W.E. Moreau, ed., *The Writings of David Thompson, vol. 1* (Toronto: The Champlain Society, 2009), p. 141.

37. Rich, *History of the Hudson's Bay Company, vol. 2*, pp. 285–86, 289.

38. Morton, *A History of the Canadian West,* p. 531; Rich, *History of the Hudson's Bay Company, vol. 2*, pp. 272, 290.

39. Quoted in Rich, *History of the Hudson's Bay Company, vol. 2*, p. 286.

40. P. Fidler, "1801/1811 Île-à-la-Crosse Journal with Astronomical Observations, May 15, 1811," [transcribed by A.H. Fender], B.89/a/2, Hudson's Bay Company Archives, Winnipeg; Macdougall, *One of the Family*, pp. 48–49.

41. Fidler Île-à-la-Crosse journal entry, 23 January 1811.

42. G. Williams, "Highlights of the First 200 Years of the Hudson's Bay Company," *The Beaver* 50, no. 2 (Autumn 1970): p. 38.

43. B.M. Gough, ed., *The Journal of Alexander Henry the Younger, 1799–1814, vol. 1* (Toronto: The Champlain Society, 1988), pp. xxxviii–xxxix.

44. Morton claimed (*A History of the Canadian West*, p. 422) that the grant "reasserted the validity of the charter and the right of the Company to the soil."

45. Quoted in Rich, *History of the Hudson's Bay Company, vol. 2*, p. 307.

46. G. Colpitts, *Pemmican Empire: Food, Trade, and the Last Bison Hunts in the North American Plains, 1780–1882* (New York: Cambridge University Press, 2014), pp. 41–42, 56–57, 105–106.

47. K.G. Davies, "From Competition to Union," in D.L. Morgan, ed., *Aspects of the Fur Trade* (St. Paul: Minnesota Historical Society, 1867), pp. 24–26.

48. G. Thomas, "Fire and the Fur Trade: The Saskatchewan District, 1790–1840," *The Beaver,* Outfit 308:2 (Autumn 1977): p. 37.

49. Williams, "Highlights of the First 200 Years," p. 42. See also C.S. Houston and M.I. Houston, "The Sacking of Peter Fidler's Brandon House, 1816," *Manitoba History*, no. 16 (Autumn 1988): pp. 23–25.

50. Williams, "Highlights of the First 200 Years," p. 42.

51. A.B. Beaudoin, "What They Saw: The Climatic and Environmental Context for Euro-Canadian Settlement in Alberta," *Prairie Forum* 24, no. 1 (Spring 1999): pp. 33–34; B.H. Luckman, "The Little Ice Age in the Canadian Rockies," *Geomorphology* 32 (2000): p. 369.

52. Quoted in P. McGuigan, "1816: The Year Without Summer," *The Beaver* 83, no. 3 (June/July 2003): p. 20.

53. Davies, "From Competition to Union," p. 18.

54. T. Binnema and G. Ens, eds., *The Hudson's Bay Company Edmonton House Journals, Correspondence, and Reports, 1806–1821* (Calgary: Historical Society of Alberta, 2012), pp. 50–52; G. Colpitts, *Pemmican Empire*, pp. 84–85; Morton, *A History of the Canadian West*, p. 532; Rich, *History of the Hudson's Bay Company, vol. 2*, pp. 302–06, 315–16.

55. Quoted in P. Goldring, "MacKintosh, William" in F.G. Halpenny, ed., *Dictionary of Canadian Biography, vol. 7*, 1836–50 (Toronto: University of Toronto Press, 1988), p. 567; Binnema and Ens, eds., *The Hudson's Bay Company Edmonton House Journals*, pp. 41–43.

56. J.C. Yerbury, *The Subarctic Indians and the Fur Trade, 1680–1860* (Vancouver: University of British

Columbia Press, 1986), pp. 83–84; Binnema and Ens, eds., *The Hudson's Bay Company Edmonton House Journals*, pp. 43–44.

57. Williams, "Highlights of the First 200 Years," p. 43; Sloan, "The Native Response," p. 299.

58. Williams, "Highlights of the First 200 Years," p. 41.

59. Davies, "From Competition to Union," p. 29.

60. Rich, *History of the Hudson's Bay Company, vol. 2*, p. 399.

61. Williams, "Highlights of the First 200 Years," p. 46.

62. J.F. Decker, "Depopulation of the Northern Great Plains Native," *Social Science and Medicine* 33, no. 4 (1991): p. 391.

63. St. Onge, "Early Forefathers to the Athabasca Métis," pp. 110, 126–28. The Athabasca Métis are the descendants of about 400 French-Canadian and Iroquois Freemen.

CHAPTER TEN NOTES

1. Quoted in H. Foster, "Long-Distance Justice: The Criminal Jurisdiction of Canadian Courts West of the Canadas, 1763–1859," *American Journal of Legal History* 34 (1990): p. 32. Simpson's assessment has since been echoed by fur trade historians. Writing a century later, for example, A.S. Morton claimed in his monumental history of the Canadian North-West that the 1820s and 1830s were marked by a "profound quiet." A.S. Morton, *A History of the Canadian West to 1870–1871* (London: Thomas Nelson, 1939), p. 624.

2. E.E. Rich, *The History of the Hudson's Bay Company, 1670–1870, vol. 2* (London: Hudson's Bay Record Society, 1959), p. 375.

3. G. Williams, ed., *London Correspondence Inward from Sir George Simpson, 1841–1842* (London: Hudson's Bay Record Society, 1973), p. xi.

4. For an alternative view, that Indian peoples faced "declining opportunities" during the Simpson era, see A.J. Ray, *Indians in the Fur Trade: their role as hunters, trappers, and middlemen in the lands southwest of Hudson Bay, 1660–1870* (Toronto: University of Toronto Press, 1974).

5. Rich, *The History of the Hudson's Bay Company, vol. 2*, p. 383.

6. The most recent biography of Simpson is J. Raffan, *Emperor of the North: Sir George Simpson and the Remarkable Story of the Hudson's Bay Company* (Toronto: Harper Collins Publishers, 2007). Because Simpson was born out of wedlock, his exact birth date is not known, but Raffan, with the help of Simpson family genealogists, has concluded that he was probably born in 1792.

7. C.P Wilson, "Sir George Simpson at Lachine," *The Beaver*, Outfit 265:1 (June 1934): p. 39.

8. Williams, ed., *London Correspondence Inward*, p. xiv.

9. Foster, "Long-Distance Justice," p. 33.

10. K.G. Davies, "From Competition to Union," in D.L. Morgan, ed., *Aspects of the Fur Trade* (St. Paul: Minnesota Historical Society, 1867), p. 20; D. Francis, *The Battle for the West: Fur Traders and the Birth of Western Canada* (Edmonton: Hurtig Publishers, 1982), p. 132.

11. G. Williams, "Highlights of the First 200 Years of the Hudson's Bay Company," *The Beaver* 50, no. 2 (Autumn 1970): p. 61.

12. T. Binnema, *Enlightened Zeal: The Hudson's Bay Company and Scientific Networks, 1670–1870* (Toronto: University of Toronto Press 2014), pp. 129–31; E.I. Burley, *Servants of the Honourable Company: Work, Discipline, and Conflict in the Hudson's Bay Company, 1770–1879* (Toronto: Oxford University Press, 1997).

13. Rich, *History of the Hudson's Bay Company, vol. 2*, p. 481.

14. Morton, *A History of the Canadian West*, p. 691.

15. Quoted in Williams, "Highlights of the First 200 Years," p. 61.

16. Of a total 125 posts (68 HBC and 57 NWC), Simpson kept 52. Burley, *Servants of the Honourable Company*, p. 6.

17. Morton, *A History of the Canadian West*, pp. 630, 698–99

18. Francis, *Battle for the West*, p. 163.

19. T.B. Smythe, *Thematic Study of the Fur Trade in the Canadian West, 1670–1870* (Ottawa: Historic Sites and Monuments Board of Canada, 1968), pp. 42, 90, 215; B. Silversides, *Fort des Prairies: The Story of Fort Edmonton* (Surrey: Heritage House, 2005), p. 20.

20. J. McKillip, "A Métis Métier: Transportation in Rupert's Land," (master's thesis, University of Ottawa, 2005), pp. 58–60.

21. D. Smyth, "The Niitsitapi Trade: Euroamericans and the Blackfoot-speaking Peoples to the mid-1830s," (Ph.D. thesis, Carleton University, 2001), pp. 472–74.

22. G. Ens, *Homeland to Hinterland: The Changing Worlds of the Red River Métis in the Nineteenth Century* (Toronto: University of Toronto Press, 1996), pp. 43–46; E.E. Rich, ed., *London Correspondence Inward from Eden Colvile, 1849–52* (London: Hudson's Bay Record Society, 1956), p. xli.

23. H.E. Ross, ed., *Letters from Rupert's Land, 1826–1840: James Hargrave of the Hudson's Bay Company* (Montreal: McGill–Queen's University Press, 2009), p. 23.

24. Francis, *Battle for the West*, pp. 164–65.

25. For an analysis of the increased fur trade family size, see J.S.H. Brown, "A Demographic Transition in Fur Trade Country: Family Sizes and Fertility of Company Officers and Country Wives, c. 1750–1850," *The Western Canadian Journal of Anthropology* 6, no. 1 (1976): pp. 67–69.

26. S. Van Kirk, *"Many Tender Ties": Women in Fur-Trade Society, 1670–1870* (Winnipeg: Watson and Dwyer, 1980), p. 123.

27. C.A. Purdy, "Orkneymen to Rupert's Land: Orkney Workers in the Saskatchewan District," (master's thesis, University of Alberta, 2010), pp. 36–38.

28. J.S.H. Brown, *Strangers in Blood: Fur Trade Families in Indian Country* (Vancouver: University of British Columbia Press, 1980), pp. 203–4; Van Kirk, *"Many Tender Ties,"* pp. 129–30. For a good discussion of the Simpson reforms, see H. Devine, "'Economy Must Now be the Order of the Day': George Simpson and the Reorganization of the Fur Trade to 1826," in M. Payne et al., eds., *Alberta Formed—Alberta Transformed, vol. 1* (Edmonton: University of Alberta Press, 2005), pp. 160–78.

29. E.I. Burley, *Servants of the Honourable Company*, pp. 92–93; C.M. Judd, "'Mixt Bands of Many Nations': 1821–70" in C.M. Judd and A.J. Ray, eds., *Old Trails and New Directions: Papers of the Third North American Fur Trade Conference* (Toronto: University of Toronto Press, 1980), pp. 127–51.

30. Quoted in Brown, *Strangers in Blood*, pp. 202–3.

31. J.S.H. Brown, "Linguistic Solitudes and Changing Social Categories" in Judd and Ray, eds., *Old Trails and New Directions*, pp. 150–51; see also J.E. Foster, "The Métis: the People and the Term," *Prairie Forum* 3, no. 1 (Spring 1978): pp. 79–90.

32. W.F. Rannie, "Evidence for Unusually Wet Summers in the eastern Prairies and northwestern Ontario," *Prairie Perspectives: Geographical Essays* 9, no. 1 (2006): pp. 85–104.

33. Burley, *Servants of the Honourable Company*, p. 49; Brown, *Strangers in Blood*, pp. 204–5, 209.

34. I.M. Spry, "From the Hunt to the Homestead," (unpublished manuscript kindly loaned to the author by Nicole St.-Onge), chap. 1, p. 14.

35. B. Kaye and J. Alwin, "The Beginnings of Wheeled Transport in Western Canada," *Great Plains Quarterly* 4 (Spring 1984): pp. 130–31.

36. McKillip, "A Métis Métier," p. 94. The Métis use of carts earned them the Indian name, "wagon people."

37. Ibid., p. 88.

38. Ens, *Homeland to Hinterland*, pp. 39–40; Rich, ed., *London Correspondence Inward from Eden Colvile*, pp. xxxvi–xxxvii; M.A. Macleod and W.L. Morton, *Cuthbert Grant of Grantown* (Toronto: McClelland and Stewart, 1963), p. 109; A. Ross, *Red River Settlement: Its Rise, Settlement and Present State* (Edmonton: Hurtig, 1972), p. 246.

39. N. St.-Onge, "Plain Métis: Contours of an Identity," *Australasian Canadian Studies* 27, no. 1–2 (2009): pp. 95–115; N. St.-Onge, "Uncertain Margins: Métis and Saulteaux Identities in St-Paul des Saulteaux, Red River 1821–1870," *Manitoba History* 53 (October 2006): p. 8.

40. Quoted in G. Colpitts, *Pemmican Empire: Food, Trade, and the Last Bison Hunts in the North American Plains* (New York: Cambridge University Press, 2014), p. 159.

41. Ibid., pp. 168–70, 186–88.

42. H. Devine, *The People Who Own Themselves: Aboriginal Ethnogenesis in a Canadian Family, 1660–1900* (Calgary: University of Calgary Press, 2004), pp. 94–99, 109–110; Spry, "From the Hunt to the Homestead," chap. 1, pp. 7–8.

43. Devine, *The People Who Own Themselves*, pp. 119–21, 139.

44. Quoted in A.A. den Otter, *Civilizing the Wilderness: Culture and Nature in Pre-Confederation Canada and Rupert's Land* (Edmonton: University of Alberta Press, 2012), p. 167.

45. A.J. Ray, "Some Conservation Schemes of the Hudson's Bay Company, 1821–50: An examination of the problems of resource management in the fur trade," *Journal of Historical Geography* 1, no. 1 (1975): p. 67–68.

46. G. Colpitts, *Game in the Garden: A Human History of Wildlife in Western Canada to 1940* (Vancouver: University of British Columbia Press, 2002), p. 16.

47. C.S. Houston et al., *Eighteenth-Century Naturalists of Hudson Bay* (Montreal: McGill–Queen's

University Press, 2003), app. 5. In 1834, for example, 7918 swan skins were traded.

48. Morton, *A History of the Canadian West*, p. 697; Ray, "Some Conservation Schemes," pp. 52–54.

49. Quoted in Ray, "Some Conservation Schemes," p. 63.

50. Rich, *History of the Hudson's Bay Company, vol. 2*, p. 480.

51. Smythe, *Thematic Study of the Fur Trade*, p. 230.

52. Rich, *History of the Hudson's Bay Company, vol. 2*, p. 486.

53. B. Macdougall, *One of the Family: Métis Culture in Nineteenth-Century Northwestern Saskatchewan* (Vancouver: University of British Columbia Press, 2010), p. 182.

54. J.S.H. Brown, "Women as Centre and Symbol in the Emergence of Métis Communities," *Canadian Journal of Native Studies* 3, no. 1 (1983): p. 40.

55. P.C. Thistle, *Indian-European Trade Relations in the Lower Saskatchewan River Region to 1840* (Winnipeg: University of Manitoba Press, 1986), pp. 88–92.

56. P.C. Thistle, "The Twatt Family, 1780–1840: Amerindian, Ethnic Category, or Ethnic Group Identity" in P.C. Douaud, ed., *The Western Métis: Profiles of a People* (Regina: Canadian Plains Research Center, 2007), pp. 77–88; Thistle, *Indian-European Trade Relations*, pp. 91–2.

57. Ray, "Some Conservation Schemes," p. 51.

58. O. Klimko, *The Archaeology and History of Fort Pelly 1, 1824–1856* (Regina: Saskatchewan Culture and Recreation, 1983), pp. 30–32.

59. Ibid., p. 38.

60. Quoted in J.F. Klaus, "Fort Pelly: An Historical Sketch," *Saskatchewan History* 14, no. 3 (Autumn 1961): p. 87.

61. Quoted in L. Peers, *The Ojibwa of Western Canada, 1780 to 1870* (Winnipeg: University of Manitoba Press, 1994), p. 99.

62. L. Peers, "Changing Resource-Use Patterns of Saulteaux Trading at Fort Pelly, 1821–1870" in K. Abel and J. Friesen, eds., *Aboriginal Resource Use in Canada: Historical and Legal Aspects* (Winnipeg: University of Manitoba Press, 1991), pp. 107–16.

63. Peers, *The Ojibwa of Western Canada*, p. 114, 118–9.

64. Quoted in Smyth, "The Niitsitapi Trade," p. 318.

65. Smythe, *Thematic Study of the Fur Trade*, p. 205.

66. G. Colpitts, "The Methodists' Great 1869 Camp Meeting and Aboriginal Conservation Strategies in the North Saskatchewan River Valley," *Great Plains Quarterly* 29, no. 1 (Winter 2009): pp. 7, 22 n. 31; R. Clow, "Bison Ecology, Brule and Yankton Winter Hunting, and the Starving Winter of 1832–33," *Great Plains Quarterly* 15, no. 4 (Fall 1995): p. 268.

67. Smyth, "The Niitsitapi Trade," pp. 441, 462–3, 477, 497.

68. On the Indian role in trapping beaver on the northern plains, see J. Daschuk, "Who Killed the Prairie Beaver? An Environmental Case for Eighteenth-Century Migration in Western Canada," *Prairie Forum* 37 (Fall 2012): pp. 151–72.

69. Smyth, "The Niitsitapi Trade," p. 273.

70. Ibid., pp. 278–89.

71. Ibid., p. 509; see also pp. 303, 338–39.

72. Ibid., pp. 361–32, 374, 397, 429, 440.

73. Ibid., p. 438.

74. Colpitts, *Pemmican Empire*, p. 208.

75. Ibid., pp. 113–20, 151.

76. Quoted in Ray, *Indians in the Fur Trade*, p. 183.

77. W. Dobak, "Killing the Canadian Buffalo, 1821–1881," *Western Historical Quarterly*, n. 27, spring 1996, pp. 41–6; A.J. Ray, "Fur Trade Pantry," p. 274.

78. Quoted in Colpitts, *Pemmican Empire*, p. 213.

79. Smyth, "The Niitsitapi Trade," pp. 512–14.

80. Quoted in Van Kirk, *"Many Tender Ties,"* p. 206.

81. Ibid., pp. 177–79. The other woman, Isabel Gunn, had disguised herself as a man and arrived at Moose Factory in 1806. When her identity was discovered, she was sent back to the Orkneys.

82. H.R. Driscoll, "'A Most Important Chain of Connection': Marriage in the Hudson's Bay Company" in T. Binnema et al., eds., *From Rupert's Land to Canada* (Edmonton: University of Alberta Press, 2001), pp. 81–107.

83. Quoted in Van Kirk, *"Many Tender Ties,"* p. 205.

84. Ross, ed., *Letters from Rupert's Land*, p. 33.

CHAPTER ELEVEN NOTES

1. Quoted in K. Pettipas, "A History of the Work of the Reverend Henry Budd conducted under the Auspices of the Church Missionary Society, 1840–1875" (master's thesis, University of Manitoba, 1972) p. 68.

2. Quoted in A.A. den Otter, *Civilizing the Wilderness: Culture and Nature in Pre-Confederation Canada and Rupert's Land* (Edmonton: University of Alberta Press, 2012), p. 168.

3. Ibid., p. xvii.

4. Quoted in C.D. Dollar, "The High Plains Smallpox Epidemic of 1837–38," *The Western Historical Quarterly* 8, no. 1 (January 1977): p. 24.

5. Ibid., p. 25.

6. A.J. Ray, "Smallpox: The Epidemic of 1837–38," *The Beaver,* Outfit 306:2 (Autumn 1975): p. 11.

7. Quoted in D. Francis, *The Battle for the West: Fur Traders and the Birth of Western Canada* (Edmonton: Hurtig Publishers, 1982), p. 161.

8. P.C. Albers: "Changing Patterns of Ethnicity in the Northeastern Plains, 1780–1870" in J.D. Hill, ed.,

History, Power, and Identity: Ethnogenesis in the Americas, 1492–1992 (Iowa City: University of Iowa Press, 1996), pp. 107–109. A.J. Ray in *Indians in the Fur Trade: their role as hunters, trappers, and middlemen in the lands southwest of Hudson Bay, 1660–1870* (Toronto: University of Toronto Press, 1974) argues that Indian tribal populations, in particular the Assiniboine, were rising up until the time of the epidemic, but that the Cree increased in numerical strength after 1837–38 (p. 192). Jody Decker maintains in "Depopulation of the Northern Plains Natives," *Social Science and Medicine* 33, no. 4 (1991) that Assiniboine numbers were declining before 1837 and that disease alone was not the sole reason for depopulation.

9. den Otter, *Civilizing the Wilderness*, pp. 170, 180, 190.

10. Ibid., p. 168.

11. H.E. Ross, ed., *Letters from Rupert's Land, 1826–1840: James Hargrave of the Hudson's Bay Company* (Montreal: McGill–Queen's University Press, 2009), p. 19.

12. den Otter, *Civilizing the Wilderness*, pp. 32–33, 169.

13. Ibid., p. 168.

14. E.E. Rich, *The History of the Hudson's Bay Company, vol. 2*, 1763–1870 (London: Hudson's Bay Record Society, 1959), p. 528.

15. R.M. Beaumont, "Origins and Influences: The Family Ties of the Reverend Henry Budd," *Prairie Forum* 17, no. 2 (1992): pp. 168, 184–85.

16. den Otter, *Civilizing the Wilderness*, p. 73.

17. N.J. Goosen, "The Relationship of the Church Missionary Society and the Hudson's Bay Company in Rupert's Land, 1821–1860," (master's thesis, University of Manitoba, 1974), pp. 66–67, 74–75; M.E. Richards, "Cumberland House: Two Hundred Years of History," *Saskatchewan History* 37, no. 3 (Autumn 1973): p. 109.

18. Pettipas, "A History of the Work of the Reverend Henry Budd," pp. 69–72.

19. Ibid., pp. 75–77, 116.

20. D. Whitehouse-Stang, "'Because I Happen to Be a Native Clergyman': The Impact of Race, Ethnicity, Status, and Gender on Native Agents of the Church Missionary Society in the Nineteenth Century Canadian North-West," (Ph.D. diss., University of Manitoba, 2004), pp. 55, 88, 106–107, 114–15.

21. Quoted in Pettipas, "A History of the Work of the Reverend Henry Budd," p 94.

22. Ibid., pp. 84–86.

23. Ibid., pp. 110–11.

24. Ibid., p. 116.

25. Whitehouse-Stang, "'Because I Happen to Be a Native Clergyman,'" p. 190.

26. The name, "Upper Nepowewin," has created confusion because the regional Cree did not use Upper and Lower Nipawin to indicate places, only the traders and missionaries. *Nipowiwinihk* was located near Codette and not today's Nipawin.

27. Pettipas, "A History of the Work of the Reverend Henry Budd," pp. 99–100.

28. Quoted in Whitehouse-Stang, "'Because I Happen to Be a Native Clergyman,'" p. 222.

29. Quoted in den Otter, *Civilizing the Wilderness*, p. 84.

30. Quoted in Pettipas, "A History of the Work of the Reverend Henry Budd," p. 105.

31. Ibid., pp. 132–39.

32. Whitehouse-Stang, "'Because I Happen to Be a Native Clergyman,'" pp. 247–48.

33. Quoted in J.F. Klaus, "The Early Missions of the Swan River District, 1821–1869," *Saskatchewan History* 17, no. 2 (Spring 1964): p. 74.

34. Ibid., pp. 61–74.

35. Ibid., p. 69.

36. W. Wheeler, "The Journals and Voices of a Church of England Catechist: Askenootow (Charles Pratt), 1851–1884," in J.S.H. Brown and E. Vibert, eds., *Reading Beyond Words: Contexts for Native History* (Peterborough: Broadview Press, 2003), pp. 237–54.

37. Pettipas, "A History of the Work of the Reverend Henry Budd," pp. 108–89, 128, 143–46, 152, 155–56, 167.

38. Goosen, "The Relationship of the Church Missionary Society and the Hudson's Bay Company," pp. 97–99, 105–15, 124–25; L.G. Thomas, "Settee, James" in R. Cook, ed., *The Dictionary of Canadian Biography, vol. 13, 1901–1910* (Toronto: University of Toronto Press, 1994), pp. 937–99.

39. Quoted in Goosen, "The Relationship of the Church Missionary Society and the Hudson's Bay Company," pp. 73–74.

40. Quoted in J.K. Galbraith, ed., *Eden Colvile's Letters, 1849–52* (London: Hudson Bay Record Society, 1956), pp. 225–26.

41. L. Dorge, "Thibault, Jean-Baptiste" in M. La Terreur, ed., *The Dictionary of Canadian Biography, vol. 10, 1871–1880* (Toronto: University of Toronto Press, 1972), pp. 676–78.

42. Quoted in Klaus, "The Early Missions of the Swan River District," p. 73.

43. Pettipas, "A History of the Work of the Reverend Henry Budd," pp. 80–81, 197.

44. Quoted in A. Ross, *Red River Settlement: Its Rise, Settlement and Present State* (Edmonton: Hurtig, 1972), p. 292.

45. C. Tellier, "Darveau, Jean-Édouard" in F.L. Halpenny, ed., *The Dictionary of Canadian Biography, vol. 7, 1836–50* (Toronto: University of Toronto Press, 1988), pp. 231–32.

46. Quoted in G. Carrière, "The Early Efforts of the Oblate Missionaries in Western Canada," *Prairie Forum* 4, no. 1 (Spring 1979), p. 5.

47. B. Macdougall, *One of the Family: Métis Culture in Nineteenth-Century Northwestern Saskatchewan* (Vancouver: University of British Columbia Press, 2010), p. 137; B. Benoit, "The Mission at Île-à-la-Crosse," *The Beaver,* Outfit 311:3 (Winter 1980), pp. 41–42.

48. Benoit, "The Mission at Île-à-la-Crosse," pp. 43-6; Carrière, "The Early Efforts of the Oblate Missionaries," pp. 5–9; Macdougall, *One of the Family*, pp. 137–38.

49. Macdougall, *One of the Family*, pp. 5–6, 28–29, 131, 142.

50. Ibid., pp. 140–57.

51. Quoted in Carrière, "The Early Efforts of the Oblate Missionaries," p. 9.

52. T. Binnema, *Enlightened Zeal: The Hudson's Bay Company and Scientific Networks, 1670–1870* (Toronto: University of Toronto Press, 2014), pp. 129–68.

53. G. Colpitts, *Pemmican Empire: Food, Trade, and the Last Bison Hunts in the North American Plains* (New York: Cambridge University Press, 2014), p. 189. Colpitts suggests that pemmican served as "an amalgam of empire."

54. *National Post* staff, "CBC hockey documentary slammed by N.W.T. Premier," Canada.com, 19 September 2006, http://www.canada.com/nationalpost/news/story.html?id=91982b5d-0fc8-422c-b28a-06cb1edaf2ec (accessed 19 August 2015). There is no mention of hockey in Franklin's published journal of his second expedition.

55. B. Peel, "Hunter, James" in F.G. Halpenny, ed., *The Dictionary of Canadian Biography, vol. 11, 1881–1890* (Toronto: University of Toronto Press, 1982), pp. 436–37.

56. Binnema, *Enlightened Zeal*, pp. 213–15; C.M. Whitfield and R.A. Jarrell, "Lefroy, John Henry" in Halpenny, ed., *The Dictionary of Canadian Biography, vol. 11*, pp. 508–10. Lefroy also enlisted HBC men to keep journals of auroral phenomenon for a major study of the aurora borealis.

57. Binnema, *Enlightened Zeal*, pp. 169–98.

58. G. Simpson, *Narrative of a Journey Round the World, vol. 1* (London: Colburn, 1847), pp. 13, 47–48.

59. G. Gillespie, *Hunting for Empire: Narratives of Sport in Rupert's Land, 1840–70* (Vancouver: University of British Columbia Press, 2007), pp. 35–59.

60. I.M. Spry, "From the Hunt to the Homestead," (unpublished manuscript kindly loaned to the author by Nicole St.-Onge), chap. 5, pp. 29, 36–7.

61. Gillespie, *Hunting for Empire*, pp. 63–68.

62. J. Cruikshank, *Reading Voices* (Vancouver: Douglas and McIntyre, 1991), p. 110.

63. J. Carnegie, *Saskatchewan and the Rocky Mountains* (Edinburgh: Edmonston and Douglas, 1975), p. 70.

64. Gillespie, *Hunting for Empire*, pp. 80–87.

65. J.R. Harper, "Kane, Paul" in La Terreur, ed. *The Dictionary of Canadian Biography, vol. 10*, pp. 389–93.

66. I.S. Maclaren, "Paul Kane and the Authorship of *Wanderings of an Artist*" in T. Binnema et al., eds., *From Rupert's Land to Canada* (Edmonton: University of Alberta Press, 2001), pp. 225–45.

67. See J. Leduc, ed., *Overland from Canada to British Columbia* (Vancouver: University of British Columbia Press, 1981); R.W. Wright, *Overlanders* (Saskatoon: Western Producer Prairie Books, 1985); D.L. Smith, ed., *Survival on a Westward Trek, 1858–1859* (Athens: Ohio University Press, 1989).

68. Smith, ed., *Survival on a Westward Trek*, p. 14.

69. W.F. Milton and W.B. Cheadle, *The North-West Passage by Land* (London: Cassell, Petter, and Galpin, 1867), p. 40 [italics have been added for emphasis].

70. Rich, *History of the Hudson's Bay Company, vol. 2*, p. 791.

71. Quoted in A.S. Morton, *A History of the Canadian West to 1870–1871* (London: Thomas Nelson, 1939), p. 818.

72. Quoted in J.M.S. Careless, *Brown of the Globe, vol. 1* (Toronto: Macmillan, 1959), p. 230.

73. Quoted in Morton, *A History of the Canadian West*, p. 827.

74. Ibid., pp. 827–31. Canada also prepared a map to illustrate its territorial claims with the western boundary set at the Pacific Ocean. But it was never sent to the Select Committee.

75. den Otter, *Civilizing the Wilderness*, pp. 198–201, 216–19, 224–27.

76. Quoted in G. Warkentin, "'Make it last forever as it is': John McDonald of Garth's Vision of a Native Kingdom in the Northwest" in C. Podruchny and L. Peers, eds., *Gathering Places: Aboriginal and Fur Trade Histories* (Vancouver: University of British Columbia Press, 2010), p. 159.

77. Quoted in G.S. Dunbar, "Isotherms and Politics: Perception of the Northwest in the 1850s" in A.W. Rasporich and H.C. Klassen, eds., *Prairie perspectives 2: Selected papers of the Western Canadian Studies Conferences, 1970, 1971* (Toronto, Holt Rinehart and Winston of Canada, 1973), p. 93.

78. Morton, *A History of the Canadian West*, p. 832.

79. F.G. Roe, "Early Agriculture in Western Canada in Relation to Climatic Stability," *Agricultural History* 26, no. 3 (July 1952): pp. 106–107.

80. Morton, *A History of the Canadian West*, p. 832.

81. Great Britain. House of Commons, *Report from the Select Committee on the Hudson's Bay Company*, 1857, p. iii.

82. Quoted in den Otter, *Civilizing the Wilderness*, p. 188.

83. J.A. Bovey, "The Attitudes and Policies of the Federal Government Towards Canada's Northern Territories, 1870–1930," (master's thesis, University of British Columbia, 1957), pp. 9–10. See also D. McNab, "The Colonial Office and the Prairies in the Mid-Nineteenth Century," *Prairie Forum* 3, no. 1 (1978): pp. 21–38.

84. Morton, *A History of the Canadian West*, p. 829.

85. *Report from the Select Committee*, 1857, quest. 4102, p. 218.

CHAPTER TWELVE NOTES

1. W.L. Morton, "The Battle at Grand Coteau: July 13 and 14, 1851," *Transactions of the Manitoba Historical Society*, 3rd. ser. (1959–60), p. 37.

2. Ibid., pp. 37–49.

3. C.M. Judd, "'Mixt Bands of Many Nations': 1821–70" in C.M. Judd and A.J. Ray, eds., *Old Trails and New Directions: Papers of the Third North American Fur Trade Conference* (Toronto: University of Toronto Press, 1980), pp. 139–41.

4. Quoted in A.J. Ray, *Indians in the Fur Trade: their role as hunters, trappers, and middlemen in the lands southwest of Hudson Bay, 1660–1870* (Toronto: University of Toronto Press, 1974), p. 207.

5. A.A. den Otter, *Civilizing the Wilderness: Culture and Nature in Pre-Confederation Canada and Rupert's Land* (Edmonton: University of Alberta Press, 2012), p. 187.

6. K. Dimmer et al., "Chief Trader King's Map" in K.T. Carlson, ed., *CURA Otipimsuak Atlas* (forthcoming).

7. B. Macdougall, *One of the Family: Métis Culture in Nineteenth-Century Northwestern Saskatchewan* (Vancouver: University of British Columbia Press, 2010), p. 181.

8. See J.S. Brown, "A Colony of Very Useful Hands," *The Beaver* (Spring 1977): pp. 39–45.

9. B. Macdougall, *One of the Family*, pp. 158–61; S. Danyluk and J. Crew, "Tracing Community Through Métis Gardens" in Carlson, ed., *CURA Otipimsuak Atlas* (forthcoming).

10. B. Macdougall, *One of the Family*, pp. 39–42.

11. Quoted in P. Hackett, *A Very Remarkable Sickness: Epidemics in the Petit Nord, 1670–1846* (Winnipeg: University of Manitoba Press, 2002), p. 199.

12. Ibid., p. 215.

13. Ibid., p. 218.

14. J. Daschuk, *Clearing the Plains: Disease, Politics of Starvation, and the Loss of Aboriginal Life* (Regina: University of Regina Press, 2013), p. 71. Measles can be a deadly disease for adults.

15. M. McCarthy, *From the Great River to the Ends of the Earth: Oblate Missions to the Dene, 1847–1921* (Edmonton: University of Alberta Press, 1995), pp. 37–39.

16. D.F. Pelly, *The Old Way North: Following the Oberholzer-Magee Expedition* (St. Paul: Borealis Books, 2008), pp. 42–46.

17. Ibid., p. 63.

18. Ibid., p. 47.

19. Ibid., pp. 47–49, 63–65, 138–41.

20. T. Binnema, *Enlightened Zeal: The Hudson's Bay Company and Scientific Networks, 1670–1870* (Toronto: University of Toronto Press, 2014), pp. 169–98.

21. Quoted in G. Williams, "Highlights of the First 200 Years of the Hudson's Bay Company," *The Beaver* 50, no. 2 (Autumn 1970): p. 61.

22. Ibid.

23. N.L. Nicholson, *The Boundaries of the Canadian Confederation* (Toronto: Macmillan, 1979), pp. 40–42.

24. E.E. Rich, ed., *London Correspondence Inward from Eden Colvile, 1849–52* (London: Hudson's Bay Record Society, 1956), pp. xliv–xlv, lviii–lix, lxxxvi.

25. A.J. Ray, "Some Conservation Schemes of the Hudson's Bay Company, 1821–50: An examination of the problems of resource management in the fur trade," *Journal of Historical Geography*, 1, no. 1 (1975): p. 67.

26. A. Ross, *Red River Settlement: Its Rise, Settlement and Present State* (Edmonton: Hurtig, 1972), p. 244.

27. G. Ens, *Homeland to Hinterland: The Changing Worlds of the Red River Métis in the Nineteenth Century*

(Toronto: University of Toronto Press, 1996), pp. 40–43, 75; Rich, ed., *London Correspondence Inward from Eden Colvile*, pp. xxxvi–xxxix.

28. Morton, "The Battle at Grand Coteau," p. 47.

29. Ens, *Homeland to Hinterland*, p. 72.

30. G. Colpitts, *Pemmican Empire: Food, Trade, and the Last Bison Hunts in the North American Plains* (New York: Cambridge University Press, 2014), pp. 177–96, 216–18, 229–33; Ens, *Homeland to Hinterland*, pp. 80, 88, 90.

31. Ens, *Homeland to Hinterland*, p. 80.

32. Colpitts, *Pemmican Empire*, pp. 197–98, 218–19, 229–31.

33. O. Klimko and J. Hodges, *Last Mountain House: A Hudson's Bay Company Outpost in the Qu'Appelle Valley* (Saskatoon: Western Heritage Services, 1993), pp. 7–12.

34. K.D. Munro, ed., *Fur Trade Letters of Willie Traill, 1864–1894* (Edmonton: University of Alberta Press, 2006), pp. 23, 42–52.

35. H. Devine, *The People Who Own Themselves: Aboriginal Ethnogenesis in a Canadian Family, 1660–1900* (Calgary: University of Calgary Press, 2004), pp. 130–32.

36. See K.D. Weinbender, "Petite Ville: A Spatial Assessment of a Métis Hivernant Site," (master's thesis, Department of Archaeology, Univ. of Saskatchewan, 2003).

37. Ens, *Homeland to Hinterland*, pp. 77–79, 90; Colpitts, *Pemmican Empire*, pp. 194–97, 218–20; Devine, *The People Who Own Themselves*, p.135; M. Weekes, *The Last Buffalo Hunter* (Saskatoon: Fifth House Publishers, 1994).

38. Curiously, the official history of Prince Albert begins in 1866 with the establishment of the Nisbet mission. G. Abrams, *Prince Albert: The First Century 1866–1966* (Saskatoon: Modern Press, 1966); D.B. Smith, *Honoré Jackson: Prairie Visionary* (Regina: Coteau Books, 2007), p. 26.

39. D. Meyer and R.A. Hutton, "Pasquatinow and the Red Earth Crees," *Prairie Forum*, 23, no. 1 (Spring 1998): pp. 102–103.

40. K. Pettipas, "A History of the Work of the Reverend Henry Budd conducted under the Auspices of the Church Missionary Society, 1840–1875" (master's thesis, University of Manitoba, 1972), p. 99.

41. Quoted in W.H. Long, ed., *Fort Pelly Journal of Daily Occurrences 1863* (Regina: Regina Archaeological Society, 1987), pp. 16, 27.

42. Ray, "Some Conservation Schemes," p. 64.

43. David Mandelbaum in *The Plains Cree: An Ethnographic, Historical and Comparative Study* (New York: American Museum of Natural History, 1940), pp. 9–11.

44. The maximum advance of the Athabasca glacier in historical times occurred in 1843–44. See B.H. Luckman, "Dating the Moraines and Recession of Athabasca and Dome Glaciers, Canada," *Arctic and Alpine Research* 20 (1988): pp. 40–54.

45. H.A. Dempsey, *Maskepetoon: Leader, Warrior, Peacemaker* (Victoria: Heritage House, 2010), pp. 131–32, 149, 157, 161, 220–22.

46. See R.H. Steckel and J.M. Prince, "Tallest in the World: Native Americans of the Great Plains in the Nineteenth Century," *The American Economic Review* 91, no. 1 (March 2001): pp. 287–94.

47. D. Christensen, *Ahtahkakoop* (Shell Lake: Ahtahkakoop Publishing, 2000), p. 62.

48. Ibid., pp. 123–24.

49. W.A. Dobak, "Killing the Canadian Buffalo, 1821–1881," *Western Historical Quarterly* 27 (Spring 1996): pp. 36–37; P. Hämäläinen, "First Phase of Destruction," *Great Plains Quarterly* 21 no. 2 (Spring 2001): pp. 101–14 argues that the bison on the southern plains were in decline by the early nineteenth century, not the 1840s as commonly assumed.

50. Quoted in G. Colpitts, "The Methodists' Great 1869 Camp Meeting and Aboriginal Conservation Strategies in the North Saskatchewan River Valley," *Great Plains Quarterly* 29, no. 1 (Winter 2009), p. 3.

51. For an examination of the loss of the commons, see I.M. Spry, "The Transition from a Nomadic to a Settled Economy in Western Canada, 1856–96," *Transactions of the Royal Society of Canada, 4th ser., vol. 6* (June 1968), pp. 187–201.

52. I. Cowie, *The Company of Adventurers* (Lincoln: University of Nebraska Press, 1993), pp. 310–11.

53. P.C. Albers: "Changing Patterns of Ethnicity in the Northeastern Plains, 1780–1870" in J.D. Hill, ed., *History, Power, and Identity: Ethnogenesis in the Americas, 1492–1992* (Iowa City: University of Iowa Press, 1996), pp. 107–14; L. Peers, *The Ojibwa of Western Canada, 1780 to 1870* (Winnipeg: University of Manitoba Press, 1994), p. 142.

54. Colpitts, *Pemmican Empire*, pp. 195–96.

55. J. Soggie, "Lost in the Red Ochre Hills," pts.1 and 2, *Folklore* (Summer 2009): pp. 12–15; (Autumn 2009): pp.12–16.

56. Cowie, *The Company of Adventurers*, p. 315.

57. Quoted in Peers, *The Ojibwa of Western Canada*, p. 156.

58. J.S. Milloy, *The Plains Cree: Trade, Diplomacy, and War, 1790–1870* (Winnipeg: University of Manitoba Press, 1988), p. 109.

59. H.A. Dempsey, *Big Bear: The End of Freedom* (Vancouver: Douglas and McIntyre, 1984), pp. 54–55.

60. P.D. Elias, *The Dakota of the Canadian Northwest: Lessons for Survival* (Winnipeg: University of Manitoba Press, 1988), pp. 16–17, 20–21, 27–34, 168–69.

61. See I.M. Spry, *The Palliser Expedition: An Account of John Palliser's British North American Exploring Party 1857–1860* (Toronto: Macmillan, 1963).

62. Binnema, *Enlightened Zeal*, p. 232–37.

63. I.M. Spry, "Palliser, John" in F.G. Halpenny, ed., *Dictionary of Canadian Biography, vol. 11, 1881–1890* (Toronto: University of Toronto Press, 1982), p. 663.

64. R.A. Jarrell, "Hind, Henry Youle," in F.G. Halpenny, ed., *Dictionary of Canadian Biography, vol. 13, 1901–1910* (Toronto: University of Toronto Press, 1994), p. 472.

65. See R.J. Huyda, *Camera in the Interior: 1858* (Toronto: Coach House, 1975).

66. A. Kunard, "Relationships of Photography and Text in the Colonization of the Canadian West: The 1858 Assiniboine and Saskatchewan Exploring Expedition," *International Journal of Canadian Studies* 26 (Fall 2002): pp. 79–83; W.L. Morton, *Henry Youle Hind 1923–1908* (Toronto: University of Toronto Press, 1980), p. 82.

67. L.H. Thomas, "The Hind and Dawson Expeditions 1857–58," *The Beaver* (Winter 1958): p. 44.

68. W.L. Morton, *Henry Youle Hind, 1823–1908* (Toronto, University of Toronto Press, 1980), p. 76.

69. Ibid., pp. 85-6.

70. H.Y. Hind, *Narrative of the Canadian Red River Exploring Expedition of 1857 and the Assiniboine and Saskatchewan Exploring Expedition of 1858, vol. 2* (London: Longman, Green, Longman, and Roberts, 1860), p. 356.

71. Quoted in F. Pannekoek, "On the Edge of the Great Transformation 1857–58" in M. Payne et al, eds., *Alberta Formed—Alberta Transformed* (Edmonton: University of Alberta Press, 2006), p. 190.

72. Ibid.

73. D.J. Sauchyn and A.B. Beaudoin, "Recent Environmental Change in the Southwestern Plains," *The Canadian Geographer* 42, no. 4 (1998): p. 347; W.F. Rannie, "Summer Rainfall on the Prairies during the Palliser and Hind Expeditions, 1857–59," *Prairie Forum* 31, no. 1 (Spring 2006): pp. 17–38.

74. Quoted in W.F. Rannie, "'Awful Splendour': Historical Accounts of Prairie Fire in Southern Manitoba Prior to 1870," *Prairie Forum* 26, no. 1 (Spring 2001): p. 29.

75. Rannie, "'Awful Splendour,'" pp. 17–18.

76. W.K. Lamb, ed., *Sixteen Years in the Indian Country: The Journal of Daniel Williams Harmon* (Toronto: Macmillan, 1957), p. 26.

77. J. Warkentin, "The Desert Goes North" in B.W. Blouet and M.P. Lawson, eds., *Images of the Plains: The Role of Human Nature in Settlement* (Lincoln: University of Nebraska Press, 1975), p. 152; see also J. Warkentin, "Steppe, Desert and Empire" in A.W. Rasporich and H.C. Klassen, eds., *Prairie perspectives 2: Selected papers of the Western Canadian Studies Conferences, 1970, 1971* (Toronto, Holt Rinehart and Winston of Canada, 1973), pp. 102–13.

78. Warkentin, "The Desert Goes North," p. 154.

79. Ironically, while searching for a more northerly route for a Pacific railway a decade earlier (1853–54), American Isaac Stevens investigated the country between the 47th and 49th parallels and suggested that the great plains had agricultural promise. G.T. Davidson, "Exploring Two Different Wests: The Stevens and the Palliser Expeditions of 1853–1860," (2000; unpublished paper kindly provided to the author). E.C. Hope, "Weather and Crop History in Western Canada" *Canadian Society of Technical Agriculturalists Review* 16 (March 1938): p. 349 argues, "There is ample evidence in reading Palliser's report that he expected to find a central desert in this region without even going into it." But this criticism really applies to Hind. Interestingly, the HBC's Dr. John Rae reached similar conclusions at the time. See I.M. Spry, ed., "A Visit to Red River and the Saskatchewan, 1861, by Dr. John Rae," *Geographical Journal* 140, pt. 1 (February 1974): pp. 1–17.

80. Hind, *Narrative of the Canadian Red River Exploring Expedition*, pp. 234–35.

81. S. Zeller, *Inventing Canada: Early Victorian Science and the Idea of a Transcontinental Nation* (Toronto: University of Toronto Press, 1987), pp. 170–80

82. Warkentin, "Steppe, Desert and Empire," pp. 120–23.

83. Quoted in G.S. Dunbar, "Isotherms and Politics: Perception of the Northwest in the 1850s" in Rasporich and Klassen, eds., *Prairie Perspectives* 2, p. 94.

84. A.I. Silver, "French Canada and the Prairie Frontier," *Canadian Historical Review* 50, no. 1 (March 1969): pp. 15–17.

85. H. Bowsfield, "Taylor, James Wilkes" in F.G. Halpenny, ed., *Dictionary of Canadian Biography, vol. 12, 1891–1900* (Toronto: University of Toronto Press, 1990), pp. 1029–31. For a fuller discussion, see A.C. Gluek, *Minnesota and the Manifest Destiny of the Canadian Northwest* (Toronto: University of Toronto Press, 1965).

86. Quoted in J. Pope, *Memoirs of the Right Honourable Sir John Alexander Macdonald* (Ottawa: Durie, 1894), p. 398.

87. See D.G. Creighton, *John A. Macdonald: The Young Politician* (Toronto: University of Toronto Press, 1952).

88. R. Gwyn, *John A: The Man who Made Us* (Toronto: Random House, 2007), p. 215.

89. Quoted in J.A. Bovey, "The Attitudes and Policies of the Federal Government Towards Canada's Northern Territories, 1870–1930" (master's thesis, University of British Columbia, 1957), p. 13.

90. Quoted in P.B. Waite, *The Life and Times of Confederation, 1864–1867: Politics, Newspapers, and the Union of British North America* (Toronto: University of Toronto Press, 1962), p. 306.

91. W.L. Morton makes this observation in *The Critical Years: The Union of British North America, 1857–1873* (Toronto: McClelland and Stewart, 1964).

92. Quoted in Pope, *Memoirs of the Right Honourable*, p. 398.

93. S.D. Grant, *Polar Imperative: A History of Arctic Sovereignty in North America* (Vancouver: Douglas and McIntyre, 2010), pp. 118, 132.

94. Quoted in Gywn, *John A*, p. 431.

95. D. Balasubramanian, "Wisconsin's Foreign Trade in the Civil War Era," *The Wisconsin Magazine of History* 46, no. 4 (1963): p. 262.

96. Great Britain did not transfer its claim to the arctic archipelago to Canada until 1880.

97. Great Britain. Imperial order-in-council, 23 June 1870, "Rupert's Land and the North-Western Territory" in D. De Brou and B. Waiser, eds., *Documenting Canada: A History of Modern Canada in Documents* (Saskatoon: Fifth House Publishers, 1992), p. 40.

98. F. Tough and K. Dimmer, "Rupertsland Transfer, 1870" in K.T. Carlson, ed., *CURA Otipimsuak Atlas* (forthcoming).

CHAPTER THIRTEEN NOTES

1. D.L. Cowan correspondence to M. Cowan on 2 July 1882, 31 January 1883, 13 October 1882, and 23 February 1885. Copies of D.L. Cowan's correspondence were generously provided to the author by American descendant William Cowan.

2. Canada's area increased almost eight-fold with the purchase of Rupert's Land and the North-Western Territory—from 384,598 square miles to 2,988,909 square miles.

3. J.A. Bovey, "The Attitudes and Policies of the Federal Government Towards Canada's Northern Territories, 1870–1930," (master's thesis, University of British Columbia, 1957), p. 27.

4. W.P.M. Kennedy, ed., *Statutes, Treaties, and Documents of the Canadian Constitution, 1713–1929* (Toronto: Oxford University Press, 1930), p. 654. For a list of blocks of land around each post see pp. 655–58.

5. A.J. Ray, *The Canadian Fur Trade in the Industrial Age* (Toronto: University of Toronto Press, 1990), pp. 3–4.

6. Ibid., pp. 20–28, 50–51, 56–57.

7. "Report with Regard to the Death of the Finlayson Brothers," Donald Finlayson papers, MG 27, RJ, ser. c-68, vol. 1, Library and Archives Canada, Manuscript Division.

8. Ray, *The Canadian Fur Trade in the Industrial Age*, pp. 6, 66.

9. T. Barris, *Fire Canoe: Prairie Steamboat Days Revisited* (Toronto: Canadian Publishers, 1977), pp. 42–46.

10. J.F. Klaus "The Early Missions of the Swan River District, 1821–1869," *Saskatchewan History* 17, no. 2 (Spring 1964): p. 95.

11. A. Ballantine, "Recollections and Reminiscences: Steamboating on the Saskatchewan," *Saskatchewan History* 18, no. 3 (Autumn 1965): p. 105.

12. D.F. Pelly, *The Old Way North: Following the Oberholzer-Magee Expedition* (St. Paul: Borealis Books, 2008), pp. 24, 29.

13. Ray, *The Canadian Fur Trade in the Industrial Age*, pp. 44, 49.

14. B. Macdougall, *One of the Family: Métis Culture in Nineteenth-Century Northwestern Saskatchewan* (Vancouver: University of British Columbia Press, 2010), pp. 176–77, 215–16, 227–29, 233–35, 243.

15. Ibid., p. 239.

16. A. Morris, *The Hudson's Bay and Pacific Territories* (Montreal: John Lovell, 1859), p. 14.

17. Quoted in D. Owram, *Promise of Eden: The Canadian Expansionist Movement and the Idea of the West, 1856–1900* (Toronto: University of Toronto Press, 1980), p. 77.

18. Ibid., pp. 4–5, 101–02.

19. C. Martin, *Dominion Lands Policy* (Toronto: McClelland and Stewart, 1973), p. 9.

20. See, for example, Canada, *House of Commons Debates* (4 December 1867), pp. 184–6, and (6 December 1867), pp. 206–07.

21. Owram, *Promise of Eden*, pp. 137–38.

22. J.G. Snell, "The Frontier Sweeps Northwest: American Perceptions of the British American Prairie West at the Point of Canadian Expansion (circa 1870)," *Western Historical Quarterly* 11, no. 4 (October 1980): p. 384.

23. G. Wilson, *Frontier Farewell: The 1870s and the End of the Old West* (Regina: Canadian Plains Research Center, 2007), p. 355.

24. B. Waiser, "The Government Explorer in Canada, 1870–1914" in J.L. Allen, ed., *North American Exploration vol. 3: A Continent Comprehended* (Lincoln: University of Nebraska Press, 1997), p. 419.

25. For an explanation for how the boundary was astronomically determined, see S. Anderson, "The North American Boundary to Lake of the Woods to the Rocky Mountains," *Journal of the Royal Geographical Society* 46 (1876): pp. 259–62.

26. T. Rees, *Arc of the Medicine Line* (Vancouver: Douglas and McIntyre, 2007), pp. 357–58.

27. Dr. T. Millman, "Impressions of the West in the Early Seventies from the Diary of the Assistant Surgeon of the B.N.A. Boundary Survey," *Women's Canadian Historical Society of Toronto* 26 (1927–28): entry for July 21st, 1874, pp. 45-46.

28. A.R. Turner, "Surveying the International Boundary: The Journal of George M. Dawson," *Saskatchewan History* 21., no. 1 (Winter 1968): pp. 1–23.

29. G.M. Dawson, *Report on the Geology and Resources of the Region in the Vicinity of the 49th Parallel, from Lake of the Woods to the Rocky Mountains* (Montreal: Dawson, 1875), pp. 292, 299, 301. In trying to explain the superficial geology of the region, Dawson scoffed at the idea that the till deposits had been laid down by a great glacier. Rather, he argued that the western interior had once been covered by an inland sea and that the surface deposits had been made by melting icebergs. Several years passed before he finally changed his mind about the reason for the deposits.

30. D.W. Thomson, *Men and Meridians: The History of Surveying and Mapping in Canada, vol. 2, 1867–1917* (Ottawa: Queen's Printer, 1972), pp. 7–19.

31. For an excellent description of the survey system and the activities of the Dominion Lands Branch, see W.F. King and J.S. Dennis, "General Report of Operations from 1869 to 1889, Together with an Exposition of the System of Survey of Dominion Lands, and a Schedule of Dominion Land and Topographical Surveys," Canada, *Sessional Papers*, 1892, no.13, pt. 4.

32. O.J. Klotz papers, diary entry for 29 July 1889, MG 30 R1B, pp. 350–51, Library and Archives Canada, Manuscript Division.

33. Thomson, *Men and Meridians*, pp. 131–40.

34. The 1870s was one of the wettest decades in climate history in western Canada. E.C. Hope, "Weather and Crop History in Western Canada," *Canadian Society of Technical Agriculturalists Review* 16 (March 1938): p. 351.

35. *Manitoba Free Press*, 7 April 1881, p. 1. For a fuller discussion of John Macoun's assessment of western Canada's potential, see B. Waiser, *The Field Naturalist: John Macoun, the Geological Survey, and Natural Science* (Toronto: University of Toronto Press, 1989), pp. 16–54. Coincidentally, by the 1870s, the idea of a Great American Desert east of the Rockies had been replaced by a new dominant image—that of the Great Plains. M.J. Bowden, "The Great American Desert and the American Frontier, 1800–1882: Popular Images of the Plains" in T.K. Hareven, ed., *Anonymous Americans: Explorations in Nineteenth-Century Social History* (Englewood: Prentice-Hall, 1971), pp. 48–79.

36. H.Y. Hind, *Manitoba and the North-West Frauds* (Windsor: Knowles and Company, 1883), p. 32.

37. C. Horetzky, *Some Startling Facts Relating to the Canadian Pacific Railway and the North-West Lands* (Ottawa: Free Press, 1880), p. 43.

38. "Report of the Department of the Interior for 1881," Canada, *Sessional Papers*, 1882, no. 18, pt. 1, pp. 4–5.

39. J. Macoun, *Manitoba and the Great North-West* (Guelph: World Publishing Company, 1882), p. 364; E.J. Chambers, *Canada's Fertile Northland* (Ottawa: Government Printing Bureau, 1908).

40. See T. Petty, "Trails of Saskatchewan," 1962, Glenbow Archives, Calgary; R.C. Russell, *The Carlton Trail* (Saskatoon: Modern Press, 1955).

41. For an account of a trip along the Carlton Trail see E.J. Skinner, "Notes of Trip, 1879," Glenbow Archives, Calgary.

42. Owram, *Promise of Eden*, p. 32.

43. A. Robb, "Edwin Watkin and the Pacific Telegraph, 1861–1865," *Ontario History* 64, no. 4 (December 1973): pp. 189–209. The Hudson's Bay Company took steps to build a telegraph between western Canadian fur trade posts in the mid-1860s, but abandoned the project when a line was completed between San Francisco and British Columbia. A. Ronaghan, "The Pioneer Telegraph in Western Canada," (master's thesis, University of Saskatchewan, 1976), pp. 12-16.

44. Waiser, "The Government Explorer," pp. 435–43.

45. S. Fleming, ed., *Report on Surveys and Preliminary Operations on the Canadian Pacific Railway up to January 1877* (Ottawa: Queen's Printer, 1877), p. 57.

46. *Report of the Canadian Pacific Railway Royal Commission, vol. 3* (Ottawa: Queen's Printer, 1882), p. 495.

47. Waiser, "The Government Explorer," pp. 443–45.

48. One of the classics in this genre is by C.E. Denny, a former mountie, who opens his book with the sentence, "Violence was in the saddle over Canada's West." *The Law Marches West* (Toronto: J.M. Dent and Sons, 1939), p. 1.

49. D. Morton, "Cavalry or Police: Keeping the Peace on Two Adjacent Frontiers, 1870–1900," *Journal of Canadian Studies* 12 (1977): p. 15.

50. S.W. Horrall, "Sir John A. Macdonald and the Mounted Police Force for the Northwest Territories," *Canadian Historical Review* 53, no. 2 (June 1972): pp. 179–91.

51. Ibid., p. 192.

52. See H.A. Dempsey, *Firewater: The Impact of the Whisky Trade on the Blackfoot Nation* (Calgary: Fifth House Publishers, 2002).

53. W. Hildebrandt and B. Hubner, *The Cypress Hills: The Land and its People* (Saskatoon: Purich Publishing, 1994), pp. 59–70.

54. Horrall, "Sir John A. Macdonald and the Mounted Police," pp. 192–99.

55. Wilson, *Frontier Farewell*, pp. 209–48.

56. D.L. Cowan correspondence to his sister on February 23, 1885.

57. J.S. Murray, "The Mounties of Cypress Hills," *Archaeology* 42, no. 1 (January/February 1988): pp. 35–37.

58. See, for example, Richard Hardisty papers, W. McKay to R. Hardisty, 28 August 1874, Glenbow Archives, Calgary.

59. G. Colpitts, "The Methodists' Great 1869 Camp Meeting and Aboriginal Conservation Strategies in the North Saskatchewan River Valley," *Great Plains Quarterly* 29, no. 1 (Winter 2009): pp. 3–27.

60. M.K. Lux, *Medicine That Walks: Disease, Medicine, and Canadian Plains Native People, 1880–1940* (Toronto: University of Toronto Press, 2001), p. 17.

61. I. Cowie, *The Company of Adventurer*s (Lincoln: University of Nebraska Press, 1993), pp. 381–82. The child was the grandchild of prominent Métis Pascal Breland.

62. J.S. Milloy, *The Plains Cree: Trade, Diplomacy, and War, 1790–1870* (Winnipeg: University of Manitoba Press, 1988), pp. 116–17.

63. Wilson, *Frontier Farewell*, p. 93.

64. J. Daschuk et al., "Treaties and Tuberculosis: First Nations People in late 19th-Century Western Canada, a Political and Economic Transformation," *Canadian Bulletin of Medical History* 23, no. 2 (2006): pp. 31–12.

65. Colpitts, "The Methodists' Great 1869 Camp Meeting," p. 7; Report of Charles N. Bell, 23 March 1874, RG 10, vol. 3609, f. 3229, Library and Archives Canada, Government Archives Division, Indian Affairs; Daschuk et al., "Treaties and Tuberculosis," p. 313.

66. Quoted in J.R. Miller, *Compact, Contract, Covenant: Aboriginal Treaty-Making in Canada* (Toronto: University of Toronto Press, 2009), p. 154.

67. G. Bell to A. Morris correspondence, 19 October 1873, RG 10, vol. 3604, f. 2593, Library and Archives Canada, Government Archives Division, Indian Affairs.

68. A. Morris, *The Treaties of Canada with the Indians of Manitoba and the North-West Territories* (Saskatoon: Fifth House Publishers, 1991), p. 173.

69. R. Brain ("Invisible Demons: Epidemic Disease and the Plains Cree, 1670–1880" [master's thesis, University of Saskatchewan, 2002]) maintains that disease played a significant role in leading Indians towards treaty negotiations, while P. Hämäläinen, ("The Rise and Fall of Indian Horse Cultures," *Journal of American History* 90. no. 3 [December 2003]: p. 852) argues that the buffalo wars critically weakened all sides and "made the Euro-American military takeover virtually effortless."

70. See J.R. Miller, *Skyscrapers Hide the Heavens: A History of Indian-White Relations in Canada* (Toronto: University of Toronto Press, 1989), chaps. 4–5.

71. R.C. Macleod, *The North-West Mounted Police and Law Enforcement* (Toronto: University of Toronto Press, 1976), p. 3.

72. Quoted in Ray, *The Canadian Fur Trade in the Industrial Age*, p. 4.

73. This notion of reciprocity is examined in Jean Friesen, "Magnificent Gifts: The Treaties of Canada with the Indians of the Northwest 1869–76," *Transactions of the Royal Society of Canada, 5th ser., vol. 1* (1986), pp. 41–51.

74. P. Erasmus, *Buffalo Days and Nights* (Calgary: Glenbow–Alberta Institute, 1976), p. 247.

75. Miller, *Compact, Contract, Covenant*, pp. 170–72.

76. Quoted in Morris, *The Treaties of Canada*, pp. 199, 202.

77. Quoted in Erasmus, *Buffalo Days and Nights*, p. 244.

78. Quoted in Morris, *The Treaties of Canada*, pp. 205, 208.

79. Quoted in Erasmus, *Buffalo Days and Nights*, pp. 247, 249–50.

80. M. Massie, *Forest Prairie Edge: Place History in Saskatchewan* (Winnipeg: University of Manitoba Press, 2014), p. 56.

81. Quoted in Morris, *The Treaties of Canada*, pp. 210–13.

82. Ibid., p. 212.

83. There is ongoing debate today whether the Cree and other Indian groups knew exactly what they were giving up by entering the numbered treaties. There is also a related controversy over whether Indians were forfeiting their right to a future share of resource development revenues or only granting newcomer access to their lands "to a plough's depth." The governing Saskatchewan Party, for example, ran ads chastising the New Democratic Party Opposition for suggesting that there be discussions over resource revenue sharing with Saskatchewan First Nations. For a discussion of the treaty relationship, see See J.R. Miller, "The Aboriginal Peoples and the Crown" in D.M. Jackson, *The Crown and Canadian Federalism* (Toronto: Dundurn Press, 2013), pp. 255–69.

84. Although Indian spirituality infused the treaty process, Euro-Canadian negotiators also used Christian culture during the negotiations. See B. Kelly, "Three Uses of Christian Church Culture in the Numbered Treaties, 1871–1921," *Prairie Forum* 33, no. 22 (Fall 2008): pp. 357–84.

85. Quoted in Morris, *The Treaties of Canada*, pp. 231, 237, 238.

86. Ibid., p. 240.

87. H.A. Dempsey, *Big Bear: The End of Freedom* (Vancouver: Douglas and McIntyre, 1984), pp. 74–80.

88. Quoted in A.J. Ray et al., *Bounty and Benevolence: A History of Saskatchewan Treaties* (Montreal: McGill–Queens University Press, 2000), p. 117.

89. A. Stevenson, "The Métis Cultural Brokers and the Numbered Western Treaties, 1869–1877," (master's thesis, University of Saskatchewan, 2004).

90. M.H. Foster, "'Just Following the Buffalo': Origins of a Montana Métis Community," *Great Plains Quarterly* 26, no. 3 (Summer 2006): pp. 188–92.

91. G. Ens, *Homeland to Hinterland: The Changing Worlds of the Red River Métis in the Nineteenth Century* (Toronto: University of Toronto Press, 1996), pp. 149–71.

92. Bovey, "The Attitudes and Policies," pp. 22–28.

93. Quoted in S. Hewitt, "Fort Livingstone: A History," unpublished Parks Canada report, Saskatoon office, n.d.

94. Owram, *Promise of Eden*, p. 102.

95. Dawson, *Report on the Geology and Resources*, p. 301.

96. Bovey, "The Attitudes and Policies," pp. 33–43.

CHAPTER FOURTEEN NOTES

1. The Ridge was located in township 45, range 27, west of the 2nd meridian. The only evidence of past

occupation—apart from the cellars and artifact scatter—are apple trees that still flower and produce fruit today. The author thanks Lyle and Terry Jones, descendants of Thomas Scott, for their tour of the family site.

2. The English Métis were also known as Country Born, English halfbreeds, and Native. The French Métis called their English Protestant counterparts, *les autres Métis or les anglais Métis*.

3. Quoted in T.D. Regehr, *The Canadian Northern: Pioneer Road of the Northern Prairies, 1895–1918* (Toronto: Macmillan of Canada, 1976), p. 2.

4. Quoted in D. Owram, *Promise of Eden: The Canadian Expansionist Movement and the Idea of the West, 1856–1900* (Toronto: University of Toronto Press, 1980), p. 182.

5. M. Zaslow, *The Opening of the Canadian North, 1870–1914* (Toronto: McClelland and Stewart, 1971), pp. 28–29.

6. For an examination of the route change, see B. Waiser, "A Willing Scapegoat: John Macoun and the Route of the CPR," *Prairie Forum* 10, no. 1 (Spring 1985): pp. 65–82.

7. The CPR was supposed to select its land from the odd-numbered sections along the main line (twenty-four miles on each side), but the "fairly fit for settlement" stipulation enabled the company to acquire some of the best farm land in the region. Ontario did not contribute a single acre of land grant even though 650 miles of CPR main line ran through the province. C. Martin, *"Dominion Lands" Policy* (Toronto: McClelland and Stewart, 1973), pp. 74–75; J.C. Weaver, *The Great Land Rush and the Making of the Modern World, 1650–1900* (Montreal: McGill–Queen's University Press, 2003), pp. 254–45.

8. G. Abrams, *Prince Albert: The First Century 1866–1966* (Saskatoon: Modern Press, 1966), p. 16.

9. For an examination of why French and English Métis left Red River during the 1870s, see G. Ens, *Homeland to Hinterland: The Changing Worlds of the Red River Métis in the Nineteenth Century* (Toronto: University of Toronto Press, 1996), pp. 158–64.

10. P. Code, "Les Autres Métis: The English Métis of the Prince Albert Settlement, 1862–1886," (master's thesis, University of Saskatchewan, 2008), pp.13, 19–20, 33, 36–37, 42–45.

11. Abrams, *Prince Albert: The First Century*, pp. 19–20, 35.

12. Editorial, *Saskatchewan Herald*, 29 November 1880.

13. A. McPherson, *The Battlefords: A History* (Saskatoon: Modern Press, 1967), pp. 35–59.

14. Quoted in L.H. Thomas, *The Struggle for Responsible Government in the North-West Territories, 1870–97* (Toronto: University of Toronto Press, 1956), p. 94.

15. By comparison, the passenger fare was $230 for a steamboat trip from Winnipeg to Prince Albert. J.H. Archer, *Saskatchewan: A History* (Saskatoon: Western Producer Prairie Books, 1980), p. 67.

16. S.D. Hanson, ed., *A Prairie Memoir: The Life and Times of James Clinkskill* (Regina: Canadian Plains Research Center, 2003), pp. ix–xiv, 16–25.

17. The transfer of government officials from Battleford to Regina took place in March 1883. See J.W. Brennan, *Regina: An Illustrated History* (Toronto: James Lorimer, 1898) for the early years of the new capital.

18. *Census of the Three Provisional Districts of the North-West Territories, 1884–85* (Ottawa: Maclean, Roger and Company, 1886), pp. 2–3.

19. Archer, *Saskatchewan: A History*, p. 67.

20. B. Macdougall, *One of the Family: Metis Culture in Nineteenth-Century Northwestern Saskatchewan* (Vancouver: University of British Columbia Press, 2010), pp. 175–76, 182, 235.

21. A.J. Ray, *The Canadian Fur Trade in the Industrial Age* (Toronto: University of Toronto Press, 1990), pp. 9, 19–20, 42; J. Daschuk, *Clearing the Plains: Disease, Politics of Starvation, and the Loss of Aboriginal Life* (Regina: University of Regina Press, 2013), pp. 128–31. Baker and Company used bull trains to deliver large quantities of goods to the region.

22. Report of Charles Bell, 23 March 1874, RG 10, vol. 3609, f. 3229, Library and Archives Canada, Government Archives Division, Indian Affairs.

23. G. Colpitts, *Pemmican Empire: Food, Trade, and the Last Bison Hunts in the North American Plains* (New York: Cambridge University Press, 2014), pp. 246–54.

24. Hugh Dempsey has suggested that "the [treaty] negotiations might have taken a different turn" if the Treaty 6 commission had not started at Fort Carlton. See H.A. Dempsey, *Big Bear: The End of Freedom* (Vancouver: Douglas and McIntyre, 1984), p. 70.

25. "Indian Affairs," Canada, *Sessional Papers*, 1877, no. 11, pp. xxxv–xxxvi.

26. D.G. McGrady, *Living with Strangers: The Nineteenth Century Sioux and the Canadian-American Borderlands* (Lincoln: University of Nebraska Press, 2006), pp. 32, 36–37, 45–46.

27. G. Wilson, *Frontier Farewell: The 1870s and the End of the Old West* (Regina: Canadian Plains Research Center, 2007), p. 312.

28. Ibid., pp. 312–18; M. Hamilton, "'Anyone not on the list might as well be dead': Aboriginal Peoples and the Censuses of Canada, 1851–1916," *Journal of the Canadian Historical Association* 18, no. 1 (2007): pp. 57–79.

29. For a fuller discussion of the bison protection ordinance, see B. Waiser, "'A legislator's view of Bison collapse: The 1877 North-West Territories Bison Protection Ordinance" in G. Cunfer and B. Waiser, eds., *Bison and People on the North American Great Plains* (College Station: Texas A&M University Press, forthcoming).

30. J.L. Tobias, "Canada's Subjugation of the Plains Cree, 1879–1885," in J.R. Miller, ed., *Sweet Promises: A Reader in Indian-White Relations in Canada* (Toronto: University of Toronto Press, 1991), p. 216.

31. F.G. Roe, *The North American Buffalo* (Toronto: University of Toronto Press, 1970), pp. 467–88.

32. "North-West Mounted Police Commissioner's Report, 1879," Canada, *Sessional Papers*, 1880, no. 4, pt. 3, p. 4.

33. "Annual Report of the Department of the Interior," Canada, *Sessional Papers*, 1880, no. 4, p. 79.

34. "E. Dewdney Report, Fort Walsh, 1879," RG 10, vol. 3704, f. 17858, Library and Archives Canada, Government Archives Division, Indian Affairs.

35. H. Forget, "1879 Diary," Amédée A. and Henriette Forget fonds, Saskatchewan Archives Board, Regina.

36. D. Laird to Minister of the Interior, June 30, 1879, RG 10, vol. 3698, f. 16142, Library and Archives Canada, Government Archives Division, Indian Affairs.

37. "Minutes of the Battleford Council, August 27, 1879," ibid.

38. "E. Dewdney Report, Fort Walsh, 1879."

39. Ray, *The Canadian Fur Trade*, pp. 34–40.

40. Quoted in J.B.D. Larmour, "Edgar Dewdney, Commissioner of Indian Affairs and Lieutenant Governor of the North-West Territories, 1879–1888," (master's thesis, University of Saskatchewan, 1969), p. 15.

41. See J.R. Miller, "The Aboriginal Peoples and the Crown" in D.M. Jackson, *The Crown and Canadian Federalism* (Toronto: Dundurn Press, 2013), pp. 255–69.

42. Quoted in W.A. Dobak, "Killing the Canadian Buffalo, 1821–1881," *Western Historical Quarterly* 27 (Spring 1996): p. 49.

43. G. Colpitts, *Game in the Garden: A Human History of Wildlife in Western Canada to 1940* (Vancouver: University of British Columbia Press, 2002), p. 41.

44. N.E. Dyck, "The Administration of Federal Indian Aid in the North-West Territories, 1879–1885," (master's thesis, University of Saskatchewan, 1970), p. 40.

45. Quoted in J.R. Miller, "Macdonald as Minister of Indian Affairs: The Shaping of Canadian Indian Policy" in P. Dutil and R. Hall, eds., *Macdonald at 200: New Reflections and Legacies* (Toronto: Dundurn Press, 2014), p. 323.

46. Daschuk, *Clearing the Plains*, p. 108.

47. Miller, "Macdonald as Minister of Indian Affairs," p. 325.

48. Canada. *House of Commons Debates* (9 May 1883), p. 1102.

49. Colpitts, *Game in the Garden*, pp. 41–53.

50. Quoted in Larmour, "Edgar Dewdney," p. 47.

51. S. Carter, *Lost Harvests: Prairie Indian Reserve Farmers and Government Policy* (Montreal: McGill–Queen's University Press, 1990), pp. 79–95.

52. Canada. *House of Commons Debates* (26 April 1882), p. 1186.

53. Ibid., (23 April 1880), p. 1695.

54. S.A. Gavigan, *Hunger, Horses, and Government Men: Criminal Law on the Aboriginal Plains, 1870–1905* (Vancouver: University of British Columbia Press, 2013), pp. 126–27.

55. I. Andrews, "Indian Protest Against Starvation: The Yellow Calf Incident of 1884," *Saskatchewan History* 28, no. 2 (Spring 1975), p. 46.

56. Tobias, "Canada's Subjugation of the Plains Cree," p. 222.

57. Larmour, "Edgar Dewdney," pp. 31–33.

58. Ibid., p. 74.

59. Daschuk, *Clearing the Plains*, pp. 100, 118, 124, 143.

60. "Report to the Minister of the Interior on the Governor General's Tour, 4 November 1881," RG 10, vol. 3768, Library and Archives Canada, Government Archives Division, Indian Affairs.

61. J.A. Macrae to E. Dewdney, 25 August 1884, RG 10, vol. 3697, f. 15423, Library and Archives Canada, Government Archives Division, Indian Affairs.

62. H. Reed to J.A. Macdonald, 23 January 1885, RG 10, vol. 3697, f. 15423, Library and Archives Canada, Government Archives Division, Indian Affairs.

63. Larmour, "Edgar Dewdney," p. 82. [italics added to quote for emphasis]

64. D.P. Payment, *"The Free People–Otipemisiwak": Batoche, Saskatchewan 1870–1930* (Ottawa: Canadian Parks Service, 1990), pp. 31–35, 151.

65. Ibid., p. 40.

66. D. Lee, "The Métis Militants of 1885," *Canadian Ethnic Studies* 21, no. 3 (1989): pp. 9–12.

67. Payment, *The Free People*, pp. 34–35, 208–10, 220; N. Schaller et al., "Climate Effects of the 1883 Krakatoa Eruption: Historical and Present Perspectives," *Vierteljahrsschrift der Naturforschenden Gesellschaft in Zuerich*, no. 154 (2009): pp. 31–40. Gabriel's Crossing was south of the one at Batoche and shortened the travel time to Fort Carlton.

68. Quoted in Lee, "Métis Militants of 1885," p. 4.

69. The Métis living at St. Albert (near Edmonton) and in the Qu'Appelle Valley also organized councils around this time.

70. RG 6, vol. 22, f. 805–900, Library and Archives Canada, Government Archives Division, Department of Justice.

71. Quoted in R. Rivard and C. Littlejohn, *The History of the Métis of Willow Bunch* (Saskatoon, 2003), p. 156.

72. Lee, "Métis Militants of 1885," p. 10.

73. A more detailed explanation of how the preliminary survey was conducted is provided by Payment, *The Free People*, pp. 262–63.

74. Hanson, ed., *A Prairie Memoir*, p. 22. There was no francophone land officer in the Prince Albert Dominion Lands office until the spring of 1884.

75. Quoted in Thomas, *The Struggle for Responsible Government*, p. 82–83. Thomas (p. 81) sarcastically suggested that "Conservative and Liberal administrations at Ottawa were witlessly assuming that nobody but an Ontario immigrant would worry about such matters [i.e., representation on council]."

76. Payment, *The Free People*, pp. 263–65. For an explanation of how quarter-sections were to be converted to river lots, see p. 291, n. 30.

77. For a list of the early electoral districts in the North-West Territories (1880–85), see Thomas, *The Struggle for Responsible Government*, p. 115.

78. The restriction on municipal organization was dropped in 1880, but the connection between electoral districts and school organization remained in place for another five years.

79. Quoted in Thomas, *The Struggle for Responsible Government*, p. 87.

80. Ibid., pp. 94, 98–99.

81. Quoted in Owram, *Promise of Eden*, p. 172.

82. Quoted in Thomas, *The Struggle for Responsible Government*, p. 123.

83. Ibid., p. 127.

84. Archer, *Saskatchewan: A History*, p. 86.

85. Canada, *Senate Debates*, (25 February 1884), pp. 143–52.

86. Quoted in Owram, *Promise of Eden*, p. 171.

87. Ibid., p. 172.

88. Abrams, *Prince Albert: The First Century*, pp. 54–55.

89. McPherson, *The Battlefords: A History*, pp. 40–41, 76; Abrams, *Prince Albert: The First Century*, pp. 22, 41–42, 52.

90. Archer, *Saskatchewan: A History*, p. 82.

91. Code, "Les Autres Métis," pp. 66–67, 78, 84–86.

92. Quoted in G.F.G. Stanley, *The Birth of Western Canada: A History of the Riel Rebellions* (Toronto: University of Toronto Press, 1960), p. 266.

93. Code, "Les Autres Métis," p. 67.

94. Political scientist and author Tom Flanagan suggests in his book *Louis 'David' Riel: Prophet of the New World* (Toronto, University of Toronto Press, 1979) that Riel can best be understood as a messianic figure who deliberately pushed the Métis towards rebellion to fulfill his chosen role as God's personal emissary, while in her book *In Riel: A Life of Revolution* (Toronto, Harper Collins, 1994) writer Maggie Siggins argues that Riel was a misunderstood revolutionary leader who served as a bridge between Indian and white cultures.

95. Quoted in Abrams, *Prince Albert: The First Century*, p. 68.

96. Stanley, *The Birth of Western Canada*, p. 310.

97. Quoted in Thomas, *The Struggle for Responsible Government*, p. 129.

98. Quoted in Ibid., p. 130.

99. Abrams, *Prince Albert: The First Century*, pp. 74–76.

100. Quoted in Code, "Les Autres Métis," p. 98.

CHAPTER FIFTEEN NOTES

1. Each cannon volley made two loud noises—one on discharge, the other on impact.

2. Quoted in E.J. Millions, "Ties Undone: A Gendered and Racial Analysis of the Impact of the 1885 North-West Rebellion in the Saskatchewan District," (master's thesis, University of Saskatchewan, 2004), p. 80.

3. Quoted in D. Light, *Footprints in the Dust* (North Battleford: Turner–Warwick Publications, 1987), p. 128.

4. K. Foster, "Moose Jaw viewed war from sideline seat," *Western People* (March 21, 1985): p. 10; S. Carter, *Lost Harvests: Prairie Indian Reserve Farmers and Government Policy* (Montreal: McGill–Queen's University Press, 1990), pp. 127–28.

5. Editorial, *Saskatchewan Herald*, 20 March 1885.

6. Quoted in Millions, "Ties Undone," pp. 37–38.

7. D. Christensen, *Ahtahkakoop: The Epic Account of a Plains Cree Head Chief, His People, and their Struggle for Survival 1816–1896* (Shell Lake, Sask: Ahtahkakoop Publishing, 2000), p. 560.

8. C. Tupper to J.A. Macdonald, 30 April 1885, John A. Macdonald papers, vol. 283, p. 129919, Library and Archives Canada, Manuscript Division. A number of books and articles on the topic make the same claim. In his 1910 history of the force, *Riders of the Plains* (Edmonton: Hurtig Publishers, 1971), mounted police historian A.L. Hayden observed, "There had been war—red war, with its many opportunities for fighting, and for many other outlets of energy so dear to the primitive mind," pp. 155–56. Historian John Jennings, meanwhile, borrowed a line from Dylan Thomas's poem, "Do not go gentle into that good night," and argued that Indians regarded the rebellion as "their last chance to 'rage against the dying of the light.'" J. Jennings, "The Plains Indian and the Law" in H. Dempsey, ed., *Men in Scarlet* (Calgary: Glenbow Museum, 1973), p. 65.

9. L. Crozier to E. Dewdney, 18 March 1885, E. Dewdney papers, box 4, f. 67, p. 1428, Glenbow Archives, Calgary, and E. Dewdney to J.A. Macdonald, 25 March 1885, Macdonald papers, vol. 107, pp. 43030–33, Library and Archives Canada, Manuscript Devision.

10. P. Ballendine to H. Reed, 8 November 1884, RG 10, v. 3548, f. 749, Library and Archives Canada, Government Archives Division, Indian Affairs.

11. D.P. Payment, *"The Free People–Otipemisiwak": Batoche, Saskatchewan 1870–1930* (Ottawa: Canadian Parks Service, 1990), p. 137, n. 69.

12. At least six Métis who fought during the spring of 1885 had been on the treaty pay lists of neighbouring reserves one year earlier. D. Lee, "The Métis Militants of 1885," *Canadian Ethnic Studies* 21, no. 3 (1989): pp. 10–12.

13. K.J. Taylor, "Kapeyakwaskonam" (One Arrow) in F. Halpenny, ed., *Dictionary of Canadian Biography, vol. 11* (Toronto: University of Toronto Press, 1982), p. 461.

14. C.W. Herchmer to E. Dewdney, 10 February 1886, Macdonald papers, vol. 212, pp. 90617-2, Glenbow Archives, Calgary.

15. Reproduced in T. Flanagan, ed., *The Collected Writings of Louis Riel, vol. 3* (Edmonton: University of Alberta Press, 1985), p. 77.

16. A. McDonald to E. Dewdney, 8 April 1885, RG 10, vol. 3584, f. 1130, pt. 3A, Library and Archives Canada, Government Archives Division, Indian Affairs.

17. B. Beal and R. Macleod, *Prairie Fire: The 1885 North-West Rebellion* (Edmonton: Hurtig Publishers, 1984), p. 139.

18. Millions, "Ties Undone," pp. 29, 31.

19. H. Devine, *The People Who Own Themselves: Aboriginal Ethnogenesis in a Canadian Family, 1660–1900* (Calgary: University of Calgary Press, 2004), pp. 146–47, 163-4.

20. P.C. Albers: "Changing Patterns of Ethnicity in the Northeastern Plains, 1780–1870" in J.D. Hill, ed., *History, Power, and Identity: Ethnogenesis in the Americas, 1492–1992* (Iowa City: University of Iowa Press, 1996), pp. 90–91.

21. Devine, *The People Who Own Themselves*, p. 145.

22. Light, *Footprints in the Dust*, p. 5.

23. P. Code, "Les Autres Métis: The English Métis of the Prince Albert Settlement, 1862–1886," (master's thesis, University of Saskatchewan, 2008), pp.100–104.

24. Quoted in Millions, "Ties Undone," p. 44.

25. G. Abrams, *Prince Albert: The First Century 1866–1966* (Saskatoon: Modern Press, 1966), p. 78.

26. C.P. Mulvaney, *The History of the North-West Rebellion of 1885* (Toronto: A.H. Hovey and Company, 1886), p. 384.

27. Thomas Clark papers, 1885 diary, 31 March 1885, Saskatchewan Archives Board, Regina.

28. See W.B. Cameron, *The War Trail of Big Bear* (Toronto: Ryerson Press, 1926). The book was later reissued as *Blood Red the Sun*.

29. Quoted in J.B.D. Larmour, "Edgar Dewdney, Commissioner of Indian Affairs and Lieutenant Governor of the North-West Territories, 1879–1888" (master's thesis, University of Saskatchewan, 1969), p. 47.

30. For a candid evaluation of the Canadian military response, see D. Morton, "Reflections on Old Fred: Major General Middleton and the North-West Campaign of 1885," *NeWest Review* 10, no. 9 (May 1885): pp. 5–7.

31. See, for example, *The Globe*, 7 April 1885. Toronto-based *Grip* magazine, a regular critic of the Macdonald government, also trumpeted the men's heroism.

32. L. Dixon, *Halifax to the Saskatchewan: "Our Boys" in the Riel Rebellion* (Halifax: Holloway Brothers, 1886).

33. As of July 1885, anyone who served west of the Lakehead during the rebellion was entitled to a 320-acre land grant on the understanding that the land had to be selected by 1 August 1886 and that homestead provisions had to be met. Instead of free land, those eligible could also select $80 in scrip. K.N. Lambrecht, *The Administration of Dominion Lands, 1870–1930* (Regina: Canadian Plains Research Center, 1991), p. 28.

34. D.N. Sprague, *Canada and the Métis, 1869–1885* (Waterloo: Wilfrid Laurier University Press, 1988), pp. 167–69; H. Adams, *Prison of Grass: Canada from a Native point of view* (Saskatoon: Fifth House Publishers, 1989), pp. 81–85.

35. G. Stephen to J.J. Hill, 18 April 1885, J.J. Hill papers, The James Jerome Hill Reference Library, St. Paul.

36. Dixon, *Halifax to the Saskatchewan*, p. 11.

37. For one soldier's diary account of the trip west, see B. Waiser, "Major Smith's Rebellion Diary," *NeWest Review* 10, no. 9 (May 1985): pp. 17–18.

38. Larmour, "Edgar Dewdney," p. 194. In looking back on the business generated by the North West Field Force, the *Qu'Appelle Vidette* (30 June 1885) sarcastically observed: "then Riel rebelled, and saved you all...Yet Dewdney says he is a rebel."

39. See W. Hildebrandt *The Battle of Batoche: British Small Warfare and the Entrenched Métis* (Ottawa: Canadian Parks Service, 1985).

40. C. Thomson, "Lakotapteole: Wood Mountain Lakota Cultural Adaptation and Maintenance Through Ranching and Rodeo, 1880–1930," (master's thesis, University of Saskatchewan, 2014), pp. 27 (n. 55), 31.

41. George Robertson testimony, "Evidence Collected at 1886 Rebellion Claims Commission Hearing at Prince Albert," E.9/29, pp. 15–17, Hudson's Bay Company Archives, Winnipeg.

42. A. Dietz, "Wapahaska: The Early History of the Whitecap Band," *Saskatoon History Review* (February 1991): pp. 43–44.

43. J.A. McDonald to E. Dewdney, 28 May 1885, RG 10, vol. 3710, f. 19550-53, Library and Archives Canada, Government Archives Division, Indian Affairs.

44. Pasquah and Muscowpetung to J.A. Macdonald, 21 April 1885, RG 10, vol. 3584, f. 1130, pt. 3A, Library and Archives Canada, Government Archives Division, Indian Affairs.

45. E. Dewdney, "Notice," 6 May 1885, RG 10, vol. 3584, f. 1130, pt. 3A, Library and Archives Canada, Government Archives Division, Indian Affairs.

46. Quoted in C.P. Mulvaney, T*he History of the North-West Rebellion of 1885* (Toronto A.V. Hovey, 1885), p. 316.

47. Ibid, p. 386; C.F. Winter, "The Surrender of Poundmaker," *The Cosmos* 1, no. 10 (October 1903): p. 84.

48. D.L. Cowan to M. Cowan, 23 January 1885. Copies of D.L. Cowan's correspondence were generously provided to the author by American descendant William Cowan. Cowan's body was not recovered for six weeks and was buried near where it was found. It was later moved to a mass grave site for the Frog Lake dead in 1909.

49. K.M. Yuill, "The Crossing of the Big Muskeg of Loon Lake, Saskatchewan, 1885" (speech before North-West Field Force Reunion, Toronto, April 1935).

50. C.W. Dunning Diary, 12 June 1885, Archives of Ontario, Toronto.

51. E. Dewdney to J.A. Macdonald, 3 June 1885, Macdonald papers, vol. 107, 43110–18, Library and Archives Canada, Manuscript Division.

52. Canada. "Annual Report of the Department of Indian Affairs," *Sessional Papers*, 1886, p. 140.

53. J.N. Sinclair, "Green Lake Claim," Rebellion Claims Commission Hearings, 1886, Hudson's Bay Company Archives, Winnipeg.

54. J.L. Tobias, "Canada's Subjugation of the Plains Cree, 1879–1885" in J.R. Miller, ed., *Sweet Promises: A Reader on Indian-White Relations in Canada* (Toronto: University of Toronto Press, 1991), 231–32.

55. H. Reed to E. Dewdney, 23 June 1885, Macdonald papers, vol. 107, 43180–83, Library and Archives Canada, Manuscript Division.

56. Lansdowne to J.A. Macdonald, 31 August 1885, Macdonald papers, vol. 106, 42559–62, and J.A. Macdonald to Lansdowne, 3 September 1885, Macdonald papers, vol. 23, 271–72, Library and Archives Canada, Manuscript Division.

57. A Regina chemist, William Pettingell, for reasons of preservation placed "certain spices and medicine in packets throughout Riel's body and his clothing" until he could be buried. F. Pettingell to D. Fisher, 20 February 1985. Copy of letter kindly provided to author.

58. B. Beal and B. Wright, "Summary and Incompetent Justice: Legal Responses to the 1885 Crisis" in B. Wright and S. Binnie, eds., *Canadian State Trials, vol. 3: Political Trials and Security Measures, 1840–1914* (Toronto: Osgoode Society for Canadian Legal History, 2009), pp. 353–60.

59. Quoted in Larmour, "Edgar Dewdney," p. 197.

60. Canada. "Rebellion Trials," *Sessional Papers*, 1886, no. 52, p, 382.

61. Ibid., p. 375.

62. Ibid., p. 370.

63. D. De Brou and B. Waiser, *Documenting Canada: A History of Modern Canada in Documents* (Saskatoon: Fifth House Publishers, 1992), p. 140.

64. See B. Waiser, "The White Man Governs: The 1885 Indian Trials" in B. Wright and S. Binnie, eds., *Canadian State Trials, vol. 3*, pp. 451–82.

65. Quoted in Beal and Macleod, *Prairie Fire*, p. 309.

66. Canada. "Rebellion Trials," p. 15.

67. Because Dewdney blamed Big Bear for spearheading Indian resistance to his policies, the lieutenant governor not only allowed the old chief's hair to be cut upon entering prison, an act considered as demeaning, but actively resisted his early release until overruled by the federal cabinet. B. Titley, *The Indian Commissioners: Agents of the State and Indian Policy in Canada's Prairie West* (Edmonton: University of Alberta Press, 2009), pp. 83–84.

68. Canada. "Rebellion Trials," pp. 249–51.

69. A. Campbell to J. Burbidge, 20 June 1885, Macdonald papers, vol. 197, 82880, Library and Archives Canada, Manuscript Division.

70. S.E. Bingaman, "The North-West Rebellion Trials," (master's thesis, University of Regina, 1971), p. 30.

71. See, for example, the *Saskatchewan Herald*, 25 May 1885: "Good and loyal Indians are among the things of the past...there are none at present."; and 22 June 1885: "... the last remnant of this fiendish band [Poundmaker] should be wiped out of existence ... put a price on their heads."

72. For a list of rebellion-related Indian convictions, see B. Stonechild and B. Waiser, *Loyal till Death: Indians and the North-West Rebellion* (Saskatoon: Fifth House Publishers, 1997), app. 5.

73. J.A. Macdonald to E. Dewdney, 20 November 1885, Dewdney papers, box 2, f. 38, Glenbow Archives, Calgary.

74. Reed's "List of Band Behaviour during the Rebellion" is reproduced in Stonechild and Waiser, *Loyal till Death*, app. 4

75. Dewdney later claimed that "the with-holding of these payments is a form of punishment." "Annual Report of the Department of Indian Affairs," Canada, *Sessional Papers*, 1887, p. 189. A May 2015 ruling by the Specific Claims Tribunal found that the Crown breached its lawful obligation to pay annuities to the Beardy's and Okemasis bands.

76. J.R. Miller, *Skyscrapers Hide the Heavens: A History of Indian-White Relations in Canada* (Toronto: University of Toronto Press, 1989) p. 188.

77. Quoted in Beal and Wright, "Summary and Incompetent Justice," p. 374.

78. D.B. Smith has provided a wonderful biography of Jackson. *Honoré Jackson: Prairie Visionary* (Regina: Coteau Books, 2007).

79. Quoted in Beal and Wright, "Summary and Incompetent Justice," p. 383.

80. Quoted in D. Owram, *Promise of Eden: The Canadian Expansionist Movement and the Idea of the West, 1856–1900* (Toronto: University of Toronto Press, 1980), p. 174.

81. Quoted in Ibid., p. 175.

82. Canada. *House of Commons*, *Debates*, 9 May 1883, 1107.

83. Larmour, "Edgar Dewdney," p. 207.

84. A. Lacombe memorandum, n.d. (July 1885), Macdonald papers, v. 107, pp. 43240–2, Library and Archives Canada, Manuscript Division.

85. Millions, "Ties Undone," p. 59.

86. Cuthbert to A.B. Perry, 20 January 1886, RG 10, vol. 3585, f. 1130, pt. 8, Library and Archives Canada, Government Archives Division, Indian Affairs.; E. Dewdney to A.G. Irvine, 1 February 1886 and A.B. Perry to E.A. Dewdney, 19 February 1886, RG 18, f. 796, Library and Archives Canada, Government Archives Division, Royal Canadian Mounted Police.

87. D. Morton and R. Roy, eds., *Telegrams of the North-West Campaign, 1885* (Toronto: The Champlain Society, 1972), F. Middle to A.P Caron, 13 June 1885.

88. S. Carter, in *Capturing Women: The Manipulation of Cultural Imagery in Canada's Prairie West* (Montreal: McGill–Queen's University Press, 1997) suggests that 1885 was a watershed in Aboriginal-white relations. This interpretation is also advanced by Millions, "Ties Undone" and Code, "Les Autres Métis."

89. L.R. Ord, *Reminiscences of a Bungle by one of the Bunglers* (Toronto: Grip Printing and Publishing, 1887), p. 35. More than 125 years would pass before the supposed bell of Batoche, kept as a war trophy in the legion hall in Millbrook, Ontario, was formally returned to the Métis community. A CBC news story suggested that the bell of Batoche is actually from the parish at Frog Lake: Karen Pauls, "Bell of Batoche may not be from Batoche, CBC documentary reveals," *CBC News*, 10 April 2014, http://www.cbc.ca/news/aboriginal/bell-of-batoche-may-not-be-from-batoche-cbc-documentary-reveals-1.2604033 (accessed 22 November 2014).

CHAPTER SIXTEEN NOTES

1. Dixon Brothers papers, Box 1, f. 4, Glenbow Archives, Calgary; D. White, "Dixon, Howard" in R. Cook, ed., *Dictionary of Canadian Biography, vol. 15, 1921–1930* (Toronto: University of Toronto Press, 2005), pp. 288–89.

2. "Annual Report of the Department of the Interior for 1887," Canada, *Sessional Papers*, 1888, no. 14, pp. xxvi–xxix; "Annual Report of the Auditor General for 1887–88," Canada, *Sessional Papers*, 1889; no. 3, pp. G1–14.

3. For an account of the incident, see M.R. Stobie, *The Other Side of the Rebellion: The Remarkable Story of Charles Bremner and his Furs* (Edmonton: NeWest Press, 1986).

4. A. Morris, *The Treaties of Canada with the Indians of Manitoba and the North-West Territories*, (Saskatoon, Fifth House Publishers,1991), p. 195.

5. J.R. Miller, *Compact, Contract, Covenant: Aboriginal Treaty-Making in Canada* (Toronto: University of Toronto Press, 2009), p. 194; H. Devine, *The People Who Own Themselves: Aboriginal Ethnogenesis in a Canadian Family, 1660-1900* (Calgary: University of Calgary Press, 2004), pp. 143–44.

6. C. Augustus, "The Scrip Solution: The North West Métis Scrip Policy" (master's thesis, University of Calgary, 2005), p. 5.

7. In 1899, under the Wilfrid Laurier government, the regulations were amended to give scrip to all children born between 15 July 1870 and the end of 1885.

8. Augustus, "The Scrip Solution," pp. 5–6.

9. L.E. Dyck, *Farmers "Making Good": The Development of the Abernethy District, Saskatchewan, 1880–1920* (Ottawa: Environment Canada, 1989), p. 23.

10. If an individual wanted to return to treaty after taking scrip, then the value of the scrip payment was deducted against future annuity payments. J.B.D. Larmour, "Edgar Dewdney, Commissioner of Indian Affairs and Lieutenant Governor of the North-West Territories, 1879–1888" (master's thesis, University of Saskatchewan, 1969), p. 214–15.

11. Augustus, "The Scrip Solution," pp. 7, 16–19, 45–51, 57–62, 75–84, 116.

12. Ibid. pp. 86–87.

13. D.P. Payment, "Monsieur Batoche," *Saskatchewan History* 32, no. 3 (Autumn 1979): p. 99. See also D.P. Payment, *"The Free People–Otipemisiwak": Batoche, Saskatchewan 1870-1930* (Ottawa: Canadian Parks Service, 1990), pp. 172, 269–81, 283–85.

14. A.J. Ray, *The Canadian Fur Trade in the Industrial Age* (Toronto: University of Toronto Press, 1990), pp. 50–95.

15. B. Macdougall, *One of the Family: Metis Culture in Nineteenth-Century Northwestern Saskatchewan* (Vancouver: University of British Columbia Press, 2010), pp. 246–47.

16. Miller, *Compact, Contract, Covenant*, p. 199. The new northern treaty boundary was aligned with the northern boundary of the provisional district of Saskatchewan.

17. One of the original handwritten copies of the treaty is permanently on loan to the University of Saskatchewan library.

18. A.J. Ray et al., *Bounty and Benevolence: A History of Saskatchewan Treaties* (Montreal: McGill–Queens University Press, 2000), pp. 144–46. For the story of how and where the new reserves were located, see M. Massie, *Forest Prairie Edge: Place History in Saskatchewan* (Winnipeg: University of Manitoba Press, 2014), pp. 59–66.

19. When Treaty 8 was negotiated in the northern Athabasca and Peace River districts in 1899 in response to the Klondike Gold Rush, the extreme northwest corner of the future province of Saskatchewan was included within the new treaty's boundaries. At Fond du Lac on Lake Athabasca in 1900, the local Métis population was given the choice of entering the treaty or taking scrip. Those who opted to be recognized as Métis all took money scrip. G. Ens, "Taking Treaty 8 Scrip: A Quantitative Portrait of Northern Alberta Métis Communities," *Lobstick* 1, no. 1 (2000): pp. 243, 247–49.

20. G. Abrams, *Prince Albert: The First Century 1866–1966* (Saskatoon: Modern Press, 1966), p. 83.

21. B. Waiser, *Saskatchewan's Playground: A History of Prince Albert National Park* (Saskatoon: Fifth House Publishers, 1989) pp. 11–12.

22. Ibid., p. 12.

23. See Massie, *Forest Prairie Edge* for the story of northern winter freighting.

24. Quoted in Ibid., p. 103.

25. B. Waiser, *The New Northwest: The Photographs of the Frank Crean Expeditions, 1908–1909* (Saskatoon: Fifth House Publishers, 1993), pp. 3–5; J.A. Bovey, "The Attitudes and Policies of the Federal Government Towards Canada's Northern Territories, 1870–1930" (master's thesis, University of British Columbia, 1957), pp. 63–71.

26. Massie, *Forest Prairie Edge*, p. 104.

27. Quoted in R.D. Francis, *Images of the West: Changing Perceptions of the Prairies, 1690–1960* (Saskatoon: Western Producer Prairie Books, 1989), p. 112.

28. D. Owram, *Promise of Eden: The Canadian Expansionist Movement and the Idea of the West, 1856–1900* (Toronto: University of Toronto Press, 1980), pp. 110–13.

29. K.N. Lambrecht, *The Administration of Dominion Lands, 1870–1930* (Regina: Canadian Plains Research Center, 1991), pp 24–26.

30. Quoted in R. Rees, *New and Naked Land: Making the Prairies Homes* (Saskatoon: Western Producer Prairie Books, 1988), p. 63.

31. P.L. McCormick, "Transportation and Settlement: Problems in the Expansion of the Frontier of Saskatchewan and Assiniboia in 1904" in G.P. Marchildon, *Immigration and Settlement, 1870–1939* (Regina: Canadian Plains Research Center, 2009), p. 97.

32. Of the total number of homesteads applications between 1872 and 1930 (the start and end of the program), only 8.8% of the entries had been recorded by 1885 and only 20% by 1900. K.H. Norrie, "The National Policy and the Rate of Prairie Settlement" in R.D. Francis and H. Palmer, eds., *The Prairie West* (Edmonton: University of Alberta Press, 1992), p. 245–46; J.H. Archer, *Saskatchewan: A History* (Saskatoon: Western Producer Prairie Books, 1980), p. 83.

33. Quoted in Owram, *Promise of Eden*, pp. 166, 179.

34. A. Lalonde, "Colonization Companies in the 1880s," *Saskatchewan History* 24 (1971): pp. 101–14; Archer, *Saskatchewan: A History*, pp. 71–72; Lambrecht, *The Administration of Dominion Lands*, pp. 25–27.

35. E.A. Scott, "Building the 'Bridge of Hope': The Discourse and Practice of Assisted Emigration of the Labouring Poor from East London to Canada, 1857–1913" (Ph.D. thesis, University of Saskatchewan, 2014), pp. 293–343.

36. Homestead cancellations outnumbered entries (255 to 149) for the Qu'Appelle agency in 1888. Dyck, *Farmers "Making Good,"* pp. 29–30, 76–77.

37. Archer, *Saskatchewan: A History*, p. 99.

38. See A.M. Penders, "The Indian Head Experimental Farm and Forest Nursery Station, Indian Head, Canada: The Making of a Canadian Landscape" (Ph.D. thesis, University of Maine, 2013).

39. The spread of tree cover on the northern plains in the late nineteenth century has been generally attributed to the coming of settlement and the stopping of fires. But C. Campbell et al. ("Bison Extirpation may have caused Aspen expansion in Western Canada," *Ecography* 17, no. 4 [December

1994]: pp. 360–62) suggest that the spread of aspen preceded settlement and was linked to the disappearance of the bison from the northern plains. For a useful "snapshot" of vegetation across central and southern Saskatchewan in the 1880s, compiled from surveyors' records, see also W.O. Archibold and M. R. Wilson, "The natural vegetation of Saskatchewan prior to agricultural settlement," *Canadian Journal of Botany* 58 (1980): pp. 2031–2042.

40. Dyck, *Farmers "Making Good,"* pp. 49, 66, 79–81.

41. C. Martin, *"Dominion Lands" Policy* (Toronto: McClelland and Stewart,1973), p. 242.

42. Dyck, *Farmers "Making Good,"* p. 70.

43. T.D. Regehr, "Western Canada and the Burden of Transportation Policies" in R.D. Francis and H. Palmer, eds., *The Prairie West* (Edmonton: University of Alberta Press, 1992), pp. 266–67; T.D. Regehr, *The Canadian Northern: Pioneer Road of the Northern Prairies, 1895–1918* (Toronto: Macmillan of Canada, 1976), pp. 6–20.

44. S.M. Evans, "American Cattlemen on the Canadian Range, 1874–1914," *Prairie Forum* 4, no. 1 (1979): p. 123, 135 (n. 13).

45. M. Mason and T. Poirier, "Ranching" in T. Poirier, ed., *Wood Mountain Uplands: From the Big Muddy to the Frenchman River* (Wood Mountain, Saskatchewan, Wood Mountain Historical Society, 2000), pp. 99–100, 104.

46. S.M. Evans, "The Origin of Ranching in Western Canada: American Diffusion or Victorian Transplant," *Great Plains Quarterly* 4, no. 1 (Spring 1983): p. 82.

47. Mason and Poirier, "Ranching," p. 86–88; B. Potyondi, *In Palliser's Triangle: Living in the Grasslands, 1850–1930* (Saskatoon: Purich Publishers, 1995), pp. 44-57.

48. W. Elofson, *Cowboys, Gentlemen, and Cattle Thieves: Ranching on the Western Frontier* (Montreal: McGill–Queen's University Press, 2000), p. 64.

49. A third of the winters between 1881 and 1907 were bad ones for the cattle industry. Ibid., pp. 80–81, 91.

50. Quoted in Evans, "American Cattlemen," p. 128.

51. W. Stegner, *Wolf Willow: A History, a Story, and a Memory of the Last Plains Frontier* (Toronto: Macmillan of Canada, 1977), p. 84.

52. G. Wilson, "Jimmy Thomson" in M. Fedyk, ed., *Fort Walsh to Wood Mountain: The North-West Mounted Police Trail* (Regina: Benchmark Press, n.d.), pp. 56–57.

53. Quoted in B. Rensink, "Native but Foreign: Indigenous Transnational Refugees and Immigrants in the U.S.-Canadian and U.S.-Mexican Borderlands, 1880–present" (Ph.D. thesis, University of Nebraska, 2010), p. 106.

54. B. Hubner, "Horse Stealing and the Borderline: The NWMP and the Control of Indian Movement," *Prairie Forum* 20, no. 2 (Fall 1995): pp. 281–300.

55. Today, there are 260 markers marking the location of the old NWMP trail. The "Road Coat Trail," from Carlyle to Eastend along Saskatchewan Highway 13, is not the same trail.

56. T. Poirier, "The North-West Mounted Police" in Poirier, ed., *Wood Mountain Uplands*, pp. 56–60; P. Fitzpatrick, "Rodeo" in Poirier, ed., *Wood Mountain Uplands*, p. 123.

57. The fate of the Indian refugees is discussed in B. Stonechild and B. Waiser, *Loyal till Death: Indians and the North-West Rebellion* (Saskatoon: Fifth House Publishers, 1997), pp. 227–30. A more detailed account is provided in Rensink, "Native but Foreign."

58. S. Carter, *Lost Harvests: Prairie Indian Reserve Farmers and Government Policy* (Montreal: McGill–Queen's University Press, 1990), p. 152.

59. This term is used to explain police behaviour in R.C. Macleod, *The North-West Mounted Police and Law Enforcement, 1873–1905* (Toronto: University of Toronto Press, 1976).

60. S.A. Gavigan, *Hunger, Horses, and Government Men: Criminal Law on the Aboriginal Plains, 1870–1905* (Vancouver: University of British Columbia Press, 2013), pp. 25–27, 33–38, 86–87, 124–25, 184–85.

61. Ibid., p. 185.

62. Ibid., pp. 75–77.

63. H.A. Dempsey, *Charcoal's World* (Saskatoon: Western Producer Prairie Books, 1978).

64. Quoted in S.D. Hanson, "Kitchi-Manito-Waya" in F.G. Halpenny, ed., *Dictionary of Canadian Biography, vol. 12 1891–1900* (Toronto: University of Toronto Press, 1990), p. 499.

65. S. Carter, *The Importance of Being Monogamous: Marriage and National Building in Western Canada to 1915* (Edmonton: University of Alberta Press, 2008).

66. Abrams, *Prince Albert*, p. 109.

67. *Prince Albert Daily Herald*, 26 May 1935.

68. W.M. Baker, "Captain R. Burton Deane and Theatre on the Prairies, 1833–1901" in W.M. Baker, ed., *The Mounted Police and Prairie Society, 1873–1919* (Regina: Canadian Plains Research Center, 1998), p. 259.

69. J. Vance, *A History of Canadian Culture* (Toronto: Oxford, 2009), p. 100.

70. Ibid., p. 121.

71. W. Hildebrandt, "Fort Battleford and the Architecture of the North-West Mounted Police" in Baker, ed., *The Mounted Police and Prairie Society*, pp. 231–41.

72. Dyck, *Farmers "Making Good,"* pp. 82, 144.

73. Canada. *House of Commons Debates* (27 April 1877), p. 1872.

74. A.I. Silver, *The French-Canadian Idea of Confederation, 1864–1900* (Toronto: University of Toronto Press, 1982), pp. 67–217; J.R. Miller, "Anti-Catholic Thought in Victorian Canada," *Canadian Historical Review* 66, no. 4 (1985): pp. 474–94.

75. M.R. Lupul, *The Roman Catholic Church and the North-West School Question: A Study in Church-State Relations in Western Canada, 1870–1905* (Toronto: University of Toronto Press, 1974), pp. 21–79.

76. Archer, *Saskatchewan: A History*, p. 104. See also A.B. Anderson, *Settling Saskatchewan* (Regina: University of Regina Press, 2013).

77. L.H. Thomas, *The Struggle for Responsible Government in the North-West Territories, 1870-97* (Toronto: University of Toronto Press, 1956), p. 180.

78. Ibid., pp. 89, 95, 97–98, 135–36. Proposed territorial electoral districts Salisbury and Kimberley became part of an enlarged Manitoba when the western boundary of the province was extended.

79. *Regina Journal*, 10 November 1887 in Thomas, *The Struggle for Responsible Government*, p. 151.

80. Thomas, *The Struggle for Responsible Government*, pp. 132–33.

81. Quoted in Abrams, *Prince Albert*, p. 81.

82. Canada. *House of Commons Debates* (3 May 1888), p. 1174.

83. Canada. *Senate Debates* (28 April 1890), p. 601.

84. *Regina Journal*, 5 July 1888 in Thomas, *The Struggle for Responsible Government*, p. 158.

85. Thomas, *The Struggle for Responsible Government*, p. 235.

86. Quoted in Ibid., p. 259.

87. Quoted in Ibid., p. 249.

88. Quoted in D. Owram, ed., *The Formation of Alberta: A Documentary History* (Calgary: Historical Society of Alberta, 1979), p. xxiv.

89. Quoted in Ibid., p. 115.

90. Ibid., pp. xxv–xxxix.

91. Quoted in Thomas, *The Struggle for Responsible Government*, p. 258.

92. P.A. Russell, "Rhetorics of Identity: The Debate over Division of the North-West Territories, 1890–1905," *Journal of Canadian Studies* 20, no. 4 (Winter 1985–86): p. 100.

93. Quoted in G. MacEwan, *Frederick Haultain: Frontier Statesman of the Canadian Northwest* (Saskatoon: Western Producer Prairie Books, 1985), p. 120. The Saskatchewan Archives Board in Regina holds a scrapbook for the 1895 Territorial Exhibition. For Haultain's visit to the Chicago World's Fair, see RG 17, vol. 757, f. 87728, Library and Archives Canada, Government Archives Division, Department of Agriculture. See also Thomas, *The Struggle for Responsible Government*, pp. 234–35.

94. Quoted in MacEwan, *Frederick Haultain*, p. 121.

95. C.J. Houston and C.S. Houston, *Pioneer of Vision: The Reminiscences of T.A. Patrick M.D.* (Saskatoon: Western Producer Prairie Books, 1980), pp. 88–89. Patrick's suggested two provinces, including boundaries, were those adopted by the Laurier government in 1905.

96. Quoted in Russell, "Rhetorics of Identity," p. 110.

97. Haultain was leader of the Opposition (Provincial Rights party) in the Saskatchewan legislature from 1905 to 1912 before being appointed Saskatchewan Chief Justice. He also served as chancellor of the University of Saskatchewan.

98. J.W. Brennan, "A Political History of Saskatchewan, 1905–1929" (Ph.D. diss., University of Alberta, 1976), pp. 28–32.

99. D.J. Hall, "A Divergence of Principle: Clifford Sifton, Sir Wilfrid Laurier, and the North-West Autonomy Bills, 1905," *Laurentian University Review* 7, no.1 (November 1974): pp. 11–19.

100. Quoted in Owram, ed., *The Formation of Alberta*, p. 270.

101. Ibid., p. 279.

102. Ibid., p. 293.

103. Ibid., p. 333.

104. D.E. Smith, *Prairie Liberalism: The Liberal Party in Saskatchewan, 1905–71* (Toronto: University of Toronto, 1976), pp. 6–8, 19.

EPILOGUE NOTES

1. All of the letter excerpts are from the Lillian Turner fonds, Glenbow Archives, Calgary.

INDEX

Liam Richards, Saskatoon Star-Phoenix

ABOUT THE AUTHOR

Bill Waiser was a member of the Department of History at the University of Saskatchewan for three decades before becoming a full-time writer and public speaker.

He has published over a dozen books, including *Loyal till Death: Indians and the North-West Rebellion*, a short-list finalist for the 1997 Governor General's literary award for non-fiction. His *All Hell Can't Stop Us: The On-to-Ottawa Trek and Regina Riot* won the 2003 Saskatchewan Book Award for non-fiction. His most recent book, *Tommy's Team: The People behind the Douglas Years*, was short-listed for the Canadian Authors Association best book in Canadian History for 2011. He is perhaps best known for his acclaimed centennial history of the province, *Saskatchewan: A New History*. As a *Globe & Mail* reviewer remarked, "Saskatchewan has found its historian."

Bill has been awarded the Saskatchewan Order of Merit, elected a fellow of the Royal Society of Canada, named a distinguished university professor, and granted a D.Litt.

Bill is a recreational runner who likes to garden, hike, and canoe. He lives in Saskatoon with his partner Marley, a retired Environment Canada Research Scientist. The couple have three children and four grandchildren.

To learn more about Bill Waiser, visit his website at www.billwaiser.com or follow him on twitter @bill.waiser